Professional
Real Estate
Development

THE ULI GUIDE TO THE BUSINESS

Second Edition

ULI–THE URBAN LAND INSTITUTE

About ULI–the Urban Land Institute

ULI–the Urban Land Institute is a nonprofit education and research institute that is supported by its members. Its mission is to provide responsible leadership in the use of land in order to enhance the total environment.

ULI sponsors education programs and forums to encourage an open international exchange of ideas and sharing of experiences; initiates research that anticipates emerging land use trends and issues and proposes creative solutions based on that research; provides advisory services; and publishes a wide variety of materials to disseminate information on land use and development. Established in 1936, the Institute today has more than 17,000 members and associates from some 60 countries representing the entire spectrum of the land use and development disciplines.

Richard M. Rosan
President

Project Staff

Rachelle L. Levitt
Senior Vice President, Policy and Practice
Publisher

Gayle Berens
Vice President, Real Estate Development Practice

Anne B. Frej
Director, Office and Industrial Development
Project Director

Nancy H. Stewart
Director, Book Program

Barbara M. Fishel/Editech
Manuscript Editor

Betsy VanBuskirk
Art Director

Helene Y. Redmond/HYR Graphics
Book Design and Layout

Meg Batdorff
Cover Design

Diann Stanley-Austin
Director, Publishing Operations

Recommended bibliographic listing:
Peiser, Richard B., with Anne B. Frej. *Professional Real Estate Development: The ULI Guide to the Business.* Second Edition. Washington, D.C.: ULI–the Urban Land Institute, 2003.

ULI Catalog Number: P38
International Standard Book Number: 0–87420–894–7
Library of Congress Control Number: 2002117393

Copyright 2003 by ULI–the Urban Land Institute
1025 Thomas Jefferson Street, N.W.
Suite 500 West
Washington, D.C. 20007-5201

Third Printing 2005

Book Web site: www.pred.uli.org

Cover credit: Artville Illustrations

Authors

Richard B. Peiser was appointed the first Michael D. Spear Professor of real estate development in the Department of Urban Planning and Design at the Graduate School of Design, Harvard University. He joined Harvard in 1998 after being on the faculty at the University of Southern California since 1986, where he served as director of the Lusk Center for Real Estate Development and academic director of the Master of Real Estate Development Program, a program he founded in 1986. Before that appointment, he was assistant professor of real estate and regional science in the MBA program of the Cox Business School at Southern Methodist University in Dallas.

Peiser has blended his academic career with professional real estate experience. A planner and entrepreneur-developer as well as an expert in real estate finance, he has also demonstrated an interest in spatial and design issues and in the economics of land development. Through various partnerships in Texas and California, he has engaged in homebuilding and apartment development as well as large-scale land development and management. His recent development and investment activities have focused on low- and moderate-income apartment development and industrial product acquisition.

His primary research has focused on developing an understanding of the response of real estate developers to the marketplace and to the institutional environment in which they operate, particularly in the areas of urban redevelopment, affordable housing, and suburban sprawl. He has published numerous articles in academic and professional journals on subjects that include new town development, urban growth, development regulation, infrastructure financing, and real estate finance.

He is editor of *Reducing Crime through Real Estate Development and Management* (ULI, 1998) and author of *Strategies and Structure of Real Estate Development Firms: Lessons from Management Research* (ULI, 1991), *Special Districts: A Useful Technique for Financing Infrastructure* (ULI, 1987), and *Financing Infrastructure to Support Community Growth* (ULI, 1984).

Peiser received his BA from Yale University, his MBA from Harvard University, and his Ph.D. in land economy from Cambridge University. He is a trustee and fellow of the Urban Land Institute, coeditor of the *Journal of Real Estate Portfolio Management*, and a faculty associate of Eliot House. He serves on the boards of American Realty Advisors and the Berkshire Income Realty, Inc.

Anne B. Frej is director of office and industrial development at ULI, where she directs research, education, and programs in the area of office and industrial development policy and practice. She recently served as project director of *Business Park and Industrial Development Handbook* and currently is directing research as background to two ULI books on logistics, distribution, and industrial development.

Before joining ULI in 2000, Frej directed real estate consulting service groups at Jones Lang LaSalle and Arthur Andersen in Warsaw, Poland. Her consulting activities there focused on providing locational advice to businesses and market feasibility studies to local and international developers active in central Europe. From 1988 to 1995, she worked as a real estate market analyst in Jakarta, Indonesia, responsible for feasibility studies and development concepts for hotels, resorts, shopping centers, and mixed-use developments in the region. She also worked as an urban planner at Kaplan/McLaughlin/Diaz Architects in San Francisco, the Historic American Engineering Record in Washington, D.C., and other private planning and architectural firms. She has a master's degree in urban and regional planning from the George Washington University and is a member of Lambda Alpha International, the honorary land economics society.

Acknowledgments

Authors

Primary Authors

Richard B. Peiser
Michael D. Spear Professor of
  Real Estate Development
Harvard Graduate School of Design
Cambridge, Massachusetts

Anne B. Frej
Director, Office and Industrial
  Development
ULI–the Urban Land Institute
Washington, D.C.

Contributing Authors
(Second Edition)

Ken Beck
Senior Vice President
ASW Realty Partners
Woodland Hills, California

Frank H. Spink
Principal
Spink Consultancy
Annandale, Virginia

Contributing Author (First Edition)

Dean Schwanke
Vice President, Development
  Trends and Analysis
ULI–the Urban Land Institute
Washington, D.C.

Research Assistants, Harvard
Design School

Benjamin Bolger
James Chang
Sofia Dermisi
Alex Duval-Arnould
David Hamilton
James Hoffman
Rick Huijbregts
Beth Miller
Andreas Savvides
Jonathan Scharfman
Kavitha Selvaraj
Dan Winters

Additional Contributors
(Second Edition)

Steve Bram
President
George Smith Partners, Inc.
Los Angeles, California

Robert Buzbee
Division Partner
South Central Region
Trammell Crow Residential
Dallas, Texas

Patty Doyle
President
Patty Doyle Public Relations, Inc.
Fort Lauderdale, Florida

David Hamilton
Anshen + Allen
Los Angeles, California

Stanley Iezman
President and CEO
American Realty Advisors
Glendale, California

Dan Kassel
Co-President
Granite Homes
Irvine, California

Allan Kotin
Allan D. Kotin & Associates
Los Angeles, California

Gerd-Ulf Krueger
Vice President, Market Research
Institutional Housing Partners, Inc.
Irvine, California

Christopher Lee
President
CEL & Associates, Inc.
Los Angeles, California

Glenn Mueller
Real Estate Investment Strategist
Legg Mason
Professor
Johns Hopkins University
Baltimore, Maryland

Somy Mukherjee
Associate
The Magellan Group
Los Angeles, California

James J. Smith
Vice President
Katell Properties
Los Angeles, California

Jo Anne Stubblefield
President
Hyatt and Stubblefield
Atlanta, Georgia

Smedes York
President
The York Properties, Inc.
Raleigh, North Carolina

Reviewers

Rene Circ
Research Analyst
First Industrial Realty Trust, Inc.
Chicago, Illinois

Paige Close
Principal, Multifamily Group
Looney, Ricks, Kiss Architects
Memphis, Tennessee

Phillip Hughes
President
Hughes Investments, Inc.
Greenville, South Carolina

David Nelson
President and CEO
The Nelson Companies
West Bloomfield, Michigan

H. Pike Oliver
Principal
INTERRA and the Presidio Group
Sacramento, California

Robert Osborne
Director of Operations
BBGM Architects and Interiors
Washington, D.C.

Robert L. Silverman
Chair
The Winter Group of Companies
Atlanta, Georgia

Steven W. Spillman
President
Pacifica Companies
Mission Viejo, California

Karen F. Thorp
Vice President, Director of Training
Liberty Property Trust
Malvern, Pennsylvania

James Todd
President
The Peterson Companies
Fairfax, Virginia

ULI Staff Contributors
Richard Haughey
Director, Multifamily Development

Leslie Holst
Senior Associate, Practice

Adrienne Schmitz
Director, Residential Community
Development

Acknowledgments

Work on the second edition of *Professional Real Estate Development: The ULI Guide to the Business* began almost five years ago while I was teaching at the University of Southern California (USC). Progress was interrupted by my unexpected move to Harvard University in 1999. Although my friends at ULI became anxious about the pace of progress on the book, the long transition from Los Angeles to Boston has had its advantages. The second edition benefits from a whole new array of contributors. Case studies presented in each chapter are all new, and the many new interviewees represent many more parts of the country.

Many of the financial spreadsheets and other information related to case studies in the book are available online. The financial analyses and accompanying information presented in Chapters 3 and 4 can be accessed through ULI's Web site, www.pred.uli.org. Additional materials are available through links to a Harvard Design School Web site, which provides more detailed spreadsheets that will be updated regularly as tax laws change and as more information becomes available regarding deal structures, financing terms, market analysis, and the regulatory environment. Although the book was originally conceived as a tool primarily for practitioners in the industry, I am grateful for its adoption as the main textbook by faculty teaching real estate development at a number of universities. It is anticipated that teaching materials will be added to the Harvard Web site over time. Color photographs of selected projects and case studies in the book, and other relevant projects will also be available there. In this way, I hope that the book's material will remain current and that readers can use it to access an ever-increasing treasure trove of materials relating to the five main property types covered in this book.

As with the first edition, some of the most important contributors have been former students of mine, at both USC and Harvard. They have given generously of their time. In true ULI spirit, they have opened their books

and provided detailed information about their projects. They have been candid about their professional successes and failures and the lessons they learned.

In every sense of the word, this book is a cooperative effort. My coauthor, Anne Frej, deserves sainthood for her gentle but persuasive pressure to get the book completed. Every chapter reflects her capable writing, additions of new material, and editing. As coauthor of the first edition of the book, Dean Schwanke deserves enormous credit for providing much of the foundation for the latest edition. His efforts in helping to create the original version of the book made the job of producing a second edition much easier.

Special recognition goes to the authors of chapters or major portions of chapters for both editions of this book. John Loper and Ken Beck were responsible for the original draft of Chapter 5 that was subsequently updated and rewritten by Ken Beck for the second edition. Dean Schwanke contributed Chapter 7 for the first edition; Frank Spink considerably revised and updated Chapter 7 in this edition. My research assistants at Harvard—Kavitha Selvaraj, Alex Duval-Arnould, Beth Miller, Sofia Dermisi, Andreas Savvides, Rick Huijbregts, Dan Winters, Jonathan Scharfman, and David Hamilton—performed many of the interviews and collected much of the new material presented in the exhibits.

Case studies are an integral element of the book. Special thanks go to the individuals who generously shared detailed project information, photographs, and site plans. The background on market analysis for the 46th Street Lofts was contributed by Gerd-Ulf Krueger and Carl Neuss from Institutional Housing Partners, and by Paul Menzies from Levin Menzies Associates. Information and text on the Gruma Corporation facility was supplied by Somy Mukherjee of the Magellan Group. Jim Smith of Katell Properties contributed detailed information about Agoura Hills Business Park. David Nelson of the Nelson Companies provided background on the development history and budget information on Northfield Commons. Robert Silverman of the Winter Properties supplied information to Andreas Savvides for the Bass Lofts case study in Chapter 4. Dan Kassel and BJ Delzer of Granite Homes provided information for the San Luis Rey land development case study as well as the Elsinore 98 case study in Chapter 3.

Several ULI staff members were instrumental in the second edition of *Professional Real Estate Development*. Adrienne Schmitz added substantive information to Chapter 3. Leslie Holst added considerable new information to Chapters 4 and 8. Rick Haughey provided insights into multifamily development issues in Chapter 4. Gayle Berens and Rachelle Levitt provided advice and encouragement throughout the entire process. Karrie Underwood assisted in a wide variety of ways, from scanning photos to tracking down information.

Many thanks go to the editorial and design team managed by Nancy Stewart. Barbara Fishel ensured that the text and exhibits were clear and concise. Helene Redmond worked under a tight deadline to create the final design. Meg Batdorff created the cover design, and Diann Stanley-Austin managed the printing production.

Participants in Harvard Design School's new Advanced Management Development Program in Real Estate have been especially helpful in the final stages. As owners and developers of all five main property types covered in this book, AMDP participants have helped provide the latest terms and conditions, rates, and other information they are seeing in the many markets where they are active. Members of the AMDP class from redevelopment agencies and nonprofit organizations have added a perspective on deal making from their point of view that every developer should appreciate.

The great thing about teaching students, from first-year graduates in planning and real estate to CEOs in the AMDP, is that I learn far more from them than I teach. I hope that learning is reflected in the pages of this book. Bright and accomplished students and executives simply will not permit stock answers. By challenging the conventional wisdom, they force me every day to rethink how I view the real estate world.

I have benefited from a cadre of speakers who have lectured to students at Harvard and USC. Their remarks are generously quoted throughout the book. I have also shamelessly taken advantage of participants in Harvard Design School's Senior Leadership Forum. This access

to the leading members of the industry, and the very generous help provided by many friends from ULI's Community Development Council and other close friends from ULI, have, it is hoped, made the new edition as current and comprehensive as possible.

More than 200 real estate professionals were interviewed at length for this book. Their comments are footnoted and they are acknowledged at the end of each chapter, but they deserve additional recognition for the wealth of practical information they added.

I have leaned on more than a few friends in the development industry for help with questions about the different product types—Jerry Frank, Jr., Bob Moss, Con Howe, Jim Perley, Jim Goodell, Ted Raymond, Bob Baldwin, Stan Iezman, Mike Keston, Martin Slusser, and Kevin Staley. A number of friends from ULI also contributed more than they are aware to the writing of this book: James DeFrancia, Ken Hughes, Pike Oliver, Bob Engstrom, Charlie Shaw, Gerry Hines, Buzz McCoy, Joe O'Connor, and Bruce Ludwig.

I note sadly the passing of three people who have had very significant influence on the book: Don Mackie, Harry Newman, and Rena Sivitanidou. Their advice and counsel are sorely missed.

I am grateful to my colleagues at Harvard and USC who have helped to mold my thinking about development and urban growth: Carl Steinitz, Jerold Kayden, Richard Marshall, Alan Altshuler, Tony Gomez-Ibanez, Bill Poorvu, Arthur Segel, Anne Forsyth, Peter Gordon, Gen Guiliano, Dowell Myers, Allan Kotin, Ehud Mouchly, and Eric Heikkila. I also owe a debt of gratitude to the terrific administrators and staff at the Harvard Design School: Molly Howard, Jessica McFarland, Janet Wysocki, Corlette McCoy, and Russell Sanna.

All of these people deserve credit for helping to make this second edition possible. They are absolved of any mistakes, the full responsibility for which is my own.

Last but not least, my wife and children have borne the brunt of my absences and preoccupation, especially during the last year. It is to them and to my parents that this book is dedicated, in the hope that the urban landscape we create in the future is better than the one we started with and as good as the best we are capable of building.

Richard B. Peiser
Cambridge, Massachusetts

Foreword

Real estate developers face an awesome responsibility. The communities and buildings they create become the fabric of our civilization. They influence people's lives in a multitude of ways. What they build affects how near or how far people come to realizing the lifestyle of their dreams. Developers play a key role in determining the financial health of cities and the everyday experiences of their inhabitants. Where people play, work, and shop, how long it takes them to get there, and the quality of the environment that they find all depend to an extent on the work of developers.

Developers face a much more complex world than they did even ten years ago. Everyone has a stake in their activities. The days are past when a developer could unilaterally decide what he wanted to build and then build it without consulting community leaders, neighbors, and others affected by the development. The political, environmental, and financial context is changing just as rapidly as the market itself. Moreover, the development industry is going through the most wrenching adjustment since the Great Depression as a result of overbuilding in virtually all segments of the industry combined with the collapse of the S&L industry and the general withdrawal of many traditional sources of development financing.

At a time when the development industry as we know it seems to be collapsing, why do we need a book on how to develop real estate? First, if sound development principles had been practiced by all the developers of real estate in the 1980s to 1990s, much of what was built never would have been conceived, let alone financed. Second, for those unencumbered by real estate workouts and tarnished reputations, now is perhaps the best time since the 1960s to be entering the development field. The industry is near the bottom of the long-term 50-year real estate cycle.

Third, there will always be a need for qualified developers, and they should have the best possible training. Development is not for amateurs. When projects go bankrupt or are poorly designed, the whole community loses, not just the developer and his financiers. Why should tenants have to put up with poorly designed spaces? Why should communities have to suffer the tax losses of ill-conceived projects and unoccupied buildings?

Successful development requires understanding not only how to develop good real estate projects but also how to determine their impacts on neighborhoods and cities. Long-term real estate values are directly tied to the quality of the urban areas where they are situated.

Developers must take an active role in protecting and enhancing the long-term economic health of the cities in which they build.

Although this book was conceived as a practical guidebook for developing five major real estate types—land, residential, office, industrial, and retail—it is intended to do much more. Successful developers must have a thorough understanding of urban dynamics, of how and why cities grow. They must be informed critics of architecture, be knowledgeable about construction, law, public approvals, and public finance, and have the normal real estate skills in financing, marketing, and property management.

Real estate development is the art—perhaps someday it will be the science—of building real estate value by managing development risk. Development expertise can be applied to much more than building new buildings and subdivisions. Development talents can be useful in such activities as buying empty office buildings and leasing them, renovating older warehouses, repositioning shopping centers by changing the tenant mix, securing development entitlements for raw land, and buying workout properties from the Resolution Trust Corporation and banks and turning them around.

Development is exciting because it is dynamic. The conditions that enabled developers to be successful in the 1970s and 1980s are different from the ones that will govern in the early 2000s. As the conditions change, so will the skills that developers require to be successful. This book presents the collective wisdom of successful and unsuccessful developers acquired throughout their careers. It is organized by property type to emphasize the different risks and concerns of particular products. The overall steps, however, are the same; hence, the sequence of steps is presented in the same order for each property type.

The challenge of building more livable cities can only be met by qualified developers working together with other real estate professionals, public officials, and neighborhood representatives. Perhaps the greatest challenge is to evolve a fairer and more efficient development process—one that reflects the needs and aspirations of all groups while eliminating the many hurdles that raise the costs of development without providing commensurate benefits. Of one thing we can be certain: the process will be different tomorrow from what it is today. Let us hope that tomorrow's developers are equipped to meet the challenge.

Richard B. Peiser

Contents

Professional Real Estate Development

THE ULI GUIDE TO THE BUSINESS

Second Edition

1. Introduction

What Is a Developer?

Real estate development is a multifaceted business, encompassing activities that range from the renovation and re-lease of existing buildings to the purchase of raw land and the sale of improved parcels to others. Developers are the coordinators of those activities, converting ideas on paper into real property. They create, imagine, fund, control, and orchestrate the process of development from beginning to end. Developers take the greatest risks in the creation or renovation of real estate—and receive the greatest rewards. Typically, developers purchase a tract of land, determine the target market, develop the building program and design, obtain the necessary public approvals and financing, build the structure, and lease, manage, and ultimately sell it.

Development is a detail business, and successful developers know that they must double and triple check everything. The clause overlooked in a title policy or the soils test skipped can come back to haunt them. They also know that they are ultimately responsible for any omissions and mistakes. Even if someone else is negligent, developers must deal with the consequences.

A developer must respond to events as they occur: a good developer is ready for the unexpected, is flexible, and is prepared to shift strategy quickly. During the approval process, for example, a developer often must negotiate with neighborhood groups that seek major changes in a proposed project. If the developer is not willing to compromise, the group could have the power to kill the project altogether. A developer must be able to address citizens' concerns without compromising the project's economic viability. The developer may change the entire equation or the entire objective to satisfy himself as well as those seeking a compromise for other reasons.

Managing the development process requires special talents—not the least of which is common sense. Developers must have a clear vision of what they want to do; they must also provide strong leadership along with that clear vision. Developers by nature have strong egos and opinions, but they must be good listeners. They depend on many other people; they cannot possibly be authorities on all the many different fields of expertise involved in a project.

Developers work with a variety of people: building professionals, including architects, planners, contractors, and consultants; people in the construction trades; tenants and customers; attorneys, bankers, and investors; city officials, city staff members, inspectors, and citizens groups; homeowners associations; and community organizers. They must be conversant in dozens of subjects, from managing people to managing buildings. No developer is an expert in all areas. Success comes from knowing the questions to ask and whom to ask, what the common practices and rules of thumb are, and how to identify worthwhile advice and information.

The spark of creativity—in design, financing, and marketing—often separates successful developers from

Pictured at left is Harrison Square, Washington, D.C.

Understanding the Real Estate Industry

The real estate industry is divided into five main product types: residential, office, commercial, industrial, and land. The market for each product type differs dramatically depending on the location. Today, rents, which used to be highest in central business districts, are often higher in suburban nodes.

Building design and density represent two other primary dimensions for categorizing different segments of the property market. Each combination represents a different building type and cost structure. For example, high-rise apartments with structured parking cost much more to build and operate than garden apartments. Rents must be higher, and to be successful, the market study must demonstrate sufficient unmet demand for units from higher-income people who want high-rise rental apartments in a given location. ∎

their competitors. Like any creative or artistic endeavor, managing the creative process and people can be extremely difficult. Too much guidance may stifle creativity; too little may lead to unmanageable results. Obtaining creative, cutting-edge work from the team without exceeding the budget is one of the fundamental challenges of managing the development process.

Real estate development is an organic, evolutionary process. No two developments are exactly alike, and circumstances in a development change constantly. For beginners, development often appears easier than it is. Most beginning developers have to work twice as hard as seasoned professionals to keep events moving in the right direction. At some point in almost every deal, developers wish they had not become involved; at that point developers realize how badly they want the deal.

Solving problems as they occur is the essence of day-to-day development, but learning to expect the unexpected and never leaving anything to chance may allow for fewer problems, less stress, and more satisfaction in one's career. Laying the necessary groundwork before an important meeting, arranging an introduction to the best prospective lender, creating the best possible setting for negotiations, and knowing as much as possible about the prospective tenant's or lender's needs and concerns before meeting with them help to ensure success.

A favorite phrase among developers is that it is better to be *lucky* than to be *good*. According to Phil Hughes, "In this business you better be lucky *and* good. Luck may be where opportunity meets preparation, but in our business the developer makes his own preparations and his own opportunities, and it is up to the developer to introduce the two."[1]

The Book's Approach and Objectives

This book is directed to beginning developers and real estate professionals who want to know more about real estate development and how to perform their jobs better. Readers are assumed to be familiar already with the real estate industry, either through their daily activities in some segment of it or through personal investment. Professionals involved in the development industry may also gain a better understanding of the role that their companies play in development: What are the rules of thumb concerning the way developers do business with them? What are the critical elements affecting the success of the development? Why does the developer, for example, care about the concrete contractor's slump test? What type of certification enables a developer to close a permanent mortgage?

This book addresses the five major types of development that beginning developers are most likely to undertake: land subdivision, multifamily residential, office, industrial, and retail. Single-family housing is not addressed except insofar as land developers sell subdivided lots to homebuilders. Each of the five product types is described from start to finish: selecting sites, performing feasibility studies, considering alternative approaches, identifying the market and designing a product specifically for it, financing the project, working with contractors, marketing the building or subdivision, and managing the completed project.

The development process, although basically the same for each product, is different in detail and emphasis. For example, preleasing is not necessary for apartment development and has no meaning for land development, yet it is critical for office and retail development. And the way a developer analyzes the market for industrial space is irrelevant for apartment development but is crucial for designing and marketing industrial buildings.

The book contains three main parts: an introduction to the development process, discussions of individual product types, and a look at trends in the industry. Chapters 1 and 2 contain an overview of the development process, entry into the business, and ways to select and manage the development team. Chapters 3 through 7 describe development of the five main product types: land development (Chapter 3), multifamily residential development (Chapter 4), office development (Chapter 5), industrial development (Chapter 6), and retail development (Chapter 7). Chapters 3 and 4 provide detailed step-by-step summaries of the core processes for development. Chapter 3 focuses on land development and for-sale property, including subdivisions. Land approval and entitlement issues, which are common to all property types, are given particular attention in this chapter.

Chapter 4 (multifamily residential) provides a detailed introduction to income property development. Because many steps are the same for all four income property types, Chapter 4 describes in detail certain steps common to all product types, such as how to calculate financial returns for the overall project and for individual joint venture partners. After reading Chapters 3 and 4, readers should then turn to the sections of the book that concern the particular product type in which they are interested. A final chapter discusses industry trends and the developer's social responsibility.

No two communities, and no two projects, are alike, and everything is subject to change. Although this book is intended to be a primer covering all aspects of development, it is no substitute for expert local advice from experienced developers, attorneys, consultants, brokers, lenders, and others involved in the process.

Information is as specific as possible, with costs, rents, and financing information included for each product type. The figures indicate the magnitude of individual items and the approximate relationship of one item to another, but they are not appropriate for actual use. Costs may be two or three times higher in cities like New York and Los Angeles than they are in small towns. In some cases, figures presented here may be useful for initial crude estimates, but local sources should be consulted for information specific to particular projects.

A wealth of information is now available from the Internet to facilitate every step of development—from market analysis and local demographics to government approvals and financing. Indeed, one of the most important trends today is the impact of the technology revolution on the conduct of the development process and on the long-term value of location in different parts of a city.

Requirements for Success

Developers take risks. At the low extreme of the risk spectrum, developers may work for a fee, simply managing the development process as agents for other owners or investors. In this role, they might incur a small degree of risk from investing some of their own money in the venture or having an incentive fee that depends on their bringing the project in under budget or with faster leasing at higher rents. At the other extreme, developers can undertake all the risk, investing the first money in the project, taking the last money out, and accepting full personal liability. Failure could mean bankruptcy.

Developers also manage risk. They minimize or eliminate risk—at least getting it down to an acceptable level—before moving forward. They attempt to minimize the risk at an early stage to make sure the risk of investment for upfront costs—when a project's prospects are uncertain—is balanced with the likelihood of success.

Beginning developers usually must accept greater risk than experienced developers do, because beginners lack a strong bargaining position to transfer risk to others. They often must begin with projects that, for whatever reason, more experienced developers have passed over. Phil Hughes argues that beginning developers often take on more risk than they have to. They need to look harder to find the right opportunity, but every project includes opportunities to reduce risk.

Many people are attracted to development because of the perceived wealth and glamour associated with the most successful developers. To be sure, development

Developers depend on a variety of professionals. The work performed or managed by the design/construction team represents the bulk of the project's total cost, and effectively managing its contributions is critical to the success of the development process.

offers enormous rewards, tangible and intangible. For many, the feeling of accomplishment that comes from seeing the result of several years of effort is worth the trouble and sleepless nights along the way.

Development's tremendous risks, however, require a certain kind of personality. Individuals must be able to wait a relatively long time for rewards. Three or more years often pass before the developer sees the initial risk money again, not to mention profit. As a rule rather than the exception, developers risk losing everything they have invested so far two or three times during the course of development. Developers live with uncertainty. Events almost never go as planned, especially for beginning developers, and projects almost always seem to take twice as long and cost twice as much as initially expected.

Development also can be extremely frustrating. Developers depend on a variety of other people to get things done, and many events, such as public approvals, are not under the developer's control. One developer recalls that when he started developing single-family houses, he often became frustrated when work crews failed to show up as promised. Only after he learned to expect them not to show up and was pleasantly surprised when they did, did building become fun. The public approval process has become much more time-consuming and costly over the last two decades, greatly reducing the developer's control over the process and adding considerably to risk, especially in the early stages when risk is already highest.

Development requires considerable self-confidence. Until beginners develop sufficient self-confidence, they probably should work for another developer and learn about the process without incurring the risk. Even after gaining enough confidence to undertake development, beginning developers often start with a financial partner who bears most of the financial risk.

Perhaps the most effective way to limit risk is to start on projects that involve leasing or rehabilitation risk but do not involve all the risks in a completely new development. Alternatively, one can begin with single-family houses or small infill commercial buildings on existing, fully entitled lots ready for building. In any event, one should start on projects where the at-risk investment can be lost in its entirety without causing undue stress.

Even the smallest projects today typically require $50,000 to $100,000 cash upfront to get a project to the point where equity and construction loan funding can be raised. A developer should never begin a project without having at least twice as much cash in hand as seems necessary to get the project to the point where other funding is available. The upfront cash is only part of the total cash equity that a developer will need to complete a project. Most lenders today require a developer to invest cash equity to cover 25 to 35 percent of total project cost. Total cash equity need not be in hand or even sufficient to purchase the land, but it should carry the project through to a point where the developer can raise other funds from investors or lenders.

Another way to reduce risk is through the terms of the land purchase (Chapter 3 discusses this method in detail). Developers can limit risk substantially by having the right kind of contract to purchase land. For example, closing on land should take place as late in the process as possible. If 60-day or 90-day closings are typical in a community, beginning developers should look for a land seller who is willing to allow 180 days. If public approvals such as zoning changes are necessary, developers can make the necessary approvals a condition of purchasing the land; the land might cost more, but the extra time is worth the difference. Doing so will allow developers to shift the risk of approval to the seller. If needed public approvals or financing fall through, developers will avoid spending their precious risk capital on sites that cannot be developed profitably. Options on property that provide control over a site without having to purchase it immediately are one of the greatest tools for developers. They are a reflection of the developer's ability to negotiate and to satisfy the owner's needs at the same time.

Raising equity for one's first deal is perhaps the biggest hurdle for beginning developers. In general, developers want equity that is available immediately. If they have to raise it before they can close on a property, sellers become nervous about their ability to close and are less willing to let them tie up the property in the first place. Options may overcome many financial obstacles with creatively constructed purchase agreements, but sellers must have confidence the necessary financing is available.

Beginning developers often do not have established sources of equity unless they have sufficient funds out of their own pocket or close family or business connections. Even if the equity funds are not guaranteed, one must have them tentatively lined up before entering into a purchase contract. In most cases, investors want to see what they are investing in before they commit funds. They should, however, be precommitted to the extent possible. The developer secures such commitments by speaking to potential investors in advance and soliciting their interest in investing in the type of property, location, and size that the developer plans to find. Investors are more eager to invest when it is clear that the developer has done the homework, that is, investigated the local market carefully to demonstrate in advance that demand for a certain product exists. The message for prospective investors is straightforward: if the developer can find a property that meets certain already identified specifications, then investors would be interested in supplying equity for the deal.

Expecting the unexpected is one lesson every person must learn en route to becoming a developer. Although problems are inevitable, they almost always have solutions. Fortunately, the development process becomes easier as developers gain experience and undertake successive projects. Instead of waiting for a bank to provide a loan, developers may discover that lenders are calling them to offer to do business.

Nevertheless, the most difficult project is the first one. If it is not successful, a beginning developer may not get another chance. Thus, selecting a project that will not cause bankruptcy if it fails is imperative. Because of increasing difficulty in obtaining public approvals and financing, a developer should not be surprised if he has to attempt five or more projects before one gets underway. For example, John Dawson, a real estate executive with McDonald's Corporation, says that out of 100 sites that he looked at, he signed earnest money contracts and paid for feasibility studies on five. None of the sites proved to be developable.

Paths for Entering the Development Field

No single path leads automatically to success in real estate development. Developers come from a variety of disciplines—real estate brokerage, mortgage banking, consulting, construction, lending, architecture, legal services, among others. Recent specialized academic programs that award master's degrees in real estate development typically look for students who are already experienced real estate professionals but who want to become developers.[2]

Most people want to learn the business by working for another developer. Jobs with developers, however, are the most competitive in the real estate industry, with many people looking for relatively few jobs. Moreover, many jobs that are available with developers do not provide the broad range of experience needed. Although

figure 1-1
You Must Control One of These to Get Started

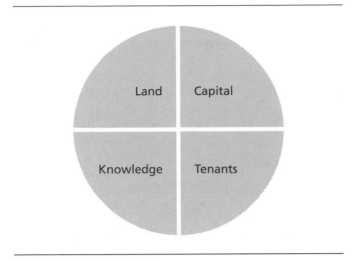

A Use Looking for a Site

All development is ultimately driven by demand. Determining who needs space—potential buyers or tenants—and what type of space they need is the starting point for all development projects. The initial market analysis should define the gaps in the market and the product or products that will fill them.

Knowledge can take several forms. Many developers capitalize on their familiarity with a particular local market gained from their previous experience in the field. Knowledge of the marketplace can give beginning developers the competitive edge they need—where space is in short supply and which tenants are looking for space, for example. The ability to convince potential lenders and investors that the market exists with supporting evidence in the form of market research data or letters of intent from prospective tenants is an invaluable asset for beginning developers, as they do not have a long track record to prove their capabilities.

In commercial development, the developer's hardest task is finding the tenant/user. It is the critical component that drives everything else to the bottom line—profit. Good money finds good projects, and finding the tenant/user is the most important task for commercial developers, whether they are beginners or seasoned. Quality tenants can help overcome resistance from neighboring homeowners or government agencies.

Many developers enter the business through contacts with potential tenants, perhaps by developing a new building for a family business or for the company for which they work. Knowing a particular tenant's needs and controlling its decision about location might enable the beginning developer who works for a firm to participate as a principal in the deal.

Knowledge about sources of financing is another way to break into the business. Assisting an established developer who needs money or a friend who has control over a tenant to find a lender or investor can enable one to become a principal in his or her first deal.

All these cases start with a use looking for a site, and the use defines requirements for the site. The developer's task is to find the site that best fits the demand.

A Site Looking for a Use

Another possible starting point is controlling a well-located piece of property. Many developers start by developing family-owned or company-owned land. Others begin by convincing a landowner to contribute the land to a joint venture in which the developer manages the development. In both cases, development is driven by supply.

The first question developers must answer is, "What is the highest and best use of the land?" Beginning developers commonly decide to develop a type of product that appears to offer the highest return (office buildings, for example) without diagnosing a demand for that product. Unless demand is sufficient, the site will not produce a financially attractive return. Thus, the beginner's first step is to perform a market analysis to determine the

larger developers usually hire people for a specialized area, like leasing or construction, the ideal job is to work as a project manager with full responsibility for one project, or to work for a small firm that provides the opportunity to see and do everything. Such jobs are the most difficult to find, but perseverance and the appropriate background will usually help beginning developers to obtain the ideal job.

Some positions in the real estate industry make it easier to move into development. Many developers start as homebuilders, then move into apartment or commercial development. Others begin by constructing projects for other developers and then for their own clients. Developers might start as commercial brokers, putting together a deal with a major tenant as anchor in a new office building or finding a site to develop for a build-to-suit tenant. Developers also might start as mortgage brokers; by controlling a source of funding, a mortgage broker could make the transition to development by overseeing the financial side of a joint venture with an experienced developer. Many experienced developers are willing to undertake joint ventures with a new partner if the partner brings a deal to the developer that strategically expands his current business.

Finding the First Deal

One of the most famous teachers of development, James Graaskamp, emphasized that to start, beginning developers must control at least one of four assets—land, knowledge, tenants, or capital. If they control more than one, the task becomes easier. If developers control land, then the task is driven by supply—a site looking for a use. If developers control knowledge or tenants, then the task is driven by demand—a use looking for a site. If they have capital, they have a choice.

Members of ULI's Community Development Council were surveyed about their experiences as beginning developers at ULI's fall meeting in Washington, D.C., in 1999. The following summary, based on 76 completed surveys, gives an idea of the background of people in the development industry who are active in community development.[a]

A Profile of Developers

All respondents were actively engaged in real estate development: 57 percent owned their own companies as individuals or in a partnership, and 16 percent were presidents of public companies (Figure A).

Over the previous ten years, respondents developed, in order of popularity by type, land, residential, retail, office, and industrial space (Figure B). In addition to development activities, respondents also had been involved in the purchase of land and completed residential, industrial, retail, and office projects (Figure C).

Career Path to Development

Respondents represented a broad range of experience, including accounting, brokerage, construction, lending, engineering, and law, among others (Figure D). Project management was the most popular path to development, representing 25 percent, 44 percent, and 31 percent,

respectively, of respondents' first, second, and third jobs. First jobs showed a wide range, indicating that accounting, brokerage, and administration all offer good entry points to development. Construction was the second most popular job (23 percent) after project management (44 percent) for respondents' second job. Many respondents have held only one or two different jobs on their way to a development career, as indicated by the 25 percent drop in total responses as one moves from first to second to third job on the table.

The most popular product for respondents' initial project was land development (Figure E).[b] The second project tended to be more evenly split between residential and land development. The most popular product type for a developer's third project was likewise evenly split—between land and office development. This progression from land and residential development to office development occurred in part because land and residential products are easier markets for beginning developers to penetrate and obtain financing for.

In running their businesses, respondents devoted their primary attention to the front end of the development process: site acquisition, obtaining regulatory approvals, market analysis, and design (Figure F). They were also personally involved in finding equity and negotiating joint ventures (Figure F).

As beginning developers, most of these individuals lacked the financial and/or practical resources to carry out projects on their own. First projects involved a partnership or joint venture (Figure G). In partnerships, the developers were most often the managing or general partner or were involved in a deal with two or three equal partners.

Lessons Learned

If they had the opportunity to redo their first project, most respondents would have done certain things differently. During planning and construction, the majority echoed the importance of select-

ing competent, experienced team members. As Randy Wheeler, a developer located in Seal Beach, California, stated, "People, people, people—good ones are hard to find. It's not just about location, location, location."

Another major concern was command of upfront scheduling and achievable goals for the approval process. One developer severely depleted his net worth by getting bogged down in a suburban traditional neighborhood development that took 30 months to get through approvals. C.W. Brown aptly summarized the concerns of most individuals interviewed: "Timeliness is next to godliness." One suggestion for dealing with this common predicament was to adopt a business strategy that is much more visible to the public and political decision makers.

figure B
Number of Projects Built in Last Ten Years

	Total	Percent
Land Development	43	52%
Residential	14	17
Retail	11	13
Office	10	12
Industrial	5	6
Mixed Use	0	–
Total	83	100%

figure C
Number of Projects Bought in Last Ten Years

	Total	Percent
Land Development	21	68%
Residential	6	19
Retail	1	3
Office	1	3
Industrial	2	6
Mixed Use	0	–
Total	31	100%

figure A
Respondents' Current Position

	Total	Percent
Owner/Developer	43	57%
Investor	4	5
Portfolio Manager/Adviser	0	–
Architect/Planner	1	1
Public Owner/Developer	12	16
Lender	1	1
Consultant/Lawyer	9	12
Contractor	0	–
Engineer	0	–
Other	6	8
Total	76	100%

Career Path to Development

Job Path	Accounting	Brokerage	Business Administration	Construction	Lending	Project Management	Student	Owner	Other	Total
1	7	3	11	4	2	16	4	1	16	64
	11%	5%	17%	6%	3%	25%	6%	2%	25%	100%
2	3	2	3	11	4	21	0	0	4	48
	6%	4%	6%	23%	8%	44%	–	–	8%	100%
3	2	3	8	3	2	12	0	0	9	39
	5%	8%	21%	8%	5%	31%	–	–	23%	100%

figure E

First Three Projects

	Land Development	Residential	Retail	Office	Industrial	Mixed Use	
1	33	23	2	3	2	0	
2	16	19	5	7	3	1	
3	16	7	6	13	2	0	
Total	65	49	13	23	7	1	158
Percent	41	31	8	15	4	1	100%

figure F

Beginners' Concentration on Phases of Development

	Primary	Secondary
Site Acquisition	16	3
Regulatory Approvals	17	7
Market Analysis	6	6
Design and Planning	9	10
Construction/Development Financing	2	6
Permanent Financing	0	1
Equity Financing	4	2
Joint Venture Structure	4	5
Construction	0	2
Marketing/Leasing	1	4
Operations/Maintenance	0	0

figure G

Structure of Deals with Other Parties for First Projects[c]

	First Project	Second Project	Third Project
Partnership	14	8	9
Joint Venture	6	9	9
Developer (Sole Owner)	5	8	7
Syndication	2	1	0

"It is a wise man who knows what he does not know," was one respondent's answer to the question about lessons learned from early projects. Knowing the intricate details of the approval process is a way to minimize confusion and one's exposure to resource-draining delays. Another dominant concern was the acquisition of land. Individuals agreed that a bad acquisition is almost impossible to rectify. Knowing the market through extensive preliminary study will alleviate the risk of getting stuck with an unworkable project.

It is crucial to recognize which obstacles are immediate, short term, and temporary, and which ones are deal breakers. It is important to maintain a critical distance from the project and allow extensive research and a conservative pro forma to generate a commitment to the deal—not an emotional excitement for building or site. ∎

Notes

a   Survey results were prepared by Rick Huijbregts and Alex Duval, graduate students at Harvard University, with assistance from Michael Peiser.

b   This result may be somewhat biased, as many survey respondents were members of ULI's Community Development Council.

c   Based on 36 responses in 1987.

highest and best use and to estimate absorption (units sold or square feet leased per month) for the site.

At a given point, every site has a highest and best use that will maximize its value. Every potential buyer analyzes a property's highest and best use before presenting an offer for a property that is for sale, hoping to turn a profit. In fact, a property's selling price is determined by many buyers deciding what the highest and best use is and bidding accordingly. The owner's valuation of the site developed to its highest and best use now determines whether to go ahead with development or to wait.

Whether to develop immediately or to wait depends on an assessment of possible changes in use or density in the future. A tract at the corner of two highways on the edge of town, for example, might eventually make a good site for a shopping center, but if current demand for retail space does not yet justify a shopping center, the most profitable current use may be single-family lots. Waiting five years, however, would offer a higher profit because the shopping center could then be justified.

When the developer already owns the site, the market study should indicate what to build, how much to build, the sale price or rental rate, and the amount of time that sales or leasing will require. While the market study is underway, the developer should investigate site conditions (how much of the land is buildable, what percentage contains slopes, whether environmentally sensitive areas are present, whether areas are prone to flooding, and so forth) and find out what public approvals are necessary.

The development strategy should be created once the developer has acquired information about the market, engineering, and environmental and public approvals needed. A large site does not necessarily need to be developed all at once. Financing capacity is usually limited by the combined net worth of the developer and his partners, including the unencumbered value of the land (land value net of loans).

The Concept of Present Value

An understanding of present value is essential for developers. (Any introductory textbook on principles of real estate finance describes present value. See, for example, William B. Brueggeman and Jeffrey D. Fisher, *Real Estate Finance and Investments,* 11th ed. [New York: McGraw-Hill, 2002].) Present value analysis equalizes the *time value* of money. Because one can earn interest on money, $100 today will be worth $110 in one year at 10 percent interest and $121 in two years with annual compounding. Ten percent interest represents the *opportunity cost* if one receives the money in, say, two years rather than now.

The present value of $121, received in two years, is $100. That is, the *discounted value* of $121 at a 10 percent discount rate, received in two years, is $100 today. If the discount rate (opportunity cost rate) is 10 percent, then it makes no difference whether one receives $100 today or $121 in two years.

The formula for calculating present value is as follows:

$$PV = FV \left[\frac{1}{(1 + r)} \right]^n$$

where PV is present value, FV is future value, r is the discount rate, and n is the number of years. Thus, the present value of $121 received in two years is:

$$PV = \$121 \left[\frac{1}{(1 + .10)} \right]^2 = \$100$$

The landowner's dilemma about developing the land immediately into single-family lots or waiting for five years to develop a shopping center is solved by applying present value analysis. Suppose, for example, that land for single-family development today is worth $100,000 per acre, whereas land for a shopping center would be worth $200,000 per acre in five years. If the personal discount rate is 10 percent, then $200,000 to be received in five years is worth $124,184 today—clearly more than the value of the land if it is developed for single-family houses. The best option is to wait.

Because of the high rates of return and high risk associated with development, most developers have personal discount rates of at least 20 percent. That is, they expect to earn at least 20 percent per year on their investment during times when expected inflation is 5 percent. Inflation is a component of the discount rate:

Real return rate + Inflation + Risk =
    Discount rate premium
3% + 5% + 12% = 20%

If inflation increases to 10 percent, then a developer's required return increases to 25 percent. The risk premium depends on the particular property and might range from as low as 4 percent for a completed office building to 15 to 20 percent for a recreational land development.

In this example, if the discount rate is 20 percent rather than 10 percent, then the present value of $200,000 is only $80,375. At the higher discount rate, the best decision is to develop the land for single-family lots today.

Which discount rate—10 percent or 20 percent—is appropriate? The answer depends on risk. At the beginning of the 21st century, land development (except for single-family houses) is considered the riskiest form of development because of uncertainties about entitlements and market absorption. Building development risk depends on local market conditions. Office development is considered riskier than industrial or apartment development because the lead time is longer and space has been oversupplied in many markets. ■

Easton Town Center in Columbus, Ohio, is a mixed-use retail/entertainment complex located about eight miles (13 kilometers) from the city's central business district. Its "town square" provides an identity for the project and reinforces its role as a retail destination.

In most cases, beginning developers must give personal guarantees to secure financing, especially for construction. Banks typically look at the net worth of the developers and partners in the deal before granting a construction loan. In some instances, however, the tenant's credit on a long-term lease may take the place of the developer's.

One advantage of developing a small part of a larger tract of land is that the rest of the land can be used as collateral for financing the first project. Defaulting on the loan, however, might entail loss of the entire site: once the land is pledged as collateral, the bank may foreclose on it after default to collect any balance owed.

Development projects that begin with a site looking for a use provide an attractive way for beginning developers to start, because they will not be required to locate and tie up land until a deal can be put together. Although such projects are perhaps the easiest way to get into development, the major problem is that land already owned may not be the best site to develop at a given time. Nevertheless, many properties can be developed profitably. Skillful developers can identify the most marketable use, determine a development strategy, and then implement it.

Improving the Chances of Successful Development

Selecting the first development project should not be left to accident, nor should beginners necessarily grab the first opportunity they see. The first deal is the most difficult and among the most important that the developer will ever undertake. Failure makes it that much harder to obtain backing for another opportunity. The first deal establishes the developer's track record, sets the tone for the quality of future developments, establishes an image in the marketplace, creates a network of brokerage and other business relationships for future deals, and builds relationships with bankers and investors. Still, every beginning developer makes mistakes. The goal should be to deliver a high-quality project that serves the needs of the local market. One should get the best advice possible but not be afraid to make a decision and move on.

A maxim of development is that it takes just as long and is just as difficult to undertake a small deal as it is to undertake a large one; therefore, developers should look for large deals. Although the maxim is true to a degree for experienced developers, it is not true for beginning developers.

A principal objective of the developer's first deal is to establish a track record. The absence of a track record is perhaps the beginning developer's greatest handicap; thus, selecting the right size project is critical. The major guidelines are to look for a project that can be put together in, say, six months and to look for one that is within the developer's financial capabilities—personal resources plus those that can be raised through family, friends, or other currently identifiable partners. A general rule of thumb is that the combined financial net worths of the partners must be at least as large as the project's total cost. In times of tight money, net worth requirements may be even greater. For example, suppose the developer has $50,000 cash and a personal net worth of $100,000. To undertake a $1 million project requires bringing in a partner with at least $900,000 in net worth. Finding partners with that much net worth may be difficult—especially those who are willing to sign personally on the construction loan[3]—but it is much easier to find partners with $1 million financial statements than those with $50 million financial statements. Further, most projects today require substantial cash equity. If lenders require 30 percent equity, for example, raising $300,000 equity for a $1 million project is much easier than raising $3 million equity for a $10 million project. If the developer has created value over and above the project cost, it may be possible to reduce the amount of cash equity required by the bank. *Value* is a function of signed leases and market rental rates. In the example above, if the appraised value were, say, $12 mil-

Beginning developers are likely to become involved with single-family residential developments. In choosing a site, it is advisable to search for land that is appropriately zoned and already served by utilities.

lion, then a 70 percent loan would provide $8.4 million, leaving only $1.6 million that the developer would have to come up with as cash equity.

In addition to preferring *smaller* deals, beginning developers should search for *simple* deals—deals that require fewer steps to bring to fruition. Smaller buildings can be developed in less time, incurring less risk and involving fewer steps. They also can be leased more quickly.[4] Although small buildings can be just as complex as larger ones, the criteria for selection should emphasize projects that do not require a lengthy and uncertain process of public approvals and complicated financing.

One exception to arguments in favor of simple deals is that smaller "problem" deals may offer an opportunity that experienced developers have passed over. For example, larger developers may decide that a site requiring special attention to curing problems with easements, boundaries, or flooding is not worth the necessary time and effort. A beginner, however, might be able to tie up the property at little cost while working out the problems. Another opportunity can be found with sites owned by local and state governments and redevelopment agencies, because large developers may prefer to avoid government red tape. Unless the site is simply put up for auction, however, the beginner might need to demonstrate a track record to convince government officials to work with him. Nonetheless, keeping officials aware of continuing interest in a project as the government works through various procedures and public hearings can give the beginner an edge when the agency finally issues a Request for Proposals or advertises the property for sale.

When money is more readily available, it becomes much easier for beginning developers to find financing. In such times, there is often more money available than "good deals"—projects that are likely to generate significant profit. Another successful strategy for beginning developers who have extensive local relationships, especially brokers, is for them to meet in advance with poten-

tial financial partners (especially local private investors) to determine what kinds of deals they are looking for. Armed with this information, beginning developers can look for deals that meet the profile of the investor's preference, such as land for small single-tenant industrial properties worth $2 million to $4 million. If a suitable property is found, the developer can tie it up and present it to the financial partner quickly. Time is critical: often the developer must "go hard" on the land purchase within 30 to 60 days, so having the financial partner ready and waiting to look at deals quickly is very important.[5]

In the final analysis, a developer's strongest assets are strength of reputation for integrity and ability to deal in good faith with a multitude of players. A large developer may be able to outlast the opposition in a contentious deal, but the best advice for a beginning developer is to avoid such situations altogether.

Managing the Development Process

Development is distinct from investment in operating properties (commonly referred to as *income-producing properties*), because it involves much more risk. Many firms and individuals invest in operating properties, buying existing properties and managing them for investment purposes. Investors often incur some risk in leasing and may make minor renovations that entail some construction risk. Developers, on the other hand, take on the full set of risks associated with development. Most developers also hold on to properties after they are developed—that is, during the operating phase—thus incurring the ongoing risks associated with operations.

Developers may take on different degrees of ownership and risk depending on their ownership structure and the complexity of the project. In the following discussion, developers who operate alone and invest only their own money are said to be *100 percent owner/developers*. They furnish all the cash equity, accept all the risk and liability, and receive all the benefits. The concept of a 100 percent owner/developer is useful for analyzing development, because if a project does not make economic sense in its entirety (as viewed by someone who has all the risks and rewards), it will not make sense as a joint venture or other form of partnership.

No generally accepted definition exists to determine who is a developer and who is not, but a developer can be defined as the person or firm that is actively involved in the development process and takes the risks and receives the rewards of development. An individual or firm that receives a commission for performing a service, such as finding tenants or money, is a broker rather than a developer.[6]

Many people involved in a development project may incur risk. Those who design, build, and lease a building for a landowner for a fee are agents of the owner and are developers insofar as they are engaged in the processes of development, but they incur no risk if the fee is fixed. If, however, the fee depends on the project's success, the individual accepts some performance risk associated with development. Development risk is associated with delivery of the entire project and thus may be distinguished from performance risk associated with individual tasks (such as contractors who accept construction risk when they have a fixed-price contract).

The major rewards in development are for the risk one takes on. Experienced developers are able to transfer some or most of the risk to others by using other people's money or by finding a lender who will give them nonrecourse financing (without personal liability). They still carry the burden of delivering a successful project, however. In almost all cases, developers will have something at risk somewhere along the line, such as front money for feasibility studies, investment in preliminary designs, earnest money, or personal liability on construction financing.

Development companies increasingly serve as development managers for major institutions. In this role, they perform all the normal functions of developers except that they bear little or no risk. The institution—a bank, an insurance company, a foreign corporation, or a major landowner—bears the risk. The developer works for a fee and usually a percentage of the profits (10 to 20 percent) if the project is successful. Historically,

---

figure 1-2

Development Phase versus Operating Phase Risk

Development Phase	Operating Phase
Acquisition risks	
Entitlement risks	
Site risks	
Financial risks	
Construction risks	
Market full lease-up risks	Ongoing lease-up risks
Operating risks	Ongoing operating risks

- Acquisition risks include title, easement, and other risks associated with obtaining control of and closing on a property.
- Entitlement risks include all risks associated with obtaining public approvals and vesting of development rights: the legal right to develop the property according to a given use, density, and design.
- Site risks include everything associated with the physical condition of the site (soils, hydrology, geology, contamination, botany) as well as off-site issues such as utility and road capacity.
- Financial risks include the cost of obtaining debt and equity financing as well as interest rate risk on the construction and permanent loans.
- Construction risks include everything associated with building the project on time and on budget at a high standard of quality.
- Market risks cover leasing up the property at a given rental rate within a given time frame.
- Operating risks include all risks associated with maintaining the property in a high-quality state, maintaining operating expenses (maintenance, repairs, taxes, management, utilities) within budget and high occupancy rates at pro forma rental and rent escalation rates (rental rates that meet or exceed the projections used to finance the project).

---

developers have preferred to own real estate rather than to manage it for others, because ownership has enabled them to amass wealth. Nevertheless, major developers increasingly have accepted roles as managers, either to keep their staffs busy during slow periods or to enter new markets with minimal risk. This approach was especially important during the real estate crash of the early 1990s. The developers who prospered during the slowdown were able to maintain cash flows by becoming service providers—property management, brokerage, tenant representation, construction, and other services to owners and tenants that provide a steady cash flow.

Real Estate Cycles

The adage "timing is everything" is especially applicable to real estate development. The importance of real estate cycles cannot be overemphasized. Like other large, capital-intensive purchases, real estate is highly sensitive to changes in interest rates. Income properties (office, industrial, and retail space, and apartments) provide insufficient cash flow to be financed when interest rates move above certain levels. For-sale developments, such as housing subdivisions, office buildings, or residential condominiums, suffer from higher financing costs and from the effect of rising interest rates on the amount of money that potential purchasers can borrow. When rates are high, buyers tend to wait for them to come back down before buying a property. The development industry is further affected by high interest rates because development firms typically are smaller than most corporate bank customers. When money is scarce, lenders tend to prefer their non–real estate customers. Even very sound projects can be difficult to finance because lenders fear the unknown development risks.

The supply as well as the demand side moves up and down. Lenders often appear to exhibit a herd mentality, all seeming to prefer the same type of product or geographic area at the same time. In Dallas, for example, during the boom of the early 1980s when money was plentiful for office buildings, some lenders began to fear that the market was being overbuilt, and money was shifted from office buildings to retail centers. From 1983 to 1986, almost every shopping center in North Dallas that was older than 15 years was renovated. But as suddenly as the money was turned on, it was turned off, as lenders across the country shared their concerns about the Dallas retail market. Similarly, in Boston in 2001, permanent financing was readily available for completed office buildings, but construction money was not. Lenders fear that the downtown office market will be overbuilt too quickly, so it is almost impossible to find a construction loan even though the office market is very tight.

Selecting the right time to enter development is crucial. Most beginning developers plunge ahead, regardless of the general economic climate, and often their success in financing the first project depends on their good (or bad) timing with respect to the cycle. Ironically, financing a project toward the end of a customer's preference

LCOR Inc. developed and owns One Penn Square West, a 25-story office building in downtown Philadelphia. Philadelphia National Bank provided the construction loan, and Kennedy Associates, a pension adviser, provided permanent financing.

James Oesch Photography

for it (when many lenders are enthusiastic about a particular geographic area and product type) is often easier. Toward the end of the positive cycle, however, risk increases as the competition for tenants or buyers intensifies. If supply becomes really excessive, those who were the last to enter the market are usually the first to get in trouble, because their costs are higher and competition is fierce for tenants.

Real estate markets are cyclical as a result of the lagged relationship between demand and supply for physical space. Glenn Mueller of Legg Mason divides the market cycle into four phases: recovery, expansion, hypersupply, and recession (see Figure 1-4). Each phase is characterized by different changes in vacancy and new construction as well as changes in rent. The position of property in the market cycle differs by property type and location. This type of analysis is helpful for understanding market timing—when the market is most favorable for new development.

A project launched early in the positive cycle means less competition for the developer. Long lead times required for finding the right site, designing the project, and receiving zoning and other public approvals mean that developers must be able to perceive new market opportunities before others do—often before they have become popular among lenders.

During the early stage of the development cycle, land is cheaper, terms are softer, and there is less entitlement and market risk.[7] During later stages, landowners push more risk onto the developer. Developers must take land down with increased entitlement and market risk. Closing times are shorter, and free-look periods are shorter or even unavailable for due diligence before contingencies are removed on purchase contracts.

How does a developer determine where a city is with respect to the economic cycle? General economic indicators, such as unemployment rates and business failures, provide information on general economic conditions. Local conditions are much more relevant than national conditions, although national conditions determine fluctuations in interest rates and credit availability. As the local market starts to approach the top of the economic cycle, rent increases slow and the supply of new space increases faster than absorption for that space. The peak of the cycle passes when new supply exceeds absorption, causing vacancy rates to increase.

Real estate cycles create windows of opportunity for financing and strong market demand in advance of a large supply. If beginning developers can synchronize their development efforts with the cycle, they can greatly improve their chances for success. The odds against beginners can only increase if they try to develop against the cycle. The biggest problem beginners face is finding a suitable project within the window of time for which the market is favorable. The favorable window (Phases I and II in Figure 1-4) may extend two to three years, but the chances for success decline significantly in Phase III, and finding money may be almost impossible in Phase IV.

Getting Started

The first step in the development process for beginning developers who do not already own the land is to select the target market, in terms of both geographic area and type of product. Staying close to the area where a developer has done business for a number of years is a major advantage, for success often depends as much on personal relationships as on skill. All real estate is local, and knowing the market is critical to getting started. On the other hand, having a specific tenant or ultimate buyer is a powerful way to begin—anywhere. Except for major projects (high-rise office buildings, shopping malls, major business parks) for which nationally recognized developers compete, local players have major advantages over outsiders. They understand the dynamics of the local area. They know the direction in which the area is growing and how buyers, tenants, and lenders feel about various neighborhoods. They know a good price and where prices have been changing rapidly. They know

Starting in Phase I—Recovery at the bottom of a cycle, the marketplace is in a state of oversupply from previous new construction or negative demand growth. At this bottom point, occupancy is at its trough. As excess space is absorbed, vacancy rates fall and rental rates stabilize and even begin to increase. Eventually, the market reaches its long-term occupancy average where rental growth is equal to inflation.

In Phase II—Expansion, demand growth continues at increasing levels, creating a need for additional space. As vacancy rates fall, rents begin to rise rapidly, pushing rents to cost-feasible levels. At this stage, demand is still rising faster than supply, and there is a lag in the provision of new space. Demand and supply are in equilibrium at the peak occupancy point of the cycle.

Phase III—Hypersupply commences after the peak/equilibrium point when supply is growing faster than demand. When more space is delivered than is demanded, rental growth slows and eventually construction slows or stops. Once the long-term occupancy average is passed, the market falls into Phase IV.

Phase IV—Recession begins as the market moves past the long-term occupancy average with high supply growth and low or negative demand growth. The extent of the down cycle is determined by the difference between supply growth and demand growth. The cycle eventually reaches bottom as new construction and completions slow or as demand begins to grow faster than new supply added to the marketplace.

figure 1-3

Physical Real Estate Cycle Characteristics

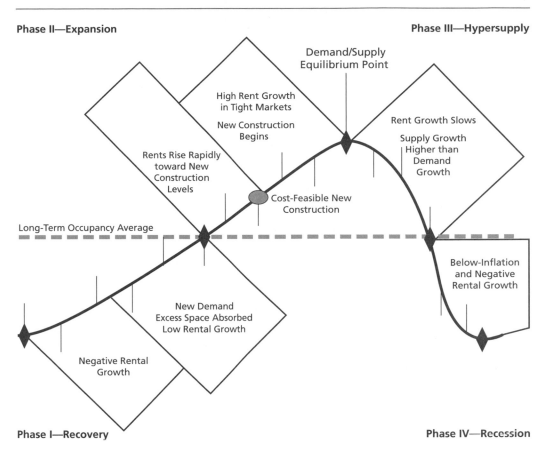

Source: Glenn Mueller, Legg Mason Real Estate, Baltimore, Maryland.

figure 1-4

National Property Type Cycle Locations

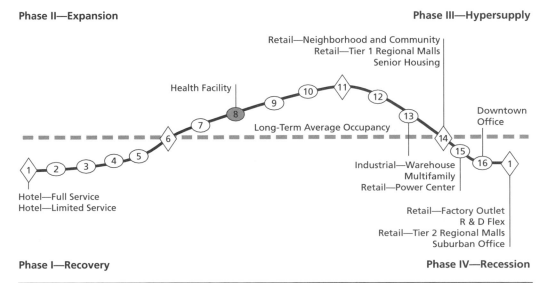

Source: Glenn Mueller, Legg Mason Real Estate, Baltimore, Maryland.

Linda S. Cornell

Linda Cornell is president and chair of the board of the Visiting Nurse Foundation (VNF) of Eastern Massachusetts, an association established in 1906 that provides more than 100,000 home health care visits annually in eastern Massachusetts. Not a typical developer, Cornell successfully oversaw the creation of the first affordable assisted living facility of its kind in the United States by a visiting nurses association.

Formally trained as a nurse, during her 15 years with VNF Cornell identified an overwhelming need in the community for affordable housing suited to low-income seniors requiring assistance with activities of daily living. With no prior real estate knowledge or development experience, she embarked on a five-year campaign to build a facility. "I was undaunted by the naysayers or enormity of the task because, to me, the mission was predicated by an unwavering absolute belief that this project was needed in the community," she says.

While serving on a state-appointed committee for economic development, Cornell gained some insight into the fundamentals of how a project concept evolves into reality. "In some respects my lack of experience was my greatest asset. With enormous community support, we sought out the best partners and consultants, assembling a superb development team that more than compensated for my deficiencies," she notes.

Compounding the challenge of developing the $14.5 million complex was finding an affordable site in a tight regional real estate market. The only suitable land available was an environmentally contaminated site, abandoned by a former industrial user. The U.S. Environmental Protection Agency provided seed money to determine the cost of environmental remediation of the site. The money was available under a brownfields pilot program to give buyers incentives to develop contaminated industrial sites.

"We took a blighted, abandoned urban property where people dumped trash and cars and successfully cleaned up the site," she says, adding "but the pieces of the puzzle we didn't have at that time were hands-on development experience and expertise in putting the financing together." Cornell searched for a partner with experience developing and raising funding for affordable housing projects. She selected a Chicago-based organization, National Equity Fund, which arranged equity of $6 million through tax credit financing for affordable housing projects to build the 97-unit complex, complete with wellness center, chapel, library, and ancillary support facilities.

The state and federal governments supported the 86,000-square-foot (8,000-square-meter) project. A partnership was established with the Massachusetts Housing Partnership Fund, which provided a first mortgage for approximately $7 million. A shared second mortgage with the Massachusetts Department of Housing and Community Development and the city of Somerville provided approximately $1 million.

When asked to define the moment she knew the project would actually materialize after years of effort, she says, "I knew at the closing of construction financing that this project would come together. The reality hit me sitting in that huge downtown boardroom with five lawyers representing the lenders and two feet of documents to sign."

Commenting on the most critical aspect of this first development experience, she says without hesitation as a veteran developer, "tight control on project costs, extremely tight control on what is going where, as it's being built, every day of construction." Total project costs exceeded the original construction budget by less than 1 percent.

In 2000, Cornell was nominated for the Phoenix Award by the Department of Housing and Urban Development for the revitalization of an urban region.

Since the project was completed, other cities with a similar vision have sought advice and support from Cornell to replicate the project's success in their communities.

Bruce H. Etkin

Bruce Etkin, currently chair of Etkin Johnson Group, started his first development in Detroit in 1974 with only two years of experience working with a general contractor after graduation from the University of Colorado in architectural engineering. Since that time, he has developed more than 4.5 million square feet (418,000 square meters) of buildings and, through strategic acquisition and development initiatives, is presently general partner of a diverse portfolio of office parks, hotels, retail centers, and residential projects totaling more than 8 million square feet (743,500 square meters) in Colorado and Michigan.

Characteristically a long-term holder of his development projects, Etkin

---

whom to call when they need information or need something done. It may take a year or longer for a newcomer to begin to understand these factors.

Newcomers *can* become insiders, however, even if they are recent arrivals. The best way is to bring in a local partner who is well connected in the community—an especially important move if public approvals are required. Another way is to use banking connections from home to open doors in the new community. Whatever the approach, newcomers have to work hard to overcome the natural suspicion of outsiders and the competitive advantage of local developers who have better information and more contacts.[8]

After deciding *where* to do business, the next question is *what* to develop. For beginning developers, the answer is simple: develop a product with which you are familiar—provided that lenders will make the money available. Even developers with no previous development attributes his sustainability to a primary emphasis on his projects' cash flow performance. "While by no means functioning in isolation, capital risk and operating risk management have distinct roles and expectations in the evaluation of our investments. . . . Cash flow is the key to maintaining responsible growth. We purposely manage our business so we do not have to develop simply to generate cash for our day-to-day operations."

Since his first project, Etkin has developed partnerships with a well-defined profile of investors. "Our investors are interested in holding investments with us for a long period of time, perhaps generations. They are not the type of investors who are attracted to an initial high rate of return with uncertain future prospects," adding "our earned participation may be greater than most in a competitive commercial market, but we see this only at the back end of the deal. This gives our investors confidence that we are in the project with them for the long term."

Using these principles, Etkin describes the core objective of his business as asset management. "Above all, property management and leasing are at the heart of our operation. Our properties are managed with absolute intensity to maximize future value, and we are committed to earning the long-term trust of our tenants, investors, and the brokerage community."

He attributes much of his success as a market leader in the early years to a practice of constantly benchmarking his product with developments in other areas of the United States. "During my forma-tive years of building, I regularly viewed other projects in other regions and listened to the nation's top developers to bring the latest innovations to our projects in Detroit."

As a self-described "dirty boot developer" in the beginning of his development career, Etkin says, "When starting the business, I hired nothing but the best lawyers, accountants, and consultants to reflect the integrity of my efforts and intentions in the industry."

Peter Pappas

Peter Pappas is president and managing partner of Pappas Properties LLC based in Charlotte, North Carolina. Before graduating from North Carolina State University in 1983, he spent six months researching the management styles and growth prospects of regional development companies. Of joining the Bissell Group of Companies of North Carolina, Pappas says, "I knew I would receive exceptional experience because the owners of the business were involved in every aspect of the business, they availed themselves to everyone, no matter how small the issue, and they were terrific mentors for all their employees." While at Bissell, it was the introduction to marketing and leasing to which he attributes his early understanding of "the most important and fundamental aspects of a commercially viable development."

He remained with Bissell for nine years, achieving senior management positions. He left in 1992 to form a partnership in a new development company, the Harris Group. In 1998, the company joint ventured with the Dallas-based Lincoln Property Company, where Pappas served as senior vice president for Lincoln Harris Corporate Services, until establishing his own company in 1999.

Pappas's interest in venturing on his own was driven by a desire to design master-planned mixed-use communities, where he believed the greatest challenges existed. His first project, Birkdale Village, near Charlotte, North Carolina, was designed with 300 residential units above and around a central main street commercial development of 400,000 square feet (37,000 square meters) of combined retail and office space. Based on his years of experience and earned reputation in the industry, Pappas was able to raise equity for the project among private sources; a conventional commercial lending institution provided the necessary construction financing.

The most difficult parts of starting a development company are "time constraints and financial requirements—balancing one's time on a day-to-day basis with equal importance on deal making and managing operations and financing when the deals always get larger and the approval periods longer."

Commenting on what it takes to be successful in the development business, he says, "Financial performance is essential, but the overall success of the development is also measured by how well a development integrates with the aesthetic and physical neighboring environment and, most important, how well it fulfills the envisioned needs of a community." The developer, he says, "earns his reputation only with a strong sense of community commitment, which must be reflected in each project while maintaining personal and corporate integrity, always
continued on next page

experience can sell potential investors and lenders on their experience with the product type if they study the local market to determine rents, competition, the regulatory environment, local tastes, local construction methods, and the types of units or buildings in greatest demand. Although beginners can successfully branch out into a new product type, they lack the background to fine-tune information about design and construction costs or to predict potential pitfalls. Beginners who do branch out cannot develop solo, however; they will probably have to bring in an experienced partner to get financing.

Identifying a product that the market lacks can make a project successful: finding that niche is the developer's challenge. Market niches are defined geographically and by product type. They can be as narrowly defined as, say, an apartment complex that has more two- and three-bedroom units than do other projects in the area or a multitenant warehouse building with front-loaded being accessible, and always being receptive to others' perspectives."

Brian R. Stebbins

Brian R. Stebbins is chief executive officer of Cooper and Stebbins, a privately held development company with offices in Texas and California. After graduating from Iowa State University in 1979 with a degree in landscape architecture, Stebbins joined Lend Lease Corporation in Dallas, an Australia-based international real estate investment and development company, as a project manager. In 1981, he relocated to Australia to manage Lend Lease's largest development division. In 1986, at the age of 29, he was enticed by New Zealand's largest publicly traded international real estate company to become chief executive officer.

With a yearning to fulfill self-expression in the development of his own projects and a longing to return to the United States, Stebbins joined long-time friend Peter Cooper in Irvine, California, in 1989; together they established Cooper and Stebbins. With the Texas economy in a significant downturn following the boom of the 1980s, Stebbins and his partner capitalized on an opportunity to purchase a 130-acre (53-hectare) site in the Dallas/ Fort Worth area when a previous commitment by one of the nation's largest real estate developers fell through.

Stebbins, provided with the opportunity to have absolute control over master planning and architectural design, envisioned the creation of a community retail development that returned to the design principles of downtowns built in this country a century ago. His design objective was to re-create the ambience of a pedestrian-friendly and relaxed retail shopping experience he believes has long since passed in the consideration of today's retail mall design. "The ultimate design objective was to re-create the authenticity and atmosphere of a central downtown heritage district so that most newcomers believed it was built a hundred years ago," says Stebbins.

While always keeping an eye on the bottom line of the $65 million Southlake Town Square development, Stebbins painstakingly participated in the design of every detail, including street-level heritage-style benches, street lamps, and signs. "Every detail is important. This place is going to be the backdrop for memories because we are going to great lengths to make it special. The experience should feel like a pair of comfortable old shoes."

Stebbins is methodical and efficient in describing the role of a developer and defining what success is: "A developer is a *creator* of product as opposed to a *processor*. The successful developer must recognize in his most embryonic vision of a block of land the real and perceived needs and requirements of the marketplace, tenants, investors, bankers, and the surrounding community and environment. Success is achieving these objectives while providing a fair and reasonable profit that reflects one's risk and effort."

To be a successful developer, Stebbins says, "requires an ability to think laterally. No matter the size or scope of a project, a developer must have the skill to be conversant in all aspects of the development—land selection, marketing, design, construction, legal, and finance. He must then be able to integrate these components into a package appealing to everyone while minimizing the financial risk. Throughout this process, the developer must present a can-do attitude; no matter what the inherent problems of any particular project may be, the developer must inspire confidence in his ability to perform to all parties concerned. Above all, a developer must conduct himself professionally and develop a genuine rapport with the people he is dealing with."

Stebbins concludes, "To conceptualize a vision, initiate the process and contribute to the realization of a shared vision, create opportunity, and enhance an environment is a pretty exciting and gratifying experience." ∎

---

garages. The phrase *designing for a specific market* is used often in this book, because that is how developers create a competitive advantage. Finding that special market, however, usually requires more than a good market study. It requires a perception of the market that other developers do not have, because if a market opportunity is obvious, another developer is probably already building to satisfy the demand. Thus, the beginner must understand the market well enough to act before other developers see the opportunity.

Stages of Development

The six main stages of development—feasibility and acquisition, design, financing, construction, marketing and leasing, and operations and management—are described for each major product type—land, apartments, offices, industrial space, and retail space—in Chapters 3 through 7.

Figure 1-5 shows the time line of development for an apartment building or small office building. The *development period* runs from the signing of the purchase contract for the land through lease-up of the building (Month 36). The development period covers all the major development risks, including financial, construction, and marketing. The *operating period* technically runs from the certificate of occupancy (when the building is ready for occupancy) until the building is sold. The *stabilized operating period* runs from the time the building is fully leased until it is sold. Stabilized operating period is the time frame used for standard appraisals of the building's value.

The six stages of development overlap considerably. In the time line, *predevelopment* covers the period from first identification of the development site to the start of construction. In the figure, predevelopment is shown as the first 12 months. Ideally, this period would be reduced to four to six months, allowing the developer to

figure 1-5

Time Line for Development of an Apartment Building or Small Office Building

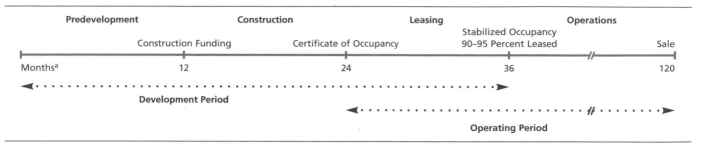

	Predevelopment		Construction		Leasing		Operations	
		Construction Funding		Certificate of Occupancy		Stabilized Occupancy 90–95 Percent Leased		Sale
Months[a]		12		24		36		120

Development Period

Operating Period

[a] Time varies widely according to a project's size, complexity, and location. Predevelopment may take two to four years or more in California but require only 90 days in some other parts of the country.

start construction at the same time the land deal is closed. It is difficult to achieve, especially for beginning developers, but the shorter the predevelopment period, the lower the cost and risk.

Four of the six stages of development occur during predevelopment: feasibility studies, design, financing, and marketing. In fact, a developer should be reasonably confident about the prospects for success on a project before he even signs the initial purchase contract. Developers rarely "go hard" (remove contingencies) on the purchase contract until they are very confident that they can obtain all necessary public approvals to build what they want and can raise all necessary financing for it. The primary purpose of predevelopment is to give the developer the necessary confidence to move forward. Before closing on a new project, a developer should be almost absolutely certain that the proposed project can be developed profitably according to his plans and objectives.

Figure 1-6 summarizes one view of the steps common to developing most types of property—determining a project's feasibility, design, financing, construction, marketing, operation, and management. It illustrates a fundamental principle of development: that development is an iterative process in which the developer obtains more and more precise information in each iteration, until he has enough confidence in the information to make a go/no-go decision. The process contains many moving parts, and knowing when they are moving in the right direction is critical. As Figure 1-5 shows, certain steps can be taken simultaneously, whereas others must be taken sequentially. For example, active preleasing for an office building begins as soon as preliminary design drawings are ready to show to prospective tenants. Preleasing occurs throughout the development period, from financing through construction. With an apartment project, leasing usually begins during construction, but it also occurs simultaneously with other steps.

Analysis of the numbers becomes more detailed and more sophisticated at each step. The initial contract for earnest money may require only a simple capitalization analysis to see whether or not land cost yields the desired overall return (net operating income divided by total project cost). Before the earnest money contract becomes

figure 1-6

The Go Decision

Existing Site

Financial Constraints

Market Information

Context Constraints

Regulatory Constraints

Driving Factors

Symbiosis

Financial Analysis

Architectural Design

Strategy

PRELIMINARY SCHEME

Documentation

Revision

Construction Cost

Line Up Financing

Construction Financing

Permanent Financing

Equity Financing

Last Check

GO DECISION

Commitment

Working Drawings

figure 1-7
The Development Process for a Corporate User

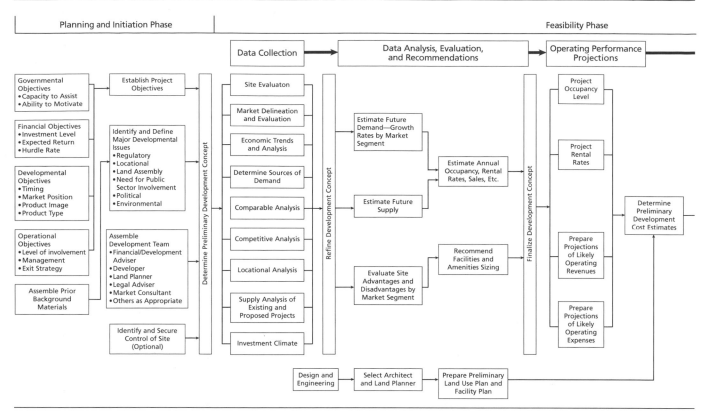

Note: The office development process for a corporate tenant with multiple location options, depicted here, goes through extensive research before starting development.

final, however, an annual cash flow pro forma is necessary, at least for the operating period. It should reflect the actual square footage planned, projected rents (based on the market analysis), and estimated construction costs. For the next iteration, a monthly cash flow during the construction period is necessary to convince the lender that enough cash will be available to complete the project. It will be based on still more accurate information about costs (from detailed design drawings) and revenues (including rent concessions and tenant improvement allowances). Finally, for a joint venture or equity syndication, a cash flow statement is necessary that combines both construction and operating periods and illustrates the timing of equity requirements, distributions of cash, tax benefits, and proceeds of sales (see Chapter 4).

The level of detail should correspond to the quality of information available at each stage. Preparing a monthly spread sheet for 60 months before reasonably accurate construction costs and market data have been assembled is a waste of time and money, yet developers need enough information to make a good decision at each stage. The information should be comparable in quality for all the different parameters, and it should be as comprehensive as possible for a given level of risk money.[9]

At each stage of analysis, certain items must be completed before moving to the next stage. For example,

before lenders consider a mortgage application, the developer usually must provide conceptual drawings, a boundary survey, title information, information about the site's feasibility, market surveys, personal financial information, and an appraisal. (Because different lenders have different requirements for appraisals, however, it may be wise not to order an appraisal until a promising lender has been identified. Otherwise, another appraisal—by someone the lender approves—might be necessary.)

The sequence of steps to be taken and even the steps themselves change frequently in development. The rate of change in the development world is one of its major sources of excitement. It also gives beginning developers a better chance to compete with experienced developers, because all developers must adapt to, and keep up with, changing conditions or they will fail.

Financing methods and sometimes even the sequence of financing steps may change over time. One major change, for example, occurred in the aftermath of skyrocketing inflation in the early 1980s. Developers traditionally obtain a commitment for a permanent loan first and then use that commitment (the *takeout commitment*) to obtain a construction loan. When inflation reached double digits in the early 1980s, however, developers suddenly could not obtain takeout commitments. Instead,

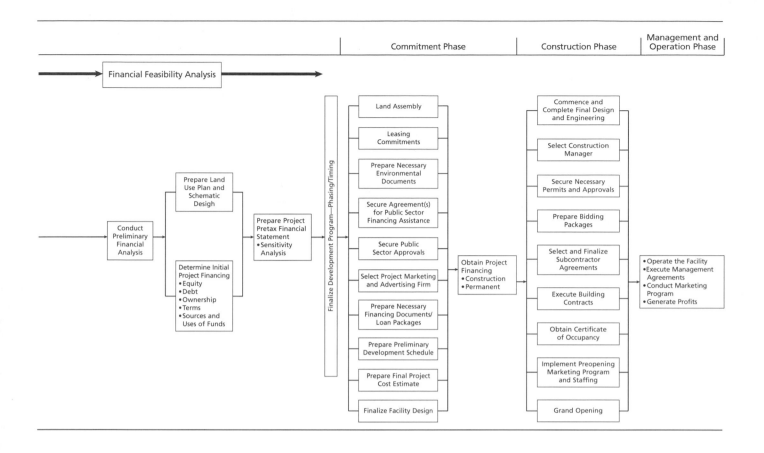

	Commitment Phase	Construction Phase	Management and Operation Phase

Financial Feasibility Analysis

Conduct Preliminary Financial Analysis

Prepare Land Use Plan and Schematic Design

Determine Initial Project Financing
• Equity
• Debt
• Ownership
• Terms
• Sources and Uses of Funds

Prepare Project Pretax Financial Statement
• Sensitivity Analysis

Finalize Development Program—Phasing/Timing

Land Assembly

Leasing Commitments

Prepare Necessary Environmental Documents

Secure Agreement(s) for Public Sector Financing Assistance

Secure Public Sector Approvals

Select Project Marketing and Advertising Firm

Prepare Necessary Financing Documents/ Loan Packages

Prepare Preliminary Development Schedule

Prepare Final Project Cost Estimate

Finalize Facility Design

Obtain Project Financing
• Construction
• Permanent

Commence and Complete Final Design and Engineering

Select Construction Manager

Secure Necessary Permits and Approvals

Prepare Bidding Packages

Select and Finalize Subcontractor Agreements

Execute Building Contracts

Obtain Certificate of Occupancy

Implement Preopening Marketing Program and Staffing

Grand Opening

• Operate the Facility
• Execute Management Agreements
• Conduct Marketing Program
• Generate Profits

---

they went directly to construction lenders, who started giving *miniperm loans*—five-year loans that covered both the construction period and the initial operating period. By doing so, lenders and developers gambled that interest rates on permanent mortgages would come down (which they did) within five years. They were also prepared to extend the loans (roll them over into new loans) if they did not. Financial markets in the early 21st century are relatively liquid and stable. Smaller developers have seen a return to traditional financing, in which they obtain a permanent takeout commitment before they apply for a construction loan. Large developers have a wide variety of financing alternatives, thanks primarily to the institutionalization of real estate financial markets. Large developers frequently have credit lines from banks that provide capital for site acquisition and even construction financing. This credit line takes the place of development and construction loans on individual properties.

Mezzanine financing provides higher loan-to-value ratios and reduces the amount of equity a developer needs. The mezzanine piece is a form of equity and may carry interest rates ranging from 11 to 13 percent or higher. Although expensive, this type of financing is still cheaper than equity financing, which often carries an implicit cost of 20 to 25 percent or more.

The development process resembles the construction of a building. The foundation must be level if the walls are to be straight. The frame must be square if the finish is to be attractive. Each step in the process depends on the quality of previous steps. Badly negotiated or written agreements with lenders, contractors, tenants, or professionals will come back to haunt the developer. At best, they will be costly to correct. At worst, they might halt completion or occupancy of the project. Lawsuits are losers for everyone involved. When disputes involve government agencies or the interpretation of public approvals, "you can't beat city hall" is very true in most cases.

Because each stage depends on the preceding one and because the developer must depend on other people to do much of the work, an adequate monitoring system is essential. A critical path chart can be assembled for each development, showing not only the events that must occur before others can be accomplished but also how much time each step should take. It also shows which events are on the critical path (those requiring the shortest time) and which events have some slack time. Critical path analysis makes it possible to calculate how much extra it will cost to shorten the path by paying workers overtime or paying extra freight charges to receive materials more quickly. The monitoring system

Three themes emerge from the advice given by members of ULI's Small-Scale Development Council: be well prepared at all times; work with experienced people, even if they are more expensive; and anticipate delays throughout the development process.

Site Acquisition

- Correctly analyze the purchase price of a site to include usable, not total, square footage.
- Anticipate problems with sellers who are not familiar with real estate and delays while a disputed estate is being settled.
- Analyze the site's physical constraints, including the availability of utilities.
- Conduct a soils test and check for hazardous waste.
- Identify the site's legal and political constraints, such as the availability of the required zoning or the existence of a moratorium on building.
- Research the market before purchasing the site.

Regulatory Process, Obtaining Approvals

- Be prepared to work with the community to resolve concerns and challenges to the project.
- Take time to understand the local political climate.
- Prepare for the local regulatory process and public hearings.
- Use qualified and experienced consultants, lawyers, and architects to give your project added credibility.
- Anticipate and do not underestimate delays in the approval process.

Product Selection, Market and Economic Feasibility

- Remember that when an opportunity is obvious, it is obvious to everyone—resulting in a great deal of competition.
- Develop toward the higher end of the market for your product type, where there is more margin for error. Low-end projects typically have slimmer profit margins.
- Choose a respected market consultant with a strong reputation in the city where your project is located.
- Decide how much time to allocate for the feasibility study. Some developers consider this step to be vital and maintain that the study should be thorough; others feel it should not be belabored.
- Make sure that extensive primary research accurately identifies all competition, whether under construction or still on the drawing boards.

Design, Site Planning, Engineering, and Construction

- Do not complete the design without paying attention to the market study.
- Work closely with the architect and the contractor.
- Be careful not to ignore important information, even if it requires redesign or additional approvals.
- Use a flexible design that can be easily adapted to different tenants' needs.
- Accept the design and recognize that it will never be perfect.
- Spend sufficient time and money to check all references before retaining contractors and subcontractors.

Construction and Development Financing

- Establish relationships with several lenders to eliminate lengthy delays.
- Deal with experienced lenders.
- Make adequate allowances for contingencies.
- Remember that it could take three to four months to process a $10 million loan—even if the lender says that it will take only six weeks.
- If the market softens, be able to cover interest out of your own pocket until the market comes back.

Permanent Financing

- Establish good communications with the lender.
- Prepare a detailed, professional presentation package for the lender.
- Secure the permanent loan before beginning construction. (Beginning developers might be forced to do so, even if they would prefer to wait until after the project is built and leased.)
- Be aware of trends in interest rates.

Equity Financing

- Investigate the financial records of sources of equity.
- Find two or three compatible partners who can provide or raise equity for the project.
- Do not give away too much equity position to secure funds, because

---

provides the best way to reinforce the written documents. For example, when an issue arises and three or four written confirmations of the contract are available (which are part of the monitoring system), it is much easier for the parties to find a solution to the issue.

The early stages of development are especially important, involving many iterations of planning and analysis before the architectural plans and other arrangements are finalized. A common mistake at each phase of analysis is to go into too much detail too soon. For example, obtaining detailed working drawings before a market feasibility study is completed is a waste of money. First, the market study should influence the design. Second, if the market is not as healthy as it appeared or if financing is unavailable or too expensive, the developer may want to abandon the project.

Projects go through several stages of risk. Developers' *at-risk capital* is the total amount of money that can be lost. During the period in which the developer makes preliminary assessments of the market and the site, the risk money typically is limited to what is spent on feasibility studies—analyses of soils, the floodplain, and the market and conceptual design. As soon as the developer goes hard on the land purchase contract, then the nonrefundable earnest money is also at risk. The money at risk escalates dramatically when the developer closes on the land, pays for financing commitments, or authorizes working drawings. These events should nothing may be left to give if you come up short.

Joint Ventures and Partnerships
- Structure a fair deal so that no partner is burdened with excessive risk and meager profits.
- Make clear who is in charge of the project.
- Avoid establishing goals that conflict with those pursued by other partners.
- Have agreements ready to cover dissolution of the partnership.
- Monitor changes in tax legislation that could affect returns.
- Establish a record of regular, honest communications with partners.

Marketing and Leasing
- Be prepared for unanticipated changes or a weakening market.
- Find a broker you trust and can work with.
- Understand the importance of marketing the project yourself.
- Create a suitable tenant mix for commercial projects.
- Be specific about tenant improvements and tenants' responsibilities in the lease, and include escape clauses for your own protection.
- Be creative about concessions. Consider buying stock in a tenant's startup company, paying moving expenses, or providing furnishings.
- Understand the implications of leasing versus sales on tenants' earnings and balance sheets.
- Advertise that you have made a deal or signed a lease.

- Recognize brokers with incentives such as dinners and awards.

Operations, Management, and Maintenance
- Pay close attention to building management and operations. Find a first-rate building manager.
- Budget properly for postconstruction maintenance.

In General
- Stick to geographic areas and product types with which you are familiar.
- Think small. Find a first project that is within your financial capabilities and can be developed in a reasonable amount of time.
- Never begin a project just because you have financing available.
- During the feasibility stage, keep investment in the project low to maximize your flexibility.
- Do your homework. Know what the holes in the market are and how to plug them—quickly.
- Never enter a negotiation that you are not prepared to leave.
- Attend to details. Whether you are designing a building or negotiating a lease, you personally must be on top of every detail. You must rely on your professional consultants, but if you do not understand the details, you should arrange for someone else to help you.
- Do not be afraid to make a nuisance of yourself. The people you are dealing with are usually very busy and hard to reach. You may have to make

several telephone calls or personal visits before you talk to them. Learn to be tenacious—nicely.
- Do not deceive yourself by ignoring facts and warning signs as they are presented to you. Be aware that self-deception occurs most often with evaluation of the market.
- Increase the time you think you need to develop a project—perhaps by twice as much. Do not promise cash payments to investors by a certain date. Be neither overly optimistic nor overly conservative in your assumptions.
- Be able to turn on a dime and switch your strategy instantly.
- Follow up *everything*. Never assume that something has been done just because you ordered it.
- If you promise something to a lender, a professional consultant, a tenant, or a purchaser, deliver.
- Communicate honestly and often with your lenders and investors. Avoid deals that show early signs of being contentious.
- Recognize that the buck stops with you. A million excuses can be found for things that go wrong in a development project, but you have the ultimate responsibility for ensuring that they go right. ∎

be delayed as long as possible, until the developer can answer as many questions as possible or obtain the best information to use to decide whether or not to proceed with the project. Developers' most precious asset is their risk capital—the money they have to spend on projects upfront to obtain control of property and to determine project feasibility. The last thing a developer wants is to have risk capital tied up in land that cannot be developed as planned. Experienced developers know that it is worth paying a little more upfront to extend the closing on land until they are certain they can proceed with development.

Because each deal has its own distinctive characteristics, limiting risk as much as the developer would like is

not always possible. In very hot markets, for example, a free look may not be possible and earnest money may be forfeitable from the first day, or the developer might have to close on the land in 60 days, before securing a firm commitment for financing the future development. Two general principles apply:

- Recognize that development is an iterative process in which each iteration brings more accurate information and puts a greater amount of money at risk.
- Spend enough money to get the quality of information needed, but do not risk more than is necessary for each level of commitment.

figure 1-8
Developer Exposure over Time

The money that a developer can lose if a project fails is illustrated here for a 160-unit, bond-financed apartment project. Exposure is greatest just before bond closing when the developer has invested $270,000 in a project that could still fall apart if the bonds fail to close.

Month	Activity	Cost	Total Investment to Date	Current Value to Date	Exposure
1	**Land optioned**	$15,000	$15,000	$0	$15,000
	Extensions	21,000			
	Architecture	10,000			
	Inducement	10,000			
7	**Inducement received**		56,000	0[a]	56,000
9	**Land closing**	388,000	444,000	403,000[b]	41,000[c]
	Architecture	10,000			
	Appraisal and market study	10,000			
10	**Fannie Mae commitment**	24,000	488,000[d]	403,000	85,000
	Architecture	15,000			
	Engineering	20,000			
	Equity syndication	50,000			
	Bond costs	100,000			
15	**Bond rate secured**		673,000[e]	403,000	270,000
16	**Bonds closed**	338,000	1,011,000[f]	0	

[a] The inducement is transferable but has a one-year limit.

[b] The land value had increased by an amount sufficient to cover sales commission costs if it had to be resold.

[c] At the time of closing on the land, the earnest money ($15,000) is recovered.

[d] The Fannie Mae commitment adds value only if bonds can be sold.

[e] Most legal costs have no value if the bonds are not closed.

[f] At bond closing, the risks are substantially eliminated, as all financing parameters are fixed.

Source: Stages of investment for August Park Apartments, Dallas, Texas, developed by Peiser Corporation and Jerome Frank Investments.

figure 1-9
Typical Months Elapsed for Development of a Small Office or Apartment Building

Stage of Development	Area with Few Regulations	Area with Many Regulations
1. Earnest Money Contract Signed	0	0
2. Earnest Money Committed	1	1
3. Market Study	2	2
4. Preliminary Design	3	3
5. Engineering Studies	5	6
6. Approvals[a]	6	24[b]
7. Financing Commitment	7	26
8. Working Drawings and Building Permits	9	36[c]
9. Land Purchase and Construction Loan Closed[d]	9	36

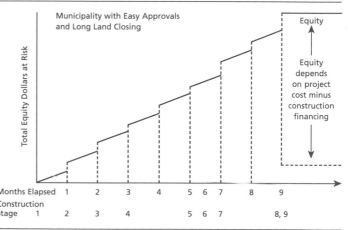

[a] Assuming no zoning changes are necessary.

[b] Environmental, political, design review, and other approvals can take two to five years.

[c] Building permits can take six to nine months after working drawings are finalized.

[d] Most sellers require closing on the land sooner than nine months, but the deal should not be finalized without tentative financing commitments and approvals in place.

Conclusion

Real estate development requires many different talents and skills for managing people and managing risk. Development is fundamentally a creative process, and managing creative people and motivating them to do their best work is one of the elements necessary for success. Development involves solving numerous problems. No matter how well planned a project is, unexpected events arise that the developer must overcome.

Beginning developers come from all facets of the real estate industry. They face a much harder road than experienced developers do, because they not only are going through the steps of development for the first time but also must establish many new relationships with advisers, consultants, professionals, financiers, and others involved in the process. For that reason, a simple, more straightforward project is preferred. The first project should not set a new precedent or require difficult public approvals or new forms of financing. Beginning developers have enough problems simply delivering a successful project. One should not take on additional burdens that even experienced developers shy away from.

Jerry Rappaport offers the following advice to beginning developers:[10]

- Use your competitive advantage, whatever it is, to *source* deals. If you find them, the money will come.
- Control over your life is a complete myth. The deal grabs you by both ankles and pulls you down.
- Take a long view of the business. You won't make it all happen in one transaction.

The key to successful development is serving the needs of a particular segment of the market in a particular location. In almost every instance, it also means serving the needs of a particular individual (whether a mayor, corporate president, business owner, landowner, or homebuyer), who must have his or her needs met in a particular manner. Above all, it requires understanding what the local market is missing. No one—not even the most experienced developer—has a monopoly on this knowledge. Beginning developers succeed by identifying an opportunity and pressing ahead. They will face obstacles that they cannot envision in advance, but perseverance, hard work, and integrity will enable them to succeed.

Notes

1. Phil Hughes, president of Hughes Investments, Inc., Greenville, South Carolina, reviewed this chapter and provided numerous suggestions that have been incorporated into the text.
2. Richard Peiser, "Can Development Be Taught in the Classroom?" *Urban Land*, July 1987, pp. 2–5. See ULI's *Directory of Real Estate Development and Related Education Programs* (9th ed.) for a list of more than 60 undergraduate and advanced degree programs.
3. The issue of net worth is significant for construction lenders, who need to be satisfied that the developer has sufficient financial resources to pay the bank back if the project goes sour. Although they may consider the total net worth of all general partners, they are more likely to prefer that one partner has net worth equal to the maximum loan commitment, because it is likely to cost more in legal fees to collect from several partners with smaller net worths than from one high-net-worth individual.

   Underwriting criteria for lenders are discussed in detail in Chapter 4. In most cases, the developer must be personally liable on the construction loan, meaning that his entire fortune is at risk in the event of a default on the loan. Banks have different criteria for determining what sufficient net worth is. Some banks may look at total assets minus total liabilities, giving real estate full value in the computation of net worth. Other banks may require liquid net worth in excess of the loan amount in the form of cash, stocks, and bonds. This hurdle can be difficult for real estate developers, most of whose net worth is often tied up in property.
4. Operating risk may be higher for smaller projects than for larger projects, however, because the loss of one tenant can jeopardize the project's cash flow. Further, a small apartment or small office project costs more to operate per dwelling unit or per square foot. Nevertheless, total development risk is lower for a smaller project.
5. When money is widely available, the market is likely to be hot, with lots of activity. In such times, sellers are more likely to demand shorter closing times and shorter free-look periods during which the buyer does feasibility studies before putting up nonrefundable deposit money *(going hard)*.
6. Phil Hughes adds that the definition of a developer ought to include the ability to control the process. He distinguishes between a full developer and a fee developer, who faces many of the same risks and rewards but does not control the project because he works for somebody else. "This is also true for 'corporate developers,' who are not satisfying themselves personally but satisfying committees and others. The whole of the corporate committee and the development manager make up the 'developer.' A developer has risk/reward and control. Otherwise, he is someone's employee."
7. Stan Ross, ULI Spring Meeting, May 11, 2000, Miami, Florida.
8. Larger developers commonly choose to diversify into a new area; they have a major advantage that beginning developers do not—staying power. Out-of-state developers might bring to a community a new concept or design that sometimes succeeds and sometimes fails. When developers from the Northeast entered the Dallas market, for example, they introduced a split-level house that had been extremely successful in the Northeast. The plan failed because local homebuyers had different tastes. To the developer's credit, the product was redesigned to meet local preferences and, in the end, did very well. If the developers had done more market research before entering the market, however, they might have avoided a costly mistake.
9. Accuracy is measured by how narrow the range is around an estimate. Statistically, it is defined by the standard deviation of the estimate. For example, a construction cost estimate of $100,000 with a standard deviation of $10,000 means that actual costs should range from $90,000 to $110,000 68 percent of the time. A standard deviation of $20,000 means that the costs should range from $80,000 to $120,000 68 percent of the time.
10. "Under the Radar Screen: Success Strategies for Small-Scale Developers," ULI Spring Meeting, May 11, 2000, Miami, Florida.

2. Organizing for Development

The Firm's Organization and Management

No matter how talented an individual, development is a team effort. A development team can be put together in one of several ways. At one extreme, a large company might include many services, from architecture to engineering. At the other end of the spectrum, a development company might consist of one principal and a few staff who hire or contract with other companies and professionals for each service as needed.

Indeed, from the perspective of organization, development can be a low-cost business that is relatively easy to enter, assuming one has the credibility and relationships needed to access significant capital. A development company can be started by just one person and with little or no investment in equipment or supplies beyond, perhaps, an office. Further, small developers are often able to compete effectively against larger developers. Although larger developers might obtain better prices in some areas and have easier access to money, they also tend to have higher overhead expenses.

The key to success for small developers is the quality of their development team and their access to capital. Small developers can often use the same professional consultants as larger developers, and beginning developers can acquire considerable credibility in the market-

Pictured at left is Mercado Plaza, a mixed-use development in Palm Springs, California.

place simply by selecting their development team members judiciously.

One way to maintain a small, lean organization is to use consultants rather than in-house staff. To select a consultant who will enhance the team:

- find the best person or company available, even if it costs a little more;
- make certain that person or company has direct experience with the particular type of product under consideration;
- select people who are familiar with local conditions; and
- consult with other developers to see how well the consultant under consideration has performed other jobs.

Finding the best team for the job takes an enormous amount of time. From the day they start in business, beginners should start obtaining names of prospects and interviewing them. Assembling a team from scratch is difficult; more experienced developers have already established a network of consultants, contractors, and professionals, and building a permanent team takes more than one project. Nonetheless, the time and effort spent in finding the best possible team is a good investment.

Forming Partnerships

The safest partnerships are those in which the partners have a long history of working together or in which all partners have faith in the honesty and integrity of their

When CIGNA invested in 1,025,545 square feet (95,300 square meters) of space at Shawnee Ridge in Atlanta, developer IDI entered into a partnership so that it could retain 10 percent ownership of the six buildings purchased by the insurance company.

©1999 Gary Knight and Associates/Courtesy IDI

fellow partners. Partnerships are frequently formed around specific projects. Developers, especially beginning developers, might have different sets of partners for each of several projects. Partnership arrangements usually evolve over time. Initial deals might involve several partners, each filling a major function—financing, leasing, or construction, for example. In subsequent deals, the number of partners might diminish as the developer becomes better able to obtain the needed expertise without giving a piece of the equity.

Landowners are often partners in a beginner's early projects because they not only supply equity for the deal but also make it possible to tie up the land for sufficient time to obtain the necessary approvals and financing. Key tenants might also be offered partnerships to induce them to lease space in the project; this policy is especially effective if the project can be designed around the tenant's specific needs. Both landowners and tenants, however, generally prefer to limit their risk, which can be accomplished by making them limited partners.

A common mistake in forming partnerships is to choose partners with similar rather than complementary skills. Partnerships that work the best are those in which everyone shares equally in the risks and returns and is equally able to cover potential losses. In most partnerships, however, one person is wealthier than the others and will understandably be concerned about ending up with greater risk, even if the partnership allocates this burden equally. One way to address this concern is to specify that a partner who is unable to advance the necessary share of capital loses his interest. Another way is to give the wealthier partner more of the return, or less of the workload, to compensate for greater potential liability.

A major source of problems in partnerships, especially general partnerships in which everyone has equal interests, is uneven distribution of the workload or lack of appropriate compensation for those partners handling the day-to-day work of creating and implementing a project or projects. The partners doing more work resent

those doing less work, and the situation can lead to difficulties. One way to address this problem is to determine responsibilities in advance. When they are unequal, the partners doing more work might be given specific compensation. For example, one partner might receive a greater share of the construction fee, with another receiving more of the leasing fee. (To save cash, it might be preferable to accrue the fees rather than to pay them as earned so long as there is adequate funding to meet expenses and provide a "living wage" to the working partners.)

Because partnerships can last for years, the choice of partners is a critical decision. Large developers who bring in less-experienced partners for specific deals generally enjoy a rather one-sided partnership, ensuring them management control; beginning developers, however, do not have the negotiating power of larger, more experienced developers.

Working out the partnership arrangement on paper in advance, preferably with an attorney, is especially important. A written agreement from the outset that defines each partner's role, responsibilities, cash contributions, and share of liabilities and sets out criteria for the dissolution of the partnership is an essential document. Many partners of general partnerships formed casually and on the basis of verbal assurances have been shocked to discover that they are liable for their partners' debts for events that had nothing to do with the partnership's purposes.

The ideal partnership combines someone with extensive development experience and someone whose credit is sufficient to obtain financing—that is, someone with a net worth at least equal to the total cost of the project under consideration. When money or economic conditions are soft, banks might require a net worth two or three times that of the project in question. If the partnership does not include someone with sufficient credit, then the partners will have to find someone to play that role before they can proceed. In the past, many savings and loan associations (S&Ls) and some life insurance companies had subsidiaries that engaged in joint ventures with developers. Few, however, worked with beginning developers. Today, individual investors or other developers with the necessary net worth and liquidity are more promising candidates for partnerships with beginners.

Bringing in any financial partner before the full requirements for cash equity and the amount of net worth are known is a mistake. If, for example, the financial partner is to provide the necessary financial statement and, say, $800,000 cash equity for 50 percent of the deal, the developer may be required to give up an unnecessarily high amount of ownership if he later finds that an additional $100,000 cash equity is needed. On the other hand, with no financial partner waiting in the wings, a prospective lender could lose interest while the developer is locating one. The ideal situation is to line up one or more prospects in advance.

Organizational Life Cycles

The life cycle of development firms resembles the product life cycle of modern marketing theory. Development firms pass through three stages—startup, growth, and maturity—and each stage is characterized by different risks and opportunities. "These risks and opportunities, combined with the firm's organizational strengths and weaknesses and the personal values of the developer-entrepreneur leading the firm, are the elements that must be evaluated in formulating a strategic plan."[1]

Startup. Startup is characterized by the establishment and attainment of two short-term goals—successfully completing the first few projects and making enough money to cover overhead. During this stage, firms are more likely to be *merchant builders,* selling their projects after they are completed and leased, rather than *investment builders,* holding them for long-term investment. "During the startup period, the developer's entrepreneurial skills are the critical ingredient. The developer has to develop contacts—with financial lenders, political leaders, investment bankers, major tenants, architects, engineers, and other consultants. Eternal optimism and the ability to withstand rejection are essential."[2]

A common pitfall during startup is to become overextended before the company has developed the staff and procedures to handle greater activity. When tenants or buyers begin to sense that a developer is not responding to their needs quickly enough, that developer's reputation is likely to suffer. The developer must build staff to handle not only increased volume but also procedures for dealing with accounting, processing, leasing, tenant complaints, lender reports, construction, property management, and project control.

Another common mistake that beginning developers make is hiring too many people too quickly. A startup business never has enough cash, and those who watch the overhead closely during startup tend to fare better than those whose first priority is projecting a high-profile image. Some of the most successful developers have built thousands of apartment units and millions of square feet of industrial and office space with a professional staff of only three or four people, contracting with consultants for virtually everything.

Growth. A firm in the growth stage has achieved a measure of success. It has instituted procedures for running the business and has assembled a team of players to cover all the major development tasks. It is beyond the point at which a single mistake on a project can lead to bankruptcy and is in a position to shape its own future through the selection of projects and their location.

Maintaining the spirit of entrepreneurship is one of the hardest challenges for growing firms. As a firm grows, its success depends on its ability to avoid the bureaucratic trappings of large organizations. The need for quick decisions entails the direct involvement of the firm's principals, no matter how large the firm becomes. When the distance between the principals and the junior staff members becomes too large, the firm either loses its ability to compete at the opportune time or blunders into situations it could have avoided had the principals exercised better oversight.

Employees who are used to the freewheeling atmosphere of a startup organization sometimes resist the increased control and the management systems that are needed to ensure proper oversight by senior management. The firm must maintain an entrepreneurial environment, one that motivates and retains qualified, aggressive people. A one-person firm succeeds because that one person accepts risk, plans the tasks, organizes the approach, and controls everything. But when the firm succeeds and the company grows, a staff is necessary to handle the workload. One of the most difficult hurdles for an entrepreneurial developer to overcome is the transition from one-person leadership to a larger organization. Not only must the right staff be in place: the founder or founders must also be able to relinquish control.[3]

Many development firms are family firms. The difficult transition in this case is from one generation to another. Often, the normal conflicts between parents and children make it difficult for the founding parent to surrender management control to the next generation, and, even after the transfer, the parent remains in the background, giving directions. Many firms never make it through this transition.

Conflict also can arise in family firms when the second generation is eager to take risks and try new projects at a time when the founding generation is becoming more interested in preserving equity and more averse to risks. The founding generation is inclined to keep developing the same tried and true projects, concentrating on managing assets, while the younger generation wants to try new projects. If the founding generation cannot find the way to let the second generation pursue its goals or have a chance to fail, the younger generation may leave the firm, at least for a time. Recognizing this dynamic, some developer-parents insist that their children work for another firm for a period before they join the family firm. Sometimes, family development companies skip a generation; the second generation leaves the business to work elsewhere while the third generation enters the business. Thus, a successful transition keeps the firm alive. Wise managers foresee the problems and plan ahead for them, recognizing their children's needs to achieve success on their own.

Maturity. Firms reach maturity after they have established a track record of successful projects and have built an organization to handle them. Mature development companies have built a network of relations with financial, political, and professional players and have financial holding power, the so-called "deep pockets." These firms tend to focus on larger, sophisticated projects that tend to be more profitable and require fewer managers than smaller, less predictable projects. They also tend to involve less competition.

Mature firms are more averse to risk, and they fully comprehend the risks that they do take. They have built up a large net worth that the owners want to protect. They do not need to assume as much risk as they did previously, as lenders and equity investors are eager to participate with them. Developers can often avoid personal liability on notes, and financial partners are willing to assume most or all financial risk in return for an equity position in the project.

Several characteristics are common to all mature firms, regardless of their size, organization, and style of management:[4]

- They know how to manage market risk, particularly in overbuilt markets.
- They know how to distribute authority and responsibility within the firm as it grows.
- They know how to evaluate the firm's effectiveness and efficiency.
- Most important, they know how to find, challenge, compensate, and retain good people.

Organizational Structure

During startup, organizational structure is less an issue than it is during growth and maturity. In the early years, most developers resist formalized organizations. Everyone reports directly to the owner, who makes all the major decisions. As firms grow, the delegation of authority, especially in financially sensitive areas, becomes essential, because the owner's time and availability are limited. In many firms, "effecting organizational change within the firm [is] a wrenching rather than an evolutionary process. A common solution [is] to hire someone from the outside—a consultant or a new CEO—to assist in establishing clear goals and to instigate the organizational changes necessary to achieve them."[5]

In most firms, the principals control the same few decisions: the sites to purchase, financing arrangements and major leases, and sale of a project. A common practice among even very large firms is that the principals retain the responsibility for making deals, "the activities that rely on the personal contacts and [the] entrepreneurial . . . mentality. The remaining development responsibilities (site acquisition, political processing, financing, design,

construction management, and marketing) are typically delegated to the development staff."[6]

Development firms are usually organized by function, by project, or by some combination of function and project. Smaller firms are more likely to be organized by project, larger ones by function. That is, owners of small firms tend to appoint one individual (the project manager, who is often a partner) to be in charge of each project, with the group working on that project responsible for all aspects of it—financing, construction, marketing, leasing, and management. In large firms, on the other hand, one group is responsible for each of these functions in all projects.[7] In some organizations, employees report to two different managers, one responsible for function and the other for geographic area or product line. A firm's organizational structure often reflects how it has grown and evolved over time. Some of the largest firms have a project manager structure because they have grown by giving partners responsibility for specific geographic areas and/or product types.

Compensation

How to compensate senior managers is one of the major issues facing the owners of a development firm. One answer is to give key individuals equity in the firm. According to John O'Donnell, chair of the O'Donnell Group in Newport Beach, California, "The reason you give employees equity is you can't pay them what they would command on the open market. Instead, you give them a stake in the future." With middle managers, "We're not basing our future on these people, so we compensate them with cash instead."[8] Orange County, California, developer Baron Birtcher adds: "Regional partners receive real equity because they are at risk. Project managers receive phantom equity."

Computed from profits like a bonus, phantom equity becomes an important incentive for project managers. Unlike real equity, however, the individual does not legally own an interest in the project and incurs no risk. If the individual leaves the company, tracking him or her down for a signature every time a legal event occurs is not necessary, and, if a partnership includes more than one property, phantom equity avoids the problem of having to create a new class of project-specific interest.

O'Donnell's firm measures the performance of each property each year and contributes the appropriate share of the manager's profit to a phantom equity account. If, for example, the property makes $100,000 and the manager has a 5 percent interest in it, the account is credited $5,000. If the property loses $100,000, the employee does not have to cover his share of the loss out of pocket, but any advances from the company to cover losses are repaid before profits are distributed. In this way, the employee does not have to worry about raising cash to cover potential liabilities.

Many firms provide for a period of five to ten years before an employee's phantom equity in projects becomes vested. O'Donnell's firm, for example, might give an employee 2.5 percent of a project after three to five years

The York Companies is a family firm with four generations active or formerly active. Smedes York is president or chair of all firms except McDonald-York, where he is a member of the board. The construction and real estate companies offer a full line of services in construction, real estate development, sales, and management of both commercial and residential real estate in the Raleigh, North Carolina, area.

York Properties

York Properties is a full-service real estate company involved in all aspects of real estate. It does not own real estate; thus, all of its work is as a third party. Some of its work is with entities owned by the York Companies. It is involved in residential brokerage through its ownership position in York Simpson Underwood.

- *Executive Committee*
  Smedes York
  Hal V. Worth III
  Joe Kalkhurst

- *Property Management*
  Lamont Farmer, manager

  Shopping centers
  Office buildings
  Apartments
  Industrial buildings
  Homeowners associations

- *Maintenance and Services*
  General maintenance
  Landscaping
  Grounds maintenance
  Security

- *Shopping Center Management and Leasing*
  Lynne Worth, vice president
  George York, vice president

- *Development and Acquisitions*
  Settle Dockery, manager

- *Commercial Brokerage*
  Joe Kalkhurst, manager

York Simpson Underwood (Residential Brokerage)

York Simpson Underwood has approximately 200 agents involved throughout the Research Triangle, North Carolina, area.

- *Board of Directors*
  Smedes York, chair
  Joe Kalkhurst
  Sam Simpson
  Speck Underwood

- *Associated Companies*
  Affiliated Mortgage
  Clark Properties
  Tri Pointe
  YSU Neighborhood Marketing Services

- *Offices*
  Cameron Village
  North Hills
  North Raleigh
  Cary
  Chapel Hill
  Southern Pines

McDonald-York (General Contractors)

McDonald-York is a general contractor that bids or negotiates contracts for all types of construction up to about $10 milllion to $15 million on a single contract.

Jack McDonald, president
Smedes York, board member

York Family Properties (Property Ownership)

York Family Properties owns various types of real estate.

Smedes York, general partner
Phil York, general partner ■

---

of employment. Each year after the employee becomes vested, he or she receives an additional 0.5 percent, up to a limit of 5 percent. Employees who become vested with 2.5 percent interest beginning in the fifth year, for example, will own 4 percent of the projects with which they are associated after eight years. If someone leaves the company, O'Donnell retains the right to buy out that person's interest at any time based on a current appraisal of the property. He also has the sole right to select the appraiser. If someone leaves the company without notice, he might buy out that employee's interest immediately. On the other hand, a long-time secretary who leaves to start a family or a manager who gives advance notice (say, three months) before leaving to start his own company might receive profit distributions for years, thus enjoying the project's full potential.

No magic formula exists for determining how much equity a developer should give away to attract top managers. Beginning developers may have to pay experienced project managers 25 percent of a project's profits, whereas established developers may need to pay only 1 to 5 percent. Employees' risks are lower with a more established developer, so their shares of the profit are lower. One major developer, for example, has three levels of participation, which are given not as rewards but as career paths. The lowest level is *principal*. Project managers who are star performers are eligible. They receive up to 10 percent (5 to 7.5 percent is typical) of a project in the form of phantom equity. The next level is *profit and loss (P&L) manager*, someone in charge of a city or county area. P&L managers are responsible for several projects and principals; they receive 15 to 20 percent of the profits from their areas. Their interest is also in the form of phantom equity. The top level is *general partner*, reserved for managers of a region, state, or several states. General partners receive real equity, are authorized to sign documents on the firm's behalf, and incur full risk.

The real estate crash in the early 1990s changed the way larger firms compensate their employees. According

figure 2-1

National Real Estate Compensation Survey, 2002

Position	Base Salary Range[a]		Potential Bonus as Percent of Salary	Actual Bonus as Percent of Salary[b]	
	High	Median	Average	Average	Highest
Executive					
President/CEO	$405,000	$290,000	91%	87%	400%
Chief Operating Officer	$336,200	$250,000	81%	77%	600%
Chief Investment Officer	$307,300	$243,400	79%	72%	194%
Top Division Executive	$226,100	$168,900	61%	58%	180%
Top Regional Executive	$220,800	$169,100	67%	58%	167%
Corporate					
Top Business Development Executive	$221,600	$177,400	63%	55%	267%
Top Human Resources Executive	$117,800	$89,000	28%	24%	150%
Benefits Manager/Specialist	$63,400	$52,300	11%	9%	36%
General Counsel	$238,900	$183,800	54%	49%	171%
Top MIS Executive/IT Director	$121,000	$94,500	27%	22%	148%
Network Administrator	$65,000	$53,000	13%	11%	60%
Communications/Investor Relations Executive	$121,600	$92,000	29%	24%	76%
Research Director	$113,500	$79,300	27%	25%	90%
Accounting/Finance					
CFO/Top Finance Executive	$258,600	$188,100	66%	62%	484%
Finance Director	$166,200	$131,100	35%	29%	100%
Controller	$111,200	$90,000	25%	23%	150%
Accounting Supervisor	$69,900	$60,000	14%	12%	52%
Financial Analyst	$67,500	$55,000	16%	14%	118%
Tax Manager	$102,900	$85,600	24%	20%	100%
Asset Management					
Top Asset Management Executive	$180,000	$144,000	47%	44%	180%
Asset or Portfolio Manager	$111,600	$82,900	36%	33%	141%
Property Management					
Top Property Management Executive	$167,200	$109,200	37%	31%	221%
Regional Vice President—Multifamily	$111,700	$91,300	23%	20%	52%
District Manager—Multifamily	$76,700	$63,000	20%	17%	96%

to Chris Lee, president of CEL & Associates in California, "We're seeing an increasing trend toward more cafeteria-style ways of constructing compensation packages. For some, benefits are important; for others, larger salaries and smaller bonuses are more important. Still others want smaller salaries and larger upside potential. It depends on the company. With regard to long-term incentive plans, firms are clearly trying to provide a way of holding onto key employees. There are tiered payout schedules extending over five to seven years or more. People who leave, therefore, will be leaving a lot of money on the table. You want to continually provide these hooks to keep people."[9]

Lee observes that truly qualified, top-notch professionals are in short supply in real estate. Firms therefore are developing very creative and highly motivating compensation packages. "Most of these talented professionals are in the boomer generation. They are moving into their fifties and are looking at the next five to ten years of their work life. They want to get as much as they can over the next decade. They are saying, 'Pay me a lot. I'm willing to stay here for ten years—just give me a good package that makes sense and I'll give you my all for the next decade, but I don't want to work year to year. I've got to find some sense of stability and security and know that I can create some value for myself for

Position	Base Salary Range[a]		Potential Bonus as Percent of Salary	Actual Bonus as Percent of Salary[b]	
	High	Median	Average	Average	Highest
On-Site Community Manager					
<300 units	$43,300	$34,900	14%	12%	38%
>300 units	$51,100	$43,600	14%	12%	35%
Property Manager					
Office/Industrial (<500,000 sf)	$64,700	$52,900	13%	11%	25%
Office/Industrial (500,001–1,000,000 sf)	$76,200	$65,000	14%	13%	48%
Office/Industrial (>1,000,000 sf)	$106,600	$89,900	17%	14%	29%
Retail (<300,000 sf)	$61,100	$52,000	12%	8%	17%
Retail (300,001–500,000 sf)	$71,800	$61,900	11%	10%	16%
Retail (500,001–750,000 sf)	$85,300	$73,700	12%	12%	18%
Mall Manager—Retail (>750,000 sf)	$112,300	$97,800	28%	23%	88%
Assistant Manager	$46,900	$35,100	11%	8%	30%
Corporate Facility Manager	$87,600	$75,600	11%	10%	15%
Marketing Manager—Retail	$64,700	$48,800	16%	21%	67%
Maintenance Supervisor	$49,300	$40,000	11%	10%	125%
Maintenance Engineer	$47,600	$34,100	8%	7%	65%
Project Management					
Development Executive	$175,800	$141,500	55%	52%	755%
Project Manager	$96,800	$82,200	30%	25%	195%
Construction Executive	$137,700	$111,300	35%	30%	110%
Leasing					
Top Leasing Executive	$173,500	$122,900	59%	52%	386%
Typical Leasing Agent	$88,200	$62,900	51%	43%	220%
On-Site Leasing Representative—Multifamily	$26,500	$22,100	14%	15%	59%
Acquisitions					
Top Acquisitions Executive	$198,800	$156,000	59%	53%	295%
Acquisitions Associate	$103,200	$82,400	28%	25%	81%

[a] Quartiles: High = 75th quartile, median = 50th quartile.

[b] Salary and/or extraordinary annual bonus awards intentionally excluded from this figure so as not to distort the results.

Source: CEL & Associates, Inc. © 2002 National Real Estate Compensation Survey, (310) 571-3113, www.celassociates.com.

the remainder of my work life.'"[10] Compensation for top performers is usually paid through bonuses rather than salary. Whereas bonuses of $50,000 or $100,000 were common in the 1990s, top performers now may see bonuses of $800,000 or more.

Lee says that personnel costs are probably 60 to 70 percent of most operating budgets, and they are the most critical component of a management or operating company. Benefit costs, especially for health care, continue to rise. Companies will pay a great deal for stars, but other workers will receive less money. Firms are also downsizing. They will use more outside contractors to fill interim needs. Lee says, "They just can't afford to pay everyone market rates [for high-end people] every day, all the time."

Strategic Planning

Most beginning developers—and even many large ones—do not have a business strategy. They respond to opportunities as they present themselves rather than deciding in advance the types of projects to pursue. Their strategy is by default rather than by design. After identifying a highly specific market, these developers look for sites that best meet the market's criteria. Such an approach helps developers build expertise that will give them a competitive advantage, and, as developers become known, brokers and landowners begin to bring suitable opportunities to their attention.

Regardless of size, however, every developer should have a strategic plan. Strategic planning helps to inculcate entrepreneurship as the firm grows. In small companies, the owner embodies the entrepreneurial spirit, but maintaining that spirit can be difficult as the firm grows. Entrepreneurship usually flourishes in a decentralized system comprising small groups with considerable autonomy. To set up a decentralized management system, a strategic plan generated by the decentralized entrepreneurial group is necessary. The plan should include budgets, a master schedule tied to the budget, and systems for approving and tracking projects. The accompanying feature box summarizes the major issues that strategic planning should address.[11]

The strategic plan helps the company to achieve its objectives faster, because everyone understands the firm's immediate goals and longer-term objectives; plans are the most effective when everyone has participated in preparing them. (Note that the business plan is strategic but the budget is tactical; that is, the budget lays out the specific tactics that will be used to follow the broad strategies laid out in the business plan.) The strategic plan culminates in an *action plan*, which should establish specific protocols for managers to follow—for example, policies for evaluating the competition and an area's long-term economic outlook.

Choosing Consultants and Contractors

Assembling a team of professionals to address the economic, physical, and political issues inherent in a complex development project is critical. A developer's success depends on the ability to coordinate the completion of a series of interrelated activities efficiently and at the appropriate time.

The development process requires the skills of many professionals: architects, landscape architects, and site planners to address project design; market consultants to determine demand and a project's economics; attorneys to handle agreements and government approvals; environmental consultants and soils engineers to analyze a site's physical limitations; surveyors and title companies to provide legal descriptions of a property; contractors to supervise construction; and lenders to provide financing.

Strategic Planning and Thinking: Planning the Business

Evaluate the present situation.
- What are the company's accomplishments?
- How do they compare with previous goals?
- Where is the company headed?
- How should it get there?
- What are the owner's or founders' interests and expectations?
- What is the external environment?
  - Market changes and trends
  - Changes affecting products and services
  - Opportunities from changes
  - New and old risks and rewards
  - Political environment
- Who are key competitors? Where do they excel?

Analyze the company's strengths and weaknesses.
- What properties has it developed, bought, marketed?
- How successful have they been?
- How has the firm done in the past?
  - Management capabilities
  - Threats
  - Opportunities
- What past decisions would be changed?

Specify goals for the strategic plan.
- What is the financial strategy?
- What is the firm's strategy regarding products?
  - Quality
  - Investor or merchant builder
- Does the company need to diversify its product?
- Does the company need to diversify its location?
- What is the company's strategy regarding land?
  - Land banking versus carrying land in slow times
  - Developed land versus raw land
- What is the marketing strategy?
- What is the strategy regarding production and construction?
- How does the company get the job done?
- What is its management and organizational strategy?

Specify an action plan—programs, steps, or tasks to be carried out—concerning risk, reward, and reality.
- What activities is the company engaged in now?
- What is the state of financial planning?

- Where do equity and debt come from?
- Are changes expected?
- How strong are financial suppliers?
- What will be its financial needs in the next 24 months, the next 36 months, or longer to meet strategic goals?
- What are the company's objectives? What measurable results is it committed to achieve?
- How strong will lines of communication and internal controls be for:
  - Financial results
  - Acquisition and development
  - Operations: property management, leasing, tenant improvements, customer relations
  - Controls and measurement
  - Responsibilities and budgets ∎

Source: Sanford Goodkin, president, Ackman Ziff Goodkin Real Estate Advisors, and chair, Horizon Strategies, LLC, Solana Beach, California.

Even the most seasoned developer finds that staying on top of all a project's technical details is difficult. Beginners especially must rely on the skillful support of an assembled team of professionals with the practical experience and technical knowledge required to deal with important issues.

Locating a Consultant

To begin the search for a consultant with particular expertise, developers should first seek the advice of successful local developers who have completed projects similar to the one under consideration. They should ask experienced developers about the consultants they use and their level of satisfaction with the consultants' work. Beginners should also remember, however, that established developers consider newcomers the competition, and it may take some time to build up the trust necessary for a frank exchange of opinions. Ralph Lewis of Lewis Homes, Upland, California, suggests that beginning developers join associations of local developers or their national organizations geared toward the real estate product of interest, be it residential, shopping centers, or business parks. The key is to become an active member in such organizations by serving on committees and making oneself known.

Developers should obtain a list of the consultants whose work has impressed public officials and their planning staffs. Certain approvals might hinge on the reputations of specific team members; indeed, part of consultants' value could lie in the connections they maintain with the public sector.

Associations of architects, planners, and other professionals are another source of potential consultants. Such organizations usually maintain rosters of members, which are useful as a screening tool because most professional and technical organizations have defined certain standards for their members. These standards might include a certain level of education and practical experience as well as a proficiency examination. Most associations publish trade magazines that provide a wealth of information about the field and are available in local public or college libraries. Such publications are likely to contain both advertisements placed by, and articles written by, consultants.

Selecting a Consultant

Strategies for selecting consultants vary according to the type of consultant being sought. The most common approach is a series of personal interviews. Beginners should not hesitate to reveal their inexperience with the issues being addressed or to ask potential consultants to explain clearly their duties. Consultants will profit by dealing with a developer, so they should be expected to take the time to explain the fundamentals.

A proper interview should address the developer's concerns regarding experience and attitudes. The developer should look for a consultant with extensive experience in developing similar projects. An architect or market consultant who has concentrated on single-family

In choosing consultants, it is important to establish who will be the project manager and what subconsultants are likely to be hired.

residential development would be inappropriate for a developer interested in an office or retail project.

The developer must be sure to ask for references and then must contact those references and inquire about the consultant's quality of work and business conduct, ability to deliver on time and within budget, receptivity to new ideas, and professional integrity.

The developer may also inspect some of the consultant's work—marketing or environmental reports, plans and drawings, and finished projects. The developer should be comfortable with the design philosophy of a prospective member of the creative team and satisfied with the technological competence of a potential analytical consultant. The technological explosion has resulted in an array of specialized computer applications tailored to solve specific problems. Software is available for everyone, from parking consultants to property managers, and can lead to more efficient use of time and reduced costs.

The developer must be certain that the chosen firm has the personnel and facilities available to take on the assignment. If a consultant appears to be struggling to keep up with current responsibilities, the project is likely to suffer from neglect.

Next, the developer should establish who will be the project's manager and request a meeting with that person, and then examine several projects for which that

Site Selection
- Brokers
- Title companies
- Market consultants

Feasibility Study
- Market consultants
- Economic consultants
- Mortgage brokers and bankers
- Engineers

Design
- Architects
- General contractors
- Surveyors
- Soils engineers
- Structural engineers
- Environmental consultants

- Land planners
- Landscape architects
- Parking consultants

Financing
- Mortgage brokers and bankers
- Construction lenders
- Permanent lenders
- Title companies
- Appraisers

Construction
- Architects
- General contractors
- Engineers
- Landscape architects
- Surety companies

Marketing
- Brokers
- Public relations firms
- Advertising agencies
- Graphic artists

Operations
- Property managers

Sale
- Brokers
- Appraisers

Throughout the Process
- Attorneys

---

project manager was responsible. Moreover, the developer is well advised to find out what subconsultants the firm would be likely to hire.

Hiring a firm is a two-way street. While the developer is sizing up the consultant, a similar process is going on across the table. Displaying a positive attitude about the project and the consultant's potential contributions is especially important. A beginning developer should not be offended when the consultant asks about his experience and competence to complete a development project, the existence of adequate financial resources to pay the bills, the feasibility of the proposal, and the ability to make timely decisions. Consultants need to be confident about a developer's ability to meet obligations.

Finally, the developer should judge whether he has established a rapport with the people being considered during the preliminary interview. The ability to get along with these people is essential for the project's completion, so if problems arise at this point, the developer should consider whether dealing with them daily is possible. Compatibility is a key to the project's success—and to preserving the developer's sanity.

If, after checking references, the developer feels uncomfortable with any aspect of the consulting firm, eliminating the firm from further consideration may be the most sensible move. If the developer's responses are favorable about the firm as a whole but not about the particular person being assigned to the project, he should raise these concerns with the firm. A larger firm should have another staff person available, but a smaller firm may not. The developer must be assured that the most qualified people will be assigned to the project.

Rates

Consultants should willingly quote a fee for their services, presenting it as a written proposal reflecting the costs for

delivery of the desired product. Developers should be careful not to choose simply the lowest price; although cost is an important factor, it must be balanced by experience and the quality of the consultant's past work. Developers should compare the proposed budgets to see how the money is allocated and identify the differences in proposals to judge whether the numbers are reasonable. They should also ensure that the prices include the same types of services. For example, a lower fee could possibly exclude services that later will be required, necessitating future additional charges. A lower quotation might also exclude the amount needed to cover unforeseen incidents.

Once a firm has been selected, most developers prefer to employ a fixed-price contract, using the figures quoted in the proposal. Payment can be made in several ways, depending on the nature of the product to be delivered. A schedule could be used to establish milestones, such as the delivery of a specified product that triggers an agreed-upon payment, or developers might find that allowing projections of cash flow to establish a monthly schedule is more advantageous. Smaller jobs might require a lump-sum payment upfront.

Like lawyers, consultants often work according to a time and materials (T&M) agreement, with developers billed according to staff members' hourly rates and the cost of materials used to complete the task. The cost of materials includes reimbursable expenses, such as telephone calls and photocopying. T&M agreements are complicated, however, and require constant monitoring to verify the amounts that are being billed.

Retainer agreements that pay the consultant a flat monthly fee should be avoided because such arrangements can be very costly in the long run. A retainer requires a monthly payment, regardless of whether or not work is completed.

Regardless of the chosen method of compensation, both the developer and the consultant must negotiate a mutually agreeable performance contract. The contract must explicitly list each duty that the consultant is expected to complete. Services not included in the agreement probably will require future negotiations that will most likely lead to additional costs for the developer. The contract should clearly spell out a schedule for the delivery of services, including a definitive date for delivery of the final product.

Working with Consultants

After the parties sign the agreement, the working relationship with the consultant begins. The developer must work closely with the consultant to ensure that everything proceeds according to schedule. The development team is made up of a group of players whose tasks are interrelated, and the tardiness or shoddy work of a single firm could set off a chain reaction and cause costly delays.

As the team leader, the developer must ensure that each consultant is provided with accurate information and that information produced by one consultant is relayed to the others. Any changes in the project's concept should be communicated immediately. The developer must be sensitive to the impact that changes in the project will have on the consultants' collective analysis; sudden change could alter requirements for the design, environmental analyses, and parking, for example. Any alterations could be costly, as consultants might demand extra compensation to address the changing elements of the project.

A healthy working relationship with consultants is vital. Developers should seek to contribute information and to ask questions throughout the process but should also show a willingness to accept consultants' ideas. Good consultants can decrease development costs and improve a project's marketability.

A developer must have the management skill necessary to coordinate consultants' efforts while ensuring that all parties respect the developer's ultimate authority to make decisions. Problems can also occur, however, when a developer's ego gets in the way of good advice. A good developer knows when to listen to and accept the advice of others.

The Design/Construction Team

The design/construction team includes an array of consultants and contractors who perform tasks ranging from site analysis and planning to building design and construction management. The work that they perform and/or manage represents the bulk of the project's total costs, and effectively managing their contributions is critical to the success of the development project.

Architects

Both beginning and experienced developers depend on architects for advice and guidance. Some developers appoint the architect to head the design portion of a project, although most developers prefer to be their own team leaders. Beyond experience with design, architects have extensive experience with the regulatory and physical constraints placed on development and are a valuable asset in communicating with other consultants and in coordinating design.

The search for an architect must be very thorough. Only those firms and individuals whose experience is compatible with the proposed project should be considered. The developer should always check a firm's credentials and make sure that it is licensed in the state where the project will be built; government planning and building departments will not approve projects unless the architect is licensed by the state.

The developer and the architect must share a common philosophy of design, and the developer must feel comfortable with the architect selected. A good architect respects the developer's opinions. At the same time, the developer must consider every decision but respect the architect's knowledge and experience. Mutual respect is essential. Some developers prefer to hire an architect whose work has withstood the test of time; others look for an architect known for innovative designs that make a distinctive statement and may give the developer a competitive advantage.

When the developer has found an architect whose work could enhance the project, the next step is to reach a written agreement. A standard contract provided by the American Institute of Architects (AIA) provides the basis for defining the relationship between developer and architect. AIA Document B151, *Agreement between Owner and Architect,* clearly outlines the architect's duties in the development process and is widely used in real estate development. Developers should remember, however, that this agreement was written from architects' perspective and seeks to protect their interests.[12] In some circumstances, modifications to the AIA agreement form are appropriate.

Sometimes architects are given responsibility for all facets of the project's design as well as selecting and supervising land planners, engineers (except soils engineers), landscape architects, and parking consultants, as well as all facets of the project's design. Few experienced developers recommend this practice, however.

The design phase lasts from the creation of the initial concept to the completion of the final drawings. The design is based on a program provided by the developer that outlines the project's general concept, most notably its identified uses and amenities. Initially, the architect prepares schematic drawings that include general floor and site plans and that propose basic materials and physical systems. A construction cost estimator or contractor should review the design to assess its economic implications. These schematic drawings are an important component in presentations to lenders. Most major design decisions are made at the schematic drawing stage. The design team should include not only the contractor but also leasing and property management representatives. If those team members are not yet named, then the developer should ask potential contractors, brokers, and property managers to review and criticize the preliminary drawings. Changes are much cheaper to make at this stage than later.

After the developer approves the preliminary design, the architect produces specification drawings, also called *working drawings*. Specifications include detailed drawings of the materials to be incorporated with the mechanical, electrical, plumbing, and heating, ventilating, and air-conditioning (HVAC) systems. Generally, drawings pass through several iterations before the final plans and specifications are finished. The developer should review these interim drawings, referred to as 25 percent, 50 percent, 75 percent, or 95 percent complete. After addressing all the developer's concerns, the architect completes final drawings.

In reviewing partially completed designs, the developer should pay particular attention to the implications for potential users by visualizing how commercial tenants or residents will react to the design, asking brokers, tenants, and other developers to identify the needs of the target groups and soliciting real estate professionals' comments on the design drawings as they progress.

The next phase of the architect's duties involves compiling the construction documents, including the package used to solicit bids from contractors. This package includes the rules for bidding, standard forms detailing the components of the bid, conditions for securing surety bonds, detailed specifications identifying all components of the bid, and detailed working drawings. The developer also relies on the architect's experience to analyze the bids and to help select the best contractor for the job.

Once construction begins, the architect is responsible for monitoring—but not supervising—the work site. The architect is expected to inspect the site periodically to determine whether contract documents are being adequately followed. Constant monitoring is beyond the scope of the architect's responsibility and requires additional compensation.

The developer also relies on the architect to confirm that predetermined phases during construction have been satisfactorily completed. The approval involves a *certificate of completion* necessary for disbursement of the contractor's fee. The AIA provides another preprinted certificate that addresses the architect's liability resulting from confirmation, noting that the architect's inspections are infrequent, that defects could be covered between visits, and that the architect can never be entirely sure that construction has been completed according to the plan.

The relationship between architect and developer follows one of two models. The *design-award-build* contract breaks the project into two distinct phases, with the architect completing the design phase before the developer submits the project for contractors' bid. The other alternative, the *fast-track* approach, involves the contractor during the early stages of design, because the contractor's input at this stage could suggest ways to save on costs, making the project more economical and efficient to construct.

The fast-track method is primarily a cost-saving device, as it uses time efficiently to reduce the holding costs incurred during design. The developer is able to demolish existing structures, begin excavation and site preparation, and complete the foundation before the architect completes the final drawings. One risk involved with the fast-track approach, however, is that the project is under construction before costs have been determined.

Several methods are available for compensating architects for their services, including T&M agreements and fixed-price contracts. The latter specify the amount that the architect will receive for completing the basic services outlined in the performance contract; any duties not listed in the contract are considered supplementary and require additional compensation. Another method calculates architectural fees as a fixed percentage (usually 3 to 5 percent) of a project's hard costs. Architects contend that this method fairly accounts for a project's complexity, thus equating cost with an elaborate development. The disadvantage of this method is that it provides little incentive to the architect to economize, as higher costs guarantee higher fees. Often it is appropriate to engage the architect on the basis of T&M during project conceptualization and then shift to a fixed-price arrangement when the project is more defined and subject to better quantification.

Regardless of the mode of calculating compensation, the architect is always entitled to additional reimbursable expenses—travel, telephone calls, photocopying, and other out-of-pocket expenses.

Landscape Architects

Landscape architects do much more than plant trees and flowers. Landscape architects work with existing conditions—topography, soil composition, and vegetation on a site—to create a distinctive site that will provide a sense of place for the project. They are responsible for working with the architect to produce an external environment that enhances the development, for devising a planting and landscape plan, and for incorporating components into the project like plants, trees, furnishings (benches, for instance), artwork, and signs. Landscape architects also can save energy costs by selecting plants that provide shade and solve drainage problems.

Landscape architects first develop preliminary plans and then manage the completion of those plans. They obtain bids, complete working drawings and final specifications, prepare a schedule, and inspect the site to verify that the contractor implements the plan correctly.

Hiring the landscape architect can be the architect's responsibility, but developers should inspect the chosen landscape architect's work to determine that they are comfortable with the design philosophy. The American Society of Landscape Architects maintains rosters and certifies its members. Landscape architects work on a lump-sum basis to complete working drawings and speci-

North elevation and section of the academic complex for Baruch College, City University of New York. The project, built on a fast-track schedule, was completed in fall 2001.

Zoning dictated the shape of the structure, which contains 40 percent of the college's total campus area in one building envelope. To minimize its bulk, architects Kohn Pedersen Fox Associates designed faceted walls with a variety of materials.

©Michael Moran

fications and, generally, on an hourly basis to supervise completion of the plans.

Land Planners

With land development projects and larger building projects, land planners allocate the desired uses to maximize the site's total potential and determine the most efficient layout for adjacent uses, densities, and infrastructure. Individual building projects usually rely on the judgment of the architect and market consultants. The land planner's goal is to produce a plan with good internal circulation, well-placed uses and amenities, and adequate open space. Land planners should prepare several schemes that expand on the developer's proposal and discuss the pros and cons of each with the developer. The developer coordinates the land planner's activities with input from marketing, engineering, economic, and political consultants to ensure that the plan is marketable, efficient, and financially and politically feasible. On land development projects, the land planner is the principal professional consultant. Reputation and past projects are the best indicators of a land planner's ability. A key characteristic to look for in a land planner is the ability to work well with the project engineer.

Engineers

Engineers play a vital role in the development of a building. Several types of engineers with specific expertise—structural, mechanical, electrical, civil—are required to ensure that the design can accommodate the required physical systems. They are generally engaged by the project architect and maintain a very close relationship with the architectural staff as the project design unfolds.

Because it is necessary for a close working relationship between these experts, the most prudent strategy is to seek input from the architect when selecting all the project engineers. Larger architectural firms often have an in-house engineering staff; smaller firms prefer to hire individual engineers project by project. The success of the design phase, which includes the overall project design and adherence to the development budget, depends on the effectiveness of this working relationship and is a point not to be overlooked.

Although the architect may make the initial recommendations, the developer should reserve the right to select engineers after inspecting their qualifications, reviewing previously completed projects of the same scope and property type, including interviewing the project's proponent, and checking their working references with various general contractors and local building inspectors.

Engineers must be licensed by each state in which they operate; plans cannot receive approvals unless signed by a professional engineer licensed in the state where the project will be constructed. Several engineering trade organizations—among them the American Society of Heating, Refrigerating and Air-Conditioning Engineers, the American Society of Mechanical Engineers, and the National Society of Professional Engineers—promote best practices and continuous learning among their members.

Landscape architects work with project architects to create an exterior environment that enhances the building's design.

The architect usually hires engineers as subcontractors and is responsible for managing their deliverables. Engineers are generally required on all projects, including new developments, renovations, or additions to existing structures. The engineer's fee schedule is usually included in the architect's budget and generally ranges from 4 to 7 percent of the overall architectural fee. As subcontractors, engineers are paid by the architect; nonpayment or default by the architect can sometimes result in a *mechanics lien* on the property.

During the initial design phase, the architect works with the engineers to develop and modify working drawings to accommodate the project's structural, HVAC, electrical, and plumbing systems. Each engineer provides a detailed set of drawings showing the physical design of the systems for which the engineer is responsible.

Structural engineers assist the architect in designing the building's structural integrity. They work closely with soils engineers to determine the most appropriate foundation system and produce a set of drawings for the general contractor explaining that system in detail, especially the structural members' sizing and connections.

Mechanical engineers design the building's HVAC systems, including mechanical plant locations, air flow requirements, and any special heating or cooling requirements such as computer rooms in office buildings or isolation wards in hospitals. They are also responsible for the building's plumbing design.

Electrical engineers design the electrical power and distribution systems, including lighting, circuitry, and backup power supplies; civil engineers design the on-site utility systems, sewers, streets, and site grading.

Effective project coordination relies on upfront communication and should be coordinated early in the process. Experienced developers generally facilitate a series of meetings with all architectural and engineering project personnel to define scope and communication channels and to discuss each discipline's goals and objectives in depth. For example, if the goal is to construct a high-efficiency building with systems that result in lower operating costs—digital thermostats, centralized off-site HVAC system controls, automatic water closets—these project aims need to be spelled out early in the process. Developers should be aware of cost tradeoffs between higher development costs and lower ongoing operating expenses and be prepared to make decisions accordingly.

Ronald Stenlund, president of Central Consulting Engineers, advises developers and their engineers to insist on two-year warrantees on all installed mechanical systems.[13] It is vital that each component, particularly for a building's heating and cooling systems, go through a full season of startup and shutdown, as a one-year guarantee is the industry standard and generally begins on the *shipping* date rather than the *installation* date. Further, maintenance people must be properly trained in the nuances of each system and gain familiarity with their operations.

The biggest concern of all developers is having their soft costs come in over budget. According to Stenlund, "Failure to achieve effective communication among the developer, architect, and engineering staff early in the process is the single most common cause for project delays, redesigns, and cost overruns. Coordinating the team early, defining expectations, and developing a congruent project vision are the three keys to minimizing this risk factor."

Soils Engineers

Experienced developers recommend completing a soils test on a site before purchasing the property. Soils engineers conduct an array of tests to determine a site's soil stability, the level of its water table, the presence of any toxic materials, and any other conditions that will affect construction. Geotechnical engineering is not an exact science, but hiring skilled, registered professionals reduces uncertainty.

A soils engineer first removes a cross section of the soil by boring the surface of the site to a specified depth. That sample is then analyzed. Laboratory tests disclose the characteristics of the soil at various levels, the firmness of each of those levels, and the presence of toxic materials. On smaller sites with no water or other potential problems, one boring test in the middle may be sufficient. On other sites, boring tests are usually completed in the middle and near the anticipated building corners. If the presence of toxic materials is suspected across the site, six or more borings may be necessary.

The soils engineer prepares a detailed report on the composition of the underlying soil, complete with an analysis of the characteristics of each layer. Soil composition is classified according to color, grain size, and firmness. Subsurface soils range from loose composition, such as gravel and sand, to solid clay and peat. The soils engineer also recommends the type of foundation system most appropriate for the site, based on the laboratory findings and tests to determine the soil's strength.

A bearing test determines the soil's ability to support the planned structure at the anticipated depth of the foundation. The soils engineer digs out a portion of the site to the designated level to complete the test. The soils engineer also determines the stability of the site's slope. During excavation, for example, digging straight down may be difficult because the remaining soil might cave in. The engineer is expected to use the results of the test to calculate the excavation angle that will leave the remaining soil intact.

Soils engineers participate with the architect and the structural engineer to design the most effective type of foundation system to support the proposed structure. They generally work on a lump-sum basis. A soils analysis can cost from $1,000 to $100,000, depending on the site's size and the number of test borings and types of tests necessary to study the soil.

Environmental Consultants

Developers must engage two basic types of environmental consultants during the life of a project—one to analyze the project's economic, social, and cultural impacts on the surrounding built environment and the second to determine, in conjunction with soils engineers, mitigation for any hazardous materials detected. Environmental reviews are often necessary for development projects of significant size and scope. They focus on impacts caused by the proposed development such as increased traffic, reduced air quality, sunshine and shading, and infrastructure requirements.

The environmental approval process varies in rigor based on state and local regulations, citizens' attitudes toward development, and the environmental sensitivity of the area in question. These reviews are often sensitive political actions and demand a great deal of diplomacy from the developer.

The financial outlay, time, patience, and perseverance required to successfully navigate a proposed project's environmental review and secure final building permits must not be underestimated. The process is governed by the appropriate level of government that first determines whether or not a developer is obligated to complete a formal environmental analysis. This process is triggered if a project exceeds various size or scale thresholds or impacts environmentally sensitive areas such as wetlands or an endangered animal's habitat. Empowered by federal legislation, including the National Environmental Policy Act of 1969, each state and locality has created its own environmental laws that all developers must adhere to.

The least stringent type of required analysis is an environmental impact statement (EIS). An EIS is simply a checklist that identifies the potential impacts a project is expected to create. A more stringent environmental impact report (EIR), based on state and local legislation, may be ordered when a project is expected to pose substantial alterations to the built or natural environment. It is advisable to analyze the legislation to understand the various thresholds that trigger a partial or full EIR, as there are times when more thoughtful design can eliminate or limit the scope of an EIR.

A developer should select an environmental consulting firm that is respected for its technical expertise, independence, and impartiality. Because the results of an environmental report can become a political issue, developers must judge the level of complexity and controversy their project is likely to create and select a consulting team that has experience in projects of a similar magnitude. To ensure impartiality, some cities provide a list of acceptable firms from which a developer may choose; in California, the public sector often randomly assigns an environmental consulting firm to the developer.

An EIR not only describes the proposed development, the site, the overall design parameters, and the project's effect on the local community but also proposes appropriate mitigation measures to offset negative effects such as increased traffic congestion, soil runoff, and construction impacts. In the case of traffic impacts, the mitigation measures may include widening certain streets, adding left-turn lanes, adding traffic signals, converting some streets to one way, or expanding public transit service to the area. Major projects may require significant off-site improvements, even new freeway interchanges.

Once a draft of the EIR has been prepared, it is submitted to various state and local agencies, circulated to concerned parties, and made available to the general public; each is allowed a specific period of time to submit its comments. These comments may lead to significant design changes.

Thereafter, the developer's environmental consultant must produce a final EIR that responds to all comments. Any mitigation measure(s) recommended by the consultant must be feasible for the developer to implement. Public bodies, usually the planning commission and/or the city council, generally include mitigation measures in their conditions for project approval. These conditions are sometimes referred to as *exactions*, which are burdens placed on the developer to make financial payments or complete on-site and off-site improvements to mitigate the project's environmental effects.

Any change to the development plan requires simultaneous changes to the consultant's analysis. A sound development strategy is to secure input from all concerned parties as early as possible, even before the draft submission of the EIR, and incorporate as many of these changes into the proposed design as possible.

The environmental review process has the potential to be a moving target and, if not managed effectively, can lead to skyrocketing development costs as a result of changes in project scope, size, massing, or use. Multiple iterations are possible based on input from independent parties, resulting in several design amendments to the original development proposal.

For complex urban projects, it is not unheard of for a developer to have to go back to square one and change the entire project, including use, height, massing, and overall square footage. As this process unfolds, it is important to maintain an eye on the market, as the time it takes to secure permits is independent of economic and market cycles and may cause the developer to miss the market or the financing window altogether.

The cost of hiring an environmental consultant varies according to the size and complexity of the project analysis. An EIR is significantly more expensive than an EIS because of the amount of work involved and the potential for change. Most consultants work on a lump-sum basis, with payment schedules tied to performance milestones.

The consultant's contractual obligations usually end with the production of the final report, although the developer might subsequently require the consultant to make presentations and answer questions at public hearings. Following contract expiration, the consultant's compensation is based on a T&M agreement. The contract with the consultant must be reviewed to determine what is and is not included in the initial scope of responsibilities.

The second type of environmental consultant a developer may have to engage is involved in detection, containment, and removal of hazardous materials. Hazardous materials have become a major concern for developers and a significant source of litigation and liability. Their presence on a site can cause major delays and increased costs for containment and soil removal as well as legal expenses. Consequently, environmental analysis, including soils analysis, should incorporate tests to determine the presence of toxic materials. Ascertaining a property's previous use(s) is important.

Environmental reports consist of three phases of analysis. Many lenders require a Phase I analysis for almost any kind of project; it simply involves a title search of previous users to determine the likelihood of toxic contamination. If the Phase I report finds contamination from, say, a gas station, dry cleaners, or industrial user, a Phase II report is required to determine the extent of cleanup. It usually includes analyzing soil samples. If the Phase II analysis finds possible off-site contamination or contamination of the water table, a Phase III analysis is required.

It is vital to inspect every development site for the presence of hazardous materials, because liability for any future cleanup falls to any and all parties named on the chain of title and may result in personal recourse to the developer—even if the contamination predated the developer's acquisition of the site in question. Because hazardous waste contamination can involve millions of dollars in cleanup costs and years of delay, prudent developers perform the necessary environmental analyses before they acquire a property.

Surveyors

Surveyors determine a property's physical and legal characteristics—existing easements, rights-of-way, and dedications on the site—and prepare a site map plotting these characteristics. This critical information reveals how much of the site can be built on and the allowable square footage.

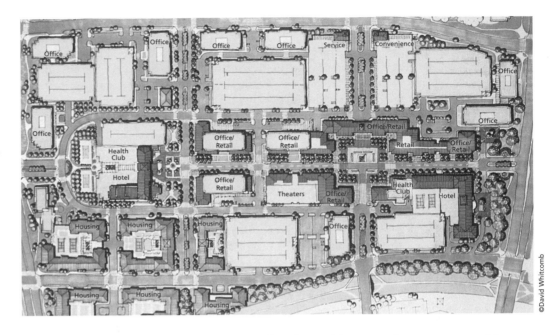

At Reston Town Center in Fairfax County, Virginia, pedestrian-scale streets, defined open spaces, ample parking, and a rich mix of uses organized into a grid of streets offer the vitality of urban life within a rapidly developing suburban context.

Developers commonly use two types of surveys: a *boundary survey,* which determines the boundaries of the site (easements and other legal requirements affect ownership of the property being plotted on a map); and a *construction survey,* which plots the location of relevant infrastructure—water, sewers, electricity, gas lines, and roads—to assist in planning connections to utility services. Surveyors also augment the work completed by soils engineers, analyzing a site's topography, likely run-off and slope, and the implications of the building's proposed location.

A good surveyor also shows all title impingements by making sure everything in the title is found in the survey. One developer suggests walking the site with the surveyor to observe any positive or negative influences on the site that can then be reconciled with the title.[14]

Costs for surveyors vary according to the type of work they perform, the detail required, and the number of surveys requested. Surveyors work on a lump-sum contract or a T&M agreement. Two surveyors should be able to complete a boundary analysis for a typical ten-acre (4-hectare) parcel in a single eight-hour day. Someone who has surveyed the property in the past will be less expensive because he has done a vast majority of the work for an earlier survey of the property.

Surveyors also can be important allies because of their involvement with the local regulatory community. In smaller communities, surveyors can represent projects to zoning boards and city councils more effectively than lawyers.

Parking Consultants

Parking is one of the major limiting factors for real estate development. High land values and restrictive local parking ordinances require a well-devised parking plan. A qualified parking consultant (usually not the architect) takes into account all the significant factors involved in designing the optimum parking for the site. The parking consultant should be included early in the design process so that the architect can incorporate parking recommendations in the overall design.

Parking consultants are responsible for many aspects of a project: evaluating the economics of a surface lot versus a parking structure; designing an efficient configuration that maximizes the available parking area; discovering whether local municipal codes can accommodate the estimated parking demand; determining whether parking should be provided free or at a competitive rate; and deciding where the points of ingress and egress will be.

Parking is an expensive undertaking, costing $1,000 to $1,200 per space for a surface lot, not including land, and $6,000 to $8,000 or more per space for a structure; underground parking may cost twice as much. Consequently, the services of a well-qualified consultant are essential. Referrals from the architect and other developers can provide a list of potential consultants whose work should be inspected by the developers before any decision is made to hire someone. Parking consultants usually work under a lump-sum contract or at an hourly rate.

Asbestos Abatement Professionals

Renovation or adaptive use of a building constructed between 1930 and 1976 is likely to run the risk of asbestos contamination. Pricing for abatement has become more competitive over the past ten years. The industry has developed more efficient methods of service delivery, and the amount of asbestos available for removal is declining.

Asbestos was used for fireproofing and insulation until 1973, when federal legislation prohibited its future use for those purposes. Asbestos was sprayed on underlying columns, beams, pipes, and ducts of buildings, above ceilings and behind walls. It was also used in building materials such as tiles.

Asbestos is hazardous when *friable* (that is, flaky or powdery); if disturbed, its fibers become airborne and are likely to be inhaled. The U.S. Environmental Protection Agency (EPA) regulates activities like renovation and demolition that could release asbestos into the air and outlines appropriate methods of disposal. Plans to rehabilitate or demolish an existing building must include the removal of any asbestos. Even the installation of sprinkler systems, electrical and plumbing repairs, and any interior reconfiguration might require some form of asbestos abatement.

Removing asbestos requires the services of qualified, well-trained professionals with extensive experience in assessing and removing asbestos; the hazards inherent in the process could lead to legal repercussions if inexperienced firms are hired to carry out the tasks. The firm selected should be bonded by a certifiable surety company. Both the consultant hired to determine the extent of the asbestos contamination and the contractor responsible for removing it should be licensed by the state. Developers may contact the regional office of EPA and the National Asbestos Council for lists of qualified asbestos abatement professionals.

Physical constraints and the characteristics of the material being removed are the most important variables in determining the cost of asbestos removal. For example, removing vinyl tiles in an easily accessible area may cost $1.00 to $3.00 per square foot ($10.75 to $32.00 per square meter), whereas fireproofing or removing acoustic material located in the ceiling plenum space and attached to mechanical or structural systems may cost as much as $30.00 per square foot ($323 per square meter) to remove.

Asbestos abatement occurs in two stages: inspection and removal. Consultants charge by the hour or by the square foot. Surveys for a typical 20,000-square-foot (1,860-square-meter) building, for example, might be around $2,500 for the physical inspection. Consultants collect about 50 samples from the building to determine what material requires removal. These tests cost about $30.00 per sample.

Estimates for removing asbestos range from $5.00 to $7.00 per square foot ($54.00 to $75.00 per square meter), based on the complexity of the job. The ideal scenario for abatement is a vacant building, but it is not always possible. Many jobs must be carried out while the building is still occupied in other areas, which can also increase the cost of removal.[15]

Construction Contractors

Construction contractors are responsible for a project's physical construction. They are required to complete an array of services (both before and during construction) on time and, ideally, under budget. They can provide a reality check on critical matters such as construction materials, local construction practices, and pricing information and can help establish a realistic budget when brought in early on a project.

Developers can select a contractor through negotiations with a particular firm or through open bidding. To find a good contractor, developers should solicit a number of contracting firms, asking them to submit proposals or general statements of qualifications. The

contractors' responses should include descriptions of past projects, references from clients and lenders, résumés outlining the experience of their major employees, and, possibly, verification that the company is bondable. These submissions can be used to select a company for direct negotiation.

In open bidding, developers send out a notice requesting bids and statements of qualifications. The problem with this approach is that contractors are reluctant to spend time bidding on a project unless they think that they have a good chance of being selected. As a result, the developer may not attract an adequate number of responses from which to choose. Two to four weeks are necessary to allow contractors to return satisfactory responses.

The most effective way to limit the number of bidders but still ensure that the targeted firms will respond is a combination of a request for qualifications and competitive bidding. After reviewing several contractors' qualifications, developers may ask the best three, four, or five contractors to prepare a bid for the project. A preference for one contractor could result in direct negotiations with a particular firm. Developers should not feel obligated to conduct protracted bidding if they have already found the best contractor for the job.

Jonathan Rose, principal of Jonathan Rose and Companies, suggests keeping in mind three points when choosing contractors:[16]

1. Find someone who is experienced in the product type being considered for the project. A specialist in assisted living facilities will likely not be an appropriate choice for multifamily housing.
2. Be certain that your project amounts to no more than one-third of the contracting firm's total workload, a good benchmark for organizational and financial stability. That is, if you have a $20 million project, look for a contractor with at least $60 million in total business at the time the contract is signed.
3. Ask for and check references to understand how the contractor has performed for past clients.

During the design stage, a contractor or a construction price estimator (also called a *quantity surveyor*) should check the architect's drawings and formulate an estimated budget for completing the project. A permanent contractor, once hired, is responsible for completing a construction cost estimate based on the construction drawings completed by the architect. If the developer chooses to put the project on a fast track, the contractor should be a helpful source of creative and cost-effective suggestions during preliminary design.

One of the contractor's tasks is to set up a projected schedule for disbursing loans from the construction lender. The contractor's major responsibility, however, is the project's physical construction, including soliciting bids from and then hiring all the subcontractors— construction workers, plumbers, painters, and electrical and mechanical contractors. The contractor is legally responsible for building a safe structure and must hire the best-qualified parties.

During construction, the developer or the contractor may alter the architect's plans, using change orders. The proposed change might result from a market-based design change or from practical problems, such as the unavailability of specified materials; the contractor may also suggest cost-saving alternatives. All change orders are subject to the architect's verification and approval. If the developer does not monitor them carefully, costs can escalate dramatically.

Two basic methods are used to determine the contractor's compensation: bids or contracts. Bids are requested to be in the form of a lump sum or some derivative of a cost-plus-fee contract. A lump-sum bid is used when the design is already established and all the construction drawings are complete before selecting the contractor. This option is rarely feasible for beginning developers, however, because they are probably not willing or able to underwrite the cost of complete drawings until the decision to construct is finalized.

Contractors' fees are based on the size of the project, the number and amount of anticipated change orders, and so on. On a $10 million project, a contractor should be expected to charge a fee equivalent to 5 percent of total hard costs—in addition to project overhead and on-site supervision costs.

A cost-plus-fee contract is a preferable means of compensating experienced contractors with excellent reputations. Under this option, all costs—labor, salaries of accountants and other such employees, travel expenses, construction materials, supplies, equipment and tools, and fees for all subcontractors—should be explicitly set forth in the contract. The costs should not include overhead and administrative expenses for the contractor's main or branch offices.

The contractor must calculate the time required to complete the project as a basis for a fixed or percentage fee. Most developers avoid a percentage fee because it fails to provide the contractor with incentives to minimize construction costs.

Often, the construction lender requires that the contractor guarantee a maximum cost when the cost-plus-fee method is used. In such cases, the architect is responsible for providing drawings with sufficient detail to allow the contractor to solicit quotes from subcontractors to calculate the maximum cost.

Guaranteed maximum cost contracts can include an incentive to save costs; perhaps 25 to 50 percent of the developer's savings could be guaranteed to the contractor if total project costs are less than the guaranteed maximum. Another model is to split the contingency fee; that is, the developer and the contractor split every dollar saved under budgeted costs, which could amount to 5 to 10 percent of a project's costs.[17]

The developer must make sure, however, that the contractor does not sacrifice quality to receive the bonus. Other types of incentive bonuses can also save costs. A

Construction of Navy Yard Metro Center, a Class A office building in Washington, D.C., helped spur the rejuvenation of an underused section of the city. Completed in July 2001, it contains 275,300 square feet (25,585 square meters) of office space, three floors of underground parking, and tenant amenities.

bonus for early completion pays the contractor a defined amount for completing the work on or before a specific date; some contracts pay a fixed amount for each day that work is completed before the deadline. By the same token, bonus clauses can be used to penalize the contractor for being late. Some contracts include a liquidated damage clause or a penalty clause to cover late completion. Not surprisingly, contractors dislike these clauses, which, they argue, destroy teamwork.

Using bonus and incentive clauses is an excellent tool for guaranteeing the contractor's performance. The developer incurs costs, however, most notably in the necessary monitoring of the contractor's performance.

A good construction job hinges on selection of an experienced and reputable contractor. Beginners especially should select a contractor with a long track record.

Real Estate Service Firms

A variety of service firms provide a wide range of real estate services that are critical in the development process. These firms are usually brought into a project to perform specific, short-term tasks.

Market Consultants

Successful real estate decisions hinge on the availability of reliable and accurate information. A market consultant provides the professional assessment of a proposed project. The resulting market study analyzes the proposed project's feasibility based on current and projected market conditions. Possessing such information reduces the risks involved with the project. Lenders, investors, and architects all use the market study.

Some developers complete their own market studies, and lenders normally accept a well-documented study by a developer for a small project. Larger projects, however, require a professional market study. Developers must have confidence in the market consultant's ability to determine the project's feasibility. A market research firm with a good reputation adds credibility to developers and their projects.

Which market consultant to hire is likely to be one of the most important decisions made during the predevelopment period. Although developers may ask other developers for recommendations, they should certainly ask lenders which consultants they respect. Lenders' opinions are particularly important, because their decisions depend on the market data proving the project's feasibility.

The requirements for specific kinds of development reinforce the importance of retaining a consultant well versed in the type of development under consideration. A local firm that knows the market area where the project will be located is usually the best choice. The databases the market consultant maintains are useful indications of the consultant's approach. Aside from being technically proficient, the consultant must be able to understand the subtle nuances of the market that are not readily apparent to the average observer. A good market consultant can identify the proposed competition and thoughtfully analyze the political situation.

Developers should ask to see several market studies that the consultant has produced and make sure that they are comfortable with the assumptions and techniques used to appraise a market. The style of writing and presentation of the report should be carefully examined, as it will be circulated among various members of the development team as well as potential lenders and investors.

The market consultant is responsible for producing a final study that should address all the factors affecting the proposed project's feasibility. As a client, the smart developer looks for a comprehensive study that will give independent evidence about the marketability of the development proposal. (The specific features of the process for various property types are discussed in the appropriate sections of Chapters 3 through 7.)

The final report should incorporate all the data into a marketing strategy to help merchandise the project. The market research firm should provide a profile of tenants or buyers to be targeted and the amenities and lease terms to be offered. The architect should receive a copy of the report so that the project's design will offer uses and sizes appropriate for the market. The market study should also provide insights into the amenities and space configurations in which tenants and buyers are interested.

H. Pike Oliver, principal of INTERRA and the Presidio Group, says, "You should not rely on a market consultant to determine whether you are going to do a deal. You should have a good idea beforehand that a project is feasible and simply use a market consultant to confirm your initial assessment and to reassure a lending institution or capital partner."[18] Good uses for market consultants include verifying third parties' qualifications, refining a niche market, obtaining data for pricing and sales rates, and confirming the project's value.

A market consultant's fee is based on the level of detail that the developer requests. Preliminary information may be obtained for less than $5,000, while a detailed report may cost from $25,000 to $75,000 or more depending on the complexity of the study. For a preliminary analysis or a quick inventory of the market, the consultant may work on an hourly basis, but larger, more complex studies require a fixed contract.

Appraisers

Appraisers produce an estimate of a property's value based on standard methodologies. Investors, potential buyers, and lenders require a professional appraisal to arrive at a market value that will set the amount of the loan for the proposed project.

Lending institutions usually employ in-house appraisers or select an independent outside firm. If the lender leaves selection up to the developer, he should ask for a list of people the lender prefers to use. A reputable appraiser adds credibility to the loan application. Professional appraiser organizations can supply references; their members must demonstrate certain minimum standards to gain admission.

The appraisal report should state the property's market value and offer supporting evidence. Three methodologies can be used to complete an appraisal: the *income approach*, the *market approach*, and the *cost approach*.

The income approach is preferred for all income-producing property, including commercial, industrial, office, and rental apartments. Value is determined by dividing the project's net operating income by an appropriate capitalization rate. The market approach uses recent information about sales of properties similar to the subject property to determine a market value. This approach is used most often with single-family residential properties, condominiums, and land sales. The *cost approach* estimates the actual cost to construct a project similar to the project under consideration. It is used to determine the value of recently completed buildings. The developer must ensure that the appraiser uses the standard techniques and professionally accepted forms to produce a credible report. Appraisal costs range from $500 for a single-family house to $10,000 for a large office building.

Attorneys

Many facets of real estate development—taxes, land use, leases, and joint venture partnerships, for example—require separate legal specialists. No single attorney can be familiar with all these topics. For zoning and other activities involving public hearings, an attorney with a proven success rate in cases involving a particular public body might be the proper choice. The ability to work behind the scenes with the local planning staff and politicians may be more important than appearing at public hearings. In any case, the law firm chosen should have attorneys with specific experience in the real estate issues likely to arise. Other developers of the type of project under consideration can recommend good attorneys.

Attorneys are essential for producing partnership or syndication agreements and contracts for consultants, acquiring property, writing up loan documents and leasing contracts, and negotiating the public approval process. The process of obtaining public approvals can be an intimidating maze for a beginning developer without an attorney and may lead to costly delays or outright rejection.

Most developers request that a partner of the law firm or a well-established attorney work on their cases, preferring to pay a little more for the top person to guarantee the best job. For technical work like syndications and contracts, highly recommended junior associates with three or four years of experience may provide the most cost-effective work from a large law firm. Attorneys generally bill clients by the hour, although fixed prices for certain transactions are not uncommon. The developer should obtain an estimate of the total cost for a given job before authorizing it.

Leonard Zax, chair of Latham & Watkins real estate group, gives the following tips for getting the best work from one's attorneys:[19]

- The scope of different attorneys' work may overlap, and important issues and transactions sometimes slip through the cracks. The development firm's general counsel is the best person to ensure legal continuity for a project. In lieu of retaining corporate counsel, it is prudent to appoint one individual already involved in the project as responsible for patching any gaps in representation.
- Distinguish legal advice from business comment.
- Clients need to understand the greater context in which their legal counsel is operating. Be aware of all matters pending between a firm you have hired and public bodies that have influence over your project.
- The most effective lawyer is not always the tough table pounder, nor is he effective by always agreeing with the developer. The most effective lawyers take time to listen to a complete idea and formulate a candid opinion of the legal elements that need to be addressed. And developers should listen to their attorney. Too many developers rush to judgment and do not have the patience to hear their counsel's entire opinion—often on complex issues that are critical to the project's success.
- Do not establish a fee structure that encourages cutting corners.

Title Companies

Title companies certify who holds title to a property and guarantee the purchaser and lender that the property is free and clear of unexpected mortgage, tax, easement, and other liens that may cloud the title. Title companies will defend any future claims against properties that they insure. The type of title policy determines the extent of the protection. Developers must read the policy carefully before signing it. Most policies follow a standard format, but many real estate investors fail to understand what protection their title policy provides, a misunderstanding that can lead to problems.

When selecting a title company, developers should make sure that the company has the financial strength to back any potential claims and should research its record of service to find out how long a company takes to obtain a clean title. Most title representatives work for a commission, and they are very accommodating because they want repeat business.

Title companies provide a number of services in addition to title insurance. They provide, free of charge, both current and potential customers with a profile of a property in which the customer is interested. That profile details who owns it, property taxes paid, liens, easements, size of improvements and the lot, grant and trust deeds, notes, and most recent sale price. Title companies also provide local data such as comparable sales information and plat maps.

A preliminary title report specifying current liens against the property can be prepared for a fee. The preliminary title is not an insurance policy but a reading of the existing title. It highlights any potential problems that a future owner may need to clear from a property before title is transferred. Standard title policies usually do not provide insurance protection for taxes or assessments not shown as existing liens, interests and claims easements not shown by the public records, conflicts in boundary lines, mining claims and water rights, and liens for services, labor, and material that do not appear in the public records. An ALTA (American Land Title Association) policy offers extended coverage that does cover such unrecorded claims; it requires a more in-depth survey that sophisticated purchasers usually demand.

Title fees, obtained from any representative of the company, are usually applicable statewide and are quoted on a scale that slides according to the sale price of the property being insured. More often than not, the seller pays for title insurance. In California in 2002, title policy fees for a $1 million policy were $2,572, for a $3 million policy were $5,672, for a $5 million to $10 million policy were $.95 per $1,000, and for a $10 million to $25 million policy were $.90 per $1,000. ALTA policies with extended coverage cost 25 percent more than standard policies, and ALTA policies in general cost 25 percent more than standard policies.[20]

Surety Companies

Developers need insurance to guard against a consultant's or contractor's failure to perform an agreed-upon task. Such a failure may have serious economic and legal consequences. For instance, a contractor's failure to meet obligations could result in a lien on the developer's property. All public works projects must, by law, be bonded for performance, because liens cannot be placed on public property. Private projects do not have to be bonded, but in most instances some form of bond is recommended. Contractors are generally required to be *bondable,* meaning that they qualify for surety coverage.

General contractors deal directly with a surety company to obtain performance and payment bonds. The developer is required to inform all contractors that bonds will be required before bids are submitted, and contractors consequently adjust their bids to pass on the cost of bonds to the developer. Bondable contractors generally establish a relationship with one surety company and fix an upper bonding limit of credit, which restricts the amount of bondable work that the contractor can perform. Construction bonds are a specialized product, offered by few insurance companies. Other developers can identify respectable carriers for a beginner, if necessary.

A surety bond involves a three-party contract in which a surety company (or, simply, a *surety*) joins with a principal, usually the contractor, in guaranteeing the specific performance of an act to the developer or municipality, also referred to as the *beneficiary.*

Bonding should not be interpreted as a negative comment on the contractor. It is rather a validation of the contractor's ability to deliver a finished product. Before issuing a bond, the surety thoroughly analyzes the contractor's firm, including the qualifications of its staff, its financial stability, its management structure, and previous experience, and inventories its equipment.

Based on these facts, the surety appraises the contractor's ability to complete the project. If the firm is deemed stable, the surety issues the appropriate bonds, and work can proceed. Even if the developer chooses not to require any construction bonds, the surety's seal of approval is an affirmation of the contractor's quality.

The three main types of bonds are performance, payment, and completion. *Performance bonds* guarantee the developer that if the contractor fails to complete the agreed-upon contract, the surety is responsible for seeing that the work is finished. The agreement allows the surety to compensate the developer equal to the amount of money needed to complete the project or to hire a contractor to finish the job. Lenders occasionally insist on bond coverage for their own protection. The general contractor, either at the developer's request or on its own, requires subcontractors to purchase performance bonds.

Payment bonds guarantee that the surety will meet obligations if the contractor defaults on payments to laborers, subcontractors, or suppliers, protecting the property against liens that might be imposed in response to nonpayment. Developers and/or lenders often require the general contractor to purchase these bonds to protect them against any future claims of nonpayment made by subcontractors or suppliers. Payment bonds usually are issued concurrently with performance bonds; both bonds often appear on the same form.

Completion bonds, often referred to as *developer off-site* or *subdivision bonds,* ensure local municipalities that specified off-site improvements will be completed. Many states require local municipalities to secure the bonds as assurance that the developer will complete the improvements.

The developer may require bid bonds during the solicitation of contractors' bids. A bid bond, issued by a surety, guarantees the developer that winning contractors will honor their accepted bids. If, for example, a winning contractor finds out that its bid was significantly lower than the others submitted, it may be tempted to withdraw the offer. In such instances, the surety pays damages to the developer, in theory to compensate for time and money lost.

In most states, surety companies must charge uniform rates. Each surety establishes its rates and underwriting standards and then files them with the state insurance department or its equivalent. For performance and payment bonds, the rate charged is the same regardless of whether 50 or 100 percent of the contract price is guaranteed; therefore, developers should ask for 100 percent coverage. Rates are based on the contract price and are calculated on a graduated payment scale. The rates for completion bonds are generally higher because they involve additional underwriting.

Opinion is divided about the need to secure the various forms of surety bonds. Performance and payment bonds cost roughly 1 percent of the construction costs, so it is up to the developer to decide whether or not bonding is worth the abated risk.

Brokers/Leasing Agents

Real estate brokers and leasing agents are hired to lease or sell a project to prospective tenants and buyers. Developers can benefit greatly from the services of a skilled salesperson who is able to quickly and completely lease or sell a project.

Developers must decide whether to sign an agreement with an outside real estate broker or to place an agent on the payroll. The decision is usually based on the type and magnitude of the project.

The use of in-house agents is most appropriate for large projects and large development firms that can carry the cost. The benefit of an in-house staff is that the developer hires the staff during initial planning and the agents become very familiar with the project, providing input during design and merchandising.

Small development firms may find it useful to retain outside brokers who are knowledgeable about the local market and who have lower carrying costs. Brokers are usually aware of potential tenants with existing leases that are about to expire; brokers from large brokerage houses may have information about regional or national tenants.

It is essential to interview representatives from a number of firms to select a firm with experience with the type of project under consideration. The developer should present the project carefully during an interview. If the broker does not respond positively to the project, another broker should be found. If developers find that prospective brokers currently represent competitive developments, they should decline to hire them because of potential conflicts of interest. Retaining a broker who has faith in the project and who can commit the energy necessary to ensure its success will be a major benefit to the development process.

The working relationship between developer and broker is defined in a contract referred to as a *listing agreement*. Under an open listing agreement, the developer may recruit several brokers and is responsible for paying a commission only to the one who sells or leases the property. In addition, if the developer completes a transaction without the broker's assistance, no commission is necessary. An exclusive listing agreement involves, as its name suggests, a single broker.

The most common form of agreement for developers is an *exclusive right-to-sell listing*. In this instance, the developer selects one broker, who automatically receives the commission no matter who sells the property, including the developer.

The broker is responsible for attracting prospective tenants or buyers and persuading them to lease or buy the project. An active broker is well informed about the market, able to identify and recruit interested parties, and prepared to comment on the project's design during its early stages, informing the developer and architect what amenities are currently popular in the market.

figure 2-2
Typical Real Estate Sales Commissions

Product Type	Percent of Total Price
Raw Land	5–10
Single-Family Houses	4–7
Apartment Building	3–5
Office Building	3–7
Industrial Building	4–6
Shopping Center	4–6
Hotels	3–6

figure 2-3
Typical Lease Commissions

Property Type	Percent of Total Lease Years						
	1	2	3	4	5	6–10	10+
Shopping Center	6	5	4	4	3	3	3
Office Building	6	5	4	4	3	3	3
Industrial Building	5	4	3	2	1	1	1

Note: Sales and lease commissions are always subject to negotiation and vary widely depending on factors such as location, market conditions, type of lease, and property value. For large assets, it is common for fees to be lower.

The marketing of a project ensures its success, but who should control the marketing process is debatable. Allowing brokers to plan, implement, and pay for the promotional campaign involves them and gives them a sense of responsibility. Developers often prefer to pay for the promotion themselves, however, to retain control over the timing, intensity, and nature of marketing.

The broker's responsibility is to negotiate leases with prospects while keeping in mind the developer's personal goals with respect to rates of return and preferred type of tenant. The developer should establish lease guidelines for the broker to follow and should readily accept leases presented by the broker within those guidelines so as to maintain credibility with the brokerage community. Developers who lose that credibility quickly lose activity on their property. Once the project is leased, the developer may retain the broker to lease space as it becomes available.

The developer should negotiate a schedule for commissions that will provide incentives to lease or sell the building as quickly as possible—for example, by providing higher commission rates early in the project to gain momentum.

Real estate brokers work almost exclusively for a commission. The broker and the developer negotiate the rate of compensation, which varies according to the type, size, and geographic location of the project. In general, commissions for property sales are based on a percentage of the total price (see Figure 2-2).

Lease commissions payable to the broker are calculated as an annual percentage of the value of a signed lease for each year of the lease. Over the term of the lease, the percentages paid to the broker are scaled down (see Figure 2-3). Half the aggregate commission typically is paid upon execution of the lease and half at move-in.

Public Relations/Advertising Agencies

Promotion spreads the word about the project to the community and differentiates it from the competition in the minds of potential users. Developers often tend to neglect promotion, hoping instead that the project will sell itself; this approach is almost invariably a mistake.

Part of the process of selecting a public relations or advertising agency involves attending presentations at which the agencies under consideration offer examples of their previous work, samples relevant to the proposed project, and promotional ideas for the project.

Public relations firms not only produce news releases, press kits, newsletters, and mailings conveying information about the project but also create situations that will give the project positive exposure in the community. Different projects and product types require different approaches to attract interest from potential consumers, and the agency chooses which tool is most appropriate for a given project. The agency should also be a source of creative ideas to market the project effectively.

Good promotional plans draw attention to the project at strategic moments—groundbreaking and topping-off ceremonies, for example. A good public relations firm can be an invaluable asset when a project is proposed in a contentious political environment. A well-conceived campaign can gain favorable publicity for the project and sell it to the community. Organized community events, complete with well-designed presentations, introduce the company and the project to the neighborhood and local politicians and leave a favorable impression.

A public relations firm can handle advertising, and an advertising agency can handle public relations. Advertising involves placing advertisements strategically to promote the project and maximize its exposure. Many different media and promotional techniques are available, including newspapers, radio and television, and outdoor signs. The advertising firm designs the advertisements and presents them to the developer for approval. Advertising firms generally work on monthly retainers plus expenses to cover radio, television, newspaper, billboard, and magazine advertising.

Property Management

Following construction and lease-up, the developer's focus becomes operational rather than visionary, with the new focus placed squarely on maximizing value until time of sale through property operations and maintenance. The two overriding goals are to maintain real rental rates and high occupancy rates. As such, this next phase of the project's life calls for sustained property management.

figure 2-4

Developing a Marketing Strategy

The developer has two choices—through an in-house staff or through a skilled outside service provider.

This decision rests squarely on the development firm's internal organizational skills, whether property management can be a profit or loss center, the amount of time this activity will command, and the opportunity costs inherent to this activity as opposed to pursuing other revenue opportunities. Each situation is unique, and the developer should reflect on the overall vision for the company and how it meshes with this activity. Maintaining property management in house provides:

- direct property oversight and quality control;
- constant tenant contact;
- a diversified organizational revenue stream;
- insight into changing tenant operational issues, which can lead to future development opportunities and higher project quality.

But in-house property management also has some disadvantages:

- Time cost is high compared with other revenue-producing activities.
- The activity is very management intensive.
- Property type organizational skills, staffing, and experience are limiting factors.
- Economies of scale place smaller developers at a competitive disadvantage compared with professional property management firms.
- Property management can be a cost center as opposed to a profit center.

Most larger developers manage their own properties through dedicated in-house staff or a wholly owned subsidiary. Smaller and/or beginning developers generally choose to use an outside source.

The key to selecting a third-party property management firm is its past experience with the type of project under consideration. Careful evaluation of firms should examine a list of all properties under their management, a client contact list, and the résumés of staff assigned to the project. It is very important to visit representative properties currently under management to get a sense for maintenance quality, staffing, and overall tenant satisfaction. An additional selection criterion is the degree of buying power the management firm commands in the marketplace, which generally is a function of the firm's size: larger management firms can purchase services less expensively by employing economies of scale, which can lead to lower operating costs.

A good source for locating a third-party property management firm is the local chapter of the Institute of Real Estate Management (IREM), which is part of the National Association of Realtors®.[21] IREM offers educational and professional development to more than 16,000 members and provides accreditation to companies through its Accredited Management Organization designation and to individuals through its Certified Property Manager and Accredited Residential Manager designations. These designations are obtained by meeting specific guidelines, including professionalism, education and training, ethics, and a demonstration of business stability. They are based on performance and must be renewed every three years.

A property manager's job begins in earnest once tenants begin to occupy the property. Daily functions include collecting rents from tenants and paying recurring expenses, maintaining common areas, and ensuring necessary repairs are carried out by soliciting bids, selecting vendors, and overseeing the quality of workmanship.

The manager should provide a comprehensive short-, medium-, and long-range strategic property plan specifying the frequency of physical inspections, maintenance needs, and a replacement schedule. This plan is particularly important for large capital expenditures such as roof maintenance and replacement, HVAC systems, and other physical and structural issues. Budgeting and planning for the year ahead will reduce unforeseen operating costs and diminish the likelihood of emergency repairs. With proper management, the ability to reduce operating costs substantially increases cash flow and the overall property investment value.

As front-line personnel, property managers address all aspects of the developer's relationship with tenants. Initially, managers should supervise the move-in process, making sure it proceeds smoothly; it is very important for tenant relationships to start off on a high note.

Effective managers maintain constant communication with tenants so that any problems that might arise can be quickly resolved with a high degree of customer satisfaction. It is important to keep in mind that it is the developer's reputation that is at stake; complaints from tenants directly to the developer are a signal that the property manager is not performing effectively.

Some contracts call for the property manager to also serve as the property leasing agent. This arrangement can be beneficial, as the management firm has the most intimate relationship with the property. A large number of vacancies, however, may call for a more aggressive leasing strategy or require the expertise of a leasing broker with broader market knowledge. Each situation is unique, and the developer must decide who is more capable of filling any vacancies that arise. High turnover rates are a sign that something—physical and/or managerial—is amiss, and the developer should take action to determine the causes and remedies.

Operations run more smoothly when the management company is given authority to sign contracts, release funds for scheduled maintenance, and implement capital improvements. The agreement between developer and property manager should specify dollar

Large properties generally offer greater opportunities for operating efficiencies. Ventana Apartment Homes in San Antonio, Texas, includes 390 units.

limits on what the manager can spend before the property owner's approval is required, with the owner's approval necessitated in all instances of projected capital expenditures.

It is important for tax, audit, and tracking purposes that funds belonging to the property owner and to the management entity be maintained in separate accounts. The management firm should set up a trust account to protect the owner's funds and prevent any commingling of funds between properties and entities. Audit reports should be prepared regularly (recommended twice per year) so the developer can verify rental collections, deposits, occupancies, vacancies, management expenses, and capital expenditures.

Property management services are generally priced as a percentage of the property's gross revenue (the exception is for very-high-end residential units, where the fee can be a fixed dollar amount per unit). In general, property managers typically negotiate a fee ranging from 1 to 5 percent of gross revenue.

The fee is predicated on the amount of management activity and degree of difficulty the project presents. When comparing bids from management firms, the developer should be careful to determine which costs are specifically included in the fee and which are additional billable expenses to the property (management and maintenance salaries are most notable). In addition, this fee does not include maintenance labor and material costs provided by outside vendors.

Some management firms offer to perform property management at break-even cost or at a loss in exchange for securing the right to all potential leasing and/or sales fees generated by the project. And some brokerage firms offer management services. Developers should proceed cautiously in this regard, as, in general, the skills required to effectively engage in each activity are very different.

Lenders

Lenders have two major concerns: the developer and the project. Lenders first evaluate the developer's experience and credibility, seeking answers to questions about whether the developer has ever defaulted on a note, how much his company is worth, whether the developer will guarantee the note, and whether the developer has the ability to deliver the project on time and within budget. Lenders then analyze the developer's project, assessing whether the project makes good economic sense and is located advantageously, whether the cost estimate is accurate, and whether the project is sufficiently preleased if the improvements are already constructed.

Some of the most important qualities that a lender looks for in a developer are honesty and organization. Demonstrating these qualities is especially important for developers without a track record or those who have not established their reputation in a given community.

Working with Lenders

Construction lenders lend money to build and lease a project. Permanent lenders finance the project once it is built through long-term mortgages. For both sets of lenders, the developer's potential gain is much less important than the lender's potential loss. Lenders tend to be averse to risks and examine a developer's ability to weather risks. For instance, can the developer withstand fluctuations in the interest rate during the development period? Does the developer have sufficient equity to cover extra costs if interest rates go up during the construction period, or if it takes an extra six months to lease the project?

Relying on their knowledge of the area, lenders weigh the developer's potential for success in a project against their own fees and exposure. For a construction loan, lenders usually require the developer to supply a market feasibility study and an appraisal. Permanent lenders are concerned about a project's long-term potential for success.

The amount of preleasing that lenders require depends on the type of project and whether the developer seeks construction or permanent financing. Apartment buildings require little preleasing for either type of financing. Office projects must be preleased 50 to 75 percent or more in soft markets or shaky economic climates. Preleasing requirements are lower in hot markets when lenders are competing for business. Preleasing commitments for retail and industrial projects fluctuate dramatically with the market.

Lenders study a project's tenant mix carefully. Strong anchor tenants with high credit ratings and a diversity of other tenants are desirable in both retail and office projects. Construction lenders are concerned about tenant mix because they depend on the permanent lender to take out the construction note. Thus, determining the criteria for tenant mix before leasing begins is a critical step. Special project types such as miniwarehouses and auto marts are harder to finance because they are considered riskier than conventional retail and industrial projects. Some lenders finance them, but at higher loan rates than for conventional projects.

Lenders are also concerned about the developer's financial capability, managerial capability, and character. Even experienced developers need to convince lenders about the economic viability of their projects. Beginning developers, those without a track record, or those who have not established their reputation in the community or real estate industry must sell themselves and their firms as well.

Financial Backing/Equity. Both permanent and construction lenders are interested in the sources of excess capital. Does the developer have enough resources to carry the project, or will the lender be expected to do so (unacceptable for lenders)? Many developers have failed because they have not planned cash flow. They are unable to finance unexpected costs. Lenders want evidence that the developer has cash available or at least the ability to raise capital in case interest rates go up

The Fairmont Plaza office building in San Jose, California, was developed jointly by the city's redevelopment agency, Kimball Small Properties (KSP), and Melvin Simon & Associates (MSA). The building is owned by KSP, MSA, and Hart Advisors (a pension fund). The land, garages, ground-level retail, and interior public spaces are owned by the redevelopment agency.

during construction or leasing is slower than expected or extraordinary cost overruns occur. Lenders also want clear evidence that the borrower understands what he wants and needs in terms of financing. For example, does the borrower want to find the cheapest loan or one with flexibility or the highest loan proceeds?

Managerial Capability. Does the developer understand real estate? In particular, does the developer understand how to work with the city, subcontractors, and leasing agents? The developer must assemble a development team that satisfies these concerns. Additionally, it is helpful if developers show a catalog with the economic results of transactions they have been involved in, such as cash in and cash out, time period, and internal rates of return. They may also want to include a description of both the good and the challenging aspects of their past development projects. An organized, thorough, and internally consistent application with necessary photos, maps, plans, and financial information creates a good first impression and is important to demonstrate a developer's managerial capabilities.

Character. First and foremost, is the developer open and honest about the opportunities and obstacles or challenges associated with the development? Lenders look for developers who share their values regarding development quality, marketing, and management. Does the developer repay debts? Does the developer keep promises? Is the developer litigious? Lenders shy away from people who go to court every time a problem occurs or may not be forthcoming when a potential problem is identified.

Developers should answer all lenders' concerns, recognizing that lenders' greatest fear is that they will be left with an uneconomic project. Developers must demonstrate their commitment, resolution, and professionalism. It is best if the developer responds to all problems before lenders point them out.

To find a lender, developers can begin by making a list of prospects. They may want to start at the bottom of the list and practice their presentations before introducing the project to a lender with which they really want to work. Some lenders are very offended to be told that a developer is shopping for a loan, and discretion is advised.

To build a reputation important to lenders, developers need to avoid common mistakes. In addition to understanding the local market and demand for their product, they must have a well-developed, thorough, and realistic budget; know the real costs of the project; set a realistic time line with milestones; and have money in reserve or access to capital. Additionally, the developer must demonstrate that he knows how to manage construction, sales, and leasing.

Fees are often based on the size of the deal. For projects under $10 million, fees are typically fixed. Lenders assess between 0 to 1 points (0 to 1 percent of the total loan amount) for the service of providing the loan.[22] Each lender who lends money to the project receives a fee as well as coverage of certain expenses such as appraisals. Additionally, if loan brokers are involved in finding a lender, they too will be paid a fee, typically 1 percent of the loan amount. If a project is anticipated to be unusually risky, an additional 1 to 2 points may be added. If the project is larger than $10 million, the fee may not increase proportionally; the net fee may actually be less. According to Steve Bram, president of George Smith Partners in Los Angeles, apartment loan rates in 2002 were priced at 225 to 275 basis points over the 12-month moving average for Treasury bills.

Sources of Financing for Real Estate Projects

Several types of financial institutions are potential sources of real estate loans.

Commercial Banks. Commercial banks are a principal source of both construction and miniperm loans. They usually prefer to lend money for a short term—one to three years—through the construction and leasing period, at which time the permanent lender pays off the construction lender. For larger developers, commercial banks may grant miniperm loans up to five years. These loans were especially attractive during periods of high inflation when developers expected permanent mortgage rates to fall. One hundred percent financing is sometimes available on a superior project, although 70 to 80 percent financing is more common today. In tight money markets, 60 to 65 percent loans are often the only financing available. Beginning developers are more likely to find a local bank than a larger national bank to fund their first few projects. Construction loans are usually made by local and regional banks because of their familiarity with local conditions. Moreover, they have the ability to oversee and properly manage the loan during the construction phase and monitor the process and progression of construction. After a developer has completed three or four successful projects, larger national banks, which tend to lend greater amounts of money, show more interest. Banks are reluctant to participate in joint ventures but will take part in participating mortgages, which offer the developer higher loan-to-value ratios while giving the bank higher yields through participation in project cash flows.

Savings and Loan Institutions. Although S&Ls were a prime source—perhaps the major source—of financing for beginning developers in the 1980s, their role today has been greatly diminished. Traditionally, they were willing to participate in joint ventures with developers and to work with beginning developers. The S&L crisis of the late 1980s, however, has made them a much smaller factor in real estate lending. They are no longer allowed to own subsidiary companies, and they cannot participate in real estate joint ventures. Today, they make primarily home loans and apartment loans.

Insurance Companies. Life insurance companies fund large projects with long-term loans, typically ten years, and provide both construction and permanent financing. Loans typically have fixed rates, unlike those from most construction lenders. Beginning developers with no track record probably will have difficulty attracting an insurance company to a project.

Pension Funds. Pension funds have become a major source of financing for real estate as they have sought to diversify their investments. Their ability to infuse large amounts of money has made them attractive financing prospects for developers. They finance both construction loans and longer-term mortgages, usually at fixed rates. Generally, pension funds finance large projects undertaken by experienced developers. Often, pension funds employ investment advisers in a fiduciary role to assess the real estate transaction. Pension fund advisers perform all the functions that a traditional real estate owner or lender performs on behalf of the pension fund.[23] They evaluate the project's location, regional and local economies, market supply and demand, projected cash flow, the developer's reputation, and the project's quality. Pension fund investments can take longer to finance because decisions do not rest with an individual as with a private investor. Instead, they are made by a committee in the organization.

Foreign Investors. Global money markets, including foreign investors and foreign banks, play a role in real estate, both in the United States and abroad. Firms from Canada, Great Britain, Germany, and Japan have traditionally been among the most active players in the United States. Asian investors were very significant players in the late 1980s to early 1990s, but their activity was sharply reduced when the "roaring tiger economies" of that period came to an end. In the early 2000s, European lenders, especially German banks, are once again the most active in U.S. markets. Foreign sources of capital will change as other European and Asian economies take off again. Although most foreign investors prefer to buy developed properties, they also have been important sources of development capital, primarily for larger firms.

Syndications and Real Estate Investment Trusts. Syndications and real estate investment trusts (REITs) provide a way of carving up real estate ownership into small pieces that many people can afford. They have been used for raising equity capital and mortgage financing for development projects. Both vehicles limit investors' liability and provide pass-through tax benefits that flow directly to the investor, thus avoiding the additional layers of taxation associated with corporate ownership. Syndications were a primary source of equity capital for development before the 1986 Tax Reform Act. The act eliminated many of the tax benefits that make syndications so attractive, and they have been in decline ever since. Public syndications are no longer a significant source of capital, although private syndications remain the best source of capital for small developers through limited partnerships and joint ventures.

REITs have become an increasingly significant mechanism for raising capital to fund development projects. REITs are entities that combine the capital of many investors to acquire or provide financing for all forms of real estate. A REIT serves much like a mutual fund for real estate in that retail investors obtain the benefits of a diversified portfolio under professional management. Its shares are freely traded, usually on a major stock exchange.

Private Investors and Joint Ventures. Probably the most common type of financial partner for a beginning developer is a private investor, who can be almost anyone. Usually, a private party puts up the necessary equity. Equally if not more important, they may be willing to sign on the construction note—something that beginning developers often require to obtain their first construction loan. Occasionally, a private investor funds a project's total cost. The profit split with private investors may range from 80/20 (80 percent to the investor) to 50/50. The developer will likely be asked to make some cash investment, ranging from 5 percent to 33 percent of the total equity required, but he may have as little as 1 to 2 percent of the equity in the deal. The developer may also be required to take on the first assignment of risk, that is, cover losses up to a certain amount. Because the investor risks a greater percentage of the equity for a lesser percentage of the profit, it is important to have complete confidence in both the project and the developer's reputation before pursuing a deal.

Investment firms also assemble equity capital from multiple investors to fund new development or to buy existing real estate. Many of these firms work with Wall Street to match up investment funds with developers that provide desired program uses or desired markets in particular locales.

The Bond Market and Commercial Mortgage–Backed Securities. The issuance of commercial mortgage–backed securities (CMBSs)—the sale of bond-like interests in portfolios of mortgage-backed loans backed by commercial real estate and sold through the capital markets to individual and institutional buyers—has grown tremendously in recent years. The CMBS market has continued to gain share in overall holdings of real estate debt, growing from less than 0.5 percent of the value of outstanding commercial real estate mortgages in 1989 to almost 14 percent in 2000.

Credit Companies. Some large U.S. corporations use their power in financial markets to establish *credit companies*. Some of these companies, such as GE Capital and General Motors Acceptance Corporation (GMAC), provide construction and redevelopment financing. Compared with banks, credit companies are subject to less federal government regulation of their lending practices. As a result, they are often willing to lend on projects that involve more risk or are more complex than those within the parameters of commercial banks. Often, however, they charge higher interest rates and have stronger recourse measures.

Mezzanine Debt. Since the 1980s, mezzanine debt has been established as an intermediate funding mechanism that usually supplements the equity investment and first mortgage. Any of the lenders identified above may use it. Typically, deals with mezzanine debt are structured with a 70 percent mortgage, 5 to 25 percent mezzanine debt, and the remainder from the developer's equity. Unlike a mortgage, a partnership interest is assigned in case the developer defaults on the loan. These loans are typically short term and have higher fees: 2 to 3 percent is common. Mezzanine debt loan rates were running 11 to 13 percent in the early 2000s (3 to 5 percent above prime). Although interest rates are significantly higher than construction and permanent loan rates, they take the place of equity, thereby reducing the most expensive money that a developer has to raise.

Construction Lenders. Several different types of lenders finance construction loans. The specific institution funding a project depends on the development team's level of experience and the type and size of the project. Most construction loans today have interest rates that float with the prime rate. Construction loan interest rates typically run 150 to 250 basis points (1.5 to 2.5 percent) over prime, depending on the developer's size, experience, and credit rating. Thus, if the prime lending rate (to a bank's best customers) is 8 percent, construction loan rates would be 10 percent, assuming a 200–basis point spread over prime.

Beginning developers should start their search for construction financing with a banker they know. They should ask for referrals and choose half a dozen potential lenders. They also may solicit the advice of other developers in the field.

Once the construction loan is closed and the construction lender begins to fund construction of the building, the developer should be aware of the lender's concerns and try to address them before they become problems. Developers should stay in close touch with their lender during construction. If a project is falling behind schedule or going over budget, the developer should inform the lender quickly and not allow the lender to hear the news from someone else. All experienced real estate lenders understand the complications that can arise during the development process. They can often advise the developer about financial strategies that can be employed while the obstacles are overcome. Regardless, it is paramount to keep lenders informed to maintain their confidence and trust in the developer.

Developers must recognize and address the varied concerns of construction lenders:

- Design—Lenders are becoming more concerned about a project's design. The general trend is toward better-quality projects.
- Permits—Developers must make sure that all permits are in place so that the project does not fall prey to delays or moratoriums. Even if building permits are obtained, entitlements (the rights to proceed) must be secured.[24]
- Brownfields—Most lenders require a borrower to indemnify and hold them free and harmless of any liability resulting from toxic or hazardous waste located on a site.
- Insurance—The builder's risk and general liability insurance must be in place; usually, lenders are named as additional beneficiaries.
- The Developer's Capacity—Lenders evaluate whether the developer's associates or partners can complete the project if the developer is suddenly injured or they must bring in another individual.
- Credibility/Integrity/Cash—Lenders analyze the developer's credibility and integrity and the status of his cash flow—anything that may prevent the completion of the project.
- Disbursements/Inspections/Lien Releases—Most lenders inspect the site monthly to verify requests for payments. If lenders have problems with lien releases (suppliers and contractors can file a *mechanics lien* against the property if they are not paid), the lender may write joint checks to the developer and contractor. A joint check must be endorsed by all payees and helps a lender to ensure that the contractor and/or suppliers are paid. The check endorsement by the contractor serves as proof of payment and protects the lender (and the developer) against frivolous mechanics liens.
- Standby Commitments—Standby commitments provide assurance to construction lenders that their loans

will be repaid. Developers often secure standby commitments when permanent financing is unavailable. Normally, the standby commitment is never exercised, because developers find permanent financing before their construction loans expire. Standby commitments are available from certain banks, insurance companies, credit companies, and REITs. Fees for standby commitments run 1 to 2 percent of the total loan amount each year that it is in force but remains unfunded (the developer has not borrowed any funds under the standby commitment). If the standby loan is actually funded, interest rates typically run 5 percent or more over the prime rate. Although standby commitments are expensive, they allow developers to proceed in situations where a construction lender demands some form of takeout commitment before it will fund the construction loan.

Permanent Lenders. The permanent loan provides the takeout (repayment) for the construction loan. Banks, insurance companies, and pension funds make permanent loans. Increasingly, permanent loans are securitized on Wall Street, where they are sold to investors in the CMBS market.

Traditionally, a developer must have a permanent loan takeout in place to obtain construction financing. Larger, more experienced developers with strong balance sheets may be able to get a construction loan without a permanent loan commitment, but beginning developers most likely will need to have a commitment for a permanent loan before they can begin construction. Permanent financing usually has fixed interest rates, and although the loan is typically amortized over 30 years, the term of the loan is often limited to ten years. At the end of that time, the note is renegotiated or refinanced by a new permanent loan.

Most of the concerns listed previously for construction lenders apply equally to permanent lenders. Permanent lenders look to the property more than to the borrower for assurance that they will not lose their investment. In most cases, developers do not sign personally on permanent loans. Thus, a strong and fully leased property owned by a financially weak party will obtain financing more quickly than an unleased property with a strong owner.

To locate permanent lenders, a developer historically needed to find out which local lenders funded projects of a size and type similar to the developer's project. Today, permanent financing is likely to come from a number of national and even international sources. A mortgage broker functioning as an intermediary can help the developer identify alternatives for permanent financing. A developer should thoroughly understand the lender's criteria, such as the percentage that must be preleased, and should compare effective borrowing costs on different mortgages—a computation (discussed in Chapter 4) that takes into account interest rates, fees, points, prepayment penalties, and other costs as well as anticipated holding time until the developer sells or refinances the property.

Once the loan agreement is operational, the developer must make prompt and punctual payments, maintain the project in good operating order, and keep all insurance and taxes up to date. If problems arise, the lender should be informed immediately. By being candid, a developer will retain the lender's confidence and find it easier to obtain financing the next time.

Mortgage Bankers and Brokers. Both mortgage bankers and brokers help developers obtain financing for their projects. In some cases, the broker assists the developer in getting financing but does not have direct access to funds, whereas the banker has direct access to funds and usually services the loan as well.[25] The relationship between the banker or broker and the client differs somewhat as well. The banker has a fiduciary relationship with the client, while a broker acts as an intermediary and merely looks for the best combination of funding for the client. A developer may use a single broker or hire different brokers to help find mortgage financing and equity financing. Brokers assist the borrower in preparing a summary package for the deal, including underwriting and research, marketing the loan to many lenders using their established relationships, and negotiating, processing, and closing complex deals and transactions.

Some developers believe that using a mortgage broker adds an unnecessary middleman and that developers who already have a banker should start there to look for financing. Others say mortgage brokers are necessary because loans can be very complex and a financial specialist such as a broker can help find more creative solutions to financing. Some also believe that it is important to give bankers or brokers exclusive rights to assemble the capital to maintain their full attention, rather than spreading this responsibility to multiple parties. In such cases, the developer may want to require the intermediary to seek other investors and split fees if necessary or to go to other bankers to access that bank's exclusive list of lenders. In some instances, a developer may ask the banker or broker to work with the developer's own established contacts for lenders, which may result in cutting the broker's fee.

Every mortgage banker or broker is not suited for every project, however. Developers should not be afraid to ask brokers and bankers for their credentials and references and should find out which projects they have financed and how well versed they are in the real estate business. Developers must also question how a prospective lender's specific system works: How do the developer and contractor request draws? Will the lender allow a land draw upfront? How often will the lender visit the site or inspect a completed building? How and when are interest, points, and origination fees paid? At the same time, developers can indicate their readiness to use a lender's services again if they prove to be satisfactory this time. Eventually, developers may want to approach lenders with the idea of starting a long-term relationship.

Once a relationship with a banker or broker is established, a developer can get the most out of the association by considering the entity as an integral part of the team whose function is to bring expertise about the capital market to the table. It is also important to provide full disclosure of both the strengths and weaknesses of the deal to the banker or broker.

Mortgage brokers' fees vary. The standard fee is 1 percent of the loan amount. The lender also charges a fee in addition to points, the application fee, the appraisal fee, and all the other standard costs of a loan.

Conclusion

Development is a team effort. The lenders, contractors, professional consultants, and other specialists described in this chapter represent the major players with whom developers must be familiar, but they are not the only ones. As development becomes increasingly complex, other talents and specialties must be found. For example, environmental and political consultants were only rarely employed as recently as ten years ago. Today, they are commonly part of the development team.

Successful development depends on the developer's ability to manage the many participants in the development process. The developer must be able to recognize quality work and must know when to ask questions, whom to ask, and what to ask. The developer must strike a delicate balance between trust in the decisions of the players on the team and constant vigilance. If mistakes are made, the developer is ultimately responsible, no matter who made them. Even if the developer is not at fault, he invariably pays for the mistakes—either directly or indirectly through delays and higher interest costs.

Notes

1. Richard Hardy, "Strategic Planning in Development Firms," *Journal of Real Estate Development*, Spring 1986, pp. 28–42.

2. Ibid., p. 29.

3. Interview with Peter Inman, Inman and Associates, Irvine, California.

4. Diane R. Suchman, *Managing a Development Company* (Washington, D.C.: ULI–the Urban Land Institute, 1987), pp. 2–3.

5. Ibid., p. 3.

6. Hardy, "Strategic Planning in Development Firms," p. 35.

7. Small homebuilding firms and industrial developers also tend to be organized by function, because the nature of their business is repetition. Repetition, especially in leasing and construction, lends itself to more functional organization, in which activities are more specialized and often require less highly trained workers.

8. John O'Donnell, chair, the O'Donnell Group, Newport Beach, California, at the USC Lusk Center for Real Estate Development spring retreat, Desert Hot Springs, California, 1989.

9. Christopher Lee, president, CEL & Associates, Los Angeles, California, January 2002.

10. Ibid.

11. For more information, see Christopher Bettin and Kenneth Reyhons, *Strategic Planning for the Real Estate Manager* (Chicago: Realtors National Marketing Institute, 1993); George S. Day et al. (eds.), *Wharton on Dynamic Competitive Strategy* (New York: Wiley, 1997); Colin Eden and Fran Ackermann, *Making Strategy: The Journey of Strategic Management* (Thousand Oaks, Calif.: Sage, 1998); Arnoldo C. Hax et al., *The Strategy Concept and Process: A Pragmatic Approach*, 2nd ed. (Upper Saddle River, N.J.: Prentice Hall, 1996); Jay R. Galbraith, *Designing Organizations: An Executive Briefing on Strategy, Structure, and Process*, Management Series (San Francisco: Jossey-Bass, 1995); and Anthony W. Ulwick, *Business Strategy Formulation: Theory, Process, and the Intellectual Revolution* (Westport, Conn.: Quorum Books, 1999).

12. See www.aia.org for more information.

13. Interview with Ronald Stenlund, president, Central Consulting Engineers, Green Bay, Wisconsin, November 2001.

14. Interview with Jonathan Rose, principal, Jonathan Rose and Companies, Katonah, New York, May 2002.

15. Interview with Douglas Hahn, senior environmental scientist, URS Corporation, Los Angeles, California, March 2002.

16. Jonathan Rose, May 2002.

17. Interview with Patrick Kennedy, owner, Panoramic Interests, Berkeley, California, March 2002.

18. Interview with H. Pike Oliver, principal, INTERRA and the Presidio Group, Sacramento, California, November 2001.

19. Interview with Leonard Zax, Latham & Watkins real estate group, Washington, D.C., December 2001.

20. Jeannie Quintal, title officer, First American Title Company, Los Angeles, California, August 2002.

21. www.irem.org.

22. *Points* are expressed as percentages (1 or 2 percent), while *basis points* are expressed as hundredths of a percent (100 basis points = 1 percent).

23. NAREIM, the National Association of Real Estate Investment Managers (www.nareim.com), is the association to which pension fund real estate advisers belong. Member organizations represent a very important class of financing sources for developers as well as jobs for real estate students.

24. In California and Hawaii, for example, construction has been halted by building moratoriums after building permits have been obtained but before significant construction (in particular, structural framing) has been completed.

25. *Loan servicing* involves collecting loan payments and sending them to the current holder of the loan. The originator often sells loans to another lender. The servicing agent does not necessarily change if the loan is sold. Servicing fees average 0.125 to 0.25 percent and are included as part of the interest rate. For example, if the quoted interest rate is 9.5 percent and the servicing fee is 0.125 percent, the servicer sends the difference (9.375 percent of the remaining loan balance) plus amortization to the loan holder.

3. Land Development

Overview

Subdivision of land is the principal mechanism by which communities are developed. Technically, *subdivision* describes the legal and physical steps a developer must take to convert raw land into developed land. This chapter examines these steps, which may apply to tracts of any size intended for any use, in the context of the development of small residential subdivisions. Subdivision is a vital part of a community's growth, determining its appearance, the mix of its land uses, and its infrastructure, including roads, drainage systems, water, sewerage, and public utilities.[1]

Many current subdivision regulations have evolved because earlier regulations did not provide adequate streets, utilities, setbacks, and development densities to create a suitable living environment. Developers and planners have often led the way toward better regulation, their projects demonstrating how improved standards lead to superior development patterns.

Each decade has brought new problems and concerns that have changed the land development regulatory process. Developers today must be more mindful than ever of the impact that their projects may have on local communities. Even when their projects conform to existing zoning requirements, developers are finding that they must justify their projects to local communities in terms

Pictured at left are the Laurel Canyon Apartments, a subdivision of the master-planned community of Ladera Ranch in South Orange, California.

of beneficial (or at least not adverse) impacts on the environment, traffic, tax base, schools, parks, and other public facilities. Thus, in the broader sphere of urban development, developers must respect the complex relationships that tie the private and the public sectors together.

Subdividing Land

The subdivision process by which land is transformed from a raw to a developed state may take place in three stages: raw land, semideveloped land (usually divided into 20- to 100-acre [8- to 40-hectare] tracts with roads and utilities extended to the edge of the property), and developed or subdivided land, platted into individual homesites and five- to ten-acre (2- to 4-hectare) commercial parcels ready for building. The latter is typical for large greenfield projects. Smaller projects and infill and redevelopment sites typically skip the second phase; together, they account for an increasing share of development. Figure 3-1 shows the structure of the land conversion industry and the roles of the various players. The process of converting raw land to semideveloped land differs from region to region, depending on the pattern of landownership, the capacity of local developers and financial institutions, and the institutional mechanisms for providing roads and utilities. To ease the conversion process, states such as California and Texas rely heavily on special districts created to finance utility services. Where such vehicles do not exist, developers must wait for the community or utility company to furnish utility service, pay for the extension of roads and utility lines

Iron Horse Lofts in Walnut Creek, California, illustrates how high-density infill housing can be achieved without compromising architectural integrity, amenities, or open space for residents. This mixed-income project on four acres (1.6 hectares) features 87 affordable rental apartments and 54 townhouse live/work lofts.

themselves, or, in some cases, form consortiums with other developers to pay for road and utility extensions.

The conversion of raw land to semideveloped land tends to be a project for larger developers. Such developers typically work with 200- to 1,000-acre (81- to 405-hectare) tracts of land, which they subdivide into smaller 20- to 100-acre (8- to 40-hectare) parcels. They provide the major infrastructure, including arterial roads, utilities, and drainage systems for the smaller parcels so that they can subsequently be subdivided into buildable lots.

In suburban fringe areas, the developer may skip the second stage and convert the raw land directly to subdivided lots. Direct conversion to subdivided lots is more likely to occur in slower growth areas and in places where municipal utility companies install the utilities. Land does not become available for development in a smooth pattern. Farmers, estate owners, and other landholders may sell parcels for reasons such as a death or retirement or because a buyer has made an attractive offer. Because large, contiguous tracts of land rarely become available at one time, leapfrog development that pushes farther away from the city center and low-density sprawl often occur.[2] A major criticism of sprawl is that it leads to uniformly lower densities and causes a city to spread out, resulting in inefficient use of roads and other infrastructure and the inability to provide municipal services such as mass transit.[3]

This process, however, may lead to opportunities for developers. The land parcels that are passed over during the first wave of development can offer creative developers opportunities for infill development. Such sites, while not without difficulties, are often better located and more competitive in terms of market potential than greenfield development sites that are farther from the city center.

Because developers are the central players in the conversion from raw land to developed land, they must understand the dynamics of market and regulatory forces. Land developers must be especially astute politically because they serve as the primary agents of physical change in a community. Residents tend to resist change and fight new development unless it offers a tangible benefit to them. As a result, developers must gain the support of those who play major roles in determining local land use: elected officials, planning and zoning boards, utility companies, regional air and water quality commissions, traffic commissions, governance boards, and citizen groups.

Developers also should be adept in dealing with multiple government jurisdictions. In fact, in some cases, they determine which municipality a new subdivision will become part of. In California, for example, adjacent municipalities may dispute which one has jurisdiction over a new subdivision. LAFCO, the Local Area Formation Commission, settles the dispute—one more government approval the developer must obtain.

Historically, developers assumed that they had the right to develop land as long as they met the restrictions imposed by zoning and other land use regulations, but this presumption of development rights has largely dissolved. Even when developers' projects conform to existing zoning, development rights may be subject to reduction, depending on the attitudes of neighboring residents and the political environment. The likelihood of obtaining necessary approvals in a timely fashion is one of the major risks that developers must evaluate before committing themselves to a project. Developers should be well versed in local politics and have an abundance of personal alliances, as even relatively problem-free tracts may require a significant amount of government processing.

Developers must become more involved in the regulatory decision-making process and must be prepared to help educate their communities and themselves. In the 1970s and 1980s, initiatives for controlling growth through caps on building permits and sewer moratoriums were popular but often ineffective and sometimes contrary to the best interests of a community, adding further to inefficiency and sprawl. In recent years, the concept of smart growth has gained support from communities as a way of addressing the issue of how to accommodate inevitable growth in a way that enhances livability, the environment, and the economy (see Chapter 8).[4]

Developers also have become advocates for affordable housing and starter homes. To hold down escalating land and infrastructure costs, they are often called on to demonstrate how new higher density concepts will create attractive and livable communities. Working with community leaders, they have developed constructive approaches that deal with the problems of growth without causing unintended side effects, such as skyrocketing housing prices.

Land Development versus Building Development

This chapter focuses on small-scale land development, typically involving 20 to 50 acres (8 to 20 hectares).

Although the techniques described here apply to any form of land development, beginning developers are most likely to become involved with single-family or townhouse residential subdivisions, small mixed-use subdivisions, and warehouse or industrial development.

Many developers engage in both land development and building development (houses, apartments, warehouses, and so forth). When they perform both activities on the same tract, they often view the two activities as a single project. They are distinct types of development, and each should be analyzed on its own merits.

Many considerations arise when a developer is in charge of both land and building development on the same property. For instance, other builders may be reluctant to buy any excess land because of the competition from the developer's own building activities, especially in light of the developer's cost advantage. Selling land to other builders may be more difficult if lots are available in other competitive subdivisions in the area. The problem of building on some lots and selling others can be alleviated by bringing in builders who will target their product to a different segment of the market.

Different parts of the country have different customs when it comes to developing small residential subdivisions. In some areas, it is customary for homebuilders to subdivide the land and build the houses together, using a single construction loan—especially for tract houses (houses of similar design by the same builder) in communities that require public hearings on house plans and on lot subdivision.[5]

In general, land development is riskier but more profitable than homebuilding because it is so dependent on the public sector for approvals and infrastruc-

figure 3-1

The Structure of the Land Conversion Industry and the Activity of Predevelopment

	Types of Land Investors				
	Buyer of Raw Land	Land Speculator	Predeveloper	Land Developer	Builder/End User
Major Function	Begins conversion	Holds the property waiting for growth to approach	Analyzes market and plans development; clears all regulatory hurdles	Installs utilities; completes subdividing program	Builds structures for sale, rent, or own use; may employ general contractor
Typical Financing	Noninstitutional		May attract institutional investment on selective basis	May be able to obtain construction loans and long-term real estate investors	
Typically Sells To	Land speculator	Other speculators. Last in line to sell to some type of developer	Land developer or end user	Other (smaller) builders or end users	
Typical Length of Tenure	10+ years	8–10 years	2–5 years	1+ years	Indeterminate

Source: Alan Rabinowitz, *Land Investment and the Predevelopment Process* (New York: Quorum Books, 1988), p. 26.

ture and because it involves a long investment period with no positive cash flow.

Project Feasibility

Although development opportunities exist for many different types of land, beginning land developers are well advised to search for comparatively problem-free tracts of land—land that is already served by utilities and is, or is likely to be, appropriately zoned. Although raw land may be available, the resources and the time required to bring utilities to a tract and to obtain the necessary public approvals generally go beyond the capabilities of beginning developers. The beginner's time and money are better spent building a track record of completed, successful smaller projects.

Market Analysis before Site Selection

Market analysis occurs at two separate times—before site selection and after site selection as the project is defined. The objective of market analysis before site selection is to identify which segments of the market are underserved. Large developers have the luxury of investigating a number of markets to select the most competitive product type and location. Beginning developers have neither the time nor the resources required to embark on such an exploration. In addition, they usually want to remain close to home in territory with which they are familiar. If possible, their projects should be near enough for them to keep a close watch over on-site progress. Further, local planning bodies and regulatory agencies tend to view local developers more favorably than out-of-towners, thereby giving local developers the home-town advantage.

This it not to say that more distant opportunities should be automatically vetoed. Opportunities can arise anywhere. Nevertheless, beginning developers have enough difficulties to overcome without the additional handi-caps of distance and unfamiliarity with distant markets, officials, and building practices.

A developer's primary market decisions concern the proposed project's use, location, and size. If a developer has no preference for a specific use, then each segment of the market—residential, industrial, commercial, or mixed-use—should be analyzed. Real estate markets are highly segmented, and a developer cannot infer from the demand for residential development that retail development is also in demand. Similarly, a developer cannot assume that because residential product is in demand in certain neighborhoods it is in demand everywhere in the region.

It used to be common practice for a developer to select a use and a target market and then find a suitable parcel of land. Today, with developable sites at a premium in so many metropolitan regions, it has become increasingly common to select the site first and then undertake market analysis to identify potential uses and target markets for that parcel. If the developer has already identified the land use for which excess demand exists, the purpose of the market analysis is to identify the particular market segment (for instance, mid-priced, single-family houses for move-up families) and the location where demand is greatest.

Major sources of information are brokers, lenders, and, in particular, builders to whom the land developer will market the developed sites. Developers should identify those firms that specialize in building their proposed product types and then should discuss their intentions with them. Because developers and homebuilders are prospective clients, they are usually eager to provide assistance. It is also possible to obtain relevant market information at little cost from other sources. Major local lenders, market research firms, and brokers often publish quarterly or annual reports for apartments, office space, single-family houses, and industrial space. A wealth of economic and market information can also be found on the Internet. Assembling this information and ana-

Beacon Centre business park in Miami, Florida. Industrial buildings can be an attractive addition to the urban environment if developed sensitively using simple decorative features, appealing signage, colorful awnings, and architectural details.

John Gillan

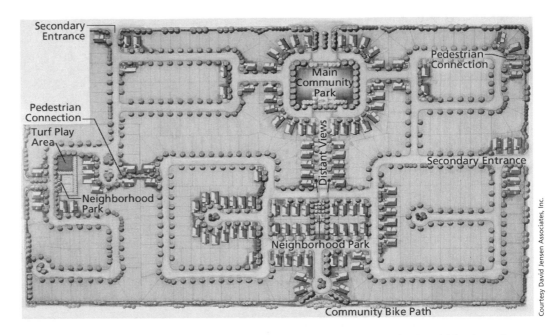

Pebble Creek at Green Valley in Henderson, Nevada, is a 67-acre (27-hectare) community targeted to entry-level first-time homebuyers. Residents have access to parks and play areas through pedestrian and bike path connections.

lyzing it can take considerable time and energy though, even at the early stages, so it may be more efficient to engage the services of a market consultant. The most important questions to which developers want answers concern the market for the proposed product type:

- Where are the desirable areas or parts of town?
- What are the hot segments of the market?
- Who are the most active buyers? What are their characteristics and preferences?
- If a builder owned land in that area, what would he build?
- For what types of building are lenders giving loans?
- For what types of building are lenders not giving loans?
- What physical features and amenities are especially popular?
- Who are the main builders?
- Who else is developing in a particular area? What are they building? How many units (or square feet) are planned for the future?
- How many units are they selling per month?
- What are the standard deal terms that builders are using to buy lots?

Major homebuilders project the annual demand for units by price category throughout their metropolitan area. They break down the number of houses sold in each market area of the metropolitan region by $25,000 or $50,000 intervals. For example, suppose it is estimated that 56 percent of all new housing units will be sold in the western part of town and that 75 percent of the units will be priced under $300,000. If the total projected demand for the city is, say, 5,000 houses in 2002, the demand for houses costing under $300,000 in the western section of town would be 2,100 units (56 percent times 75 percent times 5,000).

After estimating demand, developers should next ask themselves how much of that demand can be captured

by their project. The answer, which should be based on extremely conservative assumptions, depends on the number of similar projects selling in the market and how competitive the proposed development is likely to be. Developers must be honest with themselves. They must consider whether their site is less physically attractive or accessible or features the same level of amenities as the competition. Suppose a given area contains 3,000 lots in 20 subdivisions. If each of four developers has five of the subdivisions, each developer's share of the market captured would be 25 percent, or 525 lots (25 percent times 2,100). Many developers allocate more lots to subdivisions that possess better amenities, terrain, or management. They also look at historical absorption rates by different subdivisions and developers. Depending on the weight given to each factor, the analysis indicates that the developers should capture more or less than their prorated share. If they anticipate selling twice their share, however, then the other developers must theoretically lose market share by the same amount. Overestimating the capture rate is the single most common mistake in market analysis. In the short run, builders can steal market share from other builders, especially if they have a better design, amenity package, or location. In the long run, however, builders who are losing sales will cut prices until they regain their share.

Land developers must never forget that their product is an intermediate good that is used to produce an end product. The demand for finished lots depends on the demand for houses—not just for any houses but for houses in the price range that justifies the lot price. If demand for those houses declines, so will the demand for lots.

The ratio of lot price to house price has risen steadily over the last half century. In the 1960s, the cost of a lot rarely accounted for more than 15 percent of total house price. Today, it may vary from 20 to 50 percent. Higher ratios may be found in areas where land costs are high, such as infill sites in high-income cities and suburbs and

Site Evaluation Factors

Market Area and Competition

Location and Neighborhood
- proximity to key locations in metropolitan area
- quality of surrounding environment
- existing housing/other structures
- schools and churches
- parks and recreational facilities
- amenities
- shopping
- public improvements

Size and Shape

Accessibility and Visibility

Site Conditions
- slopes
- vegetation
- grading or fill required to build
- existing structures
- hydrology and drainage patterns
- toxic wastes
- soil properties
- wildlife/endangered species
- sensitive land

Legal Constraints
- utility easements
- private easements
- deed restrictions
- covenants that run with the land

Utilities
- water
- sewer
- electricity
- gas
- telephone
- cable television

Zoning and Regulatory Environment
- development climate
- exactions
- impact fees
- future takings
- future road widenings
- approvals needed
- citizen participation/opposition
- approval process

■

---

in high-priced metropolitan areas like Los Angeles, San Francisco, Washington, D.C., and Boston. A general rule of thumb is that builders pay approximately 20 percent of the finished house price for the lot. Thus, if they build houses that sell for $200,000, they can afford to pay $40,000 for the lot. Developers should not, however, rely on rules of thumb; they should rather carefully investigate local market conditions.

Suppose the absorption rate is ten units per month for $180,000 houses, compared with 15 units per month for $150,000 houses. Builders of the $180,000 houses will pay $36,000 per lot rather than $30,000 per lot for the less costly houses. If developers proceed with their projects under the assumption that they can sell $36,000 lots, they may be in trouble if the market turns out to favor the less expensive houses. Even if they are willing to accept the lower sale price of $30,000 per lot, their lenders may set loan covenants that prevent the sale.[6]

Developers' assessments of the market determine where they should look for land and how much they should be willing to pay for it. Market research is a critical first step, not only for selecting a site but also for determining the types of builders that should be approached. Another benefit of the preliminary market analysis is that even while looking for sites, the developer can generate interest among builders. One might focus on smaller builders (who build ten to 50 houses per year) who are likely to purchase a few lots at a time in a subdivision. The builders will tell the developer where they want to build and what the ideal lot size, configuration, and amenity package are. If the developer can meet their requirements, builders may even precommit to purchasing the lots. Such commitments can be the linchpin of the developer's first deal. A firm purchase letter from a creditworthy builder can give the beginning developer the credibility he needs to obtain financing.

Site Selection and Acquisition

In selecting a development site, beginning developers face a number of limitations that can be overcome only by doing considerable homework. To overcome the limitations:

- Choose a manageable geographic area for the search.
- Set an appropriate time frame for investigating conditions.
- Do not depend exclusively on brokers to find sites.

Because they lack the reputation and contacts of experienced developers, beginning developers are less likely to hear about deals firsthand. Deals that have been "on the street" are not necessarily bad deals, however. It may take time for landowners to realize the true value of their property. Or developers may pass on deals for other reasons: the site may be too small or otherwise inappropriate for the use the developers had in mind.

In addition to working with a network of brokers, developers should talk to landowners whose land is not currently for sale. Direct contact may generate a deal or lead to a possible joint venture or favorable terms of purchase.

Site Evaluation. The relative importance of various factors of subdivision development depends on the end user of the subdivided lots. The major site evaluation factors are summarized in the accompanying feature box, and greater detail regarding site evaluation for residential development can be found in Chapter 4.

Many physical, legal, and other factors—in fact, more than 1,000—must be considered before buying a site.[7] Among the more important items, the developer should:

- make sure all easements are plotted on a map and that any easement problems are cleared up and any purchase arrangements for easements made before closing;

- check for drainage problems and ascertain the level of the water table, which affects sewer lines, septic tanks, and foundations;
- check earthquake maps to make sure that faults do not cross the land;
- check flood insurance/floodplain maps;
- check Federal Housing Authority (FHA) requirements concerning width of roads, culs-de-sac, and other design requirements;
- investigate whether any parties are likely to delay or stop the sale;
- make sure that utilities such as water, sewer, gas, electricity, telephone, and cable television are available;
- check off-site requirements;
- check permit costs, impact fees, and exactions;
- check for appropriate zoning;
- determine whether all necessary development approvals will be granted;
- make sure that builders will be able to obtain building permits;
- check for environmental issues—especially if a lake, pond, or swamp lies on the land—and avoid wetlands, as they usually involve a time-consuming approval process;
- beware of sulfates in the soil, which eat away concrete and masonry;
- check for radon, a harmful derivative of uranium that is present in many areas;
- check historical aerial photos that may show evidence of toxic waste, such as storage tanks on the site;
- check for landfill sites close by, as methane gas could cause explosions;
- look for smoke, fumes, or odors, and check the land at all times of the day;
- always walk the land.

The developer should also carefully consider the environment where the site is located. What is the overall political climate? Will the community object to new development, or does it support growth? Is the planned development compatible with the surrounding neighborhood? Are shopping, schools, and parks nearby? If schools are an issue, what is their reputation?

Site Acquisition. In land development, as in other forms of development, purchasing a site with a three-stage contract—a free-look period, a period during which earnest money is forfeitable, and closing—is customary. Purchasers want to get as much time as they can to close with as little money at risk as possible. For sellers, the reverse is true. Sellers want the closing to occur as quickly as possible with as much forfeitable earnest money at stake as possible. The agreed-upon terms depend on the state of the market.

In slow markets, favorable terms of purchase are more likely. With fewer buyers than sellers, sellers are typically more willing to give a potential purchaser more time to investigate their property without requiring hard earnest money. In a hot market, sellers are less afraid of losing a deal and are more concerned about tying up their property when another buyer may be just around the corner. Developers must respond to market conditions accordingly.

If the site consists of multiple parcels under separate ownership, progress is further complicated by the fact that all the necessary parcels must first be acquired. Land assembly is a tricky business and usually requires sophisticated negotiation and acquisition techniques to ensure that the owner of the last or other key parcels does not insist on an exorbitantly high sale price.

The terms of acquisition set the stage for everything else. When buying land, developers are chiefly concerned about whether or not they can build what they want to build and whether they have time to check out title, physical conditions, utilities, market, financing, economics, and design feasibility.

To overcome the difficulties and potential setbacks of inexperience, a beginning developer must look harder

Checklist for Buying Land

Purchasing Agreement Data
Ownership information, environmental statements, improvements, buildable area, price, real estate agent, seller financing, escrow agent and fees, deposits needed

Condition of Title
Title report, lawsuits, existing loans, taxes, judgments or mechanics liens, building restrictions, assessments, easements, crops, other agreements

Physical Aspects
Topography, drainage, survey, special zones, environmental conditions (including soils, flood areas, wetlands, toxic or hazardous waste, vegetation, seismic faults, adjoining land), views, access, any other adverse conditions

Availability of Utilities
Gas, electric, water, wells, sewer, telephone, cable television, street lights, joint trenching, storm drainage, police, fire, trash collection, utility costs

Entitlements
Governing body; moratoriums; ordinances; zoning; redevelopment area; condemnations; special assessments, requirements, and reports; subdivision approval timetable

Development Costs
All on-site and off-site costs, all building and subdivision fees, overhead, refundable costs, cost per lot

Market Area and Proposed Product
Product type, target markets, competition, resale market, neighborhood, commercial and industrial developments, military and government installations, employment, schools, shopping, transportation, daycare, advice of experts

Financial Projections, Resale Market, and Postclosing

to find land than others who are more established. It is necessary to do more firsthand research, narrow the search to a particular area, establish strong brokerage contacts there, and find out about sites that are not yet on the market or that require too much extra work to interest larger developers. Sites with special problems that need to be solved such as easements or contamination may prove attractive but must be approached with caution, because they may be more difficult than a beginner can handle. Before deciding to tackle problem sites, beginning developers must determine whether the problem can be solved within a reasonable time frame and cost. If they cannot answer that question affirmatively with a high level of confidence, they should look for another site.

Because of the possible legal complications associated with land development, developers generally use an attorney during land acquisition, no matter how straightforward a transaction might appear to be. Each part of the country has its own terminology for the sequence of steps in property acquisition. In Texas, for example, the first step is called *signing the earnest money contract,* in California it is *going into escrow* on the purchase contract, and in Massachusetts the initial offer is an *offer to purchase* agreement. In most cases, these actions initiate a free-look period during which various contingencies have to be resolved. This agreement is binding and contains all the contingencies, at least in summary form. It stipulates that on or before a certain date, the parties will enter into a *purchase and sale agreement,* which records all aspects of the transaction.[8]

Letter of Intent. Even before submitting a purchase contract, purchasers may discuss or submit a letter of intent to sellers that sets out the business terms for purchase of the property. The letter of intent specifies the property to be purchased, its price, payment terms, timing, release provisions (for transfer of lien-free subparcels to the buyer), and other major business points. Letters of intent are especially helpful when the purchaser or seller plans to use a long, specially written legal purchase agreement rather than a standard brokers form. The letter of intent saves time and unnecessary legal expense in the beginning because it clarifies the primary aspects of the transaction. If the buyer and seller cannot come

---

Steps for Site Acquisition

Before Offer

1. Verify that a market for the property type exists.
2. Determine the price you can pay by running preliminary financial pro formas.
3. Determine whether or not the seller can sell the property for the price you want to pay. (Determine what the seller paid for the property and outstanding mortgages on the property.)
4. Find out why the seller is selling the property. (Is the sale necessary, or can the seller wait for a better price?)
5. Check the market for comparable properties in the area and their prices.

Offer

1. Ask for at least 60 days for due diligence. If a broker brought the developer the deal, the developer might expect that the broker also contacted four or five other developers and that 60 days for due diligence may therefore not be acceptable to the seller.
2. Place a refundable deposit, or earnest money.
3. Request specific due diligence that must be provided by the seller, such as existing soils reports, hazardous waste clearances, preliminary design

and engineering studies, preapproved plans, and agency approvals.

Due Diligence

1. If zoning must be changed for the project, ask for closing to be contingent on zoning approvals; if it is not approved, the earnest money is refunded. Be sure to state in the offer exactly what constitutes approval, for example:
   - general plan approval
   - zoning approval
   - conditional use permits (variances)
   - development agreements
   - tentative tract or parcel map
   - final tract or parcel map
   - grading plan approval
   - site plan approval
   - design approval
   - building permits
2. Other questions to answer:
   - Can a good title be secured?
   - How much of the site is buildable? What are the easements, slopes, soils, floodplain, drainage, and geological conditions?
   - Can you build what you want to? How many units, of what size and at what density, can be built? Can parking and amenities be built?
   - Can financing be obtained?

3. Items to accomplish before closing on the land:
   - preliminary design drawings
   - mortgage package preparation
   - commitment from permanent lenders
   - commitment from construction lenders
   - receipt of regulatory approvals or assurances that they can be obtained
   - selection of contractor and property manager (who should assist in designing the project)
4. If more time is needed, ask the seller for it. If the seller refuses, ask for the deposit money back and pull out of the deal.

Closing

1. Closing typically occurs 60 days after due diligence is complete, although longer periods can often be negotiated.
2. Closing can be made dependent on a variety of factors, including the availability of financing and the removal of toxic wastes. ∎

to agreement on the major business terms, there is no point in exchanging full legal documents. The letter of intent is nonbinding, but it does call for signatures by both parties to signify agreement on the major transaction points.

In New England, the convention is to initiate the acquisition of land with an *offer to purchase*, which is a binding agreement (unless specifically stated otherwise) that takes the property off the market while the purchaser performs due diligence. The offer to purchase must spell out all contingencies. They typically include physical inspections, environmental checks, regulatory approvals, title checks, and/or financing approval. A common mistake is for purchasers to assume they can negotiate more contingencies or other issues in the purchase and sale agreement. The latter cannot be more restrictive than the offer to purchase unless both parties agree to the changes. Three items make the offer to purchase binding: 1) specific consideration, enough to entice the seller to take the property off the market for a given period, 2) proper identification of the property, and 3) a time to close or to enter into the purchase and sale agreement. The offer to purchase should include a provision for return of the purchaser's deposit if a purchase and sale agreement is not signed.[9]

Purchase Contract or Earnest Money Contract. Whether or not a letter of intent is used initially, the purchase contract (also called *earnest money contract)* is the primary legal document for purchase of property. It sets out all terms of purchase, indemnities, responsibilities for delivering title reports (usually the seller) and other documents, performing due diligence (checking out utilities, soils, public approvals, and so on, usually performed by the buyer), and remedies in the event that the sale does not close. Signing the final purchase agreement may happen immediately in the case of a simple purchase contract for one or several lots, or it may drag on for weeks or even longer if buyers and sellers haggle over individual provisions. Although purchase contracts are almost always negotiated following due diligence, the purchaser may use the time delay in signing to line up financing or builders or to perform other critical development tasks. Until the purchase contract is signed, however, the buyer is at risk of the seller's accepting another offer. Complicated purchase contracts are appropriate in complex transactions of larger properties. Beginning developers, however, should keep it simple. Less sophisticated sellers may be scared away if they get the impression that the buyer is deliberately delaying document signing. Moreover, overly complicated legal paperwork may signal the seller that the buyer is litigious and vice versa.

Contingencies. Contingencies in the purchase contract refer to events that must occur before the purchaser "goes hard" on the earnest money. Beginning developers often make the mistake of including many unnecessary contingency clauses that only complicate the negotiations. One or two blanket clauses will suffice. The most all-encompassing clause is one that makes the sale "subject to obtaining financing." If, for whatever reason, financing is not available, then earnest money is returned. Another encompassing clause is "subject to buyer's acceptance of feasibility studies." The contract may spell out those studies to include soils, title, marketing, site planning, and economic feasibility. As long as the clause gives the buyer discretion to approve the reports, it effectively gives the buyer a way out of the contract. As soon as the buyer goes hard, though, he is subject to forfeiting the earnest money paid to the seller if the sale is not completed.

Most sellers will not give a blanket contingency for more than 30 to 60 days. Sophisticated sellers understand that such clauses amount to a free-look period. Local market conditions determine whether or not sellers will give buyers a free look; in hot markets, they are less likely to.

An important contingency in the purchase agreement is that the seller must support the developer in obtaining zoning and other necessary approvals. In areas where extensive public approvals make the allowable building density uncertain, some developers purchase sites on the basis of the number of units approved. In this case, the seller has a strong incentive to assist in the approval process. For example, if the price is $50,000 per unit and permission is given to build 100 units on the site, then the purchase price would be $5 million. If the developer receives approval for only 80 units, the price would be $4 million.

No standard amount of earnest money is required, but, as a general rule, 3 to 5 percent of the total purchase price or a payment of $25,000 to $50,000 for smaller deals is required for a 90- to 120-day closing. Because the earnest money theoretically compensates the seller for holding the property off the market, the earnest money usually bears some relation to the seller's holding cost. The amount is negotiable but has to be large enough so that the seller believes that the buyer is viable and serious about closing. Financing land is expensive—usually at least two points (2 percent) over prime. For example, if the prime rate is 10 percent and the land loan is 12 percent, then a four-month closing would incur holding costs of 4 percent (4/12 times 12 percent). Thus, a 4 percent earnest money deposit would compensate the seller for holding the property off the market.

Every developer has at least one horror story to tell about a land purchase. Most stories relate to easements, toxic wastes, title, or other problems that showed up after closing. In hot markets, sellers may sometimes try to get out of a sale because they have received a higher offer. Although each state has its own property law, buyers generally control a purchase contract as long as they strictly observe its terms. Most contracts state that a clause is waived if the buyer does not raise concerns in writing before the expiration date of the clause or contingency. If the clause (such as buyer's approval of title reports) is not automatically waived according to the contract, however, the seller may argue that the buyer failed to perform in a timely fashion and that the contract is therefore null and void. If the seller tries to get out of the contract before the expiration date, the threat of *lis pendens* (pending litigation) usually is sufficient to bring the seller back to the table. Because pending litigation makes it very difficult to sell the property to anyone else and can tie up a property, it is a last resort on the part of the buyer.

Release Provisions on Purchase Money Notes. One of the most important areas of negotiation for land development concerns the release provisions on purchase money notes (PMNs)—seller financing used to purchase the property (also called *land notes*). Release provisions refer to the process by which developers remove individual parcels in larger tracts from the sellers' land notes. Release provisions also are a major part of the negotiation with the developers' lenders (discussed in "Financing" below).

Lenders require a first lien on the developer's property. Lien priorities are determined strictly by the date that a mortgage is created. Thus, land notes automatically have first lien position, unless sellers specifically subordinate land notes to land development loans. Developers must release land from the land note before they can obtain financing from lenders. Even if developers finance development costs out of their own pockets, land must be released from the land note for the developer to deliver clear title to builders or other buyers of the lots. Buyers need clear title (free of liens from PMNs) before they can obtain their own construction financing. Buyers might view land note financing as a plus during the predevelopment period before they take down the construction loan, as long as they have the option of paying it off at any time.

Land sellers' main concern is that they will be left holding a note with inadequate underlying security. They want strict release provisions that require the developer to pay down much more on the land note than the actual value of the land to be released, which would leave more land value as security for the unpaid portion of the note. The developer's objective, on the other hand, is to achieve maximum flexibility in the location and acreage of land to be released. Ideally, the developer wants to be able to release the maximum amount of land for the minimum amount of money.

Jack Willome, former CEO of Rayco, Inc., in San Antonio, Texas, uses the following clause in purchase contracts whenever possible: "The note is prepayable from time to time without penalty; all prepayments are credited toward the next principal installments coming due."[10] Suppose a developer purchases 100 acres (40 hectares) for $1 million with an eight-year land note for $800,000, or $8,000 per acre ($20,000 per hectare). The note is amortized at the rate of $100,000 per year. Suppose the developer also negotiates a partial release provision (the clause that allows a developer to release part of the property from the note) that calls for a payment of $12,000 per acre ($30,000 per hectare). If the developer wants to sell 25 acres (10 hectares) to a builder, then he must pay the seller $300,000 (25 times $12,000 or 10 times

$30,000) to release the land. Without the above language, the developer's $300,000 payment reduces the seller's note from $800,000 to $500,000. Instead of reducing the note principal balance immediately, the special language permits the developer to pay interest only on the note for the next three years. The clause "all prepayments are credited toward the next principal installments coming due" means that the next three principal installments are paid by the $300,000 payment but that repayment of the note is not accelerated. The developer will not have to make another principal payment for three years. Without the language in the clause, the seller would probably construe that the $300,000 payment simply shortens the remaining life of the note from eight to five years. The developer, of course, wants the note to run as long as possible so that it will not be necessary to sell the land prematurely or to find other financing sources to pay off the land note.

Developers never want to release more land from the note than is necessary at any one time, because seller financing is usually their lowest-cost source of money. Thus, they should try to avoid release provisions that call for releasing land in strips or contiguous properties.[11] The release requirements should not start at one point on the property and then move in strips across the property to the other end. If releases must occur on contiguous properties, developers would be forced to release the entire property to develop or sell a tract at the other end. Sellers will rightfully be concerned if developers can release the most desirable land and then abandon the rest of the project. To get around this problem, the release provision can assign values to parcels or strips in the property that reflect market values. Thus, prime land may have a release price that is significantly higher than that for less desirable land. Alternatively, the provision may call for the developer to release two acres (0.8 hectare) of less desirable land for every acre (0.4 hectare) of desirable land.

Key Points of a Purchase Contract. A variety of clauses and provisions should be included as part of the initial purchase contract so that later renegotiations with the seller will be minimized:[12]

- Supplementary Note Procedure—This clause allows the sale of subparcels (parcels within the original tract) to builders and other developers without paying off the underlying first lien. This provision, which must be specifically negotiated, allows the developer to pass seller financing on to builders through a *supplementary note*. This note gives builders more time before they need to pay the full lot cost. Nevertheless, unless the seller is willing to subordinate seller financing, the supplementary note has first lien position, which means that builders who purchase subparcels must pay off the note before they can obtain construction financing, as construction lenders also require a first lien position. In fact, builders usually pay off the supplementary note with the first draw under the construction note.

Conversations with a variety of successful developers have produced a number of useful tips regarding land acquisition.

- Make sure that the owner is really willing to sell the land. One developer found that his bid for a site condemned by a local school district was being used only for the owner's negotiations with the school district over condemnation price.
- Do not let the seller dictate the use of the property after the sale.
- Beware of fabricated appraisals of sites that have not been physically analyzed for hazardous or other undesirable conditions.
- When rezoning is necessary, attempt to buy the land on a per-unit basis if possible so that the landowner has an incentive to help you obtain increased densities.
- If you will need a conditional use permit or variance, ask the current owner to sign a waiver to allow you to act as his or her agent in dealing with the city during the escrow period.
- If you obtain seller financing, make sure that the seller frees up some of the land so that you can build on it. You need to be able to give the construction lender a first lien on the land.
- In some states, such as California, you should use a deed of trust for purchase money mortgages so that the seller cannot claim a deficiency judgment against you if you default.
- Concerning "no-waste" clauses, be sure to read the fine print on the trust deed form because you may not be able to remove trees or buildings on the property until the note is paid off.
- Make sure you select a title company that is strong enough to back you up if you need to defend a lawsuit involving title. Some nationwide title companies enfranchise their local offices separately so that you do not have the backing of the national company.
- Make sure that the seller's warranties survive the close of escrow.
- Beware of broker commissions. A broker who casually mentions a property as you drive by it may try to collect a commission if you later buy it. ∎

- Out-of-Sequence Releases—This clause satisfies the developer's need to release certain parcels out of sequence for major utilities or amenities.
- Joinder and Subordination—This clause provides for the seller to join within 30 days any applications for government approvals made by the developer. It also provides for the seller's subordination agreements, required by any government authority for the filing of subdivision maps or street dedications.
- Subordination of Subparcels—Most sellers are unlikely to allow subordination of their note to development lenders. They may be willing, however, to allow subordination on one or two subparcels. This action can help the developer obtain the development loan without paying off the land note.
- Seller's "Comfort Language"—The seller is not required to execute any documents until he or she has approved the purchaser's general land use plan.
- Ability to Extend Closing—This clause permits the purchaser to extend the closing by 30 or 60 days by paying additional earnest money.
- Letters of Credit as Earnest Money—The developer can greatly reduce upfront cash requirements if the seller will accept letters of credit as earnest money. Letters of credit can be cashed by the seller on a certain date or if certain events occur, such as a purchaser's failure to close. For example, this type of clause might say, "Purchaser may extend the closing for 60 days by depositing an additional $50,000 letter of credit as additional escrow deposit."
- Property Taxes—Many municipalities and counties have categories such as *open space* or *agricultural land* that give the owner a reduction in taxes. When the land is developed, the owner must repay the tax savings for the previous three or five years, which can amount to a major unexpected cost to the developer if it is not provided for in the purchase agreement. For example, such a provision might say, "Seller agrees to pay all ad valorem tax assessments or penalties assessed for any period before the closing as a result of any change in ownership or usage of the property."
- Title Insurance—The seller usually (though not always) pays the title insurance policy. Many title insurance policies have standard exception clauses, however, such as a survey exception.[13] The party responsible for paying the insurance premium for deleting these exceptions is subject to negotiation.
- Seller's Remedy—If the purchaser defaults, the seller's sole remedy is to receive the escrow deposit as liquidated damages. This clause prevents the seller from pursuing the purchaser for more money if the sale falls through.

These clauses constitute only a small fraction of all those included in a standard purchase contract. They are highlighted here because they represent items that the purchaser should try to negotiate with the seller. Many sophisticated developers use a specially prepared standard form that includes such clauses. Sophisticated sellers insist on using their own standard forms, however. In this case, these clauses will probably have to be added. The assistance of an experienced real estate attorney should always be sought in the preparation of the purchase contract.

Market Analysis after Site Selection

After tying up a site, the developer should reexamine the target market for the proposed project. Special features of the selected site, as well as changes to the overall economic climate, may indicate a different market from the one identified during the preliminary market analysis undertaken before site selection.

At this stage, analysis should concentrate on location, neighborhood, and amenities. For example, suppose a developer's initial target market is buyers of move-up houses selling from $350,000 to $400,000. If sales in that price range are moving steadily, the developer may want to continue with such a program, even if several other developers are competing at the same price point. But if the developer has found that market to be saturated, he may modify plans and develop a lower-priced community. Or a more upscale product that is not represented in the market may be appropriate if demographics prove favorable.

The market analysis at this stage helps the developer 1) do physical planning by determining the specific tar-

The Vineyards at Westchase in Tampa, Florida, contains 120 single-family homes on 35- and 45-foot-wide by 80-foot-deep (10.6- and 13.7-meter-wide by 24.4-meter-deep) lots.

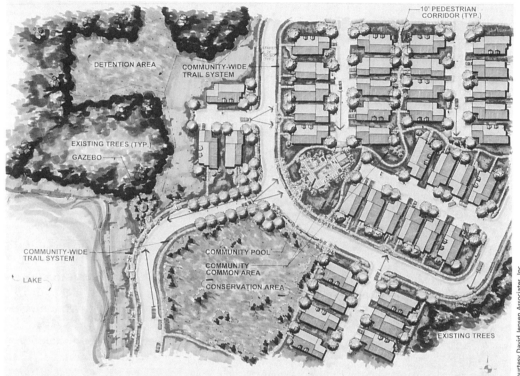

Homes at the Vineyards are oriented with the front doors facing common areas and natural amenities such as lakes and conservation areas.

get market and therefore the size and configuration of lots, amenities, and other fundamental aspects; 2) obtain a loan and supply the appropriate documentation; and 3) attract builders and subdevelopers.

Unless a subdivision is very small or the developer has already selected builders, a local market research firm that specializes in subdivision development should be hired. Ideally, the market research firm should already have a database covering all the competing subdivisions. From its analysis of the market potential of the developer's site, the market research firm should be able to assist the developer in determining the best market for the lots. From the perspective of land development, the market report should provide the total number of lots that the developer can sell per month, grouped by lot size and price range. The report should document total housing demand and supply for the market area and, from that number, project demand and supply for the specific product type and submarket area the developer's project will serve (see the accompanying feature box). The bottom line of the market study should be a projection of the number of units that can be sold each month by product type and the projected sale price. For example, suppose demand for $200,000 to $250,000 custom single-family houses on 5,000-square-foot (465-square-meter) lots is 200 houses per year (16 per month) in the submarket and two subdivisions are competing for buyers. Expected sales would be approximately five per month, assuming that each subdivision captures its share of total demand. This figure should never be assumed to be the pace of sales, however. Demand is never totally met by product that is actually developed. Many potential buyers will not purchase what is offered because it is too expensive, it is not to their taste, or any number of other reasons. Projections of the pace of sales must always be tempered by reality. Regardless of what demand statistics show, if other developers of similar projects in the general area are selling only two or three units per month, it is unlikely that a newcomer will sell twice as many. Generally, however, a homebuilder purchases (takes down) more than one lot at a time. A lot sale may include four or five or as many as 50 or 60 lots, depending on the type of project, size of builder, and market conditions.

Rolling options are a popular method for master developers to control builders' takedown of lots. These options provide for the builder to take down a designated number of lots every quarter or year. The option gives the builder an assured supply of lots while giving the land developer an out from the contract with the builder if he cannot sell as many houses as anticipated. The rolling option typically has a built-in price escalation in the lot price—perhaps a 2 to 4 percent increase per year.

Rolling options can be structured to protect the interest of the master developer, the builder, or both.[14] The master developer wants to have some assurance that the builder will meet or exceed the takedown schedule and that he cannot tie up future option increments if he is not performing. The builder wants to make sure that

What to Look for in a Good Market Study

Proper Delineation of the Market Area

The geographic area where competing subdivisions are sampled should be large enough to include the entire quadrant of the city where your project is located.

Proper Delineation of the Competing Market Product Types

Do not define a market so narrowly that you omit certain competition, which leads to underestimated supply. For example, low-cost single-family houses compete with condominiums for buyers.

The Capture Rate

The capture rate of lots for the subdivision should take into account both the total demand in the marketplace and the number of other subdivisions. In metropolitan areas with populations greater than 1 million, capture rates in excess of 5 percent for *any* project, even new towns, are suspect.

Employment and Absorption Rates

Projections of demand should be based both on employment projections and historic absorption rates in the area. Large increases relative to historic absorption rates are always suspect.

■

he has an assured supply of lots—but not before he needs them. He wants to carry as small an inventory of lots as possible and wants the ability to not exercise future options.

The builder may pay option fees, which are usually based on the value of the unexercised options. It is often a tradeoff against a reduction in the price escalation. If option fees are paid, the price escalation is lower. Higher option fees are a technique to encourage the builder to take down the option sooner (to avoid paying the option fee). Option fees are paid even if the future increments are not acquired.

As an example of a typical structure in its simplest form, suppose that a master developer has a super pad of 200 lots. The deal will provide that the builder has an option to acquire the property in annual increments of 50 lots over a four-year period. If the builder fails to take down any scheduled increment, he loses his option rights to all future increments. The builder can exercise his options more quickly and will pay value escalations and/or option fees on unexercised options.

Developed lots are an intermediate factor in the production of housing. Although a shortage of housing may exist, a surplus of lots may also exist. Therefore, the market study should examine demand and supply for both the final housing product and developed lots.

Regulatory Process

Zoning and Platting. The process of subdividing a land tract is called platting. Platting also usually involves a

The entrance to Dakota Dunes, South Dakota. To build the state's first new community in more than a century, state legislation was required to establish a local unit of special purpose government, the Dakota Dunes Community Improvement District.

zoning change. In suburban fringes, land is often zoned *agriculture* or some other nondevelopable designation that must be rezoned to allow lot subdivision and development.

Every locality has a different procedure for zoning.[15] The process can take anywhere from several months to many years, depending on how environmentally and politically sensitive the site is. Many sites are also subject to the approval of special agencies or commissions, which adds costs and time. For example, land in California that is located within 1,000 yards (915 meters) of the ocean is subject to the California Coastal Commission's jurisdiction. Fulfilling the commission's requirements may add years to the time necessary to secure approval for

a subdivision. The commission's requirements and limitations, such as anticipated density, may be extremely strict. Because even many experienced developers lack the staying power to pilot a site through the commission's process, beginning developers are well advised to avoid situations that involve lengthy and expensive approval processes.

Platting Process. Platting is the official procedure by which land is subdivided into smaller legal entities. It is the means by which cities and counties enforce standards for streets and lots and record new lot descriptions in subdivisions. The legal description of a house lot typically follows this form: "Lot 10 of Block 7143 of Fondren Southwest III Subdivision, Harris County, Texas." The legal description parallels the platting procedure. The developer submits a plat of the property showing individual blocks and lots. In this example, *III* indicates that two previous subdivisions have been platted under the name *Fondren Southwest.*

In some areas, platting requires a public hearing, even if the intended use conforms to the zoning. In other areas, no public hearing is required as long as the platted lots are consistent with the zoning and with all other subdivision regulations, such as street width, turning radius (designed for fire trucks), maximum cul-de-sac street length, lot size (total area, minimum width and depth), alleys (if any), frontyard, backyard, and side yard setbacks, number of units per acre, and minimum size of units.

The number of units permitted to be built on a given parcel usually depends on a combination of several factors, including minimum lot width and depth, alley requirements, and street rights-of-way. The target market determines whether a developer plats the greatest pos-

The U.S. Supreme Court and Development Regulations

The United States Supreme Court plays an important role in the regulation of real estate development by ensuring that state and local regulations do not infringe on constitutionally protected private property rights.

- In *Lucas* v. *South Carolina Coastal Council* (1992), the Court held that if a regulation denies the landowner "all economically beneficial" use of his land, then compensation is required under the Takings Clause of the Fifth Amendment. The only exception to this rule is when the regulation affects an activity that was already barred under state law principles of property or nuisance law.
- In *Dolan* v. *City of Tigard* (1994), the Court established standards for

regulations that require a landowner to dedicate land for public use as a condition of development approval. The government must be able to show a "rough proportionality" between the impact of the development and the public benefit that is being exacted. To date, the Court has not applied the proportionality rule to impact fees or other monetary exactions.

The Supreme Court also reviews federal regulations that affect development in areas including endangered species and wetlands.

- In *Babbit* v. *Sweet Home* (1995), the Court upheld an Interior Department regulation that requires private prop-

erty owners to obtain a permit if their actions—logging or land development, for example—harm the natural habitat of a federally protected species.
- In *Solid Waste Agency of Northern Cook County* v. *U.S. Army Corps of Engineers* (2001), the Court found that the Corps lacked the authority under the Clean Water Act to regulate a wetland that does not physically abut a navigable waterway. The precise effect of this recent decision, which may affect vernal pools and other isolated wetlands, will likely depend on lower court rulings that address various fact-specific situations. ∎

figure 3-2
City of Pasadena: Summary of Zoning Regulations for Residential Uses

| Zone | Land Use | Maximum Height (Feet) | Required Yards (Feet) | | Rear | Minimum Lot Area (Square Feet) | | Minimum Lot Width (Feet) | Maximum Building Area (%) | Parking Spaces per Dwelling Unit |
			Front	Side		Per Lot	Per Dwelling Unit			
RS 1	Single-family residential, 1 unit/acre	36	25[a]	5 minimum or 10% of lot width, 10 maximum[b]	25	40,000	40,000	100	35%	2 covered
RS 2	Single-family residential, 2 units/acre; any RS-1 use	36	25	5 Same as RS-1	25	20,000	20,000	100	35	2 covered
RS 4	Single-family residential, 4 units/acre; any RS-1 use	32	25	5 Same as RS-1	25	12,000	12,000	75	35	2 covered
RS 6	Single-family residential, 6 units/acre; any RS-1 use	32	25	5 Same as RS-1	25	7,200	7,200	55	35	2 covered
RM 16-2	Multifamily residence, 16 units/acre; any RS use	36	20	10[c,d] Corner lots require 15	10	7,200	2,750	55	40	2 covered per unit 550 square feet or larger[e,f]
RM 16-1	Multifamily residence, 14 units/acre; any RS use	36	40	10 Corner lots require 30	20	12,000	3,000	75	35	Same as RM-16[e,f]
RM 32	Multifamily residence, 32 units/acre; any RS use; group residential	36	20	10 Corner lots require 15[g]	10[g]	10,000	1,360[h]	60	60	Same as RM-16[e,f]
RM 48	Multifamily residence, 48 units/acre; any RM-32 use	60	20	10 Corner lots require 15[g]	10[g]	10,000	910[h]	60	60	Same as RM-16[e,f]

[a] Building line conformity, maximum frontyards in R districts: Section 17.20.030(F).

[b] Sideyards of corner lots: 10 percent of lot width or ten feet minimum, 25 feet maximum. See Development Standards, Section 17.20.020.

[c] Building Modulation: RM-16, RM-16-1: Additional Development Standards, Section 17.24.050(G)
RM-32, RM-48: Additional Development Standards, Section 17.24.050(M), (N).

[d] Five feet for structures not exceeding nine feet in height measured to the top plate.

[e] Parking requirements for RM zones: 1.5 covered spaces per unit smaller that 550 square feet. Developments with 20 units or more shall provide one guest parking space for each ten units. See Section 17.68.030.

[f] Compact car parking spaces in RM zones: Section 17.68.100.

[g] Interior side- and rear yards in RM-32 and RM-48 zones require an additional five feet of setback for every ten feet of building height or portion thereof above 25 feet. See additional Development Standards, RM-36, RM-48, Section 17.24.050(J).

[h] Low- to moderate-income and/or design density bonuses are available in RM-32 and RM-48 zones. See Additional Development Standards, RM-32 and RM-48 Districts, Section 17.24(D).

Source: City of Pasadena, California, Planning Department, www.ci.pasadena.ca.us/planning.

sible number of lots or creates larger lots for more expensive houses. A developer should avoid going for the highest allowable density unless previous experience has shown that the resulting density and smaller lots are consistent with target market demand or the proposed project is strong enough to attract a new market.

Replatting a previously platted area can present unexpected difficulties, especially if the developer must *abandon* (that is, remove from official maps) old streets or alleys. In Dallas, Peiser Corporation was investigating a site when it unexpectedly found that *all* abutting property owners had to agree to the abandonment of a mapped but never built alley. With 50 homeowners involved, the likelihood of unanimous agreement was almost nil. The developer passed on the site, despite having invested considerable time and money.

In addition to platting requirements, the subdivision may be subject to restrictive covenants such as single-family-only development imposed by the seller or a previous owner. Restrictive covenants should show up in the initial title search and may have a profound influence on the type of development allowable on a particular site.

Filing a Subdivision Application. Every jurisdiction has a different procedure to follow for obtaining subdivision approval. Most jurisdictions have at least a two-stage process that requires approval from the planning commission and then the city council or county supervisor. California, for example, has a two-tier process. The first tier is the *general plan,* which defines land use for all parts of the city and is reviewed every five years. Most important for new subdivisions, it defines which areas are encouraged for development and which are not. General plans also may be linked to the capital budget for a city or county. The capital budget designates planned public expenditures for utilities, roads, parks, and other infrastructure improvements. The significance of the general plan is that it is relatively easy to obtain permission for zoning changes that are in accord with the general plan. Changes contrary to it—such as development in an agricultural zone or apartments in an area designated for single-family residences—may be almost impossible to get approved. Land that is designated for agricultural use must be changed to urban use, specifying property type and density, in the general plan before a specific plan (the second tier) can be created to develop the

Regulatory Pitfalls: Multiple Jurisdictions

Be aware of opportunities and pitfalls caused by multiple, overlapping regulatory jurisdictions. Massachusetts, for example, is a "home rule" state, which means that local (city and town) authorities overlay many state approvals with their own, and vice versa. Many applicable requirements are not available on line and are not even published in the commonwealth's general laws. Developers should invest early in local expertise to:

- identify all necessary approvals;
- provide realistic time lines in light of local customs; and
- advise on the likely content (and expense) of conditions or necessary mitigation.

For example, prime waterfront property on Boston Harbor is underused and priced well below less desirable property not on the waterfront even though it has spectacular views; all necessary water, sewer, power, and transportation services; three existing, structurally sound buildings; and an adjoining public park. Why? Partly because several quirky laws apply:

- Chapter 91 (state statute and attendant regulations protecting water-

dependent uses and public access rights on tidelands)—Height limitations, lot coverage, building setbacks, and public amenities such as Harborwalk are all mandated.
- Designated Port Area (DPA) Provisions —Additional state regulatory scheme prohibiting all but marine industrial uses.
- Chapter 21E—State statute holding owners of contaminated real estate liable for cleanup after closing, even if the new owner is not at fault.
- Environmental Justice Policy of the Executive Office of Environmental Affairs—Requires special analysis of actions in low-income and/or predominantly minority census tracts.
- Article 97 of the Massachusetts Constitution (not published in the general laws of the commonwealth)—Requires a two-thirds vote of the legislature for any change in use of public land acquired for conservation or recreation purposes (the park was once part of the site).
- The Massachusetts Environmental Policy Act (MEPA)—Requires "adequate consideration of the environmental impacts" before any state agency may issue permits or funding.

- Local Zoning—Permits some uses the state prohibits and prohibits some the state requires.

But complications equate with opportunities for the patient and the astute. Chapter 91 allows for municipal harbor plans to vary from statewide requirements on a city-by-city, town-by-town, district-by-district basis, such that strategic relations with the locality can result in regulatory flexibility (including changes in local zoning). Similarly, DPA provisions in theory allow for boundary "dedesignations." It might take some time, however, to learn that the only dedesignations in 20 years have been legislatively mandated after the responsible executive agency declined to act. Similarly, Chapter 21E has new provisions and policies providing state subsidies and, ostensibly, some liability relief for prospective owners and secured lenders.

The lesson to be learned is invest strategically by obtaining early advice on the constraints and opportunities involving sites affected by multiple jurisdictions. ∎

Source: Jamy Buchanan, Buchanan & Associates, Boston, Massachusetts, 2001.

Subdivision regulations require the filing of a *tract map* for developments of five or more lots or units.

The first step in processing a subdivision is the preparation, review, and approval of a *tentative* tract map, which shows the precise boundaries of the site, the location of proposed buildings, and the dimensions of any public rights-of-way adjacent to the site. The tentative map must be prepared by a California-registered civil engineer or a California-licensed surveyor.

All applications for a tentative map require preliminary environmental review.

When an application is received, the level of review needed is determined. After the environmental review of the tentative map has been completed, no further environmental review is required for the final map unless the project is substantially changed.

After staff review, the Planning Commission conducts a public hearing during which it approves, approves with conditions, or denies the tentative map application. The tentative map will be approved if it meets the following criteria:

1. The tentative map is consistent with the general plan.

2. The site is physically suitable to the type and density of development.
3. The design of the subdivision is not likely to cause environmental damage or create serious health and safety problems.
4. The design of the subdivision and its improvements will not conflict with the use of public improvements dedicated as part of the subdivision.

A notice of the Planning Commission's hearing is mailed to all adjacent landowners. Anyone interested in the proposed project may testify at the public hearing. ■

---

property. This step takes considerable lead time when general plans are revised only every five years.

Specific plans spell out the actual zoning, density, and, in some cases, the footprint, ingress and egress, and other details of the proposed development. Specific plans are even more detailed than zoning and, once achieved, may tie the developer to a particular development scheme. Changing a specific plan often requires a new round of public hearings and subjects the developer to the full risks associated with regulatory change. These risks have grown substantially over the last decade as more and more communities have opposed growth. Any public review can be highly politicized, giving the planning commission and city council the opportunity to impose new restrictions, require more investment by the developer (exactions), or lower the allowable density of development.

Phasing. Most subdivisions larger than about 200 lots are divided into phases. Even a much smaller development may be phased, however, if the developer's company is small and has limited resources, or if a portion of the land remains unavailable until later. Each phase typically involves a single filing of the plat and subdivision restrictions. Developers finance and construct utilities, roads, and other improvements necessary to create finished lots for each entire phase. Therefore, phases should not be so large that they cannot be financed or absorbed by the market in a reasonable time frame—usually within 18 to 24 months, or one economic cycle.

The number of houses per phase shrank considerably in the 1990s after the real estate crash. Lenders who were afraid to be left holding loans on unfinished subdivisions with unsold lots reduced the size of individual phases to reduce their exposure in the event of a recession. Jo Anne Stubblefield of Hyatt and Stubblefield advises that one should not file more than the first phase of a project at the outset, especially for larger properties. Once plans are recorded, the developer may be held to them

for a phase of the project that is years away, limiting the ability to change with market conditions. Moreover, most of the regulatory process makes it advantageous to plat in smaller portions, again to preserve flexibility later if the market changes.[16]

Regulatory Concerns. Land development regulation has become so complicated in so many areas that it would take an entire book to describe the many different forms of regulation that a developer will encounter. Staying on top of new local ordinances is not enough. A developer must know which regulations are about to come into force, which are still under discussion, and which are only vague proposals. The lead times required to get a development off the ground are often long—and increasing. In Houston in the mid-1980s, for example, developers complained that it took six to nine months to obtain the necessary approvals to develop a subdivision. In southern California, developers are grateful if they can clear all the approval hurdles in fewer than three years. The more agencies involved, the longer it takes. Projects in California's coastal zone and in environmentally sensitive mountain areas have been known to take ten years or longer to secure approvals. Litigation over public approvals for larger tracts is becoming the rule rather than the exception. Tom Lee of the Newhall Land and Farming Company says that for the 15,000-acre (6,075-hectare) Valencia property, the company built $2 million for litigation and two extra years into the budget. Several years after receiving the necessary approvals, the company was sued by neighboring Ventura County.

"Political involvement," says Scott Smith of La Plata Investments, "is no longer just a good idea; it's critical. Good relationship building with the city planner, city manager, and water/sewer officials is obviously necessary, but don't forget larger issues. We work hard at developing relationships with state and national political parties—a move that may have seemed unjustified until now—when we face a ballot initiative that could kill development even of existing projects."[17]

"What has changed in the last ten years is really the intensity of competition for land entitlement. As competition for land entitlement (and associated costs) heats up, political involvement is becoming more critical," according to Al Neely of Charles E. Smith Co. "If you are not a consensus builder, you just won't make it. That means consensus at all levels, not just three or four government agencies, but community activists and advocacy groups as well. You have to engage people and get them on board."[18] Tim Edmond, president of ARVIDA, adds, "Make sure you understand fully the cost and time required for entitlements, and then add 30 percent to your estimate."[19] Jo Anne Stubblefield notes, "Too many developers underestimate the importance of regulatory compliance processes and plan inadequate time. The regulatory compliance process for the project should be laid out early, with the production of plans and the pro forma, identifying areas where the project might have a hard time. Resources must be devoted to these areas early to ensure the viability and timely completion of the project."[20]

Roger Galatas, president of Roger Galatas Interests in the Woodlands, Texas, advises that credibility with regulatory agencies is built with words *and* actions. "That means, do what you say you'll do. Successful developers must engage regulators themselves or send their most senior people. What does it say about you if you send someone junior to make your presentation to the planning board?" Galatas adds, "There are three acronyms for land development: EPA, F&W [Fish and Wildlife], and ACoE [Army Corps of Engineers]. Get to know them well—or you will get to know them too well."[21]

Four major regulatory issues affect most land developers today: vesting of development rights, growth controls, environmental issues, and traffic congestion.

Vesting of Development Rights. Historically, if developers had, or could obtain, zoning, they had the right to build what the zoning allowed. If they bought a property that was already zoned, they were entitled, without public hearings, to develop the property within the limits established by the zoning. The presumption that zoning confers the right to develop a property has been changing in many parts of the country, however. As in other regulatory areas, California has led the way. In the 1976 *Avco* decision,[22] the developer was not allowed to proceed with land development, even though he had installed streets and utilities. In other words, the developer's right to develop was not *vested,* despite having spent considerable money on improving the land. Over the years, the standard for vesting has become even more stringent. The developer must have not only received a building permit but also completed a substantial part of the foundation to obtain the vested right to proceed. A land developer who cannot deliver building permits will soon be out of business.

In California, Florida, and Hawaii, development agreements have become a popular solution to the problem of securing vested development rights. Development agreements, which are negotiated between the developer and the municipality, ensure that the ground rules under which a developer builds are the same as those that were in effect at the time the agreement was signed. Development agreements protect the developer's right to build a specified number of residential units (or square feet of nonresidential space) in exchange for providing certain facilities to the community. Although development agreements have never been tested in court, both developers and municipalities believe that they provide protection against changes in zoning, density, moratoriums, and other regulations.

Growth Controls. Growth management programs focus on guiding community development and responding to development proposals comprehensively rather than piecemeal as applications are submitted. They are used to ensure a level of quality in community development, including conservation of open space, and that infrastructure is in place to support new development as it occurs.

Growth management provisions are often incorporated in local zoning ordinances. They typically include:

- approval of zoning and subdivisions linked to capital budgeting investments in infrastructure;
- establishment of growth boundaries, which usually provide for a holding area where future development is anticipated, to limit the supply of developable land;
- ceilings on the number of housing units or square feet of space that can be constructed in the jurisdiction;
- links between development and availability of water supply or sewage treatment capacity;
- links between projects and specific public facilities, such as schools, transit, or road improvements; and
- ceilings on the number of building permits that can be issued each year.

Growth management is not a new issue. Communities have been able to limit the number of building permits that they issue annually ever since the *Ramapo*[23] and *Petaluma*[24] decisions in the 1970s. The difference today is that growth management has become more sophisticated and more widespread. Since the late 1980s, most local governments in California have used at least one growth management tool. Numerical caps on housing and population were popular in the 1970s and 1980s in certain parts of the state, but in the 1990s, their popularity decreased. The popularity of urban growth boundaries and similar techniques has grown, but adequate infrastructure is by far the most common tool used in California.[25]

Communities adopt antigrowth or managed growth measures for two main reasons: first, as a reaction to the changing character of the community (as rural or low-density areas are developed, the visual environment begins to change); and, second, in response to overburdened infrastructure—schools, sewers, parks and open space, and, most important, local roads. Traffic congestion drives many antigrowth measures. The capacity of

Dewees Island is an oceanfront island retreat northeast of Charleston, South Carolina, dedicated to environmental preservation. Sixty-five percent of the island's 1,206 acres (490 hectares) is set aside in permanent conservation.

roads and intersections has become the determinant in many communities of when and how much new development will be allowed. Developers are often required to build additional traffic lanes, install new traffic lights, and even build new freeway interchanges for major projects to receive approval.

Nevertheless, serious debates over growth and development can lead to positive changes in land use regulations, particularly in suburban areas. A growing number of local and state governments provide incentives to developers of environmentally sensitive projects; such incentives might include density bonuses, waiving permit fees, fast tracking development proposals, and infrastructure improvements such as parks, roads, and pedestrian links. The city of Austin's Smart Growth Matrix, for instance, provides developers with a range of incentives, including the waiving of permit fees and assistance with infrastructure, if their projects meet the city's objectives for development.[26]

Environmental Issues. Since the late 1970s, developers of larger projects in certain areas have been required to submit environmental impact statements and reports to receive project approval from federal and state agencies. Throughout the last two decades, the size of projects that require an EIR steadily decreased, and enforcement has become more rigorous. This trend is expected to continue, and in time, almost all development projects will be required to produce some form of environmental impact analysis. Local communities increasingly have adopted environmental measures in their zoning and subdivision regulations.

EIRs cover all potential impacts of new development on a community, including impacts on water, biodiversity, vegetation, animal habitat, archaeology, and public facilities such as roads, schools, utilities, and community services. In smaller projects, EIRs may address only the external impacts of the project beyond the site boundaries; in larger projects of 500 or more acres (200 or more hectares), the most consequential impacts may be within the site.

Roger Galatas lists a number of environmental issues requiring extensive due diligence: location in a 100-year floodplain; designation as a wetland; and presence of endangered species, cultural resources (archaeological/ Native American sites), or toxic waste. Each of these items should show up on an EIS, but the developer should not assume that an EIS protects his investment completely. Inevitably, one of these issues arises after completion of an EIS.[27]

EISs are circulated to interested parties, with comments invited. Reviewers' responses are then appended to the statement, which may be modified as a result of the comments received. Federal legislation allows litigation over the adequacy of coverage in an EIS, a step that can cause great delays.[28] Developers should never assume that because they are in compliance with federal law, they will be in compliance with state law. State laws often conflict with similar federal laws, so it is important to consult an attorney to clarify obligations. Although ultimately in a court of law the developer may be right, the cost of litigation in both time and money could break a young or undercapitalized developer.[29]

One of the most sensitive aspects of EIRs concerns hazardous waste. On a project outside Houston, for example, the EIR reported some open pools of oil adjacent to a new subdivision, but no further research was done. More than 300 houses had been built in the subdivision when it was discovered that the oil pools were toxic. The homebuyers sued the builder, the developer, the engineers, the lenders, and almost everyone else remotely connected with the subdivision. The eventual settlement was for hundreds of millions of dollars.

For land developers, sites that encompass brownfields present both constraints and opportunities. The U.S. EPA defines brownfields as "abandoned, idled, or underused industrial and commercial facilities where expansion or redevelopment is complicated by real or perceived environmental contamination." Although many of these sites are problematic because of their industrial locations and the potential cost of cleanup, several trends are helping to make brownfields more attractive for development. Amendments to the Superfund law in 1997 hold lenders harmless when financing the redevelopment of brownfield sites, and at least 35 states have enacted legislation to limit cleanup liability. As a result, insurance companies are writing policies to limit the developer's liability, and financial institutions are making loans for the development of brownfields.

A community development district formed under Florida statute administered and funded the development of all improvements and amenities at Eagle Harbor near Jacksonville, Florida. The bonds issued to fund development will be repaid through property assessments on annual tax bills.

State and local agencies are also becoming increasingly knowledgeable about cost-effective cleanup methods and frequently are willing to provide tax incentives and reduce liability for cleanups.

Value can be added to a project in the course of solving some of these environmental problems if the developer is flexible enough in acquisition. Roger Galatas notes, "We've had success in these situations by creating land trusts, environmental trusts, conservation easements, and other structures to deal with endangered species, wetlands, and cultural resources, which can then be carefully marketed as amenities for the overall development project. This matter has to be dealt with upfront, however, incorporating risk in the acquisition program and acquiring enough land to allow the developer to give up parcels to these kinds of structures without serious damage to the project's economics."[30]

Traffic. The development of single-family housing in the suburbs has been a national trend since World War II. Many people moved to the suburbs, lured by a plentiful supply of new, affordable housing. Houses were followed by shopping centers, which were eventually followed by jobs. In the 1970s and 1980s, many corporations moved their offices to suburban office parks and exurban corporate campuses.

Traffic congestion in many suburbs is as bad or worse than congestion in the cities. The low-density, semirural lifestyle that attracted many people to the suburbs has created problems of its own. Automobile-oriented development prohibits other, more efficient forms of transportation and breeds ever-increasing traffic and congestion. As a result, concerns about traffic lie at the root of growth moratoriums and slow-growth/no-growth movements. Traffic studies are a standard part of environmental impact reviews. Localities often require developers to pay for major off-site road improvements and, sometimes, for freeway interchanges to receive planning permissions. Even developers of small infill sites may be required to pay for expensive traffic mitigations.

Financing Infrastructure. Regulatory uncertainty is integrally tied to the time and cost of providing or obtaining necessary infrastructure facilities. Infrastructure facilities primarily include utilities, roads, and drainage but may also include parks, schools, treatment plants, fire and police stations, and major transportation arteries.

A variety of methods for financing infrastructure are available:[31]

- General Taxes—Historically, street and utility improvements have been financed by bonds that were repaid by general property tax revenues.
- Federal and State Grants—Historically, federal and state grants have assisted local communities in building water treatment and sewage treatment plants and other infrastructure.
- Impact Fees and Developer Fees—These fees are imposed on the developer at the time of platting or applying for the building permit and are usually computed per unit or per square foot.
- User Fees and Charges—Such fees and charges are a traditional means of obtaining revenues. Monthly fees (water and sewer fees, for example) are pledged to repay bonds issued to finance the facilities and to pay operating and maintenance expenses.
- Assessment Districts—These districts can issue bonds and impose a special tax levy on property owners who benefit from specific public improvements in the district.
- Special Districts—These districts are similar to assessment districts, except that their governing bodies are separate from the local government. They can issue bonds and levy taxes on property owners in their jurisdiction.
- Tax Increment Financing Districts—Increases in tax revenues that result from new development in a specified area are earmarked for public improvements or services in that area.

- Developer Exactions—The developer is required to install or pay for community facilities such as roads, parks, police and fire stations, libraries, and school sites in return for platting or building approval.

Developers must thoroughly understand infrastructure financing, because a major portion of the cost of land development is associated with on- and off-site roads, utilities, and other infrastructure. Developers must understand how their development will affect the revenues and costs of the local jurisdiction where they want to build. Increasingly, development approvals are tied to whether or not a new development has a positive impact on local finances.[32]

Florida's growth management law, passed in 1985, was the first in the nation to require local jurisdictions to enforce the requirement that infrastructure be in place before development could occur. These concurrency statutes followed a rash of development on the outskirts of cities where sewers and roads were inadequate to handle new development. The laws, which were intended to reduce sprawl, had the opposite effect. Because road intersections in urban areas were congested, the statute caused development to be pushed even farther out, to rural areas where road capacity was underused. Subsequent revisions lowered the standards to permit more development in currently urbanized areas. This illustration highlights a common problem in dealing with urban sprawl: attempts to reduce it often have unintended side effects that make it worse. Standards must be continuously examined for their reasonableness and, if necessary, adjusted to fit specific circumstances.[33]

Much of the slow growth movement is motivated by the belief among existing homeowners that they are required to pay an unfair portion of the cost of facilities that will be used by future homeowners in the same subdivisions. But each new generation of homeowners benefits from previous generations' investment in infrastructure.[34] Major infrastructure investment—typically, streets and utilities—is characterized by debt payments over 20- to 30-year periods, slow deterioration, and periodic replacement. When the financing life is shorter than the economic life of a facility and when a community's growth rate is more than 3 percent per year, the residents of that community pay for benefits faster than they receive them. When taxes to pay for growth rise faster than property values, dissension between current residents and future residents (represented by the developer) soon follows.

The main justification for impact fees and other development charges is that they will alleviate the burden that growth imposes on existing homeowners. Developers can expect more and more communities to impose impact fees, and those fees can reach prohibitive levels.

The appropriate level of impact fees is subject to debate. Theoretically, impact fees are imposed on developers for their share of any facilities from which they benefit, including those that have been installed and paid for earlier. In some cases, depending on negotiations between the developer and regulatory agency, facilities may be off site and may benefit other parties as much as they directly benefit the developer's project.

The legal test for impact fees is that a rational nexus, or rational relationship, can be proved to exist between the fees charged and the benefits received by the future residents of the development. The developer should not be expected to pay the entire cost of facilities that benefit other residents of the community.

Ironically, growth moratoriums and building permit caps are motivated, in part, by the lack of adequate impact fees. Residents who vote for moratoriums claim that developers are not paying their full share of the cost that they impose on a community. Developers may find that it is in their own best interest to support "you pay, you play" impact fees, although a community should not expect development to pay more than its fair share.

Unfortunately, developers have been caught in the middle of a tax revolt in many parts of the country. As development fees have become popular and developers have accepted them, communities have looked to developers to provide an ever-increasing share of the costs of urban services—so much so that, in many communities, new residents are subsidizing existing residents.

Many cities now require developers to pay for half the cost of major arterials that abut their property.[35] Further, developers often must pay for some or all of the new utility lines required to serve their property. These off-site requirements have a major impact on the location of subdivisions. Even for very large developments, the cost of bringing in water and sewer services from more than a mile away is prohibitive. Unless the municipality is able to underwrite the cost directly or through some form of special district, the amount that developers can afford to pay for off-site facilities is limited.

The first developer is often required to install infrastructure—notably roads, sewers, water, and drainage—to serve a new area. Many cities require other property owners who benefit from that infrastructure to reimburse the developer later, when those owners subdivide their own property. This procedure allows the developer to recoup the cost, albeit over the course of years. Many communities, however, do not give any interest on up-front investment to the developer. Thus, the developer's current project alone must effectively support the off-site infrastructure.

Avoiding Pitfalls. From the perspective of public policy, many regulations serve vital functions—protecting the environment, reducing flooding, controlling traffic, and ensuring that adequate infrastructure is built. From the developer's point of view, however, increasing government regulation adds considerably to the time, expense, and risk of land development.

The larger the land development project, the more likely it is to become the community's target of special regulatory concern. One way to minimize the impact of regulation is to choose infill areas located in older jurisdictions that have more established regulations. They may present other problems, however, as infill tracts are surrounded by existing development and developers may have to deal with vocal homeowners groups.

In general, developers can reduce the regulatory risk by following these suggestions:

- Stay closely in touch with city or county planning staff.
- Monitor pending ordinances and referenda.
- Join the local building industry association, which should be in touch with everything in progress.
- Once a concern has been identified that may affect the project, consult the regulatory agency's staff and, if necessary, an attorney to find out how to protect or exempt the project.
- Consider working with redevelopment agencies, which often have the power to cut red tape and expedite approvals.
- Consider using a development agreement to protect development rights.
- Select local architects, engineers, and zoning and other consultants who have worked extensively in the community.

In addition, adhering to the principles of maintaining flexibility and working with the community and homeowners should make the process smoother.

Maintaining Flexibility. Regulatory uncertainty is changing the way in which developers buy land. Increasingly, the price of land is tied to the number of units or square footage that can be built on a site, which shifts the approval risk, in part, from developers to sellers, because the purchase price is lower if developers cannot get permission to build a prenegotiated number of units or square feet. In general, most land sellers are unwilling to accept regulatory risk after closing. Either the developer must accept this risk or find a seller who is willing to defer the closing until zoning or other approvals are completed. The land price will reflect which party takes on the entitlement risk. The price should be significantly lower if the developer closes without the entitlements than it would be if entitlements are in place. Beginning developers are advised to share the risks where possible with the seller, even if it means lower profit, unless they are very confident that they can obtain zoning approval for enough units to make the project profitable.

At the same time that government approvals are becoming harder to obtain, planning commissions and city councils are requiring developers to meet specific timetables. Developers are often required to build roads and community facilities by a specific time, often in advance of selling lots. In some cases, developers must commit to building a specified number of units per year. The cyclical nature of the real estate industry, however, makes periods of boom and bust inevitable. Developers must retain the flexibility to build more units when times are good and to reduce production (and infrastructure installation) when times are bad.

Developers should also retain the flexibility, where possible, to program the mix of units for each develop-

ment phase. Because of the frequent delay between approvals and construction, developers must be able to respond to current market conditions when deciding on their final unit mix. Otherwise, developers may be forced to sell lots to homebuilders to meet a market that is no longer in demand and may be precluded from selling lots for houses in a price category that is in demand. For larger projects, developers should work in increments or stages that are small enough for them to vary the product mix as the market indicates. Many communities now require approval of specific plans that lock the developer into specific unit sizes and finishes, adding substantially to the developer's risk, as a change in the market requires a new series of public hearings to change the specific plan.

Working with the Community. The relationship between a developer and neighboring homeowners is critical to a project's success. The most common objection raised by homeowners groups to a proposed subdivision is that it will reduce the quality of the neighborhood—bringing in people who have lower incomes and live in smaller houses or exacerbating traffic problems. In urban fringe development, opposition tends to focus on spillover costs and inadequate infrastructure. The developer's best counterargument is to emphasize the quality of the new development.

Most experienced developers claim that they prefer to talk to homeowners groups themselves instead of hiring someone to represent them. Developers need to convince the community that they will keep their promises, and this trust is more likely to be gained in person.

The developer of a small project may not need to talk to homeowners groups if the project is consistent with local zoning and land use and no public approvals are required. Although doing nothing and hoping that no one will notice a project is a temptation for developers, this approach obviously is not the best one. Homeowners groups in most parts of the country are too aware of, and involved with, development for the developer to rely solely on the quiet approval of the planning commission and the city council. Such groups become particularly intransigent when they feel that they are being ignored—especially if they do not learn about proposed projects until the public hearing. If opposition coalesces at the end of the approval process, often the developer will be sent back to come to terms with homeowners groups and then to start the process again.

A better approach is to identify in advance the groups that may have an interest in, or concern about, the project and then seek them out. A developer should be careful also to identify the most influential leaders in a local community. Peiser Corporation, for example, lost a zoning case on a land development because it met with the president of the local homeowners association but not with the leader of opinion in the community, a minister, who turned against the project in part because he was not consulted initially.

Developers usually have to address concerns about the imposition of costs on property owners and the overburdening of existing roads, schools, or other public facilities in meetings with other property owners and neighborhood groups or in public hearings. In any situation where a public hearing is required for approval, the following approach is recommended:[36]

- Educate the public affected by the project.
- Talk to planning departments early in the course of the project to explore options.
- Be aware that the public hearing process is not adequate for addressing homeowners' opposition.
- Be proactive with residents: talk to the city council or legislators to get in touch with citizens groups, develop contacts with them, and, possibly, form a citizens advisory committee.
- Use graphics to communicate plans to those who are not at the public hearing.
- Know that fear of the unknown motivates citizens groups: be certain that all plans are clearly explained.
- Allocate time for the development staff to communicate with the public.

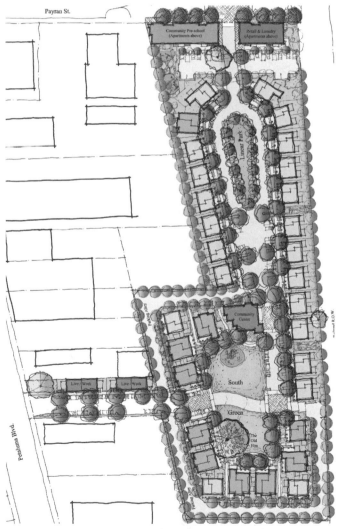

At Old Elm Village in Petaluma, California, pedestrian-oriented tree-lined streets with parallel parking, "parking alleys," and raised roadbeds help to reduce and tame automobile traffic in favor of pedestrians.

- Seek out or form homeowners groups to maintain communication within the community; and
- If problems arise, use mediators instead of lawyers.

Financial Feasibility Analysis

Financial feasibility analysis for land development is performed in two stages. The first stage is a "quick and dirty" pro forma that summarizes the project's sales revenues, expenses, interest, and profit; the second is a multiperiod discounted cash flow (DCF) analysis that provides a detailed projection of cash flows, equity and loan needs, profits, and internal rates of return (IRRs). Developers should perform both stages of analysis before they commit earnest money to a project. They should then update the cash flow analysis weekly during the feasibility period as they establish sales, price, and cost information with greater accuracy. The DCF analysis feeds into the investor return analysis, which provides a picture of the returns to the different parties who furnish the equity for the project—the investors and the developer—under a deal structure. The DCF analysis and the investor analysis are the developer's primary spreadsheets for evaluating a project's financial prospects, for obtaining a land development loan, and for raising equity from investors.

Basic Concepts. Financial analysis for land development differs from that for other property types, and developers should be aware of some basic concepts for this type of analysis.

For-Sale versus Income Property. The fundamental difference between financial analysis for land development and other property types is that land is for-sale property, whereas apartments, offices, retail stores, and warehouses are income properties. For-sale property is analyzed over the development period, which depends on how long it will take for the market to absorb the land for homes or other property types—one or two years for a small subdivision, three to five years for a larger one. This type of project is financed by equity and a land development loan. Lots or parcels are sold to homebuilders and income property developers. The land developer's profit is the difference between revenues from land sales and the costs of purchasing the raw land, planning the project, acquiring approvals, installing infrastructure, and marketing the land to end users. In contrast, financial feasibility of income-producing properties focuses on computing the value of the completed and fully leased property using a before-tax and after-tax analysis that includes permanent financing and, typically, a seven- or ten-year holding period. The development profit is the difference between the value of the completed property and the "all-in" cost of developing it.

Gross versus Net Developable Acreage. One of the most confusing concepts of the feasibility analysis for beginning developers to grasp is the distinction between gross acres, net developable acres, and net usable acres.[37] *Gross acres* refers to total acreage at the time of purchase. *Net developable acreage,* or net acreage, omits major streets, open spaces, floodplains, and major easements that are significant to the entire project. *Net usable acres* omits

figure 3-3
Approximate Residential Lot Yield Per Acre for Different Lot Sizes

Lot Size (Square Feet)	Lot Yield per Acre[a]	
	With Alleys	Without Alleys
10,000	3.0	3.3
8,500	3.6	3.8
7,500	4.1	4.4
6,500	4.7	5.0
6,000	5.1	5.4
5,000	6.1	6.5
4,000	7.0–8.0	7.5–8.5

[a]The number of lots yielded per acre is only a crude estimate for the initial calculation.

figure 3-4
Densities by Residential Type

	FAR	Net Density (Units per Acre)	Gross Density
Single-Family	0.2	8	5
Zero-Lot-Line Detached	0.3	8–10	6
Two-Family Detached	0.3	10–12	7
Row Houses	0.5	16–24	12
Stacked Townhouses	0.8	25–40	18
Three-Story Walkup Apartments	1.0	40–45	30
Three-Story Walkup over Parking	1.0	50–60	40
Six-Story Elevator Apartments	1.4	65–75	60
13-Story Elevator Apartments	1.8	85–100	75

Source: Kevin Lynch and Gary Hack, *Site Planning*, 3rd ed. (Cambridge, Mass.: MIT Press, 1985), p. 253. Density ranges for apartments have been adjusted upward.

interior street rights-of-way, alleys, and any other areas that are not actually for sale from net developable acres. Total net usable acres should equal the total area actually sold—the aggregate total area of building lots plus multifamily, commercial, industrial, and office sites.

Most rough calculations are performed on the basis of net developable acreage, which includes interior streets. When a developer investigates a new piece of property, one of the most important pieces of information about it is therefore the amount of land *not developable* because of floodplains, easements, major road rights-of-way, or dedications for schools, parks, or other community facilities. The remaining acreage is used to calculate the number of lots and the number of acres of apartments or commercial reserves to be sold separately.

A reasonably good estimate can be made of the number of lots that can be fitted on a specified property by using yield formulas. For example, 7,500-square-foot lots produce a typical yield of four lots per acre (they are called *quarter-acre* lots because of the yield, even though they are smaller than a quarter acre (43,560 square feet):

4 lots x 7,500 square feet per lot = 30,000 square feet
Estimated street right-of-way = 12,000 square feet
Total = 42,000 square feet (about 1 acre)

The yield differs from city to city, depending on the standard street rights-of-way and whether or not the city requires alleys. Most planners allow for some waste because, for example, corner lots are larger, and irregularly shaped sites are difficult to develop efficiently.

The developer should check with a local planner for lot yield, but the following rules of thumb may serve as starters. Deduct 25 percent of the acreage for streets (30 percent if alleys are required), and then divide the remainder by the lot size. (Representative densities for residential development are shown in Figure 3-4.)

Land Use Budget. The allocation of total net developable acreage into different land uses is called the *land use budget*. The total budget, including all product types,

roads, open space, and community facilities, should add up to total developable acreage. The most profitable (optimal) land use budget is determined by the marketplace, based on those product types that are being absorbed at the fastest rate and highest prices.

The land use budget should be established before meeting with the land planner. A common mistake that developers make is to let the land planner or civil engineer instead of the marketplace determine the land use budget. A rough estimate of cost may be obtained from other developers, civil engineers, and grading and utility contractors. With this information, plus sale prices and

figure 3-5
Land Use Budget for a 100-Acre Site

	Land Use Budget (Acres)	Absorption (Acres per Year)
Residential		
Single-Family (7,500-square-foot lots)	40	10
Single-Family (5,000-square-foot lots)	20	6
Apartments (30 units per acre)	10	5
Retail	15	5
Community Facilities	2	–
Parks and Open Space	8	–
Subtotal	95	
Arterial Highway Dedication	5	
Total	100	

marketing and administrative cost estimates, a developer can produce the quick and dirty analysis shown later. An example of the land use budget for a 100-acre site is shown in Figure 3-5.

The land use budget becomes the major initial input into the financial feasibility analysis. In the example in Figure 3-5, only the residential and retail land, totaling 85 acres, produces revenue (is salable). Community facilities, parks, and areas dedicated for arterial highways do not.

The absorption rate for the land is based on the number of acres that can be sold each year. In this case, it should take four years to sell out the 7,500-square-foot single-family lots, more than three years for the 5,000-square-foot lots, two years for the apartment land, and three years for the retail land. These relatively high absorption rates for the retail component are based on the location, which fronts on a new freeway in far North Dallas.

The ideal land use budget maximizes the value of the property by allocating as much land as possible to high-value uses. Developers often mistakenly allocate too much land to high-value uses such as office or retail, which command higher sale prices but have very slow absorption rates. In addition, land absorption for higher-density projects such as high-rise apartments takes longer, by definition, than it does for lower-density projects, because more units must be sold to absorb each acre of land.

Another difficulty is distinguishing between land sales to builders and other developers and those to end users. In larger projects, if enough land for 20 or 30 years of absorption has been reserved for office and retail use, it is tempting simply to assume that the unsold inventory will be sold to "land investors" at the end of the development life—say, three or five years later. The developer must, however, assume a significant discount (25 to 50 percent or more) in the retail sale price of lots to end users. Investors who buy the unsold inventory will have to wait until demand from end users warrants building out the site and so will not pay retail prices for the land.

Optimal Land Use Planning. Figures 3-6 and 3-7 illustrate the computation of land value and the allocation of land uses for a 35-acre tract of land. Suppose that retail land can be sold for a net profit of $200,000 per acre, while 7,500-square-foot single-family lots bring $80,000 per acre at $20,000 each. Suppose also that demand is one acre per year for retail land versus 40 lots (ten acres) per year for single-family lots. Note that retail absorption is much slower than single-family lot absorption.

Figure 3-6 shows the present value of land sold for retail use each year for eight years. To compare the value of retail land sold today with that sold in seven years, the value is discounted at a hefty 15 percent per year—a discount rate that reflects both the high holding cost of land and the high risk associated with land development. A retail acre sold in seven years is worth only $75,000, compared with $200,000 today. By comparison, an acre of single-family land sold today is worth $80,000. In this

figure 3-6

Effect of Present Value Factors on Land Allocation for Different Uses

Year	Present Value Factor at 15 Percent[a]	Profit on One Acre of Retail Land	Profit on One Acre of Single-Family Land[b]
0	1.000	$200,000 (1)	$80,000 (8)
1	.869	173,800[c] (2)	69,520 (10)
2	.756	151,200 (3)	60,480 (12)
3	.657	131,400 (4)	
4	.571	114,200 (5)	
5	.497	99,400 (6)	
6	.432	86,400 (7)	
7	.375	75,000 (9)	
8	.327	65,400 (11)	

[a] Opportunity cost is 15 percent annually.

[b] Parenthetical numbers indicate the order of allocation.

[c] Values are computed by multiplying value in year 0 by the factor for the year (for instance, $200,000 times .869 equals $173,800).

example, therefore, it is more advantageous to sell single-family land today than another acre of retail land in seven years.

This type of information is used to determine the land use budget. The developer should allocate land to the highest-value use as long as the present value of that year's absorption rate is greater than the next-highest-value use.

Figure 3-7 shows the allocation for a 35-acre site. The developer would allocate the first seven acres to retail use (seven years of absorption of retail land at one acre per

figure 3-7

Allocation of Land for 35-Acre Tract Using Present Value Approach[a]

Year	Retail Use (Acres)[b]	Single-Family Use (Acres)[b]
0	1 (1)	10 (8)
1	1 (2)	10 (10)
2	1 (3)	6 (12)
3	1 (4)	
4	1 (5)	
5	1 (6)	
6	1 (7)	
7	1 (9)	
8	1 (11)	
Total	9	26

[a] Given annual absorption rates of 1 acre of retail and 10 acres of single-family land.

[b] Parenthetical numbers indicate order of allocation.

year), because the present value is greater than that for single-family land sold today, even though it will not be consumed by the marketplace for up to six years (allocations 1 through 7, indicated in parentheses in the figure). The next ten acres would go to single-family land (allocation 8), however, because the present value ($80,000) is higher than the value of the retail land sold in seven years ($75,000). Ten acres is allocated to single-family use because that is the amount of single-family land that can be sold in one year. The next acre would go to retail use (allocation 9). The next ten acres would go to single-family lots (allocation 10) and then one more acre to retail (allocation 11). At this point, 20 acres are assigned to residential use and nine acres to retail use. The last allocation (12) goes to residential. Because only six acres are left to bring the total to 35 acres, the third year's allocation of residential absorption is not completely used. The final budget is 26 acres of single-family lots and nine acres of retail use.

This procedure for allocating land is an application of linear programming to real estate.[38] It works for any number of uses and can be done by hand. The only information needed is net developable acreage, sale price, development cost, and absorption rate for each land use or product type. The suggested discount rate is 5 percent above the current interest rate for development loans. The resulting land use allocation is only a guideline for the land use budget and will probably be modified by zoning, political, or environmental constraints. Nevertheless, a market-based land use allocation is the only accurate and reliable method for determining the land use budget. It should determine the land use plan, not vice versa.

Quick and Dirty Analysis. The developer analyzes financial feasibility several times during the course of a project. The first analysis is performed before tying up the property with an earnest money contract; as the deal progresses, the analysis becomes successively more thorough and complex. A good financial feasibility analysis becomes the basis for managing the project once it begins construction; therefore, the categories in the analysis should coincide with the chart of accounts.

The financial analysis illustrated in this discussion is taken from a project under development in 2002, San Luis Rey, by Granite Homes in Oceanside, California. The project consists of 111 single-family, tentatively mapped lots for which a final map will be prepared on or before the close of escrow. The average lot size is 6,800 square feet, the minimum 6,000 square feet, which is typical for the area. The property is mostly flat, with some elevation that will provide certain lots with adequate views of the adjacent San Luis Rey River. The land is currently unimproved and will be developed into finished lots by Granite Homes. Lot development will include grading, underground placement of wet and dry utilities, and construction of storm drains, streets, curbs, gutters, and sidewalks.[39]

In addition to developing the lots, Granite Homes will build and sell homes on the lots, making San Luis

Rey a combined land development/home development project. This illustration, however, evaluates the land development by itself from the perspective of Granite Homes's land development division. As such, the revenue to the land developer is derived from the sale of lots to homebuilders, regardless of whether the homebuilder is another division of Granite Homes or a third party.

Quick and dirty analysis provides the initial estimate of the project's financial performance. It summarizes projected revenues from the sale of lots, land and development costs and interest, and expected profit. All figures are aggregated for the entire project life. No time dimension for development or sales is considered. Quick and dirty analysis represents the starting point for evaluating the deal. It does not, however, give the developer all the information needed to make proper decisions.

Figure 3-8 shows the quick and dirty analysis for San Luis Rey. Granite Homes plans to develop the project in eight small phases. For simplicity, Phases 1 and 2, 3 and 4, and so on are grouped into four larger phases of 20 to 30 homes each. Sale prices for the lots range from $160,000 to $166,000, generating total revenue of $18,104,000.

Land for the project cost $9,276,500, or $83,572 per lot, reflecting the fact that the land is already entitled (it has a tentative map for 111 lots) and the developer has little entitlement risk.[40] Development costs include on-site land improvements, off-site improvements, and estimates for administration, contingency, and marketing (5 percent of revenues). Total development costs are $7,277,600. Financing costs are estimated by assuming that Granite Homes invests $4 million in equity and borrows the rest. In actuality, the development loan will be done in four phases and will not reach the $12,554,100 shown in the analysis (total development costs of $16,554,100 minus equity of $4,000,000). A principal shortcoming of quick and dirty analysis is the back-of-the envelope methodology. Interest is estimated here by assuming that it takes one year to develop the project with an average loan balance of $6,277,050, or $470,779 total interest. Profit is $1,079,121.

By traditional rules, this amount of profit is inadequate to make the deal work. Profit represents only 6.5 percent of total costs and only 6 percent of total revenue. Traditional rules of thumb suggest that these ratios should be close to 25 to 30 percent. Such rules, however, are not very meaningful because they do not provide any estimate of return on equity or take into account the holding period. For example, a 30 percent return on equity in one year would be good, whereas a 30 percent return over three years would be only 10 percent per year uncompounded and 9.14 percent per year compounded.[41] Because the time-value of money is not included in the quick and dirty calculation, comparison with other investment alternatives is not possible.

Quick and dirty analysis has other shortcomings:

- It gives no indication of how quickly lots are sold.
- It has no means of introducing inflation.

figure 3-8
Quick and Dirty Analysis

Revenue

	Lots	Price per Lot	Revenue	Total	Per Lot
Phases 1 & 2	27	$160,000	$4,320,000		
Phases 3 & 4	27	162,000	4,374,000		
Phases 5 & 6	26	164,000	4,264,000		
Phases 7 & 8	31	166,000	5,146,000		
	111			$18,104,000	$163,099

Expenditures

				Total	Per Lot
Land				$9,276,500	$83,572

Development Costs

Grading			$299,868		
Paving			675,517		
Storm sewer			345,922		
Water			304,798		
Sanitary sewer			245,118		
Off-site street paving			630,196		
Fees and permits			1,825,395		
School fees			610,833		
Indirect land development			277,554		
Financing costs (2% x maximum loan amount)			252,000		
Marketing	5% of sales		905,200		
Administration and contingencies	5% of sales		905,200		
Total Development Costs				7,277,600	65,564
Subtotal				16,554,100	149,136

Interest Calculation

Equity			$4,000,000		
Debt			12,554,100		
Average balance	50%		6,277,050		
Duration	1 year				
Rate	7.5%			470,779	
Total Expenditures				17,024,879	153,377
Profit				$1,079,121	9,722

			6.5% of Total Costs	6.0% of Total Revenue

- Computation of interest on the development loan is haphazard.
- It gives no information about when funds are needed or the amount needed.
- It has no means of computing present values or internal rates of return.

The loan calculation is the weakest part of the quick and dirty analysis. In the example above, the loan amount is chosen so that it covers all of the costs, including loan interest, which usually can be borrowed. The size of the loan depends on how quickly the lots are sold, however —one of the factors that the quick and dirty analysis

does not take into account. Whether or not the loan amount will cover 100 percent of the costs depends on the raw land appraisal, the development cost, and the borrower's credit. Today, most land development projects require some form of real equity—cash investment or significant appreciation in land value.

The main advantage of the quick and dirty analysis is that it forces the developer to make explicit assumptions concerning land uses, site planning, sales rates, prices, costs, and financing. This exercise provides a rough indication of whether or not the deal makes economic sense, and it serves as the foundation for all subsequent investigation.

Multiperiod Discounted Cash Flow Analysis. Multiperiod DCF analysis is an application of the capital asset pricing model to real estate. The cash flow analysis assigns revenues and expenditures from the quick and dirty analysis above to specific periods of time. Note that the cash flows in Figure 3-8 reflect the funding and repayment requirements of equity investors and lenders available to land developers. (Terms of the different financing sources are discussed later in this chapter under "Financing.")

The multiperiod DCF analysis for the 111-lot development at San Luis Rey is shown in Figures 3-9a through 3-9e. Its principal purpose is to compute 1) returns to the overall project (100 percent owner/developer), 2) loan requirements, and 3) returns to joint venture participants. It is a before-tax computation.

Land development financing is similar to construction financing during the development period of income property (Stage 3 analysis in Chapter 4). No permanent mortgage exists as the purpose of land development is to sell developed lots to end users—homebuilders, and apartment, shopping center, and office building developers. Another important difference from income property analysis is that the development loan is retired by the sale of lots rather than by funding of the permanent mortgage, which takes out (pays off) the construction loan.

Land development DCF analysis is used to determine the building program, phasing, and expense budget that the project can support. Like Stage 2 analysis for income properties (see Chapter 4), land development DCF analysis is rerun many times during the feasibility period and over the life of the project. The land use budget, cost, and sales assumptions are changed as more accurate information becomes available. Thus, the land development DCF analysis is the land developer's equivalent of the architect's sketch pad (just as Stage 2 analysis is the income property developer's sketch pad). The cash flow analysis for land development is used for both planning the design of the project and obtaining financing.

Several items should be noted about the methodology of the DCF analysis for land development.

Time Periods. Intervals should be selected that cover five to ten time periods of analysis. For example, for a sale of 120 lots at the rate of 30 lots per quarter, plus 12 months for development, the total time required is about two years. Quarterly time periods (three months per period) would provide eight total periods, a good starting point for analysis. For larger projects that require, say, ten years to be developed, annual periods would be appropriate for the first DCF analysis. In very large projects, such as new communities with 20- to 30-year lives, two-year intervals are preferable.

Level of Detail. The purpose of the early runs of the DCF analysis is to obtain a picture of the total project. Beginners often go into too much detail at first, forgetting that every item in the spreadsheet is subject to change. Because the developer has not yet done a detailed site plan and sales and cost estimates are, at best, rough approximations, a monthly cash flow analysis

would be meaningless. The spreadsheet can always be enhanced by adding more periods and more line items as more information becomes available. Usually, the developer should wait to prepare a monthly cash flow forecast until the site plan has been adopted, the market study has been completed, contract bids are available, and a monthly forecast for loan approval is needed.

Time Period Zero. Time period 0 represents the starting period of analysis and can be set for any time. It should always be included in cash flow analysis. For existing projects, time period 0 is recommended to be set three to six months earlier than the present date at some point where the exact amount of money spent to date is known. In projects where money has already been spent, a line item on the spreadsheet, *costs to date,* should be added that aggregates the total money spent as of time period 0. For new projects, time period 0 is normally selected as the closing date on the land. Any costs incurred before closing are simply included under the land cost or cost-to-date category.

Timing of Sales. Enough time should be allocated to develop the property and investigate the effects of slower than anticipated sales. One computer run should assume half the expected pace of sales (twice the amount of time anticipated to sell out the project) and compute the maximum loan amount needed for this downside case.

Inflation. DCF models typically include three different inflation rates—sale price inflation, cost inflation, and the inflation rate implicit in the interest rate. These rates are correlated but not necessarily the same. A 3 percent inflation rate in sale prices, for example, indicates a development loan interest rate of 7 to 11 percent (3 percent inflation plus 2 to 3 percent real rate of return plus 2 to 5 percent risk). Higher inflation assumptions make a project look better than it probably is. Lenders are rightfully cautious of overly optimistic inflation assumptions and may insist on a DCF analysis run with zero inflation in sale prices.

Development Loan Borrowings. The development loan provides bank financing for all borrowing needs after the equity. Once the loan has been reduced through the sale of lots, developers usually are not allowed to reborrow money (as they would be able to with a revolving line of credit), because the collateral for the loan—namely, the land—has been partially sold off. In San Luis Rey, the development loan does go up and down as successive phases are developed and then sold. In actuality, this ability to reborrow money would likely require separate loans on each phase or include provisions tying new borrowings to the new phases.

Loan Repayments. Loan repayments (releases) represent the amount by which the land note and/or the development loan must be repaid as property is sold. Every time a lot is sold, the land that was pledged as collateral for the development loan must be "released" from the construction loan or land loan lien by the lender. These releases are shown as *cash out* or repayment items (development loan repayments and land note repayments, Lines 115 and 116, in Figure 3-9c).

Before-Tax Computation. Before-tax rates of return may be used for evaluating the economic feasibility of a land development project as long as they are compared with before-tax returns from other investment opportunities. Unlike the development of income property (see Chapter 4), in which tax benefits are an important part of the return, land development offers no special tax benefits (such as deductions for depreciation and current interest). The Internal Revenue Service treats the land developer as a "dealer in land," and, as such, the developer must pay ordinary tax on reported profits. For example, if the developer's tax rate were 33 percent, he would pay $333 in tax on each $1,000 of profit.

Return Measures. The unleveraged internal rate of return (Line 154) assumes that all cash requirements are financed from cash equity. It is computed on Line 103 in Figure 3-9c, "profit before interest," exclusive of all financing. The unleveraged return varies from year to year but should be at least 15 to 20 percent.[42] It should exceed the cost of borrowing money so that the developer can obtain positive leverage. If, for example, the unleveraged IRR is 15 percent and the interest rate on the development loan is 12 percent, then the developer's return on equity will be higher than 15 percent. Negative leverage exists when the return is less than the loan rate. Positive leverage means that as the

figure 3-9a
DCF Results

Profit before Interest	2,278,744	Cash Flow after Financing		5,953,189
Less Interest	(325,556)	Less Repayment of Equity		(4,000,000)
Profit	1,953,189	Less Unpaid Loan Balance		
		Profit		1,953,189

Unleveraged Return[a]
Cash Flows before Interest and Financing

Net Present Value @ 15%	252,602
IRR	17.3%

Leveraged Return on Equity[b]
Net Cash Flows after Financing

Net Present Value @ 15%	661,540
IRR	25.3%

Year	Net Profit	Year	Equity	Cash Inflows
0	(9,326,500)	0	4,000,000	
1	(516,903)	1	–	
2	2,807,661	2	–	395,389
3	(444,457)	3	–	(395,389)
4	3,016,340	4	–	654,098
5	(416,903)	5	–	(654,098)
6	2,996,134	6	–	1,789,817
7	4,163,372	7	–	4,163,372
8	–	8	–	–
9	–	9	–	–
10	–	10	–	–
11	–	11	–	–
12	–	12	–	–
13	–	13	–	–
14	–	14	–	–
15	–	15	–	–
16	–	16	–	–
Total	2,278,744	Total	4,000,000	5,953,189

Note: This figure is a summary of the results of the analysis. Key outputs are the unleveraged and leveraged IRRs, which are taken from computations of cash flows and IRRs in Figures 3-9c and 3-9d, respectively.

[a] The unleveraged return is computed on the cash flows before financing (Line 154). Thus, it is an all-equity rate of return. The unleveraged return should be significantly greater than the interest rate on financing. Otherwise, no profit will be left after financing costs are paid.

[b] The return on equity is computed on cash flows after financing (Line 155). A leveraged rate of return gives the IRR on equity for the entire project (the owner/developer provides all necessary equity).

figure 3-9b
Assumptions: Sales, Prices, Development Costs, Land Note

1	Number of Time Periods per Year				4 (1 = annual, 2 = semiannual, 4 = quarterly, 12 = monthly)							
2				Q4 2000	Q1 2001	Q2 2001	Q3 2001	Q4 2001	Q1 2002	Q2 2002	Q3 2002	Q4 2002
3	Sales of Lots[c]		Total	0[d]	1	2	3	4	5	6	7	8
4												
5	Phases 1 & 2		27			27						
6	Phases 3 & 4		27					27				
7	Phases 5 & 6		26							26		
8	Phases 7 & 8		31								31	
9												
10	Total		111	–	–	27	–	27	–	26	31	–
11												
12												
13		Price Escalation	Price per									
14		per	Square	Price								
15	Sale Prices[e]	Period[f]	Foot	per Lot	1	2	3	4	5	6	7	8
16												
17	Phases 1 & 2	0.75%	–	160,000	160,000	161,200	162,409	163,627	164,854	166,091	167,336	168,591
18	Phases 3 & 4	0.75%	–	162,000	162,000	163,215	164,439	165,672	166,915	168,167	169,428	170,699
19	Phases 5 & 6	0.75%	–	164,000	164,000	165,230	166,469	167,718	168,976	170,243	171,520	172,806
20	Phases 7 & 8	0.75%	–	166,000	166,000	167,245	168,499	169,763	171,036	172,319	173,611	174,914
21												
22												
23	Sales Revenues[g]		Total	–	1	2	3	4	5	6	7	8
24												
25	Phases 1 & 2		4,352,400	–	–	4,352,400	–	–	–	–	–	–
26	Phases 3 & 4		4,473,155	–	–	–	–	4,473,155	–	–	–	–
27	Phases 5 & 6		4,426,317	–	–	–	–	–	–	4,426,317	–	–
28	Phases 7 & 8		5,381,956	–	–	–	–	–	–	–	5,381,956	–
29												
30	Total		18,633,827	–	–	4,352,400	–	4,473,155	–	4,426,317	5,381,956	–
31												
33												
34												
35	Costs[h]	Inflation	Total	[i]	1	2	3	4	5	6	7	8
36												
37	Land		9,276,500	9,276,500								
38			–									
39	Grading	223,715	299,868		49,978	49,978	49,978	49,978	49,978	49,978		
40	Paving		675,517		112,586	112,586	112,586	112,586	112,586	112,586		
41	Storm sewer		345,922		57,654	57,654	57,654	57,654	57,654	57,654		
42	Water		304,798		50,800	50,800	50,800	50,800	50,800	50,800		
43	Sanitary sewer		245,118		40,853	40,853	40,853	40,853	40,853	40,853		
44	Off–site street paving		630,196		105,033	105,033	105,033	105,033	105,033	105,033		
45	Fees and permits		1,825,395			444,015	–	444,015	–	427,570	509,795	
46	School fees		610,833			148,581	–	148,581	–	143,078	170,593	
47	Indirect land development		277,554	50,000	100,000	100,000	27,554					

Line	Land Note[j]	Data Input	Total	0	1	2	3	4	5	6	7	8
48			–									
49			–									
50	Interest per Period (Decimal)	0.075/year			0.0188	0.0188	0.0188	0.0188	0.0188	0.0188	0.0188	0.0188
51												
52		**Data**										
53		Input	Total	0	1	2	3	4	5	6	7	8
54												
55	Total Land Cost	9,276,500		9,276,500								
56	Lots Sold (enter release price/lot)	83,572	111	–	–	27	–	27	–	26	31	–
57	Downpayment		5,276,500	5,276,500								
58	Beginning Lots Released	83,572		63.1	63.1	63.1	40.9	50.5	40.2	57.0	31.0	
59	Ending Lots Released				63.1	36.1	40.9	23.5	40.2	31.0	–	–
60	Lots to Be Released			–	–	–	–	–	–	–	–	–
61	Land Note	4,000,000		4,000,000								
62	Repayment Terms					10.0%	20.0%	35.0%	35.0%			
63	Minimum Land Payments			–	–	400,000	800,000	1,400,000	1,400,000	–	–	–
64	Maximum Land Note Balance			4,000,000	4,000,000	3,600,000	2,800,000	1,400,000	–	–	–	–
65												
66	Starting Balance			4,000,000	4,000,000	4,000,000	3,600,000	2,800,000	1,400,000	–	–	–
67	Land Note Releases	83,572	–	–	–	–	–	–	–	–	–	–
68	Remaining Balance			4,000,000	4,000,000	4,000,000	3,600,000	2,800,000	1,400,000	–	–	–
69	Additional Note Payments			–	–	400,000	800,000	1,400,000	1,400,000	–	–	–
70	Ending Balance			4,000,000	4,000,000	3,600,000	2,800,000	1,400,000	–	–	–	–
71	Additional Lots Released	83,572				4.8	9.6	16.8	16.8			
72	Interest for Period[k]	1.5%	237,000		60,000	60,000	54,000	42,000	21,000	–	–	–
73												
74	Land Note Total		237,000	(4,000,000)	60,000	460,000	854,000	1,442,000	1,421,000	–	–	–

Note: Key assumptions are sales rate, sale price, costs, interest rate, and land note terms.

[c] Sales by product type are entered for each period. Units of measurement do not have to be the same. Thus, residential sales may be expressed as number of lots sold per period (lines 3 through 10); office space is expressed in acres sold per period.

[d] Each period is a quarter (Line 2). The number of periods per year should be chosen to produce five to 15 periods overall. A ten-year project is best analyzed with annual periods (ten periods), a 20-year project with two-year periods (ten periods), and a three-year project with quarterly periods (12 periods).

[e] Sale prices are expressed in the same units as sales. Thus, if residential sales are expressed in lots, sale prices should be expressed in price per lot (Lines 15 through 20).

[f] Lot prices may be escalated at a given rate per period (Lines 15 through 20).

[g] Sales revenue is computed from the number of acres or units sold per period times the price per period (Lines 23 through 30).

[h] Costs are entered by category and period. Detailed cost breakdowns for individual categories, such as utilities, are best handled in supporting spreadsheets (see Lines 35 through 47), as an overabundance of detail makes the analysis more difficult to follow.

[i] Time 0 should be treated as a separate period. Typically, Time 0 is the time of closing. Costs incurred before Time 0 should be lumped together as startup costs.

[j] The land note defines the terms, if any, of the land purchase from the land seller. The release price negotiated in the land note is $83,572 per lot. (Note that the release price is often different for different lots.) Given a downpayment of $5,276,500, 63.1 lots (Line 58) are released immediately from the note. The land note also defines the repayment terms (Line 62). If sales are slower than the terms of the note, then the developer must pay additional money to satisfy the land note (Line 69), which releases additional lots (Line 71). If lot sales occur faster than the note repayment terms require, then additional lots must be released (Line 60) to sell the lots. In the example, the sales pace is slower than the terms of the note. If releases from sales are slower than those required under the amortization terms of the land note, then the shortfall is covered by the development loan or additional equity (Line 69).

[k] Interest on the development loan typically is borrowed as part of the development loan. It may, however, be funded by cash payments rather than additional borrowing.

figure 3-9c
Cash Flow Summary

		Total	0	1	2	3	4	5	6	7	8
75											
76											
77											
78											
79	**Income**										
80											
81	Sales Revenue	18,633,827	–	–	4,352,400	–	4,473,155	–	4,426,317	5,381,956	–
82											
83	Total Income	18,633,827	–	–	4,352,400	–	4,473,155	–	4,426,317	5,381,956	–
84											
85	**Expenses**[l]										
86											
87	Land[m]	9,276,500	9,276,500	–	–	–	–	–	–	–	–
88			–				–		–			–
89	Grading	299,868	–	49,978	49,978	49,978	49,978	49,978	49,978	–	–
90	Paving	675,517	–	112,586	112,586	112,586	112,586	112,586	112,586	–	–
91	Storm sewer	345,922	–	57,654	57,654	57,654	57,654	57,654	57,654	–	–
92	Water	304,798	–	50,800	50,800	50,800	50,800	50,800	50,800	–	–
93	Sanitary sewer	245,118	–	40,853	40,853	40,853	40,853	40,853	40,853	–	–
94	Off–site street paving	630,196	–	105,033	105,033	105,033	105,033	105,033	105,033	–	–
95	Fees and permits	1,825,395	–	–	444,015	–	444,015	–	427,570	509,795	–
96	School fees	610,833	–	–	148,581	–	148,581	–	143,078	170,593	–
97	Indirect land development	277,554	50,000	100,000	100,000	27,554	–	–	–	–	–
98	Marketing[n] 5.0%	931,691	–	–	217,620	–	223,658	–	221,316	269,098	–
99	Administration and contingencies 5.0%	931,691	–	–	217,620	–	223,658	–	221,316	269,098	–
100											
101	Total Expenses	16,355,083	9,326,500	516,903	1,544,739	444,457	1,456,814	416,903	1,430,183	1,218,584	–
102											
103	**Profit before Interest**[o]	2,278,744	(9,326,500)	(516,903)	2,807,661	(444,457)	3,016,340	(416,903)	2,996,134	4,163,372	–
104											
105	Less Development Loan Interest	88,556	–	30,567	18,303	8,546	8,627	11,203	11,309	–	–
106	Less Land Note Interest	237,000	–	60,000	60,000	54,000	42,000	21,000	–	–	–
107											
108	**Net Profit**	1,953,189	(9,326,500)	(607,470)	2,729,358	(507,003)	2,965,713	(449,106)	2,984,825	4,163,372	–
109											
110	**Financing**										
111											
112	Plus Equity	4,000,000	4,000,000								
113	Plus Development Loan Borrowings[p]	4,040,593	1,326,500	607,470	–	911,615	–	1,195,008	–	–	–
114	Plus Land Note Borrowings	4,000,000	4,000,000	–	–	–	–	–	–	–	–
115	Minus Development Loan Repayments[q]	(4,040,593)	–	–	(1,933,970)	–	(911,615)	–	(1,195,008)	–	–
116	Minus Land Note Repayments	(4,000,000)	–	–	(400,000)	(800,000)	(1,400,000)	(1,400,000)	–	–	–
117											
118	**Cash Flow after Financing**	5,953,189	–	–	395,389	(395,389)	654,098	(654,098)	1,789,817	4,163,372	–
119	**Cumulative Cash Position**	5,953,189	–	–	395,389	–	654,098	–	1,789,817	5,953,189	5,953,189

Note: The cash flow summary presents net cash flows from land development (Lines 75 through 119). It is the primary table for computing cash inflows from sales, cash outflows for expenses, profit before interest, interest, net profit after interest, and cash flow after financing. It brings together the assumptions from Figure 3-9b and the cash equity and loan borrowings and interest computed in Figure 3-9d.

[l] Expenses summarizes the cost entries in Lines 85 through 101. Figures in the summary are higher in most categories because they include inflation.

[m] Even if land is contributed to the deal, its cost should be included as an expense (Lines 105 and 106).

[n] Some cost categories, such as marketing, are typically calculated as percentages of sales revenues (Line 98).

[o] Profit before interest is derived from Line 103, which sums the differences between total income and total expenses. This line gives the unleveraged cash flows, before financing, found in the results summary of the analysis.

[p] A primary purpose of the analysis is to determine the amount and timing of development loan requirements (Lines 113 through 116). Cash equity (or land equity that is considered "cash" if it is contributed to the deal) is infused into the project initially (Line 112). As money becomes available from sales, it is used to retire the development loan.

[q] Development loan repayments, called releases, are typically a negotiated ratio, usually 1.1 to 1.3 times the loan amount per lot (Line 115). Release prices are usually assigned to each lot, depending on its relative value. In this analysis, all positive cash flows are assumed to go toward paying down the development loan until it is fully retired.

figure 3-9d

Cash and Loan Calculations and IRRs

120	Cash Account and Loan Calculation										
121											
122											
123	**Cash Account**	Total	0	1	2	3	4	5	6	7	8
124											
125	Starting Cash Balance		0	0	0	395,389	0	654,098	0	1,789,817	5,953,189
126	Additions to Equity	4,000,000	4,000,000	0	0	0	0	0	0	0	0
127	Profit before Interest	2,278,744	(9,326,500)	(516,903)	2,807,661	(444,457)	3,016,340	(416,903)	2,996,134	4,163,372	0
128	Land Note	(237,000)	4,000,000	(60,000)	(460,000)	(854,000)	(1,442,000)	(1,421,000)	0	0	0
129											
130	Subtotal	6,041,744	(1,326,500)	(576,903)	2,347,661	(903,068)	1,574,340	(1,183,805)	2,996,134	5,953,189	5,953,189
131											
132	Amount to Be Financed before Interest	3,990,276	1,326,500	576,903	0	903,068	0	1,183,805	0	0	0
133	Cash Available for Loan and Interest		0	0	2,347,661	0	1,574,340	0	2,996,134	5,953,189	5,953,189
134											
135	Loan Repayments	4,040,593	0	0	1,933,970	0	911,615	0	1,195,008	0	0
136	Interest	38,239	0	0	18,303	0	8,627	0	11,309	0	0
137	Ending Cash Balance	5,953,189	0	0	395,389	0	654,098	0	1,789,817	5,953,189	5,953,189
138											
139											
140	**Loan Account**										
141											
142	Beginning Balance		0	1,326,500	1,933,970	0	911,615	0	1,195,008	0	0
143	Loan Draws		1,326,500	576,903	0	903,068	0	1,183,805	0	0	0
144	Loan Repayments		0	0	1,933,970	0	911,615	0	1,195,008	0	0
145	Trial Ending Balance		1,326,500	1,903,403	0	903,068	0	1,183,805	0	0	0
146	Average Balance		0	1,614,952	966,985	451,534	455,807	591,902	597,504	0	0
147	Interest Rate		0	0	0	0	0	0	0	0	0
148	Interest		0	30,567	18,303	8,546	8,627	11,203	11,309	0	0
149	Interest Paid from Cash		0	0	18,303	0	8,627	0	11,309	0	0
150	Ending Balance		1,326,500	1,933,970	0	911,615	0	1,195,008	0	0	0
151	Borrowings after Interest		1,326,500	607,470	0	911,615	0	1,195,008	0	0	0
152											
153	**NPV and IRR Calculations**[r]	**Quarter IRRs**									
154	Unleveraged Return	17.25%	2,278,744	(9,326,500)	(516,903)	2,807,661	(444,457)	3,016,340	(416,903)	2,996,134	4,163,372	0
155	Return on Equity	25.30%	1,953,189	(4,000,000)	0	395,389	(395,389)	654,098	(654,098)	1,789,817	4,163,372	0
156	Cumulative Return on Equity			(4,000,000)	(4,000,000)	(3,604,611)	(4,000,000)	(3,345,902)	(4,000,000)	(2,210,183)	1,953,189	1,953,189

[r] IRRs are calculated on the profit before interest (Line 154) and cash flows after financing and interest (Line 155). These IRRs are included in the results in Figure 3-9a.

figure 3-9e
Investor Return Analysis

	Cash Flows to Investors	Data Input	Total	−	1	2	3	4	5	6	7	8
164												
165												
166												
167	Cash Flows to Investors	Data Input	Total	−	1	2	3	4	5	6	7	8
168												
169	Cash In/Cash Out		5,953,189	−	−	395,389	(395,389)	654,098	(654,098)	1,789,817	4,163,372	−
170	Starting Equity Balance				4,000,000	4,080,000	3,766,211	3,841,536	3,264,268	3,329,553	1,606,328	−
171	Equity Investment		4,000,000	4,000,000	−	−	−	−	−	−	−	
172	Subtotal			4,000,000	4,000,000	4,080,000	3,766,211	3,841,536	3,264,268	3,329,553	1,606,328	
173	Cumulative Preferred Return[s]	2.0%		−	80,000	81,600	75,324	76,831	65,285	66,591	32,127	−
174	Noncumulative Preferred Return[t]	−		−	−	−	−	−	−	−	−	−
175	Preferred Return Paid		257,148	−	−	81,600	−	76,831	−	66,591	32,127	
176	Preferred Return Accrued		220,610	−	80,000		75,324	−	65,285		−	−
177	Subtotal			4,000,000	4,080,000	4,080,000	3,841,536	3,841,536	3,329,553	3,329,553	1,606,328	−
178	Reduction of Equity		4,220,610		−	313,789	−	577,268	−	1,723,226	1,606,328	
179	Ending Equity Balance			4,000,000	4,080,000	3,766,211	3,841,536	3,264,268	3,329,553	1,606,328	−	−
180												
181	Cash for Distribution[u]		2,524,918	−	−	−	−	−	−	−	2,524,918	−
182	Equity Partner	50%	1,262,459	−	−	−	−	−	−	−	1,262,459	−
183	Developer	50%	1,262,459	−	−	−	−	−	−	−	1,262,459	−
184												
185	Rate of Return Calculation											
186												
187	Equity Partner Investment		(4,000,000)	(4,000,000)	−	−	−	−	−	−	−	−
188	Preferred Return		257,148	−	−	81,600	−	76,831	−	66,591	32,127	−
189	Reduction of Equity		4,220,610	−	−	313,789	−	577,268	−	1,723,226	1,606,328	−
190	Cash Distribution		1,262,459	−	−	−	−	−	−	−	1,262,459	−
191												
192	Total Cash Flows to Investor		1,740,217	(4,000,000)	−	395,389	−	654,098	−	1,789,817	2,900,913	−
193												
194	NPV	3.0%	787,865									
195	IRR[v]		25.1%									

Note: The investor return analysis is a before-tax computation of cash flows to the developer and investors in a joint venture (Lines 167 through 195). If the landowner contributes the land to the deal, the land value is treated as cash equity for purposes of this calculation. Cash flow after financing is available to pay back investors once the loan is retired. The illustrated deal structure gives investors an 8 percent cumulative preferred return and 70 percent of the profits—the share required to give them a 20 percent IRR.

[s] Preferred returns are priority returns of cash flow to the investors. Cumulative preferred returns are accumulated into succeeding periods whenever the amount of cash available is insufficient to pay the preferred return in the current period (Line 173).

[t] Noncumulative preferred returns are not accumulated into future periods. If the amount of cash from the current period is insufficient to pay the noncumulative preferred return, it is forgotten (Line 174).

[u] The cash distribution percentages are negotiated between the developer and the equity investors (Lines 181 through 183).

[v] The investors' IRR is computed on line 195. The IRR is that discount rate for which the present value of future cash flows equals the initial investment ($4 million in Time 0). Because the periods are quarters, the IRR is multiplied by 4 to give an annualized rate of return.

Source: Dan Kassel, co-president, Granite Homes, Irvine, Califronia.

developer borrows more money, the return on equity increases. The unleveraged return in the figure is 17.3 percent per year.

Return on Equity. The return on equity (Line 155) is also an IRR calculation. In contrast to the unleveraged IRR, the return on equity takes financing into account. The developer's cash investment, plus any in-kind equity such as the value of land contributed to the deal, is represented as a cash outflow. "Cash flow after financing" (Line 118) shows cash inflows to the developer. Often, no cash inflows occur until the development loan is fully retired, although it depends on the lender's loan release provisions.[43] The return on equity should be higher than the unleveraged IRR, because the amount of equity is usually only a fraction, say 20 percent, of total project cost. The return on equity should always be higher than the loan interest rate, because equity investors have lower priority for access to cash flows than mortgage holders and thus incur more risk. If the project is financed by 100 percent equity (no debt), then the return on equity is the same as the unleveraged IRR. In the figure, the IRR on $4,000,000 equity is 25.3 percent per year.

The rate of return that constitutes an acceptable return on equity varies. Most developers require a return on equity that is 12 to 15 percent higher than what they could obtain on risk-free government bonds. If, for example, one-year Treasury bills (T-bills) are paying 8 percent, most developers want a return on equity of 20 to 25 percent.

If no equity is invested (that is, the project is 100 percent financed), then the return on equity is infinite. An infinite return does not necessarily mean that the project is economically feasible. Even if the project equity is zero, the *unleveraged* IRR should be on the order of 10 percent above the T-bill rate and preferably be around 15 percent for land development.

According to standard finance theory, the calculation of net present value (NPV) offers a better method of rank ordering projects than IRR because it provides the value in today's dollars of the wealth that a project will generate in the future. The appropriate discount rate is the developer's opportunity cost rate—the rate that can be earned in alternative investments of similar risk. The project with the highest NPV is preferred. If only one project is being considered, then the NPV should be sufficient to justify the time and risk of development, even if the developer has no equity invested in the project. For example, suppose the NPV on a four-year project with $1 million equity, discounted at 15 percent, is $200,000. Thus, the developer would have earned the equivalent of $200,000 in today's dollars over and above a 15 percent return on the initial investment. The developer should determine whether the project is worth the time and risk involved. If it would be necessary to work full time on the project for four years or sign personally on a $5 million loan, it probably is not.

Developers often must extend personal guarantees on loans, even when they have no equity invested in a project. Some developers treat their guarantee as equity and compute an IRR on that basis. Because the guarantee is a contingent liability rather than a cash investment, the appropriate return on the guarantee is not comparable with the IRR on equity when the equity is in the form of hard cash.

Relationship between Returns, Inflation, and Risk. All returns move with inflation. Return on equity has three components—a real rate of return (2 to 3 percent), an inflation premium, and a risk premium.[44] If expected long-run inflation (over the life of the investment) is, say, 4 percent and the risk premium is 10 percent, then the required return on equity would be 16 to 17 percent. The risk premium depends on the status of the real estate—whether it is fully leased, under construction, or in predevelopment—as well as on the amount of leverage (all equity versus 60 to 95 percent or more financing), the property type, location, and other factors that bear on the likelihood of success or failure (such as neighborhood opposition, competition, market and economic trends). The risk premium alone may range from 10 to 20 percent or more depending on the amount of perceived risk. The earlier the stage of development, the greater the risk. Unentitled property is considered the riskiest of all forms of development, because there is no assurance in many communities that one can obtain the necessary entitlements to build. If one cannot build on the property, it has little or no value apart from its value as agricultural or conservation land.

Although required rates of return change quickly and are hard to generalize, some rules of thumb apply. For example, pension funds making all-equity investments in fully leased investment-grade income properties (large shopping malls, office buildings, apartments) may look for returns as low as 10 to 12 percent. Projects to be developed that have entitlements but are not yet built or leased typically should offer at least a 15 percent unleveraged before-tax IRR or a 20 to 25 percent leveraged before-tax IRR. Because land with entitlement risk is considered one of the riskiest forms of real estate development, leveraged returns on equity typically range from 20 to 30 percent or more. These figures are appropriate for 2002 and 2003, when inflation is expected to be low, 3 to 4 percent. If inflation rises, required return rates will go up as well.

One of the most common misunderstandings in real estate is the relationship between IRRs, inflation, and capitalization rates (cap rates). As noted earlier, hurdle IRRs (required returns on equity) go up with inflation. This situation occurs because inflation and risk are two components of the required rate of return. Capitalization rates, however, tend to go down as inflation goes up. Because capitalization rates are simply the ratio of current net operating income (NOI) to the purchase price for income property, buyers are willing to pay more for property as inflation is expected to increase—causing capitalization rates to go down and prices to go up for the same NOI. Buyers will pay more for property today if they expect to obtain higher rents in the future and a higher sale price when they eventually sell the property. On the other hand, as risk goes up, cap rates go up as well, because buyers are willing to pay less money for property if they perceive the risks to be greater.

Design and Site Planning

Land planning begins with a marketing concept for the houses, apartments, or other buildings that will ultimately be built on the finished lots. The end product—the size, style, and quality of building—dictates how the land should be subdivided.

Good subdivision design involves much more than an engineer's efficient layout for streets and utilities. Historically, developers favored the most cost-efficient plan—the rectangular grid. Beginning in the mid-20th century, however, developers began to prefer curved streets and culs-de-sac that took advantage of natural features. Today, the grids of towns and cities are once again gaining favor over the organic forms of suburbia. In the best plans, natural features are considered as well, and the grid may bend and curve to accommodate hills and valleys, streams, wooded areas, and other important features. The new urbanist movement has shown that a grid network of streets and short blocks is not only more cost-effective but can also aid in calming traffic and promoting access for pedestrians.

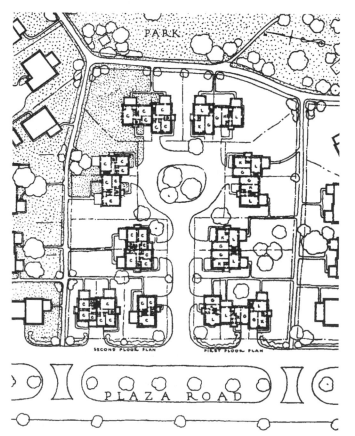

Radburn, New Jersey, pioneered numerous planning concepts, including the separation of pedestrians from automobiles.

Evolution of Subdivision Design

In the 20th century, the evolution of subdivision design was shaped primarily by three forces: the automobile, increasing housing costs, and the environment.

The Automobile. Automobiles have long been the most dominant influence on subdivision design. Indeed, private automobiles helped to create suburban growth by allowing workers to live at some distance from public transportation lines. Without the automobile, low-density single-family housing would not have been possible.

Suburban streets have always been designed to accommodate automobile circulation and parking; suburban houses have typically been designed with driveways and carports or garages—first for one car, then for two. Today, garages for three or more cars are not uncommon. Over the years, innovative methods of dealing with traffic have been tried. A three-level hierarchy of streets (local streets, collectors, and arterials) and separation of pedestrians from cars was pioneered in Radburn, New Jersey, in 1929.[45] Culs-de-sac were also first introduced in Radburn to reduce traffic on residential streets. Today, this system is being reevaluated. Because it forces all traffic onto arterials while underusing local streets, many transportation planners now realize that a hierarchical system causes, rather than alleviates, congestion. Further, a system that extensively uses culs-de-sac restricts both vehicular and pedestrian access and decreases mobility.

Increasing Housing Costs. Housing costs have risen faster than personal incomes and national inflation rates throughout the post–World War II period. This escalation in costs has been driven principally by increasing land prices, spurred by a limited supply of well-located land and by labor-intensive construction methods.

One of the few tools left to developers to help hold down housing costs is a more intensive use of land. Developers have responded to rising costs by building at ever-higher densities, thereby reducing land costs per unit. In the 1950s, a typical single-family suburban house occupied a one-acre (0.4-hectare) lot; today, a similar house is unlikely to be built on a lot larger than one-quarter acre (0.1 hectare). In the more expensive regions of the United States, it is not uncommon to find single-family lots as small as 4,000 square feet (370 square meters). The need to achieve higher densities has stimulated new methods of subdividing land—clustering houses in planned developments (sometimes referred to as *planned unit developments*, or PUDs), patio- or zero-lot-line homes, and a greater variety of attached housing at all price levels. This evolution in design has had to follow the same slow pace as major institutional and attitudinal changes. City platting ordinances had to be changed to allow new types of lots, lenders needed to be convinced of the economic viability of new configurations, and homebuyers had to accept the new designs.

In many respects, construction methods have altered little since Roman times. Although an increasing number of housing components (roof trusses, floor joists, wall sections, and cabinets, for example) are now "manufactured," much is still done by hand. The promise of the

A cluster site plan uses clustered development, open spaces, and a street hierarchy to create neighborhood enclaves. As a benefit, natural drainage is preserved, open space views are enhanced, and streetscapes are more varied.

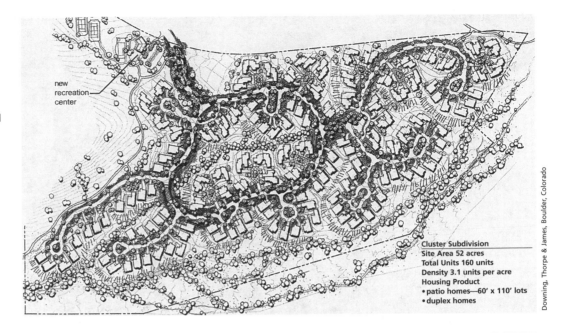

new recreation center

Cluster Subdivision
Site Area 52 acres
Total Units 160 units
Density 3.1 units per acre
Housing Product
• patio homes—60' x 110' lots
• duplex homes

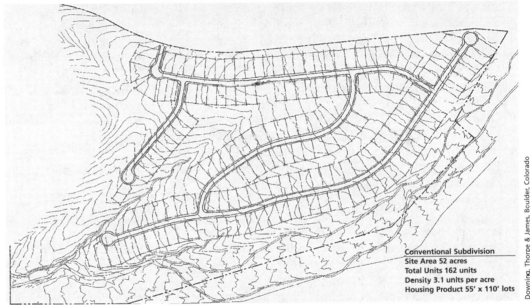

Conventional Subdivision
Site Area 52 acres
Total Units 162 units
Density 3.1 units per acre
Housing Product 55' x 110' lots

1960s that manufactured housing would greatly reduce housing costs has yet to materialize. Cost savings of 10 to 20 percent have been achieved in manufactured housing, chiefly in the areas of time and interest, but both the public and municipalities have been slow to accept it. Lenders and government agencies also have been reluctant to treat manufactured housing the same way they treat conventional, stick-built housing.

Construction quality has improved in many ways— better insulation, energy-efficient windows and mechanical systems, improved methods of waterproofing, and new materials that need little maintenance. Much of what has been gained by such cost-saving efficiencies, however, has been lost to increasing land and labor costs and to some degree to the costs of regulations related to the environment, safety, and growth.

The Environment. The third major force that has influenced subdivision design is the environment. As the environmental movement has gained acceptance, its influence has touched all aspects of the real estate development industry, including subdivision design. Environmental concerns in many communities have led to stricter open-space requirements, lower overall densities, and avoidance of building in environmentally sensitive wetlands and canyons. The effect of these concerns has been to restrict the amount of developable land and its permissible uses.

All development puts stress on land. One of the first considerations of developers should be how to develop a particular parcel of land at a reasonable profit without violating that parcel's natural features. Or if the natural features are of particular value, developers should determine which development practices, if any, will enhance the environment. Developers do not just react to regulatory policy; they help create it, for better or worse, by their actions.

Developers should be aware that homebuyers increasingly place value on environmentally sensitive develop-

At the Vineyards at Westchase, 38 percent of the total land area has been preserved as wetlands and conservation areas.

ment, resulting in a growing market for this type of product. Dewees Island near Charleston, South Carolina, for example, encompasses many land use development techniques to protect and enhance the environment, including the application of innovative water conservation measures, the protection of hundreds of acres of island habitat, and use of green building materials to save energy and reduce the level of natural resource extraction. The project has surpassed market expectations, and its property values far exceed the South Carolina sea islands' market.[46]

Environmental and conservation factors can be incorporated into the projects in many ways. For example, developers can:

- reserve open spaces that enhance natural characteristics, such as stands of trees or bodies of water;
- devise methods of protecting areas of natural beauty and reserve areas for passive recreation;
- integrate storm drainage features and water retention areas into the site plan, which, properly designed, can become major assets;
- locate open space upwind from residential areas to help reduce noise and to take advantage of lower temperatures;
- create rich landscaping and planting areas that enhance a project's appearance, control temperature and sound, and promote clean air;
- establish homeowners associations to provide for constant care of open-space areas;
- prevent erosion of steeply sloping areas; and
- avoid water and air contamination, land damage, erosion, and excessive noise during construction.

Sensitivity to Design Issues

Good developers contribute as much to the design of subdivisions as the planners and landscape architects on their team. The developer's awareness of and sensitivity to marketing issues complement the planner's skills and knowledge about layout and infrastructure design.

Considerable time and effort are required to develop a critical eye and an accurate intuition about site design. Beginning developers can take the following steps to educate themselves about subdivision design:

- become familiar with classic subdivisions and with new communities;
- visit new and old development projects locally and farther away;
- talk to other developers and architects about the types of designs that do and do not work in their projects;
- talk to brokers and sales agents at competitive subdivisions, because they usually hear customers' uncensored reactions; and
- attend planning review sessions at meetings held by professional organizations.

A developer also should be familiar with classic examples of each major building type, preferably through travel and courses in architectural history, planning, and development. Understanding architecture and urban design history is vital, because it allows a developer not only to examine structures that have survived both social and technological change but also to develop a sense of style.

Good developers supplement their knowledge of design with the opinions and tastes of homebuyers in their market area. Developers can conduct focus groups and interview homebuyers to discover what aspects they like or dislike about the design of local subdivisions and how well they meet the needs of different age groups, household types, and income segments. Dan Kassel emphasizes the close link between good design and market research. "The first thing to forget is your own preconceptions and design opinions. They are no substitute for solid market research. Your target market in any given deal is more likely than not to run counter to your own preferences in home and community design."[47]

Design guidelines provide an important tool for land developers in setting the tone and overall appearance for a subdivision. In master-planned communities such as Irvine, California, detailed urban design guidelines cover all aspects of design, from the streetscape and landscaping to individual house sites, materials, setbacks, and architecture. Although guidelines that are too severe can create monotonous subdivisions where everything looks alike, well-crafted guidelines can make the difference in establishing an attractive subdivision. When he took over a land development project from the Resolution Trust Corporation, Scott Smith of La Plata Investments found that no one had ever really taken design guidelines seriously. "We looked around and saw a bunch of bland boxes, each of which was a good enough deal on its own, but not as a community. Design guidelines aren't just quality control for individual units; they allow you to control a critical and marketable aspect of your community."[48]

Cluster Development, New Urbanist Plans, and PUDs

Among the key planning concepts with which a developer should be familiar are cluster development, new urbanism, and PUDs.

In cluster development, houses are built at higher densities in certain areas so that other on-site areas can be preserved as open space. Gross density remains the same for cluster developments as for traditional tract housing where housing is spread uniformly over the entire tract. Each cluster tends to contain houses of a similar style, and styles usually vary slightly from cluster to cluster. Cluster planning requires more design skills than conventional subdivision planning; unskilled planning or exploitation of the cluster concept can easily generate an unattractive bunching of dwellings.

Since 1980, the new urbanism has challenged cluster development, emphasizing traditional neighborhood planning that incorporates grid street patterns, narrower streets with sidewalks, small public squares and parks, narrower lots with rear garages, retail town centers, and other planning elements that create a land use pattern similar to that found in traditional cities and towns until the suburbanization of the post–World War II era. Seaside in Walton County, Florida, is a small resort community that is among the earliest examples of the new urbanist approach. These developments often rely on typographical coding rather than zoning as their planning tool. Coding, which is more design-oriented than zoning, specifies building, street, and open space "types" for each lot in the development without dictating land uses. The results are a mixed-use, mixed-housing-type community.

Whereas cluster and new urbanist development are design concepts, PUD is a legal concept. PUDs are zoning classifications typical in many jurisdictions. Some localities use other names such as *residential unit development* and *planned residential development,* but the purpose remains the same. In PUDs, traditional zoning classifications are discarded in favor of a more flexible approach that considers the project in its entirety instead of in zoning pods. The PUD is approved as an entity. It may combine commercial and residential uses, include several types of residential product, and provide open space and common areas with recreational and community facilities.

In a PUD, residential areas may be outlined and a certain number of units designated, but no detail regarding the specific site plan is required for approval. Some jurisdictions require later public review of the specific site plan; others do not. Developers have the right to build a certain number of units or a certain number of square feet of commercial or office space as long as they conform to the stipulations of the PUD ordinance.

PUDs usually involve negotiations between the developer, the reviewing agencies, and the public. The negotiations give the community an opportunity to tailor development proposals to meet community objectives. Often, the developer will be required to place more land in open space or commit more land to community facilities than originally planned. In return, the developer may receive permission to build more units than the regular zoning would allow or include a mixture of land uses.

Planning theory has been leaning toward greater mixing of uses and away from the separation of land uses that began in the 1910s. Both planners and the public have discovered that commercial, office, and residential uses can be combined on the same site to create a more functional and exciting environment.

Site Planning Processes

After the site investigation has been completed and base maps prepared, the land planner should present the developer with a site plan that describes a number of different approaches toward developing the site. The site plan, which combines information regarding the target market with the base map, must consider many different items:

- topography;
- geology;
- natural vegetation;
- drainage;
- vistas and sight lines;
- private and public open spaces;
- neighboring uses;
- easements and restrictions;
- roads;
- utilities;
- patterns of pedestrian and bicycle and other vehicular circulation—ingress and egress, sidewalks, and alleys
- market information;
- sales office location and visitor parking;
- buffers for noise and privacy; and
- building types.

The design process involves considerable trial and error. Developers must consider future users and their relationship to every aspect of the site. The site planner first produces a diagram showing constraints and opportunities with all the site's relevant features—view corridors, arterial roads, access points, streams, forests and special vegetation, neighboring uses, undevelopable slopes, and wetlands. Next, using the developer's land use budget from the market analysis, the site planner prepares several alternative layouts showing roads, lots, circulation patterns, open space, amenities, and recreation areas.

Throughout the schematic planning phase, developers must ensure that the plan will meet their marketing and financial objectives. They should mentally drive down every street, examining traffic patterns, and walk around every house, imagining the views from each window. They should consider such aspects as attractive vistas, landscaping, and homeowners' privacy. They should also envision the entrance to the subdivision, playgrounds, and street crossings.

Developers should always work closely with the planner throughout the site planning process and should not wait for finished drawings before reviewing the schematic plans. A team approach usually works best, and the contractor, civil engineer, political consultant (if needed), and sales staff should be involved as early as possible. Rough drawings of alternative schemes should be reviewed at regular intervals. Another way to develop a plan is by holding a *charrette* in which the land planners work with the public, community leaders, and other representatives to incorporate their concerns and ideas.

When the developer is satisfied with the schematic plan, the planner produces the final version. The final plan also goes through several iterations. Because it ultimately will be submitted to the city for plat approval (formal approval by the municipality of the subdivision's physical layout and lot descriptions), the final plan must show the boundary lines, dimensions, and curvatures of every lot and street. For presentations, planners usually draw a rooftop plan, showing the positioning of prototype houses on each lot. Models of the subdivision can also be a useful tool for winning public approvals and attracting buyers.

Site Information

The design process begins with the production of a base map. All subsequent design schemes are drawn on the base map. That information is in turn obtained from a variety of federal sources, including the U.S. Geological Survey and U.S. Department of Agriculture, as well as from local sources. Zoning maps can be purchased from city zoning departments or from private companies. Aerial photos, also available from private companies, are invaluable for understanding the property as well as marketing the subdivision later. City halls, local libraries, utility agencies, state highway departments, and local engineering firms are good sources for topographic maps, soil surveys, soil borings, percolation tests, and previous environmental assessments. Title companies are the source for existing easements, rights-of-way, and subdivision restriction information.

Topographic Survey. Site planning begins with the topographic map that shows the contours of the property, rock outcroppings, springs, marshes, wetlands, soil types, and vegetation. Although topographic maps are available for many counties, on-site surveys are often needed to obtain more accurate information.

The topographic map should show:

- contours with intervals of one foot (0.3 meter) where slopes average 3 percent or less, two feet (0.6 meter) where slopes are between 3 percent and 10 percent, and five feet (1.5 meters) where slopes exceed 10 percent;
- existing buildings, walls, fence lines, culverts, bridges, and roadways;
- location and spot elevation of rock outcroppings, high points, water courses, depressions, ponds, marsh areas, and previous flood elevations;
- floodplain boundaries;
- outline of wooded areas, including location, size, variety, and caliper of all specimen trees;
- boundary lines of the property; and
- location of test pits or borings to determine subsoil conditions.

Site Map. Developers should prepare a site map at a scale of one inch to 500 feet (or 1 centimeter to 50 meters) that shows the surrounding neighborhood and the major roads leading to the site. The map can be later used for advertising, brochures in support of loan applications, and government approvals. In addition to location information, the map should show:

- major land uses around the project;
- transportation routes;
- comprehensive plan designations;
- existing easements;
- existing zoning of surrounding areas;
- location of airport noise zones, if any;
- jurisdictional boundaries for cities and special districts such as schools, police, fire, and sanitation; and
- lot sizes and dimensions of surrounding property.

Boundary Survey. The boundary survey shows bearings, distances, curves, and angles for all outside boundaries. In addition to boundary measurements, it should show the location of all streets and utilities and any encroachments, easements, and official county benchmarks from which boundary surveys are measured or triangulation locations near the property.

The boundary survey should include a precise calculation of the total area of the site as well as flood areas, easements, and subparcels. Calculations of area are used to:

- determine the number of allowable units based on zoning information;
- determine net developable area (the size of this area serves as the basis for both site planning and economic analysis of the project);

CityPlace in West Palm Beach, Florida, is a mixed-use destination that fits seamlessly in its urban context. It combines street-front specialty retailing and entertainment with 582 residential units, including lofts, apartments, townhouses, and mid-rise and high-rise apartments.

- determine sale prices—often, sale price is calculated per square foot or per square meter (for instance, $2.00 per net developable or gross square foot [$21.50 per square meter]) rather than as a fixed total price; and
- provide a legal description of the site.

Utilities Map. The utilities map is prepared at the same scale as the boundary survey. It shows the location of:

- all utility easements and rights-of-way;
- existing underground and overhead utility lines for telephone, electricity, and street lighting, including pole locations;
- existing sanitary sewers, storm drains, manholes, open drainage channels, and catch basins, and the size of each;
- rail lines and rail rights-of-way;
- existing water, gas, electric, and steam mains, underground conduits, and the size of each; and
- police and fire alarm call boxes.

Concept Development. Once base maps have been prepared and accurate gross and net developable acreage calculated, the true design process begins. Before the planner begins drawing, the developer should define the target market, the end product (including lot sizes), and the approximate number of units needed to make the project economically feasible.

Base maps outline developable areas as well as important features such as lakes, stands of mature trees, and hills on the site. The developer determines which features should become focal points for the design based on the site's physical condition and specific market. For example, although a creek and its floodplain are often excluded from the developable area because of potential flooding problems, it may be the site's best amenity. The developer has the option of designating the creek as public open space and designing the plan around it or using it as a private amenity for certain lots.

The goal of site planning is to maximize the value of the developed property subject to market absorption and zoning constraints. Lots that adjoin open space or creeks or have views sell at a premium. Developers may also achieve high returns by placing higher-density products such as townhouses, multifamily housing, or zero-lot-line homes next to focal features. Lots that do not front on the focal feature will sell for more if the site plan gives them access to it. The best plans create value by using a desirable feature as a public amenity and as a generator of lot premiums—for example, a public town square with houses fronting it. The public has access to the square and its surrounding streets, while the houses that front on it have special views. A lake or pond could similarly enhance value.

If the development's use is perceived as incompatible with uses on adjacent property, the project almost certainly will arouse the hostility of local residents and will be contested at the public hearing for zoning or site plan approval. For example, if single-family houses face a developer's property, any non-single-family use is likely to draw objections from the neighbors. Although different uses on adjoining properties are actually appropriate in many situations, the burden falls on the developer to demonstrate the reason for not maintaining consistency in use or density.

Many residential tracts border major streets. Because such frontage usually sells for three to five times the value of single-family land, the developer may wish to consider placing retail, office, or multifamily uses at these locations. The risk of reserving a large amount of commercial or multifamily frontage at the edge of the development is that, in the event the market is slow, the vacant lot serves as an unattractive front entrance to the project. If frontage is retained for future development, the entrance into the residential portion of the tract should be carefully designed and landscaped. A divided parkway entrance with a permanent sign and attractive landscaping has become a common feature of many subdivisions, but more urban-style options that play down the entrance and connect seamlessly to adjacent developments are gaining favor.

As an alternative to commercial strip development or corner shopping malls, developers sometimes locate neighborhood commercial centers in the middle of the neighborhood, away from the major streets, to give the community a focal point. When situated near water features or other amenities, the center can become a popular meeting spot with the additional benefit of enhanced rental rates. Care must be taken, however, to ensure that commercial centers without drive-by visibility are able to attract a sufficient market base to support commercial uses.

Streets and Street Hierarchy

In the design of street systems for a new development, a street's contribution to the neighborhood environment is as important as its role as a transportation link. The street system should be easily understood by users so that the intended function of a particular street segment is readily apparent.

A street system should be designed as a hierarchy of streets, each with distinctive characteristics in terms of width and the level of traffic carried. The commonly used functional classification of streets includes, in ascending order, local streets, collectors, and arterials (including freeways).

- Arterial Streets—Arterial streets are seldom created as parts of new subdivisions. The primary purpose of arterial streets is mobility—movement of as much traffic as possible as fast as is reasonable—and the mobility function of arterials therefore overshadows their function of providing access to fronting properties such as residences or commercial uses.
- Collector Streets—Collector streets serve as the link between arterial streets and local streets. Typically,

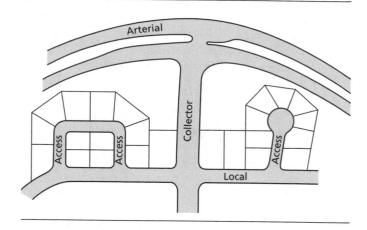

figure 3-10
Hierarchy of Streets

Source: American Society of Civil Engineers, National Association of Home Builders, and ULI–the Urban Land Institute, *Residential Streets*, 2nd ed. (Washington, D.C.: Authors, 1990), p. 26.

they make up about 5 to 10 percent of total street mileage in new developments. Increasingly, new collector streets are fronted by active properties such as neighborhood commercial centers, institutions, and multifamily residences.

- Local Streets—Local streets usually account for around 90 percent of the street mileage in new communities and are intended to provide access to the residential properties fronting them. As the preponderant class of streets in terms of mileage, they contribute much to the signature of their neighborhoods. They also constitute the backbone of neighborhood pedestrian and bicycle networks.

In designing streets for a new development, designers should select the minimum width that will reasonably satisfy all traffic needs. On most local streets, a 24- to 26-foot-wide (7.3- to 7.9-meter-wide) pavement is the most appropriate width. This width provides two parking lanes and a traffic lane or one parking lane and two moving lanes. For lower-volume streets with limited parking, a 22- to 24-foot-wide (6.7- to 7.3-meter-wide) pavement is adequate.

For low-volume streets where no parking is expected, an 18-foot-wide (5.5-meter-wide) pavement is adequate. It has been found that widening access streets a few more feet does not significantly increase capacity, but it does permit wider moving lanes that tend to encourage higher driving speeds. A wide access street also lacks the intimate scale that makes an attractive setting.

A residential collector street should be designed for higher speed than local or access streets, permitting unrestricted automobile movements. Residential collector streets 36 feet (11 meters) wide provide for traffic movement and two curb parking lanes. When parking is not needed, two moving lanes of traffic are adequate, with shoulders graded for emergency parking.[49]

In properly designed residential neighborhoods, routes carrying through traffic should be separated from routes that provide access to residential properties. Travel distances from residential collector streets should be short, traffic speeds should be low, lane capacity and design speed should not be controlling design factors, and inconvenience or minor delay should be acceptable. Further, drivers and residents expect brief delays and accept the need to decrease speed for safety.

Residential streets should not only provide safe, efficient circulation for vehicles and pedestrians but also create positive aesthetic qualities for a community and its residents. Paying attention to the aesthetics of streets helps ensure that they do not become simply a thoroughfare for vehicles. The character of a residential street is influenced to a great extent by its paving width, its horizontal and vertical alignments, and the landscape treatment of its edges. Residential streets are community spaces that should convey an image and scale appropriate to the neighborhood. For example, much of the character of older neighborhoods is derived from the mature street trees that form a canopy over entire streets, while a neighborhood with wide streets devoid of trees conveys an entirely different image. The placement of utilities and the style of traffic control devices and street lighting hardware should be carefully considered, because these features also contribute to the character of the street.[50]

Site Engineering

Adequate grading and the optimal provision of water, gas, electricity, telephone, sewage, and stormwater utility services are important elements of site design, and the cost of providing them is critical to a project's bottom line. Developers should never leave the final decision about these elements to their civil engineers; the lowest-cost site engineering is rarely the most profitable subdivision design. The developer's objective is to maximize the sale value of the lots subject to efficient site engineering. Site engineering follows from the best site design, not vice versa, although the development costs associated with design alternatives are an important part of choosing the best plan.

Grading. The grading plan, perhaps the most delicate part of the development, must contain precise details and take into consideration factors such as the amount of dirt that will be excavated from the streets, the finished heights of lots, steep areas that may require retaining walls, and graded areas that may be subject to future erosion (developers are liable for erosion even after they have sold all the lots on a site).

Grading is used as an engineering tool to correct unfavorable subsoil conditions and to create:

- drainage swales;
- berms and noise barriers;
- topsoil at a proper depth for planting;
- circulation routes for paths and roads; and
- suitable subsoil conditions for facilities.

Grading is also used for aesthetic purposes to provide privacy, create sight lines, emphasize site topography or provide interest to a flat site, and connect structures to the streetscape and planting areas.

Modern excavating contractors use laser technology for rough and fine grading of a site. By setting a rotating laser beam at a predetermined elevation, the amount of dirt to be removed from an area can be determined simply by reading the elevation of the bottom of the blade relative to that of the laser beam.

Homebuilders usually do their own fine grading of lots in addition to that done by the land developer. If the grading is unusually extensive or if homebuilders must haul dirt away from the site, however, they may ask the developer for a rebate. The land developer is contractually obligated to deliver lots that meet a reasonable standard of grading. In some cases, the developer may contract to deliver lots that are ready to build on and that require no further grading (apart from the removal of loose topsoil before setting foundations).

Storm Drainage and Floodplains. Storm drainage systems carry away stormwater runoff. In low-density developments with one-acre (0.4-hectare) lots or larger, natural drainage may suffice. In denser developments, however, some form of storm drainage system is always needed.

Gently rolling sites are the easiest and cheapest to drain; flat sites and steep sites are the most difficult and expensive. As with other environmental issues, drainage problems can come back to haunt a developer long after the lots have been sold.

If a property contains any hint of wetlands—a lake, stream, or vernal pool—a floodplain study is among the first feasibility studies a developer should perform before buying a site. Whether a flood hazard is apparent or not, developers should be familiar with where the property lies in relation to floodplains. They can do so by obtaining the Federal Emergency Management Agency's flood hazard boundary maps (see www.fema.gov). Land that is within the 100-year floodplain—that is, the area that is expected to flood once every 100 years—is usually not developable except as specialized uses such as golf courses, parks, or storage of nontoxic materials. Civil engineers can easily determine from floodplain maps the amount of land that lies within the 100-year floodplain.[51]

In some localities, land within the 100-year floodplain *is* developable, albeit with restrictions. New and existing structures in the 100-year floodplain can be mortgaged by federally insured institutions, but only if the structure carries flood insurance. To qualify for flood insurance, the lowest floor must be constructed at or above the 100-year floodplain. Some communities have adopted higher regulatory standards requiring structures to be built above the 100-year floodplain. In addition, some developers choose to build above the 100-year floodplain to reduce their risk and to lower flood insurance premiums. To alter floodplain areas, developers must apply for a permit from the EPA, U.S. Army Corps of Engineers, or any other body that has authority over the local wetlands or creek system. Any changes that developers make, however, cannot reduce the total amount of on-site water storage capacity or the flow of water through the property. For example, suppose the floodplain currently holds three acre-feet of water based on the volume of water that could be accommodated inside the floodplain without flooding other areas.[52] If developers want to channelize the flood area to enlarge a site's buildable area, they still must provide for three acre-feet of on-site storage, which may mean dredging the channel to make it deeper or digging other storage ponds.

The Army Corps of Engineers designates floodways as well as 100-year floodplains. A floodway is that portion of a channel and floodplain of a stream designated to provide passage of the 100-year flood, as defined by the Corps, without increasing elevation of the flood by more than one foot (0.3 meter). Developers may place building piers and other structures within the floodplain but not within floodways. Floodways must retain the same or better water flow rate after development as before it; otherwise, floodplain elevation is likely to rise upstream from the development, causing increased flooding in those areas. Developers can alter the floodway, but any changes must be engineered properly to preserve water flow and must be permitted by the appropriate authorities, including the Corps.

Irrespective of the frequency with which they flood, areas within a property may be defined as wetlands and thus come under the jurisdiction of the EPA as well as other federal, state, and local agencies such as the Corps and the U.S. Fish and Wildlife Service.

Wetlands come in many forms, including ephemerally wet swales, intermittent streams, hardpan vernal pools, and volcanic mud flow vernal pools. Generally, if by any standards an area can be classified as a wetland, one or more government agencies will probably do so.

In evaluating a site that contains wetlands, developers should hire a qualified biologist to conduct a preliminary wetlands evaluation report, map potential wetland sites on the property, and suggest mitigation measures and alternative approaches to the design of the property.[53]

Sanitary Sewers. The layout of the sanitary system is determined by the topography of the site and the location of the outfall point—that is, the point of connection to the sewer main. If the sewer main that connects the subdivision to the treatment plant is not located at the low point of the site, the developer may have to provide a pumping station, because, like water, sewage cannot flow uphill.

Beginning developers should avoid tracts of land for which nearby sewage and water services are not available, because the cost of bringing these services in from off-site locations can be prohibitive. When major off-site utility improvements are necessary, developers usually require sites of 300 to 500 acres (120 to 200 hectares) to support the investment. Creating a utility district to provide service or building a plant where none exists typically takes two or more years, as well as significant front-end investment.

One option available to developers whose sites do not have sanitary service is to buy or lease a package treatment plant, a small self-contained sewage treatment facility, to serve the subdivision and design the system to tie eventually into the community's system. This option works in rural areas and in communities that are accustomed to working with package treatment technology.

Septic tank systems are usually not feasible, except in rural areas. Their use depends on soil conditions. In

figure 3-11
Flood Control Channel

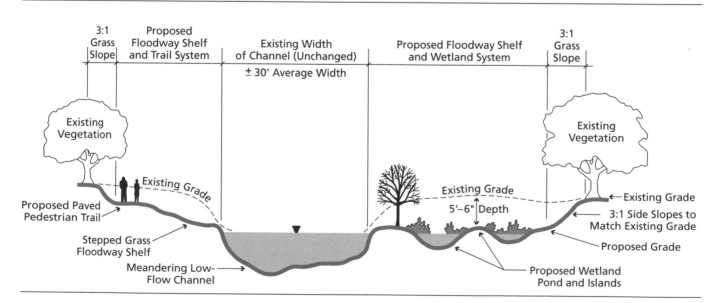

Source: Robert L. France, ed., *Handbook of Water Sensitive Planning and Design* (Boca Raton, Florida: CRC Press, 2002).

most areas, septic tanks are allowed only on lots of at least one-half acre (0.2 hectare), and a minimum of three-quarters or one acre (0.3 to 0.4 hectare) is not uncommon. If a well is included on the same site as a septic tank, even larger lots are sometimes necessary to prevent contamination of the well water.

In planning a sewer system, the developer should investigate:

- sewage capacity requirements, which vary from city to city, but 100 gallons per day (gpd) per person is common;
- available capacity of the treatment plant and connector lines;
- number of hookups contracted but not yet installed;
- the municipality's method of charging for sewer installation; and
- the persons responsible for issuing permits and establishing requirements for discharging treated sewage into natural watercourses.

Sanitary sewer lines normally are located within street rights-of-way but not under road pavement. House connections to sewers should be at least six inches (15 centimeters) in diameter to avoid clogging; all lateral sewers should be at least eight inches (20 centimeters) in diameter. Sanitary lines and water lines should be laid in different trenches, although some cities allow a double-shelf trench that contains the sanitary sewer on the bottom and the water line on the top shelf.

Water System. A central water system is standard in urban communities. Like the requirements for sewage capacity, those for water supply vary from city to city, but 100 gpd per person is common.

Water mains should be located in street rights-of-way or in utility easements. Residential mains average six to eight inches (15 to 20 centimeters) in diameter, depending on the water pressure. Branch lines to houses are three-quarter-inch or one-inch (2- to 2.5-centimeter) copper pipe connected to a five-eighths- or three-quarter-inch (1.5- or 2-centimeter) water meter, respectively. Because water lines are under pressure, their location is of less concern than it is for sewer lines, which rely on gravity flow.

Developers should consult the fire department about requirements for water pressure and the placement of fire hydrants. The fire department is likely to restrict the depth of culs-de-sac and the maximum distance between fire hydrants and structures.

Water, sewer, and drainage lines should be installed before streets are paved. If it is not possible, developers should install underground culverts where the lines cross the streets so that the utility contractor can pull the lines through later; if it is not done, streets will have to be torn up to install the lines.

Utility Systems. Electricity, gas, telephone, and data cable services are typically installed and operated by private companies. Designating the location of utility easements is an essential step in the process of land planning.

If the land planner does not specify a location, the electric company will do so with little regard for aesthetic considerations. Usually, easements run along the back five or ten feet (1.5 or 3 meters) of each lot.

Most planners prefer to place all electrical power transformers underground, but local custom usually dictates whether lines are above or below ground. The installation of transformers underground can be done at a reasonable cost and prevents vandalism and the need for frequent maintenance. Transformers located above ground can be hidden and protected from vandals by wooden lattices with thorny shrubs or similar landscaping devices.

Although electricity, gas, telephone, and cable tend to play a smaller role in site design than do public utilities such as water, sewer, and drainage, they still determine where structures can be built on each lot. The developer should talk to each utility provider as early as possible. Delays in obtaining services—which is the rule rather than the exception—can easily throw off the developer's schedule and hold up final sales.

Platting

Lot size and layout should reflect the nature of the surrounding community. It is especially important in an infill site to match the character of the new development with its surroundings. A developer should not try to suburbanize an urban community with deep setbacks, wide lots, and side garages. Alternatively, a compact development in a rural setting may not be appropriate to the community.

Two determinants of a community's layout are lot width and garage placement. Many postwar suburban subdivisions were designed with wide lots (some up to 100 feet [30.5 meters]) to accommodate a house and a two-car garage and driveway. More recently, 25- to 40-foot (7.6- to 12.2-meter) widths have become more common. The new urbanist approach embraces the concept of narrower lots, smaller frontyards, and garages at the rear of lots, typically accessed by an alley. This layout pays more attention to the streetscape and is more aesthetically appealing, because the view is not dominated by garage doors. For developers, it is desirable because it allows the placement of more houses on the same length of street.

In the past, attached townhouses tended to be sited on lots surrounded by parking lots. Today's townhouses often include individual garages that are tucked under the living space at the front or rear or separate at the rear. Garage townhouses can be very cost-effective for builders and developers because they use less land and cost little more to construct.

Sidewalks, curbing, planting strips, and catchment basins can all be adjusted to the density of the development. A single-family subdivision of 20,000-square-foot (1,860-square-meter) lots on minor streets need not be developed with the same street improvements required for a higher-density subdivision on 2,500- to 4,000-square-foot (230- to 370-square-meter) lots.

The lot layout should seek to achieve a variety of goals:

- a favorable site that does not require excessive grading or unusually deep foundation footings;
- the presence of sufficient usable area for outdoor activity (one or two larger areas are preferable to four small areas);
- adequate surface drainage away from the house, with slopes running toward the front or rear of the house; land developers should grade the lots so that they all drain toward the storm drainage system;
- minimum on-lot grading and maximum retention of specimen trees; and
- a minimum number of adjoining lots—preferably, no more than three (one on each side and one along the back).

In subdivisions with smaller lots, the side yard often plays an important role in the layout of the house on the lot. Corner lots should be 10 feet (3 meters) wider than interior lots to permit an adequate side yard on the side street. Some layouts dictate that corner lots be square with the house placed diagonally, allowing for a more private backyard. In older communities and those designed according to principles of the new urbanism, however, corner houses are usually placed perpendicular to a street.

Straight streets with rectangular lots give a more urban ambience, while curvilinear streets tend to create irregularly shaped lots and provide a more pastoral feel. A minor problem for the developer is that irregular lots may have to be resurveyed when the builder is ready to start construction, because the iron pins that mark lot corners tend to get moved or lost during construction of other houses.

If the development adjoins a busy street, that edge must be handled with great care. Ideally, the community should not turn its back on the street but should take advantage of the traffic and activity and turn it into an asset. If the project is a mixed-use development, this location could be ideal for intensive uses such as a retail district. Or it could be the site of certain neighborhood facilities, particularly if they are shared with the greater community, as might be the case for schools, libraries, or parks. If houses must be sited along a busy street, visual and sound buffering may be needed, which could take the form of service streets, landscaping, or walls. Because lots facing busy streets may yield lower prices than interior lots, the developer should consider ways to boost their appeal or possibly use them for lower-priced units.

Experienced developers, like good architects, understand which items of design create value. But even developers who have a good intuitive feel for what sells should spend time in the field investigating why people react more favorably to one design element than to another. The need for market research cannot be overemphasized. Successful developers always review the competition, use focus groups (small groups assembled to react to different schemes or ideas), and collect exit data (interviews with potential buyers who stop at subdivision sales offices).

Buyers react differently in different markets to both location and cost. For example, in western states, many buyers prefer single-level houses, while in the Northeast they are usually considered less desirable. In urban areas, buyers may like three-level townhouses, while farther from the city, only a single-family house will do. Buyers may like certain features such as deeper frontyards but not be able to afford the additional cost. Good market research can reveal buyers' preferences in the local area and specific demands of the target market.

Higher Densities

Escalating land costs have fueled a search for better-designed higher-density development. Throughout the country, land cost as a percentage of house value has risen steadily since the 1960s, from 15 percent to 25 percent on average. In certain areas of major cities, land costs may exceed 50 percent of the house's value.

In response, traditional housing types are being rescaled and redesigned for modern use. Resort bungalows and cottages, ranging from 900 to 2,000 square feet (85 to 185 square meters), are becoming year-round houses on smaller lots. They are particularly suited to move-down empty nesters and others with small households. Townhouses have emerged as a popular housing type in both urban and suburban areas, offering an alternative to those who do not want the maintenance of a single-family house. Townhouses are not always lower-priced options and can be as upscale as any other housing in some communities.

Large estate houses in exclusive gated compounds remain an American icon that appeals to certain market segments. In many areas, estate-style houses are now being rescaled to fit on quarter-acre (0.1-hectare) lots. These houses (called *small-lot villas* or *McMansions*) typically have highly designed two-story facades that face the street, giving an impression of height, volume, and quality.

Zero-Lot-Line or Patio Homes. Traditionally, local zoning codes have established minimum side yard setbacks ranging from three feet (0.9 meter) to 10 percent of the lot width. Three- or five-foot (0.9- or 1.5-meter) side yards result in unusable spaces. Windows from one house often look into windows of the next house, only six feet (1.8 meters) away. To make side yards more usable, zero-lot-line lots, which allow densities up to nine units per acre, were created. Today, most major cities and high-growth counties have modified their zoning codes to allow for them.

A zero lot line means that the house is left- or right-justified; that is, one side of the house is built on the lot line so that the side yard can be twice the normal width on the other side (10 feet [3 meters] is considered the minimum width for usable space). The side of the house on the lot line usually is a solid wall. Moreover, each lot must take care of its own drainage. If builders want to design a roof that drains water onto the next property, they must obtain a drainage easement from the owner

figure 3-12
Lot Yield Analysis for Different Zero-Lot-Line Configurations

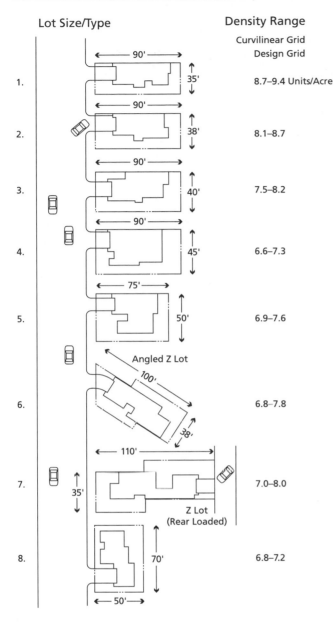

Lot Size/Type	Density Range Curvilinear Grid Design Grid
1. 90' × 35'	8.7–9.4 Units/Acre
2. 90' × 38'	8.1–8.7
3. 90' × 40'	7.5–8.2
4. 90' × 45'	6.6–7.3
5. 75' × 50'	6.9–7.6
6. Angled Z Lot 100' × 38'	6.8–7.8
7. 110' × 35' Z Lot (Rear Loaded)	7.0–8.0
8. 70' × 50'	6.8–7.2

Density ranges based on:
- Representative relatively flat 10-acre irregular site with both curvilinear and grid layouts.
- Comfortable, achievable densities.
- No recreation centers or common open space.
- 50-foot dedicated street right-of-way.
- 32-foot private street system—can increase density by ± one-half unit per acre.
- Individual characteristics and constraints of each site. Actual densities obtained will vary up and down from these generalized guidelines.

Source: Richardson-Nagy-Martin, Newport Beach, California.

of that property. In addition, a maintenance agreement, which can be made before construction while the builder or developer owns all the lots, must be recorded if using the neighbor's lot to maintain the wall on the lot-line side of the house is necessary. Creative architects have mastered the challenge of designing zero-lot-line homes (also called patio homes) by making good use of the outdoor space and developing floor plans and elevations that maximize light and space (see Figure 3-12 for various zero-lot-line configurations and associated densities).

Small-lot, high-density housing must be carefully coordinated with scattered-lot or multiple-builder land sale programs. The land plan, in fact, should be drawn up concurrently with the house plan. Planning successful small-lot communities includes other considerations:[54]

- Narrow lots do not work well on hillsides with slopes greater than 3 or 4 percent.
- Windows must be carefully placed to avoid sight lines into neighboring houses. Windows from one house should not compromise privacy in another's yard.
- Drainage requirements must be carefully studied.
- Major rooms should be oriented toward outdoor spaces to create a greater feeling of spaciousness.

Other Small-Lot Variations. Variations of the zero-lot-line concept include Z-lots, wide-shallow lots, and zipper-lots. Z-lots are shaped like a Z, with the house placed on the diagonal between its frontyard and backyard. The concept yields seven or eight units per acre (17 to 20 per hectare).

In wide-shallow developments, lots are 55 to 70 feet (17 to 21 meters) wide but only 55 to 70 feet (17 to 21 meters) deep, allowing the developer to achieve densities of seven units per acre (17 per hectare). Wider lots add proportionately to street and utility costs but may yield greater curb appeal. Wide-shallow lots usually necessitate two-story houses. If the lots are less than 65 feet (20 meters) deep, the back-to-back rear yards may be too small for privacy. Depths of at least 70 feet (21 meters) are recommended.

Zipper-lots are like wide-shallow lots except that space is borrowed from adjacent lots to avoid the problem of narrow, rectangular rear yards. Easements are used to make the rear yards of back-to-back houses abut on an angled, rather than parallel, property line. The main disadvantages of zipper-lots are the complexity of the plot plan, loss of privacy from second-story windows that overlook the neighbor's backyard, and possible resistance from buyers and government jurisdictions. Nevertheless, they offer a creative solution to high-density housing in selected markets.

With careful design, densities of seven to eight units per acre (17 to 20 per hectare) can be achieved in a single-family detached setting, and densities of 10 to 12 units per acre (25 to 30 per hectare) are possible for small senior housing units or projects without garages. Even higher densities have been achieved in traditional neighborhood developments.

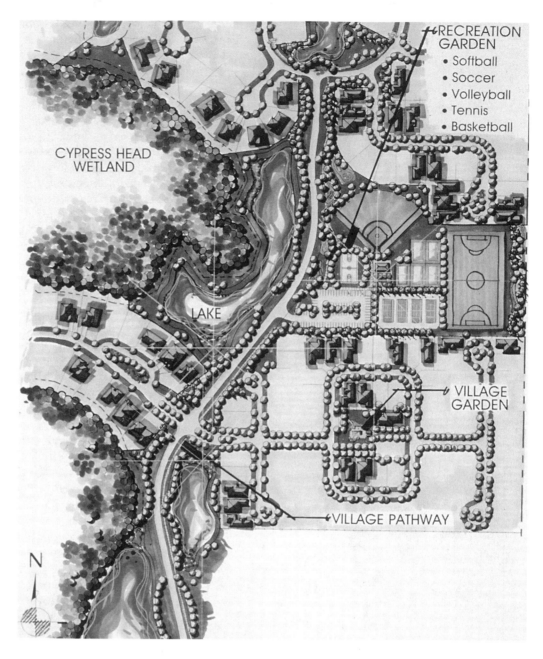

The master plan for Villa Rosa in Hillsborough County, Florida, features a series of minivillages to promote a sense of identity for residents of the community.

CYPRESS HEAD WETLAND

LAKE

RECREATION GARDEN
• Softball
• Soccer
• Volleyball
• Tennis
• Basketball

VILLAGE GARDEN

VILLAGE PATHWAY

N

Refinements in site planning and unit design are making it possible to achieve greater densities without sacrificing privacy and livability. The fact that properly designed small-lot detached housing can make, and fit into, high-quality neighborhoods needs to be made known to local planning and zoning officials and to community residents. Increased densities are one tool to be used in solving the crisis of affordable housing in areas with high land costs. Community acceptance of higher densities will be easier to secure if developers are careful to design attractive communities that enhance, rather than detract from, their surroundings.

Financing

The major difference between the development of land and the development of income property is that land is usually subdivided and sold rapidly, whereas income property usually is held and operated over a period of years. The holding period is the key to deciding the appropriate type of financing. Land development is financed by a short-term development or construction loan. Income property development is financed by both a construction loan and a permanent mortgage, the latter of which is known as a *takeout loan*. For income property development, the construction lender depends on the permanent lender to replace (take out) the construction loan with the permanent mortgage. For land development, the construction lender relies on the developer's ability to sell the finished lots within the agreed-upon time frame and at the projected price.

Success in land development—and the developer's ability to repay the development loan—thus depends on the successful marketing of the lots. Because no takeout exists for construction lenders, they must be satisfied that the developer will be able to sell enough lots fast enough to pay off the loan. Often, construction lenders require other collateral, such as letters of credit, in addition to a mortgage on the property. In addition, the amount of the loan is limited to 60 to 70 percent of the projected sale proceeds to provide a cushion in the event that sales occur more slowly than projected. Slower sales translate into greater interest costs because the balance of the development loan is reduced more slowly than the developer initially projected.

Obtaining Financing

The most difficult task for beginning developers is obtaining financing. Unless developers have enough personal wealth to finance a project themselves, they will need to convince lenders to provide them with financing. In the past, developers could obtain almost 100 percent financing without accepting personal liability. Now, however, developers must contribute equity and sign loans personally in most situations.

A developer's equity can be furnished in cash or in land. Suppose, for instance, that a developer purchased land for a project for $100,000 and the market value of that land subsequently rose to $400,000. If the total cost of the developer's proposed project is $1 million ($600,000 for development costs plus the market value of the land), the developer could probably find lenders willing to lend 70 percent of that amount. In other words, the lenders require $300,000 equity. Because the market value of the land is $300,000 greater than the original land cost, the developer should be able to use the land equity to satisfy the lender's requirement for $300,000. In fact, the loan would cover the developer's original $100,000 land cost, because the $700,000 commitment exceeds the development cost of $600,000 by $100,000.

Purchase Money Notes. The terms of the purchase money note can play a vital role in financing the project. PMNs automatically have first lien position and must be paid off before the developer can get a development loan, because the development lender must hold a first lien position on the land. If the developer can get the seller to *subordinate* the PMN to the development loan, however, it is possible to reduce or eliminate the need to raise outside equity—the hardest money for any beginning developer to obtain.

It is difficult to find a seller who will subordinate the PMN, but it is not impossible. Beginning developers should look for sellers who do not need cash immediately and who are willing to accept the risk of subordination in return for more money. The developer should expect to pay a higher land price or higher interest rate on the PMN or both in exchange for subordination. Because a subordinated PMN can be crucial for covering a beginning developer's equity requirements, it may even be worth giving the seller a percentage of the profits as added incentive to subordinate.

Even with subordination, the developer will have to negotiate with the development lender to treat the subordinated PMN as equity. Whether it is subordinated or unsubordinated, the PMN's *release provisions* are among the most important business points for negotiation with the seller. The release provisions provide for removing designated subparcels of land as collateral from the PMN so the developer can give the development lender a first lien (where the PMN is unsubordinated) or a buyer can get construction financing to build a home.

The release provisions designate which subparcels of land are to be released from the first lien of the PMN. They have two main parts: 1) land leased by the downpayment and 2) land released by future principal payments on the PMN. On larger tracts, the downpayment on the land provides for the release of the first subparcel the developer plans to develop. The land that is to be released first must be designated specifically in the purchase contract and the PMN mortgage to avoid any conflict or confusion. The unencumbered parcel provides the initial collateral for the development loan, although the developer may have to provide additional collateral such as a personal signature or other real estate. The development loan can be extended to cover other subparcels as they are released from the PMN, thereby providing construction money for development.

The land development contractor will be able to build improvements only on those parcels for which the development lender has a first lien. If the contractor begins work on any part of the land before the lender has *perfected* the lien (recorded it), the lender may halt construction until possible lien conflicts are cleared. Clearing lien conflicts can take several months, because all suppliers who have delivered material to the property and all subcontractors who have worked on the property must sign lien waivers indicating that they have received full payment. If anyone is unhappy for any reason (a common occurrence in building), he may use the developer's need for a signature on the lien waiver as leverage to get more money.

Builders' Precommitments. As part of the market feasibility stage, the developer obtains from area builders indications of interest in purchasing the lots.[55] Next, the developer must secure commitment letters from builders, which are part of the documentation the developer will have to submit to the lender to obtain a loan commitment. The commitment letter specifies the number of lots each builder will buy in the project.

Ideally, the developer will have commitments for most of the lots on a site before approaching potential lenders. Although commitments help to reduce the market risk, they do not guarantee that the lots will be sold unless they are backed by letters of credit (LCs). LCs provide guarantees to the developer that the builder's unpaid balance on the lots will be paid off by the bank that issues the LC.

Don Mackie, partner of Mill Creek Properties in Salado, Texas, notes that "most banks know that an unsecured builder commitment letter has no collateral value." Before the crash of the late 1980s, "if you had good appraisals [paper equity], a little real equity in the form of earnest money, and commitment letters from reputable builders, you could get your subdivision financed. Now, it takes major equity and a bankable builder." To be bankable, a builder's commitments must be backed by LCs. This requirement makes the developer's job substantially more difficult. Builders, who are often underfinanced, are reluctant to guarantee that they will purchase the lots. The developer must convince his lender that builders' commitments are solid or must provide proof with the LCs. The developer should know the type of documentation that lenders will require before talking to builders. If the lender requires firm commitments backed by LCs, then the developer must address that requirement as part of the deal with the builders.

Builders' Purchase Terms. The purchase terms that builders require for lots vary according to local market conditions. Downpayments range from $100 earnest money to 10 percent—or even 20 percent—of the purchase price. Builders pay the earnest money when they reserve the lots. The balance is covered by a note that sets the interest rate beginning the day the developer delivers finished lots. The contract for purchasing lots usually defines *lot delivery* as the date on which the city accepts the street dedications or the engineer certifies that the project is substantially complete.

In slow markets and in workout situations (situations in which the developer has defaulted on the loan), builders hold a stronger position than the developer. For example, in the aftermath of the oil recession of the mid-1980s, builders in Austin, Texas, could tie up a large number of lots for very little money. To generate interest from builders, developers sometimes subordinate to the construction lender the land note on builders'

Building Commitment Letter

ABC Homes

March 13, 2002

XYZ Development

Gentlemen:

ABC Homes, Inc., is prepared to enter into a contract mutually agreed upon to purchase 60 to 68 single-family lots in the _____ Subdivision of the City of _____ . This contract shall include the following terms and conditions:

1. Purchaser: ABC Homes, Inc., or assigns.
2. Purchaser shall have the right to approve the subdivision plat prior to filing such plat for approval by the City of _____.
3. Purchase Price: $40,000 per lot.
4. Takedown Schedule: Purchaser shall close 10 lots 30 days from completion of development of the subdivision and shall close 10 lots per quarter, calculated from the date of the first closing, until Purchaser has closed 60 to 68 lots. Completion of development is generally defined to mean final unconditional acceptance of the Subdivision by the City of _____, completion of installation of underground electric distribution system to service each lot, and completion of installation of the gas distribution system to service each lot.
5. The purchase price for each lot purchased, after the initial purchase, shall bear interest, payable to the seller at the final closing, from the date of the initial closing, at a rate equal to _____ prime interest rate, plus 1 percent.
6. Seller shall pay a commission equal to 5 percent of the base price of each lot to _____ at each closing.
7. Earnest money shall be in the form of a letter of credit in the amount of $150,000.

This letter expresses our desire and intent to enter into a contract with Seller to purchase the lots upon the general terms and conditions contained herein. This letter is not binding upon either Purchaser or Seller.

Sincerely,

[signature]

Executive Vice President
ABC Homes, Inc.

AGREED AND ACCEPTED THIS _____ DAY OF _____, 20 ____.

_____
XYZ Development Executives

■

model houses, allowing builders to reduce upfront costs.[56] Builders construct, say, three model houses and six *spec* houses (houses built on the speculative assumption that they will be sold while under construction). Developers give builders a rolling option so that builders are able to take down more land as the spec houses are sold.[57]

Another approach that developers use to generate interest from builders in slow markets or workout situations is to discount the initial lots. For example, if the lots normally sell for $20,000, developers may sell the first two lots to builders for $10,000 and the next two for $15,000.

Tips for Dealing with Lenders. Beginning developers must remember that each deal with a land development lender is unique. But although terms are subject to local market and economic conditions, several factors always should be considered for a three- to five-year project:

- Borrow enough money at the beginning of the project; do not think that a loan can be renegotiated later or that lots can be sold faster.
- Allow enough time on the loan to complete the project or provide for automatic rollover provisions, even though the lender will charge for the rollover option.
- Typical points for the land development loan are two points upfront and one point per year, starting in the third year. Points are calculated on the total loan request, not on the amount drawn to date. For example, two points on a $1.5 million loan request amount to $30,000.
- The loan can be structured as a two-year construction loan with three automatic renewals.

Development loans are a form of construction loan. The amounts by which the developer pays down the loan cannot be borrowed again later. If possible, developers should structure the development loan as a revolving line of credit that allows borrowing up to the limit of the credit line, regardless of repayments already made. (Doing so will likely require the provision of additional collateral as the lots are sold.)

The development lender holds a first mortgage on the entire property and must release its lien on individual lots so that the purchaser (the builder) can obtain construction financing. The *release price* is a major item for negotiation between the developer and the lender. The lender wants to ensure that the loan is paid off faster than the land is released from the mortgage, which protects his security in the event that the developer defaults on the loan. The developer, on the other hand, prefers that the release price simply be a prorated share of the development loan. For example, if the development loan is $1 million for 100 lots, the sale of one lot would retire the loan by $10,000 (1 divided by 100 times $1 million). Most lenders set the release price at 1.2 to 1.5 times the prorated share (called the *multiple*). For a multiple of 1.2, the release price is 1.2 times $10,000, or $12,000 per lot. Thus, every time a lot is sold, the developer pays down the loan by $12,000. The lender often wants a high multiple, 1.3 or greater, for releasing lots. The developer wants a multiple as low as possible, 1.2 or lower, because he needs cash flow. In return for a low multiple, the lender may require some form of credit enhancement, such as an LC or second lien on other property.

Joint Ventures

In the earlier cash flow analyses in this chapter, the developer was assumed to own 100 percent of the deal, investing 100 percent of the equity and receiving 100 percent of the cash flow. The developer also would have 100 percent of the downside risk and liability. All or any part of a land development project, however, may be packaged as a variety of *joint ventures*.

Joint ventures may be structured in a variety of legal forms, including general partnerships, limited partnerships (usually used for syndications), and corporations in which the venturing parties hold stock. Joint ventures also may be created de facto by loan agreements that give the land seller or development lender a share in the profits. In this chapter, the business side of joint ventures is the focus. The various legal forms are described in Chapter 2.

Most joint ventures involve three major points of negotiation for distributing cash flow from the venture:

1. Preferred returns on equity;
2. Priorities of payback of equity, fees to the developer, and cash flows from the venture;
3. Split of the profits.

In addition to dividing the spoils of the venture, the joint venture specifies how risk is shared between the parties—the timing and amount of equity contributions, personal guarantees on notes, allowable fees to the developer and other parties, and management control (see Chapter 6).

Developer and Landowner. One of the most common forms of joint ventures is that between a developer and a landowner. The land is put into the deal at a negotiated price; it is common that land value covers in full the equity that the developer may need to obtain development financing. The landowner may hold a purchase money mortgage subordinated to the development loan or a first priority for receipt of positive cash flow. The order in which cash flows are distributed (the order of *cash distribution priorities*) might be as follows if land value equals total equity:

- Priority 1—The landowner is returned the equity land value allowed by the lender.
- Priority 2—The landowner receives a preferred return (cumulative or noncumulative) on the equity.[58]
- Priority 3—The developer receives a development fee, some of which may be paid during the construction and leasing periods.
- Priority 4—The developer and the landowner split the remaining profits; priorities and fees are subject to negotiation.

When equity is less than land value, the landowner gets some value out of the first loan draw. If equity is greater than land value, a two-tiered partnership provides for additional equity investors.

If the landowner has a subordinated PMN on the land, the loan agreement provides for releases similar to those in the development loan agreement. Both liens must be released before homebuilders or other buyers of the lots can obtain free and clear title, which they need to obtain construction financing. For example, suppose a subdivision has both bank financing and a subordinated PMN from the seller. Suppose also that the PMN calls for repayment of $10,000 to release a lot from the note and that the development loan calls for $20,000 repayment. If the developer sells ten lots for $35,000 each, the cash flow would be:

Sales revenue:
10 x $35,000 = $350,000

Minus repayment of development loan:
10 x $20,000 = $200,000

Minus repayment of PMN:
10 x $10,000 = $100,000

Cash available for distribution: $50,000

Most joint venture agreements provide for the venture to retain *cash available for distribution* as working capital until the development loan is retired. The cash provides a safety net to cover future equity needs in the event that sales slow or costs increase. Alternatively, such cash could be given to the landowner until the land equity has been fully recovered, or it could be considered profit and divided among the joint venture parties. The landowner would prefer, of course, to receive first priority on all cash flows until recovering the value of the land equity.

Sometimes, the revenue from land sales does not cover the required loan release payments for a given parcel or series of lots. In that case, the joint venturers would be required to invest new equity into the venture to cover the cash deficit. The development loan agreement may require the lender's approval for sales below a certain price, although the developer would prefer to have full control over pricing decisions. Such pricing approval, while common, can be a recipe for disaster if the lender withholds approval of lower prices to match current market conditions.

One benefit for landowners of putting their land into a joint venture is to save on taxes, especially when they have owned the land for a long time and the initial purchase price is well below the current market value. If they sell it outright, they must pay taxes immediately on the full capital gain. If they put it into a joint venture, they can defer paying taxes until the property is sold by the joint venture. A tax accountant should be brought into the negotiations early with the landowner. Taxes can be deferred as long as the initial downpayment to the land-

owner is less than 30 percent of the total sale price, qualifying the sale as an installment sale. Taxes on the gain are paid as principal payments on the PMN are made. In a joint venture with a subordinated PMN, the principal payments are usually timed to occur when lots are sold to homebuilders or according to a prenegotiated schedule (typically three to ten years), whichever comes first. For example, suppose land originally purchased for $100,000 is put into a joint venture at the current market value of $1 million, with a PMN for $750,000. One-fourth of the $900,000 gain is taxed initially, because the downpayment is one-fourth of the sale price—$250,000 of $1 million. The rest of the gain is paid as the PMN is retired. Note that this structure works with any PMN, even if no joint venture is created with the land seller. Taxes are deferred longer, however, if the PMN is subordinated. If it is unsubordinated, it must be paid off as soon as the developer obtains a development loan.

Developer and Investor. Joint ventures between the developer and third-party investors are far more common than joint ventures with the landowner. The third-party investors (*third party* because they are not involved in the original transaction) furnish the cash equity needed to complete the deal. For example, in the deal shown above between developer and landowner, the developer purchases the land outright from the land seller.[59] The investors put up the cash needed to purchase the land, which was the landowner's equity in the first deal. The developer's arrangement with the investors might closely resemble the deal with the landowner with respect to priorities for cash distribution:

- Priority 1—All cash available goes to investors until they have received their total cash investment (*return of equity*).
- Priority 2—The next cash available also goes to the investors until they have received, say, an 8 percent cumulative (or noncumulative) return on their investment (*return on equity*).
- Priority 3—The next cash available goes to the developer until the agreed fee is reached.
- Priority 4—All remaining cash available is divided 50/50 between the developer and the investors based on the agreed-upon terms and conditions. (With institutional investors, multitiered "waterfall" provisions are more common.)

As before, every term of the deal is negotiable, including the order of priorities and the amount of personal liability on the development loan.

A common joint venture format in the 1960s and 1970s called for a straightforward 50/50 split between the developer and the investors, without any priorities. Some of the largest developers still use this format, but beginning developers will find that they must give a larger share to investors to attract their interest. In the case of a 50/50 split with no priorities, developers are able to take out profit as each acre is sold. The risk to investors is that developers may sell off the prime tracts, take all the profit, and then fail to sell off the balance of the project, leaving the investors with a loss. Today, most investors insist on receiving back all their equity before developers participate in any profit.

Developer and Lender. The lender may provide 100 percent financing for a deal in exchange for some percentage of the profits in the form of a *participating loan*. From the developer's perspective, this is perhaps the easiest form of joint venture because it involves only one other party. The lender can structure involvement in a variety of ways. The financing can be considered a 100 percent loan, or some portion can be considered equity. The difference between a 100 percent loan and, say, an 80 percent loan with 20 percent equity is that the equity portion usually receives a "preferred return" rather than "interest." The preferred return is paid when cash is available, whereas interest must be paid immediately. Some development loans have accrual provisions that allow interest to be accrued in a fashion similar to that for preferred returns. They allow the project to accrue unpaid interest into future periods until cash is available to pay it. Before the S&L crisis in the late 1980s, S&Ls served as the most common joint venture lending partner for developers. The percentage split of profits varied with the developer's experience and net worth. With stronger developers, the profit split could be 50/50. The split with less experienced developers could be 65/35 or 75/25, with the lender receiving the larger share. Joint ventures with lenders usually allow developers to receive a fee for administrative expenses. Developers like to see fees of 5 to 10 percent of construction costs, but 3 to 5 percent is more common.

Construction

The construction phase of land development consists primarily of grading the land and installing drainage systems, streets, and utilities. Although land development involves fewer subcontractors than building construction, the process can be just as complicated, not least because of the role played by the public sector. The facilities built by land developers usually are dedicated to the city to become part of the city's urban infrastructure. The city maintains the streets, and the utility company, which may also be a city agency, maintains water and sewer lines. Consequently, all facilities must be built in strict accordance with city and utility company standards.

If possible, the contractor should be part of the development team from the beginning. Even if developers choose to select a contractor after plans and specifications are completed, they should go over preliminary plans with a contractor who can offer money-saving advice for various aspects of the design layout.

The following tips are useful in dealing with general contractors:[60]

- Negotiated-price contracts are better than competitively bid contracts. On smaller jobs, developers should negotiate with two or three contractors simultaneously and take the best deal.
- A fixed fee for the contractor of, say, $5,000 to $10,000 for a $100,000 to $200,000 job (costs based on actual dollars spent, verifiable by audit) is recommended. For change orders, developers should pay the contractor the additional cost but no additional fee. Equipment is charged to the job based on direct time in operation.
- Developers should hire a member of an engineering company for which business currently is slow to be on site to check that everything is installed properly. Developers should not rely solely on the engineer's certification and should ensure that the engineer will spend enough time on site. The engineer of record (responsible for the original drawings) should certify the work (check progress three to four times per week), but the on-site engineer should check that everything is installed properly.
- The standard 10 percent retention of payment for subcontractors is recommended. Subcontractors should sign lien releases and bills-paid affidavits with every request for a draw. The general contractor must obtain these affidavits and releases from the subcontractors and suppliers before paying them.
- If the contractor is not performing satisfactorily, developers should notify the contractor in writing (by registered mail), citing the specific paragraphs of the contract that are being violated and stating the possible consequences if performance does not improve by a certain date.
- When hiring a general contractor to construct for-sale housing, developers should include a clause stating that any deceptive trade practice suits that are not warranty items belong to the general contractor, not the developer.

A developer may choose to be its own general contractor, hiring various subcontractors to do the work—for example, an excavation subcontractor to move dirt, a utility subcontractor to install water, storm, and sanitary sewer drains, a paving subcontractor to install concrete curbs and gutters or asphalt paving, and an underground utility contractor to install electricity, gas, telephone, and cable lines.

One deterrent to subcontracting in this manner is the difficulty that sometimes arises in coordinating the work of the separate subcontractors and controlling the condition of the site during the transition from one subcontractor to the next. For example, the paving contractor may complain that the utility contractor left the manholes too high or that more dirt is needed. The developer/general contractor must then choose between paying a late charge to the paving contractor, who must wait until the utility contractor comes back to correct the problem, or paying the paving contractor an exorbitant fee to fix it. If the project is coordinated correctly, the utility contractor is still on site when the paving contractor arrives, allowing any apparent problems to be solved immediately. The general contractor is encouraged to withhold

10 percent of the contract price until the city accepts the utilities.

Choosing the wrong consultant or subcontractor can be costly. Doug Boone, of Boone Communities, suggests getting recommendations for all consultants and subcontractors. "On a recent project, I got the wrong engineer. It was like a bad marriage and almost impossible to get out of in the short run. A bad consultant arrangement is the second most dangerous avoidable delay."[61] Another major problem that developers encounter is deliberate bidding mistakes. Most contracts are bid on price per unit (not as a fixed price) calculated from the engineer's estimate of quantities. If subcontractors see an area in which the quantity of an item was underestimated, they may bid lower on other items so that they get the job. They deliberately bid high on the item for which the quantity was underestimated so that the developer ends up paying more on the total contract after the correct quantity has been determined. Engineers should not be allowed to bid *and* to supervise the site; otherwise, developers will never know whether money was lost. It is better to negotiate a price-per-unit contract and then convert the bid to a fixed-price contract. The developer may pay a little more to allow for a margin of error in the quantity takeoff, but major overcharges are less likely.

During construction, it is important to remember to:

- Supervise subcontractors closely. A subcontractor who needs a piece of equipment for another job is likely to remove it unless the developer is watching closely.
- Plan drainage correctly for each lot. The usual five to ten feet (1.5 to 3 meters) of fall from one side of the property to the other is a sufficient slope. Storm sewers are normally located in the streets, so lots should slope toward the street where possible. As many lots as possible should be higher than curb height. Excavating shallow streets may save money at the front end but may cost money in the long run.
- Work closely with the electric utility contractor to determine the location and price of transformers.
- Design and execute grading carefully. Dirt slopes of up to one foot (0.3 meter) of vertical drop per three feet (0.9 meter) of horizontal distance are much cheaper to construct than concrete or timber retaining walls, but a poorly executed grading job can lead to costly repairs, back-charges by builders, and even lawsuits from homeowners.

If FHA financing is planned for houses in the subdivision, the developer should pay especially close attention to grading requirements. FHA requires that the grade between the garage and the street not exceed 14 percent, as measured from the back of the sidewalk to the garage. If the pad for the lot is too high, the house will not qualify for an FHA loan. One solution is for the builder to drop the level of the garage to meet FHA's requirements, meaning that the builder must spend more money; however, the developer usually pays the extra cost one way or another if he agrees to deliver an FHA-approved subdivision. Although FHA and Department of Veterans Affairs (VA) financing for homebuyers can greatly aid the sales pace of a subdivision, especially for lower-priced homes, developers must understand what the use of these mortgages ties them to. "Whatever you promised consumers, you must complete and deliver to the homeowners association to have access to these funds. Sometimes developers are able to get a bond or guarantee in lieu of completion, but this process can be prohibitively expensive and developers sometimes end up stuck, without money to complete amenities and without amenities to get their money."[62]

If possible, all rights for off-site road, drainage, utility, and other easements should be obtained before buying the property. The seller should assist the developer in this effort, according to specific terms that should be negotiated in the earnest money contract. The price for obtaining off-site easements can increase dramatically after closing if the neighboring landowner knows that the easement is required for development.

Marketing

Subdivision marketing begins before the developer closes on the land and continues until the last lot is sold. Various aspects of marketing, including public relations, advertising, staffing, and merchandising, are described in detail in Chapter 4. Certain items, however, are unique to land development.

Marketing for the land developer focuses on both the sale of lots to builders and the sale of houses to consumers. The primary marketing objective is selling lots to builders. Except for large-volume builders, who purchase large blocks of lots outright, most builders take down a few lots at a time. Thus, the developer's lot sales depend on builders' success in selling houses.

In most subdivisions, builders handle the sale of their houses themselves or use outside brokers. The developer is typically not involved directly with house sales; nevertheless, the developer can assist builders' efforts by undertaking advertising and public relations for the subdivision as a whole and by ensuring that the subdivision has as much marketing appeal as possible.

Virtually the entire development process can be viewed as a marketing exercise. Even before selecting a site, the developer should have identified the target market, and every step of the process, from lot design to selection of builders, should be consistent with the needs of that market.

The market determines:

- price range for the houses;
- product type or mix of product types;
- appropriate builders for a subdivision;
- design of the lots;
- types of permanent financing for builders;
- variety and quality of amenities;

Individual homes at I'On in Mount Pleasant, South Carolina, are constructed by members of the I'On Guild, a group of builders selected for their experience, enthusiasm, craftsmanship, and client and trade references.

- type of public relations campaign to be conducted;
- design of brochures and advertising material; and
- means by which homebuilders will market their houses to buyers.

Focus groups provide a useful technique for understanding the preferences of prospective buyers. Larger homebuilders use them extensively to decide what the floor plans and styling of new houses should be and the features that are important to specific submarkets. Focus groups are also useful to land developers at the beginning of a project, providing important input on lot size, siting, pricing, amenities, and other critical market information for serving a particular clientele. A number of marketing consultants have experienced focus group leaders on staff and are usually assigned the task of assembling, leading, and reporting the results of focus groups. Representatives from prospective target market groups are invited to a one- to two-hour session, often over dinner or with refreshments. Payments for participants ran from $50.00 to $100 in 2001.

Scott Smith of La Plata Investments notes that focus groups are important, even in areas where the customer base is fairly homogeneous. "A large portion of our customer base are members of the conservative Christian community, affiliated in some way with the 1,800-person workforce of Focus on the Family, which is based here. This customer group has preferences and needs as distinct as those of more identifiable ethnic or social groups,

and the close ties between neighbors and coworkers can be a word-of-mouth assist to our marketing efforts."[63]

Marketing to Homebuilders

Many different methods can be used to market a subdivision. Apartment, retail, or office sites are marketed directly to building developers. Lots in exclusive custom home subdivisions may be sold directly to homebuyers, who then hire their own custom builder or select from a list of builders approved by the developer. In some cases, a custom builder is also the developer. In most cases, however, the developer sells lots to builders who, in turn, sell to homebuyers. Builders typically market their product in one of three ways:

1. Builders may offer a range of basic plans with varying degrees of options in elevation design, interior finishes, and location within the subdivision. They may build model homes from which homebuyers select their preference. This approach is used primarily by production builders (builders of non-custom houses) for whom economies of scale can be realized by standardizing the basic units. Moreover, the costs of model homes can be amortized over a large number of lots. Depending on the market, production homebuilders typically build 25 to 100 or more houses per year in a given subdivision. Production builders are usually involved in many subdivisions in a region, or regions, or even nationwide. This method of building and mar-

keting new homes is the most common and includes homes in all price ranges.

2. Builders may build houses on spec (speculation) to be sold during or after construction. The buyer contracts for the house during construction, or, in a slow market, the house may be completed before a buyer is found. Both large and small builders, in all price ranges, use this approach. Typically, the builder selects the design, which may be customized to varying degrees for the buyer, who selects interior finishes, appliances, cabinetry, and so on. Spec building is most common when the housing market is very strong, because builders cannot afford the risk of a long sale period.

3. A custom builder may purchase lots from the developer, then sell a house to the buyer. The builder may sell a completed house or a partially completed house, giving the buyer the chance to customize it, or may contract with a buyer to build a custom home on a particular lot. Custom homebuilders typically build one to ten houses per year in a given subdivision. Most—but not all—custom builders tend to market higher-end products.

Developers' market studies should indicate the types of builders to target in marketing the development. Experienced developers suggest trying to attract a builder that has enough identity in the market to attract the public. In major markets, it means a builder who sells at least 500 houses per year. In less active markets, that number is considerably smaller. In Boston, for example, the largest builders sell 100 to 200 houses per year.

Developers should not let first-tier builders control their subdivisions. "They will want ten to 15 lots at the beginning and a rolling option on the rest. They will build four models and construct six to ten specs at a time. You need to give them enough lots for models and specs, with a one-for-one rolling option as they sell the specs.

"In pioneering areas, you convince builders by telling them how much you will spend on promotion: 'Here's what we will spend. If we don't do what we promise, we will take the lots back.' You get better absorption if you can keep traffic moving around in the subdivision. On small, 200-lot subdivisions, you must choose between selling all the lots to one major builder or working with small builders who take one or two lots each. Developers need 300 to 500 lots to run a cost-effective on-site marketing program. In a 300-lot subdivision, they would sell half the lots to the 'market maker' and the rest to three other builders. The market maker will attract many potential buyers. Smaller builders will use one of their spec houses as a model and an office."[64]

To obtain commitments from builders, developers should make contacts with potential builders as soon as the land is tied up. Savvy local builders are often more familiar with an area than market researchers, and developers should solicit their advice on the target market and its preferred products.

To broaden their markets, larger subdivisions (200 houses or more) often include two to ten homebuilders that build two or three different product types in different price ranges. A 300-house subdivision may, for example, be divided into two sections, with one production builder taking down 200 lots and two or three custom builders taking down the other 100, with the mix depending on the market. The developer should retain some flexibility for allocating more lots to one builder than to another as sales progress. A rolling option that allows builders to take down blocks of five, ten, or 20 lots at a time helps the developer avoid the problem of losing lot sales if one product type is not moving as quickly as another.

Some developers prefer to contact prospective builders directly; others prefer to work through one or several brokers who know an area very well. Developers should examine the different homebuilders who build the type and price of product market studies recommend. Beginning developers should be able to compete effectively against well-established developers by offering builders a continuing lot inventory, minimum cash upfront, and seller financing. Ideally, builders should be required to put up a 10 percent downpayment, but beginning developers may have to settle for any amount that is sufficient to hold builders' interest.

After preliminary contact with prospective builders and as soon as a preliminary plat is available, the developer should prepare a marketing package. This package should include information about the site and the neighborhood (shopping, schools, daycare facilities, churches, and recreation), and data about the site, including the subdivision plan, restrictive covenants, amenities, and the marketing program.

Terms for buying subdivision lots vary depending on the market. In softer markets, builders may put down only $1,000 cash per lot, or less, as evidence of a commitment. When the commitments are made before site development, builders are not obligated to take down or close on the stipulated number of lots until the engineer has certified that the lots are ready for building. Before then, builders have the option only to buy the lots at the specified price. The option (or purchase contract) is not a specific performance contract. In other words, if builders fail to close, they lose only their earnest money.

Once the lots are ready for building, builders are usually liable for interest on the lots that are committed but not yet closed. If a rolling option exists, builders are committed to taking down a certain number of lots at a time. Either builders may pay cash for the lots, with funds provided by the builder's construction lender, or the developer may finance the lots for builders during the period between closing and start of construction. For example, builders may commit to take down five lots immediately for model houses and have an option to purchase 30 lots every six months, beginning, say, January 1. If the builders exercise the option, the interest meter starts running on January 1 for the portion of the 30 lots not closed on that date. Six months later, if the builder does not exercise the option on the next 30 lots, they are released for sale to other builders.

If the developer wants to use the builder's credit to help secure the development loan, rolling options on lots are not sufficient. If possible, beginning developers should have a firm contract of sale for the lots covered by the development loan, either to a creditworthy builder or to a smaller builder with a letter of credit for the unpaid balance of the sale price.

Marketing Larger Parcels
In addition to single-family or townhouse lots, a larger parcel may also include nonresidential sites for commercial, apartment, office, community, or other use. Reaching potential buyers for these sites requires an approach similar to that for marketing office park and business park sites.

Two main sources of business are outside brokers and drive-bys. Experienced outside brokers require the payment of a generous commission, but many developers believe they are well worth the investment. Although advertising is not an especially effective technique, newsletters and broker parties do help to generate and maintain brokers' interest. On-site representation—a place provided for brokers to come in and talk to prospects—is desirable.

Typically, the buyer of a $1 million site puts up $25,000 to $50,000 of earnest money, in cash or by way of a letter of credit. Standard closing times range from 60 to 120 days, depending on the market. For example, buyers in Austin usually close directly into a construction loan: "Buyers almost always want the option to buy or the right of first refusal on adjoining sites. It is recommended that developers try to avoid giving these options, but they often must grant them as a component of a larger deal. This is especially important during the initial project stages when the developer is trying to encourage building construction to enhance absorption."[65]

Direct Marketing to the Public
Marketing and sales require different skills. "Our education in the school of hard knocks has taught us that marketing and sales are everything but that most developers think the two are related. They are totally separate skills, and you should be suspicious if you think you've found someone who can do both. The strategic thinking and planning of the marketing professional is a critical piece of development that very good salespeople are rarely equipped to deal with. Sales personnel need to be good deal makers. Part of the problem is that developers must learn to engage their marketing and sales team, never to think of them just as subcontractors."[66]

For most land development projects, developers are not directly involved in retail sales to the general public. If they also build homes or are engaged in condominium or recreational developments, however, they probably will be.

Marketing budgets are based on the estimated cost of marketing, promotions, sales strategies, and plans. As a guideline, a typical marketing budget is 5 to 7 percent of gross sales for nonrecreational projects and 10 to 12 percent for recreational projects. The budget includes 1 to 2 percent for advertising and the balance for commissions for the sales staff and cooperating brokers.

Most larger developers prefer to use their own in-house sales staff to handle direct marketing. Even if they use an outside brokerage firm, however, developers need their own marketing director and sufficient in-house staff to represent their interests in day-to-day negotiations. Smaller development firms should give serious consideration to using one or more local realtor firms as sales staff or as a source of sales referrals. In larger metropolitan areas, some brokerage firms specialize in new homes and have established marketing programs for builders and developers.

The sooner a marketing director is hired, the better. Before construction begins, the marketing director can help by getting to know the market area. As the person responsible for sales, the marketing director should possess an intimate knowledge of sales techniques, ability to motivate sales personnel, and firsthand experience with the types of products being sold. A minimum of two salespeople should be hired, with one or two more available to help during peak periods.

Some developers argue that salespeople should be paid on commission; others advocate a combination of salary and unlimited commission. A few rely on straight salaried staff, although salaries may need to be quite high to attract top-notch brokers. Prizes, bonuses, and competitions are proven good practices. Higher commission rates may be paid for selling certain "problem" lots or houses, and bonuses should be awarded if sales personnel exceed monthly or yearly quotas.

Marketing low-priced tract production homes requires a different approach to that for marketing high-priced custom houses. If sales are routine, the best method of compensation may be salary. For higher-priced housing, however, sales are seldom routine. Marketing for these houses may include offering special financing and a wide variety of building modifications. Further, because a buyer with a substantial amount of money usually has a greater selection of houses from which to choose, salesmanship is at a premium. A cooperative broker arrangement also is more important for higher-priced houses.

An effective sales program requires thorough training and constant motivation. Money is a good motivator, but salespeople also need to be kept enthusiastic. Good sales programs usually include:

- well-paid, well-trained, and motivated sales staff;
- regular sales meetings to discuss prospects and policies;
- a system for communicating with, and following up on, prospective buyers;
- a system for obtaining leads and referrals;
- a reporting system to inform management of buyers' objections, preferences, and attitudes; and

- a customer service system for handling the selection of options such as appliance upgrades, carpet and tile selections, and exterior elevation choices, and for taking care of closing details, occupancy procedures, and postconstruction warranty and service details.

Merchandising and Advertising

Whereas advertising is intended to reach a wide audience and to persuade people to visit a subdivision, merchandising is designed to stimulate the desire of potential buyers once they come to the site. The developer's advertising should focus on the quality of life enjoyed by the residents by emphasizing recreational opportunities, schools, and other services available in the subdivision and in the surrounding community.

Large subdivisions of 500 houses or more can support a visitors center in which all builders in the subdivision can merchandise their houses. The center should be equipped so that prospective purchasers can get an initial impression of all products available in the subdivision. Smaller subdivisions generally can support only a very modest visitors center, such as a trailer furnished as a sales center.

The developer should encourage all the builders to place their models in the same area. In this way, the builders receive the same economies of scale as those enjoyed by car dealerships that locate together along a freeway. Each builder builds two to four houses in separate but interconnected areas. The model home "park" should be large enough to show the land plan, including common spaces and pedestrian paths. The developer is responsible for the landscaping and common area maintenance. Dirty streets and unkempt construction areas generate ill will among current residents of the area and deter potential buyers.

The design of the sales office and arrangement of model units is central to the merchandising plan. Signage that is coordinated with other marketing materials should lead visitors directly to the sales office, the model houses, and the major amenities. They also should direct visitors clearly to the exits. Signs prohibiting smoking and eating should be low key, pleasant, and inoffensive.

Internet and Interstate Marketing

In recreational and larger land development properties, the developer may want to market the product to out-of-state residents. Jo Anne Stubblefield cautions that interstate marketing of land is a legal minefield and that even the establishment of a promotional Web page can trigger (sometimes costly) legal responsibilities for developers. "By and large, we've found that marketing consultants are clueless regarding the legal issues that surround the marketing of land. Tending toward zealous promotion, they are in a hurry to get to the grand opening, and push the process of establishing a Web site, mailings, and other promotions." Establishing a Web site to market land is considered the legal equivalent of advertising in a pub-lication with national subscribers. Like a mass mailing, it is interstate marketing. Stubblefield adds that about half the states require registration of a sale, full disclosure, or both. Many states claim to have "uniform acts" that are interchangeable with other states' regulations. They are almost never uniform. Each state has its own requirements for the documents to be submitted and a different schedule of fees, ranging from $250 to $500 to New York's requirement, which is calculated as a percentage of the total value of common areas of the development. To market the project in multiple states, do not rely on marketing consultants to negotiate this terrain. Get a lawyer with a national practice before even starting the marketing of the project."[67]

Development Maintenance after Completion

Among the developer's most important tasks is the creation of a proper set of mechanisms to handle long-term maintenance after the project is complete. Such mechanisms protect not only the developer's investment but also the investment and living environment of the future residents of the subdivision.

A developer's stewardship of the land may take many forms. First, a developer may make express guarantees or warranties concerning the care of streets, landscaping, and amenities when selling lots to builders. Second, a developer normally creates and records a set of deed restrictions and protective covenants. The covenants enable residents to enforce maintenance and building standards when other residents violate the restrictions. Third, a developer normally creates a homeowners association that bears the responsibility for long-term maintenance, has the power to collect and spend money on common areas, and helps to build a sense of community. Fourth, in most cases, a developer dedicates streets to the city or county. The city or county then takes responsibility for various public services, such as street cleaning and repair, parkway mowing, and trash removal. Because the types of public services available differ from city to city, a developer must make sure that all public services are provided. Garbage collection, for example, is a municipal service in some jurisdictions but is handled by private contractors in others.

Protective Covenants

Protective covenants, which embody the agreements between the seller and purchaser covering the use of land, are private party contracts between the land subdivider and the lot or unit purchasers. Covenants are intended to create and ensure a specific living environment in the subdivision. Purchasers of lots and houses in the subdivision should perceive the covenants as assurance that the developer will proceed to develop the property as planned and that other purchasers will maintain the property as planned. Strict enforcement of suitable covenants gives each lot owner the assurance that no other lot owners in the protected area can use their property

The design of the leasing center or sales office is central to the merchandising plan.

in a way that will alter the character of the neighborhood or create a nuisance. Lenders and government agencies, such as FHA and VA, often require covenants as a means of protecting the quality of the neighborhood and the condition of the houses.

Deed restrictions and covenants can augment zoning and other public land use controls by applying additional restrictions to size of lots, building envelope, location of structures, setbacks, yard requirements, architectural design, and permitted uses. Affirmative covenants can be used to ensure that certain land remains as open space and that the developer will preserve certain natural features in that space. They also may create a mechanism for assessing homeowners on the upkeep and maintenance of common facilities.

If both public and private restrictions apply, the more restrictive condition is operative. For example, Greenway Parks in Dallas abides by subdivision restrictions that were recorded in the late 1920s. The covenants stipulate a minimum side yard of five feet (1.5 meters). The zoning, however, stipulates a minimum side yard that is 10 percent of the width of the front lot. Thus, for lots with 80 feet (24.5 meters) of frontage, the operative restriction is the zoning, which requires side yards at least eight feet (2.4 meters) wide.

Covenants should take the form of blanket provisions that apply to the whole subdivision, and they should be specifically referenced in each deed. These covenants, together with the recorded plat, legally establish a general scheme for the development. They should be made superior to any mortgage liens that may be on record before recording the covenant to ensure that everyone is bound by the restrictions, even someone buying a house through foreclosure.

Although covenants are automatically superior to any future lien, many covenants and restrictions also provide for an automatic lien for payment of homeowners association fees and assessments. The documents must provide that the lien for assessments be automatically subordinated to purchase money liens.[68] Not all covenants are legally enforceable, however. Covenants that seek to exclude any buyer on the basis of race, religion, or ethnic background are both unconstitutional and unenforceable.

Usually, developers do not want to be the enforcers of covenants, unless a long-term building project requires them to keep control over an area. Subdividers may retain control over enforcement as long as they are active in the subdivision. Thereafter, however, the covenants should grant enforcement powers to the homeowners association and to individual owners. Some cities also require a provision that lets the city take over enforcement under certain circumstances.[69]

The covenants should not be recorded until developers have received preliminary subdivision approvals. Covenants frequently do not have to be recorded until issuance of the first deed. Stubblefield advises, "Don't write yourself into any covenants until you have to."

Further, if developers intend to use FHA, VA, or other sources of federal financing (such as the Government National Mortgage Association [Ginnie Mae] or the Federal National Mortgage Association [Fannie Mae]), they should ensure that the proposed covenants meet with the approval of those agencies. The FHA and VA have jointly developed acceptable model legal documents, although the same coordination has not taken place with Fannie Mae and Ginnie Mae.

Design Controls. Provisions for design control should reflect the tastes and attitudes of the target market. The types of design controls and degrees of constraint differ, depending on whether the target market is production builders or custom builders. For the developer who is selling finished sites, the best mechanism for design control is to include an "approval of plans" clause in the purchase agreements for building sites.

Even though individual designs may be attractive, incongruous styles may detract from the overall appearance of a subdivision. A design review committee should

Building Massing and Scale

The architectural image of Westpark will be perceived primarily from public spaces such as streets, parks, and greenbelts. Therefore, building massing, scale, and roof forms constitute the primary design components and require careful articulation. Emphasis should be on horizontal forms south of Alton Parkway and on vertical elements within the activity corridor.

Appropriate:
- Articulation of wall planes (required).
- Projections and recesses to provide shadow and depth (required).
- Simple, bold forms (encouraged).

Inappropriate:
- Large expanses of flat wall planes vertically or horizontally (prohibited).

Roof Pitches and Materials

Principal roof forms should be gable or hip with pitches from 4:12 to 6:12. All pitched roof materials should be clay or concrete tile from the approved color and material board to ensure a continuity of textures and colors. Minimal flat roof areas should have gravel surface with color to match roof tile. Short roof overhangs are encouraged with simple plaster fascias. Exposed rafter tails are not permitted.

Appropriate:
- Gable and hip roof forms (required).
- Combining one- and two-story elements (encouraged).
- Varying plate heights and ridge heights (encouraged).

Discretionary:
- Small areas of flat and shed roofs (limited).

Inappropriate:
- Gambrel, mansard, and "period" style roofs (prohibited). ∎

Source: Westpark Design Guidelines, the Irvine Company, Newport Beach, California.

therefore be established to approve proposed designs. Such a committee also shields the developer from accusations of arbitrariness.

Encouraging a good design is easier than discouraging a bad one. The developer's primary tool is to specify dimensional limitations on features such as yard setbacks, building heights, bulk, and signs. But size covenants may backfire. For example, the city of Highland Park, a wealthy inner suburb of Dallas, passed severe yard coverage limitations. Builders of houses that averaged 6,000 to 7,000 square feet (560 to 650 square meters) responded by building two-story boxes that completely filled the allowable building envelope. Similar boxes have appeared on small lots in Beverly Hills, California, where soaring lot prices virtually guarantee that buyers will build houses as large as possible on their lots.

Covenants that are too restrictive may lead to boring uniformity and eventual rebellion among residents. Communities have faced lawsuits over paint colors, swing sets, and other elements that were too rigidly controlled by covenants.

One of the most difficult areas to control is future alterations and additions. Materials are difficult to match or become obsolete. Costs change over time. New fire codes may prohibit the use of certain materials, such as the once popular cedar shake roofing. New technologies are developed. A covenant that was intended to ban large satellite dishes, for example, may also prohibit a discreet

12-inch (0.3-meter) dish on a roof. The covenants should therefore provide for a procedure to accommodate changes over time—a *variance*. The design review committee must consider precedents when it approves variances from the specified restrictions.

Other Covenants. Cost covenants are unsuccessful. A $60,000 minimum cost requirement, for example, may have built a mansion in the 1950s, but a cottage is all it will provide in today's market. One common method for establishing quality is to set minimum square footage standards for living areas, exclusive of garages, basements, and accessory buildings.

In cluster home, duplex, and townhouse subdivisions where houses are attached, the long-term value of a development requires a covenant that protects other owners when one house is damaged or destroyed by fire or other causes. Such a covenant should make owners of damaged property responsible for rebuilding or restoring the property promptly. The restoration should be substantially in accordance with the architecture and engineering plans and with the specifications for the original buildings.

If a subdivision includes common open space, a covenant should be included that provides for the use, preservation, and limitation on future development of the space. Open-space easements may be used to ensure long-term protection of common open space. In some cases, the granting of open-space easements to the community may be a basis for obtaining planning approval for the development.

Boats, mobile homes, campers, and trucks all require special storage areas. The developer may want to include a covenant that prohibits on-site parking of these vehicles or requires visual screening. Alternatively, the covenant may limit parking to specified areas, such as backyards. Other restrictive covenants may prohibit keeping certain types of pets or livestock on site, cutting mature trees, repairing automobiles, and parking inoperable vehicles.

Developers walk a fine line between introducing too little and too much restriction. Developers want to maintain the value of the subdivision without overly limiting their market. A potential homebuyer who cannot keep the family boat or camper on the property will probably look elsewhere for a house.

Effective Term and Revision. Although some covenants may include a definite termination date, covenants should generally be designed to renew themselves automatically and *run with the land* indefinitely. Property owners also should be able to revise the covenants with the approval of a stipulated percentage of other property owners. The developer may decide to allow some covenants to be revisable with a simple majority vote, whereas other covenants may require approval by 75 percent or even 90 percent of property owners. The developer may also want to allow homeowners to revise some covnants, such as changes in fencing, after three to five years, while others, such as "single-family use only," may be revised only after 25 to 40 years. Proposed revisions in covenants should be submitted sufficiently ahead of time to allow property owners to review them —three years for major covenants and one year for minor covenants.

Residential developers disagree about whether or not the developer should retain the power to make minor amendments to covenants. Some feel that the flexibility to adjust building lines and make modifications in design character from one phase to another is essential for the developer. Others feel that such modifications should be handled through the design review committee. Developers who frequently amend covenants risk hurting their credibility with property owners, who may doubt the developer's intentions to fulfill promises and carry out future development plans.

Enforcement. Legally, anyone who is bound by covenants may enforce them against anyone else who is bound by them. Because doing so may set neighbor against neighbor, providing a homeowners association with the power of enforcement is the best solution. Failure to enforce a covenant in a timely fashion may render the covenant void. For example, in a Dallas subdivision, the homeowners did not enforce a covenant that restricted fencing of an open-space easement running along the back of the owners' lots. Several years later, the homeowners association attempted to enforce the covenant against several homeowners who had fenced the open space. The homeowners who had fenced in the open space successfully challenged the association on the grounds that the covenant was void for lack of previous enforcement.

Community and Condominium Associations

Types. Four main types of homeowners associations exist.

Community Association with Automatic Membership. In most subdivisions in which fee simple interest in the lots is conveyed to buyers, membership in a community association occurs automatically when a buyer purchases a dwelling or improved lot. The association may hold title to real property such as open space and recreation facilities in the subdivision. It is responsible for preserving and maintaining the property. Members have perpetual access to the common property. They must pay assessments to finance the association's activities and must uphold the covenants.

Condominium Association. This approach resembles the community association, except for the form of ownership. When someone purchases a condominium, the title applies only to the interior space of the particular unit. The structure, lobbies, elevators, and surrounding land belong to all the owners as *tenants in common.* Owners are automatically members of the condominium association and have voting privileges and responsibilities for operating and maintaining the common facilities.

Funded Community Trust. This approach is an alternative to the automatic membership association. The funded community trust holds and maintains the common areas in a development. The funded trust differs from a community association in that a fiduciary organization, such as a bank, is the trustee responsible for the costs of overseeing maintenance of the property.

The funded community trust limits the ability of owners to act directly on their own behalf. The advantage of the trust is that it eliminates much of the day-to-day governance and participatory requirements of members. This form has not been used widely, primarily because banks and other institutions have been reluctant to become trustees.

Nonautomatic Association. This form of association provides for the voluntary support of homeowners. It does not work, however, if the development owns common properties, because if owners are not automatically members, assessments cannot be mandated. A nonautomatic association cannot participate in the enforcement of covenants and, therefore, can serve only as a focus of interest and social pressure for conformance.

Legal Framework. An automatic community association includes five major legal elements: a subdivision plat, an enabling declaration, articles of incorporation, bylaws, and individual deeds for each parcel.

The subdivision plat is the recorded map showing individual lots, legal descriptions, common spaces, and easements. The plat should indicate areas that will be dedicated to the association as well as those that will not be dedicated for use by the general public (often called *reserve parcels*). It also should reference and be recorded with the enabling declaration, which sets forth the management and ownership of common areas, the lien rights of the association against all lots, the amendment procedures, the enforcement procedures, and the rights of voting members.

The articles of incorporation and bylaws are the formal documents for creating a corporation with the state. The articles of incorporation set forth the initial board of directors, procedures for appointing new directors, membership and voting rights, amendment procedures, dissolution procedures, and the severability of provisions.[70] The bylaws of the association describe the rules by which the association will conduct business. They set forth the composition and duties of the board and the indemnification of officers of the association and describe the role and composition of subordinate boards, such as the design review board.

Each individual deed conveyed by the developer should reference the declaration of the association. The developer should summarize the formation, responsibilities, and activities of the association in a brochure that homebuilders in the subdivision can give to their buyers.

The developer must create the association and file the articles of incorporation and bylaws before selling any lots to homebuilders or individual buyers. Any sales that predate the establishment of the association are exempted from the association. Therefore, forming the community association is a critical part of the developer's initial activities.

The Developer's Role. Homeowners associations, protective covenants, and the common facilities managed by homeowners associations are as important to the overall success of a subdivision as the subdivision's engineering and design. If handled properly, they can serve as a major component of the developer's marketing strategy.

The developer usually donates commonly owned land and facilities to the homeowners association. The costs are covered by lot sales to builders. For the purpose of property taxes, permanently dedicated open space has no real market value and is either not assessed or taxed at all or assessed at a nominal value, with the taxes paid by the homeowners association.

During the course of development, the developer usually maintains the open-space and common facilities. These responsibilities are turned over to the association when the development is completed. Control of the association passes from the developer to the residents when the residents elect the officers of the association. The developer should design the accounts and record keeping so that the transition to the association is smooth.

The developer establishes initial assessments for homeowners that must realistically reflect the number of residents of the community at any one time. Because buyers evaluate monthly association assessments the same way they do monthly mortgage payments, the assessments cannot be too high. Although developers would like to place as much of the burden as possible on the association, they should keep the assessment competitive with that of other subdivisions.

Residents appear to be somewhat more tolerant of association dues than they are of general taxes, because the results of dues are more directly apparent. The upper limit to place on dues depends on local conditions. In Orange County, California, for example, before Proposition 13 limited property taxes to 1 percent of the house purchase price, homeowners tolerated a combined tax bill (property taxes plus special district assessments) of up to 2 percent of the house value. Homeowners may tolerate as much as an additional half percentage point per year in association dues in areas where the association owns and operates substantial common open-space and recreation facilities.

Compared with the 1970s and 1980s when homeowners associations gave boards the feeling that they must be extremely restrictive toward members, the emphasis today is much more on empowerment than enforcement. Wayne Hyatt of Atlanta-based Hyatt and Stubblefield notes that developers are beginning to see covenants as a positive method of improving quality of life, meaning that rather than simply restricting nuisances and design choices, the homeowners association can be used to establish what are essentially community development goals—activities, charities, voluntarism, and other enhancements of the way the community lives.

According to Hyatt, "There's been a sea change in the sophistication of the law and of many private developers with regard to covenant development. The emphasis today is much more on empowerment of the owner-members than on enforcement. The law has become much more precisely defined, and as the fear of uncertainty [with regard to fiduciary duties and conflict of interest] wanes, the focus of litigation has changed dramatically. Where ten years ago disputes were typically developer versus board, now they are primarily owner versus members versus board. But the reputation for disputes among members is really a reflection of society, magnified through these private governmental bodies."[71]

General Advice

All participants in the land development and homebuilding process believe that they hold the key to successful development. Lawyers, financial officers, and marketing people all believe they play the most important role. And in fact, they all do.

Scott Smith, a Colorado developer, says, "All members of the development team need to understand the process, and the finance people need to lead the show, ensuring compliance with the financial plan. Financial disasters happen when decisions are made incrementally in the field."[72]

One pitfall is trying to economize by not hiring sufficient staff. To grow his business, Doug Boone found that he needed to hire a land development manager. "It's a senior position with a six-figure salary, and I delayed hiring one. Looking back on it, I probably waited too

Do's and Don'ts for Homeowners Associations

General Advice

- The senior person on the development team responsible for the project should not serve on the board.
- Do not try to do it all yourself. Document whatever you or the association does, remain flexible and willing to "spread the risk," and never underestimate the role of the association manager.

Do:

- Observe the required corporate formalities, such as holding regular meetings, keeping a corporate minutes book, and properly authorizing and documenting all board actions.
- Purchase or renew adequate insurance.

- Require the developer to complete and convey the common areas in a timely manner.
- Order an impartial inspection of the common areas by the association.
- Maintain common areas adequately.
- Collect assessments and increase assessments as necessary.
- Enforce architectural control.
- Review the association's budget and produce quarterly and annual reports.
- Always remember to protect members' interests.
- Use due care in hiring personnel, including compliance with nondiscrimination laws.
- File tax returns and other required IRS forms.

Do Not:

- Enter into long-term contracts such as maintenance against the bylaws of the association. If it turns out not to be in the best interest of the association, you could be liable.
- Enter a dwelling unit without authorization.
- File a lawsuit after the statute of limitations expires. ■

Source: Wayne Hyatt, *Protecting Your Assets: Strategies for Successful Business Operation in a Litigious Society* (Washington, D.C.: ULI–the Urban Land Institute, 1997).

---

long to fill this key role in my business. Extremely time-intensive positions that will help you accrue experience shouldn't remain unmanned once your company's model is established."[73]

Boone advises beginning developers not to take questionable risks or undertake huge battles for their initial projects. One of Boone's first projects was a new urbanist–style traditional neighborhood development—the only type of project he could get approved in the highly restrictive town of Davidson, North Carolina. He says it was far more time-consuming in planning and implementation than a typical suburban development. "It was much more complicated to execute because success is in the details. Street layouts have to have a certain feel with quirky streets at odd angles and short vistas. If the radius is too big, you lose the feel. And you try to have different forms of housing. Mixing up house styles can be challenging to make it all fit together. It is a very tight form of development, even though my average density was only 3.25 units per acre."[74]

By building in a place like Davidson where barriers to development are high, Boone's strategy is to create a defensible position from a competitive standpoint. But in a typical suburban development, he would have been able to build a critical mass more quickly, doing probably five projects in the time he will do three with the traditional neighborhood development. "I should have asked myself, 'How can I make money and build a business to have a sustainable future?' I received a lot of recognition for getting approval in Davidson, but I might have been better off pursuing a standard suburban project."

On the other hand, some beginning developers have found rewards in tackling a challenging project such as a higher-density new urbanist development or a project on an infill or brownfield site. Vince Graham, for exam-

ple, has been involved in two major residential communities inspired by the concepts of new urbanism—Newport, outside Beaufort, South Carolina, and I'On near Charleston, South Carolina. Despite difficulties in selling the concepts to the local communities, both projects have been resounding successes in the marketplace, with higher than expected returns for the developer.[75]

Conclusion

Beginning developers will find many opportunities in land development. In some cases, land development may be combined with building development, but, in general, it should be considered a separate business to be evaluated on its own merits. Even though a developer may intend to build houses on the land after it is developed, the finished lots should provide a reasonable profit on the land development portion of the business at lot prices that are competitive with prices of finished lots in other subdivisions.

Land development is considered one of the riskier forms of development, because it is so dependent on the public sector for approvals and infrastructure support, involves a long investment period with no positive cash flow, and, especially in large projects, requires the ability to change direction to meet changing markets and other trends. Beginning developers should concentrate on smaller deals that are less complex. Problem sites, such as those containing environmentally sensitive areas, can offer attractive opportunities, but developers should be wary of getting bogged down on a site for several years in litigation and entitlement disputes.

Beginning land developers will find that obtaining financing without significant cash equity and strong financial statements is a very difficult process. Nevertheless,

Elsinore 98 is a 65-acre (26-hectare) residential subdivision of two distinct communities comprising 233 single-family lots adjacent to the Lake Elsinore recreational area in Riverside County, California. Located on the I-15 corridor between Riverside and San Diego, Lake Elsinore's regional importance has changed dramatically with new highway construction, causing a mid-1990s boom in residential construction. Elsinore's two communities, Tuscana and Castellina, are a case study in capitalizing on regional infrastructure and amenities and marketing the result to take advantage of powerful demographic trends. In executing this project, developer and homebuilder Granite Homes skillfully navigated the entitlement and regulatory processes, solving environmental problems and large-scale market changes that could easily have broken the deal irretrievably.

The Developer

Granite Homes is a mid-sized regional homebuilder based in Irvine, California. Before founding their company in 1993, partners BJ Delzer and Dan Kassel worked in industrial development in the High Desert area and in development and construction in and around Los Angeles, respectively. The company has steadily grown toward its goal of closing 250 to 300 homes per year.

The Project

Delzer and Kassel saw the potential to reenter the Lake Elsinore market after the real estate crash of the early 1990s. Although being on the leading edge of a wave can be advantageous, they also had reason to be wary of this land deal. A project on the site had been attempted almost a decade earlier by a developer who lost the project when he defaulted on bond obligations and loans. As a result, the site had a negative image—but it had major advantages as well. Grading had already been completed on the site (although a significant amount of regrading was necessary), and infrastructure had been laid in. Kassel and Delzer had determined that site work would not require large expenditures, so the mostly completed work gave them a good esti-

mate for the remaining costs. Completed access roads meant that they could expect the six model homes to go up quickly. Most important, the previous developer had shepherded his plan through most of the difficult regulatory process, and as long as no significant changes were made to the community plan, the site came with an approved environmental impact report. EIRs are a source of major uncertainty and upfront costs in this area of rapid growth, and their resolution before closing on the land was of tremendous value. And just by lying outside Orange County, the Elsinore parcels would require a much smaller purchase price (less than $8 million).

Examining the regulatory environment and financing costs in 1998, the developers concluded that they could produce finished lots in both communities for $43,000 per lot, about half the average for the same size lots in Corona, just 20 miles (32 kilometers) to the north on I-15. With changes in regional highways and job growth, they saw Lake Elsinore as the next outlying community from Corona, a suburb of Orange County. Working from numerous market studies, the developers thought they could target the lots in two communities, with prices of finished houses ranging from $170,000 (for 2,055 square feet [190 square meters]) to more than $240,000 (for 3,665 square feet [340 square meters]).

The Site and Regional Context

For most of its history, the Lake Elsinore area has been a somewhat lonely recreational outpost on the I-15 corridor. With a popular lake for small boating and other recreational activities, the area was for many years too long a commute to strong job bases in Orange and San Diego counties and the southeastern reaches of Los Angeles. Though the site is only 40 miles (64 kilometers) as the crow flies from powerful job growth in Irvine, Santa Ana, and Costa Mesa, Orange County, the commute was approximately two hours. The situation changed radically in the early 1990s with the completion of a new toll road, bringing the commute to Orange County to about an hour.

At the same time, Riverside and San Bernardino (even closer commutes) were experiencing huge job growth. Orange County land prices required very large upfront expenditures, so southern Riverside County began to see a residential boom, resulting quickly in a shortage of entitled land. Large subdivision plans on entitled parcels appeared all around the Elsinore site, which remained encumbered by the defaulted bonds. The site's location, clearly visible on a treeless hilltop adjacent to I-15, suggested easy marketing to homebuyers, especially if, as Kassel thought, they could capitalize on the approved plan and EIR and roll out their product faster than the competition.

Land Negotiations and Purchase

As negotiations on the land purchase dragged on, Kassel began to feel uneasy. The seller was difficult to deal with, and his partner was a litigator. As Kassel was preparing to close escrow on the land purchase, the water district, when Granite attempted to secure the necessary will-serve letters, stated that there might be a moratorium on new water meters. The possibility of a moratorium posed significant obstacles to the continued development of the site. One of the conditions of closing Kassel had negotiated was that he did not have to close in the case of a threatened moratorium. The seller, unwilling to abide by the contract, attempted to sell the property to another homebuilder. With no other recourse, Granite had to pursue its rights to purchase the property and ultimately sued the seller, closed on the property, and was awarded reimbursement of legal costs by the court. The purchase price for the entire parcel (approximately 60 acres [24 hectares]) was finalized at $5.4 million.

Regulatory Challenges and Mitigation

Almost immediately after the purchase, a government agency claimed the site could potentially contain habitat (coastal sage scrub) desirable to the California gnatcatcher, a threatened species. Although the project had an approved EIR, the agency considered a small portion of the property potentially able to support gnat-catchers. The small bird had not been found to be nesting on the site but was observed flying over the site and living nearby in open space. The presence of even low-grade sage scrub was enough to require the developers to file a habitat conservation plan and apply for a 10-A permit. At worst, the newly discovered condition could void the original EIR, which had already been figured into the purchase price, render a significant portion of the site unbuildable, and have a devastating financial impact on the development and Granite Homes.

After extensive biological investigation, Granite complied with the agency's requirement to submit a habitat conservation plan and apply for the 10-A permit. The costs, in both time and money, to comply with the agency's requirements were considerable. Granite was at first required to grant 29 acres (11.7 hectares) of open space to the government, but the agency then required an additional 28 acres (11.3 hectares) and a mitigation fee. The additional acreage generated a secondary land deal: Granite purchased 80 acres (32 hectares) in the same habitat area, gave the required 28 acres (11.3 hectares) to the government, and sold the remaining 52 acres (21 hectares) to another developer that needed mitigation land for its own development. Clearing the land was ultimately able to resume, but costs attributable to the challenge amounted to more than $1 million and a delay of about a year. Neither the time nor the costs had been factored into the original pro forma. The project's original timetable of 27 months was scrapped by the time home construction began in earnest. Many homebuyers were left hanging and had to make other arrangements. Fortunately, Granite's lenders and investors were understanding and, most important, patient, which Kassel credits to Granite's honesty in dealing with lenders, investors, and homebuyers.

Project Finance and Feasibility
Because part of the project's appeal was its improved lots, estimating the remaining development costs and arriving at the cost of finished lots was relatively straightforward. Even so, Granite Homes encountered significant variances over the life of the project in nearly all expenses. School fees, financing, and permits each swelled by about $1,100 per finished lot, and the gnatcatcher problem added another $5,000 per lot. (The gnatcatcher-related costs alone exceeded the contingency factor built into indirect land development costs.)

To increase absorption, Granite built two separate model complexes with three plan types each. The 125-unit Tuscana was considered entry-level homes, while Castellina's 108 lots were slated for larger houses. A private equity placement in June 1998 raised $3.3 million, and construction loans totaling slightly more than $32 million (plus just under $1 million for models) were planned at an LTV of 75 percent. An acquisition and development (A&D) loan package at 65 percent LTV totaling more than $6.5 million was also drawn. An IRR of 28 percent was projected over the initial 27-month development period. Twenty-eight percent seemed to provide a safe margin of error and a cushion of respectable returns, even in the event of escalating costs.

Design and Construction
A design reminiscent of an Italian hill town in Tuscany was chosen for the site. Architect Art Danielian of Danielian Associates, one of the premier residential development architects in southern California, was brought in to create Castellina, and Len Noble, an Irvine-based architect, designed Tuscana. The division into 108 and 125 lots was based on the original plan; it was decided that the split could serve to define the two price points that would appeal to two different types of buyers, as determined by market research. Three model plans were developed for each community, with three possible exterior treatments on each and three to five architectural options available on each plan, ranging from home offices to additional garages and bedrooms. The developer learned from demographic data that a large segment of new homebuyers comprised Latino families and that many of them prefer to live with several generations in a home. This information was taken into account in the design of two-story houses with up to seven bedrooms. Although the data required a leap of faith from both architect and developer, the information repeatedly was proved to be sound.

Direct construction costs on the project were held in check by the use of a number of novel construction technologies. Elsinore's houses were the first in Granite's history to use extruded foam exterior details, and framing for the projects has been thoroughly value-engineered, even as the project is proceeding. Scheduling of trades is critical, and Granite tries to keep at least 15 to 20 houses proceeding at roughly the same pace to consolidate work by skilled trades as much as possible between structures. Responding to the pent-up demand for the homes, the final phases were much larger—36 homes in Tuscana and 38 homes in Castellina, the largest phases Granite has built concurrently at one site. This scheduling posed additional management problems for the Granite team and subcontractors, who were not used to building 74 houses at once. More superintendents were hired and Granite focused its energy on quality and production.

Marketing
Emphasizing its experience as a developer and homebuilder, Granite Homes has developed a vision for the community. Working from the landscape and quasi-Mediterranean climate of the site, the idea of Tuscan villas is communicated across every level of marketing material and product design. The site map is rendered in aged-looking sepia, and, except for renderings of the house elevations out of context, all photography in the brochure is of historical villas and townscapes in Italy. Though visually similar, this Mediterranean lifestyle is an increasingly popular and modern twist on the Spanish vernacular popular in California for the past three decades. The impact of Spanish speakers in the massive

continued

demographic shifts of southern California is often cited as a reason for this popularity.

The importance given to market data is evident in the model units of Tuscana, where decor, approach, and even product options are continually refined based on feedback from walk-through surveys, sales personnel meetings, and knowledge of the competition. Rather than represent a stylistically consistent approach, Kassel and Delzer prefer that each model, and in some cases each room of a model, appeal to a common lifestyle. Extremely cost-conscious in direct construction and finance, the company spends freely to install surround-sound home theaters, high-end appliances, and even novelty furniture for children's rooms. Interior decoration is constantly refined to reflect popular imagery, and each bedroom is designed to appeal to competing ideals of orderliness, privacy, and luxury, depending on furniture and window treatments. Kassel's sales force insists that often the jump between merely adequate product and a closing is something as apparently frivolous as a memorable piece of furniture or fixture, which may or may not be standard in the home when purchased. The core function of Granite's marketing program is to engage the buyer.

Lessons Learned

Political processes are about friendships and trust. Decision makers support projects when they are backed by parties or individuals they trust. Building that trust is a critical process of building a development firm. "Most of the people we work with on bigger deals today are predisposed to trust us because, ten years ago, if we said we'd fax something at 4 P.M., we faxed it. Don't expect people to trust you unless you always come through on your commitments."

Due diligence means extreme diligence. Diligence goes beyond knowing what is (or might be) on or around the property. Developers should understand (if not have a relationship with) the personalities who will have approval powers over the parcel. After the regulatory challenges encountered in this project, "we discov-

ered that what normally constitutes due diligence isn't always sufficient. Do not just trust an approved or completed EIR. If necessary, send in a field biologist, and build the possible costs into your pro forma."

Take advantage of networking opportunities. The ability to talk with influential people in the market is crucial. Bob Kalmuk, chief financial officer of Granite Homes, characterizes the company as the institutionalization of Delzer's and Kassel's personal networks. Several of their networking successes were simple cold calls.

Be market driven; develop products for your market, not yourself. "Your own design sensibility is not of primary concern. When you look at the design of a community, a house, a brochure, think of your target market." The target market does not necessarily buy the same detergent as you or dress like you, and it may not even speak the same primary language as you. Find out what the market wants, how it perceives value, and what regulatory agencies will allow, and give it to them.

Use other professionals, but make deals personally. As a developer, you should conduct primary research yourself. You should also hire top professionals, consultants, and attorneys to help guide you through the maze. Regarding market research, consult salespeople who are in the forefront in the specific market(s) where you plan to compete. Although their primary responsibility is selling homes, salespeople store up critical knowledge about what sells and why. Talk to your salespeople—and your competitors— and incorporate their knowledge into design and marketing. Often, salespeople are a great resource of primary information, but they frequently are not equipped to interpret the data. The developer should not make decisions based entirely on outside opinions and projections. "If you're going to get involved with a parcel, you should personally understand the market, and you should definitely personally make the buy."

Remember that although consultants should have more experience than the developer in their area of expertise, their judgment should not supplant the developer's in the big picture. The obvious example is the architect. "Hire architects and engineers who don't fear the eraser," who understand that their solution has to satisfy the demands of the target market. Beyond just the work, be wary of consultants who do not explain their solutions. Ask why. "Don't just hire someone to make drawings for approval. Consultants should be able to explain the logic behind their solutions."

Conclusions

Overall, the success of Castellina and Tuscana is a very different scenario from the plan conceived in 1997 and 1998. Although returns are healthy—on a project that could easily have turned disastrous at the beginning—the follow-up to the original pro forma shows that both revenues and expenses increased by more than 15 percent over projections and that the time line of the development period was extended by more than a third. With few exceptions, the developer underestimated many categories of construction and regulatory expense but was saved by conservative revenue predictions. This case illustrates how hurdles in the regulatory process can be overcome by a developer who is not overextended financially and who has the time and cash to work around problems. Indeed, the developers were able to get around environmental problems and escalating costs to find the best use for the advantages of the parcel. Their awareness of long-term demographic trends enabled them to position themselves to profit from changes in the region. Although the developers showed incredible patience and flexibility in the opening rounds of this battle, the success of the overall plan is the result of ruthless adherence to a market strategy and careful evaluation of a product against market data. ∎

land development offers the opportunity to use commitments from builders as collateral for securing financing. Beginning developers will find that seller financing and joint ventures with landowners and financial institutions enable them to take part in a variety of opportunities and successfully launch a development career.

Although opportunities are always present for beginning developers, so are pitfalls. Cities are holding land developers responsible for an ever higher share of the cost of providing public facilities and solving environmental problems. In many cases, developers are becoming the de facto agents of cities in building arterial streets, libraries, fire stations, and sewer and drainage facilities and in cleaning up toxic waste and restoring environmentally sensitive land. The liability of developers for construction standards, especially streets, utilities, and drainage, extends for many years after developers have sold out of the subdivision.

Cities and land developers have always formed a kind of partnership because land development has been the primary vehicle by which cities grow in population and employment. As the burdens of responsibility shift more and more toward developers, developers must come to understand not only how to build financially successful subdivisions but also how to ensure the fiscal health of their cities.

Notes

1. The author is particularly grateful for the comments made on the earlier edition of this chapter by ULI Steering Committee member Don Mackie of Mill Creek Valley Properties, Salado, Texas, who sadly passed away in 2001. Many of his comments, made during an interview in 1987, are still highly relevant.

2. H. James Brown, R.S. Phillips, and N.A. Roberts, "Land Markets at the Urban Fringe," *Journal of the American Planning Association*, April 1981, pp. 131–144.

3. See Anthony Downs, *New Visions for Metropolitan America* (Washington, D.C.: The Brookings Institution, 1994); Reid Ewing, "Is Los Angeles–Style Sprawl Desirable?" *Journal of the American Planning Association*, Winter 1997, pp. 107–126; Peter Gordon and Harry W. Richardson, "Are Compact Cities a Desirable Planning Goal?" *Journal of the American Planning Association*, Winter 1997, pp. 95–106; J.C. Ohls and David Pines, "Discontinuous Urban Development and Economic Efficiency," *Land Economics*, August 1975, pp. 224–234; J.R. Ottensmann, "Urban Sprawl, Land Values, and Density of Development," *Land Economics*, November 1977, pp. 389–400; Richard B. Peiser, "Does It Pay to Plan Suburban Growth?" *Journal of the American Planning Association*, Autumn 1984, pp. 419–433; Richard B. Peiser, "Density and Urban Sprawl," *Land Economics*, August 1989, pp. 193–204; and Richard B. Peiser, "Decomposing Urban Sprawl," *Town Planning Review*, July 2001, pp. 275–298.

4. Smart growth is defined in different ways, but at its core, it is about ensuring that neighborhoods, towns, and regions accommodate growth in ways that are economically sound, environmentally responsible, and supportive of community livability—growth that enhances the quality of life.

5. Most communities require public hearings for subdivision approval but not for building plans, which are approved by the building department only. Public hearings are political by definition and involve much more risk—of disapproval, reduction in density, or increase in exaction cost. Building department approvals are essentially administrative: as long as one satisfies the regulations, approval is automatic.

6. The lender's release price from the loan may be higher than $16,000; thus, the developers would have to make up the difference.

7. See Ralph Lewis, *Land Buying Checklist* (Washington, D.C.: National Association of Home Builders, 1987).

8. Interview with Harlan Doliner, partner, Nixon Peabody LLP, Boston, Massachusetts, 2000.

9. Ibid.

10. Interview with Jack Willome, former CEO, Rayco, Ltd., San Antonio, Texas, 1987.

11. Ibid.

12. Interview with Don Mackie, 1987.

13. Title insurance companies do not survey property and therefore do not insure against encroachments and boundary disputes that would be disclosed by a proper survey. A correct survey, however, corresponds to the description in the deed, and if the description in the deed is wrong, the title insurance company is liable. The company insures the accuracy of the documents.

14. This paragraph and the next two are from an interview with Steve MacMillan, chief operating officer, Campbell Estate, Kapolei, Hawaii, 2002.

15. See Mike Davidson and Fay Dolnick, "A Glossary of Zoning, Development, and Planning Terms," *Planning Advisory Service Report* 491/492 (Chicago: American Planning Association, 1999).

16. Interview with Jo Anne Stubblefield, president, Hyatt and Stubblefield, Atlanta, Georgia, 2000.

17. Interview with Scott Smith, La Plata Investments, Colorado Springs, Colorado, 2000.

18. Interview with Al Neely, executive vice president and chief investment officer, Charles E. Smith Co., Arlington, Virginia, 2000.

19. Interview with Tim Edmond, president, ARVIDA, Tallahassee, Florida, 2000.

20. Interview with Jo Anne Stubblefield, 2000.

21. Interview with Roger Galatas, president, Roger Galatas Interests, LLC, the Woodlands, Texas, 2001.

22. *Avco Community Developers, Inc. v. South Coast Regional Commission*, 553 P.2d 546 (Cal. Sup. Ct., 1976). The California Supreme Court held that Avco did not have vested rights to develop.

23. *Golden v. Planning Board of the Town of Ramapo*, 285 N.E.2d 291 (N.Y. Ct. App., 1972). This case upheld regulations for timing, phasing, and quotas in development, making development permits contingent on the availability of adequate public facilities.

24. *Construction Industry Association v. City of Petaluma*, 522 F.2d 897 (9th Cir. 1975). The U.S. Supreme Court let Petaluma's residential control system stand after lengthy court battles initiated when the city was sued by homebuilders.

25. William Fulton et al., *Growth Management Ballot Measures in California* (Ventura, Calif.: Solimar Research Group, 2002).

26. See the city's Web site for more information: www.ci.austin.tx.us/smartgrowth/matrix.htm.

27. Interview with Roger Galatas, 2001.

28. Kevin Lynch and Gary Hack, *Site Planning*, 3rd ed. (Cambridge, Mass.: MIT Press, 1985), p. 124.

29. Interview with Roger Galatas, 2001.

30. Ibid.

31. See Douglas R. Porter and Richard B. Peiser, *Financing Infrastructure to Support Community Growth* (Washington, D.C.: ULI–the Urban Land Institute, 1984).

32. See Alan Altshuler and Jose Gomez-Ibanez, *Regulation for Revenue: The Political Economy of Land Use Exactions* (Washington, D.C.: The Brookings Institution and the Lincoln Institute of Land Policy, 1993).

33. A vast literature exists on the problems of urban sprawl. See Note 3.

34. See Thomas P. Snyder and Michael A. Stegman, *Paying for Growth: Using Development Fees to Finance Infrastructure* (Washington, D.C.: ULI–the Urban Land Institute, 1986).

35. The city might require the developer to pay for, say, the first one or two lanes of paving, with the city paying the rest. Alternatively, it might require the developer to pay for or install the entire arterial, with subsequent reimbursement by other developers whose subdivisions front the arterial.

36. Interview with Jim Fawcett, associate director, Sea Grant Program, University of Southern California, Los Angeles, California, 1988.

37. Although the terms *gross acres* and *net acres* are commonly used and understood, *net usable acres* is far less popular.

38. Richard B. Peiser, "Optimizing Profits from Land Use Planning," *Urban Land,* September 1982, pp. 6–10; and Ehud Mouchly and Richard Peiser, "Optimizing Land Use in Multiuse Projects," *Real Estate Review,* Summer 1993, pp. 79–85.

39. If subdivision lots are not already platted, the developer's first assessment would be how much land is developable and how many lots could be produced at a given density. For example, if a 50-acre (20-hectare) site includes two acres (0.8 hectare) that must be dedicated to widening a major frontage road plus three acres (1.2 hectares) in the floodplain, then net developable acreage is 45 acres (18.2 hectares). After examining the market, suppose the developer wants to build houses on 7,500-square-foot (700-square-meter) lots with a yield of four lots per acre (ten per hectare), with the balance of the land going toward streets, wider corner lots, and allowance for irregularly shaped parcels (180 lots altogether). The developer's knowledge of lot sale prices in nearby subdivisions provides a good initial estimate of the value of the finished lots. The sale price depends on the marketing of the lots: a bulk sale to one builder produces a lower price than a piecemeal sale to five or ten builders.

40. Entitlement risk differs from state to state and from city to city within a state. In the current litigious environment, however, even fully entitled property can be subject to lawsuits from NIMBYists or other opponents. In California, full vesting (elimination of all entitlement risk) occurs only with completion of the final map. Nevertheless, in Oceanside, the price of the land reflects the developer's assessment that there is very little if any entitlement risk in the deal.

41. The compound return is $(1 + 0.3)^{1/3} - 1 = .09139$ or 9.139 percent. The general formula is $(1 + r)^{1/n} - 1$, where r equals the total rate of return and n equals the holding period.

42. All return figures presented here are IRRs. They give the annual return on equity per year that should be made on an alternative investment (with annual compounding) to accumulate the same total amount of money by the end of the life of the project.

43. More commonly, the lot release prices on the development loan are lower than the lot sale prices, so that the developer does receive some cash flow from each lot sale after paying back the lender the stipulated amount per lot sold.

44. The rate of return on equity is the same as the discount rate used for determining the present value of a stream of future cash flows. It is also the same as the target IRR that an investor would use as his hurdle rate for making an investment.

45. Radburn was established by the City Housing Corporation, led by Henry Wright and Clarence Stein. See Eugenie Ladner Birch, "Radburn and the American Planning Movement," *Journal of the American Planning Association,* October 1980, pp. 424–439.

46. Bill Lutz, "Greenest of All," *Professional Builder,* September 1999, pp. 76–84.

47. Interview with Dan Kassel, co-president, Granite Homes, Irvine, California, 2001.

48. Interview with Scott Smith, La Plata Investments, Colorado Springs, Colorado, 2000.

49. See Walter Kulash, *Residential Streets,* 3rd ed. (Washington, D.C.: ULI–the Urban Land Institute, 2001).

50. Ibid.

51. Floodplain maps are generated from historic storm information and personal recollections of an area's residents, as well as statistical and hydrological records. Because records in most areas do not extend as far back as 100 years, the floodplain line is an educated guess, not a fact.

52. An acre-foot of water is the amount of water one foot deep that would cover one acre of land.

53. See Jeanne Christie, "Wetlands Protection after the *SWANCC* Decision," *Planning Advisory Service Memo* (Chicago: American Planning Association, 2002), pp. 1–4.

54. See Steven Fader, "By Design," *Urban Land,* July 2000, pp. 54–59+.

55. If the developer intends to build on all the lots himself rather than selling to other builders, then the financing may be more complicated. The bank would look at equity and financing needs for the entire project, including not only land but also houses.

56. Developers often provide seller financing to builders until the builders are ready to take down (close) and build on the lots. The seller financing automatically has a senior (first lien) position to any other financing such as the builder's construction loan, which the builder's construction lender will not allow. The developer, however, may *subordinate* the seller's loan to the builder's construction lender. The seller's loan, in this case, does *not* have to be retired before building occurs, thus lowering the builder's cash requirements.

57. Interview with Don Mackie, 1987.

58. The difference between cumulative and noncumulative preferred returns is discussed in Chapter 4.

59. The purchase could take place with or without a PMN. Land sellers tend to be less willing to subordinate a PMN to the development loan if they do not have an ongoing interest in the joint venture.

60. Interview with Don Mackie, 1987.

61. Interview with Doug Boone, Boone Communities, Davidson, North Carolina, 2000.

62. Interview with Jo Anne Stubblefield, 2000.

63. Interview with Scott Smith, 2000.

64. Interview with Don Mackie, 1988.

65. Ibid.

66. Interview with Scott Smith, 2000.

67. Interview with Jo Anne Stubblefield, 2000.

68. Interview with Don Mackie, 1988.

69. Houston, for example, has an administrative procedure for enforcing deed restrictions and covenants, which simplifies the process by eliminating the need for homeowners to file lawsuits to enforce covenants against their neighbors.

70. Severability provisions allow for the continued enforcement of covenants and restrictions, even if certain covenants are deemed illegal (such as race restrictions) and are thus unenforceable.

71. Interview with Wayne Hyatt, principal, Hyatt and Stubblefield, Atlanta, Georgia, 2001.

72. Interview with Scott Smith, 2000.

73. Interviews with Doug Boone, 2000 and 2001.

74. Ibid.

75. Interview with Vince Graham, principal, the I'On Company, Mount Pleasant, South Carolina, 2001.

4. Multifamily Residential Development

Overview

This chapter focuses on multifamily residential development, primarily rental income property, but also covers topics common to all forms of development. Rather than presenting separate generic discussions of the development process throughout the book, this chapter begins with a discussion of income property development and incorporates a detailed discussion of each step of the development process into its treatment of rental and condominium apartment development. (Several fundamental subject areas, such as site acquisition, the regulatory process, and site engineering, are covered in detail in Chapter 3.) Chapters 5, 6, and 7 discuss the particular applications of each step in the process to the other major income property types—office, industrial, and retail development.

Despite the apparent preference of U.S. households for owning single-family dwellings, multifamily housing continues to be an essential form for a broad range of the population. Apartments house the young and old alike, whether they are aspiring homeowners or the ever-growing number of renters by choice—those who choose to rent apartments even though they could afford to buy a single-family house. To its residents, multifamily housing offers convenience, affordability, and flexibility.

Pictured at left is Sailhouse in Corona del Mar, California.

Like other aspects of the housing industry, and like real estate in general, multifamily residential development is highly cyclical. Construction activity depends on both national and local economic conditions, the latter including local attitudes toward multifamily housing and local market conditions. Typically, in times of low interest rates, multifamily units are built by the thousands. Conversely, when interest rates are high (10 percent or above), multifamily construction slows considerably.

Major demographic trends also exert substantial influence on multifamily construction. As local growth rates influence the overall demand for units, so the composition of the population influences the demand for particular types of multifamily housing. The aging of the baby boomer generation will continue to play a leading role in the demand for housing. In the 1970s and early 1980s, the high proportion of the population aged 20 to 35 created enormous demand for adult multifamily complexes. Today, with many baby boomers in their 40s and 50s, the market for these complexes will inevitably decrease while the demand for other types of housing geared toward the active adult market, such as assisted living and continuing care facilities, will increase, offering new opportunities for developers. Additional sources of demand will come from *echo boomers*—the children of baby boomers—and new immigrant populations.

History

In the early 1980s, syndicators brought huge inflows of equity to finance apartment development in tax-driven deals offering little or no cash flow. Sale prices of apartment projects rose to uneconomic levels, often with zero and even negative cash-on-cash returns. The Tax Reform Act of 1986 effectively eliminated the market for these types of investments by limiting the ability of investors to write off tax losses against other income, and project values were accordingly adjusted downward. Developers of multifamily housing were hit hard when they discovered, too late, that they had built more units than the market could absorb. California developer Jim Perley states, "There followed a recession with a number of considerable impacts on apartment development. Apartment values dropped from the peak they had reached by as much as 70 percent in the late 1980s and early 1990s—for example, some $2 million properties were worth $600,000. With some of these properties having a 75 percent loan, it caused a big turmoil."[1]

After the real estate crash in the early 1990s, real estate investment trusts became the dominant buyers of larger apartment properties. At that time, other institutional investors such as pension funds and insurance companies also began to upgrade apartments to institutional status, giving them the same attention and place in institutional property portfolios that they previously had reserved for office and larger retail properties. The competition to buy apartment properties that were performing well resulted in higher sale prices and lower capitalization rates, making new apartment development more profitable. "It took some time for the Resolution Trust Corporation and the market to work through the inventory of problem properties. During that time, it was much cheaper to buy than to build. Now with the market coming back, prices for existing properties are starting to go up fairly quickly in places like Orange County, California. There has not been a lot of building going on, but people are out there getting their entitlements, and in the high-cost areas, building will start soon. The pressure on rents is going to intensify, which will cause more building of affordable housing as well."[2]

From the mid-1990s to the early 2000s, the multifamily sector has been doing very well. Most industry analysts agree that during this period the sector has been largely in equilibrium, apart from potential overbuilding in the luxury segment and in certain metropolitan markets. Investments in multifamily housing provided solid, steady returns in the late 1990s. Into the early 2000s, the credit quality of multifamily mortgages remained high, and delinquency rates were at near record lows.[3]

During this period, low mortgage interest rates made for-sale housing more affordable. At the same time, however, government programs that assist low- and moderate-income apartment development were substantially cut back. These cutbacks have considerably reduced the construction rate of affordable apartments. The one new supply-side subsidy program—low-income housing tax credits (LIHTCs)—was created by the Tax Reform Act of 1986 in response to the loss of incentives for the creation of low-income housing and the growing crisis in affordable housing. Tax credits are granted to each state

Residential Product Types

Single-Family Product (One to Two Units per Lot)
- Single-family houses (one unit per lot)
- Patio houses (or zero-lot-line)
- Duplexes (two units per lot)
- Townhouses (attached buildings on separate lots)

Multifamily Product (Multiple Units per Lot)
- Garden apartments (wood frame construction)
- Low-rise apartments (wood frame over concrete parking)
- Mid-rise apartments (steel or concrete)
- High-rise apartments (steel or concrete) ∎

on a per capita basis and are administered competitively through the state's housing agencies. LIHTCs have been successful in creating incentives for private developers to construct low- and moderate-income housing.

Product Types
Residential building development includes everything from single-family houses to high-rise apartment buildings and condominiums. The market can be segmented in a variety of ways:

- Rental Products—Rental apartments such as garden, low-rise, mid-rise, and high-rise units and rental houses. Tenants in rental apartments are lessees of the landlord. Their interest may range from a verbal agreement with the landlord for a month-to-month lease to a lease term ranging from six months to two or more years.
- Type of Ownership—Such as condominiums, cooperatives, and timeshares. *Condominiums* are arrangements whereby the household has individual ownership of its unit (defined as the space enclosed by the unit's interior walls) plus an undivided ownership interest in the property's common elements. In a *cooperative*, the residents of the building own shares in the corporation. The corporation actually holds the title to the building, and residents lease their units from the corporation. Since the passage of condominium legislation, cooperative forms of ownership are rarely used in new multifamily housing. *Timeshare ownership* is the right to use, or the fee simple ownership of, real estate for a specified period of time each year, usually in one-week increments. Many multifamily buildings in vacation destinations around the world use this form of ownership.
- Design—Number of stories, walk-up or elevator, and parking arrangement.
- Type of Construction—Wood frame versus concrete or steel.

Within each general product category, further distinctions can be made based on the segmentation of the target market—by income, family composition, and age.

Each segment demands different floor plans, room sizes, finish details, and amenities. The feature box on the facing page summarizes the basic design categories for single-family and multifamily products.

Product types are often confused with forms of ownership. *Apartment*, for example, is often used as a generic term covering both multifamily rental and for-sale (condominium) products. Although the form of ownership greatly influences product design, marketing, and financing, it may refer to any product type. Technically, any rental property can be designed for, or converted to, for-sale condominiums. Similarly, any for-sale product can be operated as rental property if condominium covenants permit it.

This chapter focuses on multifamily residential development—rental and condominium apartments. No standard definition of multifamily or apartment types exists, but four major categories are available:

- Garden Apartments—One-, two-, and sometimes three-story walkup buildings built of wood frame on slab, with repeated floor plans. Garden apartments are typically designed with stairways serving two to four apartments on each stairway landing. Parking is at grade or tucked under part of the building. Densities range from 16 to 40 units per acre (40 to 100 per hectare), although densities higher than 35 units per acre (85 per hectare) stretch the limits of surface-only parking.

Renters by choice, who can afford to purchase a single-family home but choose to rent, now make up a significant market for luxury apartments. Tierra del Rey is a 170-unit rental community in the waterfront Marina del Rey area of Los Angeles, California.

- Low-Rise Apartments—Three- and four-story walkup or elevator buildings with repeated floor plans that are constructed of wood frame on top of a slab or concrete deck with one or two levels of parking above grade but below the deck. Densities range from 40 to 90 units per acre (100 to 220 per hectare).
- Mid-Rise Apartments—Five to eight stories, with elevators and central halls for apartment access on each floor. Buildings are usually long and squat. Densities range from 60 to 120 units per acre (150 to 300 per hectare).
- High-Rise Apartments—Above eight stories, with densities ranging from 80 to 200 units per acre (200 to 500 per hectare). Both mid-rise and high-rise apartments are constructed of steel frame or reinforced concrete. Depending on the location of the development, parking for these buildings may be in surface lots surrounding the building, at grade but below the first floor of the building (which may sit on a podium), in a full-fledged parking structure, or in a below-grade parking garage.

The construction cost for each of these product types determines the rent that must be charged. Lower-density wood-frame garden apartments with surface parking cost less than half as much to build as high-rise apartments with elevators, a steel or concrete frame, and structured parking. Underground parking adds another $20,000 per parking space. Greg Vilkin of Forest City Development describes the array of Los Angeles–area apartment products: "Apartments that rent for $1.00 per square foot [$10.75 per square meter] per month are two- to three-story walkups at 12 to 22 units per acre [30 to 55 per hectare] because that's economically what works. The next building type is the tuck-under product [grade-level parking tucked under the second floor] at 28 to 30 units per acre [70 to 75 per hectare] with rents about $1.20 per square foot [$13.00 per square meter] per month. Next is a podium deck with one-level subterranean or podium parking with as many as 40 units per acre [100 per hectare] and rents at about $1.50 per square foot [$16.00 per square meter] per month to start justifying these projects. Developers then look at markets as densities go higher and try to match them with the appropriate apartment types. The next step involves 80 to 100 units per acre [200 to 250 per hectare], which includes two subterranean stories of parking with four to five stories of wood-frame construction on top, with rents in California of about $1.75 per square foot [$20.00 per square meter] per month to make that work. Type I high-rise apartments are at the high end of the scale, but this type of development works in only a few cities, because that's where you're going to get $2.00 to $3.00 per square foot [$21.50 to $32.25 per square meter] rent per month for the apartments."[4]

Randolph Hawthorne of Rghventures observes that "people have segmented the residential market like many other industries—for example, the way Fidelity Investments segmented the mutual funds business with specific target markets. Clearly what has happened in multifamily units now is that developers tend toward the very high rental market (renters by choice) or work on affordable housing (much of it fueled by low-income housing tax credits). So, very little new development is occurring of what would be called 'bread-and-butter' apartment complexes aimed at the typical mid-range renter."[5] → lack of middle income housing

Two trends affecting apartments in the early 2000s are a movement by aging baby boomers back to the city and increasing demand for high-end luxury apartments. "In general, a lot of people who would move into houses are now coming back to rent high-end apartments in the cities, basically for lifestyle and convenience. In bread-and-butter apartments, on the other hand, the typical renter wants a lot of space (living and storage) and reliable and secure parking."[6] According to Randolph Hawthorne, "There seems to be a demand in the high end for apartments. People find it almost easier to finance a high-end project because it's not a big increase in rent to add amenities (and in fact the cost of amenities is less than the increase in rent and generates better financial feasibility). That means you can get your development off the ground when financing is not available for other types of apartments."[7]

Getting Started

Frequently, multifamily residential developers get their start by building single-family houses. Methods of construction and issues regarding marketing and design are similar, whether a developer is building single-family or multifamily units. The differences are often ones of scale and whether the units are for rent or for sale.

Most homebuilders (that is, builders of single-family houses) act as their own general contractors, and much of their profit in homebuilding is derived from construction. Profit margins, which typically range from 10 to 15 percent over hard and soft costs, must cover construction risk.

Many multifamily developers also do their own construction, but others hire third-party general contractors. Unless they already own a construction company, beginning developers should probably begin with a third-party general contractor. Once they have developed a track record, they can consider establishing a construction division in house.

The general contractor absorbs the construction risk and earns the construction profit, which typically runs from 5 to 8 percent of hard construction costs. The development profit, which typically runs from 8 to 15 percent of total cost, is in addition to the contractor's profit. The development profit represents the difference between total development cost and the capitalized value—the market value—of the property when leased.

In general, developers bring a wide variety of backgrounds, approaches, and concepts to their first projects. The key to success, however, is skillfully executing the steps in the development process and paying attention to every detail.

Project Feasibility

Project feasibility encompasses a number of activities that a developer must perform before committing to a given project. As feasibility analysis progresses, the developer must acquire more information that will indicate whether it makes sense to proceed further. During the feasibility period, the project may be canceled at any time, usually limiting losses to the costs of the feasibility study plus the cost of tying up the land. Positive information, however, usually justifies making the next increment of expenditure to acquire additional information.

Project feasibility includes four major activities:

- market analysis
- site selection/engineering feasibility
- regulatory approvals
- financial feasibility.

In some cases, these activities are performed sequentially; more often, they overlap. Developers must be satisfied, however, that all four activities have been completed satisfactorily before making a final go/no-go decision. Moreover, developers must treat the findings of their research objectively and not become enamored with their site or concept.

Developers rarely close on a site (finalize the acquisition) until they are certain that the project will go ahead; in practice, that means when all financing commitments

figure 4-1
Time Line of Events

Ideally, the developer does not close on the land until he is ready to start construction. In most cases, however, the land seller will not wait that long.

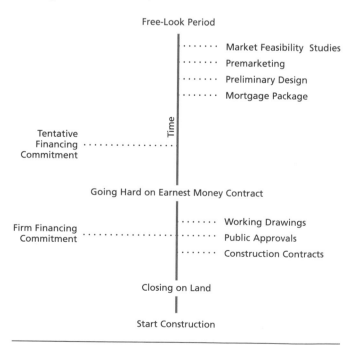

Experienced residential developers offer the following pointers for obtaining the most useful market data:

- A developer should not rely on the architect to do the market research. Decisions on project features such as unit mix, unit sizes, and amenities should be based on solid market research and on the tastes and preferences of the target market.
- The results of market analysis should be balanced with a developer's assessment of his ability to deliver a particular project.
- The determination of how much market share can be captured is critical. Capturing more than 2.5 percent of any market that absorbs more than 15,000 housing units per year is an ambitious undertaking. Although a developer in a small town may capture 50 percent of a market, the same developer in a large metropolitan area probably would not capture more than 5 percent.

- In an unfamiliar market, a new developer may estimate his potential market share by studying what success other developers have had in the area with a similar type of product and sales promotion program.
- It is extremely important to identify the idiosyncrasies of an unfamiliar market. It is likely that the proposed project must be modified somewhat to meet local tastes. ∎

---

are in place for both debt and equity, and major permissions have been received. For beginning developers, most of the steps taken during the feasibility period are aimed at securing financing and ensuring that no unexpected surprises show up later during construction or lease-up.

Market Analysis

Market analysis should precede site selection because the choice of sites depends on the market that the developer wants to target. High-quality market information is essential to determine accurately what to build, whom to build for, and how much to build.

No matter how familiar a developer is with the local submarket, an up-to-date market study is indispensable, both to support loan applications and to verify current rents and unit types that are most in demand (number of bedrooms, amenities, configurations, quality, for example). The primary benefit of analyzing the market before selecting a site is that such an analysis will help to identify the niches in the market.

The more clearly a developer defines the target market, the more specific the requirements are for a site. For example, when a developer knows who the prospective homebuyers or tenants are—their preferences, their income level, their family situation—then the developer has the facts needed to make careful decisions. Particular market needs imply particular site requirements. If a need for high-end apartments is identified, for example, a developer should be willing to pay more for a superior site with special amenities such as views, trees, water features, or recreational opportunities.

Developer Marvin Finger's niche is the high-end rental market in major cities around the country. The Finger Companies concentrates on developing inner-city sites in the affluent parts of town, focusing on upscale residential communities. "We identify the employment base and the retail locations where affluent renters would likely spend time. Further, we bracket the price of the land to what we can afford based on the final product appropriate to that market."[8]

The market study in the early stages does not need to be as comprehensive as it will have to be in the future. Market information is not only time-consuming but also expensive to obtain, and a developer should concentrate on specific issues:

- What geographic submarkets have the greatest need for apartments?
- What product type is in greatest need?
- What product types are attractive to renters and why?

The design of the Caruth at Lincoln Park reflects the traditional architecture and scale of its surrounding high-end neighborhood in Dallas, Texas. The 338-unit rental apartment project features pedestrian-scale streets, sidewalks, and below-grade or alley-access garages.

Institutional Housing Partners (IHP) undertook an analysis of the economic and market potential for a 79-unit loft condominium development in the San Francisco Bay Area in August 2001 as background to investment in the project. Straddling the border between the cities of Emeryville and Oakland, California, the subject property consisted of a 13-acre (5.3-hectare) site with an existing 115,000-square-foot (10,700-square-meter) manufacturing facility to be converted into single-family lofts. Levin, Menzies & Associates of San Francisco purchased the property in December 2000, obtained entitlements, and served as the developer for the project. Plans called for 12 below-market-rate units to satisfy local requirements and 67 market-rate units ranging from 800 square feet to 2,250 square feet (74 to 209 square meters), with pro forma prices ranging from $290,000 to $560,000. Planned amenities included gated parking, a signature lobby/entry area, in-house fitness center, and landscaped interior courtyard.

IHP undertook extensive in-house field and data research to 1) assess the status of prices for loft-style units in the San Francisco and Oakland areas, 2) identify all proposed projects that could effectively compete with the 46th Street Lofts, and 3) establish detailed assessments of pricing and sales absorption for the project.

An overview of the regional housing market consisted of analysis of the market for new lofts in nearby San Francisco and analysis of new home sales and the resale market for attached and detached housing for communities throughout the region (Figure A). Analysts concluded that although sales momentum had declined in the area, supply and demand in the resale market were stable.

A competitive project analysis determined that the main competitive pressure would come from future developments in the immediately surrounding area of Emeryville, although additional competition would come from other loft developments in the Jack London Square and downtown Oakland areas, several miles away. Ten proposed projects with a total of 750 units identified in Emeryville were ranked in terms of competitiveness and plotted on an area map. A micropipeline analysis was then undertaken using an estimated sales schedule for each project. The analysis pointed to a very strong absorption rate for the subject project, in part because of dormant demand for new attached and loft units.

A product pricing analysis was a critical component of IHP's investment decision-making process, particularly in light of potentially softening market conditions. Drawing from data provided by market consultants, internal data, and field research, IHP developed its own pricing schedule in which final unit pricing was determined based on the sum of the base price and potential price premiums (Figure B). Unit base prices were derived from sales data on comparable loft projects, and price premiums were based on individual unit locations in the building, views, and whether a patio was included (Figure C).

figure A

San Francisco Bay Area Housing Market Analysis, Months of Inventory by Price Segment

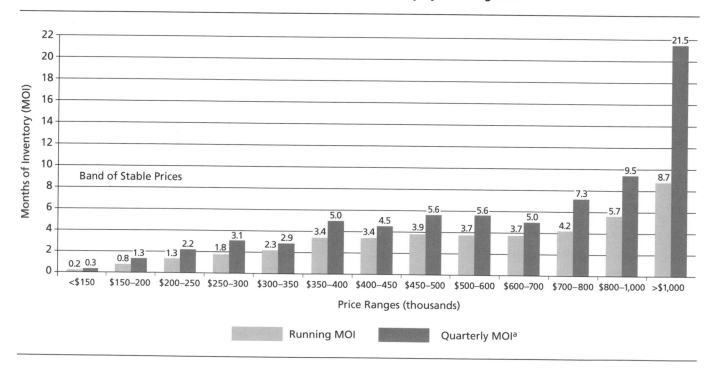

Band of Stable Prices

Price Ranges (thousands)	Running MOI	Quarterly MOI[a]
<$150	0.2	0.3
$150–200	0.8	1.3
$200–250	1.3	2.2
$250–300	1.8	3.1
$300–350	2.3	2.9
$350–400	3.4	5.0
$400–450	3.4	4.5
$450–500	3.9	5.6
$500–600	3.7	5.6
$600–700	3.7	5.0
$700–800	4.2	7.3
$800–1,000	5.7	9.5
>$1,000	8.7	21.5

[a]Quarterly months of inventory on a seasonally adjusted annualized basis.

Product Price Mix Analysis

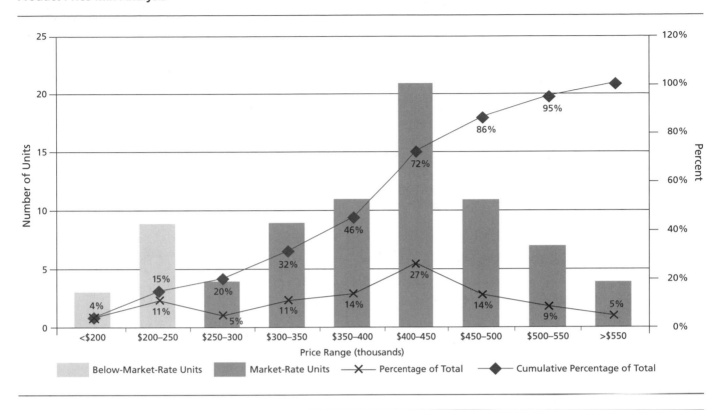

Analysis of the anticipated price and size mixes for the 46th Street Lofts indicated that the property would be well positioned for target buyers—convenience-driven urban professionals and first-time homebuyers. With nearly 75 percent of proposed units priced below $450,000, the region's entry-level price range, the project was expected to experience significant demand, even in a weak economy.

The overall conclusion of the research was that the proposed project economics and pro forma were solidly supportable and that any erosion in housing market conditions would not be of a magnitude to threaten the economic vitality of the project. ∎

Sources: Institutional Housing Investors, Irvine and San Francisco, California, and Levin Menzies & Associates, San Francisco, California.

figure C

Percent of Price Premium to Potential Unit Revenue: Comparison of 46th Street Lofts with Comparable Property

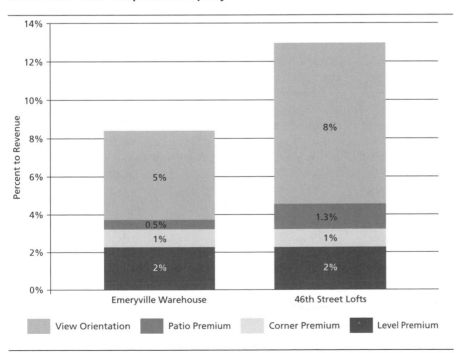

- Who is the target market? What are the demographic characteristics (age, income, household size) of renters who have the greatest need for apartments?
- What types of units or unit sizes are expected in this market? What is the appropriate rent range?
- What types of features, amenities, and services do renters expect?

The focus should be on *greatest need* rather than on vacancy rates or hottest areas, but a low vacancy rate points to a need. Need is measured by the relationship between demand (the absorption rate for new units) and supply of units (existing and anticipated) for a particular submarket. The submarket is identified not only by geographic area but also by product type and renter profile.

Developers often confuse existing supply with need. Certainly, historic absorption rates of existing supply are an important source of information for predicting future absorption, but because a particular product type is absent from an area does not necessarily mean that demand exists for that product type. "Often a product type is not there because *no supply* is equivalent to *no demand*."[9]

In summary, the goals of the preliminary market analysis before site selection are to:

- identify holes in the market—market niches where demand exceeds supply, locations and circumstances that offer special opportunities to build a project serving a particular market;
- define the target market for the project as narrowly as possible—number of units needed with particular design, amenity, and cost characteristics (number of rooms, size, and mix of units);
- develop a market strategy—whether to compete directly with other projects or to look for market niches.

Once a site is selected, the submarket should be analyzed in much greater detail. By collecting submarket information on rents, unit sizes, types of renters, levels of activity, and vacancies for each unit type, a developer will be able to determine how best to position a project. A project-by-project catalog of existing multifamily developments in the submarket should be created and used to decide whether to engage in direct competition with other local properties or to cater to a market niche that shows need and little competition.

Developer Marvin Finger says that once a site is placed under contract, "market analysis goes right to the top of the list of due diligence. In my firm, we send in-house staff people to interview property managers and analyze the current needs of tenants in properties that we consider to be in the same market and price range. Often we follow that up with a professional management company to confirm our findings."[10]

Location, site, and market potential determine the appropriate product to be developed. An urban locale demands a different type of residential development from a suburban one. The typically higher price of urban land requires higher densities. Greater automobile ownership in suburban communities necessitates more parking. A historic neighborhood might have specific height and architectural controls that dictate development parameters for a particular site. A waterfront site with panoramic views is better used for luxury condominiums than for entry-level housing.

The identified market segment should suggest special types of development. If the research detects strong demand from young families with small children, then the project should be planned with this market segment in mind, and the greatest percentage of units should be large enough for such households. If the target market is young, first-time renters, a moderately priced project with few amenities and maximum unit space for the dollar might fit the bill. A growing elderly population might suggest a need for a retirement community and elder care facilities. Amenities, features, design, and unit size should reflect residents' needs and should be determined through market research.

Although it is frequently easy to continue developing and marketing rental products that have leased well in the past, it can be rewarding, both financially and in terms of serving a public need, to develop a new type of product. Comparable residential projects might not currently exist in the immediate market area, but if the demand analysis shows a need, the analyst should explore the possibilities. In an overbuilt market, consideration of less standard types of development may lead to better opportunities but will require looking beyond the immediate market area for examples of successful comparable projects.

Traditionally, the largest multifamily housing markets have been those at both ends of the housing cycle: young singles and couples, and older empty nesters. In addition to these age-related cohorts, lifestyle niches provide further market potential. They include people in all income and age brackets who traditionally would purchase a single-family home but for any number of reasons choose multifamily living instead. In many instances, they make up target markets for more innovative product types.

Demand and Supply. A formal market analysis increases in importance as developers move farther away from familiar locations and product types. Beginning developers are unlikely to have the firsthand knowledge of local market conditions required to compete successfully and therefore need to make an extra effort to collect reliable market information before making even basic decisions about site selection.

Market Area. The developer's first task is to define the geographic study area. The study usually starts with the metropolitan area (data are available for metropolitan statistical areas [MSAs]) or the city where the project is to be located. Ultimately, it will focus on the narrow submarket area where the project will compete directly with other similar projects.

For rental apartments and condominiums, the submarket is defined as the area of generally comparable population characteristics and is usually limited to one

Designed to complement downtown redevelopment activities, the Landing at Jack London Square in Oakland, California, offers upscale rental housing overlooking the estuary in the city's urban core.

or two neighborhoods. Although the employment center or corridor that the project serves generally defines the broader market, the *primary market area* is usually restricted to a radius of two or three miles (1.5 or 2 kilometers) around the project and may even be smaller, especially if freeways, railroads, or other physical barriers exist between neighborhoods.

A *secondary market area* should also be defined. This area includes apartment projects that may not be directly competitive but offer an alternative to renters who are less sensitive about location.

The importance of defining the correct market area cannot be overemphasized. All too often, beginning developers omit competing projects or include so large an area that absorption rates are overestimated. In addition, many market areas are hard to define because they have no particular identity in the marketplace. This lack of identity poses problems not only for market definition but also for future lease-up and sales, because projects perform better in areas that have distinctive identities. Creating a market identity where none exists can be quite a challenge.

Various factors are considered in delineating the target market area for a proposed development:

• Travel Time from Major Employment Centers—With traffic congestion a serious problem in most metropolitan areas, housing decisions are usually based on proximity to employment. By identifying major employment centers and making assumptions regarding acceptable commuting time, market analysis can define a target market area.

• Mass Transportation Facilities and Highway Links—Commuting patterns and times are based largely on ease of access; thus, the target market's geographic size is influenced by the availability of mass transit, the location of transportation corridors, and the speed at which they operate at peak travel times. Convenience of transportation is an especially important consideration for multifamily development.

• Existing and Anticipated Patterns of Development—Most urban settings contain areas of both growth and decline. Growth areas might be distinguished by desirable attributes, such as proximity to employment, availability of affordable housing, physical attractiveness, and/or outstanding community facilities.

• Socioeconomic Composition—An area's income, age, household characteristics, and other demographic characteristics influence housing choice and location (but note that it is illegal in the United States to target market segments based on race, religion, or ethnicity).

• Physical Barriers—Natural features like rivers, bluffs, and parklands as well as manmade features like highways or intensive development can sometimes form a wall through which the market's boundaries do not penetrate.

- Political Subdivisions—Municipal boundaries can be especially important when adjoining jurisdictions differ markedly in political climate, tax policies, or status, or hold different attitudes about growth. School district boundaries are important if households with school-age children represent a target market segment. For easier data collection, it is sometimes necessary to manipulate a target market area to conform to a political jurisdiction such as a county or planning district in a county or city.

Demand Factors. On the demand side, the market study measures the number of households with particular age, size, and income characteristics. Market research firms employ many statistical techniques to refine their estimates of the number of households, but their basic approach is the same and takes into account the following factors:

- employment growth in *basic* industries (manufacturing and other industries that generate sales outside the city);
- employment growth in *service* industries (retail, local government, real estate, professionals, and others whose activities support the local community);
- percentage of growth expected to occur in the submarket;
- socioeconomic characteristics, such as population, age, education, income distribution, and household size and characteristics—families with children, couples without children, singles, divorcees with children, and so on;
- in- and out-migration.

Each factor must be carefully analyzed so that the developer understands the characteristics of the target population groups. From these statistics and other market surveys, the market analyst estimates the number of new households moving into an area or being created by marriage or divorce from within the area (by income, family composition, and age). From the total number of households, the number of those who will need apartments or condominiums is computed based on historic ratios combined with new information about income and preferences. These aggregate *absorption rates* (units absorbed per year) are then broken into absorption rates for individual product types and unit types. For example, a study that indicates demand for 500 apartments per year for a given market area is incomplete. It should subdivide that number according to product type: say, 350 adult units, 100 of which are luxury units, and 150 family units, 50 of which are luxury units.

Supply Factors. The supply of housing includes the existing housing stock, the units currently under construction, and the units that may be under construction in the future. The vacancy rate is usually considered the most important indicator of market need. Submarket vacancy rates, however, can be very misleading. For example, vacancies may be 40 percent in older buildings without central air conditioning but as low as 5 percent in newer buildings. Equally important, a 15 percent vacancy rate in a submarket with only 100 total units may be quickly absorbed, especially if a new company is planning to move into the area; elsewhere, however, 15 percent may indicate a very soft market. A more meaningful measure is *total number of months it will take to absorb the existing and planned inventory,* given the estimated demand as measured by the absorption rate expressed in units per month. This computation is illustrated in the next subsection.

Information about the existing housing stock and vacancy rates can best be determined by personal inspection and interviews with managers of surrounding apartment complexes. Even though such information may be proprietary, most managers are willing to cooperate, especially if the developer promises to reciprocate when the project is completed. Other sources of information include local real estate boards, local homeowners and apartment associations, public utility companies, mortgage companies, lending institutions, and the FHA.

The most common mistake that developers make in estimating supply is to ignore units on the drawing board—that is, projects that have not been announced and do not yet appear on any standard sources, such as city building permits. Often, local brokers, bankers, and architects are the best-informed sources concerning planned units. Of course, many such units may never be built and some planned projects may never get off the ground, but the most likely estimate of the number of units that will be built should be included in the projections of supply.

Net Market Absorption and Months to Absorb Current and Projected Inventory. The end product of the market analysis is the number of months required to absorb the current and projected inventory of units in that submarket. This figure should be broken down according to the different unit types planned for development. For example, the market study may show a short six-month inventory of one-bedroom units but a long 24-month inventory of three-bedroom units. The number of months to absorb the inventory should preferably be 12 or fewer for apartments. Twelve to 18 months is considered soft but not impossible; longer than 18 months should be avoided unless the developer has truly strong reasons to believe that his product will be absorbed significantly faster than the competition.

To illustrate, suppose that the market analysis indicates demand for 1,200 middle-income adult apartments per year in a quadrant of the city where a developer wishes to build. Suppose further that the current inventory of existing vacant units is 500 apartments with another 500 units under construction and that the developer is aware of 400 units on the drawing board. Realistically, the developer probably has learned of only half of all units planned (for a total of 800), but of the planned units, perhaps only 60 percent (480) will actually be built. Thus, the total supply of units is an estimated 1,480 and the number of months to absorb the projected inventory is 15:

Vacant units	500
Units under construction	500
Planned units estimated to be built	480
Total estimated supply	1,480
Total estimated annual demand	1,200
Total estimated monthly demand	100

Number of months to absorb projected inventory =

Total estimated supply ÷ Total estimated demand =

$\frac{1,480}{100} = 14.8$ months.

If the developer plans to begin construction immediately and to begin leasing in 12 months, the current and projected competition should be only about three months of inventory.

What is a reasonable number of months of absorption of inventory? Although no widely accepted guidelines exist, the developer should attempt to scale the project so that it can be leased within 12 months from the date it opens for occupancy. A soft market is usually one that has 18 months or more of projected inventory (including vacant, under-construction, and planned units).

The rationale for determining a reasonable number of months of absorption is the amount of interest reserve provided in the development budget for leasing the project. For an average-size apartment development relative to the local market, it is customary to include a 12-month leasing reserve plus some cushion in the form of a contingency reserve in case leasing takes 16 to 18 months. Although a larger reserve gives both the developer and the lender additional protection and comfort in case the market turns sour, competition usually limits the amount of the reserve. If the reserve is too large, the project will appear to be more costly than the competition, which in turn will scare off investors and lenders. It is a two-edged sword. Although reserves should be as large as possible, they cannot be too generous or the overall construction budget will be too high relative to the competition.

Capture Rates. The percentage of total demand in the submarket that a project absorbs (units leased or sold per month) is the *capture rate.* A fundamental principle of market analysis is that, in the long run, a project will capture its prorated share of total supply. If a project has 200 units and total supply currently available for leasing is 1,000 units, the developer's expected capture rate is 20 percent of the total supply. This capture rate is multiplied by the demand. In the above example, if demand is 100 units per month, the developer's prorated capture rate is 20 units per month. At this rate, it should take ten months to lease-up 200 units.

The most common mistake in market analysis is to assume that one's project is better than the competition and will achieve a higher capture rate than that indicated by the prorated share. The fallacy here is that competitors faced with losing market share will eventually cut prices to attract more tenants. In the long run, projects are unlikely to capture more than their prorated share, no matter how much better they are than the competition. This situation is exactly what happened in the recession of the late 1980s and early 1990s. Although it took longer than expected for owners to slash rental rates—often because their loan agreements stipulated that rents be a given rate or higher for loan funding—eventually rents were sliced by half or more to lease-up properties with high vacancies. Although a superior project may beat the competition even if its rents are 10 to 20 percent more, at a 30 to 50 percent discount, competitors will take away tenants. Therefore, no matter how superior one's property is to the competition, the market study should compute absorption based on a prorated capture rate. It is acceptable to include higher capture rates as well, but the financial analysis should be based on the more conservative prorated capture rate for estimating absorption.

Market Study Guidelines. Market studies serve two purposes: they facilitate internal decision making, and they provide documentation for lenders and investors. Lenders and investors are suspicious of market analyses, because developers often perform them as ex post facto justifications of decisions already made. Lenders and investors also know it is easy to find someone to write a market study showing that an area has a strong market.

The following guidelines should be observed for the market study to be most useful to lenders, investors, and developers:

1. Give specific directions to the market research firm concerning boundaries of both primary and secondary areas to be researched and the types of product to be researched. The larger the boundaries and the greater the number of product types, the more expensive the study will be.
2. Be aware that general statistical information is by itself inadequate for making market decisions. Critical differences exist between market studies that collect general statistics on the market and those that gather data on specific projects. The latter type is significantly more expensive but is essential unless developers are *certain* that the market is good and the competition is weak. General statistics—housing inventory, vacancies, average rents, average unit sizes, number of housing starts the past five years, number and dollar volume of permits, number of completions—are a useful starting point, but they must be supplemented with survey data from projects in the specific market area. Even if the market research firm has a data bank with project-by-project information, the data should be updated to reflect the latest market conditions.
3. Although vacancy rates may be helpful indicators of market demand in areas where rates are very low, in general, developers should not base their decisions about whether or not to proceed with a project on them alone. The preferred indicator is the number of months of inventory in the marketplace—the time it will take at projected absorption rates to consume the existing supply of units, units

under construction, and units on the drawing board. The number of months of inventory correlates directly with the amount of interest reserve that developers will need.

4. Developers should be sure to hire the best firm to undertake the market study. Firms that specialize in rental apartments and condominiums for particular market areas have information at their fingertips that other firms charge thousands of dollars to replicate. Developers certainly do not want to pay a firm to collect raw data from scratch. They should evaluate firms on the basis of their information sources and track records: How accurate have they been in their projections? Which banks and other financial institutions rely on their studies?

A good study of the market for multifamily residential development should include:

1. Figures for the total yearly demand for the metropolitan area, the city, and the submarket where the project is located. *Demand* refers to the number of multifamily units the marketplace will absorb during the period in which the project will be under construction and leasing.
2. Figures for total supply on a project-by-project basis. The data on each project should include:
   • target market, location, developer, completion date;
   • number of units by type (one bedroom, two bedroom, and so on);
   • square footage of each unit type;
   • rent or sale price for each unit, along with premiums and concessions;
   • vacancies (if possible, by unit type);
   • amenities of complexes; and
   • amenities of individual units (appliances, fireplaces, and so on).
3. An assessment of how many units (for rent or for sale) the market will absorb each month by unit type. Developers should guard against anticipating unreasonably large capture rates.

Geographic information systems (GIS) data make market analysis today much more sophisticated than it was even in the 1990s. "Fifteen years ago most clients didn't rely on market analysis and feasibility studies as much as they do today."[11] Randolph Hawthorne observes that a coherent marketing strategy is best developed in the feasibility stage. "That's clearly a plus, so that by the time you have a property that's coming out of the ground, you have information for marketing and leasing the units."[12] Market analysis today relies much more on focus groups and interviews to determine tenants' needs. Forest City, for example, has found that its upscale market is becoming much more service driven than it was before—watering plants, maid service, trash collection, concierge service, everything from ordering food to laundry service to personal trainers.[13]

Site Selection

According to an old real estate adage, the worst reason for developing a parcel is that you already own it. Ideally, developers first come up with an idea and then locate a suitable site. Many sites, however, are developed by owners who want to do something with their land. Although owning a plot of land may not by itself be a good reason for developing it, a site should not be eliminated from consideration just because a developer owns it. Almost every site is developable for some purpose. The developer's challenge is to identify the *highest and best use*—the use that maximizes the property's land value.

During the acquisition process (see the guidelines in Chapter 3), the ability to buy more time can be crucial for beginning developers. For example, when Peiser Corporation and Jerome Frank Investments purchased a site in Dallas for a 160-unit apartment project, they had what seemed to be a comfortable 120-day period during which to close. The project was economically attractive only if the partnership could obtain permission to issue tax-exempt housing revenue bonds available for low- and moderate-income housing. Approval from the city council was needed to issue the bonds. Because housing revenue bonds were a new program for the city of Dallas, the city council kept postponing the hearing date to allow more time to work out the details of the bond program. Fortunately, the partnership had negotiated the right to extend the closing by up to three months at a cost of $5,000 per month, and the extra time allowed the partners to receive the necessary approvals. Options to extend the closing are especially important in hot markets where the seller may receive a higher offer from another buyer.

Location and Neighborhood. It has often been said that the success of a real estate project depends on three factors: location, location, location. Location has many dimensions and has been the subject of considerable debate and comment in professional and academic journals.[14] Location can be categorized by macrolocation factors and microlocation factors.[15] *Macrolocation* refers to a property's proximity to major urban nodes, *microlocation* to a property's immediate environs. A property's long-term value depends not only on its current macrolocation and microlocation but also on how they are changing over time.

Both macrolocation and microlocation influence multifamily residential development. Macrolocation determines what part of the city offers the best long-term potential to preserve and enhance value—proximity to downtown and suburban employment centers, major growth corridors, medical centers, regional shopping and entertainment, regional parks, and recreation. Microlocation determines how well a site is situated in its immediate neighborhood —access to freeways or arterial roads, schools, parks, shopping, daycare and health care facilities. Ideally, a site is visible from a major road yet situated to ensure privacy, a sense of security, and a low noise level.

The ability to foresee changes in the urban fabric before others is one of the hallmarks of the most successful developers. Whether their predictions are based on careful research, intuition, luck, or some combination of all three, successful developers understand the dynamics of location well enough to survive over the long term.

An important component of their success is tied to the health of the cities or suburbs where they build. If the level of public services in a city declines, real estate values decline as well. Successful developers understand how much they depend on the physical and financial health of the communities where they build—which is why so many of them are active in public affairs.

It takes a lifetime of practice to fully understand all the dimensions of location that affect real estate value over time. Trends in public investment, private investment, design, demographics, and personal preferences are critical components of location. The rate of change in most American neighborhoods is very slow—often 30 to 50 years from peak to trough. It is much faster in poorly designed or poorly built neighborhoods, however, which often cycle downward within 15 to 20 years after they are built. On the other hand, some neighborhoods seem only to increase in value, often for reasons having to do with not only location but also the availability of shopping, open space, and other amenities, and ongoing investment by private owners to renovate and improve their properties.

The character of adjacent areas also affects the use of an undeveloped parcel. If adjoining areas are compatible, they can enhance the desirability of a proposed multi-family project. When they are deleterious or conflicting, developers should proceed very cautiously.

For many years, it has been common practice to place higher-density residential areas closest to commercial and industrial districts. Doing so serves as a buffer to single-family areas and allows the multifamily residential areas to benefit from proximity to the higher-capacity streets and more extensive commercial and employment districts required for heavier population densities. In turn, cluster and attached housing is often located as a buffer between multifamily housing and lower-density single-family development.

More recently, however, these planning practices have come into question. Local governments increasingly are willing to view development proposals in terms of integrating rather than separating different uses, a point illustrated by the increasing flexibility of land use controls through the widespread acceptance of mixed-use zoning and concepts that have long been associated with good planning but popularized by the new urbanists. Such development plans permit the mixing of previously separated uses, provided they are properly designed. The result is often a more varied, efficient, and attractive development.

A good site for multifamily development is one that has positive synergy with surrounding land uses. For example, a multifamily site in an established or emerging suburban business core offers residents the convenience

Special efforts to preserve natural features such as vegetation, water features, and wildlife habitats can pay off in marketing dividends for a project.

The Heritage at Freemason Harbour in Norfolk, Virginia, was developed on former public parking lots in the historic Freemason neighborhood.

of employment and commercial services within easy driving or walking distances. A site in an area with several other successful apartment projects may also be more desirable than one that lacks such neighborhood development. The best locations are naturally more costly than those with detrimental surroundings but are usually worth the expense, particularly for high-end development. When selecting sites for multifamily uses, developers should look for sites with positive synergy with surrounding uses and avoid those where uses are not likely to be compatible.

In considering compatibility, developers should be aware of potential liabilities that could be incurred from building residential units too close to conflicting uses. Proximity to large storage tanks of gas, oil, and other flammable material should be avoided. Fire protection must be considered in heavily wooded or fire-prone areas. Generally, protecting the public from such hazards rests with the municipality through its police powers (including zoning), but developers also need to protect themselves against possible liability by examining the potential conflicting uses near a given site.

Size and Shape. The best size for a site varies according to local market conditions, including lease-up rates, acceptable unit densities, and preferred amenity packages. For example, suppose a developer wants to build a project that can be leased within 12 months from its completion. If 15 units can be leased per month (180 units per year) and the product being built has an average density of 24 units per acre (60 per hectare), then the ideal site would be 7.5 acres (3 hectares). The size of a site is also influenced by property management considerations. Although the optimum number of units varies with each project, many developers consider 150 or 200 units the minimum number necessary to support a full-time on-site maintenance staff, and they look for sites that are large enough to accommodate that many units. In Los Angeles, where the availability and cost of land make it very difficult to assemble sites large enough for 200

units, developers often build several smaller complexes in a neighborhood that are run as a single project with shared property management and maintenance staffs.

Design options increase as the size of the site increases. A site that is too narrow prevents the inclusion of double-loaded parking or back-to-back units, which increase efficiency and reduce costs.[16] A site that is too deep, however, may require a loop road or a costly turnaround for fire trucks. One should always draw a preliminary site plan to see how a site can be laid out before going hard on an earnest money contract.

Beginning developers should look for individual tracts that are large enough to accommodate the type of product they want to build. They should avoid tracts that require assembling several parcels under different ownership. The process of land assembly is virtually a development business in itself, offering its own risks and rewards. Problems in assembling tracts include multiple closings, extra legal costs, multiple lenders, and the possibility that key parcels will not close. Incomplete assembly carries costly penalties for developers, who may have to pay exorbitant prices for outparcels or spend extra money on design and construction to squeeze as many units as possible on an inadequate site.

Accessibility and Visibility. In evaluating a residential site's accessibility, a developer should ask several questions:

- How will prospective tenants approach the property? What will they see as they drive to the site that may make it more or less desirable? (In brochures and advertisements, developers often select the most attractive, although not necessarily the shortest, route to a project.)
- How will visitors enter the property? Will they be able to turn left across traffic? Can approval for a median strip or curb cuts be obtained if necessary?
- Will the current transportation network support the additional traffic generated by a new development?

- What is the heaviest traffic burden that the planned project will create? Will that burden prevent residents from exiting the project easily?
- During peak hours, are exit roads clogged with traffic?
- How long will it take residents to travel to work, schools, shops, and recreational facilities?
- Is the site served by public transportation?
- Is road construction planned? If so, rentals will be severely impaired during the construction period.
- Are existing roads adequate for the type of development planned? (In general, high-density development requires collector and/or arterial street access, whereas lower-density development can be undertaken on smaller interior streets.)

Visibility is critical for marketing and leasing, for if prospective residents cannot see the project, they will not know it is there. A developer can enhance a project's visibility in several ways, including using special design elements, special landscaping features, striking colors, off-site signage, and nighttime lighting, especially of the frontage. The aim should be the creation of an appealing, distinctive project.

Site Conditions. Apartment and condominium development offers somewhat more latitude with respect to the physical characteristics of a site than do other types of development. A developer of multifamily residential projects is less constrained by slopes and by the size and shape of parcels because residential building pads tend to be smaller and more flexible than, say, pads for office or industrial buildings. Nonetheless, a developer must still carefully evaluate every potential aspect of a site, including its slope, geology, soils, vegetation, and hydrology.

Slope and Topography. Developers have always been attracted to hilltops and other places offering views. Moderately sloping sites are preferable to steep or flat land. Slopes create opportunities for more interesting design, such as split-level units and varied rooflines. They also help to reduce the amount of excavation needed to provide structured parking in denser developments (densities greater than 35 units per acre [85 per hectare] usually require some form of structured parking).

Improvement costs, on the other hand, rise sharply on slopes greater than 10 percent. Retaining walls, special piers, and other foundations can add to the time and cost of construction. Further, some cities—San Diego, for example—have adopted hillside development ordinances that restrict development of steeply sloping sites. Allowable densities are reduced on slopes greater than 15 percent, and development is forbidden on slopes greater than 25 percent.[17] Flat land may also create additional expense. Sewers must slope downward to create flow; thus, pumping stations may be required if a site is entirely flat or if part of the site lies below the connection point to the city sewer line.

Geology, Hydrology, and Soils. In earthquake-prone areas, a geologic survey is essential. If a site is crossed by fault lines, it may be unbuildable. The same is true of a site in an area with abandoned subterranean mines. Even though building around the fault line or mine may be possible, obtaining insurance may be impossible. Moreover, proximity to a fault line creates an intractable marketing problem.

If a site contains, or borders on, a creek or wetlands area, a floodplain study must be conducted. Areas that are wet only part of the year may be considered vernal pools, which may be protected under the North American Wetlands Conservation Act of 1989.[18] Standing water on a site may also indicate the presence of an underground stream, which must be located, because some portion of the site will almost certainly be unbuildable. A developer should be able to obtain a rough approximation of how much land lies in the floodplain or wetlands area by hiring a civil engineer who has done previous work in the immediate area.

Like floodplains, soil conditions are problematic. Even if a site looks clean, a developer should always hire a geologist to take soil samples of a site before purchasing it. Geologists usually take at least one core sample near each corner of a property and one or more in the center to determine what type of soil is present, its viscosity, its plasticity, and the depth of the water table and underlying bedrock.

Good soil like sandy loam is moderately pervious to water. Clay soils, however, expand and contract with water, which may cause foundations to crack. Impervious soils cause increased water runoff. If rock is located near the surface of a site, excavation may cost ten to 20 times more than for a site with deep soil.

Vegetation. Plant cover provides useful information about soil and weather conditions.

> Red maple, alder, tupelo, hemlock, and willow indicate wet ground that is poorly drained. Oak and hickory grow on warm, dry land, spruce and fir in cold, moist places. Pitch pine and scrub oak are signs of very dry land and of good drainage. Red cedars mark poor soil. This list can easily be extended in any locality. It is a list worth learning and using as a predictor of site constraints.[19]

Special efforts should be made to preserve mature trees. Large, healthy trees face several dangers. Heavy foot traffic or parked cars under a tree compact the soil and may kill the tree. Workmen often do not like saving trees because it makes their work more time-consuming and costly. Trees often die during construction because of paint or chemical poisoning. Even if they survive construction, they often die later because their root systems have been disturbed or because the amount of water they receive has been altered. A developer should consult an arborist about saving trees, and should clearly mark and place a protective barrier around trees that are to be preserved.

Other forms of vegetation also may require special handling. Grasslands, particularly in coastal areas, are a crucial component of erosion control. Many kinds of grasses, vines, shrubs, and wildflowers provide wildlife habitats or are included on the endangered species lists, and their preservation becomes a legal issue.

Stormwater. In the past, stormwater runoff has been handled in the most convenient method possible: the rapid disposal of surface water through closed, manmade systems. Stormwater runoff has often been mismanaged under this philosophy, aggravating the velocity and volume of runoff problems downstream and increasing the pollution of local streams. Potential legal issues concerning the effects of stormwater management on adjacent properties during and after construction have led many jurisdictions to adopt stormwater management standards restricting the runoff's quantity and velocity after development to no more than predevelopment levels. Many areas also require filtration of stormwater before its release.

The preparation of a functional and aesthetic stormwater runoff plan requires coordination among the project's architects, engineers, planners, and landscape architects. Much of the runoff can be handled through passive design elements, including proper grading and landscaping materials rather than engineering systems. Such considerations need to be part of the early design plan. Recent trends in stormwater management encourage eliminating large stormwater ponds in favor of smaller "rain gardens" located throughout the development. Local stormwater management regulations may vary by jurisdiction.

Existing Buildings. Developers should proceed with caution before demolishing existing buildings on a site. Most cities have laws that protect historic structures, and some cities have laws that restrict the eviction of tenants. Before purchasing a site for complete renovation or redevelopment, developers should make certain that they can evict the current tenants. Eviction can take a long time—often four to six months or more—and can be expensive, especially if relocation assistance is required from the developer. Relocation payments may run as high as $3,000 to $5,000 or more per tenant. In extreme cases, the developer may be required to find or build the tenant a comparable unit.

Environmental Issues. Environmental due diligence is required now for every development site (see Chapter 3). A preliminary Phase I investigation, performed for as little as $500 to $1,000, gives the developer a history of the property and indicates the need for further investigation, if any. Every potential lender requires at least a Phase I report, so a standard part of purchase contracts is that the offer is subject to the buyer's determination that no significant environmental problems exist.

Most urban infill sites have at least one environmental issue. In most cases, no remediation is necessary, but if dirt must be removed or, in the worst case, groundwater is contaminated, cleanup costs can be enormous. The seller is responsible for cleanup, but once the buyer has closed, he becomes part of the chain of title and may be liable in the future. In any case, the cleanup must be completed before lenders will finance new construction. Because environmental problems are so prevalent, lenders seek environmental insurance policies and guarantees from companies to indemnify them from problems. The

insurance can be costly, but it has made many sites developable that were not so before.[20]

Easements and Covenants. An easement is one party's right to use the property of another. The land for whose benefit the easement is created is called the *dominant tenement.* The land that is burdened or used is called the *servient tenement.* Generally, unless easements are created with a specific termination date, they survive indefinitely. Only the beneficiary of the easement—the dominant tenant—can extinguish them. Subsequent owners of property that have existing easements may have to purchase the easement back from the current beneficiaries.

Protective covenants, also called *deed restrictions,* are private restrictions that *run with the land;* that is, once created, they remain in force for all future buyers or heirs. Deed restrictions may be created by a property owner at any time. Once created, however, they remain in force unless all parties subject to the covenants agree to remove them.

Developers usually establish deed restrictions at the time they subdivide, or *plat,* a property. Some covenants expire automatically after a number of years under state statute as in Houston, Texas, but others never expire. To be enforceable, covenants usually must be filed with the county recorder and thus will appear in a title search.

Developers must carefully review any and all deed restrictions, for deed restrictions can kill a project even after developers have invested many months of time and money. In Dallas, for example, one case involved a subdivision that still had single-family-only restrictions in place despite the presence of many nonresidential uses. A developer bought property in that subdivision, assuming that the existing nonresidential uses effectively voided the restrictions. Although the developer may have been able to overturn the restrictions in court, he found that no bank would lend him money on a site that had restrictions against the intended use. The developer lost the property.

A dominant tenant who knows that the servient tenant must have a release from an easement to proceed with development enjoys a powerful bargaining position and can exact almost any price for that release. Land sellers usually have more rapport with the dominant tenant than the developer, as a new buyer, has. Therefore, developers should enlist sellers' assistance to clear up any easement problems before closing on the land.

Several important points should be kept in mind regarding easements:

- Easements, especially utility easements, often do not show up on plats. Double-check with the utility companies, and check the deed.
- Never rely on a site plan provided by the seller. Always order a title survey before going hard on the contract. The title survey will indicate any recorded easements.
- Pipeline, utility, and other *easements in gross*[21] usually give the utility company the right to make repairs within the easement at any time. If, for instance, a concrete driveway has been built over the easement,

a utility company may still enter the property with minimum notice to repair or maintain the utility line without liability or obligation to restore any damage done to the owner's improvements. Where possible, developers should try to locate easements in greenbelts, pedestrian pathways, and other open spaces.

Utilities. Water, sanitary and storm sewers, electricity, gas, cable television, and telephone service are critical factors in site selection. Before purchasing a site, a developer should always confirm that services are not only nearby but also available. It is not unusual, for instance, for a major water line to run adjacent to a property but be unavailable to that property because the line's capacity is already committed or because the city is concerned about a loss in water pressure. To verify that service is available, a developer should never simply take the word of the land seller and should instead visit the appropriate city departments or pay a civil engineer to do so.

Water and sanitary sewer services are the most costly utilities to bring in from off site. When water and sanitary utilities must be brought in from off site, the developer should undertake the work rather than wait for the city or utility company to do it to ensure that the work is performed speedily. Electricity, gas, and telephone services are usually provided by private utility companies. Except for remote sites, these utility companies usually provide service to the site at no cost to the developer. Each locality has its own fee structure and method of handling utility services.

A developer should ask several questions about utilities:

- How long will it take to obtain service?
- How much will it cost?
- When is payment due?
- When does one have to apply for service?
- Are public hearings involved (they may cause delays and increase the political risk)?
- Is the provision of service subject to any potential moratoriums?
- Are easements needed from any other property owners before services can be obtained?
- Is the capacity of the service adequate?

Some municipalities with scarce water have responded by imposing high water hookup fees on residential building permits. Others have imposed strict requirements for conserving water, including flow-restricting devices on plumbing features, installation of drought-tolerant landscaping, and, in some extreme circumstances, partial or total moratoriums on development until new water supplies are available. Developers should check the availability of water at a site and, if it appears that supplies are limited, understand fully what will be required before a supply can be hooked up to a site.

Regulatory Issues. Securing the necessary regulatory approvals has become the developer's primary concern in many communities. The regulatory process has become increasingly difficult in recent years, and the ability to pass safely through the regulatory minefield plays an increasingly important role in determining a developer's success.

The increasing complexity of development regulation has created a whole new field of development—developers who bear the risk of obtaining necessary approvals and entitlements (see Chapter 3). Even where land is appropriately zoned, no guarantee exists that developers will be able to build what they want to build. New players in the regulatory process, such as design review boards and neighborhood planning committees, must approve developers' plans before a building permit is issued. New setback, parking, environmental, air quality, and fire code regulations affect the density that developers can achieve on a parcel, irrespective of the allowable density under the zoning.

The regulatory process is described more fully in Chapter 3. The following issues arise more frequently with multifamily development.

Zoning. Zoning determines the building envelope and the density for a site. Specific issues that are usually covered in the zoning code include the number of units allowed, parking requirements, height limitations, setback restrictions, floor/area ratios, and unit size requirements. Some zoning codes give actual density constraints (for instance, up to 24 units per acre [60 per hectare]), whereas others stipulate minimum land area per unit (for instance, 1,500 square feet [140 square meters] of land per unit). The other major zoning constraint for apartments is parking. A common requirement is one parking space per bedroom (up to two spaces for a three-bedroom apartment) plus spaces for visitors. A developer may petition to change the zoning or obtain a variance, but it is often a long and arduous process, especially if higher densities are involved.

Many suburbs are very hostile to multifamily housing, and NIMBYism (the "not-in-my-backyard" syndrome) tends to focus as much or more on multifamily development than any other product type. Jerome Frank, Jr., advises, "For a beginning developer, it's very difficult—unless the land is already zoned—to find and develop a piece of property that needs rezoning. Find land that's already zoned and pay for the zoning."[22] Marvin Finger adds, "There has been a definite trend toward more restrictive zoning from the relevant boards; over the last 15 years, there has been a greater supply of multifamily housing, and much of it is not pleasing. Even extremely low-density upscale developments represent nothing but evil to the surrounding single-family owners. To overcome this perception, you have to employ the premier professional, who would probably be an attorney, to negotiate your case in that neighborhood. It cannot be done in house."[23]

Fire Codes. Fire codes have particular importance for residential construction, because residential buildings are usually wood frame and therefore especially prone to the risk of fire. Fire codes determine the number of stairways each unit requires as well as the maximum distance each unit must be from a fire hydrant. The codes directly affect the number of units that can be placed on a site as well as the cost of building them.

Many communities encourage developers to install fire sprinklers in their apartment projects by imposing stringent requirements on wood frame construction without sprinkler systems. Beginning developers should consult architects who are familiar with local fire codes and the type of product under consideration to determine the best way to meet fire regulations.

Rent Control. Developers considering multifamily rental housing projects must consider the degree of rent control prevailing in the area and local politicians' general attitudes about rent control. Rent control ordinances often restrict potential developers' and investors' ability to obtain the rent required to make the project feasible.

Apart from the obvious economic disadvantages of rent control that restricts rent increases, developers find financing harder to obtain for projects in communities with rent control. Rent control laws differ dramatically from community to community. Most rent control laws exempt new projects. Many laws also allow the landlord to raise rents to market rates when a tenant moves out (called *vacancy decontrol*). Until recently, some communities, such as Santa Monica and Berkeley, California, did not allow rents to be raised to market value, even when a unit was vacated. Not surprisingly, few new rental units were built in these cities. Vacancy decontrol has helped to reignite development in these cities. Instead of developing rental apartments, however, developers are building mostly for-sale condominiums, which promise greater profit because of the lack of construction of condominiums for so many years.[24]

The threat of rent control can hurt developers almost as much as its enactment. Even if existing rent control regulations exempt new buildings, the possibility of a future referendum or a vote by the city council to place new buildings under rent control creates uncertainty about one's ability to raise rents. This uncertainty makes it more difficult for developers to raise the necessary equity and debt financing at favorable rates.

Building Codes. Building codes are legal documents that set minimum requirements for sanitary facilities, electrical work, lighting, ventilation, construction, building materials, fire safety, plumbing, and energy conservation. They are local laws that vary from city to city. The United States has no uniform building code, but one of four separate model codes is generally used as the basis for a municipality's set of regulations. Although the trend is toward greater uniformity, developers must still deal with a diverse set of codes that is often applied inconsistently.

A major problem for developers is that governments do not accept responsibility for review of the plans. Although one department may review and stamp a plan *approved,* the local government's field inspectors, who exercise considerable control over a project, often interpret the codes differently and do not advance an opinion before construction. To make the process of obtaining permits as smooth as possible, developers should work with local architects. Any questions about interpreting the local

For teachers only, Casa del Maestro is a 40-unit apartment community that provides quality affordable housing in the cost-prohibitive market of Santa Clara, California.

building code should be addressed as early as possible in meetings with those in the building department who check plans. During construction, it is helpful for the developer to build a strong working relationship with code enforcement officials—in particular, building inspectors.

Condominium Conversions. Condominium conversions —the conversion of rental units to for-sale units—provide an attractive entry point for beginning developers because seller financing is often available. The development process is shorter and less risky than in other types of multifamily residential development, and the amount of money developers must raise is also usually smaller. The major risk involves carrying interest for the units during the sale period and renovation expenses for upgrading the units.

Condominium conversions are subject to special regulations in many communities. Concern about preserving their rental housing stock has caused cities such as New York to pass laws that limit or complicate condominium conversion. Not surprisingly, restrictions on conversion often are found in communities with strict rent control laws. Rent control can reduce the incentive for developers to build new units and reduce the value of existing apartment complexes, thus increasing the premium for converting them to condominiums.

Before entering the conversion business, developers should carefully investigate local procedures, which can be time-consuming and intricate. The advice of a local attorney who specializes in condominium conversion is critical and should be sought before developers commit to a project.

Developers should also be wary of litigation over construction defects. This litigation resulted in frenzied activity in California in the 1990s among attorneys who organized condominium associations to sue their developers before a ten-year time limit on construction lawsuits expired. Attorneys told directors of condominium associations that if they did not take action against the developers in a timely fashion, the directors would be liable for failing to protect the interests of the condominium owners. As a result, a majority of all condominium projects built or converted within the previous ten years became involved in lawsuits against the developer, contractor, and architect. The extraordinary litigation risk associated with condominiums caused new construction to fall dramatically, impacting high-cost areas like Orange County and Los Angeles County where condominiums had provided the major source of for-sale housing under $200,000. Changes in the laws to remove liability for directors, combined with tighter construction supervision, have restored condominium construction activity somewhat, but concerns about litigation still overshadow the market.

Exactions and Impact Fees. To recover what is perceived as the public cost of new development, local ordinances often require developers to dedicate land, improvements, or fees as a condition of approval. In the past, these dedications were primarily for the basic infrastructure necessary to serve the development site, such as on-site roads and utilities. Now, however, dedications or exactions are often required for off-site improvements above and beyond the immediate infrastructure needed for a development site.

Today, exactions may be required for improvements to arterial streets, flood control facilities, sewage treatment plants, schools and parks, fire and police stations, open space, or almost any other public necessity.[25] Developers are required to share the costs of infrastructure needed by the proposed subdivisions even if the improvements are not situated directly on the new development site. Also known as shared infrastructure costs, they are an alternative to development exactions, impact fees, and growth fees. Despite many alternatives for financing capital improvements, including taxes, general obligation bonds, revenue bonds, tax increment financing, user charges, special assessments, and special districts, the trend has been toward more widespread use of exactions by local governments.[26]

Some local governments have adopted standards by which to measure exactions, while others determine exactions project by project, thereby complicating a developer's ability to predetermine a project's feasibility. When no standards exist to measure exactions, developers can use exactions levied on similar developments in the area to price exactions for a feasibility analysis and as a basis for negotiating equity.

In small developments, which characterize the lion's share of multifamily housing developments, it is more likely that exactions will be made through impact fees rather than dedication of land and infrastructure improvements. Impact and other permitting fees, however, especially for schools, may be extraordinarily high—more than $25,000 per unit in some California communities in 2002. A requirement for dedication of parks, schools, and other public facilities would be too great a burden for a small site. Instead, fees are combined with those obtained from other small developments to provide the necessary public improvements at some off-site location.

Financial Feasibility Analysis

The next important step in feasibility analysis is financial feasibility. In essence, this analysis is the one lenders want to see to make sure the project will live up to its performance expectations. How one analyzes the financial feasibility of apartments is similar to the process used for all income property. The steps of financial analysis begin with a simple back-of-the-envelope capitalization and end with a multiyear discounted cash flow analysis that includes returns to investors or joint venture partners.

Evaluating financial feasibility for all income property development involves several stages of analysis, each more detailed than the previous one, from land purchase to a final go/no-go decision on a property. How much analysis is necessary before purchasing land? Experienced developers working in their own area know from past experience what they can spend. They know the local market and therefore know when they see a good deal.

Beginning developers, however, must overcome several handicaps:

- lack of experience in determining a workable price;
- lack of visibility in the brokerage community, hence hearing about deals only after larger players have rejected them; and
- less staying power, so they must be more careful about which deals to pursue.

Sophisticated developers perform a sequence of financial analyses for income properties, starting with simple capitalization analysis and ending with monthly cash flow analysis of the development period. The main difficulty that developers face in terms of financial feasibility studies is understanding what type of analysis is appropriate at what stage. Too much detail too early is a waste of time and money. Too little detail gives insufficient information on which to base informed decisions.

Analysis of any income property involves five stages:

- Stage 1 (the pro forma statement)—Simple capitalization of pro forma NOI;
- Stage 2—DCF analysis of annual cash flows during stabilized cash flows of the operating period;
- Stage 3—Combined analysis of the development and operating periods;
- Stage 4—Monthly cash flows during the development period;
- Stage 5—DCF analysis for investors.

This chapter concentrates on Stages 1, 2, and 3, and a before-tax version of Stage 5. Of all the stages of analysis, Stage 2 is the most important. It is known by various names, including *DCF analysis* and *justified investment price analysis*. Appraisers do a form of Stage 2 analysis when they compute the unleveraged returns on a building from the time of stabilized occupancy to final sale in seven or ten years.[27]

figure 4-2

The Development Period and the Operating Period

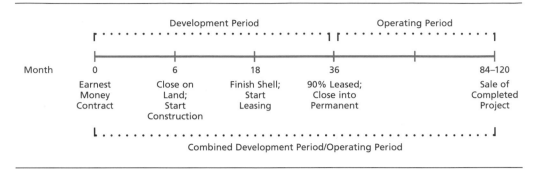

As part of the general framework, it is helpful to distinguish the development period from the operating period (Figure 4-2). The development period runs from the time the developer purchases the land through lease-up of the property. Although the operating period begins when the property is put into service, appraisers and lenders typically evaluate the property from the time it reaches stabilized occupancy, normally 90 or 95 percent, when the permanent mortgage is funded through final sale. Stage 2 analysis is used to evaluate this operating period (although in some cases the permanent mortgage may be funded in stages).

Stage 2 analysis is the developer's version of the architect's sketch pad. Just as the architect tries many versions of a building before settling on the final design, the developer goes through many iterations of Stage 2 analysis. For the first iteration, rents, expenses, costs, and other assumptions are crude estimates based on cursory evaluation. By the time developers are ready to commit to the earnest money contract (that is, remove any contingencies that may allow them to get back the full purchase deposit on the land), they should have the best information possible about the property's expected performance. This information forms the basis for computing expected returns to the developer and investors, assuming the property is purchased at the given price. If the property is to be built, then the total estimated project cost from inception to stabilized occupancy is used instead of the purchase price.

The stages of analysis correspond to major hurdles in the course of financing a project. Stage 1 is the developer's first cursory analysis based on simple pro forma income and cost estimates. Stage 2 justifies the overall value of the investment as an operating real estate venture and is given to mortgage brokers and lenders who will provide permanent financing. Stage 3 gives the developer a picture of the overall development, from inception through final sale. Stage 4 is given to the construction lender in support of the estimated construction loan required and interest reserves during construction and lease-up. Stage 5 is given to potential investors in support of the returns they will receive if they invest in the property under a specific deal structure.

Stage 1—Simple Capitalization. Figure 4-3 illustrates the stages of analysis for a new 200-unit apartment complex, Shady Hollow, in Dallas, Texas (see www.pred.uli.org for more information). The complex has one-, two-, and three-bedroom units averaging 958 square feet (90 square meters) that rent for an average of $1,021 per month. Estimated development costs total $14,849,637. Project cost and operating information are adapted from data for a new property under construction by Trammell Crow Company in Mesquite, Texas, a suburb east of Dallas. (That project, Alexan Town East, is a three-story wood-frame building with surface parking. The 224-unit project has 90 carports and 72 detached garages. Net density for this type of project runs 20 to 22 units per acre [49 to 54 per hectare] in Dallas and Austin.[28])

Stage 1a—Rental Summary. Stage 1 analysis is used to develop the two simple return measures common to all income properties—overall capitalization rates and cash-on-cash returns. To compute these ratios, begin by projecting NOI, project development costs, and leverage (maximum mortgage amount) for the proposed project. Figure 4-3a shows the rental summary. Rents per square foot for one-bedroom units ($1.22) are substantially higher than for larger two- and three-bedroom units. Usually, rent per square foot decreases as units become larger. Three-bedroom units in Dallas in 2002, however, were in comparatively short supply, so rents per square foot for three-bedroom units were $1.07 per square foot versus $.97 per square foot for two-bedroom units. These rents are estimates that the developer believes can be achieved in Shady Hollow when the project comes on line in 2004. They are based on a careful analysis of comparable properties in the market area of Shady Hollow.

Stage 1b—Pro Forma NOI. The first step is to create a pro forma statement that estimates rents and expenses for the stabilized project. Inputs include the type and size of apartments to be built and market rents for the apartments (see Figure 4-3b). The other needed inputs are estimated vacancy rate and operating expenses. Both income and expense estimates should reflect local conditions and any specific features of the project. Income and expenses should reflect conditions as they will be

figure 4-3a
Stage 1a: Rental Summary

4 Unit Type		Number of Units	Rent per Square Foot	Square Feet per Unit	Total Square Feet	Rent per Month per Unit	Total Annual Rent for Unit Type
5							
6							
7	A-1 1-Bedroom	80	$1.22	725	58,000	$884.50	$849,120
8	B-1 2-Bedroom	90	$0.97	1,050	94,500	$1,018.50	$1,099,980
9	C-1 3-Bedroom	30	$1.07	1,300	39,000	$1,391.00	$500,760
10							
11							
12							
13	Total Rental Income	200	$1.07	958	191,500	$1,020.78	$2,449,860
14	Other Income (parking, concessions)						$40,000
15	Total Income	200	$1.08	958	191,500	$1,037.44	$2,489,860

figure 4-3b
Stage 1b: Pro Forma NOI

3		Factor	Annual Revenue/Cost
4	Income		
5	Gross Potential Rent (from Figure 4-3a)		$2,489,860
6	Less: Vacancy	5.00%	$124,493
7			
8	Adjusted Gross Rent		$2,365,367
9			
10			
11	Total Cash In		$2,365,367
12			
13			
14	Expenses		
15	Property Management	3.50% of Adjusted Gross Rent	$82,788
16	Controllable Costs (salaries, maintenance, repairs, marketing)	$2,200 per unit per year	$440,000
17	Real Estate Taxes	2.60%	$390,000
18	Insurance	$275 per unit	$55,000
19			
20	Total Expenses		$967,788
21			
22	Net Operating Income		$1,397,579

at the time that leasing begins; for example, if the project is expected to require a year to design and build, rents and expenses should be projected as of a year from now. For Shady Hollow, the pro forma indicates total income of $2,365,367 and NOI of $1,397,579 (see Figure 4-3b).

Stage 1c—Maximum Loan Amount. The project's pro forma NOI is the basis for determining the size of the permanent mortgage for the project. Lenders use two common criteria: debt coverage ratio (DCR) and loan-to-value (LTV) ratio to determine the maximum loan amount. The maximum loan amount is the lesser of the resulting loan amounts computed by the two methods.

The debt coverage ratio is a tool used to measure the financial risk of an investment. It is calculated by dividing NOI by the debt service for the project. A DCR of 1.0 means that NOI equals the debt service for the project. For income-producing properties, most lenders re-

figure 4-3c
Stage 1c: Maximum Loan Amount

3 Pro Forma NOI and Value	
4 Pro Forma NOI (from Figure 4-3b)	$1,397,579
5 Capitalization Rate	9.00%
6 Value (NOI/Cap Rate)	$15,528,657
7	
8 Loan Terms	
9 Interest Rate	6.5%
10 Amortization (years)	30
11	
12 Using Loan to Value	
13 Maximum LTV	70.00%
14 Maximum Loan Based on LTV	$10,870,060
15	
16 Using Debt Coverage Ratio	
17 Monthly NOI	$116,465
18 Maximum DCR	1.25
19 Maximum Monthly Payment (NOI/DCR/12)	$93,172
20 Maximum Loan Based on DCR	$14,740,810
21	
22 Maximum Loan (Lesser of LTV or DCR Result)	
23 Maximum Principal	$10,870,060
24 Monthly Payment	$68,706
25 Annual Debt Service	$824,474

quire a DCR of at least 1.2. The DCR represents the cushion by which the NOI could fall before the property had insufficient cash flow to pay the debt service on the mortgage. The greater the cushion, the less risk of default. Lenders prefer as much cushion as they can get. Developers prefer more leverage (to obtain as large a mortgage as they can get), because it reduces the requirement for equity.

The DCR can be applied directly to NOI to determine the maximum payment that can be assumed for the loan. Given the lender's requirements for amortization and interest, it is then possible to calculate the maximum loan that could be serviced by the project's income, less the required coverage. In this case, a DCR of 1.25 would allow monthly payments of $93,172 (monthly NOI divided by 1.25). Assuming an interest rate of 6.5 percent and 30-year amortization, $14,740,810 is the maximum loan a lender would allow (the present value of $93,172 for the given rate of interest and term (months): PV(PMT = $93,172, i = 6.5/12, n = 30 x 12).

To establish the maximum loan available using the LTV ratio, it is necessary to first determine the project's value. The value can be calculated by applying a capitalization rate to the pro forma NOI. The capitalization rate is determined by the market and by the recent selling price of similar properties. It reflects the relationship between a property's income and its value. The lender ultimately requires an appraisal to verify the income and assumptions about the capitalization rate used to establish the value. The value is then multiplied by the LTV ratio to determine the maximum loan amount. In this case, a capitalization rate of 9 percent yields a value of $15,528,657. With an assumed maximum LTV ratio of 0.70, the most the lender will lend is $10,870,060.[29]

Lenders typically look at both criteria when underwriting a loan and use the more restrictive one. When interest rates are low, LTV tends to be more restrictive, and when interest rates are high, DCR tends to be more restrictive. In this example, LTV is more restrictive, so the maximum loan on the property would be $10,870,060 (see Figure 4-3c).

Stage 1d—Development Costs. Development costs are the other part of the equation needed to evaluate a project's feasibility. An overall static cost estimate for the project must be calculated. The estimate should include the cost of acquiring the site, construction costs, and soft costs such as legal and accounting fees, architecture and engineering, and contingencies. Eventually, the developer will have firm cost bids for building the project. The initial financial feasibility analysis, however, relies on the developer's experience from other

figure 4-3d
Stage 1d: Development Costs

5	Development Costs			
6	Number of Units		200	
7	Total Square Footage		191,500	
8				
9	Land	$6,000	per unit	$1,200,000
10		Rate	Number of Months	
11	Land Carry[a]	8.00%	3	24,000
12	Approval Fees	300	per unit	60,000
13	Construction Hard Cost	$56.00	per s.f. gross area	10,724,000
14	Soft Costs			
15	Architecture and engineering	$1,600	per unit	320,000
16	Legal	$125,000	total	125,000
17	Appraisal and title	0.50%	of hard cost + $20k	73,620
18	Marketing	$1,000	per unit	200,000
19	Taxes during construction	2.6%		348,530
20	Insurance during construction	$275	per unit	55,000
21	Loan origination costs	2%	permanent loan amount	217,401
22	Total Soft Costs			1,339,551
23	Developer Overhead	3%		402,150
24				
25	Contingency	5%		536,200
26				
27				
28	Total Development Cost, Excluding Interest and Operating Reserve for Lease-up			$14,285,901
29				
30	Estimate of Construction Interest[b]			
31	Permanent Loan	$10,870,060		
32	Construction Interest	7.50%		
33	Construction Period (months)	12		
34	Average Draw	65.00%		
35	Estimated Construction Loan Interest			529,915
36				
37				
38	Total Project Cost before Operating Reserve			$14,815,817
39				
40	Estimate of Operating Reserve[c]			
41	Gross Potential Rent (monthly)	$207,488		
42	Lease-up Period (months to reach stabilized occupancy)[d]	12		
43	Average Occupancy during Lease-up	48%		
44	Estimated Rent during Lease-up		1,182,684	
45	Estimated Operating Expenses during Lease-up		967,788	
46	NOI during Lease-up		214,896	
47	Construction Interest during Lease-up		815,255	
48	First-Year Operating Reserve Required			600,359
49				
50				
51	Total Project Costs			$15,416,175

Notes

[a]Land carry refers to interest paid to the land seller as part of the land purchase contract.

[b]This calculation is a preliminary estimate of interest during construction. A more accurate estimate will be made as part of the Stage 3 analysis, and even more accurate estimate in Stage 4 (not shown).

[c]Operating reserve during lease-up represents the subsidy that will be required to cover operating costs and debt service before the project reaches break-even occupancy.

[d]Based on market studies, the project is projected to lease at a rate of 16.6 units per month. The project will then take 12 months to be fully leased (200 ÷ 16.6 = 12).

figure 4-3e

Stage 1e: Simple Ratios

5	Net Operating Income	1,397,579
6	Total Project Cost	15,416,175
7		
8	**Overall Return (Overall Cap Rate = NOI/Total Project Cost)**	9.1%
9		
10	Net Operating Income	1,397,579
11	Annual Debt Service	824,474
12	Cash Throw-off (CTO or BTCF)	573,105
13		
14		
15	Total Project Cost	15,416,175
16	Permanent Mortgage	10,870,060
17	Equity	4,546,115
18		
19	**Cash-on-Cash Return (CTO/Equity)**	12.6%
20		
21	**Development Profit**	
22	NOI	1,397,579
23	Overall Cap Rate at Sale	8.5%
24	Capitalized Value	16,442,108
25	Total Project Cost	15,416,175
26	Development Profit	1,025,932

similar projects and information provided by contractors and consultants.

The costs should also include the developer's overhead and costs associated with the initial marketing and lease-up of the project. As an initial rough estimate, interest costs can be approximated by assuming an average draw and length of the loan. The operating reserve during lease-up can be approximated by assuming a lease-up period and computing the rent lost from vacancies during that time. Figure 4-3d shows total development costs for Shady Hollow before interest and lease-up of $14,285,901. With estimated interest during construction of $529,915 and an operating reserve during lease-up of $600,359, project costs total $15,416,175.

Stage 1e—Simple Ratios. Stage 1 analysis is sometimes called a *back-of-the-envelope analysis,* because the simple returns can literally be computed on the back of an envelope. Still, the overall return (NOI divided by total project cost) and cash-on-cash return (cash flow after debt service divided by equity) are the two most commonly cited measures of return in the industry. For an apartment project, returns in excess of 10 percent are desirable. As inflation picks up, the initial cash-on-cash return may go down to 6 to 8 percent as developers look to the future for higher cash flows and profit from sale of the complex. For Shady Hollow, the over-all return is 9.1 percent (1,397,579 ÷ 15,416,175). The cash-on-cash return is 12.6

percent (573,105 ÷ 4,546,115).[30] Both figures compare favorably with other deals (see Figure 4-3e). Figure 4-3e also shows development profit of $1,025,932, which represents the difference in the market value of the project at stabilized occupancy minus total project costs to reach that point.

In summary:

Total Project Cost (Figure 4-3d)	$15,416,175
Less: Mortgage (Figure 4-3c)	10,870,060
Equity	$4,546,115
NOI (Figure 4-3b)	$1,397,579
Less: Debt Service (Figure 4-3c)	$824,474
Cash Flow after Debt Service	$573,105

Stage 2—Discounted Cash Flow Analysis. Discounted cash flow analysis of the operating period is the most important of the five stages. It is used by lenders, appraisers, and investors to determine projected returns of the proposed development. Even if the developer plans to sell the project as soon as it reaches stabilized occupancy, Stage 2 analysis is the most widely used methodology to evaluate an income property investment or development (see Figure 4-4).

To calculate operating cash flows, the pro forma NOI is extended over time, usually seven or ten years, showing growth in both rents and expenses. In this case, rents are assumed to increase at a rate of 3 percent per year and expenses at 5 percent per year.

Pension funds, appraisers, and many institutional investors focus on the unleveraged before-tax returns, because those numbers give the "pure" real estate value of the property (without financing or income tax considerations). Pension fund retirement accounts do not pay tax and often buy properties on an all-cash (unleveraged) basis. Both leveraged and unleveraged analysis can be done on the same spreadsheet simply by changing the assumptions about the mortgage and income taxes.

Developers use Stage 2 analysis to determine whether the proposed project offers an attractive rate of return. The DCF analysis is performed many times as more detailed and accurate information becomes available about design, development costs, and anticipated rents. The initial runs of Stage 2 analysis may focus on the unleveraged returns for the project—the internal rate of return on all-equity financing of total project cost, annual cash flows representing the full NOI (with no mortgage or debt service), and the adjusted sale price at the end of the seven-year holding period. The IRR represents the relationship between the present value of the cash flows from operations and sale, and the capital invested. This return should range from about 11 to 15 percent, depending on the type of property, its location, and interest and inflation rates. (The higher the inflation rate, the higher the overall return.) The unleveraged rate of return is computed on NOI for each year of ownership, starting from the time the building is fully occupied and ending with the sale of the project. The unleveraged (before-tax) return for Shady Hollow is 10.8 percent. Although this figure is unusually low for a to-be-developed deal, the historically low interest rates in 2002 generate extremely favorable leverage and very attractive cash-on-cash returns.[31]

Note that in the example, Stage 2 analysis begins *after* the building reaches stabilized occupancy. All the interest subsidies during lease-up are included in the total investment cost. In this case, we assume that the building is fully leased even though it is not yet built. Alternatively, we could assume that Year 0 figures include all development costs through construction, up to the certificate of occupancy, and Year 1 (and 2 if needed) are the lease-up years. In this case, the project does not reach stabilized income for a full year until Year 2 or 3. Such an assumption lowers the apparent returns but more accurately reflects what happens in a new development where the building must be constructed and leased from scratch. These nuances are considered in the more detailed analysis of Stage 3 and discussed later in this chapter.

Appraisers calculate the present value of the future cash flow stream at a discount rate determined by the market (usually 11 to 13 percent). The concept of present value represents the reverse of future value. Just as one dollar will likely be worth more in the future, one dollar in the future is worth less than one dollar today.

The discount rate is used to discount future values to present value. It also represents the investor's required rate of return. The resulting present value represents the value of the building once it is fully leased. The difference between the discounted value and the development cost (equal to the net present value) is the developer's profit, also known as net present value. Using the NPV method of DCF analysis, a prospective investment must show a positive NPV to justify the investment. The unleveraged net present value at 10 percent is $636,801. This amount is the development profit for Shady Hollow, assuming that the unleveraged rate of return in the marketplace is 10 percent. If it is lower, then the development profit will be higher.

The unleveraged IRR in Figure 4-4 is 10.8 percent, which is lower than historic unleveraged IRRs for a project yet to be developed. IRR requirements change directly with changes in interest rates and inflation.[32] In the mid-1990s, occupied apartment projects needed to produce an unleveraged IRR of 11 to 12 percent and new development projects on the order of 14 to 15 percent to compensate for the added risks. Both these rates were lower in 2002 as a result of historically low interest rates, low inflation, and the stock market collapse, which caused money managers to shift money into real estate, pushing prices up and return rates down.

Although the unleveraged IRR is important, developers are primarily interested in the return on equity (ROE). The return on equity also is expressed as an IRR and takes into account the financing (leverage) and personal income taxes of the owner/developer. Stage 2 analysis focuses on the returns on the project as a single, undivided investment where one individual (the owner/developer) puts up all the equity and receives all the cash flow.

Figure 4-4 shows the leveraged analysis of the project with mortgage financing. Developers focus on the leveraged before-tax and after-tax returns on equity because investment in the project must compete with returns available from other investments such as stocks and bonds. Shady Hollow's before-tax IRR is 19.15 percent, the after-tax IRR 15.43 percent. With low-risk money market accounts paying 2 to 4 percent in 2002, Shady Hollow's return more than adequately compensates for the risk of to-be-developed real estate.

The DCF analysis of a project should be updated at each of the following three times:

1. *Before a developer submits the earnest money contract*—By setting up the DCF model at this stage, subsequent updates will be easy to accomplish. To create a DCF model, a developer needs the following information in addition to that used for simple capitalization:
   • assumed density, based on what the developer plans to build or on densities of similar projects in the vicinity of the site;
   • more accurate figures for soft costs with financing points, interest, and legal, marketing, administrative, architecture, and engineering costs.

figure 4-4

Stage 2 Analysis

3	Project Costs										
4	Total Project Cost	$15,416,175									
5	Total Project Cost before Operating Reserve	$14,815,817									
6	Land Cost	$1,200,000									
7											
8	**Financing Assumptions**										
9	Equity	$4,546,115									
10	Mortgage Principal	$10,870,060									
11	Interest Rate	6.50%									
12	Amortization	30									
13	Annual Debt Service	$824,474									
14											
15	**Depreciation Assumptions**										
16	Building Basis	$13,615,817									
17	Life (in years)	27.5									
18	Acceleration Factor	1.0									
19	Straight line (calculated)	$495,121									
20											

21	**Mortgage Calculation**			1	2	3	4	5	6	7	8
22											
23	Beginning Balance[a]			10,870,060	10,748,563	10,618,928	10,480,612	10,333,033	10,175,570	10,007,561	9,828,300
24	Ending Balance			10,748,563	10,618,928	10,480,612	10,333,033	10,175,570	10,007,561	9,828,300	9,637,034
25	Amortization of Principal			121,497	129,634	138,316	147,579	157,463	168,009	179,261	191,266
26	Interest			702,977	694,840	686,158	676,895	667,011	656,465	645,213	633,208
27											

28	**Depreciation Calculation**										
29											
30	Beginning Balance[b]			13,615,817	13,120,696	12,625,575	12,130,455	11,635,334	11,140,214	10,645,093	10,149,972
31	Less: Annual Depreciation			495,121	495,121	495,121	495,121	495,121	495,121	495,121	495,121
32	Ending Balance			13,120,696	12,625,575	12,130,455	11,635,334	11,140,214	10,645,093	10,149,972	9,654,852
33	Cumulative Depreciation Taken			495,121	990,241	1,485,362	1,980,482	2,475,603	2,970,724	3,465,844	3,960,965
34	Cumulative Straight Line			495,121	990,241	1,485,362	1,980,482	2,475,603	2,970,724	3,465,844	3,960,965
35	Recapture			–	–	–	–	–	–	–	–
36	Remaining Book Value			14,320,696	13,825,575	13,330,455	12,835,334	12,340,214	11,845,093	11,349,972	10,854,852
37											
38											
39											

40	**Annual Cash Flows**			1	2	3	4	5	6	7	8
41											
42	Gross Rent	(inflation rate)	3.00%	2,489,860	2,564,556	2,641,492	2,720,737	2,802,359	2,886,430	2,973,023	3,062,214
43	Vacancy	(vacancy rate)	5.00%	(124,493)	(128,228)	(132,075)	(136,037)	(140,118)	(144,322)	(148,651)	(153,111)
44	Adjusted Gross Income			2,365,367	2,436,328	2,509,418	2,584,700	2,662,241	2,742,109	2,824,372	2,909,103
45											
46	Operating Expenses	(inflation rate)	5.00%	967,788	1,016,177	1,066,986	1,120,335	1,176,352	1,235,170	1,296,928	1,361,775
47	Other Expenses			–	–	–	–	–	–	–	–
48	Total Expenses			967,788	1,016,177	1,066,986	1,120,335	1,176,352	1,235,170	1,296,928	1,361,775
49											
50	Net Operating Income			1,397,579	1,420,151	1,442,432	1,464,365	1,485,889	1,506,939	1,527,444	1,547,328
51											
52	Annual Debt Service			(824,474)	(824,474)	(824,474)	(824,474)	(824,474)	(824,474)	(824,474)	(824,474)

53			1	2	3	4	5	6	7	8
54	Before-Tax Operating Cash Flow		573,105	595,677	617,958	639,891	661,415	682,465	702,970	722,854
55										
56	**Tax Calculation**									
57										
58	Net Operating Income		1,397,579	1,420,151	1,442,432	1,464,365	1,485,889	1,506,939	1,527,444	1,547,328
59	Interest		(702,977)	(694,840)	(686,158)	(676,895)	(667,011)	(656,465)	(645,213)	(633,208)
60	Depreciation		(495,121)	(495,121)	(495,121)	(495,121)	(495,121)	(495,121)	(495,121)	(495,121)
61										
62	Taxable Income (loss)		199,482	230,190	261,153	292,350	323,758	355,353	387,110	419,000
63	Passive Loss Offset[c]		–	–	–	–	–	–	–	–
64										
65	Taxable Income		199,482	230,190	261,153	292,350	323,758	355,353	387,110	419,000
66	Passive Loss Carryforward		–	–	–	–	–	–	–	–
67										
68	Taxes	28.00%	55,855	64,453	73,123	81,858	90,652	99,499	108,391	117,320
69										
70	**After-Tax Cash Flow**									
71										
72	Before-Tax Operating Cash Flow		573,105	595,677	617,958	639,891	661,415	682,465	702,970	722,854
73	Taxes		(55,855)	(64,453)	(73,123)	(81,858)	(90,652)	(99,499)	(108,391)	(117,320)
74										
75	After-Tax Operating Cash Flow		517,250	531,223	544,835	558,033	570,763	582,966	594,579	605,534
76										
77										
78	**Sale Calculation**									
79										
80	**Before-Tax Cash Flow from Sale**									
81	Sale Price (cap rate of 8.5%, using next year NOI)	8.50%							18,203,863	
82	Commission	4.00%							(728,155)	
83	Adjusted Sale Price								17,475,709	
84	Remaining Mortgage Balance								(9,828,300)	
85	Before-Tax Cash Flow from Sale								7,647,409	
86										
87	**Taxes**									
88	Adjusted Sale Price								17,475,709	
89	Remaining Book Value								(11,349,972)	
90	Total Taxable Gain								6,125,736	
91	Passive Loss Carryforward								–	
92	Total Gain								6,125,736	
93	Total Depreciation Taken								3,465,844	
94	Recapture Tax (25%)	25.00%							(866,461)	
95	Capital Gain								2,659,892	
96										
97	Tax on Capital Gain	20.00%							531,978	
98										
99	**After-Tax Cash Flow from Sale**									
100	Before-Tax Cash Flow from Sale								7,647,409	
101	Total Tax (recapture plus capital gain)								(1,398,439)	
102	After-Tax Cash Flow from Sale								6,248,969	

continued

figure 4-4
Stage 2 Analysis *continued*

	Return Measures	Investment	1	2	3	4	5	6	7
103									
104									
105									
106	**Return Measures**	**Investment**	**1**	**2**	**3**	**4**	**5**	**6**	**7**
107									
108	**Unleveraged IRR**								
109	Project Cost	($15,416,175)							
110	Net Operating Income		1,397,579	1,420,151	1,442,432	1,464,365	1,485,889	1,506,939	1,527,444
111	Adjusted Sale Price								17,475,709
112	Total Before-Tax Cash Flow	($15,416,175)	1,397,579	1,420,151	1,442,432	1,464,365	1,485,889	1,506,939	19,003,152
113									
114	Unleveraged IRR	10.81%							
115	Net Present Value (10%)[d]	$636,801							
116									
117									
118	**Before-Tax IRR**								
119	Equity	($4,546,115)							
120	Before-Tax Operating Cash Flow		573,105	595,677	617,958	639,891	661,415	682,465	702,970
121	Before-Tax Cash Flow from Sale								7,647,409
122	Total Before-Tax Cash Flow	($4,546,115)	573,105	595,677	617,958	639,891	661,415	682,465	8,350,378
123									
124	Before-Tax IRR	19.15%							
125	Net Present Value (12%)	$1,785,317							
126									
127									
128	**After-Tax IRR**								
129	Equity	($4,546,115)							
130	After-Tax Operating Cash Flow		517,250	531,223	544,835	558,033	570,763	582,966	594,579
131	After-Tax Cash Flow from Sale								6,248,969
132	Total After-Tax Cash Flow	($4,546,115)	517,250	531,223	544,835	558,033	570,763	582,966	6,843,548
133									
134	After-Tax IRR	15.43%							
135									
136	**Simple Return Measures**								
137	NOI/Project Cost		9.1%	9.2%	9.4%	9.5%	9.6%	9.8%	9.9%
138	Before Tax Cash Flow/Equity		12.6%	13.1%	13.6%	14.1%	14.5%	15.0%	15.5%
139	Tax Shelter/Equity		–	–	–	–	–	–	–

Notes

[a] The permanent mortgage balance was determined based on value and cash flow. During the development period, only interest would be paid on the construction loan. Amortization would begin upon the funding of the permanent loan, after stabilization.

[b] The depreciable basis is the total project cost, excluding land costs and operating losses during the lease-up period. The remaining book value includes the land cost. Personal property is included in the depreciable basis here for simplicity. It can be tracked separately. Moreover, apartment buildings may be brought on stream at different times in successive months as construction is completed. A separate depreciation spreadsheet may be added to account for these nuances. This level of accuracy, however, is inappropriate for early Stage 2 analysis, as other assumptions are at best good approximations.

[c] Current tax laws treat real estate as passive income and limit the amount of loss one can take. Passive losses can be taken only against other passive income (with minor adjustments for small investors). In this example, rules limiting passive loss do not apply, because taxable income is positive. Stage 3 (Figure 4-8) shows the treatment if taxable income is negative. See Brueggeman and Fisher, *Real Estate Finance and Investments,* for more information.

[d] Net present value equals the present value of future cash flows, less the initial investment. The unleveraged NPV represents the development profit.

The purpose of the analysis at this stage is to reconfirm that the project is worth the time and investment required to proceed with the feasibility studies.

In addition to determining whether or not the project is feasible, this first computation of DCF provides an estimate of how large the negative cash flows will be during lease-up of the project. If, for exaple, a 16-month lease-up is anticipated for the project to reach 95 percent occupancy, then the average occupancy rate during the first year would be 35.6 percent and during the second year would be 91.2 percent. Thereafter, it would be 95 percent (see Figure 4-5).

Subtracting the average occupancy rate for each year from 100 percent produces the average vacancy rate—in this case, 64.4 percent (100 minus 35.6) and 8.96 percent (100 minus 91.04) for the first and second years, respectively. The figures for average vacancy rates are used in the DCF analysis to determine cash flows in the first two years or until the project reaches stabilized occupancy. The first one or two operating years usually have negative cash flows that represent additional equity that must be infused into the project. They become part of the cash flow stream for computing the internal rate of return. Most developers add the negative cash flows into project cost under a heading *operating reserve during lease-up.*

2. *After a developer signs the earnest money contract but before going hard on the contract*—By this time, the developer should have formed a firm concept of the proposed project. With the architect, the developer should lay out the site and prepare a site plan and building program that defines the number of units obtainable, the mix of units, and average unit sizes. From the developer's own market study and with the input of a professional marketing consultant, the developer should focus clearly on a target market for the project. Equipped with this information, the developer can arrive at more detailed projections of rental income based on a breakdown of unit types and more accurate rents per unit.

The decision to go hard on the earnest money contract usually hinges on the findings of consultants' studies, especially those regarding soils, floodplains, utilities, easements, and zoning. The main purpose of the studies is to uncover any factors that may affect what can be built and how much it will cost. This information is critical before the developer's at-risk investment is increased through nonrefundable earnest money. Any information that affects costs or densities should be fed into the DCF model to determine whether the project is still feasible.

3. *After a developer goes hard on the land purchase contract but before closing on the land*—The developer wants to accomplish as much as possible before having to close on the land. At the very least, the developer wants to have a tentative financing commitment. To obtain the financing commitment, most beginning developers should use a mortgage broker unless they have already established good personal contacts with institutions that

---

figure 4-5

Calculating the Average Occupancy Rate

If lease-up is expected to take 16 months to reach 95 percent occupancy, then the average occupancy rate for each year is computed thus:

Year 1:
$$\frac{12 \text{ months}}{16 \text{ months}} \times 95\% = \frac{71.25\%}{2} = 35.62\%$$

Year 2:
$$\frac{(71.25\% + 95\%)}{2} = 83.215\% \times \frac{4 \text{ months}}{12 \text{ months}} = 27.71\%$$

$$95.000\% \times \frac{8 \text{ months}}{12 \text{ months}} = 63.33\%$$

Average Occupancy = 91.04%

---

offer permanent financing. (The contents of the mortgage package and the procedure for finding financing are explained in "Financing" later in this chapter.)

The following information is needed to produce both the mortgage brochure and the next iteration of the DCF:

• market studies that define unit mix, unit size, amenities, and rent per unit;

• architectural and engineering conceptual design drawings, developed from the market study information, that have sufficient detail to be used to obtain construction cost estimates within 5 percent of the final bid;

• construction cost estimates from two or three general contractors (unless the developer has an in-house construction staff or a contractor as part of the team). For purposes of comparison, the contractors' bids should follow the 16 categories laid out on the standard form issued by the American Institute of Architects. The developer should be especially careful to specify what the bid will and will not include.

Stage 3—Combined Analysis of the Development and Operating Periods. Some time before the developer makes a firm commitment on the earnest money, it is important to compute a more refined estimate of cash flows during the development period and the operating period.[33] This stage of analysis provides measures of return for the entire life of the proposed project. Stage 3 is more accurate than Stage 2, which assumes that equity is invested at the time of stabilized occupancy, whereas in fact it must be invested before construction begins. Because the time frame is extended one to two years before Stage 2 analysis and the initial years produce little if any cash flow, the IRRs for Stage 3 are necessarily lower than for Stage 2. Nevertheless, they represent the most accurate picture of how the project will perform.

Stage 3 evaluates cash flows quarterly during the development period, taking into account the anticipated construction schedule and projected monthly lease-up rate. It also shows when equity and debt funds will be needed and how long they will accrue interest before the project's cash flow can support the debt service. In this example, costs are projected quarter by quarter.

Stage 3 is the most complicated of the spreadsheets presented here. It has three parts. Figure 4-6 shows the quarterly cash flows during the development period (construction and lease-up). Figure 4-7 shows the sources and uses of cash accumulated by year for the development period. It summarizes project costs and identifies separately the capitalized costs from the first-year operating loss. Both are project costs that need to be funded but are treated differently when calculating income taxes. Total project cost, total capital cost, depreciable basis, operating reserves, and cash result-ing from the permanent loan takeout are inputs to Figure 4-8.

Figure 4-8 shows the operating period cash flows for Stage 3. The quarterly figures from Figure 4-6 are summed to obtain annual numbers and brought forward to Figure 4-8. This analysis resembles Stage 2 analysis except that the construction and lease-up years (1 and 2) are included, whereas Stage 2 analysis assumed that the first year already had stabilized occupancy. Note that the cash flow for Year 1 is zero, because all the equity is invested before Year 1 and all costs are covered by construction draws.

Stage 3 provides a much more refined estimate of construction interest and operating reserves during lease-up than Stages 1 and 2. (A detailed explanation of Stages 1 and 2 can be found at www.pred.uli.org.) In Stage 3, the estimate for construction interest is $268,867, compared with $529,915 in Stage 1. Operating reserves are $376,412, compared with $600,359. The resulting total capital cost is substantially lower than in the initial Stage 1 estimate —$14,931,180 versus $15,416,175, or $484,995 less:

	Stage 1d (Figure 4-3d)	Stage 3 (Figure 4-7)	Difference
Construction Interest	529,915	268,867	261,048
Operating Reserve	600,359	376,412	223,947
	1,130,274	645,279	484,995
Total Project Cost	$15,416,175	$14,931,180	$484,995

The construction interest is lower in Stage 3 analysis primarily because equity is assumed to be invested in full before the construction lender starts to fund the construction loan. (Lenders usually require that the entire equity be invested before any funding of the construction loan.) With equity funding the initial phases of construction, the average construction loan balance is far less than the 65 percent assumed in Stage 1d (Line 34). Similarly, the operating reserve is also lower in Stage 3 because the construction loan ending balances each year are lower in Stage 3, never reaching the maximum of $10,870,060 on which interest was computed for the entire year in Stage 1. Less conservative is the assumption that units pay rent from the beginning of the quarter in which they are leased (an assumption that should probably be revised in subsequent runs).

The lower figures for construction interest and operating reserves in Stage 3 give the developer ammunition to discuss the amount of reserves actually needed with the construction lender. The lender wants to be as conservative as possible, ensuring that sufficient interest reserves are available to protect the developer in the event of construction delays or slower lease-up. The developer must have these resources available but would prefer not to have to set them aside if they are not needed: an estimate that is too conservative raises the total project cost unnecessarily and may make the project uncompetitive.

The IRRs shown in Figure 4-8 for Stage 3 analysis indicate that before-tax IRR is 19.6 percent and after-tax IRR is 17 percent. These figures are more accurate estimates of the project's performance than Stage 2 analysis, where before-tax IRR was 19.15 percent and after-tax IRR was 15.43 percent, because they take into account quarterly construction draws and projected lease-up. Normally, IRRs for Stage 3 analysis would be lower than in Stage 2 because the positive cash flows from stabilized performance occur in Year 3 rather than Year 1. They are almost the same in this illustration, however, because the more accurate estimates of construction interest and operating reserve during lease-up produce lower overall development cost.

Stage 4—Monthly Cash Flows during the Development Period. Stage 4 analysis (not shown) focuses on just the development period and refines the cash flow projections to support the request for the construction loan. Stage 4 analysis resembles the quarterly analysis in Figure 4-6 except that projections are made monthly rather than quarterly. The schedule in Figure 4-6 assumes that the project will be built during the first four quarters and that it will be leased over the next four quarters. The estimated lease-up time (12 months) was calculated from the anticipated absorption of apartments based on the market study. The project reaches stabilized occupancy after the second year.[34]

A primary purpose of the monthly analysis of the development phase is to estimate the amount of the loan that needs to be set aside to cover interest expenses and operating losses during construction and startup. Based on the quarterly cash flow computation in Figure 4-6, the total project cost is estimated at $14,931,180 (Figure 4-7, Line 51). With positive cash flows after interest of $192,084, total project cost after the first year of operation (Figure 4-7, Line 53) is $14,739,096.[35] We get to the same total project cost at the end of Year 2:

Permanent Mortgage	$10,870,060
Equity	4,169,704
Total Funding	$15,039,764
Less Cash Proceeds from Permanent Loan Takeout	484,995
Total Capital Costs	$14,554,769
Plus Cash Flow from Operations after Interest (Line 14)	184,328
Total Project Cost after First-Year Operations	$14,739,097

A monthly Stage 4 analysis would provide an even more accurate estimate of these figures. It is not uncommon for developers to stop at Stage 3, presuming that quarterly cash flow analysis will be sufficiently fine-grained to give them a reasonably accurate picture of their funding needs. But monthly projections are recommended because they give both the developer and the lender the most accurate picture of funding needs and serve as a useful tool for monitoring cash flows once construction begins.

Stage 5—Discounted Cash Flow Analysis for Investors: Joint Venture–Syndication Analysis. In Stages 1, 2, and 3, we look at the real estate project in its entirety. We assume that all equity and all subsequent cash flows are invested or received by a single owner or developer entity. The final step in the analysis is to divide the cash flows for the whole project into the investor's and developer's shares.

Stage 5 is the joint venture–syndication analysis. It is used to structure the deal between the developer and the equity investors. The developer uses Stage 5 to determine the best combination of preferential returns and profit splits to attract the required equity for the project. He will likely experiment with a number of different deal combinations before making a final selection. Because different types of equity investors are accustomed to different deal structures, the final structure depends on whom the developer is approaching for equity.

Although the final version of Stage 5 for the offering package is usually prepared by an accountant on an after-tax basis, the developer's analysis typically focuses on *before-tax* cash flows and IRRs to the investor. The project's viability hinges on attracting sufficient equity capital, so the investor's IRR is one of the key measures of return.

Stage 5 analysis should be done before a firm commitment for the earnest money is made for the land. If the investor's IRR is below 15 percent (and higher if inflation exceeds 3 to 4 percent or the deal is unusually risky), the land price or purchase price is too high. Alternatively, investors can be given a greater share of the profits, but if too little money is left over for the developer, the deal is not worth doing.

Figure 4-9 shows the before-tax Stage 5 analysis for Shady Hollow. The cash flows in Figure 4-9, Line 11, are taken from the Stage 3 combined analysis in Figure 4-8, Line 88. Note that although Stage 5 analysis is illustrated here using cash flows from Stage 3, it can just as easily be tied to Stage 2 analysis. In that case, before-tax cash flows from Stage 2 (Figure 4-4) are substituted in Stage 5 (Figure 4-9, Line 11).

The investor who puts up the equity typically requires a preferred return. The preferred return is most often cumulative, which is to say that if funds are not sufficient to pay the preferred return, the deferred return is added to the equity balance and accrues interest. In this case, the investor receives an 8 percent cumulative preferred return and takes 80 percent of the remaining cash flow

as paydown of the equity. The other 20 percent is split evenly between the developer and the investor. When the property is sold, the first distribution goes to pay down any remaining equity and unpaid (accrued) preferred return. The remaining balance is then split 60/40: 60 percent to the investor and 40 percent to the developer. Under this structure, the developer receives some cash flow throughout the operating period. The investor's before-tax IRR is 16.85 percent.

Some investors may insist on receiving all the cash flow until they receive back their initial equity investment and preferred return. No deal structure is "typical." It is up to the developer to devise a structure that will attract the necessary equity.

When a single large investor is involved, the deal is negotiated directly between the developer and the investor. Institutional equity investors typically require 75 to 80 percent of the profits. Developers can often raise money more cheaply from private individuals. A common structure with private individuals during the 1980s was a 6 to 10 percent preferred return and a 50/50 split of the profits after return of equity. As money for real estate became scarce in the late 1980s and early 1990s, investors required as much as 80 to 90 percent of the profits. *Lookback IRRs* of 20 to 25 percent were also common; in essence, the investor had to achieve a 20 to 25 percent IRR before the developer received a share of the profits. These returns are difficult to achieve except when properties are purchased at deep discounts or perform especially well. They require getting in and out of the deal in a short time— two or three years at most.

As money became more available in the mid-1990s, terms of deals with investors became less stringent. Still, many investors lost money, especially in nonresidential property. In today's environment, it remains difficult for developers to obtain the traditional 50/50 deal with investors.

What to Watch For. Financial analysis is a necessary but often misused tool. Experienced developers sometimes scoff at the latest DCF and IRR techniques because the old rules of thumb (such as capitalized value should exceed cost by a comfortable margin, say 15 to 20 percent, or cash-on-cash return should be 10 to 11 percent) work just as well when a project is obviously a good investment. Stage 2 analysis can easily be misused to overestimate a project's returns. Beginning developers especially should be aware of the major pitfalls:

- underestimating costs;
- overestimating rents;
- underestimating operating expenses, especially after five years;
- underestimating or omitting a reserve for replacements;
- underestimating or omitting expenses for tenant turnover, such as repainting, carpets, draperies, and appliances;
- overestimating rent escalation;

figure 4-6

Stage 3 Analysis, Part 1

Cash Flows during Development Period, including Initial Lease-Up Activities

		Data	Total	Time Zero	Development Year 1 Total	Development Year 2 Total
4	**Development Costs**					
5	Land	$1,200,000	1,200,000	1,200,000	0	0
6	Land Carry	$24,000	24,000	$24,000	0	0
7	Approval Fees	$60,000	60,000	$60,000	0	0
8	Construction Hard Costs	$10,724,000	10,724,000		10,724,000	0
9	Soft Costs					
10	Architecture and engineering	320,000	320,000		320,000	–
11	Legal	125,000	125,000	125,000	–	
12	Appraisal and title	73,620	73,620	73,620	–	
13	Marketing	200,000	200,000		100,000	100,000
14	Taxes during construction	348,530	348,530		174,265	174,265
15	Insurance during construction	55,000	55,000		27,500	27,500
16	Loan origination costs	217,401	217,401	217,401	–	–
17	Developer Overhead	402,150	402,150		201,075	201,075
18	Contingency	536,200	536,200		268,100	268,100
19						
20	Total Development Costs, excluding Construction Loan Interest and Operating Reserves	$14,285,901	$14,285,901	$1,700,021	$11,814,940	$770,940
21						
22						
23	**Operating Income (Loss) during Lease-Up**					
24	Months to Reach Stabilized Occupancy	12			0	0
25	Apartments Leased per Quarter				0	200
26	Cumulative Number of Apartments Leased				0	200
27	Vacancy Resulting from Lease-Up (percent of gross potential)				0	38%
28	Stabilized Vacancy (percent of gross potential)	5.00%			0	5%
29	Overall Vacancy Rate				0	39%
30	Gross Potential Rent for Quarter (from pro forma NOI)	622,465	2,489,860		0	2,489,860
31	Vacancy Loss ($)		(964,821)		0	(964,821)
32	Adjusted Gross Rent		1,525,039		0	1,525,039
33	Total Revenue		1,525,039		0	1,525,039
34						
35	Operating Expenses		967,788		–	967,788
36						
37	Net Operating Income		557,251		0	557,251
38					0	
39	Combined Cash Flow during Development Period before Interest		(13,728,650)	(1,700,021)	(11,814,940)	(213,689)

			Lease-Up				
Quarter 1	Quarter 2	Quarter 3	Quarter 4	Quarter 5	Quarter 6	Quarter 7	Quarter 8
$2,681,000	$2,681,000	$2,681,000	$2,681,000				
320,000							
50,000		25,000	25,000	25,000	25,000	25,000	25,000
43,566	43,566	43,566	43,566	43,566	43,566	43,566	43,566
6,875	6,875	6,875	6,875	6,875	6,875	6,875	6,875
50,269	50,269	50,269	50,269	50,269	50,269	50,269	50,269
67,025	67,025	67,025	67,025	67,025	67,025	67,025	67,025
$3,218,735	$2,848,735	$2,873,735	$2,873,735	$192,735	$192,735	$192,735	$192,735
				50	50	50	50
				50	100	150	200
				75.00%	50.00%	25.00%	0.00%
				0.00%	0.00%	0.00%	5.00%
				75.00%	50.00%	25.00%	5.00%
				622,465	622,465	622,465	622,465
				(466,849)	(311,233)	(155,616)	(31,123)
				155,616	311,233	466,849	591,342
				155,616	311,233	466,849	591,342
				241,947	241,947	241,947	241,947
				($86,331)	$69,286	$224,902	$349,395
($3,218,735)	($2,848,735)	($2,873,735)	($2,873,735)	($279,066)	($123,449)	$32,167	$156,660

continued

figure 4-6

Stage 3 Analysis, Part 1 *continued*

Cash Flows during Development Period, Including Initial Lease-Up Activities

		Data	Total	Time Zero	Year 1 Total	Year 2 Total
40						
41	**Construction Loan Balance and Interest Calculation**					
42		Data	Total	Time Zero	Year 1 Total	Year 2 Total
43						
44	Maximum Loan Balance (from financing calculation)	10,870,060				
45						
46	Equity Sources	4,546,115	4,546,115	1,700,021	2,846,094	0
47	Equity Account Ending Balance		4,546,115	1,700,021	4,546,115	4,546,115
48						
49						
50	**Construction Loan Account**					
51	Beginning Balance				6,220,404	10,192,330
52	Loan Draw					
53	Construction draw		9,739,786		8,968,846	770,940
54	Operating deficit		86,331		0	86,331
55	Trial balance		10,385,065		9,094,139	10,385,065
56	Additional equity required		0		0	0
57						
58	Ending Balance before Interest					
59	Average Loan Balance					
60	Total Construction Loan Interest	7.50%	1,010,446		268,867	741,579
61	Interest accrued during construction period		268,867		268,867	0
62	Interest accrued during operating period		741,579		0	741,579
63	Interest paid during operating period		451,498		0	451,498
64	Trial ending balance		10,385,065		9,237,713	10,385,065
65	Additional equity required		0	0	0	0
66						
67	Ending Balance		10,385,065		9,237,713	10,385,065
68						
69	Total Additional Equity Required		0		0	0
70	Cash Flow after Interest		192,084		0	192,084

Quarter 1	Quarter 2	Quarter 3	Quarter 4	Quarter 5	Quarter 6	Quarter 7	Quarter 8
2,846,094	0	0	0	0	0	0	0
4,546,115	4,546,115	4,546,115	4,546,115	4,546,115	4,546,115	4,546,115	4,546,115
0	376,134	3,258,629	6,220,404	9,237,713	9,692,602	9,999,595	10,192,330
372,641	2,848,735	2,873,735	2,873,735	192,735	192,735	192,735	192,735
0	0	0	0	86,331	0	0	0
372,641	3,224,869	6,132,364	9,094,139	9,516,779	9,885,337	10,192,330	10,385,065
0	0	0	0	0	0	0	0
372,641	3,224,869	6,132,364	9,094,139	9,516,779	9,885,337	10,192,330	10,385,065
186,320	1,800,502	4,695,496	7,657,272	9,377,246	9,788,970	10,095,962	10,288,697
3,494	33,759	88,041	143,574	175,823	183,543	189,299	192,913
3,494	33,759	88,041	143,574	0	0	0	0
0	0	0	0	175,823	183,543	189,299	192,913
0	0	0	0	0	69,286	189,299	192,913
376,134	3,258,629	6,220,404	9,237,713	9,692,602	9,999,595	10,192,330	10,385,065
0	0	0	0	0	0	0	0
376,134	3,258,629	6,220,404	9,237,713	9,692,602	9,999,595	10,192,330	10,385,065
0	0	0	0	0	0	0	0
				$0	$0	$35,602	$156,482

figure 4-7

Development Cost Summary

3				Year		
4	**Uses**		**Total**	**0**	**1**	**2**
5						
6	Total Development Costs		$14,285,901	$1,700,021	$11,814,940	$770,940
7	Capitalized Construction Loan Interest	4 quarters	268,867	0	268,867	0
8	Total Capital Costs		$14,554,769	$1,700,021	$12,083,807	$770,940
9						
10	**Cash Flow from Operations**					
11	NOI		557,251	0	0	557,251
12	Construction Loan Interest during Operations		741,579	0	0	741,579
13	Permanent Loan Debt Service		0	0	0	0
14	Cash Flow from Operations after Interest		(184,328)	0	0	(184,328)
15	Total Uses		$14,739,097	$1,700,021	$12,083,807	$955,268
16						
17	**Sources**					
18	Construction Loan Ending Balance		10,385,065	0	9,237,713	10,385,065
19	Permanent Loan Ending Balance		0		0	0
20	Equity Ending Balance		10,792,252	1,700,021	4,546,115	4,546,115
21						
22	Construction Loan Sources		10,385,065	–	9,237,713	1,147,352
23	Permanent Loan Sources		–	–	–	–
24	Equity Sources		4,546,115	1,700,021	2,846,094	–
25	Additional Equity Required		–	–	–	–
26	Positive Cash Flow after Interest		192,084	–	–	192,084
27	Total Sources		14,739,096	1,700,021	12,083,807	955,268
28						
29	**Check**					
30	Equity for Capital Investment (equity sources plus cash flow from operations minus positive cash flow after interest)[a]		4,169,704	1,700,021	2,846,094	(376,412)
31	Equity for Capital Investment (total capital costs minus loan sources)		4,169,704	1,700,021	2,846,094	(376,412)
32						
33	**Summary**					
34						
35	**Capital Costs**					
36	Total Development Costs, excluding Interest		$14,285,901			
37	Interest Accrued during Construction (Figure 4-6, Line 61)		$268,867			
38	Total Capital Costs		$14,554,769			
39						
40	**Depreciable Basis**					
41	Total Capital Costs		$14,554,769			
42	Land Cost		$1,200,000			
43	Depreciable Basis (capital cost minus land)		$13,354,769			
44						
45	**Operating Reserve**					
46	Operating Loss during Lease-up (Figure 4-6, Line 54)		$86,331			
47	Interest Accrued during Operating Period (Figure 4-6, Line 62)		$741,579			
48	Interest Paid during Operating Period (Figure 4-6, Line 63)		($451,498)			
49	Total Operating Reserve Funded by Construction Loan		$376,412			
50						
51	**Total Project Cost (capital costs plus operating reserve)**		$14,931,180			
52	Positive Cash Flow after Interest		192,084			
53	**Total Project Cost after First-Year Operations**		$14,739,096			
54						
55						
56	**Cash Proceeds from Permanent Loan Takeout**					
57	Permanent Mortgage Amount		$10,870,060			
58	Construction Loan Ending Balance		10,192,330			
59	Cash Proceeds from Permanent Loan Takeout		677,730			

Note

[a]Equity for Capital Investment provides a helpful check for Stage 3. It is necessary not to double-count this equity, because it comes not only from new equity but also from positive operating cash flows during lease-up. Lines 30 and 31 in this figure should be equal for each year.

- assuming a sale-year capitalization rate that is too low (which increases sale value); and
- not allowing a sufficient interest reserve during lease-up or assuming an insufficient lease-up time.

Errors in analysis are compounded by developers' natural optimism—the predilection to assume several optimistic or aggressive assumptions simultaneously. Making one optimistic assumption, such as too short a lease-up period, may not alter the results too much, but when two or three such assumptions are made, the resulting returns may represent a *very* optimistic and unrealistic case. For example, if three assumptions that each are likely to occur only 25 percent of the time are used together, the resulting case has only a 1.5 percent likelihood of occurring (0.25 x 0.25 x 0.25). Thus, one must be very careful about selecting assumptions for the variables that represent *average* or *most likely* values.

The other common mistake is going into too much detail too early in the analysis. It is inappropriate to analyze monthly cash flows when first looking at a project because the data for costs and rents are so crude that the extra detail does not help. In fact, it may make it harder to see what is going on. A basic rule of financial analysis is that the level of detail should be no greater than the accuracy of the information analyzed. Therefore, Stage 4 monthly cash flow analysis is appropriate only after considerable time and money have been spent collecting the best possible information about operations and development costs. Until that point, it is a waste of time.

Last, one should always use common sense. The various measures of return should correlate with standard rules of thumb. Good projects typically meet the following measures of return, although they vary according to the degree of risk and current interest and inflation rates:

Measure of Return	New Development	Stabilized Property
Cash-on-Cash Return		
(Cash Throwoff/Equity)	8–10%	8–10%
Overall Return (Overall Cap Rate:		
NOI/Total Cost)	10–11%	9–10%
Unleveraged IRR	12–15%	10–12%
Before-Tax Leveraged IRR	20–25%	15–20%
After-Tax Leveraged IRR	15–20%	12–15%
Investor's Before-Tax IRR	16–20%	14–18%

These rules of thumb are rough guidelines. Returns may be higher or lower, depending on the risk associated with a particular deal and the general economic environment and geographic location. The returns also vary with inflation and interest rates. In 2002, with inflation very low and interest rates the lowest point in 40 years, it was possible for cash-on-cash returns to exceed 10 percent, even though unleveraged IRRs were below 11 percent. As interest rates increase, expected returns are likely to resemble the historic relationships shown above.

Financial analysis is an iterative process. Stage 2 analysis is performed many times in the course of collecting better and better information about a project. Fortunately, once the model is set up, it is a ten-minute exercise to introduce better information and rerun it. But one must double-check that the assumptions and results make sense. Simple measures of return for cash-on-cash returns and capitalization rates still apply. Avoid the trap of creating so complicated a spreadsheet that key numbers become lost in pages and pages of analysis.

The Go/No-Go Decision. Each stage of project feasibility requires a go/no-go decision. A decision to go forward does not commit the developer to construction; it does, however, cause the developer to ascend to the next level of investment and risk. Each level may involve substantial or very little commitment. For example, some projects may have all necessary regulatory approvals already in place, thereby allowing the developer to apply directly for a building permit as soon as construction drawings and financing have been obtained. Other projects may require little investment in feasibility studies, because the physical aspects of the site are already known, the lender does its own appraisal, the market has been proved through past experience, preliminary engineering is unnecessary, or the architect provides preliminary design drawings on spec.

The importance of holding down front-end costs cannot be overemphasized. It is pure risk money, because the odds are still heavily against a project's proceeding, even after a developer has decided to go hard on the land. The key to success is knowing what information is required and how to obtain it at the lowest cost. A developer must walk that fine line between spending money unnecessarily and doing insufficient investigation to evaluate the property properly.

The two most important decisions—especially for small developers with limited resources—involve purchase of the land and the beginning of construction, both of which usually require the largest financial commitments.

The DCF analysis provides data that influence the go/no-go decision to purchase the site:

- expected dollar profit
- IRR
- amount of money needed
- amount of equity needed
- length of the commitment.

The decision to purchase is not made solely on the basis of the DCF analysis, however. The developer must also weigh other available investments, the amount of risk involved in the project, and a host of other considerations, including:

- Does the developer have the personnel and capital resources to carry through the project?
- Is this really the project that the developer wants to spend the next three years or so working on?

figure 4-8

Stage 3 Analysis, Part 2

Combined Annual Before- and After-Tax Cash Flows during Development and Operating Periods

				Development Period			
	Mortgage Calculation	Year 0	Year 1	Year 2	Year 3	Year 4	Year 5
5	Beginning Balance[a]	10,870,060			10,870,060	10,748,563	10,618,928
6	Ending Balance	10,870,060			10,748,563	10,618,928	10,480,612
7	Amortization of Principal				121,497	129,634	138,316
8	Interest				702,977	694,840	686,158
9							
10	**Depreciation Calculation**						
11	Beginning Balance[b]			13,354,769	12,859,648	12,364,527	11,869,407
12	Less: Annual Depreciation			495,121	495,121	495,121	495,121
13	Ending Balance			12,859,648	12,364,527	11,869,407	11,374,286
14	Cumulative Depreciation Taken			495,121	990,241	1,485,362	1,980,482
15	Cumulative Straight Line			495,121	990,241	1,485,362	1,980,482
16	Recapture			0	0	0	0
17	Remaining Book Value			14,059,648	13,564,527	13,069,407	12,574,286
18							
19	**Annual Cash Flows**		Year 1	Year 2	Year 3	Year 4	Year 5
20	Gross Rent	3.00%		2,489,860	2,564,556	2,802,359	2,886,430
21	Vacancy Rate	5.00%			5.00%	5.00%	5.00%
22	Vacancy ($)			964,821	128,228	140,118	144,322
23	Adjusted Gross Income			1,525,039	2,436,328	2,662,241	2,742,109
24							
25	Total Cash In			1,525,039	2,436,328	2,662,241	2,742,109
26							
27	Operating Expenses	5.00%		967,788	1,016,177	1,066,986	1,120,335
28	Total Expenses			967,788	1,016,177	1,066,986	1,120,335
29							
30	Net Operating Income			557,251	1,420,151	1,595,255	1,621,773
31	Less: Construction Loan Interest			741,579			
32	Less: Annual Debt Service			0	(824,474)	(824,474)	(824,474)
33	Plus: Operating Reserve Funded by Construction Loan[c]			376,412	–		
34							
35	**Before-Tax Cash Flow**			192,084	595,677	770,781	797,299
36							
37							
38							
39	**Tax Calculation**						
40	Net Operating Income			557,251	1,420,151	1,595,255	1,621,773
41	Less: Interest			(741,579)	(702,977)	(694,840)	(686,158)
42	Less: Depreciation			(495,121)	(495,121)	(495,121)	(495,121)
43							
44	Taxable Income (loss)			(679,448)	222,054	405,295	440,495
45	Less: Passive Loss Offset			0	222,054	405,295	52,100
46							
47	Taxable Income				0	0	388,395
48	Passive Loss Carryforward			(679,448)	(457,395)	(52,100)	0
49							
50	Taxes	28.00%			0	0	108,751
51							
52							

Investment Period						
Year 6	Year 7	Year 8	Year 9	Year 10	Year 11	Year 12
10,480,612	10,333,033	10,175,570	10,007,561	9,828,300	9,637,034	9,432,959
10,333,033	10,175,570	10,007,561	9,828,300	9,637,034	9,432,959	9,215,216
147,579	157,463	168,009	179,261	191,266	204,075	217,743
676,895	667,011	656,465	645,213	633,208	620,399	606,731
11,374,286	10,879,165	10,384,045	9,888,924	9,393,804	8,898,683	8,403,562
495,121	495,121	495,121	495,121	495,121	495,121	495,121
10,879,165	10,384,045	9,888,924	9,393,804	8,898,683	8,403,562	7,908,442
2,475,603	2,970,724	3,465,844	3,960,965	4,456,085	4,951,206	5,446,327
2,475,603	2,970,724	3,465,844	3,960,965	4,456,085	4,951,206	5,446,327
0	0	0	0	0	0	0
12,079,165	11,584,045	11,088,924	10,593,804	10,098,683	9,603,562	9,108,442

Year 6	Year 7	Year 8	9	Year 10	Year 11	Year 12
2,973,023	3,062,214	3,154,080	3,248,703	3,346,164	3,446,549	3,549,945
5.00%	5.00%	5.00%	0	5.00%	5.00%	5.00%
148,651	153,111	157,704	162,435	167,308	172,327	177,497
2,824,372	2,909,103	2,996,376	3,086,267	3,178,855	3,274,221	3,372,448
2,824,372	2,909,103	2,996,376	3,086,267	3,178,855	3,274,221	3,372,448
1,176,352	1,235,170	1,296,928	1,361,775	1,429,863	1,501,357	1,576,424
1,176,352	1,235,170	1,296,928	1,361,775	1,429,863	1,501,357	1,576,424
1,648,020	1,673,933	1,699,448	1,724,493	1,748,992	1,772,865	1,796,023
(824,474)	(824,474)	(824,474)	(824,474)	(824,474)	(824,474)	(824,474)
823,546	849,459	874,974	900,019	924,518	948,390	971,549
1,648,020	1,673,933	1,699,448	1,724,493	1,748,992	1,772,865	1,796,023
(676,895)	(667,011)	(656,465)	(645,213)	(633,208)	(620,399)	(606,731)
(495,121)	(495,121)	(495,121)	(495,121)	(495,121)	(495,121)	(495,121)
476,005	511,802	547,862	584,159	620,663	657,345	694,171
0	0	0	–	0	0	0
476,005	511,802	547,862	584,159	620,663	657,345	694,171
0	0	0	–	0	0	0
133,281	143,304	153,401	163,564	173,786	184,057	194,368

continued

figure 4-8

Stage 3 Analysis, Part 2 *continued*

Combined Annual Before- and After-Tax Cash Flows during Development and Operating Periods

53	**After-Tax Cash Flow from Operations**					
54	Before-Tax Cash Flow		192,084	595,677	770,781	797,299
55	Less: Taxes		0	0	0	108,751
56						
57	After-Tax Cash Flow		192,084	595,677	770,781	688,549
58						
59	**Sale Calculation**	Year 1	Year 2	Year 3	Year 4	Year 5
60						
61	Sale Price: End of Year 9, Based on Year 10 NOI	8.50%				
62	Less: Commission	4.00%				
63	Adjusted Sale Price					
64	Less: Remaining Balance on Mortgage					
65	Cash from Sale before Tax					
66						
67	**Taxes**					
68	Adjusted Sale Price					
69	Less: Remaining Book Value					
70	Total Taxable Gain					
71	Less: Passive Loss Carryforward					
72	Total Gain after Passive Loss					
73	Total depreciation taken					
74	Recapture tax	25.00%				
75	Capital Gain					
76	Tax on capital gain	20.00%				
77	Total Tax from Sale					
78	Cash from Sale before Tax					
79	Less: Tax					
80	Cash from Sale after Tax					
81						
82						

		Year 0	Year 1	Year 2	Year 3	Year 4	Year 5
83	**Return Analysis**	Year 0	Year 1	Year 2	Year 3	Year 4	Year 5
84	Equity (loss)	(4,546,115)	0	0			
85	Cash Proceeds from Permanent Loan Takeout			677,730			
86	Before-Tax Cash Flows from Operations		0	192,084	595,677	770,781	797,299
87	Cash Flow from Sale before Tax						
88	Total Before-Tax Cash Flow	(4,546,115)	0	869,814	595,677	770,781	797,299
89	**Before-Tax IRR**	19.63%					
90	Equity (loss)	(4,546,115)	–	–			
91	Cash Proceeds from Permanent Loan Takeout			677,730			
92	After-Tax Cash Flows from Operations		0	192,084	595,677	770,781	688,549
93	Cash Flow from Sale after Tax						
94	Total After-Tax Cash Flow	(4,546,115)	0	869,814	595,677	770,781	688,549
95	**After-Tax IRR**	16.99%					

Notes:

[a] The permanent mortgage balance was determined based on value and cash flow. During the development period, only interest would be paid on the construction loan. Amortization would begin upon funding of the permanent loan, after stabilization.

[b] The depreciable basis is the total project cost, excluding land costs and operating losses during lease-up. The remaining book value includes the land cost. Personal property is included in the depreciable basis here for simplicity. It can be tracked separately. Moreover, apartment buildings may be brought on stream at different times in successive months as construction is completed. A separate depreciation spreadsheet may be added to account for these nuances. This level of accuracy, however, is inappropriate for early Stage 2 analysis, because other assumptions are at best good approximations.

[c] The operating reserve includes funds needed to cover operating costs and debt service during lease-up.

823,546	849,459	874,974	900,019	924,518	948,390	971,549
133,281	143,304	153,401	163,564	173,786	184,057	194,368
690,264	706,155	721,572	736,454	750,732	764,334	777,181

Year 6	Year 7	Year 8	Year 9	Year 10	Year 11	Year 12
			20,576,377			
			823,055			
			19,753,322			
			9,828,300			
			9,925,022			

			19,753,322			
			10,593,804			
			9,159,518			
			–			
			9,159,518			
			3,960,965			
			990,241			
			5,198,553			
			1,039,711			
			2,029,952			
			9,925,022			
			2,029,952			
			7,895,070			

Year 6	Year 7	Year 8	Year 9
823,546	849,459	874,974	900,019
			9,925,022
823,546	849,459	874,974	10,825,040

690,264	706,155	721,572	736,454
			7,895,070
690,264	706,155	721,572	8,631,524

figure 4-9

Stage 5 DCF Analysis, Return to Investors

			Development Period				Investment Period			
		Year 0	Year 1	Year 2	Year 3	Year 4	Year 5	Year 6	Year 7	Year 8	Year 9

#											
3	Initial Equity	$4,546,115									
4	Cumulative Preferred Return	8.00%									
5	Investor Priority Payback of Equity	80.00%									
6	Investor Share of Remaining Cash Flow	70.00%									
7											
8				Development Period				Investment Period			
9		Year 0	Year 1	Year 2	Year 3	Year 4	Year 5	Year 6	Year 7	Year 8	Year 9
10											
11	Before-Tax Cash Flow	($4,546,115)		$869,814	$595,677	$770,781	$797,299	$823,546	$849,459	$874,974	$10,825,040
12											
13	**Preferred Return**										
14	Beginning Equity Account Balance			4,546,115	4,141,215	3,929,712	3,564,588	3,154,883	2,697,959	2,191,061	1,631,309
15	Preferred Return Earned			363,689	331,297	314,377	285,167	252,391	215,837	175,285	130,505
16	Preferred Return Paid Currently			363,689	331,297	314,377	285,167	252,391	215,837	175,285	130,505
17											
18	**Unpaid Return Account**										
19	Beginning Balance			0	0	0	0	0	0	0	0
20	Deferred Preferred Return			0	0	0	0	0	0	0	0
21	Deferred Preferred Return Paid			0	0	0	0	0	0	0	0
22	Ending Balance			0	0	0	0	0	0	0	0
23											
24	**Equity Account Balance**										
25	Beginning Equity Account Balance			4,546,115	4,141,215	3,929,712	3,564,588	3,154,883	2,697,959	2,191,061	1,631,309
26	Equity Payback			404,900	211,504	365,123	409,706	456,924	506,898	559,751	1,631,309
27	Ending Balance			4,141,215	3,929,712	3,564,588	3,154,883	2,697,959	2,191,061	1,631,309	0
28											
29	**Equity Payments Recap**										
30	Preferred Return Paid Currently			363,689	331,297	314,377	285,167	252,391	215,837	175,285	130,505
31	Deferred Preferred Return Paid			0	0	0	0	0	0	0	0
32	Equity Payback			404,900	211,504	365,123	409,706	456,924	506,898	559,751	1,631,309
33	Total Payments on Equity			768,589	542,801	679,500	694,873	709,315	722,735	735,036	1,761,814
34											
35	**Remaining Cash Flow**										
36	Before-Tax Cash Flow			869,814	595,677	770,781	797,299	823,546	849,459	874,974	10,825,040
37	Total Payments on Equity			768,589	542,801	679,500	694,873	709,315	722,735	735,036	1,761,814
38	Remaining Cash Flow			101,225	52,876	91,281	102,426	114,231	126,725	139,938	9,063,226
39											
40	**Investors' Share of Remaining Cash Flow**			70,858	37,013	63,897	71,698	79,962	88,707	97,956	6,344,258
41											
42	**Investor Cash Flow Recap**										
43	Investment	(4,546,115)									
44	Total Payments on Equity			768,589	542,801	679,500	694,873	709,315	722,735	735,036	1,761,814
45	Investors' Share of Remaining Cash Flow			70,858	37,013	63,897	71,698	79,962	88,707	97,956	6,344,258
46	Before-Tax Investor Cash Flow	($4,546,115)	$0	$839,447	$579,814	$743,397	$766,571	$789,276	$811,442	$832,992	$8,106,072
47											
48	**Investor Before-Tax IRR**	16.85%									
49	**Net Present Value at 15.0%**	1,255,607									
50											
51	**Developer Cash Flows**										
52	Before-Tax Cash Flow to Developer	$0	$0	$30,368	$15,863	$27,384	$30,728	$34,269	$38,017	$41,981	$2,718,968
53											
54	**Net Present Value at 15.0%**	$1,012,067									
	Discount Rate:	15.00%									

- Is the project worth the developer's time, effort, and risk?
- Is the project of such a scale that the developer can survive major delays and unforeseen difficulties? If not, is this project worth risking the loss of all the developer's assets?

Design

The developer's conceptualization of design should be based entirely on the target market. The rental apartment and for-sale condominium markets are segmented into many submarkets, with each niche demanding specific elements. Submarkets vary enormously by demographics, level of competition, and preferences related to unit mix, unit finishes, parking arrangements, and amenities. No matter how good the pro forma for a project might look, if the product does not satisfy the market's needs at a price that customers can afford, the project will not succeed.

Each building type, from suburban garden apartments to downtown lofts, offers a different set of problems and opportunities for design to meet the needs of the submarket. Luxury garden apartments, for example, typically include some or all of the following design features: generously sized bedrooms and kitchens, tile bathrooms that feel like a master suite, tile or wood entries, vaulted ceilings, nine-foot-high (2.7-meter) ceilings, fireplaces, balconies, microwave ovens, trash compactors, washer/dryers, club facilities with exercise rooms and tennis courts, double-glazed windows with energy-efficient air cavities or plastic separators for soundproofing, security systems, elevators, and attached garages with direct access for residents. Property management services might include grocery shopping, pet sitting, dry cleaning delivery, and trash pickup. Although each of these features and services increases development costs, renters of the highest-end apartments will pay for all of them, and the increased rent more than justifies the additional cost. In fact, competition may make it difficult to rent the project if it does not have these features and services.

In comparison, renters of lower-end apartments are unwilling to pay for many such features, because they are cost-conscious and may have an absolute limit on rent they will pay. Even so, in some areas (Texas, for example), even the lowest-end garden apartments contain club rooms and swimming pools, private balconies, outside storage, cable television, Internet wiring, and central heat and air conditioning.

The developer is responsible for establishing the development program within which the architect will work. The developer should choose an architect experienced with the particular product that the developer wants to build but should not let the architect define the product to be built. The architect should not be allowed to dictate unit mix, unit sizes, and amenities; these decisions should be made jointly and on the basis of the results of the market analysis for the geographic submarket area where the developer is building. Design decisions should take costs and ease of maintenance into consideration. Although the architect's mission is to design the project, the developer must also have sufficient design skills to give the architect the required guidance. The developer's ability to mentally visualize the design and floor plans is vital to success. Fortunately, computer-aided drawing (CAD), which most architects use, helps developers visualize the drawings through three-dimensional computer renderings. CAD is also very helpful for marketing, because it allows potential customers to visualize the new development as it is being built. CAD enables viewers to "walk through" a proposed project, looking at every room from any number of viewpoints.

Time spent scrutinizing the plans during design is among the most important the developer will spend on the entire project. The developer should mentally walk through every unit, look out every window, and envisage every view inside and outside the apartment. What does a guest first see when opening the front door? That view is the same first impression that renters or buyers will receive when they open the door to see model units. It is less expensive and easier to fix something with the architect during design than it is out in the field or, worse, after the building is built.

Multifamily residential buildings are among the most complex buildings to design. And increased demand for higher densities increases the complexity every year. They must accommodate all the functional needs of a large number of people at a relatively high density while protecting the privacy of individuals and families. At the same time, they must provide a sense of ownership and sense of place and community. Multifamily residential design is often the result of a series of compromises between notions of ideal living conditions (derived from single-family housing concepts) and the economic realities of higher-density dwelling.

Unit Mix

The mix of units by size and type should be based on the results of the market study. Unit types most often range from studio apartments through two- and three-bedroom units with two baths; some include extras such as sunrooms, dens, and lofts. In many markets, apartment developers are seeing increased demand for luxury units for downsizing empty nesters. In projects designed for lower-income renters, family-sized units should predominate. If the target market is young singles just starting out, demand likely will be strongest for a mix of split two-master-bedroom roommate units and one-bedroom units for singles. In very-high-rent urban locales, studio units are popular, but in more distant suburban areas, demand is almost nonexistent for such small units.

Nationally, unit sizes have increased in recent years. In 1999, the median size of a new multifamily unit was 1,105 square feet (105 square meters), compared with a median of 955 square feet (90 square meters) in 1990 and only 882 square feet (80 square meters) in 1985. Further, the percentage of new units constructed with three or more bedrooms has increased consistently. In 1985, three-bedroom units accounted for only 7 percent of new multi-family units, nearly three times the percentage only 15 years earlier.[36] Much of the increase can be attributed to the demand by more affluent renters-by-choice who require features such as home offices. Certain niche markets also play a role in determining unit types. For example, apartments housing students require special floor plans that include three- and four-bedroom units, because typically the majority of students share a unit. More difficulty in getting approvals because of neighborhood opposition to higher density and increasing land and permitting costs also contribute to larger units as developers are forced to pursue higher-income tenants.

Site Design

A good site plan respects the natural characteristics of the site and its surroundings. The primary determinants of the site plan are the desired and permitted density, parking layout, and requirements for emergency access. The density of the project in turn is determined by zoning and the market. Generally, one-story apartments or townhouses yield seven to 12 units per acre (17 to 30 per hectare), two-story garden apartments with surface park-ing comfortably yield 12 to 18 units per acre (30 to 45 per hectare), and three-story garden apartments with surface parking yield up to 30 units per acre (75 per hectare). Structured parking, usually accommodated in one or two levels under the apartments or in a separate structure, is required to achieve densities greater than 40 units per acre (100 per hectare).

Fire codes typically permit a maximum distance of 150 feet (45 meters) between a fire road or hydrant and a building. Local fire officials should be consulted early in the design process to determine requirements.

As a reasonable guideline, approximately one-third of the site plan for a garden apartment project should contain building area, one-third should be allotted to parking areas, and one-third should be open space. Any plan that provides less than that amount of open space may seem overly crowded. In garden apartments, the open space often takes the form of courtyards, which work well as interior focal points of activity if they are large enough to provide separation between units. The size of a courtyard should increase with the height of the buildings that enclose it; as a rule, the narrowest dimension of a courtyard should be at least equal to the height of the buildings surrounding it.

A mix of unit types and sizes in a multifamily development helps create distinctive streetscapes and an eclectic neighborhood character.

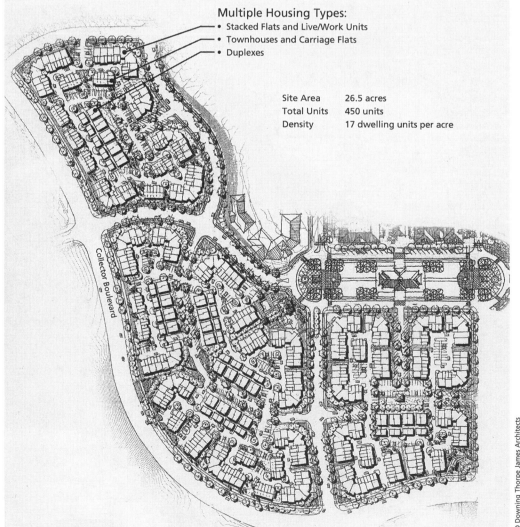

Multiple Housing Types:
- Stacked Flats and Live/Work Units
- Townhouses and Carriage Flats
- Duplexes

Site Area	26.5 acres
Total Units	450 units
Density	17 dwelling units per acre

Traditional forms of multifamily housing have yielded to new configurations, making for greater flexibility for both residents and developers. New forms appeal to renters from diverse market segments, many of whom perceive multifamily housing as the optimal lifestyle, offering more freedom and convenience. Paige Close, an architect with Looney Ricks Kiss in Memphis, Tennessee, says, "In 1995, fully 80 percent of our work was in garden apartments in suburban locations. By 2000, 80 percent was in downtown urban infill projects. This change points to why multifamily housing is one of the most exciting building types in the country."

Townhouse Forms
Buildings with townhouse-like exteriors can contain multiple types of units, including a mix of stacked flats and two- or three-level units, each with private outdoor spaces. Achievable densities are greater than those of traditional townhouses. Communal or individual garages underneath the buildings decrease the acreage dedicated to parking, allowing for better, more attractive site design.

Mews with buildings back to back or facing each other can be clustered tighter than traditional townhouses. Piggyback units—for example, a flat on the first level facing front and a two-story unit above it—also allow increased densities. Such designs work well on small infill parcels and introduce the possibility of multiple unit types in a single structure.

Four- and Six-Plexes
New garden apartments often consist of small buildings designed to look like a large single-family house, each containing four to six flats. Elevations incorporate traditional residential design elements, and site plans resemble those of single-family neighborhoods. Surface parking is minimized by the use of attached garages, and the surface parking that remains is in landscape-screened groups of three or four spaces—not the concrete sea found at earlier garden apartments. Such projects can successfully overcome difficulties in rezoning because of their single-family look.

Courtyard Buildings
Buildings oriented around courtyards provide desirable private outdoor space and views for residents, away from the noise and traffic of urban surroundings. Courtyards and buildings erected over structured parking or with aboveground structured parking are a more efficient use of expensive land and result in higher densities than typical garden "breezeway" apartments. Designs of up to four stories in wood-frame construction include internal corridors and elevators.

Mid-Rises
Buildings of five to eight stories may provide the density that an expensive urban site requires. The design of mid-rises is following a trend toward fitting in the urban fabric of downtown districts, many of which have design guidelines requir-ing new construction to incorporate a mix of uses, be oriented toward the street, and use traditional masonry elements in the exterior facade. Parking is usually structured, at grade or below.

High Rises
Like mid-rise buildings, high rises today are more varied in height and shape, allowing for more corner units, private terraces, and more diverse streetscapes. In the largest cities, high-rise apartments are viewed as the most desirable housing because of their security and on-site services. Responding to a very discriminating market, new buildings imitate the graciousness of pre–World War II luxury high-rise apartment buildings with their high ceilings, large, well-defined rooms, and quality finishes.

Scattered-Site Low-Income Housing
The size, shape, and location of low-income housing is changing. Massive, old-style public housing projects isolated from the larger community are turning into human-scale projects integrated into mixed-income neighborhoods. Local housing authorities are involved in projects that scatter low-income housing on small —usually infill—sites throughout the community. Some public and private developers have combined low-income units with market-rent units in the same project. ■

Parking. Parking—its dimensions, arrangement, and location—is more important than building coverage in the design of a project. One parking space per bedroom is standard. Typically, 1.75 to 1.8 parking spaces per unit is a recommended standard, and two spaces per unit is mandatory with for-sale condominiums in most areas. One-bedroom condominiums generally do not sell as well as two-bedroom condominiums except in dense urban areas, where parking standards may be even lower. Even where standards are lower, however, the availability of parking is often a requirement for units to sell well.

Each car needs 300 to 350 square feet (28 to 33 square meters), including driveways. Consider, for example, a three-story apartment building with two-bedroom units averaging 900 square feet (85 square meters). The build-ing footprint for the unit is 300 square feet (28 square meters) or 900 (85) divided by three stories. If, as is often the case, two-bedroom units require two parking spaces, then for each footprint of 300 square feet (28 square meters), 600 to 700 square feet (55 to 65 square meters) of parking is necessary. In addition to parking for the apartment units, guest parking and dedicated spaces for the project's leasing office are advisable.

The placement of parking is a critical design element. When a project is oriented to the periphery to take advantage of views or to allow direct access from units to green space, parking clusters should be located in the center of the project. When the surroundings are not to be featured, a project should be turned inward to face the common greens and site amenities, and parking should be placed on the periphery.

Avalon at Arlington Square in Arlington, Virginia, includes a mix of apartment products and exterior elevations, including multifamily buildings with elevations reminiscent of a single-family house.

Parking should not invade interior open spaces, which are any project's best feature. If possible, pedestrian circulation should be kept separate from vehicular access, although walking distances between parking and units should be as short as possible. For access to interior courtyards, breezeways should be located between every two or three units.

Concrete parking areas and driveways are cost-effective in the long run. Although they cost more initially, they look better and are cheaper to maintain than asphalt parking.

Parking costs vary for many reasons, but the following guidelines are probably a reasonable starting point: surface parking at $2,500 per space, structured above-ground parking at $8,500 per space, podium parking supporting residential units at $15,000 per space, and underground parking at $20,000 per space.[37] These costs may be as much as 50 percent higher in high-cost areas on the East and West coasts.

In most parts of the country, garages for luxury garden apartments are considered essential, and the developer must attempt to justify the cost of constructing them. For example, if above-grade structured parking for two cars costs $17,000 to construct, then the developer needs approximately $170 (or 1 percent of the construction cost) additional rent per month to cover interest, amortization, and minor maintenance. In most areas, the developer is lucky to collect $50.00 per space.

Carports are built less often today than they were in the 1960s and 1970s, but they remain a solution to the problem of covered parking, especially in areas with severe climates. Care should be taken to make them structurally sound, because flimsy carports have collapsed in heavy winds, rains, and snow, damaging the cars below. Underground garages and hillside cutouts for parking are especially expensive to build, because fireproofing, waterproofing, air handlers, and drainage or sump pumps are required.

Amenities and Landscaping. The selection of amenities begins with the market analysis. A good market analysis answers several questions: What are comparable properties in the market area offering? Do projects with certain amenities have an edge in marketing, or do lower-priced projects with fewer amenities attract more residents? And perhaps the most important: Will residents pay for the amenities?

Amenities help sell the product. What some communities consider standard, even essential, other communities view as luxurious. Generally, if amenities are wanted and used, residents will pay a reasonable price for them —unless operating costs do not correspond with residents' income levels. Therefore, the developer should design not only what the residents like but also what they can afford.

Swimming pools and outdoor Jacuzzis are standard amenities in many areas. Interesting shapes and heavily landscaped pools can add much to the appearance and

The higher densities common at multifamily developments make it economically feasible to provide a range of amenities for residents. The swimming pool at Avalon Corners in Stamford, Connecticut, provides an attractive focal point for the development.

- Be flexible when targeting a market. In the event that the market for a project turns out to be very different from the developer's initial expectation, the presence of basic features with a broad market appeal will help sales or rentals.
- Common areas for stairs, elevators, corridors, lobbies, laundries, and so forth should occupy no more than 18 to 20 percent of total heated rentable areas.
- Property managers can make many useful contributions to the design process and should be included in all design review meetings.
- Do not put family units on the third floor.

- Renters look primarily at total rent, not rent per square foot. Design units to meet the affordability requirements of the target market.
- Condominiums often end up as rental units because of changing market conditions. Make sure a project will not bring financial ruin if units must be rented rather than sold.
- Where possible, buildings should enclose a project's open space, creating courtyards free from cars. Views of cars detract from the courtyard environment and may reduce attainable rents.
- Avoid creating canyon-like areas and barracks-like buildings.

- Avoid placing air-conditioner condensing units in areas where children will play.
- Plan ahead for trash disposal. Make containers easy to reach, easy to clean around, and screened if possible.
- The U.S. Postal Service requires that mail boxes be grouped together. Place mail boxes near the manager's office so that the manager can see tenants as they come and go.
- Provide storage facilities near the pool for outdoor furniture during the winter.
- The leasing office should be visible from the street, be easy to find, and have reserved parking close by. ∎

---

marketability of a complex. Because of its prominence, the pool area deserves special attention, and its design should not be left to a pool contractor. In complexes designed for families, a wading pool for children separate from the adult pool should be provided.

Pools should be carefully landscaped so that planting areas do not catch chlorinated pool water. Other landscaping should be as maintenance-free as possible. Focal planting areas with seasonal color should be located near the project's entrance, the leasing office, the pool, and courtyards. The landscaping plan and sprinkler system should be designed as an integral part of the site plan. Detailed plant design may be left until later, but the general plan should be completed before construction begins. Indeed, many local governments require a landscaping plan before they issue a building permit.

Tennis courts are very land-intensive and are usually included only in larger projects. Depending on the particular market niche, a play area for children or a daycare center may be a valuable amenity to include. Most projects should allow some space for play areas even if the development is geared largely to a singles market, as some of the residents will likely be part-time parents.

Demand is growing in many markets for an on-site business center, including computers with Internet access, printers, fax and copy machines, mailing and shipping services, and even concierge services and meeting space. Many new high-end apartment communities provide a business center with some or all of these services for residents to take advantage of these facilities for personal and business use.

If the project incorporates a clubhouse, it should be centrally located, usually at one of the edges of a courtyard. Where possible, the leasing office is best situated near the clubhouse and should be visible to passing street traffic; studies have shown that up to 70 percent of rentals

Community facilities at Avalon Corners include a clubhouse, business center, fitness center, and billiard room.

Sensitivity to neighborhood context is enhanced by variations in rooflines and creativity in facade elements.

are the result of drive-by traffic. Some projects separate the leasing office from the clubhouse so that the business of running the development does not infringe on the sense of community provided residents. In some larger properties, developers even separate the marketing function from resident services for existing tenants.

Landscaped areas can serve as buffers, are usually visually attractive, add to the project's overall market appeal, and serve as passive recreational areas. A six-foot (1.8-meter) walking trail surrounding the property can be used for walking, running, biking, or skating and costs little to construct and maintain. Gardening is an increasingly popular hobby, and as a result, some new developments include community gardens as well as private outdoor space adjacent to units. Integrating landscaped areas with active recreational facilities such as pools and children's play areas yields the most attractive site plan.

Landscape design must consider the climate, terrain, and cultural influences of the region where the project is located. The best landscape designers effectively use hardy indigenous plants that provide interest during all seasons. Easier maintenance is possible through careful planning.

Xeriscaping, a method of landscaping that relies on proper plant selection and planning to conserve water, minimizes the use of chemicals and reduces the amount of labor-intensive maintenance by carefully considering the site's climate, soil, existing vegetation, and topography. Such methods can be applied to any kind of climate or site.

Exterior Design

The choice of exterior materials and architectural designs should closely relate to the target market's preferences and the character of the local community. The style and materials of a new project should be compatible with existing development in the surrounding area. A project in a new developing area should aspire to set the tone for future development.

Regional traditions and climate play very important roles in the exterior design of apartment buildings. Brick is a common material throughout the South and along the East Coast. Stucco is very popular in the Southwest, whereas wood siding is most common in the northern United States.

Economies of scale can be achieved by minimizing and repeating building types. The fewer the number of building types, the greater the potential for minimizing costs. Wall segments and roof trusses can be prefabricated in groups, and labor costs fall when more work can be done by semiskilled workers. At the same time, however, marketability may require considerable variety in appearance. Long, straight walls and rooflines should be avoided. Individual buildings should not extend more than 200 feet (60 meters).

Marvin Finger states that his development company never goes to the architect with a generic design. "We go to the neighborhood and select the prominent features of the building elevations of that upscale community and then we take that to the architect to enhance and work into the proposed facade."[38]

The building's exterior should express the individuality of the apartment units within. Useful as private outdoor space, balconies are often instrumental design elements in denoting individual apartments. Six feet (1.8 meters) is usually considered the optimal depth for a usable balcony—anything larger may cause excessive shading of windows below and anything smaller may be useful only for storage, which is unsightly. Inset balconies are visually more attractive and can be useful in establishing privacy. Such balconies in combination with an L-shaped plan allow two rooms to open onto one balcony.

The roof should help to establish a residential character as well as to shed rain and snow. The silhouettes of various roof forms can create a friendly, village-like impression. Like the rest of the exterior of the building, roof design is determined partly by regional traditions and styles. Apartment buildings are large, wide buildings, and a shallow roof slope (say, less than a five-inch rise for every 12-inch horizontal run [12.5-centimeter rise for a 31-centimeter horizontal run]—called a *5 in 12 pitch*) may prove visually unsatisfying. The extra cost of a steeper slope can represent a cost premium of up to 10 percent over roofs less than 12 feet (3.6 meters) high, however.

Utility meters, transformers, and trash bins, always potentially unsightly, should not be overlooked during design. A bank of meters, for example, can be quite obtrusive. Utility companies prefer that meters be grouped together and often have a say in their placement. Now that electricity and gas have become deregulated in some areas, negotiations with competitive companies could facilitate the placement of meters. Submetering also allows for optimal placement of meters away from visible areas.

Interior Design

One of the chief objectives in designing an apartment interior is to make a relatively small space seem larger than it is. Large windows and angled walls that lead the eye around corners can help in this regard. L-shaped units offer greater design opportunities than do square or rectangular units. Higher ceilings can be an especially effective means of increasing the impression of space. A cost analysis should be done, however, to determine the cost of an increase in the exterior building envelope. The traditional eight-foot (2.4-meter) ceiling height has been replaced with nine or even ten feet (2.7 or 3 meters)

as the current standard, especially in luxury apartments and condominiums. High, vaulted, or coffered ceilings also are commonly used for high-end developments.

Windows are important not only for the views they offer but also for the light and ventilation they permit. Natural ventilation of an apartment requires that windows be placed on at least two exposures, not necessarily in the same room and preferably on opposite walls. In any room, natural lighting is improved when light comes from more than one direction.

Most markets today demand laundry facilities in the units and fully equipped kitchens with dishwashers, garbage disposals, wood cabinetry, and built-in microwave ovens. Adequate kitchen and storage areas make apartments more livable. The kitchen for a one-bedroom apartment should provide a minimum of 16 linear feet (5 meters) for counters and appliances. Each bedroom should offer a minimum of 12 linear feet (3.6 meters) of closet space, and guest and linen closets should provide another four linear feet (1.2 meters) of storage. These standards can be met in a floor plan of 700 square feet (65 square meters) in a one-bedroom apartment and 1,000 square feet (95 square meters) in a two-bedroom apartment. In smaller units, some compromises may be necessary.

Every room should have a ceiling light, and every wall should have at least one wall plug. Phone and cable connections and security devices should be placed based on interior design for likely furniture arrangements.

Fully equipped kitchens, wooden cabinetry, fireplaces, and high ceilings are some of the features that help distinguish luxury condominiums and apartments. Avalon Court North in Melville, New York, raised the bar on amenities in its marketplace.

Consumers demand more and better-appointed baths. At least one bathroom for guests' use should be accessible from the hall, without walking through a bedroom.[39] In most markets, two-bedroom units should have two baths. In higher-priced developments, master baths must compete with those in new single-family homes. Amenities include large soaking tubs, separate showers, and double vanities. Quality at the lower end has risen correspondingly.

Successful developers worry about every detail. In small apartments, for example, circulation is critical. One should pay careful attention to how the doors will open so as to minimize conflicts and obstructions. In larger developments, full-scale mock-ups of prototypical units are often built. Such mock-ups serve two main purposes: first, they allow discovery of problems in the design; and second, subcontractors can use the mock-ups to familiarize themselves with the plan, make decisions about the placement of wiring, plumbing, and ductwork, and correct potential conflicts between subcontractors. For example, a plumbing pipe may interfere with the best route for an air-conditioning duct. Such conflicts often do not become apparent until the construction stage. The cost of building mock-ups is more than repaid in terms of time saved and aggravation avoided during the course of construction.

Finish materials in an apartment should be chosen for ease of maintenance and also to reflect the tastes of the market. Linoleum or vinyl tile is commonly used in kitchens, baths, and entries, although ceramic tile or stone may be used in higher-end apartments. Other rooms are typically carpeted, with the quality of the carpet varying with the market. Many urban projects now include hardwood floors to replicate the feel and ambience of loft buildings.

Certain optional features can add value to the unit in terms of additional monthly rents. Bookcases, paneling, ceiling fans, built-in computer desks, and undercabinet lighting all can increase a unit's sense of quality but are desirable only if they are supported by the market. Fireplaces, for instance, take up space, and many tenants of smaller apartments are reluctant to pay the increased rent charged for such amenities. The appropriateness of amenities such as washer/dryers or washer/dryer hookups also depends on the market. In condominiums, they are almost essential; in apartments, they are optional. To recover amenity costs, the developer should be able to increase an apartment's monthly rent by at least 1 percent of the construction cost of any amenities. For example, units with a $1,000 fireplace should be able to command rents at least $10.00 per month higher than those without fireplaces. Otherwise, the amenity is not cost-effective.

Separate HVAC systems for each unit should be provided for most garden and mid-rise developments. Mechanical systems can be contained in the walls, ceilings, or roof spaces of the unit but require an outside compressor. The compressor can be located on the roof, where it must be screened and integrated with the roof design, or on the ground outside the unit, where its noise is more noticeable and where it may create an obstruction. High-rise projects typically use a combined compressor and HVAC unit or a central plant for service to the entire building.

With technological advances in communications and increasing numbers of workers telecommuting from home, up-to-date wiring systems are essential. Units should be prewired for cable television, security systems, Internet connections, and multiple telephone lines, with outlets in all rooms. Some developers report the need for as many as eight separate telephone lines per unit. Retrofitting wiring in a completed building is very expensive and difficult, but more and more developers see the wisdom of building smart buildings, with all systems integrated and controlled by computer. Such technology is essential in luxury apartments and before long will be an expected feature in lower-end projects as well. Greg Vilkin notes, "One amenity we are putting into every unit is Category 5 wire so that we have high bandwidth throughout the building. It's absolutely critical and a nonstarter in most urban locations if you don't have high bandwidth access."[40]

Ray Kimsey observes, "Today, developers are paying more attention to the characteristics of the particular market for which they are designing, which will determine what kind of features go into the apartment layout. For example, they design high-end, multifamily apartments with baths, finishes, and trim that you would see in expensive homes, whereas 15 years ago an expensive condominium would not be that dissimilar from an average-price apartment."[41]

Design Issues

Privacy and Security. The layout of apartment buildings needs to provide privacy for each apartment, regardless of the project's density. Fortunately, many of the techniques employed in the design of the site, units, and building exteriors are devices for creating visual separation between units. Building codes also provide useful criteria: for example, a code might stipulate that a wall with windows should be separated from a facing wall with windows by at least 30 feet (9 meters), that a wall with windows should be separated from a facing wall without windows by at least 20 feet (6 meters), and that two outside walls without windows should be separated by a minimum of 10 feet (3 meters). Vertical and horizontal projections such as walls and balconies should be placed to help screen views into bedrooms from other apartments or from common spaces.

Security is becoming an increasingly important issue in site design. A plan that minimizes the number of entries to a project provides greater control of traffic and therefore better security. Entries to units should not be hidden from view, and walkways and breezeways should be visible from several points. Exterior lighting can do much to create a feeling of security for tenants. At the same time, exterior lighting should be designed so that light does not shine directly into apartment units or adjacent properties or cause glare for passing motorists.

Electronic security systems for individual units as well as project entrances are increasingly common in some parts of the country, most notably in California, Florida, and Texas. Gated community entrances are another growing and somewhat controversial trend. Although the gate lends an air of security as well as prestige to some communities, research does not indicate that crime rates are lower in gated communities. Jerome Frank, Jr., notes, "People are very concerned about covered parking or garage parking and related issues of security. People like to see a security gate. They are a maintenance hell and don't provide much security, but it works psychologically." He adds, "Many higher-density apartments deal with this issue by putting parking in the middle. How traffic is handled—vehicular and pedestrian—has to be worked out in terms of planning for overall circulation (proximity of parking to housing and the length of walk to one's unit, for example)."[42]

Design elements can be used to create a sense of ownership. Studies of successful subsidized housing projects have shown that tenants take better care of their apartments when a transition area of "semiprivate" space that they can assume ownership of is provided between the outdoor public space and their private apartment. This concept can also work well for luxury apartments. The semiprivate space may range from an inset doorway to a fenced-in front patio. Inside the unit, a transition space should also be provided. Units that open directly into the living room do not rent as well as those with a foyer or at least some kind of separation—perhaps simply a different floor material—from the living room.

Privacy for individual apartments is increased by fences, walls, and plantings used as screens between patios, buildings, and the street. With duplex or two-story arrangements, garden apartments take on characteristics of townhouses. High-end apartments in Irvine, California, for example, are being designed so that the second-floor unit has a ground-level entry with an interior staircase. The second-floor living room opens onto a high-ceilinged foyer to create a sense of space. The private ground-floor entries have special appeal if the unit is to be converted to condominium use.

Rental Apartments versus Condominiums. Rental housing and for-sale (condominium) housing differ in their design in a number of respects. Security and privacy are even more important issues in condominiums. If rental and for-sale units are combined in the same complex, they should be physically separated, because their proximity hurts the sale of condominiums. Renters are not confronted with the long-term investment of a mortgage and are less likely to be critical of a less-desirable location within the complex as a whole. Many condominium complexes forbid investor-owned units, because owner-occupants do not want to live next to renters.

Some condominium developers recommend higher bedroom counts in the unit mix. In general, there should be a smaller number but a greater variety of dwelling units per building in a condominium, compared with a rental project. In condominium projects, units should be

Tree-lined brick walking streets provide an alternative to the automobile in the Davidson Mews section of Austin Ranch.

larger, by at least 20 to 25 percent. Kitchens need additional countertop space and cabinets. Baths must have better appointments and offer the feel of a master suite. Closets and general storage areas also must be larger.

One-quarter to one-half more parking space per condominium unit is often required, compared with rental units. Moreover, condominium spaces should be identified and separated from rental unit spaces. Assigned spaces can, however, create management problems as a result of the misuse of those spaces.

As a general rule, condominium units are difficult to sell before they are completed, because buyers have trouble visualizing the final result. Furnished model units are thus worth the time and expense they require, because they help buyers to picture how their individual units will function.

Designing to Save Costs. Developers must make many decisions that involve tradeoffs between construction costs and operating costs. For example, the use of exterior wood siding may save construction costs, but because such siding needs to be repainted every five to six years, its use may increase maintenance costs. High-maintenance materials also depress the sale value of a rental project, because proper accounting for operating expenses indicates the extent to which replacement reserves and maintenance expenses reduce net operating income.

Some elements of design have changed considerably over the last 30 years. Separate water, electricity, and gas meters were rare until soaring utility bills in the 1970s virtually mandated separate metering and separate heating and air-conditioning units. The additional cost was justified not only by tenants' paying for their own utilities but also by renters' preferences for separate HVAC controls and the advantage of separate meters for future conversion to condominiums.

Design Process
Preliminary Plans. Some developers believe that the safest way to deal with local government officials is to tell them

Native materials such as limestone and red granite, old-growth landscaping, and traditional architectural features help create a signature style at Austin Ranch.

very little until documents are submitted for project approval. This policy is not, however, wise. If any public review is required, the developer should meet with an official of the reviewing agency before drawing up preliminary plans. A preapplication conference is a useful means of meeting the planning staff and learning their likes and dislikes. In turn, the planning staff can inform the developer of the requirements that must be met and the factors to consider during the planning stage. The conference also gives the developer the chance to involve the staff in the project, thereby encouraging a sense of cooperation that is likely to make the entire project proceed more smoothly.

Even in cases when the developer can apply directly for a building permit, it is possible to obtain valuable information from members of the planning department before starting to draw up design plans. For example, the fire inspector at one building department informed Peiser Corporation and Jerome Frank Investments of proposed changes that their architect had not heard of regarding the regulations governing fire walls. The changes made it more economical to use sprinklers than floor-to-rafter fire-rated partitions. Six months later, when they returned for plan approval, the proposed changes had taken effect. Thus, the fire inspector's forewarning saved Peiser and Frank the time and money that would otherwise have been necessary to redraw the plans.

A developer should not spend too much money on preliminary plans in case, as often happens, the project does not proceed. At the same time, however, sufficient care should be taken so that the plans satisfy government agencies and financial backers. Further, the most creative part of the design process often occurs in drawing preliminary plans. The preliminary plan phase sometimes is divided into a rough concept planning phase and a refined schematic phase. Rough concept plans consist of floor plans and elevations that may be prepared for testing the market for financing and for tenants, whereas refined schematic drawings represent the last opportunity for major design decisions. Refined schematic drawings also are used to solicit lenders and tenants. Once the plans are approved, most major features of a project cannot be changed.

A collaborative design process is important for ensuring that the design is as functional and marketable as possible. Regular meetings should be held with property managers, construction superintendents, and leasing managers to obtain their input and to have them critique the latest plans. Beginning developers should ask mentors and other developers to review the plans as well. They may see problems in the design that others do not.

Many communities now have design review hearings open to the public. The developer should meet with design review board members (often local architects) as soon as possible to learn about their primary concerns. Neighbors, especially in infill areas, will have strong opinions about the design, including facades, ingress, egress, parking, materials, landscaping, elevations, open space, and views. Developers should be prepared to answer their criticisms. It is advisable to meet with them sooner rather than later in the design process. In this way, the developer can learn about their concerns in advance. The meetings can help to establish a rapport if the neighbors feel that their concerns are being addressed. In addition, the neighbors may understand the compromises and tradeoffs better if they are part of the process rather than being asked to react to final plans.

Final Plans. Final plans and specifications become part of the official contract package used by the contractor and submitted to the lender and the city building department. They include the construction drawings and material specifications required to build the project.

Unless a developer is certain that the project will go ahead, final plans and specifications should not be ordered until all feasibility studies are completed, all predevelopment approvals—such as zoning changes—are in place, and a tentative financing commitment is received. Final plans and specifications, which typically cost three or four times as much as the preliminary plans, represent a major increase in at-risk investment. They must be completed in their entirety before plans can be submitted to the city for a building permit.[43] And in cities such as Los Angeles, the building permit process is so lengthy (six months or more) that a developer cannot afford to make any major changes to the plans once they have been submitted.

Because the drawings and specifications become contract documents, the more precise and well coordinated they are, the better. At the same time, items such as air-conditioning equipment should not be specified too exactly in case the contractor can make a cost-saving substitution.

Change orders during construction are the single largest source of construction cost overruns. Unfortunately, they are unavoidable, and prudent developers carry up to a 5 percent construction contingency for these unexpected events. The fewer changes that are made, the fewer opportunities the contractor or sub-

contractor has to raise the contract price. If the developer has done his homework properly during preliminary plans, the process of obtaining final drawings should be routine. The time for intensive review and refinement is during preliminary plans, and both the architect and engineer should be able to produce final plans and specifications with little interruption from the developer. The contractor should be involved as early as possible in reviewing the drawings so as to minimize problems in the field and provide cost-to-value assistance to the entire development team.

Design Trends. Atlanta architect Ray Kimsey points out a number of changes that have occurred in apartment design in recent years:[44]

- The entire design team is much more involved with issues relating to building codes and zoning codes.
- Building departments that looked at residential construction very casually before 1985 are now taking a closer look.
- Multifamily construction increasingly is viewed as a commercial enterprise with high demand for fire safety and protection; local municipalities are imposing many more requirements for sprinklers to be installed in multifamily projects.
- Much more attention is paid to accessibility for handicapped individuals since passage of the Fair Housing Act of 1988.
- Much more stringent zoning reduces the availability of easily rezoned land outside some key urbanized areas.
- The percentage of conventional, suburban garden apartment projects has gone down tremendously. On the other hand, the percentage of urban infill projects has risen dramatically, with many projects located where mass transit is available (especially in Atlanta, Denver, Washington, D.C., Boston, and Chicago).
- In the case of building exteriors, the emphasis today is on long-term asset management. Fifteen years ago, apartments were built in the same way as a single-family residence. More attention is being paid to ex-

---

Do's and Don'ts for Dealing with Architects

- The developer should keep a direct line of communication open with the design architect. Intermediaries are a liability in the initial phases of design.
- Establish team milestones to ensure the project stays on schedule.
- Use an initial design workshop to streamline the concept design phase.
- Always use a qualified contractor who has experience and legitimate references and involve him from the very beginning of the design process.

- Pay very careful attention to the circulation of the building and site plan. Sometimes the investment in a computer simulation helps to clarify unresolved issues about circulation.
- Invest in design that creates a particular ambience and sense of identity, but keep cost considerations in mind.
- Identify the norms for the region when choosing amenities and functional systems.
- Always have a furniture plan drawn up for each apartment type proposed

by the architect. Sometimes the design may seem very good, but the configuration and dimensions of the rooms will not allow for even the most typical furniture, like couches and larger beds, to be located well in the unit. ■

Sources: Jan Van Tilberg, Van Tilberg, Banvard & Soderbergh, Santa Monica, California; and Paige Close, Looney Ricks Kiss Architects, Memphis, Tennessee.

terior maintenance costs and to the full life cycle of materials used for the exterior.

Financing

Rental apartment projects, like other income property developments, have traditionally relied primarily on three types of financing: construction loans, permanent loans, and equity.

For-sale condominium projects, like land development, usually involve only equity and a construction loan, the latter covering the construction and sales period. Buyers of individual condominium units obtain their own permanent loans. By contrast, in rental apartment projects, the developer uses the permanent loan to *take out* the construction loan as soon as the apartment reaches a specified level of income or occupancy. The amount of the construction loan usually equals that of the permanent loan, because the construction lender will lend up to, but no more than, the amount that the permanent lender will fund. The construction lender looks to the permanent lender's funds to retire the construction loan.

Equity makes up the difference between total project cost and the amount of the construction and permanent loans. In the 1960s and 1970s, construction and permanent loans often covered 100 percent of project costs, and developers were not required to contribute additional equity. After the real estate crash of the late 1980s and early 1990s, however, stiffer loan coverage requirements usually demand that equity cover 15 to 30 percent of total project costs.

Equity is the most expensive source of funding because equity investors receive returns only after other lenders have been repaid. Equity investors therefore have the riskiest position, and they require much higher rates of return to compensate for the risk. Construction lenders usually require developers to invest most or all of the needed equity in a project before they begin to fund the construction loan. Even after the construction loan has been retired by the permanent mortgage, equity investors receive cash flow only to the extent that property produces cash flow over and above the annual mortgage debt service. If a shortfall occurs, developers (or their investors) are responsible for injecting additional equity to cover the shortfall so that the bank always receives its full monthly debt service payment when it is due. Otherwise, the permanent mortgage goes into default, and lenders can begin foreclosure proceedings on the project.

For beginning developers, the task of finding lenders is perhaps the hardest job after finding equity investors. Lenders look chiefly at track record, credit, and the project itself. By definition, beginning developers lack a track record, and they rarely have the financial net worth of more experienced developers. Thus, the project must be well above average in terms of its market feasibility, design, and economic appeal to capture a lender's interest. Beginning developers can improve their chances

of securing loans by joint venturing with experienced developers and/or wealthy individuals. Beginning developers should also bear in mind that smaller localized lenders are more likely than large banks to consider their requests. Many developers begin as homebuilders, which allows them to build relationships with lenders that carry over to subsequent larger projects. Lenders are just as concerned about the way developers handle their business (meet deadlines, handle draw requests, build within budget, and so forth) as they are about the size of developers' previous projects, although they must be satisfied that the developer has the competency to complete larger, more complicated projects. (See Chapter 2 for a review of the various financial institutions that provide construction and permanent financing for real estate.)

Construction Loans

Traditionally, developers obtained a permanent loan commitment before obtaining a construction loan commitment, even though construction financing occurs before permanent financing. The construction lender approves the construction loan on the basis of the promise that the loan would be retired by the permanent loan at some specified date. In the early 1980s, however, when interest rates soared, open-ended construction loans without permanent takeouts became common. Floating-rate *miniperms*—three- to five-year construction loans that carried over into the operating period—were granted on the expectation that permanent rates would come down. This drop in fact occurred as permanent loan rates fell from the high teens to 12 percent, so developers who used miniperms fared well.[45] The provision of open-ended loans, however, generally depends on the track records and financial statements of developers. Beginning developers usually must have a permanent takeout commitment unless they possess a very strong financial statement and an excellent credit history.

The construction loan is characterized by its short term, installment draws, variable interest rate, and single repayment when the project is completed and the construction loan is taken out by the permanent loan.[46] The developer files draw requests with the construction lender each month as work progresses on the project. The lender funds the request by transferring money into the developer's project account. This money is then available for the developer to pay the contractor (see Figure 4-10).

The limit, term, and interest rate of the construction loan are defined by the loan agreement. Interest payments are added to the loan balance so that the developer does not have to make out-of-pocket payments. If the project is not fully leased and the permanent loan is not funded within the stated term limit, the construction lender is technically able to *call the loan*—that is, demand immediate payment from the developer. In practice, however, the construction lender does not want to have to foreclose on a bad construction loan as long as a reasonable likelihood exists that the project can be completed successfully. If the developer has kept them regularly informed about the project's progress and reasons for delay,

figure 4-10
Calculating Interest for a Construction Loan

Suppose a developer has a $1 million construction loan with 2 points ($20,000) paid upfront (out of loan proceeds). Assuming 10 percent annual interest, interest on the construction loan and the draw schedule are as follows. The bank will accrue interest monthly. The loan must be repaid at the end of the 12th month.

Month	Beginning Balance	Interest Charges	Current Draws	Ending Balance
0			$20,000	$20,000
1	$20,000	$167	40,000	60,167
2	60,167	501	80,000	140,668
3	140,668	1,172	80,000	221,840
4	221,840	1,849	100,000	323,689
5	323,689	2,697	100,000	426,386
6	426,386	3,553	100,000	529,940
7	529,940	4,416	100,000	634,356
8	634,356	5,286	100,000	739,642
9	739,642	6,164	100,000	845,806
10	845,806	7,048	100,000	952,854
11	952,854	7,940	80,000	1,040,795
12	1,040,795	8,673	0	1,049,468
Total		$49,468	$1,000,000	

Total amount to be repaid to the bank: $1,049,468

Effective yield to the bank: 14.49%

the construction lender will probably be willing to extend the construction loan term by six or 12 months. Such extensions almost always require the payment of an additional one or two points.

Construction loans suffer from a high degree of uncertainty: delays caused by weather, labor troubles, and material shortages; cost overruns; bankruptcies by contractors and subcontractors; and leasing risk (lease-up rates and rents that fall below expectations). Consequently, lenders providing construction funding take special precautions to ensure their protection.

Moreover, construction lenders have become increasingly suspicious of the viability of permanent commitments. Permanent loans sometimes contain such stringent covenants that developers must meet before funding is provided that takeout loans are unlikely to materialize. In negotiating permanent takeouts, developers must take care that they have bankable commitments—that is, commitments that construction lenders will lend against.

The lender's security comes from two sources: the project and the developer's credit. The developer typically is required to sign personally on the construction loan and must show a net worth at least equal to the loan. During economic downturns, the credit requirements may become even more stringent, and the developer may have to prove a liquid net worth (cash, stocks, and bonds) equal to the amount of the loan.

For apartments, the construction loan usually has a term of one to two years, which must cover both the con-

struction and lease-up periods. Interest rates depend on the developer's credit and typically range from 1 to 3 percent over prime with one or two points upfront.[47]

If total project cost exceeds the amount of the construction loan, construction lenders require a beginning developer to put the necessary equity into the project on the front end, before the developer can draw down on the construction loan. Any necessary equity must therefore be raised before construction can begin.

Interest is calculated each month on the average daily balance. Developers can make precise calculations of their interest requirements (as illustrated in Figure 4-10), but banks have their own method for computing interest. For example, if a total loan amount is $1 million with a one-year term at 10 percent interest, a bank may apply a standard factor as high as 0.75 to determine the average loan balance, even though a developer may show the average loan balance to be 0.50 of the final amount. This factor is used to determine the interest reserve, or $75,000 in the above example ($1,000,000 x 0.75 average balance x 10 percent interest x 1 year).

Institutional lenders require a first lien on the property. Existing loans automatically have a superior position to subsequent loans under the rule of *first in time, first in priority*. Thus, any prior loans such as seller financing or land development loans must be paid off, releasing the senior liens, at the time of the first construction draw.

Construction loan draws are tied to stages in the construction process, called *percent completion*, based on an appraisal of the work completed to date. The appraisal is done by the developer, the architect, or an inspector hired by the lender. If the value as measured by percent completion is lower, additional draws will not be permitted, irrespective of the dollar amount expended by the developer. The developer makes a detailed line item budget of off-site expenses such as street improvements and traffic signals, on-site expenses such as asphalt and landscaping, and direct construction expenses for the whole project. For example, he may tell the lender he is 50 percent done with concrete and wants 50 percent funding of the line item for concrete. The lender's inspector may check and say that only 40 percent of the work has been done. Then the developer negotiates or explains why 50 percent is done, and the two parties come to terms.

Construction loans have traditionally been made by *institutional* lenders, namely, commercial banks and sometimes insurance companies and pension funds. Institutional lenders are subject to close scrutiny by the Federal Reserve, which carefully monitors loan balances and reserves. If a loan is not repaid on time or if interest payments are not made, the loan is placed into a separate category that requires significantly higher *loan reserves* (cash balances held by the bank to offset potential losses).

In the wake of the real estate crash of the late 1980s, the Financial Institutions Reform, Recovery, and Enforcement Act (FIRREA) was enacted in 1989. Among other things, it regulates the amount of bank reserves required to cover high-risk real estate loans. The average equity reserve was initially 3 percent but has been raised to 6 percent to minimize defaults. The rates are variable and depend on whether the loan is standard, development, or speculative. Many law firms specialize in compliance with FIRREA.[48]

Because higher loan reserves drag down a bank's earnings, banks are eager to avoid any construction loans that involve unnecessary risk. This caution makes it especially difficult for new developers to obtain financing, because lenders are even more reluctant than before the real estate crash to lend money to developers who do not have lengthy track records.

The task of finding a construction lender is much simpler if a developer has a takeout loan commitment for the permanent loan. Jerome Frank, Jr., states that it might be worthwhile to join forces with someone who has the credit history and relationship with a bank. He emphasizes that finding the lowest loan rate is less important than establishing a relationship with a good banker: "A quarter to a half point in interest is not going to make or break the deal. The most important thing for the developer is not going to be the rate but the time—making sure that he negotiates enough time for himself to get it done." Frank adds that developers should watch out for future balloon payments. "Make sure you are not caught with a short balloon that requires refinancing. Try to build in the ability to renew or extend the loan at the beginning and buy yourself time."[49]

Randolph Hawthorne observes that the tension always remains between the construction lender and the permanent lender about who is going to finance the lease-up risk. "People are pretty skilled at building competently without significant time overruns. The real risks in both the affordable and higher-income side are what the demand is and how quickly the property will lease-up initially, which have a huge effect on the pro forma. In times of optimism, you see a lot of open-ended construction loans, the so-called *miniperms* without a forward commitment for permanent financing. When markets get soft or when people get concerned about regulatory pressures, they do not seek open-ended construction loans but look for forward commitments and permanent financing instead."[50]

Karl Zavitkovsky says it is important to distinguish between loans provided by small banks and loans provided by big banks. Smaller regional banks originate loans that they plan to keep on their own balance sheets, whereas large banks syndicate the loans to other banks and get them off their books as soon as possible. Large developers like JPI and Trammell Crow Company depend on banks with high-volume credit facilities—those that deal in $15 million to $20 million and larger syndicated transactions. "Smaller banks tend to underprice the big institutions, because they do not have the portfolio exposure limitations of big banks. Big banks issue loans with flexible pricing language that reserves the right to ratchet up the interest rate, say from LIBOR [London interbank offered rate] plus 200 to LIBOR plus 225 to syndicate it.[51] Even with these types of tools, it is almost impossible to syndicate speculative loans because of current attitudes in large financial institutions."[52]

Permanent Financing

Permanent financing—a long-term mortgage on the completed project—is a critical ingredient in the development process, especially for projects undertaken by beginning developers who are unlikely to receive construction financing without a permanent loan takeout. Permanent loans take many forms. In addition to bullet loans and the standard fixed-rate, adjustable-rate, and variable-rate mortgages, lenders make participating loans and convertible loans.[53] Participating loans give lenders a participation in cash flows after debt service and sometimes a participation in residual cash flows from sale. These participations, called *kickers,* raise lenders' IRRs above the loan rate by an additional 2 or 3 percent—an amount sufficient for lenders to consider funding 80 to 95 percent of a project's costs. A comparison of a standard bullet loan with two lender participation loans is shown in Figure 4-11, showing how these different approaches change the loan terms, cash flows, and yields. The best approach depends on the developer's situation and preferences. The summary statistics indicate that the participating loan with owner priorities gives the highest return to the developer, as measured by net present value—$427,000. The participating loan with lender priorities gives the highest return to the lender—12.52 percent.

Another popular variation on standard mortgages provides a *note rate,* which is higher than the *pay rate.*

figure 4-11

Comparison of Bullet and Participating Loans for a Prototypical Income-Producing Development

Bullet loans are standard fixed-rate mortgages, amortizable over 30 years but with a five-, seven-, or ten-year call (repayment) provision. Participating loans, commonly made by pension funds, give the lender a participation in annual cash flows and proceeds from sale. The developer or the lender may receive a priority cash flow before the participation is calculated.

Assumptions (000)

Project Cost	$11,000
Net Rentable Square Feet	93
Depreciable Basis of Building	$9,500
Depreciation Method	31-1/2 years SL
Initial Gross Potential Income	$1,674
Income Appreciation Rate	4%
Vacancy Rate	5%
Initial Operating Expenses	$419
Expense Inflation Rate	4%
Ordinary Tax Rate	28%
Costs of Sale	4%
Holding Period	5 years

Loan Terms (000)	Bullet Loan	Participating Loan with Developer Priorities	Participating Loan with Lender Priorities
Required Debt Coverage Ratios	1.20	1.15	1.15
Maximum Loan-to-Value Ratio	75%	90%	90%
Loan Amount	$8,788	$10,546	$10,546
Note Rate	9.60%	8.75%	8.75%
Loan Fee	0%	0%	0%
Loan Amortization (years)	30	30	30
Cash-Flow Kicker to Lender	–	50%	50%
Owner's Threshold Cash Flow		$20	–
Lender's Threshold	–	–	$20
Reversion Kicker to Lender	–	50%	50%
Owner's Threshold Reversion	–	$200	–
Lender's Threshold Reversion	–	–	$200
Land Sale Price	–	–	–
Land Lease Payment Rate	–	–	–
Land Repurchase Price	–	–	–

After-Tax Cash Flows from First Year of Operations (000)	Bullet Loan	Participating Loan with Developer Priorities	Participating Loan with Lender Priorities
Annual Tax Liabilities			
Net Operating Income	$1,172	$1,172	$1,172
Less: Interest	844	920	920
Less: Depreciation	302	302	302
Less: Land Lease	–	–	–
Less: Lender Participation	–	78a	98
Taxable Income	$26	($128)	($148)
Taxes Paid (saved)	$ 7	($36)	($41)

continued

figure 4-11

Comparison of Bullet and Participating Loans for a Prototypical Income-Producing Development *continued*

Annual After-Tax Cash Flow	Bullet Loan	Participating Loan with Developer Priorities	Participating Loan with Lender Priorities
Net Operating Income	$1,172	$1,172	$1,172
Less: Land Lease	–	–	–
Less: Mortgage Payment	896	996	996
Less: Threshold Amount Paid to Developer	–	20	–
Less: Threshold Amount Paid to Lender	–	–	20
Cash Flow Subject to Participation	$275	$156	$156
Less: Lender Participation	–	78[a]	78
Before-Tax Cash Flow	$275	$98[b]	$78[c]
Less: Taxes Paid (saved)	7	(36)	(41)
After-Tax Cash Flow	$268	$134	$119

After-Tax Cash Flows from Sale (000)	Bullet Loan	Participating Loan with Developer Priorities	Participating Loan with Lender Priorities
Tax Liability upon Sale			
Net Sale Price	$13,160	$13,160	$13,160
Less: Adjusted Tax Basis	9,492	9,492	9,492
Taxable Capital Gain	$3,668	$3,668	$3,668
Tax on Capital Gain	1,027	1,027	1,027
Tax Savings from Lender Payments	–	402	458
Total Tax Liability	$1,027	$625	$569
After-Tax Cash Flows upon Sale			
Net Sale Price	$13,160	$13,160	$13,160
Less: Land Purchase Price	–	–	–
Mortgage Balance	$8,466	$10,092	$10,092
Threshold Amount Paid to Owner	–	200	–
Threshold Amount Paid to Lender	–	–	200
Cash Flow Subject to Participation	$4,694	$2,868	$2,868
Less: Lender Participation	–	1,434	1,434
Threshold Amount Paid to Owner	–	200	–
Before-Tax Cash Flow	$4,694	$1,634	$1,434
Less: Tax Liability	1,027	625	569
After-Tax Cash Flow from Sale	$3,667	$1,009	$865

Summary Statistics for Developer and Lender (000)	Bullet Loan	Participating Loan with Owner Priorities	Participating Loan with Lender Priorities
Developer:			
Sale at End of Year	5	5	5
Owner's Equity Contribution	$2,211	$454	$454
Undiscounted Before-Tax Net Cash Flows	$4,348	$1,915	$1,615
Net Present Value of Cash Flows Discounted at 20%	$227	$427	$327
Lender:			
Loan Amount	$8,788	$10,546	$10,546
LTV Ratio	75%	90%	90%
Effective DCR	1.31	1.18	1.18
Lender Yield	9.59%	12.05%	12.52%

Notes
[a] Calculated below.
[b] Includes threshold amount paid to owner.
[c] Includes threshold amount paid to lender.

The note rate is the nominal interest rate on the mortgage, say 12 percent. The pay rate (used to determine the monthly debt service) is lower, at, say, 10 percent, because the initial cash flow from the property will not cover mortgage payments at the note rate. The difference in interest payments between the 12 percent note rate and the 10 percent pay rate is accrued until the property is sold. The advantage of a lower pay rate is that the borrower can obtain a larger loan than if the mortgage payment were calculated from the note rate, because the lower interest rate reduces the mortgage payment (see Figure 4-12 for an illustration of the calculation).

The types of permanent financing are much better today than they were in the early 1990s because of Wall Street's greatly increased involvement in the mortgage market. *Conduit loans* (so called because the loan originator in effect has a conduit through Wall Street directly to investors) have significantly increased the amount of mortgage money in recent years. Mortgage brokers, banks, and other lenders prenegotiate the sale of a package of mortgages, say $100 million, to a Wall Street underwriter under certain terms. They then proceed to originate the mortgages to borrowers or to buy existing mortgages from other originators. The Wall Street underwriter sells the package of mortgages to investors, using the proceeds to reimburse the originator. Sales of commercial mortgages in the secondary market, of which conduit loans represent one form, are a relatively new phenomenon. They follow years of evolution of single-family residential mortgage sales in the secondary market through quasi-governmental organizations like Fannie Mae and Ginnie Mae.

In the case of a conduit loan, the original borrower is known as the *sponsor*. Typically, this individual is the owner of a completed project, a large-scale building, and is seeking new sources of capital. The owned building is put up as collateral for the loan. The *originator* is the institution that loans the money against the building at a discounted rate to the sponsor. The *issuer* could be that lending institution or another institution that securitizes and issues a bond against the collateral.[54]

The popularity of different types of permanent mortgages changes frequently, sometimes every few months. The basic alternatives for permanent loans, however, remain the same—a fixed-rate or adjustable-rate mortgage for 65 to 80 percent of value, or some form of participating mortgage for 80 to 95 percent of value that gives the lender higher returns to cover the additional risk associated with higher leverage.

Financing Issues
Personal Guarantees and Loan Funding. Although standard practices differ from area to area and from time to time, most developers must personally guarantee their construction loans. Often, they must also guarantee some part of their permanent loans (such as the top 25 percent),[55] at least until their projects reach some threshold level of debt coverage or occupancy.

Lenders' requirements with respect to personal liability depend on the lending environment. After the real estate

---

figure 4-12
Mortgage Calculation: Pay Rate versus Note Rate

Suppose a mortgage has the following terms:

Mortgage Amount	$1,000,000
Term	30 years
Note Rate	12%
Pay Rate	10%

The monthly payment under the note rate would be:
PMT (PV = $1,000,000, i = 12/12, n = 30 x 12)[a] = $10,286.13

The monthly payment under the pay rate would be:
PMT (PV = $1,000,000, i = 10/12, n = 30 x 12) = 8,775.71

Difference in Monthly Payments (accrued) $1,510.42

The borrower would pay the lower amount, $8,775.71, and would accrue the difference of $1,510.42 per month. Suppose the borrower wanted to retire the mortgage after five years (60 months). The borrower would calculate the mortgage balance under the note rate:

PV (PMT = $10,286.13, i = 12/12, n = 300)[b] = $976,632.18

Next, the borrower would calculate the accrued interest:
FV (PMT = $1,510.42, i = 12/12, n = 60) = 123,354.71

Total Payment to Retire Mortgage $1,099,986.89

To retire the mortgage, the borrower would pay the combined amount, or $1,099,986.89.

To check the calculation, the present value of the monthly payments plus the present value of the combined payment at retirement, discounted at the note rate, should equal the initial mortgage of $1,000,000:

PV (PMT = $8,775.71, i = 12/12, n = 60) =	$394,512.64
PV (FV = $1,099,986.89, i = 12/12, n = 60) =	$605,487.36
Total	$1,000,000.00

Notes
[a] PMT = the mortgage payment; PV = the mortgage amount; i = the interest rate; n = the term; all represented as monthly figures.
[b] The ending balance on a mortgage is calculated on the remaining number of payments: 30 – 5 years = 25 years x 12 months = 300 months remaining on the mortgage.

---

crash in the 1990s, lenders became much more conservative in their lending practices and generally required developers to personally guarantee development loans. With more money for lending than good projects to loan on in the early 2000s, lenders have reduced their requirements to compete for business from experienced developers. Beginning developers, however, should be prepared to sign personally on their construction and development loans. They should be able to avoid personal liability on standard permanent loans for fully leased properties.

How do developers trade out personal liability? No developer wants to be a perpetual guarantor of the loan,

Applications for both construction and permanent financing should be accompanied by a mortgage package—usually a notebook or file—that includes many of the following items as appropriate:

Introduction
- Letter of transmittal;
- Loan application (supplied by lending institution and filled out by ownership entity and each major principal);
- Good faith deposit; and
- Mortgage loan submission sheet summarizing the major aspects of the project and terms of the loan request.

Property Description and Rationale
- Description of the physical aspects of the property;
- Acquisition, title, and zoning;
- Environmental reports;
- Attachments, including location maps, aerial photographs, surveys, floodplain maps, and so forth; and
- Community profile.

Economics
- Financial forecasts or historical operating statements for the project;
- Projected or current rent roll;
- Survey of competitive projects;
- Supply and demand information;
- Information about market rents and comparable sales; and
- Market vacancy rates.

Development Plan
- Land comparables showing sale prices of similar tracts of land in the area;
- Overall development plan;
- Complete engineering data covering soil tests, bearing strength, grading, road specifications, drainage, floodplain surveys, and so forth; and
- A copy of the purchase option.

Buildings
- Plans and specifications of proposed buildings; and
- Architectural drawings.

Credit Information
- Credit report on entity and principals;
- Financial statements of borrower and principals;
- Copy of the purchase money mortgage from seller (if any); and
- Financial statement of the landowner. ∎

Source: Steven M. Bram, president, George Smith Partners, Inc., Los Angeles, California.

---

and many developers refuse to agree to unconditional liability and negotiate for some performance criteria that release them from personal liability. Some alternative compromises include:

1. Lenders cannot call on the guarantor directly in the event of default. They must instead foreclose on the defaulting property and obtain a legal decision against the guarantor. Because judicial foreclosures can be time-consuming and expensive, lenders may prefer to take over the property immediately in return for releasing the developer from some or all of the liability under the guarantee.
2. The note limits the amount of any deficiency over time. For example, if the loan is current for three years, then the guarantor's liability reduces to, say, 50 percent of any deficiency.
3. The note states that if all the land improvements have been installed within budget and if the project has been completed, the developer's (guarantor's) liability reduces to zero after three years.
4. The developer places money in escrow to cover potential losses. Suppose a developer undertakes a project appraised at $12 million but requiring only $10 million in costs. The developer may borrow the full $12 million, leaving $2 million in escrow to eliminate any personal liability. This solution, of course, involves added interest costs, which in turn add to the project's risk.

Personal liability is defined to mean either the "top half" or "bottom half" of the loan. Suppose the developer guarantees the top half of a loan. If a project with a $10 million loan sells for $7 million, guarantee of the top half means that the developer owes the deficient $3 million. If the developer guarantees the bottom half, then nothing is owed unless the project sells for less than $5 million. In some cases, ambiguously worded loan documents that fail to specify whether the developer is guaranteeing the top or the bottom half of a loan have caused the developer and lender to end up in court. The prospect of a long court battle to satisfy the deficiency has motivated some lenders to settle with developers.

Beginning developers find it difficult to eliminate personal liability altogether, but they can negotiate to limit it. If they can limit their liability to a specified amount, they can sell pieces of that liability to their investors along with pieces of the transaction. It is hard enough, however, to raise equity without also asking investors to accept liability for potential losses.

Closing. Obtaining the funding (closing) for a permanent loan may involve almost as much work as originally securing the lender's commitment to provide that funding. The loan commitment document specifies the requirements for permanent loan funding. Typical requirements include a certified rent roll showing the property's actual cash flow as well as all signed lease documents. Loan closing can be an exasperating process, and any issues not clearly spelled out in the original commitment can come back to haunt the developer at closing. For example, loan documents may be ambiguous as to whether a project must be 90 percent leased, 90 percent occupied, or 90 percent occupied and paying rent. Lenders usually take the most restrictive interpretation, so developers are well advised to ensure that qualifying standards are described precisely.

Some loan commitments require that a project have attained certain rental objectives, say, 80 percent occupancy for a specified period—one month, six months, or 12 months. The shorter the period for qualification, the better for the developer. Lenders may also require that releases, credit reports, or other paperwork be obtained from all tenants. Such procedures should be confirmed at the outset, thereby allowing the property manager to obtain the necessary documentation as tenants sign new leases. It is much more difficult and can be costly to obtain such documents later.

Closing on condominium loans can pose a different set of problems. When markets are soft, sales may not reach targets set by permanent lenders, and developers may find themselves obliged to give investors unsold units in lieu of a cash return. If a developer subsequently decides to consolidate ownership and to convert a project to a rental project, the price of, or interest rates on, those units may be very high.

How difficult loan closings are depends on the local real estate market at the time of closing. When conditions become soft, lenders naturally become more concerned about the safety of their investments and thus more rigorous in the enforcement of the various requirements for closing.

Equity: Joint Ventures and Syndications. Developers use a variety of joint venture formats to raise equity, provide loan guarantees, and secure financing. This section focuses on joint ventures with equity partners.

Syndications are a form of joint venture in which equity from a number of smaller investors is raised through a private or public offering subject to regulations of the Securities and Exchange Commission. Investors in syndications receive a security interest similar to what they own in stocks or bonds, whereas joint ventures of only a few parties typically, but not necessarily, involve direct real estate interests. Every joint venture deal is different. Nonetheless, certain formats are more common, such as those described by the following three developers.

Tips on Joint Ventures and Deal Packaging

- In drawing up the partnership agreement, be very clear as to the rights and duties of each partner. Use arbitration to solve disputes.
- Beware of "dilution squeeze-down" provisions that allow investors to squeeze the developer out if a project does not generate a given level of current return.
- Some developers recommend overborrowing if possible because it allows them to withdraw money from a project without tax. Overborrowing increases the risk of default, however.
- Make sure that investors have no right to tell the developer how to run the project.
- If investors commit money to be paid in the future, make sure that the money is available by persuading investors to post letters of credit. ∎

Harry Mow, former board chair of Century West Development in Santa Monica, California, recommends keeping it simple. "If you cut too sharp a deal with your investors, you probably won't get them to invest in another deal." Mow, whose company does its own construction, adds a 15 percent fee to the hard and soft costs (excluding land and financing costs). The fee pays the superintendent, the project manager, corporate overhead, and the costs of raising equity. If the construction loan is sufficiently large to cover the 15 percent fee, it is paid to them in installments during construction. Otherwise, it is left in as a loan to the partnership until the property is sold, when they receive it out of sale proceeds. Cash flow from operations and sale of the property is distributed in the following order:

- First, the limited partners receive back their capital.
- Second, the limited partners receive a 6 percent cumulative return.
- Third, the limited partners and the general partners split the remainder equally. The developer also receives a 5 percent or 6 percent management fee and a 6 percent brokerage fee for selling the property.

Richard Gleitman, president of R.J. Investments Associates of Sherman Oaks, California, gives his equity partners—who tended initially to be friends and business associates—50 percent of the profits and an 8 percent noncumulative preferred return. He recovers all cash advances for land, entitlements, or other initial expenses for a project from the equity partners when they make their initial investment. Gleitman creates the joint venture before the close of land escrow as soon as he has reliable financial projections. Gleitman's firm charges a minimal contractor's fee—2 to 3 percent of hard costs—and a larger management fee—4 to 5 percent—that help cover the cost of using the largest, most active outside broker in an area to sell a project.

In his first deal, Paul Schultheis, president, Real Property Investment, Inc., of Arcadia, California, raised $400,000 in cash, splitting profits 50/50 with investors after they received back their capital. Because he had no previous direct experience, Schultheis brought in a builder and a broker/marketing director as general partners. He and his brother acquired the land, secured planning approvals, and performed the front-end work. The broker received 10 percent of the general partners' share of the deal; the three other partners received 30 percent each. Today, Schultheis gives neither the broker nor the builder any interest, as he is now able to pay for their services in cash.

In structuring joint ventures with investors, the priorities of payback and cash distributions are even more important than the final split of profits. Priorities simply refer to who gets what and when. As indicated in the previous examples, it is common for investors to receive back their investment before the developer shares in any profit. When both the investor and the developer have money invested in a project, the investor may receive, say, the first $100,000 as a priority before the developer receives the next $100,000 of cash flow. Priorities become a way of dealing with risk—the person who bears the most risk receives money back last. Risk is higher because, if a loss occurs, there may be no money left to pay back lower priorities.

Preferred returns are similar to interest on money invested in a savings account. The difference is that they are paid only if cash flow is available—like dividends—whereas interest must be paid currently whether cash flow from a project is available or not (if not, then the general partner must cover the interest from other sources). The basic concept behind preferred returns is that the investor will be paid back as a top priority at least the equivalent interest on his investment that he would earn in an interest-bearing account. Although many deals have no preferred returns, beginning developers are advised to include them because they make raising equity a little easier. Investors like the notion that they will receive back their initial equity plus a preferred return before the developer receives any profit. It is customary for the developer to receive a "development fee"—3 to 5 percent of total costs (sometimes excluding land) during construction to cover overhead. But any significant profit to the developer carries a lower priority than the investor's return of capital and preferred return.

One of the simpler and more common deal structures has four priorities (similar to Harry Mow's structure described above):

1. Investors receive a current preferred return.
2. Investors receive unpaid but accrued preferred returns.
3. Investors receive back their equity.
4. Investors and the developer split the remainder according to a *profit split* ranging from 80/20 (80 percent to the investors) to 50/50.

The payment of preferred returns can be structured as *cumulative* or *noncumulative*. In the case of a cumulative preferred return, any unpaid preferred return in one period is accumulated until funds are available to pay it in a later period. A noncumulative preferred return does not accumulate in this fashion, and unpaid returns during a period of insufficient cash flow are forgotten and left unpaid.

The *current* preferred return is that amount owed each year, found by multiplying the preferred return rate by the equity. For example, if the preferred return rate is 8 percent and the equity is $1 million, the current preferred return is $80,000. Figure 4-13 shows how the cash flows and IRRs would differ for the same deal under the two different preferred return structures. Both deals illustrate a 10 percent preferred return with a 50/50 split of the remaining profits. Note that the cumulative preferred return is accrued in Years 1 and 2, because the cash flows of $5,000 and $8,000 are insufficient to cover the 10 percent preferred return of $10,000; the

outstanding sum is finally paid off in Year 5. Because of the accumulation provision, the total cash flow to the investor is $104,000, compared with $100,500 in the non-cumulative case. The investor's IRR is 17.02 percent, compared with 16.60 percent. The developer's total cash flow is less in the cumulative case, $54,000 as opposed to $57,500, because the investor receives more from the same total project cash flows.

In some deals involving cumulative preferred returns, the *accrued return balance* earns interest. Many developers, however, prefer not to pay such interest because it further reduces their share of the proceeds without enhancing the marketability of their deals. Another variation gives accrued preferred returns a lower priority, and they are paid *after* the investor's equity is paid back. This twist further helps the developer, because current preferred returns are reduced as investors' equity is paid back (from annual cash flows that exceed the *current* preferred return).

Developer Fees. One of the most delicate issues in raising equity is when and how much the developer will receive. Both investors and lenders want assurances that their position is ahead of the developer's—and that they get back their money as well as a reasonable return on their money *before* the developer receives significant profit. They want assurances that the developer has strong incentives to work hard on their behalf throughout the development process.

This situation creates potential conflicts of interest, which generally are resolved in favor of the investors. When Peiser Corporation first raised equity, a popular refrain (uttered mainly to themselves) was "developers have to eat too." Lenders and investors unfortunately like to see very thin developers. They believe that the more money the developer receives on the front end of a deal, the less incentive there is to work hard on their behalf. Therefore, they want to see virtually all the developer's compensation, both in fees and profit share, deferred until the end (final sale of the project). The developer, on the other hand, needs to at least cover the out-of-pocket costs for managing the deal and for performing all the functions necessary to complete it properly. As a rule, lenders allow the developer to take out 3 to 6 percent of the construction cost to cover direct overhead costs—in addition to any on-site construction superintendents.

Developers can receive fees from a number of different activities in the course of a deal. The fees fall into two main categories: 1) compensation for specific achievements, and 2) share in the upside profits. Even when fees are earned, their timing of payment to the developer is subject to priorities as described above. The developer, for example, may earn fees totaling 10 percent of the development cost during construction and lease-up of the project. He may be allowed to receive (or take out) only half of those fees during the construction and lease-up period. The other 5 percent may be subordinated to the investors' receiving back all their equity plus an 8 percent preferred return.

figure 4-13

Cumulative versus Noncumulative Preferred Returns

		Year 0	Year 1	Year 2	Year 3	Year 4	Year 5	Total
	Project's Cash Flows							
1	Equity Investment	($100,000)						($100,000)
2	Cash Flows from Operations		$5,000	$8,000	$10,000	$15,000	$20,000	58,000
3	Cash Flows from Sale						200,000	200,000
4								
5	Total	($100,000)	$5,000	$8,000	$10,000	$15,000	$220,000	$158,000
6								
7	**Cumulative Preferred Return**							
8	Preferred Return Owed	10.00%	$10,000	$10,000	$10,000	$10,000	$10,000	$50,000
9	Preferred Return Paid		5,000	8,000	10,000	10,000	10,000	43,000
10	Unpaid Preferred Return		5,000	2,000	0	0	0	7,000
11								
12	Preferred Return Accrued		$5,000	$7,000	$7,000	$7,000	$2,000	
13	Accrued Return Paid		0	0	0	5,000	2,000	7,000
14	Accrued Return Balance		5,000	7,000	7,000	2,000	0	0
15								
16	Return of Equity		$0	$0	$0	$0	$100,000	$100,000
17	Equity Balance	100,000	100,000	100,000	100,000	100,000	0	0
18								
19	Cash Flow for Distribution		$0	$0	$0	$0	$108,000	$108,000
20	50% to Investor		0	0	0	0	54,000	54,000
21	50% to Developer		0	0	0	0	54,000	54,000
22								
23	Net Cash Flow to Investor	($100,000)	$5,000	$8,000	$10,000	$15,000	$166,000	$104,000
24	Investor's IRR	17.02%						
25								
26	**Noncumulative Preferred Return**							
27	Preferred Return Owed	10.00%	$10,000	$10,000	$10,000	$10,000	$10,000	$50,000
28	Preferred Return Paid		5,000	8,000	10,000	10,000	10,000	43,000
29	Unpaid Preferred Return		5,000	2,000	0	0	0	7,000
30								
31	Preferred Return Accrued		$0	$0	$0	$0	$0	
32	Accrued Return Paid		0	0	0	0	0	0
33	Accrued Return Balance		0	0	0	0	0	0
34								
35	Return of Equity		$0	$0	$0	$5,000	$95,000	$100,000
36	Equity Balance	$100,000	100,000	100,000	100,000	95,000	0	0
37								
38	Cash Flow for Distribution		$0	$0	$0	$0	$115,000	$115,000
39	50% to Investor		0	0	0	0	57,500	57,500
40	50% to Developer		0	0	0	0	57,500	57,500
41								
42	Net Cash Flow to Investor	($100,000)	$5,000	$8,000	$10,000	$15,000	$162,500	$100,500
43	Investor's IRR	16.60%						

The developer's share of upside profits is, by definition, something that is paid on the back end of a deal—usually when it is sold. Most joint venture agreements also allow the developer to take out cash if a project is refinanced, although even here, the cash is often subordinated to return of capital and preferred return to the investors.[56]

An infinite number of deal structures are possible. Joint ventures with institutional investors (firms that invest money on behalf of their own clients, such as pension fund advisers) are described in detail in Chapter 6. These investors have a preidentified partner who will negotiate with the developer about the fees.

Beginning developers usually are not able to attract institutional investors. The advantage of starting with smaller deals is that they require less equity. It is much easier to raise $100,000 or $200,000 than $1 million or more. In either event, the developer usually raises money from family or friends, who will look to the developer to fashion a fair deal. The developer must decide what to offer them. Because of his inexperience, the investors, however friendly or supportive personally, want the developer to defer as much compensation as possible.

Simpler deal structures are recommended, primarily because they are easier to explain to potential investors. For tax reasons, it is advantageous to set fees that can be expensed immediately rather than being amortized over five years or, in some cases, never expensed at all. Therefore, a tax accountant is an essential member of the developer's team, even before the process of raising equity begins.[57] In addition to the developer's fee, other common fees include:

Front-End Fees

Acquisition fee	1–2 percent of acquisition cost
Organization fee for partnership	1–3 percent of equity raised
Financing fee	1–2 percent of financing raised (usually shared with outside mortgage brokers, if used)

Fees Paid during Construction or Lease-Up

Development fee	3–5 percent of hard costs or total cost; may include or exclude land
Construction fee	4–8 percent of construction cost (usually paid to contractor)
Leasing fees	4–6 percent commissions on leases (shared with outside brokers)

Fees Paid upon Sale of the Project

Sales fee	4–6 percent commission on sale price (shared with outside brokers)

Profit

Preferred return	Same as investors (6–10 percent) on equity invested[58]
Profit share	20–50 percent of profit (usually after investor receives back all equity plus preferred return)

Investors' Primary Concerns. Investors are most concerned with the following five aspects of joint venture deals:

1. Preferred Return Yields—These yields tend to approximate the interest rate on money market accounts plus 1 to 3 percent. In the early 2000s, preferred returns typically range from 6 to 10 percent times the equity account balance at the beginning of each year.

2. Share of Residual Profits—In deals sold privately and in joint ventures with financial institutions or large investors, profit splits range from 75/25 (75 percent to investors) to 50/50. In public syndications, however, the profit split is usually 80/20 (80 percent to investors) or at best 70/30. The percentage to investors is higher because stockbrokers and financial planners who sell the deals claim that investors are reluctant to buy into projects that offer lower profit shares.

3. Downside Liabilities—Most syndications and joint ventures are structured as limited partnerships that restrict investors' downside liabilities. Unless investors sign notes for more than their direct equity investment, their downside risk is limited to the loss of their equity.

4. Cash Calls—Cash calls occur when a partnership requires additional equity from the investors to meet its obligations. Sophisticated investors tend to be more concerned about the handling of cash calls. Most partnership agreements have provisions that penalize partners for not making cash calls. For example, consider a partner, Smith, who has invested $50,000 out of total equity of $100,000 for a 50 percent interest. Suppose each partner makes a $10,000 cash call. Smith fails to come up with his $10,000, so the other partner, Jones, must come up with $20,000. In a prorated dilution arrangement, Jones would have invested $70,000 out of $120,000, reducing Smith's interest to $50,000 out of $120,000, or 41.67 percent. A penalty clause might reduce Smith's ownership by, say, 1 percent for each $1,000 he fails to produce, giving him a 31.67 percent interest. In the extreme, although not uncommon, case, Smith could lose his entire interest.

5. Developer Fees—The treatment of front-end fees differs considerably between private offerings and public syndications (including Regulation D private offerings to 35 or fewer "nonqualified" investors).[59] Stockbrokers and financial planners selling public syndications and Regulation D private offerings focus on the ratio of front-end fees to total equity raised and frequently will not offer a deal where front-end fees account for more than 25 percent of total equity. By comparison, in private joint ventures, front-end fees often exceed 25 percent of total equity, especially for new apartment projects in which the developer also is the contractor. The construction fee alone may exceed 25 percent of the equity, as it is based on total construction costs. For example, a 6 percent construction fee on a $1 million construction cost is $60,000. If $200,000 equity were needed, this fee alone would be 30 percent of the equity raised.

The Advantages of Private Offerings. On the surface, public offerings and Regulation D syndications may appear to be better deals for the investor. For three reasons, however, they usually tend not to be. First, developers dislike giving away more profits than necessary and so prefer to engage in private ventures. The deals sold by outside brokers are therefore often those for which a developer could not raise private money and may consequently be of dubious worth. Second, Regulation D offerings and public offerings involve much greater expense for legal work, due diligence, and broker commissions. Third, developers must make a certain level of profit or they will not stay in business. If they must take lower front-end fees and a lower share of residual profits, they usually compensate by "selling" the project to the syndication at a higher price.

For example, Harry Mow's company, Century West, packages deals in which the front-end load on a $1 million deal with 80 percent financing is 45 percent of the equity rather than the 25 percent syndicators prefer. A public syndication offering has a lower ratio of fees to equity but a higher total project price to the partnership, and therefore higher risks to the investors.

In addition to the higher front-end load in private offerings, Century West receives 50 percent of the residual profits after the investor receives a 6 percent preferred return. Despite the seemingly higher fees, Century West's deals were very well received by investors who appreciate the opportunity to buy into projects at cost rather than at a higher price that includes development profit.

Economically, the ratio of front-end fees to total equity raised is much less important than the investor's expected returns. Unfortunately, brokers, financial planners, and others who sell real estate securities focus on such ratios rather than on the likelihood that investors will achieve certain levels of return. Nevertheless, for public offerings through securities brokers and financial planners, developers must package their deals in accordance with current terms in the syndication market to raise the equity.

Government Programs and Working with Nonprofit Organizations

Government programs are no longer as fruitful a source of financing as they used to be, but they still can provide helpful financing to new developers. Over the years, numerous government programs have been created to generate low- and moderate-income housing. Many of those programs have been curtailed in recent years, but housing support programs are available from all levels of government—federal, state, and local.

In the 1980s, the dominant program was tax-exempt housing revenue bonds. Housing revenue bonds grew out of industrial revenue bonds, which were originally introduced to foster new industrial development in depressed areas. Interest rates on both industrial revenue bonds and housing revenue bonds were typically 2.5 percent below conventional interest rates; such favorable interest rates were possible because the bonds were rated AAA and guaranteed by the federal government.

To qualify for tax-exempt status, developers originally had to set aside 20 percent of the units in a project for low- or moderate-income tenants (that is, tenants whose incomes were no higher than 80 percent of the median income for the area) and had to meet the U.S. Department of Housing and Urban Development's (HUD's) income requirements under Section 8 of the Housing Act of 1937. A state or local housing agency had to be created to issue the bonds. Especially in areas where median incomes were very high, many developers found that they could make good profits on projects funded with housing revenue bonds.

The 1986 Tax Reform Act changed the law, however. Although tax-exempt status was still available, tenant income requirements became stricter: 20 percent of the units in a project henceforth had to be dedicated to renters with incomes below 50 percent of the area median income, or, alternatively, 40 percent of the units had to be rented to persons with incomes below 60 percent of the area median income. Previously, the requirement for low-income units was much less damaging to cash flows: 20 percent of the units had to be dedicated to renters earning 80 percent of the area median income. The rent that families could afford with incomes at 80 percent was much higher than at 50 percent. Nevertheless, tax credit programs and housing *setaside* allowances—money collected by cities from impact and linkage fees on commercial properties—provide helpful sources of financing for new developers.[60]

The Tax Reform Act of 1986 created low-income housing tax credits as an alternate method of funding housing for low- and moderate-income households. Tax credits are granted to each state on a per capita basis and are administered competitively through the states' housing agencies. Developers may use the credits for new construction, rehabilitation, or acquisition of residential properties that meet the following minimum requirements:

- Twenty percent or more of the residential units in the project are both rent restricted and occupied by individuals whose income is 50 percent or less of the area median gross income, *or* 40 percent or more of the residential units in the project are both rent restricted and occupied by individuals whose income is 60 percent or less of area median gross income.
- Properties receiving tax credits must stay eligible for 15 years.

Developers who receive the credits may use them or sell them to private investors to generate equity.

Building under government programs can be very time-consuming and frustrating. Government financing programs involve much more paperwork and many more hurdles than private financing. The programs often contain vague guidelines that cause differences in interpretation. Associated legal costs can also be onerous. Bond deals, for example, involve as many as nine different parties, each represented by its own attorney. The developer pays everyone's fees, and because most of the

Derek M.D. Chen, Jerome A. Fink, and David S. Kim formed the Bascom Group in early 1996 to purchase value-added real estate in southern California. Bascom's primary objectives were to 1) capitalize on the recovering southern California economy by investing in multifamily rental properties with a three- to five-year turnaround; 2) diversify its portfolio in southern California by location and industry; and 3) provide investors with attractive current *cash-on-cash yields* and total investment returns.

Bascom creates single-purpose limited liability companies (LLCs) to own and operate each property to protect its entire portfolio in the event that any single property defaults or has issues that could affect other properties in the portfolio. These LLCs are capitalized from several sources, including 1) private and institutional investors contributing pari passu (equally) or preferred equity and subordinated debt (for example, second mortgage loans and mezzanine financing); and 2) traditional institutional lenders funding senior mortgage debt (for example, a primary mortgage loan). A typical structure requires 5 to 10 percent Bascom-sponsored equity, 10 to 15 percent institutional coventure partner equity or mezzanine financing, and 80 percent senior mortgage debt. The equity typically requires a minimum preferred return of 9 to 12 percent and allows for Bascom to participate in the profits after the preferred returns are paid currently. This equity structure aligns Bascom's interest with that of the passive investor by creating an incentive for Bascom to maximize the total return to the investor. The senior mortgage debt is typically a three-year bridge loan based on total cost (property plus renovation cost) with a LIBOR-based interest rate, which is similar to a construction loan. The lender retains funds for renovation (lender holdback) and releases it to the sponsor as work is completed, allowing Bascom to purchase and renovate the property with much less equity.

Bascom targets multifamily properties located in infill areas with high barriers to entry that offer value-added opportunities. Targeted properties need renovation or suffer from poor resident profiles relative to the competing trade area, below-market rents, high expenses, high vacancies, poor management and marketing, and undercapitalization. Although these myriad problems may seem overwhelming and tend to scare away traditionally conservative investors, they can be overcome with well-planned strategy and effective implementation. Simply put, Bascom seeks "the worst property on the best block."

One such property, La Paz Apartments, in Pico Rivera, California, had an occupancy rate of 52 percent before close of escrow, coupled with a poor resident profile, below-market rents averaging $643 per unit, poor management, and a desperate need for renovation. After the close of escrow in August 1998, a professional, third-party, fee-managed property management company was assigned to the property; a complete renovation program was implemented, with the majority of resources devoted to apartment interiors; the property's name was changed to Courtyard Apartment Homes; and the majority of the former resident base was removed through enforcement of community rules and regulations, cooperation with local law enforcement agencies, and eviction for nonpayment of rent— all done to remove the stigma caused by years of neglect. Between January 1999 and December 1999, the occupancy rate rose from 55 percent to 96 percent. In fall 2000, average market rents were $835 per unit, with significant improvement in the quality of residents and new ancillary income programs such as utility charge-backs to residents. In addition, net operating income increased substantially, providing equity investors with very desirable returns.

Bascom's value-added deals involve a certain amount of risk. At each step in the process, from purchasing to renovating to operating to disposition, Bascom's principals have learned that surprises will happen and risk cannot be totally eliminated, even through the most conscientious due diligence or management. The tenant profile may be worse than anticipated and higher-than-expected rollover may result. The cost of renovation may increase because of labor shortages in a recovering market or increases in the cost of materials or simply because of surprises found after work begins. Property managers must be closely monitored to ensure high service standards and fair treatment of residents. Although the use of high leverage can magnify a deal's potential total returns, it can also hurt cash flow if interest rates rise more than expected. Clear roles, goals, and expectations for investors, lenders, property managers, and even residents are paramount to ensure that each investment meets the mutually agreed-upon pro forma. Finally, and most important, it is clear that frequent reporting and the open disclosure of any critical issue or surprise are critical to maintaining a trustworthy relationship between investors and lenders.[a] ∎

[a]In fall 2002, Bascom was in the process of selling some 2,500 units to a pension fund through a sale/buyback arrangement. The pension fund viewed the renovated and retenanted apartments as core assets carrying a significantly lower hurdle rate of return (12 to 13 percent leveraged IRR), compared with the high-yield returns (25 percent plus) on the equity raised for buying and renovating the units originally. Bascom will continue to operate the properties and have an interest in the upside. The sale/buyback structure motivates Bascom to get the highest price possible from the acquiring pension fund.

Source: Interview with David S. Kim, managing director, the Bascom Group, Irvine, California, September 2002.

attorneys do not work directly for the developer, monitoring their time and fees is difficult.

Yet despite the added costs, bond programs generated many thousands of housing units throughout the United States. The sale of tax credits for low-income housing remains an important source of funds for apartments, although it must be supplemented by other forms of subsidies (that development agencies and HUD may provide) to make low- and moderate-income apartments financially feasible. Beginning developers who are interested in low- and moderate-income housing development should investigate the financing programs available in their area by contacting local housing departments, redevelopment agencies, state housing finance agencies, HUD, and Fannie Mae. A number of low-income housing programs, including LIHTCs, give nonprofit organizations an advantage in obtaining money, the result of government policies to encourage the growth of community-based nonprofit organizations. The nonprofit organizations are intended to assist depressed neighborhoods in building a cohort of skilled leaders to develop housing and community facilities. The nonprofit organizations often lack development expertise and are eager to form joint ventures with private developers to build housing. Although financing for low-income housing limits the amount of profit a developer can earn, the limits are high enough to make such housing development attractive. Many cities are eager to build low-income housing and will smooth the way for developers to build it—although neighboring homeowners may fight equally hard to keep it out. Still, the financing programs provide beginning developers a source of money that may be easier to qualify for than private banking sources. Moreover, tax credits, once obtained, are easily sold to investors (because of the virtually guaranteed tax write-offs) and effectively take care of equity requirements, the hardest money for beginning developers to raise. Although nonprofit partnerships offer special opportunities for financing, they also bring much greater complexity, paperwork, time, and the need to apply for multiple loans. Experienced nonprofit organizations can greatly assist beginning developers in the process, while inexperienced nonprofit organizations may make their lives impossible. As with any partnership, success depends on the personalities of the people involved.

Greg Vilkin notes that tax credits are the modern syndications of today. "The use of tax credits has become an excellent way to bring capital into the market." Syndications are taking advantage of Section 47, which covers historic tax credits, and Section 42, which covers LIHTCs. Forest City is syndicating those properties with institutional investors—typically corporations that can take advantage of the tax credits.[61]

Construction

General contracting is distinct from development (see Chapter 2 for a general discussion of construction contractors). Many general contractors engage in development, and many developers, especially of residential products, engage in construction; nonetheless, they are two different businesses, each with its own set of risks and rewards. In general, if a project makes economic sense only if the developer can earn a contractor's profit, then it is not worth pursuing. Many projects undertaken by developers to keep their contracting arms busy have led those developers into bankruptcy.

Most major difficulties faced by developers who perform their own construction arise from the fact that they must run another business—a labor- and detail-intensive business—that leaves them insufficient time to pay adequate attention to their development activities. Most of the major benefits of an in-house construction company stem from the developer's ability to take care of construction problems rapidly and to exercise control over costs of change orders. Construction does offer a relatively easy entry into development, and many homebuilders draw effectively on their construction background to make the transition into apartment development.

Residential construction differs from nonresidential construction in many ways. Typically, residential construction involves smaller subcontractors, a smaller scale of construction, and a less skilled, nonunion workforce. The architect's role is also more limited in residential than in nonresidential development. Usually, the architect is not involved in the residential bidding process and does not manage subcontractors' work for compliance with plans and specs. Any time that the architect does spend is usually priced on an hourly basis instead of a fixed-fee basis, thus raising costs for developers who keep changing their minds.

Managing and Scheduling the Job

In construction, one quickly learns that delays are the norm rather than the exception. Most problems occur around scheduling different subcontractors or material deliveries—hence the importance of employing a good construction manager who can monitor the work of subcontractors as well as deal with architects, engineers, and city inspectors. A job superintendent—ideally, one with at least three or more years of experience on comparable projects—should always be on site to monitor subcontractors. This person handles the purchases from major suppliers and manages the contracts with all subcontractors who do the labor, giving the developer full control of construction while minimizing the number of direct employees.

One benefit of developing multifamily residential projects containing several buildings rather than one large building is that, with proper scheduling, the first units can be occupied and producing income well before the last units are completed. The contractor can facilitate early completions by paying subcontractors on the basis of buildings completed rather than on percentage of contract completed. The subcontractors, on the other hand, may prefer to run their crews from building to building. For example, a framing contractor may prefer to frame the first story of all buildings before starting the second story. Therefore, the developer may need to negotiate a rolling completion schedule as part of the subcontractor's contract.

Jerome Frank, Jr., states that one way to ensure cooperation between the construction and property management teams is to have the construction company and the management company belong to the same entity and under one roof rather than a fee construction and/or fee property management company. "If they are separate companies, the two end up not talking to each other much, and the developer has to spend extra time coordinating two different entities. There should also be good communication with the superintendent who handles site inspections, and the developer should have a business relationship with building department officials."[62]

Frank adds that a developer must be personally involved in negotiating contracts and working with each subcontractor. Preconstruction meetings are also important. Such meetings are the time when the superintendent talks directly to the people who head the different trades—both bosses and foremen who will actually be on the job. The meeting allows people to meet and get to know each other, leading to a smoother operation. While construction is in progress, the developer should convey orders through the superintendent. "Do not try to jump in there and micromanage," says Frank.

Inspections

Construction involves numerous inspections, all of which must be correctly performed if the developer/contractor is to guard against liability. In addition to city building inspectors, the construction lender usually requires an outside inspector to verify that work is completed in conformance with plans and specs. The developer should ask the lender for recommendations for an inspector and then consult with other builders on that inspector's reputation. Most lenders will cooperate with a developer to find a mutually agreeable inspector.

Jerome Frank, Sr., recommends that developers hire an outside inspector on any project above $2 million, even if the bank does not require it. Inspectors not only protect developers and the bank from lawsuits by independently verifying that work is correctly performed but also help to ensure that subcontractors' work conforms to plans. Moreover, developers should undertake several inspections to protect themselves, including an independent engineering inspection of all foundations (to check that they are level and correctly located and elevated and to test the strength of cable tendons and concrete) and a verification that soil has been properly compacted. "These and other inspections done by an independent firm cost a little more but save money in the long run."[63]

On government-funded projects, a government inspector may work on the site. When changes or additional requirements are made in the middle of a job, Frank advises, "Never do work unless you get a change order approved by the proper authorities or you will never get paid for it." Dan Kassel, co-president of Granite Homes in Irvine, California, hires an inspector to videotape homes during construction. This record of the quality of work underneath the wallboard is available in case they later get sued for construction defects. The inspector also helps to ensure that the work—especially that that is eventually covered up—is performed properly. The developer's liability, as well as the contractor's, can extend many years after the completion of a building.

Subcontractors and Draws

Typically, apartment subcontractors are smaller than nonresidential subcontractors and are not bonded. To be competitive, most builders rely on nonunion subcontractors but also appreciate that they sometimes will go out of business or fail to complete a job. Developers should not automatically avoid working with a financially weak subcontractor. They should, however, check on the subcontractor's clients, suppliers, banks, and record and make sure that the subcontractor pays social security taxes. "Just be careful," cautions Frank. "Check his insurance coverage. If he doesn't have liability insurance, then you arrange for him to get it and charge him for it."

Every time a subcontractor makes a draw, the developer/contractor should have the subcontractor sign a *lien waiver* and an affidavit showing that suppliers, taxes, insurance, and other bills have been paid and then attach the lien waiver to the check stub and file it in the job's folder.

The purpose of the lien waiver is to prevent subcontractors from subsequently claiming nonpayment or one of their suppliers from filing a lien. Liens, even completely unwarranted, can delay loan closings and sales. If a lien is filed, a developer can post a bond for the amount of the lien or leave money in escrow to cover the potential liability.

One of the most difficult problems in construction is removing a subcontractor whose work is substandard. To reduce the associated delays, some developers require subcontractors to sign a stringent subcontract that provides for their removal for slow work or nonperformance.

Insurance

A good insurance agent who specializes in construction is invaluable to a contractor. Developers/contractors must be familiar with many different types of insurance: worker's compensation insurance, subcontractor's general liability insurance, builder's risk insurance, completed operations insurance, and contractor's equipment floater. Like the general contractor, subcontractors must each have their own builder's risk insurance that covers, say, the theft of material from a site. It is important to get a copy of their insurance and check copies of their workmen's compensation, general liability, and builder's risk insurance before they begin work. It is the superintendent's responsibility to make sure that documents are in.

It is also advisable to take out completed operations insurance, which protects builders from claims for injury or damage caused by building collapse or structure failure after its completion. It does not, however, cover faulty workmanship.

Marketing

Marketing begins while a project is still on the drawing board and does not end until a project is sold. In the residential development business, developers do not attempt to create a market where one does not already exist. On the contrary, their foremost objective is to identify the specific market segment for which more housing is needed and then to design the best possible product to serve their needs. Marketing is the process of finding the renters or buyers and then attracting them to the property at a time when they are in a position to make a decision.

Marketing serves a number of objectives:

- analyzing what market to pursue and what product to build;
- persuading—through careful presentation—buyers and renters that the product meets their specific needs;
- packaging the product and offering assistance to enable those people to buy or rent it; and
- ensuring afterward that the product meets their expectations.

Insufficient predevelopment market research can result in a product that has been built for a certain market but does not appeal to that market. In such cases, developers must determine which market the product does appeal to and then repackage it to attract that market. Although almost any product will sell or rent at a low enough price, its developer is unlikely to turn a profit if prices must be discounted.

Jerome Frank, Jr., says that developers can do two things for marketing and public relations: "You can market your company's history—for example, if you are Lincoln Properties or a similarly large company, you talk about the 'Lincoln style.' But what you're really selling is the company's management style." Alternatively, developers can sell the personality of the property, promoting the uniqueness of the development. "Find something in every development that you like and get excited about, for example, beveled mirrors over the fireplace or an abundance of closets, so that your manager gets really excited about it also. Some developers spend a lot of money on clubrooms and swimming pools and in many ways waste money. Potential residents might be attracted to these amenities at first but find interior features in the units are more important in the long run. The integrity of the management company is very important for dealing with clients. The developer has to exhibit a continued commitment to constantly train the property's managers."[64]

Market analysis is vital not only for predevelopment feasibility studies but also throughout the life of a project. Ongoing market analysis assesses the accuracy of the original analysis of the target market and identifies any important changes in market projections, rents, prices, and even the target market itself. Typically, 12 to 24 months elapse from completion of the first market study to the leasing of a project, and, in the interim, major changes may have occurred in the market. The developer must constantly monitor the market, especially by watching neighboring projects, to remain up to date on current rental activity, pricing, concessions, and preferred physical characteristics and amenities. Changing market strategy in midstream can substantially increase construction and operating costs, but failing to respond to market changes can be fatal.

Developing a Market Strategy

A marketing strategy is the philosophy the team supports and consistently follows throughout the life of the project. The strategy focuses on what is to be done, why, and the projected outcome. The cornerstone of any market strategy is its target submarket. Once it has been identified through market analysis, every aspect of development—from design through property management—should reinforce the appeal of the project to that submarket.

After the development program and marketing strategy are established, preparation of project objectives can help the marketing team understand the strategy as well as the basic facts about the product and the market. The property's advantages should be clearly defined. What makes the property different, better, or more marketable than its competitors? In short, what makes it special from the point of view of marketing? A project's distinctiveness may be its affordability, location, aesthetics, units, lifestyle, or other characteristics that make it outshine the competition.

The marketing plan ties into the established marketing strategy and can be thought of as a blueprint for the advertising campaign, public relations efforts, and leasing activities, including hiring and managing the leasing staff and preparing budgets and schedules for each component.

The plan also specifies the design of all elements to create a coordinated image for the project. Based on the target market's profile and the project's distinctive selling points, it defines an overall theme to be carried out in all community design elements, including the name, logo, signage, sales displays, interior design, brochures, and other print and media materials.

The Marketing and Leasing Budget. The marketing and leasing budget should cover all aspects of marketing. It should include appropriate amounts for exterior and interior marketing-related features, preleasing activities, general marketing, and promotional materials and events. A typical marketing budget includes:

- Exterior Marketing—Directional signs, identification signs, banners, and flags;
- Interior Marketing—Model apartments, sales displays;
- Preleasing—Flyers, voice mail setup, staff, signs for construction and leasing, advertisements in appropriate publications, a Web site;

- Recognition Marketing—Advertising campaign, staff, promotion materials, public relations, press releases and other print media, community involvement in charitable events, memberships in community organizations;
- Other—Nominations for awards, move-in gifts, good will gestures to outside leasing agents and contractors.

Leasing and Selling. Prospective residents are sophisticated home shoppers, and the leasing staff should be chosen accordingly. Staff should comprise well-trained professional sales personnel experienced in dealing with clients.

The old rule of one leasing agent for every 100 units in a new project is considered inadequate today. With staffing at that level today, agents do not have time to give prospective residents the service and attention they need. If the leasing center is understaffed, sales are lost. Using additional personnel is cost-effective when compared with the cost of losing leases.

Because apartments turn over regularly, marketing is a continuous and long-term effort. Therefore, a well-trained, professional sales staff contributes a great deal to the project's marketability. Some developers use in-house teams of leasing and sales agents, providing them with greater control over the leasing and sales process—but also entailing greater management responsibilities. Another alternative is to use leasing companies that specialize in grand openings and initial lease-up. Because they are rewarded according to the number of leases signed rather than the long-term performance of the project, the developer should monitor tenants' credit-worthiness very carefully. Another solution is to engage the services of an outside agency to take ongoing responsibility for marketing and leasing the project.

Pricing. Pricing, the most important tool for influencing leasing in the short run, cannot be based on pro forma projections. Rents must reflect current market conditions at the time the property is being leased, especially the prices charged by neighboring projects. Pricing should be monitored weekly, or even daily. Conditions change quickly, and a vacant unit costs a developer much more than a slight reduction in rent.

Funding requirements for permanent mortgages usually specify a target NOI that must be met for the mortgage to be fully funded. This target implies an average rent level. In declining markets, the developer may be obliged to obtain rents that are above market rate.[65] In such cases, the developer must find other incentives to make the *effective* rental rate (including all concessions) in line with the current market. To make a project more competitive, a developer can:

- Reduce the amount of the deposit required.
- Offer accruing deposits, where tenants make little or no initial deposit and earn deposit credits at the rate of $20.00 or $30.00 per month, which they receive at the end of six months or so. This incentive also helps improve the punctuality of payments.
- Provide free cable television or other services that normally carry a monthly charge.

- Install additional appliances such as microwave ovens, ceiling fans, and washer/dryers. (Such appliances represent a permanent capital improvement to the unit.)
- Offer privileges at health or other clubs.

Point-of-sale incentives are also invaluable tools for selling condominiums. The amount and type of sales incentives depend largely on local market conditions. In very soft markets, free vacations and even cars have been offered as special incentives; more commonly, prospective buyers are tempted by household appliances or additional decorating allowances for carpet, wallpaper, window coverings, or light fixtures.

Public Relations

The purpose of public relations is to create a favorable public image. The result of good public relations is free advertising.

Public relations plays an important role on site and off site. Developers who enjoy good off-site public relations are active in their communities with civic groups, the local chamber of commerce, churches, and other organizations. Developers who promote on-site public relations ensure that visitors to their sites receive a positive general impression—a neat and orderly site and sales office, polite staff, among other things.

Public relations experts are particularly useful to developers by virtue of their relations with local news media. Through their contacts, they should be able to obtain coverage for announcements and news releases about a new property. Potentially newsworthy events include purchasing the land, obtaining financing, closing loans, ground breaking, the grand opening, the first families to move in, attaining certain lease hurdles, human interest stories about tenants (especially stories that highlight a special feature of the project, such as units for the handicapped), and special events. Other stories may be crafted about the product itself, featuring such elements as the design of the interior or exterior.

Public relations firms may also stage special events for a developer. Useful events include press parties, previews of a complex for community leaders and media representatives, and sponsored community events aimed at fundraising. Award competitions are another fruitful source of favorable publicity and provide third-party endorsement for a project.

Newsletters are a particularly effective public relations tool. Their frequency depends on the size and the level of activity in an individual project. Apartment properties may issue only one or two newsletters per year, while master-planned communities may publish one per month. Newsletters, which function essentially as direct-mail pieces, should be sent to residents, area employers, brokers, prospects, neighborhood stores, and community facilities. They are helpful for attracting prospective buyers and tenants and for informing current residents about what is going on in the neighborhood and property. Most important, newsletters suggest to residents that the developer cares about them—an attitude that they pass

A developer who hires a public relations firm to work on behalf of his organization should expect that firm to undertake the following tasks. A designated individual on the developer's marketing staff could also undertake these tasks.

- Develop a program.
- Compile fact sheets and biographies for the developer's company, projects, product(s), and principals. Assist in developing a company Web site.
- Identify potential story lines: announcements of new products and openings, for example, personnel appointments, awards, design features.
- Write simple, concise releases that include all pertinent facts and affix a dollar value if at all possible. Post on the Web site.
- Develop a local, regional, and national press list for print, broadcast, and the Internet. Identify reporters who wish to receive news via E-mail, fax, or mail.
- Make personal contact with news media representatives on the press list.
- Establish contacts with national trade publications and consumer magazines and newspapers.

- Try to place interview articles for the development company's principals.
- Obtain media kits and editorial calendars from all appropriate national and trade publications.
- Plan regular visits to local, regional, and national media as appropriate. Invite media representatives to visit the developer's offices and projects.
- Obtain dates of awards competition; coordinate design and marketing awards.
- Try to place the company's principals as speakers for local, regional, and national conferences.
- Develop a photograph file of people and projects and a graphics file of renderings, logos, and so on. Scan images and save on computer or disk to accompany E-mail distribution of articles.
- Develop a mailing list of the developer's old, present, and potential clients for promotional mailings (if not handled by the marketing director).
- Reprint articles about the developer's projects that appear in magazines and newspapers. Use them, accompanied by a letter, for direct mailings

to client list. Post articles on the company Web site.
- Develop a company newsletter. Post newsletter on the company Web site.
- Establish contact with the public relations directors of all the developer's clients and coordinate projects to secure mention for the developer's projects in client news releases and advertisements.
- Call, E-mail, or send thank you notes to press who feature the developer's projects.
- Plan special events to attract people and attention to the developer's projects.
- Encourage the developer's participation in professional organizations and community organizations and activities.
- Personally participate in organizations and attend programs, seminars, and conferences that affect or support the developer's activities. ∎

Source: Patty Doyle, president, Patty Doyle Public Relations, Inc., Fort Lauderdale, Florida.

---

on to others. Newsletters tend to combine product and sales information with human interest stories. Usually, an advertising agency does the creative design and a public relations firm writes the copy, though many public relations firms handle the whole production process.

A successful public relations campaign waged by a large development firm should target different publics with different messages:

- Land Sellers—Building faith in the developer's ability to perform.
- Lenders—Building faith in the developer's capacity to deliver what he promises and to repay loans.
- Government—Announcing that the company takes care of consumer complaints and is a good citizen in its dealings with the public sector.
- Future Employees—Creating the impression that the company is a fun and profitable place to work.
- Competitors—Conveying a sense of mutual respect and a shared readiness to work together in industry and civic organizations to address common problems.
- Customers—Establishing the developer's preoccupation with satisfying the demands of customers.
- Media—Conveying respect and a willingness to share information.

Advertising

The primary purpose of advertising is to motivate potential tenants and buyers to visit a project. Advertising is vital but can be very expensive. Discussions with other local developers, property managers, and advertising agencies can help to identify the best media for advertising the project. Advertising agencies typically recommend that the advertising budget equal about 1 percent of the developer's hard costs. This amount is variable, however, depending on market conditions and the property's size, nature, and visibility.

The most prestigious advertising agency in a city may not necessarily be the best for a beginning developer who requires considerable personal attention. A developer should interview at least three firms, obtain recommendations from their clients, and then select a firm that is genuinely interested in his account. Advertising agencies provide various services, including developing a long-range advertising strategy, planning individual programs, selecting the best media for presentation, preparing copy and design layouts, and monitoring the performance of its efforts.

Advertising for a project typically employs a common logo, theme, and style. A well-crafted logo can be used not only in advertising but also on signage, brochures, stationery, and even as a design motif. A project's name likewise plays an important role in creating an image for a project. New developers should promote a project's name first, with the developer's name of secondary importance. Names should be descriptive, not misleading. For example, a complex should not be named "Forest Hills" if it sits on a Kansas-like prairie.

The most cost-effective media for advertising vary by project and location. Some typical outlets include neighborhood newspapers, metropolitan newspapers, radio and television, Web sites, and temporary signs.

Brochures. Developers should ensure that advertising brochures are begun at least two months before they will be needed. The brochures should be ready to be mailed to local employers, brokers, community leaders, and apartment locators during construction as part of premarketing. Despite the need for early preparation, brochures should not tie developers to specific figures; therefore, they should not contain prices (which change continually) or bound floor plans (people always want the floor plan that has already been rented or sold out). Prices should be listed on a separate page that can be easily changed. The square footage of a unit should be omitted from a floor plan unless its inclusion is a very competitive advantage. Special features and amenities, however, should be emphasized.

Many developers opt for a folder with a high-quality printed cover and pockets inside for inserts. The jacket is the major printing expense; inserts can be changed and updated as needed. Brochures can be of all shapes and colors. When people are shopping for apartments, they pick up a number of materials and are more likely to notice distinctive brochures. Brochures that fold into the shape of, say, a door key or a house may cost extra to print but are more memorable.

Newspaper Advertising. Layout and copy for newspaper advertisements should be simple and specific and should not exaggerate the project's attributes. The name of the developer and clear directions to the project should be included; in this respect, maps are helpful and allow prospective tenants to be directed along the route that creates the most favorable impression as they approach the project.

Classified advertisements, the least expensive form of newspaper advertising, are a must for rental housing. At the same time, however, the quantity and similarity of classified advertisements make it hard for any one project to stand out.

Radio and Television. Radio advertising is useful for drawing attention to grand openings of larger projects and groups of projects by one developer. To select a station, first check listener profiles and pick a station whose general programming is similar to the tastes of the target market. In addition to spot advertisements, live remote broadcasts work well during times when many people are out driving. Radio advertisements may generate considerable traffic on site. If a developer is not prepared to handle a large number of people on site, the advertisements may do more harm than good.

Television is the most expensive medium. It probably is not cost-effective in large metropolitan areas, but it may be effective in smaller markets for grand openings.

Signs. Billboards help establish name identity and may be useful as directional signs near a project. Transit advertising—such as bus banners, bus benches, and commuter station posters—can also be an effective way of keeping the developer's name in the public eye. Direction signs are probably the most effective signs of all. Removable "bootleg" signs are an inexpensive and efficient means of bringing people to the project from major arterials within a two-mile (3.2-kilometer) radius for special events.

Web Sites. A good Web site can be an excellent way to advertise a property and supplement more traditional print materials and advertising. The Internet is used increasingly as a marketing tool to reach potential renters and buyers. Smaller developers may wish to have their properties linked to Web sites and Internet apartment rental services that provide information on a variety of properties. In this way, individual properties that might not be able to attract any attention on their own can piggyback on the larger service to gain visibility in the Internet marketplace. Web sites dedicated to one property or a group of related properties involve much more than making an initial investment and waiting for customers to access the information. Web sites require ongoing maintenance to ensure that information is up to date and accurate. To their advantage, Web sites make it possible to customize the information and provide more details such as floor plans, photographs, and virtual tours.

Merchandising. Whereas advertising is intended to tell people about a project and entice them to visit it, merchandising is concerned with on-site displays and practices. Visitors' first impressions are critical to a project's success. Particular attention should be paid to the condition of entrances, signs, landscaping, and buildings. A pleasant environment should be created as soon as possible, even while construction is still in progress. A well-designed and carefully located entrance not only helps merchandising but also bolsters a project's future identification in the neighborhood. Entrance signs and nameplates should be modest, designed to blend with the character of the community. Generous landscaping may be expensive, but it is also cost-effective—as a visit to any successful project demonstrates. Restrictive signs (prohibiting, say, walking on the grass) should be pleasant and inoffensive and should be designed, where possible, to relate to other merchandising features.

Sales Office. The sales office should be easy to find and should open up to attractive views of interior courtyards or other features of the project. Colors and furnishings should be consistent with the project's theme and chosen with the target market in mind. In the sales office, brochures, models, and maps should be placed so that visitors can view them at their leisure. Drawings of the apartment site plan and unit plans make attractive and informative wall hangings. Graphics give visitors an impression of what an uncompleted project will eventually

© Rick Alexander & Associates, Inc.

look like. Perspective drawings are important. Visualizing a project from two-dimensional plans is difficult for most people. Small models of the project, although expensive, make attractive focal points and can help renters and buyers see how their apartments are located with respect to major amenities, access, security, and views. Aerial photographs also help to show a project's relationship to off-site facilities such as schools, churches, libraries, daycare centers, shops, and parks.

Model Units. Model units play an important part in selling and leasing by giving customers a sense of what the unit will look like and what they can do to personalize it. Model units should be close to the sales office, offer pleasant views of either the project or the surrounding area, and benefit from afternoon sunlight (afternoon is the most popular time for visitors).

Although decorating a sample of every unit type is unnecessary, those units that are decorated are likely to lease or sell more quickly. Decor for the models should be selected to appeal to the target market. Current trends in decorating are moving away from standard furniture toward lavishly decorated units with smaller furniture that makes units look larger. Doors are often removed to add to a sense of spaciousness. Many decorators use art, decorative objects, plants, and mirrors extensively. Nonstandard built-ins, however, should be avoided because they may mislead customers and because the model units may be moved to different locations in the complex once the project is leased. Moods may be en-

hanced through the use of background music, colors, and lighting.

Condominium Sales. Marketing for condominiums is similar to that for single-family houses. Despite their desire to sell units during construction, developers have found that few buyers will commit themselves before they have seen the completed lobbies and amenities.

For smaller projects, an in-house sales staff is often uneconomical, and many developers use outside brokers, who are paid on commission. Developers who own other apartment houses or condominiums find that word-of-mouth advertising can be very effective. Some developers send out announcements to tenants or owners at their previous projects every time they open a new project. Paying a referral fee of, say, $50.00 to tenants or owners in other projects often helps to generate sales, although in some states this practice violates real estate license laws.

John Math recommends that to sell 50 to 100 condominium units, a developer should hire a sales manager plus one salesperson. For projects of 100 to 200 units, two salespeople should be hired. Their total compensation should amount to 1.5 to 3 percent of gross sales. Many successful salespeople prefer to work totally on commission. If a developer expects them to be in the office during certain hours of the day, they should receive a salary plus commission or draw against commission.[66]

Many condominium developers and lenders restrict non-owner-occupied units under the assumption that absentee owners take less care of their property and thereby depress sales to owner-occupants, who will pay the highest prices. At the same time, developers need to be flexible and prepared to respond to changing market conditions. When condominium sales are slow, some companies decide to operate the projects as rental units. Paul Schultheis, a developer in Arcadia, California, undertook a condominium project during a downturn in the market: "We set up an intensive marketing budget with an all-out push for 90 days. Only three of the 16 units were sold. We decided to change direction and set the building up as apartments. Now we own a deluxe-deluxe apartment house." In many cases, however, projects conceived as condominiums do not work financially as apartments and subsequently lose money or go through foreclosure.

Operations and Management

No matter how well it is designed and built, an apartment project will be profitable only if it is well managed. Further, management must be competent at many levels for a project to succeed:

- initial marketing and lease-up (often assigned to an outside source);
- ongoing marketing and leasing;
- collecting rents, handling accounts, and keeping records;
- making ongoing reports to owners;
- maintaining and repairing units, readying them for new tenants;
- maintaining and repairing building systems and common areas;
- maintaining landscaping and building exteriors;
- hiring and training new staff;
- keeping residents informed about apartment policies and operating activities of interest to them;
- initiating services for residents;
- dealing with residents' complaints;
- maintaining good relations with brokers, community organizations, and local government;
- maintaining good relations with managers of neighboring apartments to share information and work together on security and other common problems; and
- developing budgets and operating plans.

The nature of the relationship between the developer and the property manager depends, in part, on the property's size, the extent of the developer's property portfolio, and the nature and structure of the businesses. The manager can be the developer, the developer's employee, a subsidiary or in-house department of the development/property company, or an individual or third-party management company under contract. Most large apartment property companies, including REITs, manage their own properties through an in-house department or owned subsidiary company.

©Rick Alexander & Associates, Inc.

Effective property management helps achieve the goal of stable occupancy with low turnover and high-quality tenants who pay market-rate rents punctually.

For most apartment projects, the decision whether or not to use an outside property manager is based on the developer's willingness to invest time in the project. Properly addressing residents' needs and maintaining the property are extremely time-consuming. Most developers prefer to delegate these responsibilities to a qualified property manager.

Although the operation and management of condominiums is the responsibility of unit owners through their condominium association, the legal framework for the condominium association must be established by the developer (see Chapter 3).

Even though most developers would prefer not to be in the management business, many feel that only by managing their own projects can they get the service they need. Beginning developers usually do not have an organization in place, however, and must therefore rely on outside managers. Greg Vilkin notes that property management fees have dropped as larger management companies compete for business. "You are not going to make money if you do management, as you can hire someone at a 3 percent fee. They consider 3 to 3.5 percent of gross rent what it costs them to do it."[67]

In selecting outside managers, beginning developers should look for companies with a good reputation for managing a particular type of property in terms of size, design, and tenant characteristics. It is also useful to investigate on-site procedures for accounting and collecting rents. An audit should be performed at least twice a year, preferably quarterly. The auditor, who should appear unannounced, reviews collection reports, rent rolls, and individual leases and inspects vacant units to ensure that no "skimming" is occurring.

The management company should prepare monthly reports that show gross potential income, actual income, and line-by-line expenses. The reports should also detail which units are vacant and which are not producing revenue. Cash receipts should be deposited daily. Monthly cash collection reports should be reviewed and approved by off-site staff.

The larger the property and its operating budget, the more likely it can accommodate specialists on staff such as equipment engineers, gardeners, painters, or guards. Many developers consider 150 or 200 units the minimum number necessary to support a full-time maintenance staff consisting of a property manger, assistant manager, maintenance worker, and porter. Management of smaller properties can be a more formal undertaking at the beginning, possibly by employing a resident manager, which may be less expensive in the short run but mostly inadequate for today's markets. In many urban areas, however, assembling a site that will support 150 units is very difficult, so developers have learned how to cope with smaller complexes.

A key change in the business in recent years is the much greater emphasis on property management in all development phases. The developer should endeavor to have as much good information as possible on future operations and maintenance, including but not limited to costs, to make informed design decisions. Property managers can make many useful contributions to the design process and should be included in all design review meetings. The increasing importance of residents' personal and property security can be addressed in part by improving design. Property managers' perspectives, based on experience with defensible space, can be valuable in this effort.

Hiring Staff

Property management is one of the fastest-growing specializations in the real estate profession, "emerging as a managerial science. Today, [property managers] must have at their fingertips the knowledge, communication skills, and technical expertise needed to be dynamic decision makers. They also must be versatile, because they may be called on to act as market analysts, advertising executives, salespeople, accountants, diplomats, or even maintenance engineers. Interpersonal skills are needed to deal effectively with owners, prospects, tenants, employees, outside contractors, and others in the real estate business."[68]

According to Randolph Hawthorne, property management has become much more professional in recent years. "Firms have gotten larger (some of that was the REIT phenomenon and some the efficiency that was gained), with the biggest change in the profile of the on-site rental manager. It's not unlike being given a $15 million asset to manage; rather than simply collecting rents and fixing the toilets, there is a lot more—leasing,

reporting, optimizing the income stream. A lot of it is driven by the availability and ability to use computers and related programs, and that requires staff to have higher skills—management, computers, people skills, awareness of operations and maintenance. That translates into paying more for qualified people, which has put a strain on the availability of people that come into the business."[69]

Beyond hiring and training, a third component of effective customer service is feedback and reward. Leading apartment management companies tend to stress the bottom-up "culture of service" in their organizations, based on closely monitoring residents' satisfaction and compensation schemes that reward employees for keeping residents satisfied.

Turnover

The most volatile element in net operating income is usually the turnover rate. Although turnover sometimes offers a good opportunity to raise rents for units renting near the market rate, turnover can be costly in terms of rent lost during vacancies and of the renovations and cleanup required to prepare an apartment to rent again. In general, after a property has reached stabilized occupancy, the focus turns to keeping the property stable.

"It's good to raise rents, but the more important key number you should watch is turnover. Reward your management for renewing leases of existing tenants. Make sure that there is not a lot of turnover. That's a key thing to watch; stabilization, during the long run, keeps turnover and maintenance costs down."[70] Every turnover entails a minimum loss of two weeks of rent plus up to $500 for cleaning and carpet shampooing. In garden apartments, for example, turnover rates average 55 percent per year and can reach as high as 70 percent. In soft markets, turnover can exceed 100 percent.

Turnover occurs for many reasons, some of which— a tenant's changing jobs, for example—lie outside the developer's control. But the developer can reduce turnover caused by poor construction, design, maintenance, or management. Residents become disenchanted if their refrigerator leaks, if their unit is too noisy, or if they cannot find parking.

Property management experts stress the importance of communication to reduce turnover. Owners should communicate often and regularly with managers and staff so that all parties understand their goals, objectives, and concerns. On-site managers should communicate regularly with residents, answering questions and reducing uncertainty among tenants. For example, if a swimming pool must be emptied to make repairs, tenants should know when they will be able to use it again.

Problem tenants can create difficulties for an entire complex. Controlling noise and other irritants among neighboring tenants is critical for maintaining low turnover. The property manager can set the stage for tenants from the beginning by going over a written list of rules

Bass Lofts is an adaptive use multifamily project by Winter Properties, Inc., an Atlanta-based development firm specializing in the redevelopment of historic properties and the revitalization of urban neighborhoods. The 120,000-square-foot (11,150-square-meter), three-story former high school built in the 1920s offers unconventional living space to the city's rapidly growing population of young professionals.

Eighty-five apartments are located in the former high school itself, while an additional 18 units were developed in the freestanding red brick gymnasium, a separate structure built in 1949. To increase the project's feasibility, 30 new units were built adjacent to the school. Amenities on the seven-acre (2.8-hectare) site include a swimming pool, health club, gated parking, and additional phone lines for computer modems and faxes. In addition to these modern conveniences, many original elements of the buildings were retained and integrated into the apartments. Several gymnasium units feature 30-foot-high (9-meter-high) ceilings, and most school units have irregularly shaped rooms. Others still contain blackboards and built-in cupboard space. Original classroom doors and transoms, school clocks, the trophy case, and a 1930s-era Works Progress Administration (WPA) mural in the auditorium have been preserved where possible. In the gymnasium, the basketball court floor and bleachers have been retained and the building's red brick walls left exposed.

Site

Bass Lofts is located on a seven-acre (2.8-hectare) site just east of downtown Atlanta in an area known as Little Five Points. That area experienced some decline during the 1960s and 1970s, but in the 1980s, the area began to experience a resurgence as young, middle-class residents began to move back. The area is considered a funky, trendy, and largely retail/entertainment district of the city that attracts a wide range of people.

The project sits on a plateau overlooking Euclid Avenue; it is bounded by a small expanse of open space and trees surrounding the parking areas. Private, single-family homes abut three sides of the site, which is conveniently located near theaters, restaurants, and supermarkets. Downtown is easily accessible by car, and the project also is within walking distance of a Metropolitan Atlanta Rapid Transit Agency station.

Development and Design

Winter Properties purchased the former Bass High School in 1996 after beginning planning two years earlier. The company's strong track record of historic redevelopment in Atlanta and its reputation for quality helped the project win neighborhood support. Although the community generally supported the project and welcomed the high-income residents it would attract, traffic was a concern.

The developer's original plan called for the development of 103 units in the school and gym structure and an additional 60 to 70 new units in a separate building; negotiations with neighbors resulted in scaling the project back to 30 new units. In addition, parking was divided into two distinct areas to provide for better traffic distribution.

The project was delayed 18 months when, while it was already under contract to Winter Properties, the Atlanta School District requested use of the school as a temporary elementary school. The developer complied; in return, the school district made some minor renovations. In December 1997, Winter was able to begin construction.

Although structurally sound, the building presented significant problems, and the developer's decision to use the school's existing window frames and sashes made the job more complex. Each ten-foot-high (3-meter-high) window was double reglazed, retaining the beauty and scale of the original building while also significantly increasing its energy efficiency. Large amounts of asbestos in the window caulk and abatement of lead-based paint on the windows added significantly to the project's cost, doubling the original cost estimate. Besides abatement costs, all the building's mechanical systems were deemed inadequate and replaced. And, as is often the case in preservation projects, a new roof was required.

Many original finishes were left intact and incorporated into the project, both to differentiate Bass Lofts from other residential projects and to satisfy require-

Bass Lofts combines the reuse of a historic school with adjacent new construction.

ments for historic tax credits. The U.S. Department of the Interior, which administers the tax credit program, required the developer to preserve the basic elements of the school, resulting in the loss of several thousand square feet of living space on the first floor of the classroom building, where the original 14-foot-wide (4.3-meter-wide) corridor and all of the lockers, which have been welded shut, had to be retained. On the second and third floors, the developer was able to narrow the corridor, thus creating somewhat larger units on those floors. In the auditorium, the developer was required to preserve ten rows of the original seats.

Winter Properties voluntarily left many other attributes of the school in place. All units in the school building have the original wooden floors, and many sport the original doors and transoms. In some units, the original chalkboards and built-in cabinets were left in place. A vault in what had been the principal's office now holds a water heater, and the school nurse's station has been converted to a kitchen. In the auditorium, besides the seats that were preserved, the developer also restored a mural depicting women dancing that was painted during the Great Depression as a project of the WPA. The developer still was able to put 17 units in the auditorium, with four units built directly on the stage. Eight two-level units were developed in the former gymnasium; they feature 30-foot-high (9-meter-high) ceilings, the original basketball court floor, bleachers, and red brick walls. In addition, ten units were built on the sides of the gymnasium. The addition of patio spaces for these units creates an outdoor area for tenants.

Combined with the historic touches are the amenities that upscale residents have come to expect in a modern apartment complex. The basement of the school houses a 1,500-square-foot (140-square-meter), fully equipped exercise room and a laundry room. Each unit also features modern wiring that includes six phone lines for computers and fax machines. Both the buildings and the parking areas are served by a key card electronic secu-

High-quality interior features and on-site amenities have helped Bass Lofts achieve better than expected rents.

rity system. Each unit also is individually metered for gas and electricity.

The 30 new units are housed in two separate buildings located behind the former gymnasium. The three-story structures were finished with stucco of the same color as the brick used in the former school, and they feature large palladium-style windows like those in the existing structure. Including the new units helped bring in the revenue necessary to make the project feasible.

Financing

Although Winter Properties's track record and reputation made financing easier to obtain, it can still be difficult in a market such as Atlanta, where many lenders are unfamiliar with historic preservation and adaptive use projects. Market research indicated that the developer could obtain monthly rent of about $930 for a one-

bedroom apartment, a rent similar to that for garden apartments in more upscale sections of the city. In fact, the project has performed better than expected, with one-bedroom rents nearing $1,000 and rents for the two-bedroom, two-level gymnasium units topping $1,600 per month.

The developer was able to obtain a construction and acquisition loan with the interest rate tied to LIBOR, resulting in significant savings in interest. The project ultimately came in on time and near budget. Cost overruns resulting from unexpected additional abatement costs were absorbed by the interest savings and the high contingency budget, which the developer insists is always a necessity in adaptive use projects.

In addition to federal historic preservation tax credits, the developer used local *continued* redevelopment tax abatement programs that freeze property taxes for a specific period of time. Further tax relief was achieved by donating the facade of the school to Easements Atlanta, Inc. Under this program, the owner agrees to leave a historic building's facade intact. The building's facade is then appraised, and the value is treated as a charitable contribution.

Marketing and Management

Leasing began in January 1998. Marketing initially was done primarily through signs posted on the site and through RentNet on the Internet. As often is the case in central city locations, attracting the family market can be difficult, in large part because of concerns about school quality; marketing therefore targeted single young professionals and empty nesters. One reason the units were equipped to handle modern telecommunications was the developer's belief that the space could be marketed successfully to high-tech live/work tenants. Although some tenants fit this category, tenants ultimately have been a more eclectic mix of single and divorced urban professionals. The average age of tenants at Bass Lofts is 33. Because of the city's well-known traffic congestion, easy access to downtown was a strong selling point, but the unconventional layout and distinctive features of the project have been its biggest draw. By September 1998, the project was fully leased. During its first four years of operation, the project has seen turnover in apartments of about 25 to 30 percent per year; many of these cases are of tenants transferring into larger or smaller units in the development. Rents have been raised semiannually at 2.5 to 3 percent.

Winter Properties believes in the ability of historic rehabilitation projects to energize people and foster a sense of community among them. One function of the on-site manager at Bass Lofts is to encourage neighborliness by organizing informal social gatherings; the gatherings have been quite successful, consistently attracting a cross section of tenants. Tenants themselves also have begun to organize

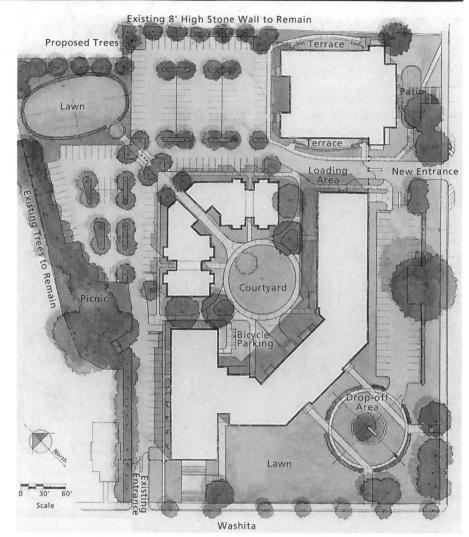

Bass Lofts site plan.

events, making a genuine neighborhood of the project.

Experience Gained

Prior experience and reputation can be important in developing adaptive use and historic preservation projects. Winter's reputation went far in assuring tenants and local residents that a quality project would be developed.

Because historic preservation projects invariably entail unforeseeable circumstances, the budget should always include a significant contingency fund. The biggest risk, according to the developer, is not the market but cost overruns.

Working with local planning authorities and residents is critical to the success

of a project. Without their support, a developer is likely to experience significant delays related expenses.

In negotiating with planning officials and residents, calculate the costs and benefits of concessions accurately. Developers who do not fully appreciate the financial effects of certain concessions may soon find their projects over budget.

An architect with experience in historic preservation is important to the success of such a project. The architect, general contractor, and various subcontractors should be engaged early in the project and made part of the development team. ∎

Project Data

Land Use and Building Information

Site Area	7.013 acres
Dwelling Units Planned	133
Dwelling Units Completed	133
Gross Density	19 units/acre
Off-Street Parking Spaces	226

Land Use Plan

	Percent of Site
Buildings	24%
Roads/paved areas	36
Common open space	40
Total	100%

Residential Unit Information

Unit Type	Average Size (Square Feet)	Number of Units	Initial Rent Range
School	748	68	$630–1,175
Auditorium	1,090	17	$950–1,600
Gymnasium	1,191	18	$750–1,660
New Units	1,035	30	$860–1,620

Development Cost Information

Site Costs

Site acquisition	$1,143,213

Site Improvement

Excavation/grading	$124,332
Sewer/water/drainage	31,226
Paving/curbs/sidewalk	250,180
Landscaping/irrigation	67,950
Fees/general conditions	76,068
Other	217,871
Total	$767,627

Construction Costs

Superstructure	$1,556,764
HVAC	411,374
Electrical	641,834
Plumbing/sprinklers	851,528
Finishes	3,091,518
Graphics/specialties	2,500
Fees/general conditions	818,845
Total	$7,374,363

Soft Costs

Architecture/engineering	$341,745
Project management	535,000
Marketing	15,960
Legal/accounting	88,667
Taxes/insurance	24,595
Title fees	17,124
Construction interest and fees	381,460
Other	80,092
Total	$1,484,643

Total Development Cost	**$10,769,846**
Total Development Cost per Unit	**$80,976**
Construction Cost per Gross Square Foot	**$65.65**
Construction Cost per Rentable Square Foot	**$81.38**

Developer

Winter Properties, Inc.
1330 Spring Street
Atlanta, Georgia 30309
404-223-5015

Architect

Surber Barber Choate & Hertlein
1776 Peachtree Street, NW
South Tower, Suite 700
Atlanta, Georgia 30309
404-872-8400

Construction

The Winter Construction Company
1330 Spring Street
Atlanta, Georgia 30309
404-588-3300

Development Schedule

3/1994	Planning started
11/1996	Site purchased
12/1997	Construction started
1/1998	Leasing started
10/1998	Lease-up completed

Stable occupancy with low turnover and high-quality tenants who pay market-rate rents punctually is every property manager's goal. The following advice will help achieve it:

- If you make promises, deliver.
- Check the credit and criminal history of new tenants through credit agencies, applicant screening services, and Web-based services.
- Make vacant units ready for occupancy quickly; ready units lease more quickly and reduce vacancy loss. The manager's challenge is to balance the need to respond promptly to current residents' requests for service with the need to prepare newly vacated units for occupancy. It may be necessary to use outside contractors to ready units if a large number of units must be prepared or a large number of service requests are pending.
- The property manager can help minimize the possibility of receiving a large number of move-outs in any one month by carefully monitoring lease expiration dates and staggering expiration dates for new leases accordingly.
- Collect the first month's rent plus a security deposit from new tenants to guard against their leaving without giving notice.
- Work hard to hold on to current tenants in a slow market. For lease renewals, meet with tenants 45 days before their lease is due to expire.
- Deal with problems quickly and efficiently; unresolved problems will only grow.
- Remember that fewer callbacks by tenants on maintenance and repairs means greater tenant satisfaction and fewer turnovers.
- Even when cash flow is low, try to minimize cutbacks on maintenance, repairs, and replacements, because they can lead to a lower standard of maintenance. ∎

and regulations for the apartment house before tenants move in and asking tenants to sign the rules signifying that they understand them. When problems arise between tenants, the manager should first try to reach an amicable solution with both parties. Moving a tenant to a different unit sometimes solves the problem. If one party is at fault and an amicable solution does not work, the lease should be used to enforce the rules of the property, up to and including eviction. Timely response and firm enforcement of rules are vital for maintaining good tenant relations.

Selling the Property

The life cycle of property management has three stages: lease-up, stabilizing income, and positioning the property for sale. The third stage usually involves a different management approach from the first two.

When the time comes to sell a project, on-site staff should be informed about the developer's goals and given some financial incentive to motivate them to help put the apartment in the best possible physical and financial condition for sale. It is an intense period when rents are raised and vacancies are filled. Experienced developers recommend that residents not be informed of a pending sale, but each tenant should receive a letter immediately *after* the sale. In Texas, for example, the law requires that tenants be notified within 48 hours of a sale about the status of their security deposits, which are transferred with the asset.

Cash flow is generally the most important consideration for buyers. Some steps will increase short-term cash flow at the expense of long-term profitability. For example, some developers become less selective about tenants to increase their occupancy and the rent roll when they get ready to sell a property. Other owners cut back on operating expenses and capital expenditures. Sophisticated buyers will use their own experience with respect to operating costs so that sellers' attempts to artificially reduce costs will have little impact on the sale price. Short-term efforts to raise cash flows are not advised, but many sellers do it. If a sale does not go through, the owner will have to deal with the consequences of the short-term strategy, such as getting rid of unreliable or troublesome tenants.

Conclusion

Beginning developers will find multifamily residential development one of the easier points of entry into the development industry, especially if they have some background in homebuilding. Like other types of development, multifamily housing is rapidly evolving. The process begins and ends with market analysis. If the depth, characteristics, and preferences of the target market are not correctly identified, delivering a product that best serves the market's needs is impossible.

Jim Perley notes that a beginning developer has to adapt to new situations and to try to predict the flow of situations. "You are trying not only to make money but also to develop a good product. It is also important to build equity and develop a good staff to make a difference."[71] Marvin Finger also emphasizes the people side of the business. "The three components of multifamily development are location, product, and management. If you don't have the location, the product and the management will not make a difference and you'll never be successful. If you have the location, you can miss on the product somewhat if it is reasonably designed. But you must have the people if the product is to be sold. Renters rent from an individual when they sign the lease agreement. They have made a bond with an individual. It's very important not to have turnover in the office. You must groom and build an organization that is somewhat permanent, because people create relationships. When these relationships are not in place anymore, tenants will take their business elsewhere. People are key in the management business."[72]

To obtain financing today, new projects must demonstrate solid cash flows and produce real economic returns. This trend should offer long-term benefits to developers who face less tax-motivated competition. REITs and pension funds have helped to generate more money for apartment development in recent years by buying new and existing properties and making forward commitments to buy projects under development. In many areas, rents have lagged behind other cost-of-living increases, resulting in fewer apartment starts throughout the 1990s. As the echo boomers begin to enter the workforce, apartment demand will likely go up, putting pressure on rents to rise more quickly. Developers are also finding opportunities to build apartments for new niches, such as luxury renters in upscale communities who want to stay in the same community but no longer want a large suburban home to maintain.

More stringent fire codes, parking requirements, density restrictions, and standards for amenities are raising the cost of apartment construction. At the same time, the scarcity of land, rising neighborhood opposition to development, stricter environmental regulations, and growing difficulties with public approvals are raising the price of land for apartments. Historically, rents have lagged behind inflation in the general economy. Rents will have to rise more sharply than they have in the past for apartment units to remain financially attractive—a trend that is likely to increase pressures for rent control in many communities. Although new apartment construction on suburban greenfield sites remains the easiest way for beginning developers to start, smaller urban infill projects, conversions of older industrial and office buildings to apartments, and affordable housing programs such as tax credits offer appealing opportunities for beginning developers. Their most important goal should be to build a track record of successful projects in which tenants, investors, and lenders are pleased with their performance. There are advantages to working on smaller, simpler projects than larger complicated ones. Completing three smaller projects over two to three years will take a beginning developer farther than completing one large project over the same period.

Notes

1. Interview with James Perley, Western America Properties, Los Angeles, California, 2000.

2. Ibid.

3. Jun Han and Mark Gallagher, "Outlook for the New Millennium," Urban Land, January 2000, p. 42.

4. Interview with Greg Vilkin, president, Forest City Development, Los Angeles, California, 2000.

5. Interview with Randolph Hawthorne, Rghventures, Brookline, Massachusetts, 2000.

6. Interview with Jerome J. Frank, Jr., Jerome Frank Investments, Dallas, Texas, 2000.

7. Interview with Randolph Hawthorne, 2000.

8. Interview with Marvin Finger, the Finger Companies, Houston, Texas, 2000.

9. Interview with Joan Betts, vice president, Fidelity Mutual Life Insurance Company, Atlanta, Georgia, 1987.

10. Interview with Marvin Finger, 2000.

11. Interview with Ray Kimsey, Niles Bolton Associates, Atlanta, Georgia, 2000.

12. Interview with Randolph Hawthorne, 2000.

13. Interview with Greg Vilkin, 2000.

14. Interested readers should refer to Homer Hoyt, The Structure and Growth of Residential Neighborhoods in American Cities (Washington, D.C.: U.S. Federal Housing Administration, 1939); D. Grether and P. Mieszkowski, "Determinants of Real Estate Values," Journal of Urban Economics, 1974, pp. 127–146; Edwin S. Mills, "Studies in the Structure of the Urban Economy," in Resources for the Future (Baltimore: Johns Hopkins University Press, 1972); Denise DiPasquale and William C. Wheaton, Urban Economics and Real Estate Markets (Upper Saddle River, N.J.: Prentice Hall, 1995); D. Thimothy and W. Wheaton, "Intraurban Wage Variation, Employment Location and Commuting Times," Journal of Urban Economics, Vol. 50, No. 2 (2001), pp. 338–367; and Sewin Chan, "Spatial Lock-In: Do Falling House Prices Constrain Residential Mobility?" Journal of Urban Economics, Vol. 49, No. 3 (2001), pp. 567–587.

15. See Richard B. Peiser, "The Determinants of Nonresidential Urban Land Values," Journal of Urban Economics, 1987, pp. 340–360.

16. Double-loaded parking has parking stalls on both sides of the driveway. Back-to-back apartment units adjoin the back of another unit along the rear wall. This shared wall can accommodate plumbing for both units and reduces the total amount of outside wall per unit, thereby saving money.

17. The San Diego general plan requires at least one acre (0.4 hectare) for lots with an average slope of 15 percent or less, two acres (0.8 hectare) for an average slope of 15 to 25 percent, and four acres (1.6 hectares) for an average slope greater than 25 percent. Interview with Neal LaMontagne, County of San Diego Department of Planning and Land Use, 2000.

18. NAWCA contains no specific definition of vernal pools. The U.S. Fish and Wildlife Service uses the "Classification of Wetlands and Deepwater Habitats of the United States" (December 1979) for defining types of wetlands, which is also used for NAWCA. Typically, a vernal pool is a shallow, intermittently flooded wet meadow, generally dry for most of the summer and fall. Interview with David Buie, U.S. Fish and Wildlife Service, 2000.

19. Kevin Lynch, Site Planning, 3rd ed. (Cambridge, Massachusetts: MIT Press, 1984), p. 81.

20. Interview with Greg Vilkin, 2000.

21. An easement in gross is an easement that does not benefit another specific tract of real estate but benefits a specific individual or business by permitting him to use land. An example is a right-of-way for a power company.

22. Interview with Jerome J. Frank, Jr., 2000.

23. Interview with Marvin Finger, 2000.

24. Cities that prohibit vacancy decontrol also typically prohibit (or make it very onerous to move) any rental units from the housing stock for conversion to condominiums.

25. For an excellent discussion of exactions, see James E. Frank and Robert M. Rhodes, eds., Development Exactions (Washington, D.C.,

and Chicago: Planners Press and the American Planning Association, 1987).

26. For a good overview of alternatives for financing infrastructure improvements, see Robert W. Burchell, David Listokin, et al., *Development Impact Assessment Handbook* (Washington, D.C.: ULI–the Urban Land Institute, 1994).

27. Stage 2 analysis is standard throughout the real estate industry and is taught in most real estate graduate schools and executive training courses. Most real estate finance textbooks describe DCF analysis in detail; see, for example, William B. Brueggeman and Jeffrey Fisher, *Real Estate Finance and Investments,* 11th ed. (New York: McGraw-Hill, 2002).

28. Robert Buzbee, division partner for the south central region, Trammell Crow Residential, provided project cost and operating data for Alexan Town East. Although costs, unit sizes, distributions, and operating costs reflect Trammell Crow Residential's experience in Dallas in late 2002, interest rates and terms of deal structures have been adjusted to represent those that a beginning developer would be likely to obtain. Trammell Crow Company has extremely favorable financing available because of its size and reputation.

29. Loan-to-value ratios dropped to 60 percent in the aftermath of the recession of the early 1990s. Conservative underwriting by lenders has kept the LTV ratio in the 65 to 70 percent range in the early 2000s. Historically, LTVs have been as high as 75 to 80 percent for fixed-rate apartment loans, although they are not likely to return to such levels in the near future.

30. Equity is $4,546,115 (from Figure 4-3e).

31. Unleveraged discount rates are published for pension fund investors and life insurance companies. Institutional investors looked for unleveraged returns of 8.5 to 10 percent on "stabilized" apartment projects in 2002.

32. When interest rates are well below overall capitalization rates, cash-on-cash returns on equity skyrocket as leverage (debt/total project costs) increases. Because inflation is a component of the IRR (along with risk and real return rates), the IRRs required by investors also are lower.

33. Some time before the developer goes hard on earnest money, it becomes nonrefundable.

34. Time Zero typically is considered to be the time when the developer closes on the land. When closing occurs a long time before start of construction, it is simpler to assign Time Zero as the start of construction and to include land carrying, design, and other interim costs as "costs to date." "Apartments leased" in Figure 4-6 is the average for the quarter (50 units leased each quarter).

35. In Quarters 7 and 8, cash flows exceed interest payments by a total of $192,084 (Figure 4-6, Line 70).

36. See the U.S. Census Bureau Web site, www.census.gov/const/CSS/ Table 8.

37. Interview with Ron White, president of residential development, Hillwood Development Corporation, Dallas, Texas, 2000.

38. Interview with Marvin Finger, 2000.

39. Peiser and Frank broke this rule successfully in August Park in Dallas, designing a 732-square-foot (68-square-meter) two-bedroom/one-bath unit in which the second bedroom could substitute for a den. The cost savings and concomitant lower rent were very appealing to single-parent families and young couples without children in a lower-rent part of Dallas.

40. Interview with Greg Vilkin, 2000.

41. Interview with Ray Kimsey, 2000.

42. Interview with Jerome J. Frank, Jr., 2000.

43. For large projects, demolition and foundation permits are sometimes obtained before the other building permits. Only foundation drawings must be submitted.

44. Interview with Ray Kimsey, 2000.

45. An important element of developers' success with miniperms was that new construction fell dramatically with sky-high interest rates in the early 1980s. Those developers who were able to obtain miniperm loans benefited from significantly less competition as their properties came on stream.

46. Both construction and permanent loans are called *mortgages,* because they are backed by the collateral of the property.

47. A *point* represents a front-end fee equal to 1 percent of the loan amount. Points are usually paid out of the loan proceeds. On a $1 million loan with two points, the lender receives $20,000 in fees, and the developer receives the net amount of $980,000. Points are a normal part of the developer's financing costs and should be included in soft costs.

48. Interview with Richard Klein, senior vice president of corporate development, Environmental Industries, Inc., Calabasas, California, 2000.

49. Interview with Jerome J. Frank, Jr., 2000.

50. Interview with Randolph Hawthorne, 2000.

51. *LIBOR* is the interest rate offered by a specific group of London banks for U.S. dollar deposits of a stated maturity. LIBOR is used as a base index for setting rates of some adjustable-rate financial instruments.

52. Interview with Karl Zavitkovsky, managing director, Bank of America, Dallas, Texas, 2001.

53. See Brueggeman and Fisher, *Real Estate Finance,* Chapters 4 and 5, for how to calculate a mortgage.

54. Interview with Karl Zavitkovsky, 2001.

55. *Top 25 percent* means that the developer guarantees the first 25 percent of loss. For example, if the loan is for $1 million and the lender loses $300,000, the developer is responsible for the first $250,000 of the loss.

56. Refinancing often occurs when a project achieves certain rental objectives, such as major lease rollovers at higher rents. If, for example, the developer refinances a project for $5 million that previously had a $4 million mortgage, $1 million in cash is left over after paying off the old mortgage. This cash from refinancing is especially attractive, because it does not create any immediate tax consequences and therefore is available in its entirety for distribution. The joint venture agreement specifies how the money is to be distributed. It may call for splitting the entire proceeds of refinancing 50/50 between the developer and the investors, or after the investors receive, say, $500,000, or only after the investors receive back all their equity.

57. Real estate tax accounting is a highly specialized area. Although non–real estate accountants are familiar with depreciation rules, the categorization of upfront fees requires a specialist. Too often, beginners select advisers who do not have the necessary familiarity and experience in the technical aspects of real estate partnership tax and law.

58. Many investors require the developer to make some sort of equity investment in the form of cash or a *contribution* such as land that has appreciated in value over and above its cost. The developer's equity can be treated one of two ways: 1) identical to the investor's equity, so that priorities of preferred return, repayment, and profit

are identical to the investor's (called pari passu), with all distributions based on one's prorated share of total equity, or 2) subordinated to the investor's equity, in which case the investor receives priorities ahead of the developer (see Chapter 5 for an illustration).

59 Regulation D private offerings are not subject to the intense review by public agencies that public offerings receive. Public offerings must be offered to no more than 35 "nonqualified" investors, who are defined as investors with personal net worths less than $1 million or incomes less than $200,000 per year. A Regulation D private offering may be offered to an unlimited number of "qualified" investors.

60. Linkage fees require developers of office buildings to contribute money to city-controlled accounts, which is then available to low-income housing developers. The fees are justified on the grounds that office buildings attract people such as clerks and janitors who cannot afford market-rate housing. Providing such housing is therefore "linked" to the new office space. Linkage programs have not been universally successful. Los Angeles, for example, introduced a linkage fee in the early 1990s just as new downtown office construction stopped altogether for ten years. The few buildings that went ahead were able to waive the linkage fee as part of inducing the developer to proceed with development.

61. Interview with Greg Vilkin, 2000.

62. Interview with Jerome J. Frank, Jr., 2000.

63. Ibid., 2000.

64. Ibid., 2000.

65. Permanent lenders have been stung by artificially inflated rental rates and usually require full disclosure of all rental concessions.

66. Interview with John Math, October 2001.

67. Interview with Greg Vilkin, 2000.

68. Floyd M. Baird, Marie S. Spodek, and Robert C. Kyle, *Property Management*, 6th ed. (Chicago: Dearborn Trade, 1999), p. 1.

69. Interview with Randolph Hawthorne, 2000.

70. Interview with Jerome J. Frank, Jr., 2000.

71. Interview with Jim Perley, 2000.

72. Interview with Marvin Finger, 2000.

5. Office Development

Overview

Office development is one of the most competitive segments of the development industry. Office development firms come in all sizes, ranging from one-person companies to large international development firms and real estate investment trusts (REITs). Office users are likewise characterized by their diversity, occupying spaces that can range from 500-square-foot (46.5-square-meter), or smaller, executive offices to urban complexes and suburban campuses that contain several million square feet.[1]

This chapter focuses on the types of office buildings most frequently built by beginning developers—buildings costing under $10 million and typically ranging from 5,000 to 100,000 square feet (465 to 9,300 square meters). Small office buildings and large office complexes tend to involve the same issues, although scale does make a difference in the time involved. The particular problems and perspectives in developing larger office projects are noted where they differ significantly from those encountered in smaller projects.

Office developers usually begin with a market analysis or a tenant, although sometimes a developer begins with a site in search of a use, with an office development the single most suitable use for the site. Speculative ("spec") developers determine a target market, find a suitable site, design the building, find lead ten-

ants, obtain necessary public approvals, arrange financing, construct the building, and lease it. Developers who begin with a tenant construct the building to the tenant's specifications.

Categorizing Office Development

Office developments tend to be categorized by class, building type, use and ownership, and location.

Class. Perhaps the most basic feature of office space is its quality or class. The relative quality of a building is determined by a number of considerations, including age, location, building materials, building systems, amenities, lease rates and terms, occupancy, management, and tenant profile. Office space is generally divided into three main classes:

- Class A—Investment-grade buildings that offer an excellent location and first-rate design, building systems, amenities, and management. Class A buildings command the market's highest rents and attract credit-worthy tenants. They are typically new, highly competitive buildings, although sometimes older buildings are renovated and repositioned as Class A properties. In some markets, Class A+ space is a distinct class, consisting generally of one-of-a-kind trophy or signature buildings that feature outstanding architecture, building materials, location, and management.
- Class B—Buildings with good location, management, and construction and little functional obsolescence or deterioration. Class B space is found generally in

figure 5-1

Characteristics Determining Office Classifications

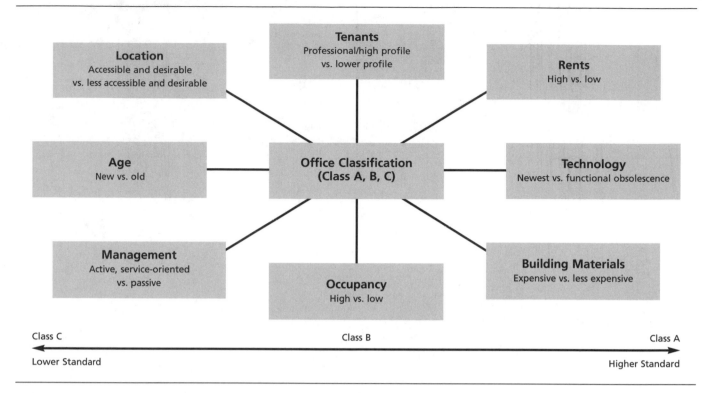

well-located buildings of an earlier generation that have been maintained to a high standard.

- Class C—Buildings that are substantially older than Class A and Class B buildings and that have not been modernized. Class C buildings are often functionally obsolete and located in less desirable locations than Class A or Class B buildings.

Building Type. Categorization of the office market by building type includes:

- High Rise—Typically higher than 15 stories;
- Mid-Rise—Four to 15 stories;
- Low Rise—One to three stories;
- Garden Office—One to five stories with extensive landscaping;
- Research and Development (R&D)—Typically one or two stories with up to 50 percent office/dry laboratory space and the remainder workshops, storage, and perhaps some light manufacturing (office/industrial hybrid);
- Flex Space—One- or two-story buildings that can accommodate warehouse and light industrial activities as well as offices.

Use and Ownership. Office buildings can also be classified in terms of their users and owners. Buildings can be single-tenant or multitenant structures. A single-tenant building may be leased from a landlord or owned

by the tenant. In the latter case, it is referred to as an *owner-occupied building*. A building designed and constructed for a particular tenant who occupies most or all of the space is called a *build-to-suit development*. A single- or multitenant building designed and developed without a commitment from a tenant is considered a *spec building*.

Location. In most urban areas, at least four distinct types of office nodes can be found, distinguished by their location; each location is distinctive in terms of the physical characteristics of the offices themselves and of typical users.

- Central Business District—The largest concentration of major office buildings occurs in the downtown or central business district (CBD) of most large cities, although the CBD's share of metropolitan office space is declining in most cities. By 1999, the central city share of office space dropped to 58 percent, while the suburban share grew to 42 percent.[2] Typical tenants in downtown offices include law firms, insurance companies, and financial institutions that require high-quality prestigious space.
- Suburban Locations—The increasing decentralization of offices in the past 20 years has led to greater diversity in office locations outside the city center. Suburban office nodes of both large and small office buildings are often found in business districts or in clusters near freeway intersections or major suburban shopping

centers surrounded by low-density residential development. Characterized by low- to mid-rise office buildings, suburban offices traditionally offered lower rents than the CBD. Tenants typically included regional headquarters offices and smaller companies and service organizations that did not require a location in the CBD. Increasingly, however, suburban locations are attracting major law firms, accounting firms, and corporate headquarters. As a result, the difference in image, quality of construction, and even rents between the CBD and prime suburban office nodes has gradually lessened.

- Neighborhood Offices—Small office buildings are frequently located in suburban areas, away from the major nodes, where they serve the needs of local residents by providing space for service and professional businesses. Neighborhood offices can be integral parts of neighborhood shopping centers or freestanding buildings.

- Business Parks—Office space is also found in business parks, developments with several buildings accommodating a range of uses from light industrial to office. Business parks vary from several acres to several hundred acres or more, so they tend to be located in suburban areas. Office buildings in business parks are generally small to medium with one to three stories. Flex space and R&D office buildings, with capabilities for laboratory space and limited warehouse space, are typically located in business parks.

The last 20 years have witnessed an increase in the number of offices located outside these traditional nodes. In a study for the Brookings Institution, Robert Lang found that considerable development has taken place in highly dispersed clusters with fewer than 5 million square feet (465,000 square meters) of space. Termed *edgeless cities,* these small clusters of offices lack a well-defined boundary and can extend over wide areas.[3]

Class A office buildings are distinguished by an excellent location and first-rate design, building systems, amenities, and management.

Trends in Office Building Development

The office market is a highly cyclical business that is subject to boom and bust periods. The playing field for office development comprises many elements, and unforeseen changes in basic forces can influence office markets in unexpected ways.

Market Trends. In response to increased demand and readily available financing during the early to mid-1980s, the United States experienced a major boom in office construction. Many office buildings were built by developers using cheap money generated by partnerships more interested in tax write-offs than in positive cash flows. S&Ls, banks, pension funds, and insurance companies were also keen to fund office projects to generate fees and keep funds from lying fallow. Even marginal projects were funded, as developers and investors were willing to believe projections about demand and rents that—at least in hindsight—were extremely optimistic and unwarranted. As a result, much more space was constructed than the market could absorb within a reasonable period of time.

During the early 1990s, the national office vacancy rate hovered near 20 percent, with many markets significantly higher. Only after ten years of economic expansion with relatively little new office construction did the national vacancy rate fall to the "normal" range, around 10 percent.[4]

In contrast, the office supply glut of the early 2000s resulted mainly from an economic recession that led to employee layoffs and corporate cost cutting. Office tenants who expected continued economic expansion and leased more space than needed were caught by surprise, leading to a large amount of office space for sublease in many markets. The result was higher vacancy rates, lower rents, and a market working in favor of tenants rather than landlords.

Regional Economic Growth. A shifting economy creates uneven regional office development patterns. A good knowledge of trends in the local economy and the forces that drive employment growth is critical in understanding the office market and discerning new opportunities for development.

The migration of people and firms to the southern and western United States in recent decades has provided many opportunities for developers. Many major companies have moved their corporate headquarters and other functions into the Sunbelt, promoting increased office construction in those areas. The rate of movement to Texas and other oil states slowed in the late 1980s because of the recession there, but certain cities in those areas such as Austin, Texas, have since attracted significant technology employment. In the 1990s, for example, the greatest absolute growth in high-tech jobs took place not in California or Massachusetts, the traditional high-tech leaders, but in Texas and Georgia.[5]

Cities in the Northeast, such as Boston, New York, and Washington, D.C., enjoyed a boom during the late 1980s as a result of expansion in technology-based industries, pharmaceuticals, financial services, and government services, but by the early 1990s many of these industries were in decline. During the late 1990s, renewed expansion of high technology as well as a booming stock market and resurgence in the financial sector led to increased demand for office space, rising rents, and lower vacancies in cities along the East and West coasts.

Influence of Technology. Rapid technological changes have also affected the workplace. "Smart buildings" have become a reality, as office tenants require more extensive and sophisticated telephone and computer network systems integrated into the design of buildings. Increased demand for advanced telecommunications cabling and services—phone systems, computer networks, data transmission, voice- and videoconferencing, and other communications technologies—is an important consideration in the design or upgrade of office buildings. The demand for office space and the character of office functions are also likely to be affected by growth in the number of workers able to telecommute from home via personal computers, modems, fax machines, and other technology.

Changing energy technology is altering the way that office buildings are designed and managed. Since the oil embargoes of the 1970s, energy conservation and energy management have become important aspects of building design and property management. The shortages experienced during the early 2000s, of both crude oil and electricity, have only heightened these issues. Energy management systems that control heating and ventilation can substantially reduce operating expenses and are becoming increasingly critical components of an office building. Many utility companies encourage the use of cogeneration and off-peak cooling systems through special financial incentives and technical assistance. With the advent of computerized systems and the Internet, remote monitoring and control of HVAC systems has become practical even for relatively small office buildings. The advantages of such systems include not only lower operating costs but also more efficient billing of tenants. Typical office leases include provisions defining operating hours (e.g., between 8 A.M. and 6 P.M. on normal business days), and building owners may charge for occupancy costs outside those hours. Modern tracking systems provide an easy mechanism for tracking and billing tenants for use outside standard operating hours. For tenants in key industries, backup generators that provide uninterrupted supply may be a critical requirement to be negotiated in an office lease.

In addition, state or locally mandated energy conservation requirements affect the design of buildings. Building codes typically restrict the size or type of windows permitted in a new building to achieve a minimum R-factor in the perimeter wall, require solar water heating, specify insulation levels, or require water-conserving plumbing fixtures and landscaping. All these rules and regulations must be considered when designing an office building and computing its budget.

Sprawl. The rapid development of suburban offices has created traffic congestion in many cities throughout the country—ironically, one of the problems that origi-

Wellesley Gateway is a corporate headquarters facility with downtown-standard building materials and landscaping on a highly visible suburban site in Wellesley, Massachusetts.

nally motivated companies to move to the suburbs. The dispersed and low-density nature of suburban offices also makes them difficult to serve by mass transit, because mass transit works best where employment is highly concentrated.

Resolving suburban traffic congestion is a major issue today. In fact, suburban traffic problems and a reaction against sprawl have begun to regenerate interest in inner-city locations.[6] Beginning developers may find attractive opportunities in inner-city and infill development, not the least because the time and cost of public approvals may be lower in such areas. Moreover, many urban areas have a rich resource of vacant or underused historic buildings that are ripe for redevelopment if a developer can find a financially feasible use.[7]

Corporate Campuses. A countertrend to the move back to the city has been the move of major corporations into private corporate campuses and out of the broader commercial real estate market. During the 1990s, for example, Sears vacated its namesake tower in Chicago and relocated to a suburban campus. In southern California, the Disney Company continued to add to its corporate collection of architecturally interesting office buildings in suburban Burbank, with the final design of architect Aldo Rossi joining earlier buildings designed by Robert Stern and Michael Graves. In Kansas City, Sprint has created a new 240-acre (97-hectare) headquarters campus in the suburb of Overland Park.

Corporations' choices of office space often significantly impact the local office market. For example, Sprint's decision to consolidate its facilities in a corporate-owned campus significantly impacts the suburban office market as the company vacates space it had occupied in scattered locations in the area. Most market surveys in tracking office space specifically exclude owner-occupied buildings from the inventory of commercial office space, yet developers should be keenly aware of the impact of major corporations in their market.

Project Feasibility

Market Analysis

The first task for developers contemplating office development, like any type of development, is to conduct an initial market analysis. This exercise tests the developer's belief that a market exists for additional office space. It also provides direction for site selection and design by indicating the type of space and amenities that office users are looking for. The market analysis also provides critical input for the financial analysis, which will ultimately be used to demonstrate the feasibility of the project and provide investors and lenders with the information they need to provide funding.

The market analysis usually requires the assistance of a market research firm, although the developer should be sufficiently familiar with the market to make an initial determination that the project is likely to be feasible. Before selecting a firm, developers should carefully evaluate the extent of survey information available in house to each of the major market research firms. Established market research firms usually maintain or have access to substantial databases. Major brokerage firms also maintain data on major tenants and buildings in most cities. They know when tenants' leases expire, what the terms of those leases are, and who will decide whether or not to renew the leases. These firms also know what the current trends in the market are and what segments of the market have the largest unmet demand (or the smallest oversupply). Some firms will provide this information only if they receive an exclusive listing on a property, but leasing decisions have their own criteria separate from market research decisions and developers must decide whether they wish to accept such conditions or pay for the data.

Demand. Analysis of demand for office space begins with an analysis of the economic base of the local metropolitan area. Specifically, this step involves studying existing employers and industries in the market and their potential for growth, with particular focus on the sectors of the economy that generate demand for office space. Employment projections should take into consideration new firms moving into the area as well as the expansion of existing firms. In general, state or national projections are likely to be more accurate than local projections, but they may be less useful than a local projection in determining demand for office space in a

Sheridan Plaza at Inverness in Englewood, Colorado, is targeted to small to medium tenants who require on average less than 3,000 square feet (280 square meters). Features include underground parking, a fully equipped conference room, a high-tech telecommunications center, an on-site tenant relations manager, and high-quality exterior and interior finishes.

particular location. Moreover, projections are likely to reflect recent trends and may not anticipate short-term changes in the economy, such as an unexpected boom in a growing industry or a recession in the national economy.

Projected employment growth is key to the demand for office space. It should be broken down by industry and ultimately should yield office-based employment growth projections for the local economy. The U.S. Department of Commerce, through its Bureau of Economic Analysis, provides employment projections for metropolitan areas. A number of commercial forecasting firms offer employment estimates as well. Local governments and chambers of commerce are additional sources for employment figures and projections, although they should be carefully analyzed to ensure that they are realistic and not subject to boosterism or exaggeration. Any forecasts for employment growth to significantly exceed past trends or the metropolitan trend should be carefully examined. Good reasons may exist for a particular submarket to outperform the region or the state, but for one submarket to outperform means other submarkets will have to underperform.

A viable market analysis helps to define the preferences and requirements of potential tenants. Approximately 95 percent of tenants in a new building come from existing businesses located within a 60-mile (97-kilometer) radius of the site. Companies seek new space primarily for one of five reasons:

- to accommodate additional employees or a new subsidiary;
- to expand an existing business into a new area;
- to improve the quality of their office environment;
- to consolidate dispersed activities into a single space; and
- to improve their corporate image (thereby improving both sales and customer contacts and enhancing employees' morale).

The market analysis should also focus on whether the market contains headquarters, regional, or branch office users. The type of tenant to be targeted will affect the architectural design with respect to office depths, corridor widths, parking, and amenities. A large institutional tenant, for example, may be more concerned about its ability to use the space efficiently. On the other hand, in a market dominated by small corporate headquarters, the image of a building, its amenities (for instance, the availability of on-site recreation facilities or restaurants), and its ability to provide distinctive identities for tenants will be major concerns.

Potential users' space requirements inevitably affect the design and type of facility, including average floor area, number of entrances, and the location of hallways and elevator cores. The bay depth—the distance between the glass line and the building core—is particularly important. Large users frequently desire large bay depths for greater efficiency, but small users require smaller bay depths to increase the proportion of window offices. Space requirements are themselves influenced by a potential tenant's employee mix; 250 square feet (23 square meters) per employee is often considered the norm but space requirements per employee can vary greatly. Secretaries generally require 100 to 150 square feet (9 to 14 square meters), while a typical president's office might occupy 400 square feet (37 square meters) or more. Office cubicles for clerical employees may be as small as 60 to 90 square feet (5.5 to 8 square meters). *↳ Space Requirements*

The first step in any market study is to carefully define the competitive market area, which can be both the region and the submarket. For regional employment, a step-down approach can be used to allocate employment growth from the region to the local market. In terms of supply, it is most important to look at local or submarket data. Office buildings compete most closely with other buildings that are in the immediate vicinity. Rents, amenities, parking, and services can vary considerably between submarkets, though regional conditions may affect all submarkets. It is therefore important to understand how a particular development will fit into its competitive environment.

Once a market researcher has collected data on potential tenants and the expected employment growth calculated for a specified time period, the following equation can be used to estimate the total square footage demanded:

Number of projected employees x Gross space per employee = Projected office space demand

The amount of space required per employee is not a constant factor and is, in part, a function of the type of business, the type of employees occupying the space, and overall market conditions. For example, legal and other professional firms traditionally require large offices with libraries and support space, resulting in an average of three employees per thousand square feet (95 square meters) of rentable office space. A telephone call center with small workstations and little support space might generate six employees for every thousand square feet (95 square meters).

The demand for space is also affected by market rents. When space is readily available and rents are relatively low, employers tend to use space less efficiently than when rents are high and availability is more limited. In some industries, the trend has been to decrease space per employee so that employers can expand their staff without leasing additional space. Haworth, a manufacturer of interior office systems, reports that employee work areas and cubicles have been reduced in size over the last 15 years:[8]

	1985 Cubicle Standards (Square Feet/ Square Meters)	2000 Cubicle Standards (Square Feet/ Square Meters)
Managers	115/11	64/6
Technical	82/7.5	48/4.5
Clerical	43/4	36/3

One purpose of an office market study is to estimate the net rentable square footage demanded per year, given anticipated market rents and availability. The time dimension—absorption per year—is one of the most important parts of the market analysis. Without it, the analysis is meaningless.

Two rules of thumb are useful in estimating the demand for office space. First, all Class C space greater than 50 years old will likely be replaced within the next 20 years at a rate of 5 percent per year. Second, most firms that wish to move are looking for 10 to 20 percent more space than they currently occupy. Understanding the current inventory of space and current tenants' needs makes it possible to estimate a baseline projection of future needs, even in a stable market with little anticipated growth.

Supply. After establishing market demand, the developer must focus on the competitive supply of office space in the market.

Either the developer or a market analyst should undertake a thorough survey of existing, planned, and potential office projects in the market area. Such an inventory should identify the following information for each competitive building:

- location;
- gross and net building area;
- scheduled rent per square foot per month;
- lease terms;
- tenant finish allowances;
- building services;
- amount of parking provided and parking charges (if applicable);
- building and surrounding area amenities (restaurants, conference facilities, health clubs, and so forth); and
- list of tenants and contact persons.

This information can be used to help determine the market niche in which a proposed development will compete. It provides the basis for estimating rents, concessions, design features, and desired amenities. As for demand, the definition of the appropriate market area should take into account regional and metropolitan supply. The submarket definition—areas that include the primary competitors for the subject project—is especially important. All competitive buildings in this area—and in particular, those actively leasing—should be carefully monitored.

A variety of published and online services sell office supply data. *Black's Guide* (published annually by Black's Research Service, Inc., Redbank, New Jersey) provides a good overview of the type and amount of office space available in many cities. F.W. Dodge also offers a comprehensive supply database and a construction forecast for the top metropolitan areas in the country. CoStar is an online office market database with data on existing inventory, current construction, vacancy rates, rental rates, and top lease and sale transactions for all classes and types of offices. Market data can be purchased for the entire U.S. market or for individual markets.

From the analysis of supply, the developer can determine total existing supply plus the future supply of office space. By subtracting the expected supply from the expected demand for office space, the deficit or surplus of office space for a particular period can be determined. This knowledge allows the developer to estimate the market conditions that will prevail when a proposed building comes online. If demand is increasing faster than supply, vacancy rates should be falling, creating a more favorable market for the developer. Alternatively, if supply is increasing faster than demand, vacancy rates should be increasing.

The vacancy rate resulting from turnover, sometimes referred to as the *natural* or *stabilized* vacancy, is inevitable. The total square footage of supply should be adjusted by the natural vacancy rate, which tends to be higher in faster-growing cities. A very rapidly growing city may have a natural vacancy rate of more than 10 percent, whereas the rate in a stagnant city may be only 3 percent. In the equation below, market supply, natural vacancy, and total demand are expressed in square footage. Care should be taken to be consistent in terms of how space is measured; either net rental square footage or gross square footage may be used, but not both:

$$\frac{\text{Total market supply} - \text{Natural vacancy}}{\text{Total demand per year}} \times 12 = \begin{array}{l}\text{Months of}\\ \text{existing inventory}\end{array}$$

For example, suppose the natural vacancy rate in a city is estimated at 5 percent or, say, 50,000 square feet (4,650 square meters) of the total inventory of 1 million square feet (93,000 square meters). If total existing market availability is 150,000 square feet (14,000 square meters) and annual absorption is 100,000 square feet per year (9,300 square meters), then the market contains one and one-half years (18 months) of existing supply. When the natural vacancy of 50,000 square feet (4,650 square meters) is taken into account, the excess supply drops to one year. Suppose another 200,000 square feet (18,600 square meters) is on the drawing boards of local developers, according to the information collected from bankers, brokers, and city planning staff. Not all this space will actually be built, so only some percentage of it, say 50 percent, should be added to total market supply. If another 100,000 square feet (9,300 square meters)—50 percent times 200,000 (18,600)—is added to the existing supply of 100,000 square feet (9,300 square meters), the total existing and planned supply becomes two years:

$$\frac{150,000 - 50,000 + 100,000}{100,000} \times 12 = \begin{array}{l}\text{24 months of existing}\\ \text{and planned inventory}\end{array}$$

Should a developer build in a market that has two years of existing and planned inventory? No firm guidelines exist for determining what constitutes a soft market, although a market with less than 12 months of inventory is generally considered a strong market, 12 to 24 months a normal market, and more than 24 months (18 months in slower-growing areas) a weak or "soft" market. With a building that will enter the market in 12 months, a developer will face a 12-month existing inventory in the above example. If the building adds 50,000 square feet (4,650 square meters) to the inventory, then in 12 months the inventory will be 150,000 square feet (14,000 square meters). If the developer captures a prorated share (33 percent) of the total inventory available, the building will take 18 months to lease.

A common mistake is to assume that a proposed project will capture an unrealistically large share of the entire market. Developers, optimists by definition, usually believe that they can outperform the market because they have properties with superior location, product design, cost advantages, or leasing personnel. Obviously, not everyone can outperform the market, and it is a grave mistake to plan on doing so. Developers should have sufficient cash available to cover situations in which leasing takes longer than indicated by the prorated capture rate. In the example, the developer should expect to take 18 months to lease the building but should also be able to cover a slower lease-up of 24 to 30 months.

Subleased Space. Subleased space is an important feature of the office market and should be recognized in assessing supply. For various reasons, tenants may lease space that they later find they do not need. This space, although technically leased, is often available, formally or informally, and thus part of the competition faced by new development. It is extremely important that a market analysis take this subleased space into account when calculating available inventory.

It is important to understand the difference between occupied and leased space. Market research historically focused on leased and unleased space to measure vacancy because leases were easier to measure. One way to identify *occupied* space is to knock on doors or check with building managers (if they will tell you) to see which spaces in a building are actually occupied. Fortunately, major brokerage firms and market research firms in most major cities continually monitor occupancy so that more accurate measures of vacant space available for lease can be obtained.

One fallout from the collapse of the dot-com and telecom bubbles of the early 2000s was the availability of large blocks of subleased space. Many high-tech firms, flush

An inventory of competitive buildings should include a review of on-site amenities as well as amenities and services found in the surrounding area.

with cash from stock offerings and planning on growth through expansion, built or leased space far in excess of their current needs. In the late 1990s, some firms engaged in defensive leasing to ensure their future ability to expand in especially prime locations where a shortage of space was anticipated.[9] As these companies saw their stock value plummet, they found they needed to conserve capital. As a result, companies started to lower their growth projections and put unused space back on the market. In some markets where the vacancy rate had been low, unanticipated subleased space and new product coming online in response to a tight market had the effect of significantly affecting vacancy rates in a very short time. Space available for sublease can be a useful indicator in assessing the trend for commercial real estate, just as short selling is for the stock market.[10]

Effective Rental Rates. One of the most important distinctions to understand in office market analysis is the difference between quoted (*face*) rents and *effective* rents. With a glut of office space in the 1980s, many techniques were introduced to maintain the appearance of future rent levels while effectively reducing tenants' rent. Typically, permanent lenders require that developers achieve a certain rent level as a condition of funding or as a condition of releasing the developers' personal guarantee on the construction loan. To meet these conditions in a soft market, developers may offer tenants free rent for a specified period or an extra allowance on their space improvements (called *tenant improvements*) to induce them to lease space, as long as the rent in the lease meets the lender's requirements for funding the mortgage or releasing the developers' personal liability.

Such concessions remain common practice in some markets, although lenders have become more sophisticated in how they review lease agreements before funding a loan. Like tenants, they now focus on effective rents. In strong office markets, building owners no longer offer free rent, except perhaps during an initial period when tenant improvements are being completed. In such cases, however, tenants are often required to pay operating expenses during this period.

Rental concessions are harder for market analysts to identify than asking rents. Brokers and leasing agents have incentives to overstate rents or understate concessions because they do not want future prospects to know what they gave away on earlier deals. Hence, analysts may be misled and report that rents are higher than they actually are.

Scheduled rental rate increases also change the effective rent. For example, a lease with flat rent for ten years has a lower effective rate than a lease with annual 2 percent increases. A lease with annual 2 percent increases is likely to have a lower effective rate than a lease with annual increases tied to the consumer price index (CPI), because the CPI historically has increased more than 2 percent per year.

The market study should provide the information necessary to compute rental rates and the estimated absorption rate during lease-up as well as the types of

Calculation of Effective Office Rent

Suppose a developer has an office space of 1,000 square feet with a nominal rent of $24.00 per square foot for five years ($2.00 per month). Concessions include six months of free rent and $3.00 per square foot in extra tenant improvements. The developer's discount rate (opportunity cost of money) is 12 percent or 1 percent per month.

To find the effective rent, the developer must convert the lease and the free rent to present value, which can be computed per square foot or for the total leased area.

Present value (*PV*) of lease per square foot:	
PV ($2/month, 1%/month interest, 60 months)	$89.91
Less:	
Present value of free rent per square foot:	
PV ($2/month, 1%/month interest, 60 months)	11.59
Extra tenant improvements	
(already stated as present value)	3.00
Present value of effective rent	$75.32
Convert present value to equivalent monthly rent:	
PMT ($75.32 PV, 1%/month interest,	
60 months)	$1.67
	x 12 months
Effective annual rent per square foot	$20.04

∎

concessions necessary to compete with other options available to prospective tenants. These numbers will be used directly in the financial analysis.

General Advice on Office Market Research. Allan Kotin, an adjunct professor in the Master of Real Estate Development program in the School of Policy Planning and Development at the University of Southern California, emphasizes several points about office market research:[11]

- The larger the tenant, the more difficult it is to determine what the tenant is actually paying in rent after taking into account rent concessions such as free rent, expense caps, free parking, and extra tenant improvements.
- A problem with assessing the impact of larger tenants is their susceptibility to consolidations or changes in business plans from swings in the economy. Such actions can result in their putting large amounts of space on the sublease market, which has an effect that is hard to measure and often missed in market analysis.
- Major markets are stratified by scale as well as by quality, rent, and location. A 10 percent vacancy rate may be very misleading if the largest space available is only 20,000 square feet (1,860 square meters). The market for 50,000-square-foot (4,650-square-meter) tenants is very different from that for 100,000-square-foot (9,300-square-meter) tenants.

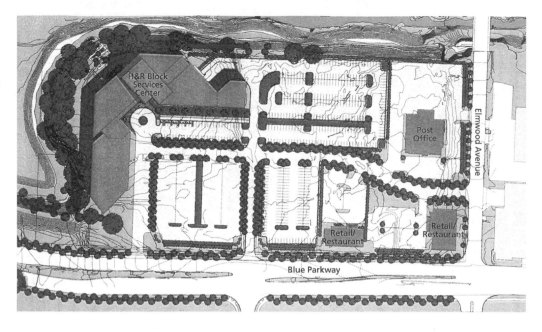

The site of the H&R Block Services Center in Kansas City, Missouri, was transformed from unusable low-lying terrain to a park-like setting with mature trees that enhances the immediate area.

- For major buildings, control of a single large tenant is far more important than generic measures of space.
- Despite the sophistication of market analysis, the fact remains that many small and medium firms decide where to rent space on such distinctly unscientific grounds as "where the boss lives."

Site Selection

Site selection is a crucial step in the project feasibility analysis, because an office project's location directly impacts the rent and occupancy levels it can achieve. All a site's qualities affect the office building's potential for attracting tenants. Developers should compare the locational, access, and physical attributes of alternative sites to identify potential opportunities and obstacles to development. This comparison should include a review of the rent and occupancy characteristics of the buildings located around each site. It should also note any differences in zoning or allowable development potential.

In general, office uses can support the highest rents of any land use type and thus are often located on the highest-priced land. Thus, high land prices should not be a deterrent in the search for a site; a high price is usually indicative of the desirability of the location for office uses. Similarly, developers choosing sites based on a lower price can find themselves unable to compete in the market, even at lower rents.

The site should be able to accommodate an efficient building design. Office buildings are less flexible in terms of size and shape than are industrial, retail, and residential buildings. Back-office users, such as clerical and data-processing operations, prefer floor plates (that is, area per floor) in excess of 20,000 square feet (1,860 square meters). Small office users, such as professional firms and smaller companies, prefer buildings with more window area and floor sizes ranging from 16,000 to 20,000 square feet (1,500 to 1,860 square meters), although smaller floor plates are not uncommon. The most efficient buildings are 100 feet wide and 200 feet long (30 by 60 meters).

Such a shape allows a core of about 20 by 100 feet (6 by 30 meters) and a typical office depth of around 40 feet (12 meters) between the core and the exterior wall. Such plain rectangular boxes, however, may lack sufficient design appeal to win the public support needed for approvals. Prospective tenants also respond negatively to plain boxes if they do not offer the type of image they want to present to their clients.

Because of high land values, the cost of parking structures is often warranted, and parking structures are even less flexible than office buildings in terms of layout. Structured parking modules with efficient layouts should be designed in bays that are 60 to 65 feet (18 to 20 meters) wide, with a minimum of two bays; therefore, a parking structure needs to be at least 180 feet (16.5 meters) long to efficiently accommodate internal ramps.[12] Freestanding parking structures are much less expensive to build than structures that are integrated into the office building itself, because the structural systems required for parking are different from those required for office buildings. Except in urban settings with very high land values, an office building site should, whenever possible, be large enough to accommodate a freestanding parking structure. It is not uncommon to have one parking structure serve several office buildings.

Topography can play an important role in site selection. Hilly sites may require extensive grading, which will increase construction costs, but they may also provide excellent opportunities for tuck-under parking that requires less excavation than for a flat site.

Access is another primary consideration in site selection. Sites should have access to freeways and roads that feed into the regional transportation system. Parcels located on major highways or frontage roads may have great visibility but may not be accessible from those highways; therefore, developers should check with local municipal, county, state, and federal transportation authorities about access before proceeding. A traffic study is useful for the design of access points and internal circulation of an office project and is usually a requirement for public approvals. Access to public transit is also important, particularly as traffic congestion continues to worsen. With many metropolitan roads now at or near capacity, the availability of choices beyond just the automobile can be a strong marketing tool.

Jim Goodell, president of Goodell Associates, recommends that office buildings be located in areas with a sense of place. "A synergy exists between office buildings and activities such as restaurants, shopping, entertainment, hotels, and residential uses. A mixed-use environment generates benefits that translate into higher rents and better leasing."[13] The terms of site acquisition are essentially the same for office buildings as for the other product types and are discussed in detail in Chapters 3 and 4.

Regulatory Issues

Historically, office developers were concerned only with local zoning and building codes. Floor/area ratios (FARs), height limitations, building setbacks, and parking requirements were the primary determinants of how much space could be built on a particular site.

Today, zoning ordinances may set the upper limits of office development, but the rules are often more complex and less clear than suggested by zoning alone. Communities often have wide discretion in reviewing projects not only for compliance with zoning but also for environmental and community impacts that are difficult to quantify. In some cases, specific impacts, such as increased traffic at a particular intersection, can be addressed by constructing off-site improvements such as traffic signals or turn lanes. Others, such as increased regional congestion or lack of affordable housing, are difficult to mitigate for a project but may be mitigated through the payment of impact fees.

Over the last two decades, developers have encountered new regulations aimed at office buildings. Some of these initiatives were motivated by a local community's need to control negative impacts of office development such as traffic, others by a community's need to raise tax revenues. As a result, public regulation of office development has been somewhat ambivalent. On the one hand, cities want office development because it is clean and generates jobs. Office developments generally have a positive fiscal impact; that is, they generate more in tax revenues than they require in public services. The direct fiscal benefits of office developments, however, pale in comparison with retail uses and the sales tax they generate. Shrinking local tax revenues from other sources have led many cities to look toward office development as a way to fund public projects and even social programs such as affordable housing. The result has been a host of impact fees and new requirements, such as linkage programs that require developers to build up to 200 units of low-income housing for every 1 million square feet (93,000 square meters) of office space constructed.

The results have backfired in some cases, particularly when the economy weakens and employers can be selec-

tive. San Francisco for a time experienced an exodus of businesses from the city's core to outlying areas when it instituted a combination of very high impact fees, exactions, and housing linkage programs. In another instance, Beverly Hills inherited all the traffic but none of the tax revenues when it refused to approve a major hotel that was eventually built across the street in the city of Los Angeles.

Certain cities are in such distinctive and attractive locations that they can extract above-average concessions from developers, but even these cities have suffered a slowdown of new business development when the cost of their exactions made development unprofitable. After all, developers pass on the regulatory costs to future tenants in the form of rent or operating expenses. If rents become too high, present and potential tenants will seek space elsewhere. Further, with the office development slowdown in the early 1990s, many cities that depended on office development to generate tax revenues found that they needed to look to other sources, most likely higher property, sales, or business taxes.

Government bodies continuously revise local building codes covering building safety and public health, spurred in some cases by litigation or the threat of litigation. As more information is gathered about the effects of fire, wind, earthquakes, tornadoes, and hurricanes, local and national building codes are updated. Many government agencies have enacted stringent energy codes. The trend toward stricter building codes is likely to continue.

Zoning and Land Use Controls. In addition to the typical zoning restrictions on building setbacks, height, and site coverage, the regulations specifically affecting office development concern FARs, building massing, solar shadows, and parking requirements. FARs are often used to set an upper limit on building densities. This ratio between building floor area and site area is obtained by dividing the gross floor area of a building by the total site area. Some cities—Los Angeles, for example—have passed citizen-sponsored initiatives that dramatically reduce allowable FARs. Such reductions give cities unusual leverage in negotiating with developers for facilities or services the city wants.

Some cities, including New York, award FAR bonuses to developers who provide plazas, subway connections, pocket parks, galleries, and other public amenities in high-density commercial districts. Trump Tower in New York City, for example, originally had a floor/area ratio of 15. Because the design of Trump Tower incorporated special features, such as a pedestrian arcade, landscaped terracing, and interior retail space, the developer received a FAR bonus of 3. After purchasing additional air rights from an adjacent building, the total allowable FAR reached 21.6 times the buildable lot area.

Building massing and solar restrictions are intended to prevent city streets from becoming dark canyons. Most zoning ordinances include provisions that carefully define allowable building envelopes and shapes to stop buildings from casting permanent shadows and to prevent the glass on buildings from reflecting excessive heat onto other structures. In addition, some government agencies regulate the types of materials, styles of architecture, location of entries, and various other design aspects of office projects. Developers must recognize and work within these restrictions to determine the maximum envelope that their buildings can occupy.

One special regulatory device that has been used with urban office development is transferable development rights (TDRs). TDRs allow for the sale of development rights on a property from one owner to another. If one owner wants to retain a two-story building on a site zoned for ten stories, that owner may sell the right to build the additional square footage to another landowner. Once sold, however, the original owner cannot build any more square footage than that for which zoning rights were retained.

TDRs have not been as widely adopted as planners expected. Some of the obstacles to establishing a working TDR program include finding areas to receive higher-density development, calibrating values for development rights, and creating a program that is simple enough to understand and administer but complex enough to be fair. TDRs work well with historic landmark buildings, including older office buildings. Historic buildings often do not take the fullest advantage of a site's development potential. In addition, designation of older buildings as historic landmarks can complicate and even prevent major changes to their structure and exterior facade. TDRs are one technique for owners to receive compensation for their loss of development rights.

Parking requirements for office buildings vary by location, but they typically stipulate a minimum of three to four spaces per 1,000 square feet (95 square meters) of gross floor area. Developers often find, however, that they must provide more spaces than required. Many lenders finance only suburban office buildings with at least four spaces per 1,000 square feet (95 square meters), because they know from experience that parking difficulties will drive away tenants. In fact, many users, such as call centers, want up to six spaces per 1,000 square feet (95 square meters). At the same time, however, communities wishing to encourage use of mass transit may restrict parking. Some cities have proposed that developers provide mandatory off-site parking for some portion of the parking requirement for buildings in congested downtown areas. In Los Angeles, for example, the Community Redevelopment Agency has required that 40 percent of the parking for buildings in the downtown core be located in remote facilities, with on-site parking limited to only one space per 1,000 square feet (95 square meters) of office space. Developers are concerned that such a requirement causes tenants to search elsewhere for office space, because employees will not tolerate the additional travel time from the off-site parking to their offices. On the other hand, lower parking requirements can save money, and lenders will still provide financing if all developers are subject to the same restrictions. One concept that can satisfy local government's desire to limit parking while at the same time providing the ability to meet tenants' future needs is *deferred parking*. Deferred parking is shown on the approved development plan but need not be built until demand for parking is proved.

Local communities have also become increasingly concerned about the aesthetics of commercial development, office developments in particular. Although developers and their architects do not always appreciate the opinions of regulators, local planning staffs and officials believe that office buildings are important to a city's image, so they are not shy about expressing their preferences about building massing and shape, exterior materials, and finishes.

Transportation. One of the most politically sensitive areas regarding office development is the impact that such development has on traffic. Congestion was once a problem only for central city areas. Today, many suburbs experience congestion that is as bad as or worse than that in older downtown areas.

Most large office developments and many small ones are now required to provide a traffic impact study during the approval process. Because office development generally contributes large traffic loads during peak hours, traffic mitigation measures are becoming a common requirement for approval. These measures can range from widening the streets in front of a building to adding a traffic signal or widening streets and intersections surrounding a site. Satisfying off-site infrastructure requirements can be extremely costly and time-consuming, not least because of the need to work with public agencies and other property owners.

An office developer may be required to undertake any of the following actions:

- restripe existing streets;
- add deceleration and acceleration lanes to a project;
- construct a median to control access;
- install signals at entrances to a project or at intersections impacted by the project;
- widen streets in front of a project;
- widen streets between a project and major highways or freeways;
- build a new street between a project and a major highway; and/or
- contribute to construction of highway or freeway interchanges.

Instead of requiring certain improvements through exactions, some areas have created impact fee programs to cover traffic improvements. Impact fees are typically assessed per peak trip generated or translated into a fee per square foot. Fees can run as high as several thousand dollars per peak trip generated. The number of expected peak trips generated by the project thus becomes a critical factor in the cost of the project.

Several creative solutions have emerged to reduce peak traffic trips, such as adding retail components to a project, providing residential facilities on or adjacent to the site, and providing links with public transportation sys-

Because office markets are constantly evolving, buildings should have the flexibility to meet tenants' shifting demands.

tems. Mixed-use developments appeal to planners and local officials, and on-site retail services offer benefits to tenants. Nonetheless, adding a significant retail component to an office project is likely to increase rather than mitigate traffic impacts if the retail portion needs to attract a wider customer base to be viable.

Transportation demand management (TDM) programs (sometimes called *transportation system management* or TSM) have become a popular mechanism for reducing the generation of traffic. A number of cities have passed ordinances requiring developers of projects with a certain number of employees to implement ride-sharing programs, such as carpools and vanpools. A TDM plan may also include reduced-price passes for public transit and preferential parking spaces for individuals who carpool. The developer is often responsible for ensuring that these programs are implemented, as TDM programs are often a condition of approval. The cost may be borne ultimately by the office tenant. Encouraging commuting by bicycle or by foot is another strategy some cities encourage. In Boulder, Colorado, for instance, bicycle storage and showers for employees are a requirement for any office development, and good connections to the city's network of bike trails are important not only for approval but also for marketing the project.

Financial Feasibility

The financial feasibility process involves gathering market data from the market study, cost data for various alternatives, and financing costs, and entering these data into the financial pro forma. Financial feasibility analyses for office projects use methods similar to those employed for other income properties (see Chapter 4).

One useful source of information for estimating operating costs for a new office building is *Experience Exchange Report: Income/Expense Analysis for Office Buildings,* an annual study published by the Building Owners and Managers Association (BOMA) and the Institute of Real Estate Management (IREM) that provides detailed break-downs of operating costs and revenues for different types and sizes of office buildings in different locations and metropolitan areas.

The key to accurately estimating revenues for office projects is to make *realistic* projections regarding lease-up time, vacancy rates, and achievable rents. Developers and analysts have a strong tendency to make overly optimistic projections.

Cap rates are very important in underwriting an office building, because a project's debt capacity is a function of its value. Cap rates reflect current market conditions and vary over time, as commercial real estate—office buildings in particular—is perceived as a more or less attractive investment. During the 1980s, pro forma cap rates of 8.5 percent were not uncommon. During the recession of the early 1990s, cap rates often exceeded 10 percent, and distressed properties could be acquired at considerably higher cap rates. (As cap rates rise, values fall.) The effect of cap rates can be quite dramatic. Cap rates are lowest when markets are strong and highest when markets are weak, thus compounding the effects of changing occupancy and rental rates that respond to market conditions.

Cap rates tend to be lower in major metropolitan areas and higher in secondary markets, reflecting a perception of higher risk associated with smaller markets as well as a smaller pool of potential buyers. Developers should consult local mortgage brokers and lenders to determine current appraisal and underwriting criteria before considering a project.

Design and Construction

General Principles

Office buildings need to be adaptable to changing requirements over time. Tenants may use a building for 50 years or more, with succeeding generations of tenants moving in and out of the space many times. Further, the office market is an ever-changing market, and a well-designed building should have the flexibility to meet the shifting demands of its tenants. For tenants today, flexibility is especially important as they look for ways to expand and contract as their needs change.

The market analysis should help provide the design parameters for the project, although some design elements, such as the placement of halls, corridors, and fire walls and space requirements for restrooms, corridors, and stairwells, are usually dictated by local building and fire codes. For example, suppose an analysis indicates that the average office tenant leases 4,000 square feet (370 square meters) and has a workforce of 16 employees, each of whom occupies an average of 250 square feet (23 square meters). These figures would be the basis for designing the building's size, parking, elevators, building depth, and interior air-circulation requirements.

As a general rule, total project costs are broken down into the following percentages:

Building shell and interior	45%
Environmental and service systems	25
Land and site improvements	18
Fees, interest, and contingencies	12
Total	100%

These numbers differ depending on regional requirements, construction methods, and special fees required by local government bodies. In high-rent districts, land is likely to represent a larger portion of the costs, as much of the increased rent can be attributed to the property's locational advantages.

Among the most important design decisions to be determined at the outset are those concerning the shape of the building, the design modules, and the bay depths that will be used.

Shape. A square is the most cost-efficient shape for a building in terms of providing the most interior space for each foot of perimeter wall, but it often generates the lowest average revenue per square foot because tenants pay not only for floor area but also for windows. Rectangular and elongated shapes tend to offer higher rents per square foot but cost more to build because they provide more perimeter window space and shallower bays. Developers prefer rectangular buildings for multitenant speculative space because the interior and perimeter spaces can be more balanced.

Changing tastes and the desire for more striking architecture produced a strong movement away from the glass boxes of the 1970s toward more articulated office buildings. Although nonrectangular shapes may be less efficient in terms of the ratio of perimeter wall to floor area, they often create more interesting office shapes and more corner offices. In most markets, such offices generate higher rent if they are designed correctly.

Design Modules and Bay Depths. Office buildings are designed using multiple modules of space, which allows for the repetition of structural and exterior skin materials. Although the design module is most visible on the exterior of the building, it should evolve from the types of interior spaces planned. The market study should suggest the types of interior design (for example, open-plan or executive offices) that are in the greatest demand in the target market.

The most common design module is the structural bay. Defined by the placement of the building's structural columns, the structural bay can be subdivided into modules of three, four, or five feet (0.9, 1.2, or 1.5 meters) that provide a grid for coordinating interior partitions and window panels for the exterior curtain wall. The structural bay determines the spacing of window mullions, which in turn determine the possible locations of office partitions. The space between the mullions determines whether interior space can be easily partitioned into offices of eight, nine, ten, 12, or 15 feet (2.4, 2.7, 3, 3.6, or 4.6 meters) (see Figure 5-2).

The market analysis should also provide design guidelines for the bay depth, which is defined as the distance from the glass line to the interior core. This distance is calculated by adding the depths of the exterior offices, hallways, support areas, and interior offices. Typically, offices are ten to 14 feet (3 to 4.3 meters) deep, and hallways are five to six feet (1.5 to 1.8 meters) wide. The width of the hallways plays an important role in setting the tone for the building: wider, more spacious hallways are associated with higher-class buildings.

The bay depth is typically about 40 feet (12 meters). Multitenant buildings with many small professional tenants, however, generally require smaller bay depths—say, 36 feet (11 meters)—to permit a larger number of window offices. Institutional users, on the other hand, prefer 40- to 50-foot (12- to 15-meter) bay depths, which are more efficient to build and tend to cost less. Some firms, such as law offices, can use large amounts of interior space for libraries and file storage. Some office designers claim that 42.5 feet (13 meters) is the ideal amount of space for perimeter offices, interior clerical workstations, and support areas. One alternative is an asymmetrical design, with the core offset to allow flexibility in marketing and layout. The bay might be 40 feet (12 meters) deep on one side of the core and 50 to 60 feet (15 to 18 meters) on the other.

Institutional users are more likely to prefer open-space plans and thus are less concerned about the number of window offices. Some tenants, particularly design and media firms, prefer more creative space marked by large open floor plates, exposed mechanical systems, open ceilings, and a lack of floor-to-ceiling partitions. Large bay depths offer an advantage in such a layout, as private offices do not require prime perimeter locations. Greater depth also provides greater flexibility in laying out workstations, and few, if any, private offices require prime perimeter locations. Some firms, in fact, choose to locate private offices in interior locations so that their open spaces can benefit from views and daylight.

Ceiling Heights. The vertical dimension is also important in designing office buildings. Traditionally, office buildings have been designed with floor-to-floor heights

figure 5–2
Relationship of Module to Interior Office Size

Module Size	Interior Office Width
3-foot	9, 12, and 15 feet
4-foot	8, 12, and 16 feet
5-foot	10 and 15 feet
5½-foot	11 and 16½ feet

Examples of Structural Bay Modules

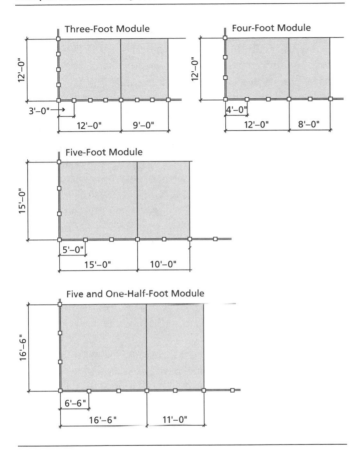

Note: Multiples of the module size determine where interior walls are joined to the exterior window wall system.

of about 12.5 feet (3.8 meters), which allows nine-foot (2.7-meter) ceilings and 3.5 feet (1 meter) above the ceiling for structural and mechanical systems. Recently, both dimensions have been increasing, with the floor-to-floor height growing to accommodate indirect lighting fixtures and the ceiling-to-floor height increasing to accommodate the deeper structural systems needed for increased column-free bay depths. A floor-to-floor height of 14.5 feet (4.4 meters) has become common for typical floor heights in Class A buildings when the total height of the building is not constrained by zoning or other codes. Additional construction costs resulting from increased areas of exterior walls and interior finishes must be balanced against the potential for increased rents obtained from spaces with higher ceilings.

Site Planning

The overall design, or curb appeal, of a building is significantly influenced by the building's location on its site. Generally, a building should enjoy maximum exposure to major local streets, and signage should be visible from those streets. Good site planning provides a logical progression from the street to the parking lot or structure to the building's entrance. The trip from the car to the entrance of the building provides visitors and prospective tenants with their first close look and impression of the building.

Parking. In theory, an office building in which each employee occupies an average space of 250 square feet (23 square meters) needs four parking spaces per 1,000 square feet (95 square meters) of rentable space, assuming that all employees drive separate cars. Workers who carpool, ride with their spouses who work elsewhere, or take public transportation reduce the parking requirement. Visitors, on the other hand, increase the parking requirement. Consider, for example, a doctor who has 1,000 square feet (95 square meters) of office space and employs two nurses. If the doctor has on average two patients in examining rooms and two patients in the waiting room at any one time, the office needs seven parking spaces. But doctors are busy at different times, and one doctor's inactivity may ease the parking burden for another doctor's crowded waiting room. Thus, the type of tenants expected in the building and the building's location influence the amount of parking needed.

Lenders often prefer that buildings provide at least four parking spaces per 1,000 square feet (95 square meters) of rentable space, even though local zoning may require less. Locations served well by public transportation require less parking. According to John Thomas of Ware Malcomb Architects in Irvine, California, many developers reduce the parking ratio as a project becomes larger.[14] For example, developers commonly provide four parking spaces per 1,000 square feet (95 square meters) for the first 250,000 square feet (23,235 square meters) of office space (1,000 spaces) but then provide only two parking spaces for each additional 1,000 square feet (95 square meters). Experienced developers, however, cite inadequate parking as one of the most common flaws of projects undertaken by new developers. Both the availability of parking and its proximity to offices play key roles in developers' ability to attract and hold tenants. If representatives of prospective tenants have trouble finding parking places when they visit a building, the tenants are unlikely to rent there.

Marshall Kramer, Walker Parking Consultants, recommends that developers look to their parking as an additional source of revenue. In urban locations, visitor parking spaces can potentially generate more revenue per square foot than the office space itself. The cost of building underground parking can represent 20 percent of the cost of the entire project. Some developers have presold their garage structures, raising a significant portion of the construction cost. Whether tenants are willing

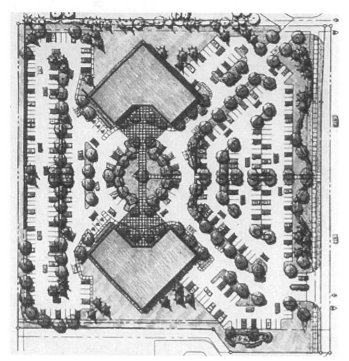

The planting plan for Sheridan Plaza at Inverness includes a heavily landscaped central plaza with a fountain and seating.

to pay for parking and how much are functions of the market. It is common practice to oversell parking spaces. For example, if a garage has 100 spaces, lease commitments might include 120 spaces. This practice is usually not a problem, because tenants are always coming and going, and at any given time, a certain number of employees will be traveling in and out of the office. Tenants may require assigned parking spaces, which limits the operational flexibility. Again, the need for assigned parking is market-driven. Building operators should in general avoid assigning parking spaces or charge a significant premium for them. Security is also a big issue with garages, particularly for high-profile trophy buildings. Some building operators have decided not to offer visitor parking, requiring visitors to park on the street or in public facilities.[15]

Landscaping. The importance of landscaping to a project's overall appearance cannot be overemphasized. Landscape design can tie diverse buildings together; it can define spaces; it can form walls, canopies, and floors. Concealing, revealing, modulating, directing, containing, and completing are all architectural uses for plants. Trees, shrubs, and ground cover may be used to control soil erosion, to mitigate unpleasant sounds, to remove some pollutants from the air, to control glare and reflection, and to slow the effects of erosive winds.

Landscaping elements include not only vegetation such as plants and trees but also rocks, berms, streams, retaining walls, and trellises. Ground cover and low-lying plants can provide lush backdrops as well as help control foot traffic. Vines that grow well in shady areas help to protect steep banks from erosion. A reasonable landscape budget accounts for 1 to 2.5 percent of total project costs.

Preserving existing trees can improve a project's image, assist with marketing efforts, and increase the project's long-term value. Mature trees can easily be destroyed, however, if precautions are not taken during construction. Contractors should build boxes around trees to be protected, and soil should be left undisturbed within a ten-foot (3-meter) radius of a tree's trunk. Many trees have survived construction only to die later because their roots were buried too deep in the final grading. Some trees can survive two or three feet (0.6 or 0.9 meter) of fill dirt, but gravel or stone should be spread to a depth of six to eight inches (15 to 20 centimeters) over their roots to ensure air circulation. Tree wells with at least a two-foot (0.6-meter) radius should be left around the tree trunk, extending to the original ground level. The developer should call on the expertise of landscape architects to design the landscape and save existing trees where possible and appropriate.

Plantings and trees should be chosen to enhance the development for both the short and long term. Developers should also bear in mind the size of plantings and trees at maturity. Plants beneath office windows should be chosen so as not to obstruct views. Landscape maintenance costs must be assessed with the landscape architect during design. For example, ground cover may be more expensive to install than grass but will not require weekly mowing.

Exterior Design

Exterior design concerns aspects such as exterior building materials, signs, and lighting. Prospective tenants and visitors gain their first impression of a building from its exterior, so the look of the building can be an invaluable marketing tool.

Building Materials. The building materials used in an office building generally are part of two distinct systems: the structural system and the skin system. The structural system supports the building, and the skin protects the interior space from the weather. Usually, the skin hides the structural material and is the only material visible to the casual observer. An office building can be built using one of five structural systems:

- Wood Frame—Generally used for one- or two-story garden offices;
- Concrete Tilt-Up—Generally used on one- to three-story buildings and typically employed in flex buildings and garden offices;
- Masonry—Typically used for low-rise buildings;
- Reinforced Concrete—Used for both low- and high-rise buildings;
- Steel—Used for both low- and high-rise buildings.

Each of these systems can be combined with another to produce economical hybrids, such as a lightweight steel frame building with wood truss floors or a masonry building with metal trusses or prestressed concrete floor units. Wood-frame construction is used predominantly for residential construction and infrequently for office development. In some suburban settings, however, a residential feel may be appropriate, especially for one- or two-story projects that cater to small businesses. Concrete tilt-up construction offers an advantage in that the concrete panels serve as both the structural system and the skin (see Figure 5-3).

The exterior of an office building can be covered with:

- Exterior Insulation Finish System—Synthetic stucco that can be formed into many shapes;
- Precast Concrete—Usually cast off site and shipped to the site and usually not part of the structural system;
- Tilt-up Concrete Panels—Cast on site and used as part of the structural system, limited to three stories;
- Glass Curtain Wall System—A combination of vision and spandrel glass hung in front of the building frame;
- Metal Panels—Aluminum or steel finished in a factory;
- Stone—Granite, marble, or slate in large panels or small tiles;
- Storefront System;
- Residential Materials—Including wood or stucco;
- Brick.

figure 5-3
Exterior Skin Materials

Material	Cost per Square Foot	Characteristics/Comments	Aesthetics	Long-Term Maintenance	Energy Efficiency
Plaster (Decorative Lime Plaster)	$30–50	Used on highly articulated surfaces. Can create optical illusions with it. Limited installers.	Excellent	Good	Fair
EIFS (Exterior Insulation and Finish Systems)	$14	Used to add architectural details at minimal cost. Fails under certain conditions; water penetration has led to lawsuits.	Very good	Very poor	Good
Flexirock	$14.50	Has more texture and character than stucco; looks more like concrete.	Good, depending on installation	Good, depending on installation	Fair
GFRC (Glass Fiber Reinforced Concrete)	$36–38	Best for mid-/high-rise office buildings. Can be used to achieve substantial design articulation with integral color.	Very good	Excellent	Good
Thin Shell GFRC	$28		Good		
Precast Concrete Panels	$34	Heavier than GFRC but can achieve same detail.	Very good	Excellent	Good
Concrete Tilt-up Walls	$15	Combines structure and skin—no studs in perimeter wall. Usually limited to three stories. Paint, leave natural, or sandblast.	Very good, depending on design	Excellent	Good
Metal Panels (Alucobond)	$25	Used for high-tech, precise look. Can be finished in wide range of standard or custom finishes.	Excellent	Good (may corrode)	Poor if installed without foam backing
Plaster System (Basic)	$13	Most economical surface system. Quality generally depends on installer.	Fair, depending on design	Fair—surface cracking will appear. Needs maintenance	Fair
Masonry (Decorative)	$13	Combines structure and skin. Substantial variety to achieve various looks. Height limitations.	Very good, depending on design	Excellent	Good
Storefront (Basic)	$16–18	Used for retail stores and low-rise office buildings where large glass areas are not present.	Fair (very utilitarian)	Excellent	Depends on glass: high-performance glass excellent, tinted or clear glass poor
Glass Curtain Wall	$27–28	Used for large expanses of glass in combination with various mullion systems and glass colors. Interesting geometry can be achieved.	Good to excellent, depending on design of glass mullion geometry	Excellent	Depends on glass: high-performance glass excellent, tinted or clear glass poor
Stone Veneer (Granite and Marble)	$50	Used to give building a sense of elegance and permanence. Minimum long-term maintenance.	Excellent	Excellent	Fair, depending on thickness

Source: John Thomas, Ware Malcomb Architects.

An attractive exterior design helps establish an office building's image, such as that at International Business Park in Dallas, Texas.

Materials may be used in combination; for example, a tilt-up building might incorporate a storefront system or precast elements for architectural variety. John Thomas, a designer at Ware Malcomb Architects, uses more expensive and tactile materials such as stone in places where people come in direct contact with the material, such as on the ground floor and building lobbies, and less expensive materials elsewhere on the facade.

Signage. Signs not only serve the necessary function of identifying a building and its tenants but also help create the overall impression for visitors to a building. Although tenants will negotiate for sign privileges, developers should retain sign approval as a condition in their tenants' leases. Total acquiescence to a tenant's preconception of its signage needs may damage the environment that attracted the tenant to the development in the first place. Restrictions should be specific to a building and should stipulate the size, shape, color, height, materials, content, and location of all signs. Typical sign restrictions include the following:

- No lettering shall be affixed to the building without written approval.
- Signs shall mean any structure, component, fabric, device, or display that bears lettered, pictorial, or sculptured material, including forms shaped to resemble any human, animal, or product designed to convey information or images that are exposed to public view.
- No sign or lettering shall be formed or constructed of paint or similar material applied to the face or other surface of a building within the complex.
- No sign shall be constructed or erected on the roof of any building in the complex.
- No sign shall be constructed so that the top of the sign is 15 feet (4.5 meters) higher than the adjacent finish street grade.
- No sign shall be constructed or erected with more than 72 square feet (6.7 square meters) of surface area per sign facing, and no sign shall consist of more than two such faces.
- No more than one sign shall be constructed on a building site.

The best approach is to develop a comprehensive signage program. The developer's architect should work with an interior designer and graphic artists to create a signage program for individual tenants and for common areas of the exterior and interior. A comprehensive signage program includes designs, materials, and color schemes for:

- project identification at the entry to the development;
- building identification;
- directory of major occupants;
- directional signs for vehicular and pedestrian traffic;
- building location directories; and
- interior building service signs.

Some developers hire a single sign maker to coordinate the signs for an entire project. This policy allows the developer to obtain specifications easily when a sign must be changed. The system for doorplates should allow for easy replacement of old signs when tenants change. Coordinating the installation of signs should be the responsibility of the on-site building manager.

Exterior Lighting. Exterior lighting can greatly enhance the security of building entrances and parking lots, thereby increasing marketability. Inadequately illuminated areas hurt the image of a building and may pose a liability problem. Lighting can also highlight architectural and landscaping features of a project. The developer should work with an electrical engineer and architect to design exterior lighting that will not only accomplish the desired effects but also be energy-efficient. Mercury vapor, sodium vapor, quartz, and fluorescent lights may all be used in exterior lighting fixtures; they use only a fraction of the electricity used by incandescent lights, although at the cost of light quality and color rendition. Many local jurisdictions have also become concerned about light pollution, and they require the use of high-cutoff lights and limit the use of architectural illumination that lights the sky. How the lights will be controlled—manually or by a timer or photocell—must also be considered.

Lighting standards for parking lots should be placed around the perimeter of the lot or on the centerline of double rows of car stalls. To prevent cars from hitting them, lighting standards should not be placed on the line between car stalls but should instead be placed in planter medians. The Illumination Engineering Society recommends a minimum illumination level of 0.5 to two footcandles for outdoor parking areas and five footcandles for structured parking.

Interior Design

Interior design begins with the determination of the building envelope, design modules, and bay depths, all of which determine how the various interior elements of the building are laid out and how the building functions. The interior design must accommodate various systems—elevators, plumbing, HVAC, lighting, wiring, life safety, for example—and the overall design must provide flexibility for the targeted tenant type.

Ways of Measuring Space. Office buildings contain a certain amount of shared common areas, such as lobbies. Tenants are very sensitive to the amount of common space in a building, because developers typically charge tenants for their prorated share of common space in addition to their usable space. To design an office building appropriate to its market, the developer, architects, and brokers must understand how to calculate rentable areas. The tenant pays rent at the stated rental rate multiplied by *rentable square feet*. Rentable square feet can be measured in many ways. BOMA provides standard methods of measuring different types of area: gross building area, rentable area, and usable area.[16]

For commercial buildings, *gross area* is measured from the outside finished surface of the permanent outer walls of a building. It is the sum of all enclosed floors of a building, including basements, mechanical equipment floors, and penthouses.

Rentable area is measured from the inside finish of the permanent outer walls of a building or from the inside of the glass line where at least 50 percent of the outer building wall is glass. Rentable area includes all areas within outside walls except vertical penetrations (elevators, stairs, equipment shafts, and atriums). According

An inviting lobby is a wise investment that can help market an office building.

figure 5-4

Typical Space Requirements per Employee

Job Function	Space per Employee (Square Feet)
Upper Management	280
Senior Management	193
Middle Management	142
Senior Professional	114
Technical/Professional	92
Senior Clerical	84
General Clerical	73

Source: "Benchmarks III," *Research Report No. 18* (Houston: International Facility Management Association, 1997).

to local definitions, it may also include elevator lobbies, toilet areas, janitorial rooms, and equipment rooms.

Usable area is measured from the inside finish of the outer building walls or glass line to the inside finished surface of the office side of the public corridor. Usable area for full-floor tenants is measured to the building core and includes corridor space. An individual tenant's usable area is measured to the center of partitions separating the tenant's office from adjoining offices. Usable area excludes public hallways, elevator lobbies, and toilet facilities that open onto public hallways.

The rentable/usable ratio (R/U ratio) is the rentable area divided by the usable area. Tenants normally pay rent on their usable space plus a prorated portion of the common space. Their rentable area is derived by multiplying the usable area by the R/U ratio. For example, if a tenant rents 1,000 square feet of usable space in a building with a 1.15 R/U ratio, the tenant pays rent on 1,150 square feet:

Usable square feet x R/U = Rentable square feet

1,000 usable square feet x 1.15 = 1,150 rentable square feet.

Tenants have become very sensitive to the R/U ratio, often referred to as the building *efficiency ratio, core factor,* or *load factor.* The average R/U ratio for high-rise space is about 1.15. Garden office and low-rise space average around 1.12. Developers with especially inefficient buildings (with R/U ratios greater than 1.2) sometimes arbitrarily reduce the ratio so that their buildings appear competitive. All developers should be careful to calculate pro forma project rental income on the actual rentable area and not the gross building area, which is more appropriately used to estimate construction costs.

Despite the BOMA standards, many geographical markets calculate rentable areas slightly differently, depending on local customs and market conditions. Both brokers and architects should be familiar with local measurement customs and should assist developers in designing a building that meets market standards.

Crate & Barrel's new corporate headquarters north of Chicago includes offices and merchandising space for review of sample projects.

© Hedrich Blessing/Courtesy Perkins & Will

Space Planning. Effective space planning involves five basic components: the space itself, the people who will use it, their activities, future uses, and energy efficiency.

The amount of space and its functionality are controlled by a building's exterior walls, floors, ceiling heights, column spacing and size, and the building core, which includes elevators, stairs, bathrooms, and mechanical equipment.

Typical space allotments for different types of employees are shown in Figure 5-4. In a single-tenant building, the tenant is responsible for improving the lobby and interior hallways. In a multitenant building, however, the developer improves the lobby, restrooms, and hallways that serve each suite, and individual tenants are responsible for improvements of hallways and facilities only within their own suites. Developers prefer tenants that occupy entire floors, because hallways and elevator lobbies fall within the rentable space of such tenants.

Optimum floor size depends on the type of tenant for which the building is planned. For multistory buildings, optimum floor sizes range from 16,000 to 25,000 square feet (1,490 to 2,325 square meters). Larger floor plates are better suited for larger users such as institutions and clerical operations; smaller floor plates are generally used for multitenant and professional uses. Smaller floor plates cost more but provide space for more offices with windows.

Many modern office layouts use the open-space planning approach, which not only helps to reduce the cost of office design changes but also costs less than closed offices for initial construction. Partitions in open-space plans are movable, and a variety of furniture/wall systems are available that are attractive and use space efficiently. Further, the tenant pays for them, although the developer may contribute the standard tenant improvement allowance for walls and flooring. The quality of soundproofing varies by product.

Money spent to make a building's lobby inviting and attractive is a wise investment. Bathrooms likewise can help recover high-quality decoration costs, because both tenants and visitors use them. Developers should avoid using color schemes that will soon seem outdated. Instead, they should opt for materials that can be replaced at low cost or employ neutral colors that will blend with future color schemes.

Elevators. Elevators are one of the most critical items to consider in setting the tone for a multistory office building. Tenants' and visitors' initial impressions are shaped first by a building's lobby and then by the quality of the interior finish of elevator cabs. Materials used in the lobby—such as carpet, granite, marble, brass, and steel—can also be used effectively inside the elevator.

Waiting time for elevators should average no more than 20 to 30 seconds; longer waits can play a significant role in a tenant's decision not to renew its lease.

Elevator capacity depends on the kind of tenants that occupy a building. Buildings occupied by larger companies with staff who work regular hours tend to need high-capacity elevators to accommodate peak-hour demand—sufficient capacity to move as many as 30 percent of the employees in a five-minute period. Buildings with a larger percentage of professional staff tend to have lower peak-period demand, because more tenants keep irregular hours. On the other hand, professional tenants are more conscious of time lost waiting for elevators.

The following rules of thumb are useful for gauging elevator capacity:

- Buildings with two floors require one or two elevators, depending on the nature of the local market and the size of the floors.
- Buildings with three to five floors require two elevators.
- Ten-story buildings need four elevators.
- Twenty-story buildings need two banks of four elevators.
- Thirty-story buildings need two banks of eight elevators.
- Forty-story buildings need 20 elevators in three banks.

Lighting. Because it can define spaces, highlight features, and create different atmospheres, lighting plays a critical role in how users and visitors perceive office space. The absorptive or reflective qualities of selected colors and fabrics may alter the need for lighting in different areas.

Four types of artificial light are available for interior applications:

- Fluorescent—Fluorescent fixtures are expensive but have the advantage of long bulb life (18,000 to 20,000 hours) and reduced energy consumption.
- Incandescent—Less costly than fluorescent fixtures, incandescent fixtures provide superior color-rendering properties but have a short bulb life (750 to 2,000 hours) and are more expensive to operate.
- High-Intensity Discharge—This type of lighting includes mercury vapor (frequently used outdoors), metal halide, and high- and low-pressure sodium lamps. Although they are excellent for illuminating outdoor spaces and are very energy-efficient, high-intensity discharge lights offer poor color-rendering properties.
- High-Intensity Quartz—Sometimes called *precise lighting*, high-intensity quartz lighting is a new product that is often used in upscale environments. Multifaceted, mirrored backs reflect the light onto specific objects or areas, making high-intensity quartz fixtures appropriate for task-oriented lighting.

Direct lighting is most frequently used in offices. Installed in a grid pattern across a drop ceiling, this solution offers equal levels of illumination across large spaces when the specific activity to be carried on is unknown—most often the case in speculative office buildings. Direct lighting is available in integrated ceiling packages, which can integrate lighting, sprinklers, sound masking, and air distribution. Heat recovery is more efficient when air-distribution outlets are linked to the lighting fixtures, because the lighting fixtures contribute heat to the system. Moving fixtures, however, is more expensive with integrated systems.

Indirect lighting uses walls, ceilings, and room furnishings to reflect light from other surfaces. The ceiling material plays a critical role in indirect lighting. Acoustical tiles, which are designed to absorb sound, often have poor light-reflecting capabilities. Indirect lighting works best with smooth ceiling textures. In recent years, indirect lighting has become more common for general office lighting as a way to reduce glare on computer monitors. Indirect lighting generally requires higher ceilings to reduce "hot spots" on ceilings and to improve the overall efficiency of the lighting layout.

Lighting is measured in footcandles. Acceptable office lighting ranges from 50 to 70 footcandles. Lamp efficiency is measured in lumens per watt, which is the ratio of light output (lumens) to the electrical energy consumed (watts). Another useful measure is the *coefficient of utilization*—the ratio of light from the lamp reaching the work surface to the total lamp output. The coefficient of utilization indicates the combined effect of fixture efficiency, room shape, and surface reflections on light emitted by lamps.[17] The electrical engineer, interior designer, and architect all play important roles in designing the lighting system to suit each tenant's needs.

Heating, Ventilation, and Air Conditioning. A building's HVAC system is one of the major line items in its construction budget. Several different types of HVAC systems are available:

- Package Forced-Air Systems—These electrical heat pumps, usually located on the roof, heat and cool the air in the package unit, then deliver it through ducts to the appropriate areas of the building. The units are inexpensive to install and work well on one- and two-story buildings.
- Variable Air Volume Systems—In these systems, a large unit on the roof cools the air and delivers it through large supply ducts to individual floors. Mixing units control the distribution of the air in each zone. This system offers great flexibility as many mixing units can be installed to create zones as small as an office, but it is more expensive to install than forced-air systems. Rooms are heated by a heating element in the mixing units or by radiant heater panels in the ceiling.
- Hot- and Cold-Water Systems—In these systems, a chiller and water heater is centrally located to provide hot and cold water to the various mixing units in the building. The air is heated or cooled in these mixing units and delivered to the local areas.

To choose an HVAC system, the developer should seek the advice of the architect and mechanical engineer. The developer should also solicit opinions regarding the control mechanisms. These computers, which are an extremely important component of all HVAC systems, can control the timing, level, and operations of the HVAC system and can even bill each tenant separately. Besides heating or cooling the air, the HVAC system provides fresh air from the outside. The American Society of Heating, Refrigerating and Air-Conditioning Engineers (ASHRAE) has published a standard that specifies the minimum ventilation rate for different occupancy and building types. The final authority on building ventilation is the local code authority, however, which may or may not have adopted ASHRAE standards.

ASHRAE also recommends desirable ranges for relative humidity and specifies a maximum allowable air velocity to prevent draft. Standards for air movement for each room depend on the local climate and the glazing, lighting, and orientation of the building. The amount of air conditioning likewise depends on such factors as the design of the building, orientation of the building to the sun, the climate, and the types of uses in the building. The output from an air conditioner is measured in Btu (British thermal units) or in tons (one ton equals 12,000 Btu). Typical air-conditioning requirements for office buildings are shown in Figure 5-5.

A well-designed HVAC system divides the building into zones, each controlled by a thermostat. These zones should cover areas with similar characteristics, such as orientation to the sun, types of uses, and intensity of uses. Areas such as conference rooms, waiting rooms, computer rooms, lunchrooms, kitchens, and restrooms have different loads and should, if possible, be in separate airflow zones from the general office uses. A standard rule of thumb is one thermostat zone per 1,200 square feet (110 square meters). Usually, each zone has one mixing damper that controls temperature by mixing hot and cold air.

Energy management through computer-controlled systems is now standard in medium and larger buildings. Variable air volume systems allow one to balance loads and automatically adjust airflow. The most common form is scheduling systems that raise or lower temperatures in different rooms according to a schedule. Sensors can also monitor changes taking place in a room, such as changes in occupancy, and adjust room temperature.

Sick building syndrome continues to receive attention as a serious health concern, and more building owners and insurance companies are being exposed to lawsuits on this subject. Generally, this problem and mold and moisture damage can be traced to some degree to poor humidity control and leaks in a building. ASHRAE's *Humidity Control Design Guide for Commercial and Institutional Buildings*[18] was written to provide guidance on humidity control to the entire building team.

Performance-based measuring of air circulation became the dominant technique for determining air circulation standards in the 1980s. In this system, contamination rates are measured by the presence of 34 specific contaminants, among them mold, carbon dioxide, and other human- and nonhuman-generated elements, found in air-cleaning devices used on recirculating systems. The system has proved very complicated to impose, and opinions are split about how to proceed in standardizing the system for measuring interior air quality. Ultimately, the common dilemma faced by those trying to set ventilation standards stems from the fact that maximizing ventilation to minimize illness increases energy consumption.[19]

Michelle Addington, associate professor of architecture at Harvard Design School and an expert on energy/environmental systems and building technology, further cautions about any condition that causes condensation or standing water. Humidity-caused condensation is the problem. Where it causes a "wetting incident"—such as in kitchens, drip trays, or fan coils—and condenses on a wall surface, mold grows quickly. Mold itself is not the problem, but when parts of the mold become airborne and can be breathed in, sick building syndrome may result.

Technology. Technology is changing the economics of office buildings in a variety of ways:

- Design—E-mail allows information to be communicated much more efficiently. The acceptance of the same

figure 5-5

Typical Air-Conditioning Requirements for Office Buildings

	Btu per Square Foot	Square Feet per Ton
High-Rise Building		
Exterior Office	46	263
Interior Office	37	325
Low-Rise Building		
Exterior Office	38	320
Interior Office	33	360
Small Suite Office	43	280

Source: *Building Construction Cost Data* (Kingston, Massachusetts: R.S. Means Company, Inc., 2002).

computer language simplifies the exchange of drawings among consultants, contractors, brokers, and tenants.
- Energy—Buildings are consuming less energy as well as producing some of their own energy.
- New Revenue Sources—Every part of a building is being examined for the potential to generate revenue; for example, income can be received from communications towers mounted on roofs and from signage in highly visible locations.
- Maintenance Costs—Mechanical rooms are kept cleaner, with filters changed more often and air monitored. Recycling chutes in high-rise buildings eliminate the need for recycling bins on every floor.

Energy Efficiency. A building's energy efficiency depends on its site orientation, the design of its windows, and the type of mechanical equipment and energy control systems it contains. Energy efficiency, which measures all the components that use energy, can be determined by calculating the energy efficiency ratio. The ratio is calculated by dividing the amount of energy used by the amount of energy expended.

A popular way to measure the energy efficiency of different designs is the *U-value*. U-values measure the rate of heat loss expressed in Btu per hour per square foot per degree difference between interior and exterior temperature. The U-value is the reciprocal of the total resistance of construction multiplied by a temperature or solar factor.

A film of air exists along the interior and exterior walls of any building. The U-value measures the resistance of the construction to the air and indicates the amount of Btu gained or lost in the building. All wall and roof construction components—including air space and paint—must be entered into the calculation to determine the U-value. U-values must be recalculated throughout the building whenever materials change.

As a general rule, U-values should be a minimum of 0.09 for insulated exterior walls and 0.05 for insulated roofs. The specific requirements of insulation depend on the local climate. The architect and mechanical engineer can provide recommendations for insulation.

Glass reflection plays an important role in determining energy use and is measured as the *shading coefficient*. The shading coefficient equals the amount of solar energy passing through glass divided by the total amount of solar rays hitting the glass. The lower the coefficient, the larger the amount of heat reflected away from the building's interior. Lower shading coefficients tend, however, to be more expensive to obtain. Moreover, a very low shading coefficient adversely affects the quality of light for building occupants.

Developers must decide how they wish to trade off construction and operating costs. Higher construction costs can purchase greater energy efficiency and thus lower operating costs. Lower initial installation costs may mean higher operating costs.

Many states and local government agencies have their own energy efficiency requirements. The state of California, for example, has an extensive set of energy regulations, called *Title 24 regulations,* which provide a tradeoff between window areas and heat loss through the windows. The regulations restrict the amount of energy loss allowed in a building and regulate the types and amounts of insulation, glazing, and lighting fixtures.

Green Building Design. A modest but increasing trend has occurred toward sustainable or "green" building design for office buildings. Green buildings (also known as *high-performance buildings*) emphasize reduced energy consumption through the use of techniques that bring natural light deeper into office space and the use of efficient HVAC systems. In addition to energy conservation, green building design may incorporate more environmentally friendly approaches toward construction, including use of recycled materials and renewable resources. Green buildings may also employ a greater use of natural materials and avoid synthetic materials, such as plastics and synthetic carpets, that emit toxic gases.

All the building systems and construction technology for the Condé Nast building at Four Times Square in New York City were evaluated for their impact on energy reduction, environmental sensitivity, and occupants' health, making it the first project of this size to adopt state-of-the art standards for energy conservation, indoor air quality, recycling systems, and sustainable development processes.

Green buildings can be defined a variety of ways, but the LEED (leadership in energy and environmental design) rating system developed by the U.S. Green Building Council has become the accepted standard.[20] Based on this set of guidelines, buildings are awarded points for incorporating criteria in six categories: sustainable sites, water efficiency, energy efficiency, materials and resources, indoor air quality, and innovative design processes. Depending on the total number of points received, buildings are awarded different levels of certification.

For example, Four Times Square in New York City was promoted as New York City's first green office tower. It incorporates several energy conservation features in the building:

- Photovoltaic (solar) panels laminated into the curtain walls. Electricity is collected and fed back into the building's electrical distribution system.
- Fuel cells, which provide 400 kilowatts of electrical energy to the buildings, reducing peak load and maintaining energy efficiency. Fuel cells produce electricity using nothing more than gas and air, with only heat and water as byproducts.
- Gas-fired absorption units that produce a relatively low level of emissions and do not use refrigerants.
- Low-noise air handlers on each floor that limit noise to adjacent uses and are designed to allow the air volume to vary as the outside air temperature drops or as the interior load is reduced.[21]

According to Tom McCaslin and John Wong of Tishman Construction Corporation, the builders of Four Time Square, the effort to create a green building generally adds to the construction cost. Some tenants, however, will pay a premium for a green building.[22]

Some of these first costs can be recovered later through energy savings. A green building also can provide good publicity and promote the firm as environmentally friendly, as well as boost employees' morale.

Life Safety and Security. Life safety and security have become increasingly important considerations in the design and marketing of an office building. Protecting the building, its contents, and its tenants and visitors involves planning from the beginning to ensure that security principles are integrated into a building's overall design.

The ability to control access in and out of a building is essential and can be secured by several methods:

- lobby security controls and on-site security guards;
- surveillance systems;
- entry-card systems;
- keyed elevators;
- alarm monitors; and
- building perimeter barriers.

Access to the building from parking garages should also be controlled. For parking structures adjacent to the main building, users find it most convenient if entrances lead from each floor of the garage directly into the building; this arrangement, however, makes access difficult to control. Greater security is obtained if all users of parking are required to enter the building through its main lobby. This method requires installing a separate set of elevators and stairs for the building and the parking structure. Parking garages located below a building should also have separate elevators to maintain security. Staircases should provide access only to the building's lobby.

Security and safety are enhanced by the inclusion of *life safety systems* in a building. Life safety systems can include fire sprinklers, alarms, sensors, fire hoses and extinguishers, automatic shutoff systems for the HVAC system, and other monitoring and control systems. The addition of these systems can lower fire insurance rates in some situations.

Fire codes differ from city to city, and developers should check with the local fire authorities to obtain the current codes. Some fire codes require compartmentalization, which involves providing special firewalls between office suites and corridors and exits for tenant suites. Such compartmentalization is usually required for suites larger than 3,000 square feet (280 square meters).

Tenant Leasehold Improvements

As part of the lease for office space, the developer usually provides a set allowance for tenant improvements that covers buildout of the interior space, including ceilings, walls, flooring, and electrical and telephone outlets. In the early 2000s, the allowance was typically $25.00 to $30.00 per square foot ($270 to $325 per square meter) of leased space. The allowance provides for only a minimum level of improvements and is usually insufficient to cover all the costs of tenant improvements, so the tenant is responsible for costs over and above the tenant improvement allowance. Because leases typically do not require the tenant to pay rent during the improvement phase, it is incumbent on the developer to ensure that work is done on schedule.

Tenant Improvement Process. Steps in the process of completing tenant improvements in a small office building parallel the steps involved in constructing the building itself: budgeting, preliminary planning, including design and construction drawings, approvals and permits, contractor selection and bidding, and construction.

- Step 1: Fix the Budget—The budget is determined by the quality the tenant wants and the resources available. Someone on the developer's staff must have a good appreciation of construction costs so that the budget will be realistic and the tenant will understand the quality of the improvements provided. The budget usually exceeds the developer's allowance and the tenant typically is required to pay any costs above the tenant improvement allowance, although in some cases the lease rate may be adjusted as an alternative.
- Step 2: Prepare a Space Plan and Design for the Improvements—The space planner/interior designer may be under contract to the developer or to the tenant. If the designer is under contract to the developer,

The Can Company complex in Baltimore, Maryland, provides eclectic spaces for tech-related companies.

the developer maintains greater control but will be liable for all costs if the tenant backs out of the lease.

The design firm is usually selected in one of two ways: 1) the developer selects a design firm and then recommends that firm to all tenants, or 2) the developer approves three or four firms and then allows tenants to select from the approved list.

The tenant usually has the option of choosing another firm, and larger tenants that lease a large amount of floor space in a building often do so. The developer, who pays for the work out of the tenant improvement allowance, retains the right to approve the designer, however. Only a large developer with a series of ongoing projects would be able to maintain a space planner on staff.

The developer ultimately owns the tenant improvements and thus has a strong interest in controlling quality and design. But because the object is to lease space and satisfy the tenant, the developer needs to be flexible in evaluating a tenant's proposals.

- Step 3: Have Plans Approved—Plans are submitted to the local building department for approval and permits. Whenever improvements involve safety or require electrical work or partitions, building permits are required. Requirements for permits vary by municipality, so it is important to check local codes.
- Step 4: Select a Contractor—The options for selecting a contractor are similar to those for selecting a space planner. Generally, the developer selects a single contractor—usually not the general contractor for the building—to do all the tenant improvements in the building, but some developers prefer to approve three or four contractors and then submit the drawing to each for bids. Because the continuing happiness of the tenant is of paramount importance to the developer, the developer usually works with the contractor to see that the bids are within the tenant's budget. If the tenant feels that the bid is too high, the lease usually allows the tenant to secure additional bids, although the developer again retains the right to approve the contractor.
- Step 5: Oversee Construction—The developer must maintain close contact with the contractor during construction to make certain that the project is proceeding smoothly and that the tenant will be able to move in on time. The developer should carefully monitor any claims for change orders so that the project remains within the tenant's budget. The tenant may be required to pay its share of the cost at the start of construction, but usually payments are phased. If the project will be completed in less than two months, it is common for the tenant to pay one-half (either to the developer or to the contractor, depending on the agreement) at the start of construction, with the balance due at completion. On longer jobs, a smaller initial payment and regular progressive payments may be made.

Work Letters. Work letters serve as the formal agreements between the developer and the tenant concerning the amount and quality of improvements that the landlord will provide. They specify the work the landlord will do before the lease commencement date as well as the schedule of costs.

Building standard installation (the *building standard*) includes the list of items installed in every tenant suite: partitions; doors and hardware; size and pattern of acoustical ceiling tiles; floor coverings; size, shape, and location of lighting fixtures; electrical receptacles; switches; telephone and data outlets; plumbing connections; HVAC; painting and wall coverings; and window coverings or venetian blinds. If the tenant wants items above the building standard, the work letter also specifies them, their cost, and method of payment.

A standard tenant improvement work letter is created for improvements throughout the building. This document lays out the minimum improvements that will be constructed in every tenant space. The job is bid to the contractor on a job or per-unit basis—for example, so many dollars for the cost of each light fixture or for each square foot of partition space.

Level of Tenant Improvements. The quality of tenant improvements, the tenant improvement allowance, and the standard tenant improvements have a definite bearing on the success of marketing the building. The developer is trying to please two parties—the prospective tenants and the brokers—and must be aware of what both the tenants and the brokers perceive as the quality of standard tenant improvements in relation to the market.

Typical items specified in a tenant improvement work letter include:

- size and type of ceiling tiles used;
- number of linear feet (meters) of wall for every 100 square feet (10 square meters) of rentable space;
- number and type of doors per 100 square feet (10 square meters) of rentable space;
- type of wall coverings and color of standard paint;
- quality and type of floor covering—normally, several choices of colors and different carpet weights are allowed;
- number of HVAC registers, mixing units, and thermostats per 100 square feet (10 square meters) of rentable space;
- specifications for the telephone system, including the installation of conduit and boxes and the provision of equipment rooms (this item is negotiable, and many businesses have their own systems and installers);
- type and extent of alarm and security systems;
- type and extent of computer wiring.

A developer should avoid stating the tenant improvement allowance in dollars, which allows tenants to design their own improvements and may result in spaces that are incompatible with each other and that fall below the building standard. Instead, by using a standard tenant improvement work letter, the developer can establish the basic quality and style of improvements for every space. Compatible colors and materials will make individual tenant spaces easier to re-lease when tenants move out. With a tenant improvement work letter, the tenants have a starting point from which they may pay for extra improvements.

Some common upgrades in tenant spaces include:

- kitchen bar consisting of a microwave, small refrigerator, and sink;
- full kitchen and lunchroom with a sink, disposal, microwave, refrigerator, and dishwasher;
- executive bar in office with a refrigerator and sink;
- executive bathroom containing a sink, vanity, toilet, and sometimes a shower;
- climate-controlled computer room;
- fireproof safes or fireproof file rooms;
- built-in fixtures such as shelves, cabinets, worktables, bookshelves, counters, and other cabinetry.

Pitfalls and Suggestions

The architect and interior designer may want to carry exterior and lobby finishes into each tenant's suite. Doing so can provide continuity throughout the building, but it may wed every tenant to the particular color scheme. A better alternative is to create a series of coordinating colors that will harmonize with the materials used in the lobby and common areas yet allow each tenant to choose a particular color for its own suite.

The spacing of columns and window mullions can lead to many problems in the design of interior spacing. Columns in the middle of a window or in the center of an office can cause challenges during buildout and leasing. For example, in instances when interior walls abut the windows between two window mullions, it can be difficult to create an acceptable junction that prevents sound from carrying from one room to another. When a wall must be built between mullions, one alternative is to end the wall six to 12 inches (15 to 30.5 centimeters) from the window. The wall is turned parallel to the window until it can be fastened to the mullion in a perpendicular joint. This solution produces oddly shaped spaces, but it does provide a soundproof seal between offices. A flexible scheme for spacing window mullions and columns is essential for meeting the particular needs of each tenant.

Availability of plumbing is also important to the flexibility of the design. Any suite larger than 3,000 square feet (280 square meters) should be able to have plumbing for a sink installed at minimal cost.

When existing spaces are remodeled, building parts such as light fixtures, ceiling tiles, metal studs, and air-conditioning components can be reused, thereby reducing expenses.

Financing

Significant capital is required to develop an office building, no matter the size or scale, and developers generally use funds from outside parties to finance their projects. For beginning developers, the process of financing a project is difficult, because they do not yet have a track record. They may also find that small office buildings do not fall into the categories favored by institutional investors and are therefore one of the most difficult types of real estate to finance.

Historically, office developers depended on local financial institutions and investors to finance their projects. A typical scenario for an undercapitalized developer with an office project was first to solicit wealthy individuals in the community to invest in its ownership and, after a sufficiently large portion of the total cost was accumulated, to approach a local bank for a construction loan. At the same time, the developer would secure long-term permanent financing that would be funded after the building was completed and fully leased.

Today, real estate capital markets offer a greater variety of financing sources. The role of local banks as the primary source of construction loans has been taken over by well-capitalized regional, national, or international banks. The local partnerships that were once a significant source of equity investment for office developments are now overshadowed by national and global REITs, pension funds, and property trust companies. The shift from private to public sources of capital for real estate development began in the early 1990s, when lending from banks, S&Ls, and other traditional sources of capital was severely curtailed and developers started going to the public markets to raise equity capital.

The most common form of securitized commercial real estate debt is commercial mortgage–backed securities (CMBSs), which are put together by banks, mortgage companies, insurance companies, and investment banks. A mortgage-backed security has as its collateral a pool of commercial mortgages—from a single mortgage to several hundred. Bonds backed by these mortgages are structured in tranches having varying risk and maturity profiles based on the characteristics of the underlying loans and the investment preferences of buyers of CMBSs. Securitization in the form of REITs has also broadened the sources of equity capital for office developments. Other sources of long-term office development financing are pension funds, credit companies, foreign investors, and municipal bonds. Beginning developers, however, are unlikely to deal with many of these sources, and they will need substantial preleasing and equity to be able to secure financing.

Construction Loans

Construction financing for office buildings is similar to that for other income properties, except that the lender is more concerned about leasing. Both construction and permanent lenders require some preleasing, typically from 20 to 50 percent of the space in a building. Banks typically require personal guarantees as well. With a strong market and a financially strong developer, the bank may forgo the preleasing requirement altogether, but banks typically require new, inexperienced developers to have 40 to 50 percent of the building preleased in normal markets and 50 to 70 percent in soft markets. These requirements change often, so developers should check with prospective lenders for their latest requirements.

The major problem encountered by many developers is failing to leave enough cushion for cost overruns and slower leasing. Developers should be wary of clauses in their loan documents that may allow the lender to increase reserve requirements and adjust the terms accordingly.

The terms of construction loans range generally from six months to three years. Reflecting their higher risk, the interest rate is usually higher than on permanent loans. Construction loan rates usually range from 0.5 to 2 percentage points above the prime rate (the short-term interest rate banks charge their most credit-worthy commercial customers), but they may be even higher, depending on market conditions and the bank's assessment of the credit risk posed by the project or developer. Upfront loan fees *(points)* are also common on most construction loans. Most construction loan agreements call for interest to accrue through the construction period. When construction is complete and the building is leased up, the developer obtains a permanent loan or sells the project and, at that point, pays off the total loan amount, which includes the accrued interest and the principal balance.

Permanent Loans

With office buildings, like other types of income property, the permanent mortgage is funded once the building reaches some negotiated level of occupancy—usually, a level sufficient to cover debt service on the mortgage. This point normally occurs when the building achieves 70 to 80 percent occupancy at rents stipulated in the loan commitment. Often, the loan commitment provides for funding the mortgage before the building is fully leased. In those cases, the developer must post a letter of credit for the difference between the amount that the leases will carry and the full loan amount. Alternatively, the permanent lender may fund the mortgage in stages as the building is leased.

"Documentation for the permanent loan can be a nightmare," warns Judith Hopkinson, formerly of Berkeley Development Corporation. "There are lots of pitfalls. If you take down the permanent loan before the project is finished, the draws for tenant improvements can take forever to process." She says that it often takes 60 days or more to receive payments.[23]

Significant capital is required to develop an office building. Developers, particularly those just starting out, need substantial preleasing and equity to secure financing.

Lenders are well aware of the tricks that developers have used to get tenants into a building while showing leases with high nominal rents. For example, if a developer gives away 12 months of free rent and $10.00 per square foot ($110 per square meter) in additional tenant improvements to a tenant that signs a five-year lease at the market rate, say $30.00 per square foot ($325 per square meter), the lender would see only the lease showing $30.00 per square foot ($325 per square meter). Similarly, a developer who plans on funding the permanent loan in two years may sign a lease with stepped rent, rising from $20.00 per square foot ($215 per square meter) in the first two years to $30.00 per square foot ($325 per square meter) in the third, fourth, and fifth years. When the lender analyzes that lease two years later, the rental rate is then $30.00 per square foot ($325 per square meter).

Bob Kagan, of Levin Menzies and Associates, says that "a big issue in financing office buildings is the appraisal. Even when a building is fully leased with good tenants, the appraiser may decide that the rents are above market and use a lower rent to determine the value of the building. Lenders are also looking at value per square foot rather than a capitalized value. For example, in San Francisco, buildings have been trading at $300 to $400 per square foot ($3,230 to $4,305 per square meter), even though the cost to develop the same space would be around $200 per square foot ($2,150 per square meter). In such a market, lenders won't appraise the buildings for more than about $250 per square foot ($2,690 per square meter), regardless of comparable sales. Lenders are wary of financing properties based on high prices that are not sustainable."[24]

In a volatile or weakening market—such as San Francisco in the early 2000s—lenders look for a debt coverage ratio of 1.4 and a loan-to-value ratio of 65 percent or less. In a less volatile market—such as San Diego during the same period—lenders accept a 1.25 DCR and 70 percent LTV.

Because lenders find it difficult to discover what concessions developers have made to attract tenants, they now perform more due diligence than they did a few years ago to determine effective rents. If the lender has to foreclose on a property, effective rental rates in the marketplace will determine lease rates for the space. If five-year leases are expected to roll over at a time when effective rents are $1.75 per square foot ($18.85 per square meter) per month, tenants that have leases with face rental rates of $2.25 per square foot ($24.20 per square meter) will expect either a reduction in rent or new concessions that bring down the face rate to the prevailing effective rate. Further, lenders today are more cognizant of the potential for a tenant to become bankrupt and threaten to vacate its lease if the landlord will not agree to lowered rent. Lenders are interested in determining not only the current rent that the tenant is paying but also the effective rent, and even the market rent. The lender is likely to use the lowest of these rents to underwrite a permanent loan.

Lenders may also deduct amounts from the cash flow to cover capital costs and leasing reserves. Even when a tenant has a long-term lease that extends beyond the term of the loan, the lender may require reserves for leasing costs and tenant improvements so that funds will be available in the event the tenant defaults.

Lease Requirements

Developers must execute leases that satisfy the construction and permanent lenders' requirements. Different lenders have different concerns, so knowledge of their requirements is essential if the building is to be financed without the need to renegotiate initial leases. In addition to some of the more common areas of concern among lenders listed below, developers should work with experienced attorneys before executing any leases and should not rely on standard lease forms.

Lenders require assignable leases so that they can take assignment of the rents (that is, receive rent directly) in the event of default. A major concern is not being able to get control of a building's cash flow after default and before foreclosure. Proper maintenance of the building and service of the tenants are essential to protect the interests of lenders.

Lenders prefer clauses that require tenants to pay rent even if the building burns down or is destroyed by an earthquake. Sophisticated tenants, however, will not agree to such clauses, even though insurance is available

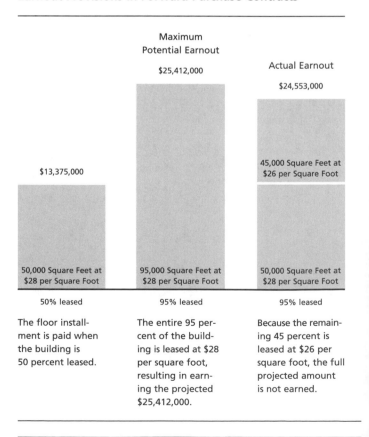

figure 5-6
Earnout Provisions in Forward Purchase Contracts

Maximum Potential Earnout
$25,412,000

Actual Earnout
$24,553,000

$13,375,000

45,000 Square Feet at $26 per Square Foot

50,000 Square Feet at $28 per Square Foot

95,000 Square Feet at $28 per Square Foot

50,000 Square Feet at $28 per Square Foot

50% leased	95% leased	95% leased
The floor installment is paid when the building is 50 percent leased.	The entire 95 percent of the building is leased at $28 per square foot, resulting in earning the projected $25,412,000.	Because the remaining 45 percent is leased at $26 per square foot, the full projected amount is not earned.

to cover rent when calamities occur. In the event of a calamity, lenders want to receive condemnation and insurance awards first and only then pay the developer. Owners, on the other hand, usually want the insurance money to restore the building, especially if they are obliged to make such restoration under the terms of certain leases.

Lenders do not like rental rates to be offset against increases in pass-through expenses. For example, most leases require tenants to pay increases in operating costs over some base figure. Increased costs are *passed through* to tenants. Lenders dislike exclusions for increases in management fees and similar items because they reduce the ability of owners to cover these increased costs.

Mortgage Options

Bullet loans (standard 30-year self-amortizing mortgages with a ten- to 15-year call) are probably the most common form of permanent financing for office projects. Interest rates are usually lower for short-term mortgages because of the lower interest-rate risk to the lender over time. Occasionally, when inflation and long-term interest rates are expected to fall in the future, interest rates are higher for shorter-term mortgages than for longer-term ones. Other common forms of financing are participating mortgages, convertible mortgages, and sale-leasebacks —all of which are forms of joint ventures with lenders (see Chapter 4).

Standby and Forward Commitments

Although experienced developers can generally obtain open-ended construction financing without a permanent takeout, beginning developers almost always need a takeout commitment before they can obtain construction financing.

Standby commitments are one alternative. They represent permanent loan commitments from companies such as credit companies and REITs that are sufficient to secure construction financing but are very expensive if they are actually used. Standby loans, if funded, may run three points or more above prime. Companies typically charge one or two points per year for the commitment while it remains unfunded. Developers use the commitment to start construction and then look for permanent financing once the building is partially leased. Ideally, the standby commitment is never funded because it is replaced by a bullet loan or another type of mortgage.

Standby commitments can be dangerous. Many developers were forced to call on their standby lenders to fund their commitments in the recession of 1973 and 1974. A number of REITs that had expected to fund only a small portion of their commitments were unable to fund them all. Even those mortgages that were funded had such high interest rates that many projects defaulted.

Another alternative to a permanent mortgage is a presale or forward commitment by an institution to purchase the building. The developer negotiates the sale of the property in advance of construction. The construction loan may be borrowed against proceeds from the sale.

The presale price is determined by capitalizing the net operating income at the market capitalization rate.

A forward commitment often includes an earnout provision whereby the developer is paid part of the purchase price and the balance is paid as the leasing is completed (see Figure 5-6). Suppose, for instance, the negotiated purchase price for a building is determined by capitalizing the gross rent from executed leases on 95 percent of the building's rentable area at 10.467 percent, which equates to approximately an 8.5 percent cap rate on the NOI. Consider a building with a rentable area of 100,000 square feet, face rents of $28.00 per square foot, and expenses of $5.00 per square foot. The purchase price would be calculated as follows (with k representing the overall cap rate):

Gross rent (100,000 square feet at $28 per square foot)	$2,800,000
Vacancy (5%)	−140,000
Adjusted gross income	$2,660,000
Expenses ($5 per square foot)	−500,000
NOI	$2,160,000

$$\frac{NOI}{k} = \frac{\$2,160,000}{0.085} = \$25,412,000$$

$$\frac{Adjusted\ gross\ income}{k} = \frac{\$2,660,000}{0.10467} = \$25,412,000$$

An earnout would provide for the purchaser's paying the capitalized value on that portion of the building that is leased at the time of closing, say 50 percent, and paying the balance later as leases are signed on the remainder of the building.

For example, if 50 percent of the building is leased at $28.00 per square foot, the purchaser would pay $13,375,000 ($28 x 50,000 square feet ÷ 0.10467) at closing. The balance would be paid as the developer leases the rest of the building. If the remaining 45,000 square feet is leased at $26.00 per square foot instead of $28.00, the developer would receive $11,178,000, for a total of $24,553,000. Therefore, the developer would have failed to "earn out" the full projected amount of $25,412,000.

Equity

Lenders normally require 20 to 30 percent of the development cost to be funded by equity sources. The amount of equity required depends on the strength of the development team, the difference between the project cost and the value of the project, the strength of the market, and the overall health of the financial lending industry.

Joint ventures with lenders and tenants offer one of the easiest methods for covering a developer's equity requirement. Since the 1980s, major lenders and major tenants have increasingly asked for, and received, a share of the equity ownership. The packaging of their interest takes a variety of forms. Lenders have preferred participating loans, which give them a share of the cash flows during operations and profits from sale while shielding them from liability and downside risk. As major tenants have gained a better understanding of the value of getting a development project off the ground, they too have started to seek a share in the ownership of buildings. Developers have obliged as the oversupply of new office space has increased competition for tenants.

Several forms of joint ventures with lenders that were initially conceived for office buildings are now used for all property types (see Chapter 4).

Marketing and Leasing

Marketing an office building is a process that begins in the initial planning phases and continues through the stages of attracting prospective tenants or buyers and successfully completing negotiations with them. The crux of a marketing plan is to identify the target market segment (discussed earlier under "Market Analysis") and then to convince that segment of the desirability of the building.

The key to the successful marketing of a project is to focus on the criteria that are important to the target market and to emphasize the provision of these features to prospective tenants. Important features might include:

- exceptional location and access;
- competitive rental rates;
- efficient floor configuration;
- outstanding building services;
- distinctive design;
- a high standard of tenant improvements; and/or
- special amenities and features.

A basic element of the marketing program is the effective communication of the building's attributes to prospective tenants at a time when they are in a position to lease or buy. Office buildings are not leased in a vacuum, and the reality is that in anything but an overheated market, an office building—no matter how well conceived and executed—cannot generate its own market.

Marketing Strategy

A systematic approach to marketing produces superior results. Guided by the market analysis and controlled by a strategic marketing plan and budget, the developer should undertake a variety of initiatives to attract and satisfy the needs of prospective tenants.

The marketing strategy lays out a basic plan for publicizing the project and defines the roles of members of the marketing team. It should include a description of the project and its target market and a realistic analysis of the project's relative position in the marketplace. It must also include a statement of the developer's financial goals and investment strategy, including exit strategies. A leasing plan with guidelines for rental rates and potential concessions is also essential.

Preleasing is something of a Catch-22. Lenders, of course, want to see a building preleased before they fund a construction loan. Preleasing also reduces the developer's risk, and developers usually start marketing space when the building is still in the design phase. But tenants are reluctant to lease a building that may not be ready for occupancy for more than a year, especially when business conditions are volatile and there is no shortage of space for lease. The larger the building and the longer the construction schedule, the more difficult preleasing becomes. A developer with a good track record, a sizable equity investment in the project (preferably cash), and significant other assets may convince a lender to fund a loan without any preleasing, but a lender will require guarantees, at least from the developing entity and most likely from the developer personally.

A good location often attracts a build-to-suit tenant. The developer must be willing to adapt the building to the tenant's distinctive requirements, which may later pose problems if the building must be leased to another tenant. Nonetheless, the advantages of build-to-suit projects —especially the advantage of a committed tenant— outweigh their disadvantages.

Advertising. Advertising is an integral element of the marketing strategy that promotes the image of the project and attracts the interest of prospects. Whether the developer coordinates the marketing activities with in-house staff or through the services of a professional agency depends on the size of the project and the resources available. In all cases, however, the advertising must be well conceived and well designed to convey the appropriate image of the project.

Advertising should be unified by a theme and a style. A name, logo, and identity design—to be used in all printed materials, including ads and letterhead—can be developed early during the project conceptual planning phases to ensure continuity in image from design to marketing.

Although some developers believe that newspaper advertisements are more likely to enhance public relations than to attract new tenants, advertising in publications can be an effective method of marketing the office building. Advertising in trade journals and magazines can be especially productive if the reading habits of prospective tenants are accurately determined. Periodicals aimed directly at prospective tenants and guides that list office buildings are also effective marketing tools. Newsletters too are an efficient means of keeping brokers and prospective tenants aware of the building and its progress.

Direct-mail advertising can be an effective tool for reaching specific audiences. Some developers aim their direct-mail campaigns more at the local brokerage community than at prospective tenants. They use direct mail to supply brokers with promotional brochures and floor plans.

Signboards on the project site should announce the amount of available space, a contact, and a telephone number. For signs to attract the attention of passersby, they should be perpendicular to the road, and the letters should be large enough to be read easily by passengers inside a vehicle driving by the site. The design of the sign should convey the tone of the building. Regular sign maintenance is necessary.

The key to successfully marketing an office project is to focus on the criteria that are important to the target market. Some important features to publicize include exceptional location, competitive rental rates, and distinctive design.

The Internet can also be used as an effective tool to advertise an office development. An individual Web site for a property or a listing that is accessed through a broker's Web page can be relatively easy to set up and keep up to date. At a minimum, a Web page should include an overview of the project, building data, typical floor plans, a summary of technical specifications, proposed lease terms, and a location map. Photos illustrating construction progress and updates on leasing activity can also help sell the project to prospective tenants before its completion.

Public Relations. Public relations firms assist the office developer with news releases, promotional ads, and special ceremonies. Newsworthy items include groundbreaking, land closing, signing of leases with major tenants, securing public approvals, construction progress, building completion, first move-ins, and human interest stories on individual tenants. Many newspapers will print announcements of lease signings, hirings, and promotions at no charge. These announcements help to keep the name of the firm before the public.

Public relations events are designed to obtain press coverage and to generate interest in the project. These events, which include press parties, functions for brokers, and community events, may be costly, however, and may not be effective in reaching the right group of tenants, especially in the case of small buildings. Support for community or charitable organizations is also a good way of attracting media attention and has the added benefit of contributing to the local community.

Merchandising. Merchandising is just as important for office leasing as it is for house sales, and the developer must address the same questions: Is the site free from trash and excess clutter during construction? Does the completed building have a high-quality image? Does the lobby create the appropriate atmosphere?

Ideally, the leasing office should overlook the construction site. At the very least, the leasing office should include an executive office, a staff office, an open area for support staff, and a conference room. In terms of decoration, the office should contain the standard tenant improvements to show prospects how attractive their space will be without added expense for extras or upgrades.

Models, pictures, and other graphic aids should be displayed to generate interest and to facilitate movement throughout the sales office. Scale models are useful in obtaining financing and gaining public approvals as well as helping prospective tenants to visualize the space. Floor plans serve a similar purpose and give potential tenants something tangible as a reference after they have left the site. Computerized presentations incorporating virtual reality tours of the offices can also be quite helpful.

Brokers

A fundamental issue in the marketing process is whether to use an in-house team or outside brokers for leasing. Each choice has its pros and cons. With an in-house team, the developer has greater control over the process. For a beginning developer, however, the cost and management obligations from this structure may be prohibitive. Arrangements with real estate brokerage agencies can provide market experience and access to a professional sales force, but it does mean that the developer has less control over marketing and leasing.

Working with Outside Brokers. A real estate brokerage firm can bring an in-depth knowledge of such factors as major competitors and major tenants looking for space and can be very helpful in the marketing of office buildings. Such firms frequently have large databases that list key items in recently executed leases, including lease rates, terms, concessions, and tenant improvement allowances. Brokers also play an important role in spreading the word about a new development through their contacts with development agencies, chambers of commerce, business organizations, and other community groups. Jim Smith, of Katell Properties, estimates that 90 percent of office tenants come through the brokerage community.[25]

In hiring outside brokers, developers should consider several points:

- What is the size and competence of the broker's leasing staff?
- How many competitive buildings is the broker working on? Brokers with many clients may not be able to devote sufficient time to a new developer's project. They may also refer prospective tenants to other projects that they are handling. A younger or smaller agency with fewer clients may offer better service but may have fewer contacts.

Brokers may have a contract with the developer that ensures them the exclusive right to negotiate all deals for the developer's building. Alternatively, the developer may opt for an *open listing,* which allows any broker to act as the primary broker on a deal. Some developers prefer not to grant an exclusive authorization and right to lease to one broker until the mid-point of construction.

Developers should keep outside brokers informed about their projects through presentations, breakfasts, monthly news releases, and events at the properties being marketed. Some developers give as much as 20 to 30 hours of instruction on their products to brokers. The more members of the brokerage community see of the project, the more likely they are to show it to prospective tenants.

Traditionally, a broker brings a prospective tenant to the developer and assists in negotiating the commercial terms of the lease. In some situations, developers may prefer to negotiate the lease themselves or with the use of legal counsel.

Commission rates for brokers are typically expressed as a percentage of rental income. Commissions depend on market traditions as well as current conditions and the competitiveness of the market. As a rough guide, however, a beginning developer could expect a broker to request a 6 percent commission rate in the first year of the lease. In most cases, this structure calls for a declining percentage of income for the later years of the lease. For example, a deal for a five-year lease may command a staggered commission, starting at 6 percent in the first year and dropping to 3 percent in the fifth year.

The typical payment schedule for brokers' commissions is half upon lease signing and half upon occupancy or at the time rental payments begin. In cases in which a substantial period of free rent is offered at the beginning of a lease, it is common for a developer to pay one-third of the commission at the signing of the lease, one-third at occupancy, and one-third at the commencement of rent.

Using In-House Brokers. Some developers prefer to employ an in-house staff of leasing agents. Such a staff can provide continuity over time in a marketing program. Although costly in terms of salaries, an in-house staff can also substantially reduce the cost of leasing space because in-house brokers receive lower commission rates (typically, 3 to 4 percent of the full value of the lease).

figure 5-7

Typical Breakdown of Gross Rent for Office Space

Base Rent	$15.00
Energy	1.10
Cleaning	1.08
Management	1.00
Administrative	0.45
Grounds and General Maintenance	1.20
Elevators	0.15
Security	0.05
Insurance	0.40
Property Taxes	2.00
Total Expenses	7.43
Total Gross Rent	$22.43

Source: Ken Beck, senior vice president, ASW Realty Partners, Woodland Hills, California.

An effective in-house brokerage department offers its employees many of the same training programs used in outside brokerage firms. For example, some companies have weekly education sessions for salespeople covering self-motivation, product presentation, listening, negotiation techniques, overcoming objections, obtaining commitments, following up with a prospect, and closing deals.

The decision to use in-house brokers or outside brokers depends largely on market conditions and the size and expertise of a developer's staff. Even development firms that employ in-house brokers recognize the importance of cooperating with outside brokers.

Types of Leases

Three general types of leases are used in office projects: gross leases, net leases, and expense stop leases. Each type of lease has advantages and disadvantages for the tenant and landlord.

Gross Leases. Under a gross lease, the landlord pays all operating expenses and thus absorbs the risk of paying rising expenses. Small tenants that want constant rent payments that will not increase over time prefer this type of lease. A typical rent breakdown is shown in Figure 5-7.

Net Leases. Three variations of net leases are common, but it is important to remember that definitions can vary from market to market. Under a net lease, the tenant typically pays a base rent plus its share of certain building operating expenses, such as utilities. Under a net-net lease, the tenant pays everything that it would in a net lease plus ordinary repairs and maintenance. Under a net-net-net lease (called a *triple-net lease),* the tenant pays all the building's ongoing operating expenses, including capital improvements.

Developers should ascertain the local definition of the various types of net leases so that no confusion exists in dealing with prospective tenants and brokers. Ultimately, the lease itself, which is a product of negotiation between owner and tenants, defines which expenses fall under the responsibility of the tenant and which the owner will be responsible for.

A net lease allows the developer to pass through to tenants several, if not all, of the variable expenses associated with leasing real estate—namely, increasing operating costs, maintenance, taxes, utilities, and insurance.

Expense Stop Leases. Expense stop leases involve sharing expenses between the tenant and the landlord. The landlord pays a stated dollar amount for expenses, and the tenant pays any expenses above that amount. Normally, the expense "stop" is determined by an estimate of expenses for the first operating year. Thus, the tenant pays any increases in expenses above the stop over the term of the lease after the second year of the lease term. An expense stop shifts the responsibility for increased expenses to the tenant in much the same way a net lease does. It is also possible to structure a lease so that the tenant is responsible for the increase in utility costs but not other expenses.

Lease Rates and Terms

Tenants pay rent at the stated rental rate multiplied by *rentable square feet;* in addition, they are charged for their prorated share of public common area space. Many tenants are knowledgeable about building efficiency and its effect on total rent, and for this reason, the individuals who market a building must know and understand a building's R/U ratios when quoting rental rates and lease terms to prospective tenants.

The base rent that can be charged depends on market conditions. If local vacancy rates exceed 15 percent, tenants enjoy a strong bargaining position, and the base rent may have to be lowered accordingly.

The lease document sets forth the terms and conditions under which the tenant's rights to use the space are granted. Most office developers have their own standard lease forms that provide the starting point for negotiations with prospective tenants. Many corporate tenants also have their own forms, and negotiations with corporate tenants often begin with determining which form will be used as the starting point.

Lease negotiation usually focuses on four major issues: rent, term, tenant improvements, and concessions such as free rent or moving expenses. Rental rates vary with the amount of space a tenant takes and the stage in the project's life that a tenant signs the lease. Lead tenants (the first tenants to lease space in a building) not only receive lower rental rates but also are sometimes given an equity interest in the building.

The lease term for the lead tenant often runs ten to 15 years, with rent escalations every year or every five years. The rest of the tenants usually have three- to five-year leases; the shorter term allows the landlord to renegotiate the terms of the lease to match inflation and

gives tenants greater flexibility. Bob Kagan, of Levin Menzies and Associates, says that firm is not typically a long-term holder; it prefers short leases that give a future buyer an opportunity to increase rents when leases roll over.[26]

Because of the nature and risk involved in long-term leases, several adjustment provisions have been created to allow the rent to be adjusted to better reflect the market value of the leased space. For instance, *dollar stop* or *full stop* clauses charge the tenant for any increases in operating expenses during the term of the lease. An estimated dollar amount (the dollar stop) for real estate taxes and another amount for other operating expenses and insurance are determined at the beginning of the lease. The actual experience for the year is compared with the dollar stop. Any difference between the actual cost and the dollar stop is debited or credited to the tenant on a prorated basis.

Under CPI (consumer price index) clauses, rent is adjusted annually based on a specified government price index, usually the CPI or the wholesale price index, which is tied to the cost of living in the United States. Varying percentages (from 20 to 100) of the rent are indexed to the CPI. During inflationary periods, developers tend to prefer CPI leases. Tying the rent to an index protects developers from the effects of inflation. In softer markets, CPI leases are harder to negotiate. In periods of low inflation, fixed increases may be more common. Tenants are often willing to accept annual 3 percent increases, which in recent years has provided larger rent increases than a straight CPI adjustment, as the CPI has ranged from 1 to 2 percent in the same time period.

Buyers of a project give some, but not full, value for future rent escalations. Because the current market usually does not fully capitalize future escalations in rent, some developers adopt a strategy of holding buildings for sale until the escalations occur. Frequently, developers need to find institutional partners to help them carry a building for the first two or three years.

The key to successful lease negotiations is being able to respond to the tenant's needs. Does a tenant require free rent for certain periods, low initial rent with later escalations, or above-standard tenant improvements? Everything is negotiable, including the cost of above-standard tenant improvements. Generally, smaller tenants prefer higher tenant improvement allowances, because they often lack the cash to pay for the improvements in advance; larger tenants often prefer free rent for certain periods.

Every lease should specify the following information:

- location of the space in the building;
- size and method of measuring the space;
- options for expansion, if any;
- duration of lease term, renewal options, and termination privileges;
- rent per square foot (per square meter);
- services included in the lease and costs associated with those services;

Agoura Hills Business Park is located in the city of Agoura Hills, a suburban community 40 miles (64.5 kilometers) northwest of downtown Los Angeles, California. Agoura Hills lies near the western end of an area known as the Conejo Valley, which spans western Los Angeles and eastern Ventura counties along U.S. Highway 101 (the Ventura Freeway). The Conejo Valley has attracted a large number of high-tech and biotech firms, the best known of which may be Amgen in Thousand Oaks, the largest city in the Conejo Valley. Other companies in the immediate vicinity of the Agoura Hills Business Park include Teradyne Corporation, J.D. Power & Associates, State Farm Insurance Company, and Castle & Cook.

Background and Site Selection

Agoura Hills Business Park was initially developed in the 1980s as a joint venture between Ahmanson Commercial Development (a subsidiary of Home Savings) and Katell Properties. During the late 1980s, the first five buildings of the business park were completed—three buildings that had been built for and sold to Teradyne—and two multitenant office buildings that had been acquired by Equity Office Properties, a REIT.[a] Those original

The entrance to Agoura Hills Business Park presents a corporate image.

five buildings were straightforward two-story concrete tilt-up structures with surface parking. Ahmanson retained ownership of this final site, which had not been developed when the southern California office market entered a prolonged slump in the first half of the 1990s. When Ahmanson decided to dispose of the site, Katell agreed to purchase it in

1997, just as the southern California office market was picking up.

Katell was very familiar with the site and expected development to be uncomplicated. The 3.5-acre (1.5-hectare) site has freeway frontage and excellent access, and was already zoned for office development in an area where entitled property is scarce and barriers to entry high. The relatively flat site sits slightly above the freeway, providing good visibility. Katell expected to develop the property along the same lines as the first five buildings—a two-story tilt-up structure in a landscaped campus environment with ample parking. The buildings would present a professional image, with large, flexible floor plates designed to appeal to high-tech and corporate users.

Approvals

The property had been zoned for office development, and the only requirement —other than typical building permits— was a site plan and architectural review. Initially, Katell expected that this process would be easy, as the intent was for the building to continue the design character set by the first five buildings in the busi-

Project Cost Summary

	Total	Per Square Foot	Percent of Total
Land Acquisition Costs	$793,722	$11.67	6.78%
Land Use/Permit Consultants	132,445	1.95	1.13
Architecture and Engineering	804,091	11.82	6.87
Hard Costs	5,553,491	81.67	47.44
Tenant Improvements	1,836,000	27.00	15.68
Leasing Commission and Costs	640,947	9.43	5.47
Permits and Fees	674,830	9.92	5.76
Project Overhead	243,422	3.58	2.08
Project Contingency (2.0%)	213,707	3.14	1.83
Construction Loan Fees and Costs (1.25%)	160,370	2.36	1.37
Construction Loan Interest (8.75%)	654,274	9.62	5.59
	$11,707,300	$172.16	100.00%

ness park. As it turned out, this design did not meet Agoura Hills's expectations for the site. Agoura Hills has attempted to retain something of a rustic character, and many in the city, including the planning director, felt that the existing buildings were out of character with the town. The tilt-up buildings were too monolithic and the surfaces too plain. Although an explicit objective of the design criteria was that buildings should be compatible with surrounding development, the planners wanted this building to be different—more articulated, different materials, and preferably not tilt-up construction.

Katell, however, was committed to a tilt-up design. A frame structure with stucco walls and tile roofs would be easier to get approved, but it would not convey the corporate image Katell was looking for. Tilt-up construction offered cost advantages over steel frame and—with proper attention to detail—could provide the image needed to attract corporate and high-tech tenants. The decision to

Ample parking is an important marketing feature of the development.

press forward with a tilt-up design, however, cost Katell a two-year delay. The building was redesigned twice before finally gaining approval. The final design

remains a concrete tilt-up structure, but it incorporates articulated form, detailing, and inset stone that enhance the appearance and mask the stark look of many tilt-up structures. These enhancements also offset much of the cost advantages of tilt-up construction.

Design and Construction
The site plan itself is very straightforward, with parking around the perimeter of the site and the building in the center. The structural system consists of exterior tilt-up concrete panels, with a 30-foot by 30-foot (9-meter by 9-meter) grid of structural columns providing the interior structure. The structure consists of two wings joined by a lobby that provides access to the single elevator, a staircase serving the second floor, and restrooms. Each wing of the building is potentially bisected by an exit corridor, providing a logical division of each floor into two, three, or four separate spaces. Depths are relatively large, ranging from 45 to 60 feet (13.7 to 18.3 meters), and are intended to appeal to larger users. Nonetheless, the flexible leasing plan can accommodate users as small as 5,000 square feet (465 square meters).

continued on next page

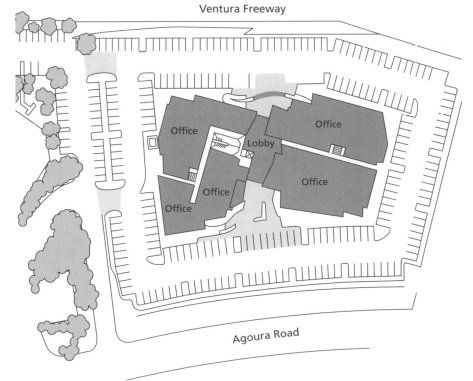

Site plan.

Marketing and Tenants

Katell began construction without any preleasing. The difficulty of preleasing a building, when most tenants looking for space would rather lease space that is already available than wait a year, was particularly true of generic office space such as Agoura Hills Centre. Katell felt very confident about the Conejo Valley market as a result of its success in the adjacent Teradyne project, although lease-up had been slowed by the national economic slowdown.

Katell Properties relies on the local brokerage community for marketing and lease-up. In a highly competitive market like Los Angeles, commercial brokers are an invaluable resource.

As part of its budget, Katell included a 12-month reserve for lease-up. Although the developer would rather not spend the reserve, it does provide a reasonable time to market and lease the building.

Financing

Katell obtained a construction loan of $9.75 million from Tokai Bank, a lender it had dealt with previously. The loan required an initial $1.3 million in equity, which was applied to site acquisition and various soft costs. The rate is LIBOR plus 250 basis points, plus a loan fee of 1.5 percent. The lender did not require any preleasing as a condition of funding, although it did require a personal guarantee for 50 percent of the loan principal.

Experience Gained

In hindsight, it might have been wiser to consult earlier with the city and present an initial plan that the city would have found acceptable. Persisting with a tilt-up design cost Katell considerably in terms of time and architectural fees. The two-year delay cost money directly—for the carrying costs of the land—but it also incurred opportunity costs. Had the developer completed the project two years earlier, he would have been able to devote his time and resources elsewhere. The fact that the economy and the office market turned during that time compounded the loss to the developer.

There is no reason, however, to believe that this project will not be successful. The changes made to mollify the city did in fact improve the appearance of the building and reinforce its corporate image. The building is very well located in a desirable area, home to many growing technology firms.

Financial Projections

Katell uses simple capitalization as the primary tool in evaluating the feasibility of a simple income property such as Agoura Hills Centre. Such an approach is particularly appropriate before leases are in place and it becomes highly spec-

Operating Pro Forma

	Square Feet	Rent per Year	Rent per Month	
Gross Rent	68,000	$27.60	$2.30	$1,876,800
Parking Revenue				
Tenant	839	–	0.00	0
Visitor	50	–	0.00	0
Vacancy	5.00%			93,840
Effective Gross Income				$1,782,960

Expenses	Per Square Foot	
Operating Expenses	$7.00	$476,000
Nonoperating Expenses	0.20	13,600
Reserve	0.10	6,800
Total Expenses		496,400
Net Operating Income		$1,286,560
Estimated Costs	$172	$11,707,300
Return on Costs		10.99%

Cap Rate	9.25%	9.00%	8.75%
Valuation	$13,908,757	$14,295,111	$14,703,543
Value per Square Foot	204.54	210.22	216.23
Value Created	$2,201,457	$2,587,811	$2,996,243

Net Operating Income				$1,286,560

	DCR	Interest	Amortization (Years)	Amount	
Debt Service	1.25	7.00%	25	$10,431,568	884,738
Cash Flow after Debt Service					401,822
Equity Required					$1,275,732
Return on Equity					31%

A location northwest of downtown Los Angeles with access to many growing technology firms was a plus in marketing the development.

ulative to project the terms of various leases, future rollover costs, and so on.

The cost is first projected based on estimated square footage, with more detail as information is provided. Total projected cost is $11.7 million. In this case, the land is a relatively small part of the total, less than 7 percent of total costs. Direct construction costs (excluding tenant improvements) are a little less than half the total cost.

The next step is to project operating income. Without any leases in place, the projection is based on market analysis; expenses are based on similar properties. Because the property is new, only a small reserve is included. NOI can then be compared with total project cost to determine the return on costs (the ratio of income to costs). The return on costs can be compared with cap rates for similar buildings. For the project to be feasible, there must be a spread between the return on costs and the cap rate. For Agoura Hills Centre, the return on costs is about 11 percent, while market cap rates are around 9 percent. This 2 percent spread indicates that the project will generate positive value.

Another way of looking at it is to cap NOI to determine the value of the stabilized building, which can be compared with project costs. In this case, the stabilized project has a value of $13.9 million to $14.7 million, depending on the cap rate used. Value added is $2.2 million to $3 million.

Looking at the return on equity, it is estimated that the project can support $10.4 million of debt based on a DCR of 1.25, at 7 percent interest and 25-year amortization. Subtracting the loan from total costs, the project requires $1.3 million in equity. Return on equity for the first year is projected to be 31 percent.

Straight capitalization does not give a true indication of the overall return on equity, which would require a discounted cash flow. Simple capitalization does, however, provide a direct and quick method to evaluate project feasibility. ∎

Note

[a] Equity Office sold the properties to Lowe Enterprises in August 2000.

Source: Based on interviews with Jim Smith, vice president, Katell Properties, and documents provided by Katell Properties. Additional information is available at www.katellproperties.com.

Project Data

Developer	Katell Properties
Architect	Nadel Architects Inc.
Contractor	Keller Builders, Inc.
Site Area	3.5 acres (150,000 square feet)
Gross Building Area	68,000 square feet 0.45 FAR
Gross Leasable Area	67,000 square feet
Usable Floor Area	60,000 square feet (depending on final tenant layout)
Parking	230 spaces 4 per 1,000 square feet
Building Height	30 feet to top of parapet 35 feet to top of mechanical screen wall
Lease Depths	35 to 60 feet
Construction Cost	$5,550,000 (site work and cold shell) $82 per square foot gross building area
Total Development Cost	$11,700,000 $172 per square foot gross building area

- interior work to be performed by the developer under the base rent;
- operating hours of the building;
- the landlord's obligations for maintenance and services;
- the tenant's obligations for maintenance and services;
- escalation provisions during the lease term;
- number of parking spaces, their location, and terms of their use (for example, whether designated or undesignated);
- allowable use of the leased space permitted by local zoning ordinances and building rules;
- date of possession and date that rental payments are due; and
- sublease and assignment privileges, if any.

The calculation of effective rent shown on page 221 highlights the difference between nominal and effective rents. Although the nominal rent in the example is $24.00 per square foot, combining tenant improvements picked up by the landlord, free rent, the fixed-rent period, and CPI escalators results in an effective rent of $20.04—well below the nominal rent. Tenants and brokers compare different lease alternatives on the basis of effective lease rates after taking into account the particular concessions for each building.

Operations and Management

Management of an office building means not only maintaining the property and ensuring that it is operated efficiently but also enhancing its value as an asset. For a beginning developer, management is likely to focus on the day-to-day operations that are normally handled by the property manager. The functions of a property manager include maintaining good tenant relations, collecting rent, establishing an operating plan, creating a budget, maintaining accounting and operating records, hiring contractors or vendors to provide all services to the building, paying bills, overseeing leasing, developing and managing maintenance schedules, supervising building personnel, providing security, addressing issues related to risk management, coordinating insurance requirements, and generally preserving and attempting to increase the building's value.

Larger buildings have property managers on site, while several smaller buildings may share a property manager. For office building owners that lack the in-house capabilities to manage the property, the services of a well-staffed professional management company are essential. Firms that specialize in property management can offer the advantages of advanced management techniques and systems that individual property owners generally do not possess.

The agreement between the developer and the property manager should spell out the duties and responsibilities of each party. The management contract may include the authority to sign leases and other documents, to incur expenses, to advertise, and to arrange banking/trust agreements. Also included are provisions on record keeping, insurance, indemnification, employees, and management fees. Most management fees are quoted as a percentage of gross income collected monthly over the term of the lease, both new and renewal. Fees typically range from 1 to 6 percent of gross income collected.

The property management function has been upgraded in many development firms to the same level as new development. *Asset management* has become the catchphrase for managing properties to their fullest potential. Although beginning developers may find that hiring outside management for their properties is more convenient or helps their credibility in the search for financing, most developers manage their own buildings, not only for the fees they generate but also to develop and maintain close ties with tenants. Indeed, some developers have strongly promoted their asset management capabilities to institutional owners such as pension funds. Other developers are expanding their property management activities by buying existing properties. Asset management counterbalances a slowdown in new office development while adding to the developer's base of tenants. Development companies that perform property management well are able to generate much of their new development business from the expansion of existing tenants.

Budgeting and Accounting

The management staff usually provides a range of accounting information, including an annual projection of income and expenditures, updated quarterly with reports to explain any variances. The income side should include rents as though the project were fully occupied, plus garage and parking fees, escalation charges, and miscellaneous income. The gross possible income is adjusted for anticipated losses from vacancies, turnover, and delinquencies. Management staff should also detail expenses, which include but are not limited to electricity, water and sewer, fuel, payroll, employee benefits, cleaning supplies, repairs, decorating, advertising, management fees, administrative costs, taxes, insurance, security, window washing, landscape services, trash removal, and snow removal.

The property manager should prepare a monthly (or quarterly) statement of operations showing the rent roll (that is, all tenant data, including income, directly allocable charges, and lease expirations) and a disbursement statement for all funds expended.

Keeping Tenants Satisfied

The first step toward ensuring the satisfaction of tenants is the coordination of an effective program of tenant improvements. Many developers have their own in-house project manager who undertakes this time-consuming and tedious phase of construction. Thereafter, developers should abide by several policies that will help to create and maintain tenants' satisfaction. First, they should demonstrate a concern to uphold the reputation of their company and its projects. Second, they should ensure that any express guarantees or warranties that were offered

Addressing management concerns during design ensures that building features and systems are responsive to tenants' and investors' long-term needs.

to the tenants are honored. Third, they should ensure that the lease agreements and protective covenants spell out each service and maintenance function that each party will provide. And fourth, they should create an organization to attend to maintenance and the provision of services. Four items are key to the successful maintenance of any office building: maintenance and janitorial services, elevator service, HVAC systems, and security. Tenants usually take these items for granted and notice them only when problems occur.

If the lease gives the tenant responsibility for maintenance or landscaping, the developer should retain the right to order the work if the tenant fails to do so. (This approach is necessary because the condition of one building in a multibuilding complex may affect the rentability of other buildings.) Under this type of agreement— called a *condition of premises clause*—the developer must notify the tenant in advance, giving the tenant the opportunity to comply. If the tenant still fails to respond, then the developer can do the work and charge the tenant for the cost.

One of the most important management tools is the lease agreement. Developers should ensure that leases contain clauses stipulating that:

- tenants must not alter the building without the landlord's consent;
- tenants must not do anything that might increase the costs of fire insurance or create noise or nuisance;

- tenants must not use the building for immoral or illegal purposes; and
- if tenants remove floor, wall, or ceiling coverings, they must restore the surfaces to the condition that existed when they first took possession of the space.

Despite their responsibilities for enforcing such policies, however, property managers should remember that their most important function is to keep tenants happy.

Selling the Completed Project

At some point in the life of almost every project, the project will be sold. The decision to sell depends on such factors as the needs of the equity partners, the term of the construction or permanent loan, the market for office building investments, and the developer's analysis of alternative investment opportunities.

Office buildings are commonly sold at one of three points in their development: 1) when stabilized occupancy occurs, 2) after the first full year of occupancy (when the first CPI or fixed adjustments occur), or 3) after the leases are renewed. The developer's goal is to sell the project at the point when the building will provide the highest return according to the developer's investment objectives. Two common objectives are to secure the highest return and to hold the property for a long-term investment. Usually, the highest internal rate of return is achieved if the building is sold as soon as it reaches stabilized occupancy. In competitive markets, however, most developers prefer to wait until just after the leases first roll over or until the first rent escalations have occurred. At this point, the highest net present value (at a discount rate of 12 to 15 percent) is often reached. On the other hand, long-term investors usually plan to hold buildings for at least seven years.

Developers can take several actions to position a building for sale:

- hire a building inspection team to thoroughly inspect a building's mechanical and other systems and to prepare a report that can be shown to prospective buyers;
- prepare summaries of a project's income and expenses and ensure that accounting records are in order;
- make sure that a building is clean and has a well-landscaped and well-maintained appearance or curb appeal;
- prepare a summary of all outstanding leases on a building; and
- create a marketing brochure that describes a project's noteworthy qualities—its tenants, management, location, and position in the market.

Conclusion

Offices are at once one of the more challenging and more straightforward types of development that a beginning developer can undertake. Office space itself is somewhat generic: it is designed as flexible space that can

Valencia Town Center Drive, opened in 1998, integrates a new main street with a mix of uses with an existing major shopping mall. Office buildings housing more than 3,000 people help to create a vibrant working, shopping, and living environment.

serve primarily the needs of the service and financial sectors, both of which have grown and will continue to grow in relative importance to the economy. Even when space is designed carefully for specific tenants, the space needs to accommodate changes over fairly short time periods. Lease terms are typically only five years, and a landlord has to be prepared for tenants to move out at the end of their terms. Flexibility can be constrained within fairly tight limits, however.

Nonetheless, rents are highly dependent on location. Although offices can be built most anywhere, firms want to be located where their employees want to work. Tenants are willing to pay far more for a location on the right side of town within walking distance of restaurants and services if that is what it takes to attract and retain key employees. In prime locations, office space can generate higher land values than any other use.

More than anything else, a concentration of office buildings defines the urban core, at least since the industrial era. When department stores and other retailers followed consumers to the suburbs, offices remained concentrated in the urban core. Today, central business districts no longer have the preeminence they once had, and office buildings are widely dispersed throughout metropolitan regions. A large concentration of office space defines today's *edge cities* that lie at major highway intersections at the periphery of every major American city. At the same time, most cities have created redevelopment agencies or other mechanisms to stimulate office

development and are looking for fresh ideas and creative developers to revitalize their downtowns.

Office buildings do not have the noxious characteristics of industrial space and in fact can be good neighbors for residential areas: office users are typically quiet, especially during evenings and weekends when nearby residents are most likely to be at home. Office development is relatively compact and uses less land per employee than industrial or even retail development. But office buildings do generate high peak traffic volumes. They also do not generate significant sales tax revenue—a prime consideration for most local governments. Nonetheless, local officials often embrace office development as an economic development tool, and office buildings constitute a primary use in redevelopment areas.

The barriers to entry for office development are relatively low. Yet because individual office buildings tend to be rather large, they typically take two or more years to build and lease-up, and the market may be quite different when a project is completed from when it was begun. Although construction lenders are more cautious in the early 2000s than they were in the 1980s, many office markets were overbuilt when the Internet and telecommunications industries contracted. Growing segments of the economy demand the newest office space—in emerging locations and with the best technologies. Those same segments are the most likely to suffer during an economic slowdown, as seen in the meltdown of the dot-com and telecommunications industries in 2001. Markets can weaken and turn in the time that it takes to construct a major office building.

Notes

1. John Loper, while a student in USC's Master of Real Estate Development program, wrote the original draft of this chapter in the first edition of the book published in 1992. It has been revised and updated by Kenneth Beck, senior vice president, ASW Realty Partners, Woodland Hills, California. For more detailed background on office development, see Jo Allen Gause et al., *Office Development Handbook*, 2nd ed. (Washington, D.C.: ULI–the Urban Land Institute, 1998).

2. Robert Lang, *Office Sprawl: The Evolving Geography of Business* (Washington, D.C.: The Brookings Institution, 2000).

3. Ibid.

4. This figure represents a significant increase over what had been considered "normal"—5 percent in the 1970s and early 1980s.

5. Joel Kotkin, www.REISource America, December 29, 2000.

6. See Christopher B. Leinberger, "The Beginning of the End of Sprawl," *Urban Land*, January 2000, pp. 74–77+.

7. See William H. Hudnut III, "Promoting Reuse," *Urban Land*, December 1999, pp. 69–75.

8. William Drebs, "Space Squeeze" (Holland, Mich.: Haworth, Inc., 2000).

9. See Diane Anderson, "The Race for Office Space," *The Industry Standard*, January 11, 2000; and Joe Gose, "How Dot.Coms Pushed Office Markets to New Heights," *Barron's*, June 5, 2000.

10. Stock market analysts interpret increases in short-selling as an indicator that more investors are betting the market is likely to fall. Similarly, increases in space available for sublease indicate a likely drop in rents as property owners vie for tenants.

11. Interview with Allan Kotin, adjunct professor, School of Policy Planning and Development, University of Southern California, and Allan D. Kotin & Associates, Los Angeles, June 2002.

12. Individual full-size parking spaces range from 8.5 feet wide by 16 feet long (2.5 by 4.9 meters) to 10 feet wide by 18 feet long (3 by 5.5 meters). Compact spaces are somewhat narrower and/or shorter, while spaces for the handicapped are wider. Two-way aisles for perpendicular parking vary from 24 to 27 feet (7.3 to 8.2 meters) wide. A double-loaded parking module requires a 60- to 63-foot (18.3- to 19.2-meter) cross section for two parking places and an aisle, plus the space required for the structure itself. The simplest design requires a minimum of two modules (a combined width of 130 feet [40 meters] or so) with continuously ramped floors that provide circulation between levels. Generally, the maximum slope for parking bays is 5 percent, requiring 100 feet (30 meters) of ramp to rise 5 feet (1.5 meters), one-half the floor-to-floor height of a typical parking structure. With circulation and parking along the ends of the structure, the minimum dimension for the entire structure is about 130 feet by 190 feet (36.5 by 57.9 meters). Many local jurisdictions have adopted specific parking requirements, which should be consulted.

13. Interview with Jim Goodell, Goodell Associates, Los Angeles, California, June 1989.

14. Interview with John Thomas, Ware Malcomb Architects, Irvine, California, October 2001.

15. Interview with Marshall Kramer, Walker Parking Consultants, Elgin, Illinois, January 2002.

16. BOMA International, *Standard Method for Measuring Floor Area in Office Buildings* (Washington, D.C.: BOMA International, 1996).

17. See Bernard R. Boylan, *The Lighting Primer* (Ames, Iowa: Iowa State University Press, 1987).

18. L. Harriman et al., *Humidity Control Design Guide for Commercial and Institutional Buildings* (Atlanta, Ga.: American Society of Heating, Refrigerating and Air-Conditioning Engineers, 2001).

19. See D. Michelle Addington, "The History and Future of Ventilation," in *Indoor Quality Handbook*, ed. J. Spengler, J. Samet, and J. McCarthy (New York: McGraw-Hill, 2001).

20. U.S Green Building Council, www.usgbc.org.

21. David S. Chartock, "4 Times Square: New York's First Green Office Building," *Construction News*, June 1998.

22. Interview with Tom McCaslin and John Wong, Tishman Construction Corporation, New York, New York, September 2000.

23. Interview with Judith Hopkinson, former COO, Ameriquest Capital, Orange, California, and regent, University of California, November 2002.

24. Interview with Robert Kagan, Levin Menzies and Associates, San Francisco, California, September 2001.

25. Interview with Jim Smith, Katell Properties, Los Angeles, California, January 2002.

26. Interview with Robert Kagan, September 2001.

6. Industrial Development

Overview

Industrial development involves site planning, subdivision design and platting, and the construction of utilities and internal streets. Consideration must be given to access, parking, building design, and landscaping.

Beginning developers may start out with a building for lease or a site that is suitable for one or more industrial users. If a build-to-suit tenant or buyer has not been pinned down, they might proceed with a speculative building that can be leased or sold in the future. Depending on market conditions, more profit can potentially be made on a speculative building than on a build-to-suit project, because negotiations over lease terms with a potential major tenant can be tough. Speculative buildings are much harder to get financed, however. Construction lenders typically will not proceed unless the developer has deep pockets, with other collateral available, and is willing to sign personally on the loan.

Beginning industrial developers should be wary of some possible pitfalls:

- paying too much for land;
- underestimating the amount of competition;
- building the wrong product for the market, which can usually be avoided by involving the right consultants in the development process from the beginning; and

- using an architect who has no experience in the type of product chosen; developers should find someone who knows the local market, can provide a market-oriented, functional design, and knows how to maximize its flexibility.

Business parks offer developers the flexibility of deciding whether to sell unimproved land parcels or completed buildings. Generally, they are completed in phases, which helps to minimize risks associated with changing market conditions.

Today's business parks are the product of an evolutionary process that had its antecedents in the manufacturing-oriented industrial estates and parks of the late 1800s and early 20th century. The first planned industrial estate was begun in 1896 in Manchester, England, when a private company, Trafford Park Estates, purchased a 1,200-acre (485-hectare) country estate on the Manchester ship canal.[1] Trafford Park Estates remained the world's largest planned industrial estate until the 1950s, when larger facilities were developed in the United States and Canada.

The first planned industrial districts in North America were created in Chicago. Their focus was on manufacturing, and the catalyst for their development was access to rail lines and plentiful supplies of electric power and steam. Chicago's Central Manufacturing District, built in 1902 on 260 acres (105 hectares), had uniform four-story buildings designed for *gravity flow production*, in which manufacturing of an item began on the top floor and continued on lower floors until it was finished on the bottom floor, ready for delivery. Private rail sidings, grid-iron streets, landscaping and planting strips, and ornamental street lighting were located there. The Clearing Industrial District, built in 1909 on 530 acres (215 hectares), introduced 40-acre (16-hectare) superblocks that eliminated interior grade rail crossings and provided a variety of site sizes and depths. The Pershing Road District, built in 1910 on 91 acres (37 hectares), consisted of buildings with a handsome facade along the freeway and railroad access in the rear.[2]

The one-story industrial building typology became popular primarily because of the advent of the assembly line. Henry Ford's introduction of the mechanized manufacturing plant caused a shift from multistory buildings to large single-story structures designed to accommodate horizontally organized factories.[3] Industrial development during the 1920s and 1930s was centered around railroad yards and lines, with every site enjoying some form of rail service. Significant industrial developments during the next 30 years included Slough Estates in England (1920); the Los Angeles Central Manufacturing District (1922); the New England Industrial Center in Needham, Massachusetts (1949); and Stanford Industrial Park in Palo Alto, California (1951).[4]

In the 1950s, the first business parks appeared, with a focus on office rather than industrial uses. A decade later saw the advent of specialized R&D parks that benefited from links between universities and business. These settings combined a variety of functions, from offices to laboratory research to light manufacturing.

Light industrial uses such as manufacturing and warehouse/distribution facilities are still integral parts of many business parks today, but the proportion of office space and new uses such as call centers is growing. Heavy industry, once a significant element of planned industrial districts, is seldom included. Economies have shifted away from heavy manufacturing, and communities concerned about potential environmental impacts prefer lighter, higher-tech businesses as employment generators. Zoning often restricts the location of heavy industry in business parks and closer-in areas, while at the same time, large manufacturing companies generally prefer to locate at stand-alone sites farther outside the city where land is cheaper.

In the 1950s and 1960s, business park locations shifted from rail-oriented urban sites to suburban areas with freeway and airport access. Proximity to housing, shopping, cultural amenities, and educational facilities became more important, and communities began to appreciate their benefits. At the beginning of the 21st century, the outward movement of industrial facilities such as warehouses and business parks has continued as new parks are developed on the edges of major metropolitan areas. At the same time, older inner-city industrial sites with good freeway access are becoming attractive again because of the scarcity of greenfield sites in the suburbs and the availability of existing buildings and infrastructure at infill locations.

Product Types

Industrial development encompasses a broad range of product types and settings. No universally accepted typology exists for categorizing industrial real estate, and the same terms are often used to refer to different types of buildings.

Building Categories

All types of industrial properties have common characteristics despite variations in functions and use. Three primary categories of buildings are typically used to categorize industrial real estate: warehouse/distribution, manufacturing, and flex. Within these categories are a variety of subcategories that have distinctive physical characteristics to accommodate specialized functions.[5] These buildings may be located in industrial areas or master-planned business parks, or they may be stand-alone structures.

Warehouse/Distribution. Warehouse/distribution buildings focus on the storage and distribution of goods. Within the category are five major subtypes of facilities: regional warehouses, bulk warehouses, heavy distribution buildings, refrigerated distribution buildings, and rack-supported distribution buildings. Some differences exist in these types in terms of size, ceiling heights, and loading requirements, but in general, they have similar requirements: large, flat sites with space for maneuvering trucks and access to transportation facilities.

Warehouse/distribution buildings have low employee-to-area ratios—typically one or two employees per 1,000 square feet (95 square meters). As a result, only a small amount of employee parking is needed. Most have a minimal amount of office space—5 to 10 percent of total floor area. In some buildings, however, as much as 10 to 20 percent of the area may be allotted to office uses, chiefly to accommodate the purchasing, accounting, and marketing staff of a distribution or manufacturing company. Typically, these buildings have an attractive front elevation with ample windows for the office portion of the building and provide good truck access to the rear or side of the building. Dock-high and/or drive-in doors are provided to serve the warehouse functions.

In recent years, ceiling heights of warehouse/distribution buildings have increased from 26 to 28 feet (8 to 8.5 meters) clear to 36 feet (11 meters) or more clear in state-of-the-art buildings. The extra clearance provides room for higher stacking. Plentiful truck bays, preferably on opposite sides of the warehouse, are critical for moving merchandise in and out, as the value-added of bulk warehouses is the ability to move goods faster with minimal storage time.

Compared with the 1990s, today's warehouse/distribution buildings have become substantially larger. Previously, buildings of 400,000 square feet (37,175 square meters) were considered large. In the early 2000s, spaces from 750,000 to 800,000 square feet (70,000 to 74,350 square meters) are being occupied by single tenants. One reason behind the demand for larger spaces is the

Flex buildings generally feature well-designed exterior facades with lots of glass.

Courtesy Spieker Properties

consolidation of distribution businesses. Many sophisticated third-party logistics companies now handle transport of merchandise and parts for other companies.[6]

Some communities oppose the development of warehouses because they bring lower tax benefits and more truck traffic than other types of industry. On the other hand, such buildings generate relatively little daily automobile traffic and can be attractively landscaped.

Manufacturing. Manufacturing structures are large facilities designed to accommodate the equipment for manufacturing processes. Light manufacturing buildings can be up to 300,000 square feet (27,880 square meters), heavy manufacturing buildings more than 1 million square feet (93,000 square meters).

Floor-to-ceiling heights range from 14 to 60 feet (4.3 to 18.3 meters) and average 20 to 24 feet (6 to 7.3 meters). Large bay doors with at-grade or dock-high parking for large trucks and ample room for trucks to maneuver are usually a necessity. With the exception of assembly-related facilities, parking ratios are usually low—as low as one and one-half parking spaces per 1,000 square feet (95 square meters) of building area, although the ratio depends on the number of employees. Because of their minimal parking requirements, traditional industrial buildings frequently cover 45 to 50 percent of a site.

The development of heavy manufacturing facilities has slowed considerably in the recent past, their place taken by clean light manufacturing industries that have contributed significant demand for new industrial space. Because they focus on technology-based activities, these industries typically produce fewer of the undesirable side effects that limited the location of the older heavy industries. Manufacturing facilities often are designed specifically for a company's manufacturing process. Consequently, fewer tenants are interested in taking over another company's manufacturing facility. Nevertheless, these manufacturing plants often have special equipment such as heavy-duty cranes, which some companies find very valuable. Once a new tenant is found, it is likely

to stay there longer because of the specialized design and equipment.

Flex. No clear-cut definition of flex space exists, although some define it as anything between offices and warehouses, usually combining some part of both office and warehouse uses. Flex buildings typically are one- or two-story buildings ranging from 20,000 to 100,000 square feet (1,860 to 9,295 square meters). The pattern for internal uses has been about 25 percent office space and 75 percent warehouse space, but this proportion is changing in favor of more office space in many markets. External designs are generally clean, rectangular shapes with an abundance of glass on the front facade. Building depths vary, so developers need to understand the market to determine the best configuration.

Specialized R&D flex buildings fall into two distinct categories. One category includes facilities in which research is the primary, or only, activity. Design of the interior spaces frequently is unique to the specific research that will be carried out there. The other type of R&D building is intended to serve multiple uses. This type of structure, which may have one or two floors, often has office and administration functions in the front of the building and R&D or other high-tech uses in the rear.

Offices in R&D buildings typically have open floor plans to promote teamwork and collaboration, and to facilitate easy rearrangement of spaces and furniture for rapidly changing work groups. Many tenants are small startup companies; others are subsidiaries of major corporations. Activities range from the creation and development of new technologies and products to the development, testing, and manufacture of products from existing technology.

The design of tenant improvements is more important for R&D uses than for other industrial uses and is usually tailored to the needs of specific tenants. The percentage of space allocated to laboratories, research offices, service areas, assembly, and storage varies widely. Hard-to-rent space in the center of buildings is well suited

The corporate headquarters for Compaq Computer Corporation in Houston, Texas, consists of six manufacturing and 13 administrative buildings.

for laboratories and computer rooms where environmental control is critical.

Multitenant. Multitenant buildings cater to customer-oriented smaller tenants such as office, showroom, and service businesses that require spaces of 800 to 5,000 square feet (75 to 465 square meters). The buildings are generally one story, with parking in the front and roll-up doors in the rear for truck loading. They provide parking ratios of two to three spaces per 1,000 square feet (95 square meters) and turning radii in loading areas that are large enough for small trucks. Leased spaces are built so that they can be divided into modules as small as 800 square feet (75 square meters). Frequently, 25 to 50 percent of the interior is improved, leaving the balance of the building as manufacturing, assembly, or warehouse space.

Some developers build all the tenant improvements for a project along with the base building, while others initially build just the shell and wait to build tenant improvements as space is leased. The first method limits flexibility and increases upfront costs; the second can be expensive if materials for tenant improvements cannot be bought at bulk prices. A middle course is to buy materials in bulk at the start of tenant space buildout and then put improvements in place as needed. Methods for building tenant improvements frequently depend on a project's marketing scheme and anticipated absorption rate.

Exterior designs vary. Some markets require a more upscale look that can be supported by higher rents. In other markets, multitenant buildings are considered economy space so the most cost-effective combination of construction materials is used.

Office/Tech. Office/tech buildings are used primarily for office space. They may provide limited truck access and warehouse facilities. Users of such buildings generally look for large volumes of space to house employees and have only limited interest in space for laboratories or computer facilities. Large paper processors, such as insurance companies and banks, require large office spaces and desire low rental costs for their back-office functions; hence, they prefer the cost advantage and efficiency of office/tech industrial buildings. High parking ratios (three and one-half to four spaces per 1,000 square feet [95 square meters] of net rentable area) are important to office/tech users.

Freight. Freight facilities are not always included as a category of industrial real estate, but they are assuming an increasingly important role in supply chain management. The freight forwarding processes involving the transfer of goods from trucks to trucks and from planes to trucks require specialized buildings, each of which has special requirements in terms of loading capabilities, building configurations, and space buildout.

Telecommunications. Two types of telecommunications facilities have emerged since the late 1990s—data warehouses and switch centers. These types of buildings can be developed through the conversion of an older building that has access to fiber-optic cable or the construction of a new building solely for telecommunications use.

Categories of Business Parks

Business parks are multibuilding developments planned to accommodate a range of uses, from light industrial to office space, in an integrated park-like setting with supporting uses and amenities for the people who work there. They can range in size from several acres to facilities of several hundred acres or more.

Most business parks offer a conventional mix of warehouses, flex space, and offices to meet the needs of a range of occupiers. Over the past 20 years, however, more specialized types of business parks have emerged. Although each of them can be categorized by a distinctive function and design characteristics, product types and their users overlap considerably. The primary categories include:[7]

- Industrial Park—Modern industrial parks contain large-scale manufacturing and warehouse facilities and a limited amount of or no office space. The term *industrial park* connotes a setting for heavy industry and manufacturing, but it is still sometimes used interchangeably with *business park*.
- Warehouse/Distribution Park—Warehouse and distribution parks contain large, often low-rise storage facilities with ample provisions for truck loading and parking. A small portion of office space may be included, either as finished space built into the storage areas or housed in separate office structures. Landscaping and parking areas are included, but, because of the relatively low ratio of employees to building area, a wide mix of on-site amenities for employees is not available.
- Logistics Park—Such business parks focus on the value-added services of logistics and processing goods rather than warehousing and storage. As centers for wholesale activity, they may also provide showrooms and demonstration areas to highlight products assembled or distributed there.
- Research Park—Also known as R&D and science parks, research parks are designed to take advantage of a relationship with a university to foster innovation and the transfer of technology. Facilities are typically multifunctional with a combination of wet and dry laboratories, offices, and sometimes light manufacturing and storage space. Biomedical parks are a specialized version.
- Technology Park—Technology parks cater to high-tech companies that require a setting conducive to innovation. They rely on proximity to similar or related companies rather than a university to create a synergistic atmosphere for business development.
- Incubator Park—Incubator parks or designated incubator sections of research or technology parks meet the needs of small startup businesses. Often

supported by local communities through their economic development agencies or colleges, they provide flexibly configured and economically priced space and opportunities for shared services and business counseling.
- Corporate Park—Corporate parks are the latest step in the evolution of business parks. Often located at high-profile sites, they may look like office parks, but often the activities and uses housed there go beyond traditional office space to include research labs and even light manufacturing. Supporting uses such as service-oriented shopping centers, recreational facilities, and hotel/conference centers are provided as a focus rather than an afterthought.

Rehabilitation and Adaptive Use

Older industrial areas of cities offer opportunities to beginning developers, notably the presence of underused buildings suitable for rehabilitation and small infill sites. Communities throughout the country have established programs to encourage the redevelopment of older industrial areas. Redevelopment agencies and economic development agencies may offer incentives such as tax abatement and financing to developers who build in designated redevelopment areas. Renovation of older industrial areas offers many opportunities to developers:

- upgrading low-tech, light industrial buildings to make them competitive with newer facilities;

©Assassi Productions/Courtesy HLKB Architecture

Praxair Distribution's renovation of a warehouse in Ankeny, Iowa, is designed to house office, conference, and training facilities as well as warehousing and distribution uses.

- redeveloping low-tech, light industrial buildings for higher-tech R&D and office uses;
- rehabilitating major older plants, such as automobile plants, into multitenant warehouses and office/tech buildings;
- removing heavy industrial facilities and reusing the land for business parks; and
- adapting obsolete multistory urban warehouses to commercial and office uses.

The strong economy of the late 1990s and early 2000s motivated many developers to look at underperforming older industrial buildings for their potential reuse. Many of the more easily resolved problem properties have been taken, leaving properties that are likely to have more serious difficulties. Despite these issues, developers have access to a large pool of bargain-price properties by performing suitable due diligence before buying industrial property.

Some of the potential issues surrounding the rehabilitation of older buildings include cost overruns, title problems, building code problems, poor street and utility infrastructure, and unforeseen construction problems. A major concern that must be addressed is the cleanup of contaminated sites. The answer to which party in the ownership chain is responsible for environmental remediation and what constitutes a suitable cleanup for various planned uses is still evolving.

Reengineering older industrial buildings with historic character is a special challenge. Architectural features should be retained as much as possible, and additions and improvements should be sympathetic with the existing design. New roofing and insulation, new windows with energy-efficient double- or triple-paned glass, the repair and cleaning of exterior wall surfaces, and painting and other cosmetic improvements are common exterior changes. A significant portion of the budget for internal redesign may be required to bring a building up to current fire and safety codes: enclosing stairways, adding sprinklers and fire alarm systems, installing or upgrading new wiring and plumbing, and upgrading or installing the HVAC system.

Project Feasibility

Market Analysis before Site Selection

The market analysis that precedes site selection for industrial development serves three purposes: to identify the types of users that will be served, to identify the type of product to be built and thus the parameters of the site to be purchased, and to identify where the product should be located. The process is similar to that for office development insofar as the market group to be analyzed consists of employers engaged in producing goods or services.

Just as for office development, the developer should be familiar with basic data about the local economy and its relation to the regional and national picture. The items that should be checked include:

- national, regional, and local economic trends;
- growth in employment and changes in the number of people engaged in job categories (as measured by Standardized Industrial Classification codes);
- socioeconomic characteristics of the metropolitan area, including rates of population growth and employment patterns;
- local growth policies and attitudes toward office and industrial development;
- forecasted demand for various types of office and industrial facilities;
- current inventory by industrial subtype;
- historic absorption trends and current leasing activity; and
- historic vacancy rates and current space available.

This information is available from a host of sources, including government and commercial Web sites, local universities, market analysts, data service firms, chambers of commerce, and major real estate brokerage firms. In addition to evaluating statistics, the developer should consult local brokers, tenants, and other developers to verify the accuracy of the information obtained. A developer who is unfamiliar with the local area should consider hiring a market research firm with experience in industrial real estate.

Few market data sources segment industrial space beyond the categories *warehouse/distribution, manufacturing,* and *flex,* and in many cases, secondary market data are lumped into a single category labeled *industrial,* making it difficult to assess the performance of individual subtypes. One method of obtaining a rough idea of the various property types when the information is not broken down is to segment properties by size categories, such as "under 5,000 square feet" or "larger than 25,000 square feet" (or "under 1,000 square meters" or "larger than 2,500 square meters").

Before searching for specific sites, a developer must become thoroughly familiar with industrial development patterns throughout the metropolitan area. During this investigation, the developer wants to learn as much as possible about local market conditions and which types of industrial tenants are expanding or contracting. A developer or industrial company looking for a large, single site is concerned with a number of issues:

- availability and cost of land;
- labor quality and cost;
- tax structure and tax incentives;
- utilities and waste disposal;
- energy rates; and
- comparative transportation rates.

Market preferences, land costs, labor costs, utility costs, and transportation costs can differ dramatically within the same city or region. Companies with markets outside the city have different criteria for site selection from those with markets primarily inside the city. The developer's market analysis before site selection should

Sample Market Analysis for a Multitenant Warehouse

This sample market analysis for warehouse space in Dallas indicates the steps to be taken in a market analysis for industrial properties. In this example, the analysis focuses on the Valwood submarket, a prime location for industrial space in the Dallas, Texas, metropolitan area.

A space inventory for Dallas and the Valwood submarket (Figure A) provided a historical sketch of how the submarket has evolved in recent years. At the time of the survey, vacancy rates remained comparatively low, 6 to 7 percent, although some upward movement was obvious in Valwood.

Characterization of submarket rents and lease terms was obtained through a survey of brokers and a review of leasing comparables (Figure B). Discussions with brokers also permitted a breakdown to be made of industrial tenants in Valwood by industry group (Figure C). The breakdown indicated that rents were at attractive levels and unencumbered by concessions or high tenant improvement allowances.

Projections of warehouse space absorption in the Dallas metropolitan area were based on changes in gross metropolitan product and population. Total employment growth was also considered an indicator of demand in the market. These

continued on next page

figure A
Space Inventory for Dallas and Valwood

Type	Valwood Square Feet (Millions)	Valwood Percent Vacant	Dallas Square Feet (Millions)	Dallas Percent Vacant
Flex	9.1	5.6	37,464	9.0
Warehouse	42.6	7.6	202,185	7.2
All	51.7	7.1	239,650	7.5
Year				
1989	39.6	12.1	NA	NA
1990	39.3	10.0	192,391	13.0
1991	39.5	11.0	192,952	12.0
1992	39.3	9.4	192,648	11.0
1993	39.5	6.0	192,949	10.0
1994	39.8	4.5	192,180	8.0
1995	41.1	5.0	192,548	7.0
1996	41.6	7.6	202,186	7.2
1997	44.3	6.8	213,248	6.4

NA = Not available.

Source: M/PF Research and RREEF Research.

figure C
Industrial Tenants by Industry in the Valwood Submarket

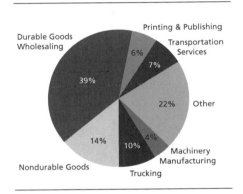

Source: Cognetics Real Estate, Inc., and RREEF Research.

figure B
Warehouse Rents and Lease Terms for Valwood

	Multitenant* Less than 20,000 Square Feet	Multi-tenant* 20,000–40,000 Square Feet	Single Tenant* 100,000 Square Feet or More
Annual Rents per Square Foot (double net)	$3.50–4.25	$3.25–3.50	$3.00–3.25
Term	3–5 Years	3–5 Years	5–10 Years
Escalations	Flat for 3–5 years; mid-term increase for longer terms		
Free Rent	1–2 months/lease term		
Tenant Improvements	$0.50–1.00 per square foot overall $2.00–3.00 per square foot office		
Expenses	$0.85–1.05 per square foot		

*Rents and terms for "new" warehouse properties with minimum 24-foot clear heights and office buildout of 10 to 15 percent (under 10 percent for single tenant).

Source: RREEF Research.

figure D

Warehouse Construction Pipeline in the Valwood Submarket

Building Name	Square Feet	Developer	Completion
Completed Early 1998			
2515 Tarpley Road	36,000	Group R.E.	3/1998
1808 Monetary Lane	67,200	Industrial Prop.	3/1998
Speculative	75,000	Off Valwest Parkway	3/1998
	178,200		
Under Construction			
Frankford Trade Center #6	709,920	Argent/Meridian	7/1998
Luna Distribution Center III	260,000	Billingsley Co.	8/1998
Luna Distribution Center IV	260,000	Billingsley Co.	8/1998
	1,229,920		
Planned			
Frankford Trade Center 1–14	2,433,774	Argent/Meridian	
Luna Distribution Center II	250,000	Billingsley Co.	
	2,683,774		

Source: RREEF Research.

projections were then used to model metropolitan area warehouse absorption in Dallas. *Fair-share capture* was used to estimate what share of metropolitan absorption could be captured by the Valwood submarket. The area's locational advantages suggested a capture rate of 10 to 15 percent in the near term and 15 to 20 percent in the long term. Net absorption in Valwood was estimated to be 9 million to 10 million square feet (836,400 to 929,400 square meters) over the next ten years.

Warehouse space construction in Dallas was found to be occurring in a number of submarkets, including Valwood. Six projects totaling approximately 1.5 million square feet (139,400 square meters) were anticipated to be completed in 1998, and another 2 million to 3 million square feet (185,900 to 278,800 square meters) was expected to enter the market in 1999 to 2001 (Figure D).

A final step in the analysis was to present an outlook and a projection of rents for the submarket. To accomplish these tasks, warehouse space absorption and construction volume were compared and measured by projected vacancy rates. These projections showed an upward trend in submarket vacancy through 2001. It was concluded that warehouse construction in Valwood would outpace absorption, even though the Dallas economy was expected to expand at a healthy rate. The imbalance in supply was expected to correct itself by 2002 as development activity eased and absorption remained positive, but the threat of continued additions to supply remained a long-term concern.

In light of these trends, submarket rents in Valwood were expected to experience only modest growth (Figure E). Larger properties of 100,000 square feet (9,300 square meters) or more were not anticipated to realize any increase in rents, because much of the increase in supply was occurring in this property segment. The near-term prognosis for warehouse space in the under 25,000- and 25,000- to 40,000-square-foot (2,325- and 2,325- to 3,720-square-meter) category was more positive because of a lack of supply in these segments (Figure F). ■

Source: Adapted from a case study by Marvin F. Christensen, RREEF Funds, San Francisco, California, in *Real Estate Market Analysis: A Case Study Approach* (Washington, D.C.: ULI–the Urban Land Institute, 2001).

assess the target market's preferences regarding such factors as access to transportation and location.

Local Links. Local links are critical to many companies. Firms that have frequent contacts with suppliers, distributors, customers, consultants, or government agencies consider the following in choosing a location:

- accessibility to firms with which they do regular business;
- the number of trips to be made to and from their business inside the metropolitan area;
- congestion in and around the site;
- commuting time for employees and public transportation available; and

- vehicle cost, including taxes, maintenance, and fuel per mile traveled.

Clustering and Agglomeration. A number of industries —food distribution, garment manufacturing, printing, wholesale flower marts, machinery parts and repair, commercial groceries and kitchen supplies, for example— tend to cluster together. The clustering, known as *agglomeration* or *co-location*, often relates to time-sensitive products (such as perishable foods) or to the interdependency of firms in a particular industry. High-tech firms tend to congregate in research parks near major universities, where they can take advantage of resources such as laboratories, libraries, professors and graduate students,

figure E

Completions, Absorption, and Vacancy in the Valwood Submarket, 1990 to 2007

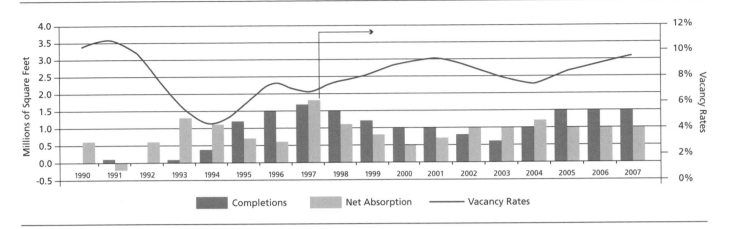

Source: M/PF Research and RREEF Research.

figure F

Projected Change in Warehouse Rents in the Valwood Submarket, 1999 to 2007

	100,000 Square Feet and More		Multitenant 25,000–40,000 Square Feet		Multitenant 25,000 Square Feet and Less	
	Rent Range	Percent Change	Rent Range	Percent Change	Rent Range	Percent Change
Current	$3.00–3.25		$3.25–3.50		$3.50–4.25	
2Q 1999	3.00–3.25	0	3.25–3.50	0	3.65–4.40	3–5
2Q 2000	3.05–3.30	0–2	3.30–3.55	0–2	3.80–4.60	3–5
2Q 2001	3.15–3.40	2–4	3.45–3.70	3–5	3.90–4.75	2–4
2Q 2002	3.30–3.55	3–5	3.60–3.85	3–5	4.00–4.90	2–4
2Q 2003	3.45–3.70	3–5	3.75–4.00	3–5	4.10–5.05	2–4
2003–2007	Changes in rent will depend on future levels of construction and absorption.					

Note: Rents are calculated using the mid-point of the forecast range.

Source: RREEF Research.

and large pools of highly educated and skilled labor. Venture capital is also attracted to universities because of the commercially valuable discoveries they generate.

Proximity to Airports. Airports exert a strong attraction for industrial users. In many cases, businesses locating near an airport use cargo and passenger services regularly. In other instances, this "airport effect" is the result of good highway access, available land, and favorable zoning.

Foreign Trade Zones. A foreign trade zone is a site in the United States in or near a U.S. Customs port of entry where foreign and domestic merchandise is generally considered to be in international commerce. Firms located in foreign trade zones can bring in and assemble

parts from abroad and export the finished product without paying customs duties until the goods leave the zone. They also can store goods within the zones without paying duty until the goods leave the trade zone. Many foreign manufacturing firms transport their products to a warehouse in the trade zone, store the products until they are ordered by a customer or distributor, and pay the import duties when the product leaves the warehouse to be delivered to the customer. Thus, the firms can have a readily available supply of stock without having to pay the associated import fees until the product is actually needed.[8]

Access. Access is fundamental to all types of industrial properties, although requirements vary by type of use. Virtually all industrial uses depend on trucking, so connections to major interstate highway systems are essential. In recent years, the growing "need for speed" in distribution, particularly of high-value goods, has made proximity to highways and airports more important than ever. Although rail service has remained an important factor for some manufacturing and industrial processes, smaller and lighter industrial users depend less on rail accessibility.

Quality of Life. The more intangible factors surrounding quality of life should not be forgotten in site evaluation. Livability is increasingly an important aspect of business location decisions. The presence of affordable housing, quality schools, and recreational and cultural resources strongly influence a company's ability to attract skilled workers.

Site Selection

Selecting the correct site is crucial to the success of an industrial development, and it is important to ensure that as many criteria as possible are satisfied. Location directly influences a development's marketability, the rate at which space can be absorbed during leasing, the rents that can be achieved, and the eventual exit strategy.

Evaluating Specific Land Parcels. Because they lack the staying power necessary to survive the many unpredictable delays of the approval process, beginning developers should avoid buying land that is not ready for immediate development. Obtaining zoning changes or variances and conditional use permits, installing major off-site infrastructure improvements, or waiting for the completion of planned transportation improvements tends to require more time and capital than most beginning developers have.

It is especially important that water, gas, electricity, telephone, and sewer services with appropriate capacities be available at competitive rates in a site for industrial use. The site should be flat to accommodate the large pads that are needed for industrial buildings and should have a minimal amount of ledge rock, groundwater, or peat with soft ground.

The presence of oil wells, natural gas, contaminated soils, high water tables, or tanks, pipes, or similar facilities can cause major problems and should be carefully studied to determine present and potential dangers.

When searching for sites for office and high-tech uses, developers should also consider the following criteria:

- distinctive terrain and vegetation, such as a water feature, that can help market the project;
- the standards of development in the surrounding area and the level of commitment among neighbors to maintain high standards;
- proximity to residential and commercial areas;
- proximity to recreational and cultural amenities;
- availability of shopping, hotels, restaurants, daycare facilities, and fitness centers;

Dowe Business Park in Union City, California, built by Chamberlin Associates in the mid-1980s, has successfully weathered downturns in the market by offering a range of building types that satisfy a wide market.

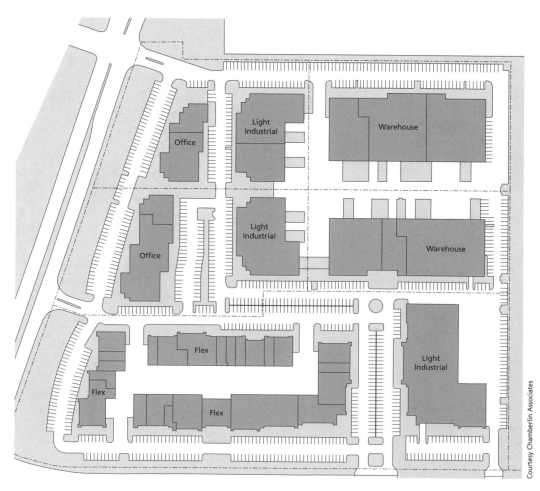

Courtesy Chamberlin Associates

- proximity to mass transit and availability of active transportation management associations and car pools;
- proximity to educational and technical training facilities such as universities, community colleges, or technical schools; and
- accessibility from freeways, arterials, or mass transit routes.

Despite the desirability of proximity to amenities such as shopping and recreation, industrial tenants who use trucks frequently prefer to be located in exclusively industrial areas rather than in mixed-use areas surrounded by residential development. Nearby apartments can be a negative factor, especially if the area has above-average crime.

Finding and Acquiring the Site. Public agencies such as local planning departments, redevelopment agencies, and economic development agencies possess a considerable amount of information useful to developers in the search for potential sites. If the target area lies inside an incorporated city, the municipal planning department, county planning department, or regional planning council is the relevant authority. Most communities have comprehensive plans or master plans that indicate the areas favored for industrial development.

Real estate brokers specializing in industrial properties are another good source for information about potential sites. Developers should first narrow down their target area and then work with brokers familiar with it to obtain information on sites that may not currently be on the market.

Remaining sites in business parks that are approaching buildout should also be considered as potential sites. Extra land around existing industrial buildings, often used for storage, also may present opportunities to expand a building for current tenants or to build another one. Owners of such properties may be interested in becoming a partner for the addition or may prefer to sell the land outright. If the land is in the back of the property, care must be taken with respect to access and visibility to ensure that the new building is leasable.

Infill sites offer developers the advantages of readily available streets, sewer, water, and other public services. But existing streets may be narrow and congested and neighboring homeowners may resist new traffic, especially trucks. Space may be too constricted to allow for the creation of the high standards that tenants now expect of business parks. The developer should consult with local neighborhood groups and property managers of neighboring industrial and other properties to learn about potential problems in advance.

Site acquisition for industrial property follows the same four steps as for other forms of development: investigation before the offer is made, offer, due diligence, and closing (see Chapters 3 and 4).

During due diligence, developers should pay special attention to hazardous wastes, especially if existing industrial uses are present nearby. Waste spilled locally may

be spread by the water table to an otherwise clean site: a small amount of solvent or gasoline can still show up as hazardous waste two or three years after it was spilled. Appropriately licensed engineers should perform water and soil tests; if necessary, developers should ensure that enough time is allowed to verify that no toxic waste is present by paying for an extension to the option. Sellers typically give buyers 60 days to perform due diligence for soils and toxic waste and 30 to 60 days for everything else.

Most developers face a standard dilemma during site acquisition. They need time to execute thorough due diligence, while the seller wants to close as quickly as possible. Both desires are perfectly reasonable, but protracted periods of time before closing are usually not met well by an eager seller and they can kill a deal. At the same time, rushing into a purchase to find out later that the site requires major environmental cleanup or going ahead without financing fully in place may be too high a price to pay to win the property.

As described in detail in Chapter 3, site acquisition generally takes place in three stages: 1) a free-look period; 2) a period during which earnest money is forfeitable; and 3) closing. The agreed-upon terms depend on market conditions. In a hot market, acquisition can be difficult for most developers and nearly impossible for those with contingencies on the approval of financing. The buyer who pays all cash eliminates most financing-contingent buyers from the race.

In mid-1997, Howard Schwimmer, executive vice president for Daum Commercial Real Estate Services, faced one of the hottest markets ever experienced in Commerce, California, but following a few basic tenets, he was able to successfully negotiate the purchase of a 240,000-square-foot (22,300-square-meter) industrial property that had fallen into foreclosure. Recognizing that complicated contracts and legalese in the first stage of an acquisition are usually not well received by a seller, Schwimmer submitted a letter of intent stating his ability to close the deal in three weeks with cash. A week or two after the seller accepted the first letter of intent, the parties agreed to a purchase and sale agreement that included an environmental review contingent on the transfer of the deed. The property was located on a parcel adjacent to contaminated ground, and lead had migrated onto the seller's property. The lead was discovered during the environmental inspection; further testing and abatement extended the closing date by two months.

During this time, the buyer was able to conduct thorough due diligence and to leverage the project more favorably. The property was successfully acquired at a price considerably below the market rate.[9]

Engineering Feasibility. Preliminary engineering investigations are an integral part of preliminary site planning. In the case of purchasing existing industrial buildings, engineering studies are among the first steps of feasibility analysis. A civil engineer usually leads the site investigation under the developer's direction. Chapter 3 provides a comprehensive review of the site evaluation process for all types of development. As far as industrial development is concerned, perhaps the two most significant aspects of this process are utilities and environmental regulations.

Utilities. Because of the low ratio of workers to building area, employee-related utility needs of industrial facilities are fewer than those for office or retail uses. Many manufacturing and some R&D facilities, however, use enormous amounts of water. Because most water is discharged eventually into the sewer system, both water and sewage services are affected. The capacity to service such customers can be a good draw, especially in areas where the availability of water is limited.

A developer should meet with the local water company as early as possible to discuss plans. The developer will learn about the utility company's current capabilities and limitations, and the utility company will learn about future expansion needs. The developer's engineer can obtain preliminary information on flow and pressure from the utility company. Fire departments usually require that the water system and fire hydrants be installed and activated before construction can start on individual buildings.

Some local agencies require the installation of lines to reclaim water for irrigation and some industrial purposes. Two parallel systems, domestic and reclaimed, must be installed on every lot in areas such as Irvine, California.

The developer should meet with the sewer company to determine the following information:

- capacity of sewage treatment facilities;
- capacity of sewer mains;
- whether gravity flow for sewage and drainage is sufficient or if pumps are necessary;
- the party responsible for paying for off-site sewer extension;
- the due date for payments and impact fees;
- quality restrictions on sewage effluent: some sewage treatment plants impose severe restrictions on the type and quantity of chemicals that firms can discharge into the general sewage system;
- discharge capacity for sewage effluent;
- flow standards; and
- periodic service charges: although the rate structure for service charges does not directly affect the developer, it will influence prospective purchasers of property, especially heavy users such as bottling plants.

Cities that use water consumption as the basis for sewer system service charges may penalize projects that consume a large quantity of water to irrigate landscaping. In such cases, the developer may attempt to negotiate treatment costs based on anticipated discharge rather than on water consumption.

Industrial land developers usually must front the costs for water and sewage lines and for treatment plants and then recover those costs as part of the sale price or rental income. They may also be reimbursed by developers of other subdivisions and owners of other properties that subsequently tie into the water and sewage mains. Most cities that provide for reimbursement by subsequent developers, however, do not permit the original developer to recover carrying costs. Moreover, because of the unpredictable timing of such reimbursements, developers cannot rely on them to help meet cash flow requirements.

For business parks with multiple buildings, developers should provide the local companies that supply electricity, telephone service, and gas with information about the type and size of buildings in their plans so that the utility companies can project the estimated demand from the project. Electricity can be a big issue, especially for manufacturing and R&D users. The projected demand is used to design the local distribution system as well as the systems that will feed the local systems.

The frequency of power outages and gas curtailments during the winter should be investigated, because this factor can deter potential tenants and buyers. Frequent outages also may influence the developer's choice of target market or may change his decision to purchase the site altogether.

Environmental Regulations. Many federal environmental statutes can affect industrial development:

- The *National Environmental Policy Act* requires that projects using federal funds must produce an environmental impact statement for approval.
- The *Clean Air Act* requires the provision of information on anticipated traffic flow and indirect vehicle use.
- The *Clean Water Act* severely restricts discharge of any pollutant into navigable and certain nonnavigable waters.
- The *Occupational Safety and Health Act* requires employers to provide safe working conditions for employees.
- The *National Flood Insurance Act* limits development in flood-prone areas and requires developers who build in flood-prone areas to meet standards concerning height, slope, and interference with water flow. The act requires that a project not impede the water flow speed and volume that exist before development in any floodway traversed by the project.
- The *Comprehensive Environmental Response, Compensation, and Liability Act,* also known as *Superfund,* addresses issues concerning toxic waste.

In addition, each state and local municipality may have its own environmental laws that affect industrial development.

Concerns about toxic waste, water supply, sewage treatment constraints, and sensitive environmental areas are forcing developers to perform very careful site investigation before closing on a tract. Although laws in most states give developers some recourse against prior owners in the chain of title for problems such as toxic waste, such protections are of little use if developers cannot proceed with their plans.

States are working to ease the liability put on developers when they engage in projects that come with environmental wildcards and potentially massive costs. In

The three main goals of business park and building design are functionality, economy of construction, and easy long-term maintenance. Shown here is the Short Run facility, Phillips Plastics Corporation, New Richmond, Wisconsin.

Massachusetts, the attorney general's office has successfully negotiated a number of covenants not to sue with developers reclaiming brownfields. According to Raymond Bhumgara, the state has recognized that future owners of sites should not be held liable for contamination that they did not cause.[10] These covenants protect developers from being financially responsible for cleanups after taking ownership of a parcel and then having to pull out of the project.

The recent trend in urban adaptive use, the conversion of industrial properties to residential or live/work spaces, generates new concerns for industrial developers. These conversions can have a positive effect on economic development in underperforming neighborhoods but simultaneously cause incompatible uses in a single zone. Developers consequently must create environmental impact reports to show, among other things, traffic and noise effects on adjacent properties. In the past, individuals creating industrial projects did not have to consider how the building's use would affect residential occupants. The gradual infiltration of residential uses into industrial zones is increasing the sensitivity of environmental requirements in these newly created mixed-use areas.

Market Analysis after Site Selection

Once a site has been secured with a signed earnest money contract, the second, more detailed phase of the market analysis begins. The purpose at this stage is to investigate the immediate market area for information about rental rates, occupancy, new supply, and features of competing projects.

An important step before beginning this stage of market analysis is to define the property type or types most likely to be developed at the site to focus the research and determine which other properties constitute potential competition. This often overlooked step can help narrow the amount of research and reduce unnecessary effort.

Industrial Supply Analysis. The first task in identifying future supply is to identify properties that are currently under development or construction. A drive through the submarket and follow-up calls to brokers and active developers can yield information on project sizes, completion dates, costs, and rents. Information on proposed projects that have not yet broken ground can be obtained from local planning and building departments.

Estimating the amount of additional space to the industrial supply beyond two or three years is difficult. Industrial buildings take a relatively short time to build, and when vacancy rates are low, the amount of construction can increase quickly. It is useful to look at factors such as the amount of land available for industrial development in the submarket and estimate the number of years before the available land supply is exhausted, given the likely pace of development. Some market analysts and data providers use econometric models to forecast new construction. These numbers may not be entirely accurate, but they provide a picture of future conditions.

Developers should also keep in mind that the public sector may influence future supply. Cities and redevelopment agencies offer incentives to industrial tenants that they do not offer to office and retail tenants. If developers are not offered the same benefits as those available to others, they are at a competitive disadvantage.

An analysis of potential competitors helps to assess the strengths of the proposed project compared with its competition. Again, a good place to start to collect this detailed data is from real estate brokers or management companies involved in the marketing of industrial developments who may be willing to provide plans or brochures and marketing materials on individual properties.

The developer should collect information on competing projects for the following items:

- overall site area and the size of individual lots and buildings if it is a multibuilding development;
- schedule, including date when marketing was initiated;
- occupancy levels at the date of the survey (acres sold, total square feet leased for each type of facility, percentage of space occupied);
- estimated annual land absorption;
- estimated annual space absorption by property type;
- initial and current sale prices and lease rates per square foot (land and buildings);
- lease terms and concessions;
- tenant allowances to finish interior space;
- building characteristics and the quality of architectural and landscape design, level of finish, quality of materials, signage, overall park appearance, and maintenance;
- development cost per acre;
- major highway access, rail availability, and utilities;
- amenities such as retail services, restaurants, open space, recreation, daycare, and health and conference facilities; and
- developer or current owner.

Industrial Space Demand Analysis. Demand models for industrial space often emulate office demand models, where a change in employment is a prime determinant of potential space absorption. Multiplying the estimated number of new employees in a metropolitan area by the space allocated per employee provides an estimate of future space requirements. (It is important to keep in mind that space ratios are different for different types of industrial space.)

Analysts should also review other measures of metropolitan growth such as gross metropolitan product or changes in total population or households. Growth in gross metropolitan product is a good indicator of absorption of warehouse or distribution space, because it is a measure of the output of a local economy. Another indicator is manufacturing output as measured by the Federal Reserve Board's Index of Manufacturing Output.[11] Sometimes demand is tied to growth in another nearby city. Warehouse space along the U.S. border in

southern California is correlated with the growth of warehouse space in Mexican cities just south of the border.

After space demand is calculated for a metropolitan area, a final step is to estimate what share of the area's absorption will be captured by the submarket where the property is located. Often, the concept of fair share is used. For example, if a submarket holds 8 percent of a metropolitan area's industrial space inventory, then its fair share is 8 percent. Another method is to examine the historical share of net absorption in the submarket in relation to the metropolitan area's net absorption over time. This information should provide an overview of how well the area stacks up against other locations. If a submarket is overbuilt, a developer may choose to sit on the land for months before beginning construction.

Allan Kotin observes that market analysis for industrial space has more pitfalls than for other types of development. Industrial zoning is far more permissive with respect to land use than is commercial, office, or residential zoning. Industrial zoning often allows any of the other uses except, perhaps, residential and may therefore lead to overestimation of the size of the market. "There is a blurring of key distinctions in the general category that can lead to such errors," notes Kotin. "Nominally industrial space that is half finished as office space and rents for $.90 to $1.00 per square foot ($9.70 to $10.75 per square meter) per month cannot be averaged with traditional industrial space that is 10 percent finished and rents for $.45 per square foot ($4.85 per square meter)."[12] Developers must look at the type of use and the degree of finish to determine rents accurately.

Industrial development provides a back door into both office and retail development, and market analysts sometimes mistakenly include absorption figures for office and retail users in their estimates of demand by industrial users. The distinction between product types can be made primarily by the amount of tenant improvements. Care must be taken to isolate the percentage of nonindustrial users. Office users in industrial buildings are often tempted to move back into higher-image office buildings, especially if office markets are soft. This phenomenon occurred during the early 1990s in California, Texas, and other depressed real estate markets when office rents fell precipitously following the real estate crash of the late 1980s.

Another pitfall to be wary of is the incubator approach. Incubator industrial space is a frequently abused concept. Originally, incubator space was intended to house small firms that have the potential to grow into large ones. In practice, however, users are often marginal firms. Those firms in incubator space that actually grow and prosper are in the minority; thus, potential tenants should be carefully scrutinized. Other issues involved in analyzing the market for industrial development arise from the different ways of measuring rents. Some tenants have full-service leases, in which the landlord pays all expenses, while others have triple net (NNN) leases, in which the landlord pays no expenses. Some tenants have modified industrial gross leases in which the tenant pays direct utility costs, internal janitorial costs, and insurance, but the landlord pays for common area maintenance. If developers mistakenly interpret modified industrial gross leases as full-service gross leases, rent estimates will be too low. And if they interpret modified industrial gross leases as triple net leases, estimates will be too high.[13]

Regulatory Issues

The approval process for industrial parks is similar to that for residential subdivisions (see Chapter 3). Although the basic procedures for platting industrial subdivisions depend on the local area, most communities begin with some form of tentative approval, such as the tentative tract map in California. After appropriate review by the public, the developer is eligible to obtain a final tract map. The final tract map (also called the *subdivision plat*) indicates the lot lines, setback requirements, allowable floor/area ratios (FARs), and other restrictions that determine the developer's buildable site and its density.

The approval process for individual buildings may be as simple as obtaining a building permit or as complicated as the process for a full-scale business park. Normally, if the developer is building within the envelope of the existing zoning and subdivision restrictions, the approval process is similar to that for individual commercial and office buildings. If variances or changes in the zoning are sought, however, the approval process may be lengthy and expensive. Planning commissions and city councils tend to be especially concerned about traffic—traffic through neighborhoods, turning traffic, truck traffic, curb cuts, and more—as well as noise, fumes, and other negative effects of the planned development. Some communities are eager to attract the employment opportunities that industrial development generates, while many others are more concerned about keeping out truck traffic and preserving the character of business districts and residential neighborhoods.

Zoning. Several basic types of zoning districts commonly are used for industrial and business park development. Most common are the *by-right districts, planned unit developments* (PUDs) or *floating districts,* and *special districts.*

- By-right districts are the most traditional type of zoning district. Uses permitted by zoning regulations can be built by right without requiring further approvals.
- PUDs are known as floating districts because they can be applied anywhere the locality approves them. PUDs have flexible land use controls that can increase site coverage and provide for a mixture of uses. They also give the developer flexibility by not requiring precommitments for the exact acreage to be zoned for industrial or commercial purposes and by delaying precise subdivision layout until sales occur.
- Special districts are approved by the local jurisdiction for a specific tract of land. The special district is then adopted as part of the local zoning ordinance. Provisions of the district are site specific and address issues such as land use, design, transportation, and landscaping.[14]

Zoning restrictions determine the size and placement of the structures that can be built on a given site. Typical zoning regulations for industrial buildings include:

- front, side, and rear setbacks;
- height restrictions;
- access requirements;
- parking ratios;
- parking and loading design; and
- landscape requirements and screening regulations.

Most communities have maximum FARs for their industrial zones. In addition, landscape coverage ratios may be predetermined for the entire site or for the parking areas.

Although zoning ordinances have traditionally separated land uses from one another and limited the mix of uses in business parks, a move toward greater commingling of different land uses has occurred in recent years. The recognition that business parks often end up

Existing wetlands at Prairie Stone Business Park near Chicago, Illinois, were preserved, supplemented, and enhanced to become a focal point for the development.

Courtesy Homart Development Co.

as sterile work settings without basic services or amenities for employees has led some communities to allow plans that include shopping facilities, restaurants, hotels, and even residential uses.

Covenants, Conditions, and Restrictions. Covenants, conditions, and restrictions (CC&Rs) are private land use controls and standards commonly used for business parks. CC&Rs take the form of a legally enforceable instrument filed with the plat or deed of individual buildings. They supplement municipal regulations such as zoning and subdivision controls and apply to virtually every aspect of a business park's development, including site coverage, architectural design, building materials, parking requirements, signage, and landscaping.

Design guidelines can be included as part of the CC&Rs or as a separate document. They establish very specific uniform guidelines and criteria regarding bulk, height, types of materials, fenestration, and overall aesthetic design of the building. Subdivision restrictions sometimes require facilities for employees such as outdoor lunch areas, recreation areas, and open space.

Public/Private Negotiations. Increasingly, developers are required to negotiate agreements with local municipalities to secure approval for proposed projects. These agreements are especially helpful in volatile political climates in which pressures for no growth may cause city councils to change development entitlements unexpectedly. Public/private negotiations are also required when a developer seeks to work with a public agency on publicly owned land or in redevelopment areas.

In California, public/private contracts take the form of development agreements that usually take considerable time to negotiate.[15] The agreements protect developers from later changes in zoning or other regulations that affect development entitlements and lend an air of certainty to the regulatory process by delineating most rights, requirements, and procedures in advance. Once adopted, no surprises related to approval should occur. Most agencies, however, require something in return, such as special amenities, fees, or exactions.

The use of public/private negotiations to shape the form of industrial developments is widespread, though not routine. In high-growth areas, public displeasure with the negative impacts of development has led to direct public involvement in negotiations with developers over specific projects. Many municipalities and counties have realized that well planned industrial facilities such as business parks can provide significant revenues from property taxes. Some communities have therefore established redevelopment agencies to supervise negotiations with private developers and to represent the community's interests as development proceeds.

The public sector's role can include:

- sharing risks with the developer through land price writedowns and participation in cash flows;
- creating utility districts and contributing toward off-site infrastructure;
- participating in loan commitments and mortgages;

- sharing operating and capital costs;
- reducing administrative red tape; and
- providing favorable tax treatment.

The role played by private developers is also expanding. Their functions may include paying for major off-site infrastructure and building freeway interchanges.

Development and Impact Fees. Some stages of the regulatory process require public hearings, and virtually all require some form of fee. The developer should understand the full range and scope of charges before closing on the land. Some of the more common fees that are assessed on industrial development projects include:

- Approval and Variance Fees—Either a lump sum or a charge for the actual time spent by government personnel on processing an application;
- Plan Check Fees—Generally, a percentage of valuation;
- Building Permit Fees—Generally, a percentage of valuation;
- Water System Fees—Possibly based on amount of water used, meter size, frontage on water lines, or a combination;
- Sewer System Fees—Usually based on expected discharge;
- Storm Drainage Fees—Usually based on runoff generated or on acreage;
- Transportation Fees—Based on trips generated or on square footage (some areas have freeway fees, county fees, and local transportation improvement fees);
- School Fees—Even industrial buildings are charged school fees per square foot in some areas;
- Fire and Police Fees—Usually based on square footage; and
- Library, Daycare, and Various Other Fees.

The types and amounts of fees vary drastically from one city to another. The developer must learn each city's and each agency's particular system of imposing fees. Because the fees can be imposed by a multitude of agencies, the developer should check with every agency that possibly could set fees. In many jurisdictions, the building department handles a majority of the fees and can be a good source of preliminary information.

State and Local Incentives. State and local governments have developed a variety of incentive mechanisms to encourage industrial development:

- Publicly owned business incubator parks are designed to accommodate small startup companies; publicly owned research-oriented parks cater to high-tech companies.
- Enterprise zones, created by many states to encourage new industry in economically depressed urban areas, offer incentives to companies that locate in the zones. These incentives include various combinations of property tax abatements, industrial development bonds, exemptions from income and sales taxes, low-interest venture capital, infrastructure improvements, and special public services.

- State and local grants offer revolving commercial loans, loan and development bond guarantees, infrastructure projects that aid particular industries, and even venture capital funds.
- Tax increment financing is useful in areas with low tax bases. The difference between new taxes generated by development and the original taxes is reserved for infrastructure improvements for the designated area. Redevelopment agencies frequently use tax increment financing as a source of revenue for their projects.

Industrial development bonds were very popular in the late 1970s and early 1980s, but the 1986 Tax Reform Act severely restricted the types of projects that could qualify for tax-exempt financing. Originally intended to bring manufacturing to depressed areas, bonds were used instead to provide tax-exempt financing for a number of activities, in both industrial and commercial development. Some communities abused industrial development bonds by using them to finance activities such as fast-food restaurants and other businesses in areas in which conventionally financed development was already occurring. Businesses complained that the bonds gave certain firms an unfair cost advantage and questioned the contention that industrial development bonds actually stimulated much development that would not otherwise have occurred. Despite these problems, a number of cities have used industrial development bonds effectively to generate development in once stagnant areas.

Financial Feasibility

As with other product types, financial analysis for industrial development is performed several times during the feasibility period. At the very least, it should be updated three times before closing on the land: 1) before submit-

ting the earnest money contract; 2) before approaching lenders, and 3) before going hard on the land purchase.

At each stage of development, more information is known with greater certainty and accuracy. Data from the market study, design data, and cost estimates are incorporated into the financial pro formas as the information becomes available. Developers should not wait until these studies are done, however, before performing financial analysis; cruder information based on secondary sources may be used at earlier stages. For example, as soon as the size of the building to be built is estimated, the construction cost can be estimated from average costs per square foot for similar projects. Contractors and other developers usually will share this cost information.

The method of analysis for business park development is different from that for industrial building development:

- *Business park development* is a form of land development and follows the approach for analyzing for-sale property described in Chapter 3.
- The stages of analysis for *industrial building development* are similar to the five stages of DCF analysis for income-producing property described in Chapter 4.

For building development, the major decision tool is the DCF analysis, a five- to ten-year pro forma showing the property's operations from the completion of construction to sale. It incorporates rental rates, rent concessions, lease-up time, and expected bumps in rents over the holding period.

Internal rates of return are computed on the before- and after-tax cash flows. Industrial developers like to see IRRs on total project cost of 13 to 15 percent for an all-equity (unleveraged) case in which zero mortgage is assumed. A 15 percent unleveraged IRR typically produces a leveraged IRR (with a 70 to 75 percent LTV ratio) on equity in the high 20s. Leveraged IRRs on equity need to be 20 to 30 percent to entice investors.

The developer should use the financial pro forma to perform sensitivity analysis to test the impact of various assumptions on the results:

- For industrial building development, what effect do leasing schedules have on the IRR?
- How sensitive is the IRR to changes in assumptions with respect to rental rates and concessions, construction costs, financing costs, interest rates, release assumptions, and inflation assumptions?
- For industrial park development, what effect does lowering land prices to sell the land faster have on the IRR?
- What is the effect on the IRR if more money is spent upfront on items such as amenities, roads, utilities, and entrances to permit faster sales or higher prices?

Because in-depth examples of multiperiod cash flow analyses for both land development and building development are included in Chapters 3 and 4, none are included here.

© Aerpic

The design of the roadways at the ConAgra Corporate Campus in Omaha, Nebraska, reflects the topography of the site and provides opportunities for future growth.

Design and Construction

This section deals first with design considerations for business parks and second with building design for the major industrial building types.

Site Design

Site design for a business park must consider a variety of interrelated variables, from lot layout to street systems to landscaping plans. Flexibility is a key issue. The site plan should easily accommodate new buildings, changes in traffic flow, and division into smaller parcels.

The planning process generally follows three general stages: concept planning, preliminary planning, and final planning. Each stage involves the collection and analysis of information about the site and the identification and evaluation of alternatives. Throughout the entire process, the developer and project planning team should maintain a meaningful dialogue with relevant public agency representatives, because they can assist in compliance and in facilitating public support.

Platting and Lot Size. Lots 200 to 300 feet (60 to 90 meters) deep are popular for a variety of industrial uses. Large single users may require deeper lots of 500 feet (150 meters), which can be subdivided if necessary. Lot width is variable and depends on the needs of the user. If parking requirements are minimal, building coverage may range from 50 to 70 percent of the total lot area. For example, a 20,000-square-foot (1,860-square-meter) building in an area limited to 50 percent coverage would occupy a 40,000-square-foot (3,720-square-meter) site. If the remaining 20,000 square feet (1,860 square meters) were all used for parking, at 350 square feet (32.5 square meters) per parking space on average, then approximately 57 spaces would be possible, for a parking ratio of 2.9 spaces per 1,000 square feet (95 square meters).[16]

Parking. The amount of parking required for individual buildings in a business park is dictated by zoning requirements and users' needs, although frequently these two requirements differ. Most jurisdictions' zoning and building codes require a minimum number of parking spaces based on the square footage of different uses being built, expressed as a ratio of spaces to 1,000 square feet (95 square meters) of leasable space. Ratios have been increasing in recent years, and they now range from one to two spaces per 1,000 square feet (95 square meters) for warehouse uses to three, four, or more spaces for R&D flex buildings and other predominantly office uses.

Street Design and Traffic. The location of external roads provides the basis for internal street systems in business parks. The ideal street layout for a business park provides easy access to the nearest major highway or freeway and discourages unrelated traffic. A public highway that runs through the middle of a park reduces the developer's expenditure on internal roads and enhances the value of frontage sites, but it also tends to divide rather than unify the development, bring heavy unrelated traffic through the middle of the park, and increase the possibilities of accidents.

The more points of ingress and egress in a development, the better. For instance, assume that a 160-acre (65-hectare) business park is being developed with an employment density of 20 persons per acre (50 per hectare). With 3,200 employees at 1.1 per car, approximately 2,900 cars would be in circulation. Three planned access points probably could accommodate that volume in just over an hour. If, however, a half-hour traffic jam occurs at the park nightly and the competing industrial park down the road does not have a traffic jam, the owner of the first park faces a serious marketing problem.

Within the site, roads must be designed to permit maximum flexibility in shaping development parcels, because changes in demand could require modifications in site design at some point in the future. Contemporary business parks typically are not designed around the grids common to earlier parks. Today, streets are more likely to curve and follow land contours.

Because traffic is a chief concern of most communities, developers should understand the impact that their proposed developments will have on traffic. *Trip generation* refers to the number of vehicle trips that originate from a given source. Figure 6-1 gives some standard figures for trip generation for different types of industry.

One lane of pavement typically handles 800 to 1,200 trips per hour, depending on the street layout and traffic control at intersections. For purposes of design, developers should estimate the percentage and directional distribution of truck traffic. Overdesigning the traffic system is better than underdesigning it, as the intensity of future uses is unknown.

Design considerations include road thickness, pavement type (concrete or asphalt), road curvatures, and sight distances for stopping, passing, and corners. Standard drawings of the following items are available in most agencies:

- typical street sections;
- commercial entrances and private driveways;
- culs-de-sac and turnarounds;
- intersections, interchanges, and medians;
- guard rails, bridges, and bridge approaches;
- signalization, signage, and lighting;
- drainage, curbs, and gutters;
- erosion control features;
- sidewalks, paved approaches, and pavement joints;
- safety features; and
- earthwork grading.

Standards are subject to constant revision. The developer usually relies on the civil engineer to ensure that street and utility designs conform to the latest standards.

Culs-de-sac need a paved turnaround of 100 feet (30 meters) in diameter to allow trucks with 45-foot (13.7-meter) trailers to turn around without backing up. Roadway widths depend on the amount of traffic the roadways handle, median design, and the absence or presence of parking. Some designers prefer that the major roads leading into a project have no parking and that interior access roads allow limited parking. Street parking can be advantageous to some businesses, because it can provide space for overflow visitor parking.

Walks and Landscaping. A carefully designed pedestrian system can be an attractive selling feature, particularly if it is connected to a nearby retail or recreation area. If the business park includes significant open space, then a pathway system (perhaps including a jogging path)

figure 6-1

Vehicle Trips per Weekday

	Per 1,000 Square Feet of GFA	Per Developed Acre	Per Employee	Per Employee
	Average	Average	Average	Range
General Light Industry	6.97	51.80	3.02	1.53–4.48
General Heavy Industry	1.50	6.75	0.82	.75–1.81
Industrial Park	6.96	63.11	3.34	1.24–8.80
Manufacturing	3.82	38.88	2.10	.60–6.66
Warehousing	4.96	57.23	3.89	1.47–15.71
Miniwarehouse	2.50	38.87	56.28	17–19.40
Office Park	11.42	195.11	3.50	2.92–3.85
R&D Center	8.11	79.61	2.77	.96–10.63
Business Park	12.76	149.79	4.04	3.25–8.19

Source: Institute of Transportation Engineers, *Trip Generation*, 6th ed. (Washington, D.C.: Author, 1997).

figure 6-2

Characteristics of Motor Vehicles Typically Used in Business Parks

Typical Dimensions in Feet

Type of Motor Vehicle	Wheelbase	Front Overhang	Rear Overhang	Overall Length	Overall Width	Height	Minimum Outside Turning Radius[a]	Minimum Inside Turning Radius[b]
Passenger Car	11	3	5	19	7.0	–	24	14.9
Single-Unit Truck	20	4	6	30	8.5	13.5	42	27.8
Intermediate-Size Semitrailer Combination	13 + 27 = 40	4	6	50	8.5	13.5	14	17.7
Large Semitrailer Combination	20 + 30 = 50)	3	2	55	8.5	13.5	45	16.6
Semitrailer/Full Trailer Combination	9.7 + 20 + 9.4[c] + 20.9 = 60	2	3	65	8.5	13.5	45	21.4

Note: Dimensions may vary slightly, depending on the vehicle manufacturer.

[a] To the path of the left front wheel.

[b] To the path of the right rear wheel.

[c] Distance between rear wheels of front trailer and front wheels of rear trailer.

Sources: Wolfgang S. Homburger, ed., *Transportation and Traffic Engineering Handbook,* 2nd ed. (Englewood Cliffs, New Jersey: Prentice-Hall, 1982); and Patrick Meehan, "Industrial Park Guidelines," *Landscape Architecture,* November/December 1985, p. 90.

The following basic criteria must be considered when designing the landscape for a business park:

1. Streetscape—Whether dealing with one parcel or a multitenant park, the objective is for the project to look good from the street, for the street to look good from the project, and for the street to serve pedestrians as well as vehicular traffic. Design elements include berming, pedestrian paths, sidewalks, and trails.
2. Entry Landscape—Monumental signage clearly marks and identifies a business park site. For an individual parcel, a site sign might be included in addition to exterior building signs. Standards set for the park dictate the type and placement of signs.

3. Circulation—Site circulation, whether vehicular or pedestrian, should be direct and clearly marked. Way-finding devices include signage, berming, tree planting, seasonal planting, site furnishings, and artwork.
4. Front Door—Landscape architecture can reinforce the significance of a main entrance through paving materials and patterns, plantings, fountains, and plazas. Each choice comes with a cost; when projects are subjected to cutbacks, the last thing to go is usually the identity at the front door.
5. Service Areas—Service areas include truck docks, loading areas, dumpsters, recycling areas, and outdoor mechanical, electrical, and communications equipment. When building orientation does not permit complete screening,

other methods can be employed, such as commercial and evergreen fences, walls, and berming. Certain plant materials work better for this type of screening, and the landscape architect can recommend what is most appropriate for the site.
6. Stormwater Management—Local codes contain requirements for stormwater management that typically state water must be retained on site for a period of time before it can be released. Various retention methods can be used, from wet ponds to dry ponds to underground storage. The site's size, topography, and budget help determine which is the most practical and cost-effective choice. ■

Landscaping and design highlight this front door at Audubon at the Branches in Reston, Virginia, with a curved sidewalk, lighting along the path, blooming flowers, and mature trees.

©James Oesch Photography/Courtesy Donnally, Lederer, Vujcic

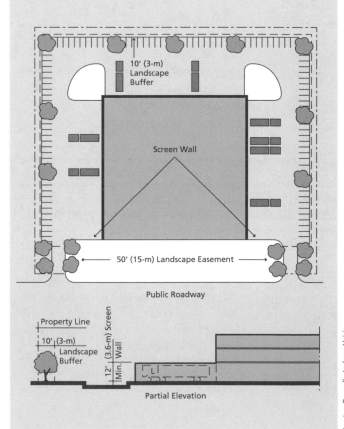

Loading bay screen.

Courtesy Donnally, Lederer, Vujcic

through the space, away from heavy traffic, is also an attractive amenity.

In designing aesthetic features such as berms and slopes, developers should be aware that mowing equipment cannot handle slopes steeper than three to one (three feet horizontal to one foot vertical [0.9 to 0.3 meter]). Care also must be taken to avoid interfering with drivers' visibility by landscaping and berms at road intersections. Where industrial uses adjoin residential uses, deep lots, berms, fences, landscaping, or open space can help to create a buffer.

Truck and Rail Access. Well-designed truck access, docks, and doors are critical to the operation of most industrial facilities. The distance of the truck apron from the truck dock affects the on-site maneuverability of trucks. The current maximum length for a tractor and semitrailer can be somewhat longer than 70 feet (21.3 meters). Therefore, the current recommended standard for a truck apron is 120 feet (36.5 meters) from the truck dock; some developers provide as much as 150 feet (45.7 meters).

The path from the truck areas to the street should be scrutinized to ensure adequate turning radii for truck maneuverability. Developers should separate truck loading areas from passenger car areas to improve safety and to ensure that noise from loading and operating trucks does not interfere with R&D or office tenants.

According to David Hasbrouck, industrial buildings now have truck courts to fit 53- to 55-foot (16.1- to 16.8-meter) trailers, compared with 43- to 48-foot (13.1- to 14.6-meter) trailers ten years ago. Truck yards have increased from 120 feet to 135 feet (36.5 to 41.1 meters) in depth.[17]

Most tenants do not require access to rail. If such access is contemplated, however, railroad officials should be contacted early in the design process to determine design requirements, reciprocal switching limits, frequency of switching service, and general rates. Some business park designs allow rail spurs to be installed later if a new tenant desires rail access. Developers must obtain the necessary easements and rights-of-way initially. It is extremely difficult if not impossible to do so later.

Amenities. Support services are an important amenity for tenants of business parks. In smaller parks, service kiosks can be installed. For example, the developer of Braker Center, an R&D park in Austin, Texas, placed a kiosk containing automatic teller machines, a Federal Express station, and post office services at the entrance to the main parking lot. In larger parks, a retail service center may be warranted. Specific uses vary widely; popular amenities include delicatessens, cafeterias, or full-service restaurants. Larger business parks can support small retail centers that cater to their industrial tenants and provide services such as printing, office supplies, computer supplies, and food services. Availability of hotel and restaurant facilities also is important to large-scale industrial parks, if permitted by zoning. Car repair shops and gas stations can also provide useful services to tenants.

Today's warehouses and distribution centers are state-of-the-art facilities with generous clear heights, easy truck access and loading, advanced fire protection systems, and above-standard column spacing.

Building Design and Construction

Design elements for industrial buildings are tailored to both the functional aspects of each particular building type and to economic considerations. Beginning developers should study carefully the design and construction of other buildings that serve the same market. They should speak to tenants to discover which features they require and to contractors about ways to save money. Finally, they should choose an architect who specializes in the particular industrial building type that they are planning and talk to contractors and other developers who have previously worked with that architect. An architect who is an expert designer of office/warehouse space is not necessarily also an expert in R&D space. As with other product types, a team approach to design and construction is the most effective, and, ideally, the contractor and the leasing agent should be part of the design team and work with the architect to obtain a design that is both functional and marketable.

The design of industrial buildings aims to combine functionality, economy of construction, and easy long-term maintenance. Designers of industrial buildings have pioneered many construction techniques that have been gradually adopted by other product types. Tilt-wall construction, for example, was developed to assist the low-cost construction of large expanses of wall. The technology has been adapted successfully to both retail and office development. The need for open, column-free spaces leads to a structural system largely based on efficient roof construction. Because industrial buildings are typically one story high, the roof is the primary load carried by the columns.

Bay Depths and Ceiling Heights. Bay depths of a building depend on two elements: the stacking plan of the proposed buyer or tenant, and the construction system used. With wooden roof systems, bay depths are based on a four- by eight-foot (1.2- by 2.4-meter) roof system.

Thus, the structural system and design of the building should be based on multiples of four feet (1.2 meters). Bay depths between columns are commonly 24 feet by 48 feet (7.3 by 14.6 meters). Increasingly, large users look for bay spacing in excess of 48 feet by 48 feet (14.6 by 14.6 meters) to accommodate more efficient racking and storage systems. Concrete block buildings are designed with the same system (three 16-inch [40-centimeter] concrete blocks equal four feet [1.2 meters]). Preengineered metal systems frequently feature multiples of four feet (1.2 meters) or five feet (1.5 meters).

The developer must assess the efficiency of an industrial building's design from the perspective of the buyer or tenant. A minimal number of columns is very important to tenants. The difference between two and three rows of columns can substantially affect the efficiency of stacking systems.

The height of the building likewise depends on prospective tenants. Smaller industrial buildings and small multitenant buildings frequently are 16 to 24 feet (4.8 to 7.3 meters) floor to ceiling. The floor-to-ceiling height is measured as the minimum distance between the lowest structural member in the roof and the finished floor. Buildings with 24-foot (7.3-meter) ceiling heights were popular in the 1980s and 1990s because they could readily accommodate a mezzanine (a nine-foot [2.7-meter] first-floor ceiling height, four feet [1.2 meters] for floor structure and air-conditioning ducts,

Comparison of Industrial Building Types

Warehouse/Distribution Buildings

- Clear heights of 24 feet (7.3 meters), but moving toward 30 feet (9.1 meters) and higher.
- Large interior column spacing (40 feet x 40 feet [12.1 x 12.1 meters]).
- Docks that are 4 feet (1.2 meters) above ground level (truck bed heights vary from 3'-8" to 4'-8" [1.1 to 1.4 meters]).
- Dock-high doors that are 9 or 10 feet (2.7 or 3 meters) wide and 10 feet (3 meters) high and double doors that are 20 feet (6 meters) wide and 10 feet (3 meters) high.
- Grade-level doors of 10 feet (3 meters) wide by 12 or 14 feet (3.6 or 4.2 meters) high if trucks are to drive into the warehouse.
- A minimum of 120 feet (36.5 meters) of space in front of the dock for truck movements. Some developers prefer to make this distance 125 to 130 feet (38.1 to 39.6 meters) to allow for a double row of parking in the space if the building is later converted into a more intense use.
- On average, one dock for every 10,000 square feet (930 square meters) for warehouse buildings and one for every 5,000 square feet (465 square meters) for heavy distribution buildings.
- Trailer storage—an attribute often overlooked.
- Truck ramps that optimally slope no more than 5 percent.
- Screening for loading docks and truck parking areas.
- Security features such as fencing, gates, and guard facilities.

- A parking ratio of one to two parking spaces per 1,000 square feet (95 square meters).

Manufacturing Facilities

- Clear height rarely exceeding 30 feet (9.1 meters).
- Separate entrances for cars and trucks, separate employee and public parking, overhead doors, and loading facilities. A mixture of dock-high doors and at-grade doors is usually an advantage.
- Parking ratios of two to four spaces per 1,000 square feet (95 square meters) with an average of about three and one-half spaces per 1,000 square feet (95 square meters).
- Emphasis on landscaping features for visitors and employees.
- Emphasis on security for employees.
- Interior column spacing conforming to manufacturing equipment requirements.
- Gas for processing.

Flex Facilities

- One- or two-story buildings designed for maximum flexibility.
- Office space of 12 to 14 feet (3.6 to 4.2 meters) slab to slab for cabling and other building systems.
- Clear height 10 to 18 feet (3 to 5.4 meters) in warehouse area.
- Parking ratio of 4 to 5 spaces per 1,000 square feet (95 square meters).
- Curb appeal in building design.
- Campus setting, preferably.

R&D/Flex Buildings

- A combination of offices and laboratories.
- Smaller bay depths and lower clear heights (14 to 16 feet [4.2 to 4.8 meters]) than for typical industrial buildings.
- One- to two-story buildings with 25 to 75 percent office space.
- Specialized rooms and systems.
- Higher employee density than warehouse or manufacturing/assembly space.
- A parking ratio of four spaces per 1,000 square feet (95 square meters).
- High curb appeal.
- Design features such as the extensive use of glass.
- Loading capability, including drive-in doors or docks.

Multitenant/Showroom Buildings

- Customer access in the front and truck access in the rear or intermixed traffic when units are back to back.
- Ample visitor parking and provisions for pedestrian access.
- Generous use of glass and architectural features.
- Easily divided space.
- Clear height of 16 to 18 feet (4.9 to 5.5 meters).
- Parking at two to three spaces per 1,000 square feet (95 square meters).
- Truck access at grade.
- A comprehensive signage program and unified entrance design. ■

a nine-foot [2.7-meter] ceiling height on the second floor, and two feet [0.6 meter] for the air-conditioning ducts). Today, large industrial buildings and warehouse buildings are 30 to 32 feet (9.1 to 9.7 meters) or higher floor to ceiling. Because the roof must slope to allow rainwater to run off, the ceiling may be several feet higher. Clear heights above 30 feet (9.1 meters) present more expensive structural issues and should be constructed only if the costs can be justified by demand. Although some taller warehouses are being constructed, David Hasbrouck says that most tenants cannot use the higher cubic footage.[18]

Older buildings near international airports are attractive to tenants who are part of the *just-in-time* delivery chain, which has led to the conversion of cheap older airfreight buildings. According to Izzy Eichenstein, warehouse tenants in the vicinity of Los Angeles International Airport look for a minimum of 22-foot (6.7-meter) clear buildings and wide turning radii for trucks. Requirements for sprinklers have also become more stringent since the early 1990s.[19]

Foundations and Floor Loading. Foundation design depends on the dead and live loads of each part of the building. If tilt-wall construction is used, a concrete beam with steel reinforcement, called a *spread footing* or *continuous beam,* is poured along the line of the wall. The beam may be one foot to four feet (0.3 to 1.2 meters) wide, depending on the load, and 12 to 24 inches (0.3 to 0.6 meter) deep.

In areas with good soil and no earthquakes, *spot footings* may be poured under each point where panels join. Spot footings typically are four feet (1.2 meters) square and range in depth from 12 inches (30.5 centimeters) in good soil to 18 or more inches (45 or more centimeters).

In areas subject to freezing weather, the beam, or footing, must extend below the frost line, because soil tends to expand when frozen. In Michigan, for example, footings are three to four feet (0.9 to 1.2 meters) deep, and in Alaska they may go down five feet (1.5 meters) or more, depending on the depth of the frost line. Areas with permafrost require special construction.

In areas with poor soils, a grade beam is used rather than a continuous beam to distribute the load over a greater area and to prevent cracking. Steel reinforcement is an integral part of the grade beam design, whereas a continuous beam requires fewer reinforcing bars *(rebar)* and is tied together only to the extent necessary to prevent movement during the concrete pour. The beams may be formed with plywood or by the dirt itself.

The slab is poured separately from the foundation beam, leaving a three- to five-foot (0.9- to 1.5-meter) *pour strip* around the perimeter. The pour strip slab is poured before the walls are formed. In earthquake-prone areas, the pour strip ties the foundation and walls together into a monolithic unit through steel rebar that comes out of the footings, tilt panels, and slab.

Floor slabs that will support 250 pounds per square foot (1,222 kilograms per square meter) provide flexibility for buildings with changing tenants and unpredictable floor loading requirements. This level of floor loading capability can accommodate different weight loads and a wide variety of users over time.

Wall Systems. Three basic wall systems are in use today: concrete tilt-up, masonry, and preengineered metal panelized construction. Tilt-wall construction now dominates industrial building construction in most parts of the country, although masonry is still popular for smaller buildings and in parts of the Northeast where unions have helped to slow the adoption of tilt-wall construction.

Concrete tilt-up buildings are constructed of large concrete panels poured on top of the slab, tilted up, and fastened together to create the walls of the building. Each panel is engineered with rebar and various steel fasteners to connect it with the adjacent panels and roof structure. These panels, which can contain windows and doors, are generally six to eight inches (15 to 20 centimeters) thick, 16 to 24 feet (4.8 to 7.3 meters) wide, and as tall as the building (20 to 40 feet [6 to 12 meters]). This type of construction is very economical, because the panels act as the structural support system, the interior wall, and the exterior wall. To prepare for tenants, paint is applied to inside walls, and the outside face of the wall is painted, sandblasted, or finished with gravel to provide a textured appearance. Concrete tilt-up construction is one of the fastest methods of building industrial buildings, because the walls are all poured at once, and, as soon as they are dry, they can all be put in place in one or two days.

The wall subcontractor begins by laying the gravel or finish stone inside the form and then pouring the concrete on top of it. The subcontractor should ensure a uniform consistency of the concrete aggregate, or the final color or density of the wall will be inconsistent. Samples of concrete are taken during the pour and broken after seven and 28 days to test the concrete's strength. Curing time can be hastened if necessary by adding chemicals to the concrete mix. In seven to 10 days, the concrete panels are cured, at which time they can be lifted into place on the foundation.

The height of the wall and the kind of exterior aggregate used determine the thickness of the wall. Window and door openings are framed directly into the wall panels. On a 24-foot-wide (7.3-meter) panel, at least two feet (0.6 meter) of concrete is needed on each end of a continuous window to prevent cracking. Bottoms of windows on office spaces should be no more than 36 inches (0.9 meter) from the floor.

After the walls are lifted into place, they may be welded or bolted (bolting requires considerable accuracy) to small steel plates that are cast into both the wall and the foundation before the concrete is poured. Temporary steel braces are used to support the walls immediately after they are lifted into place and before roof braces are installed.

Panels often break during lifting. James Westling, head of construction for O'Donnell, Armstrong, Brigham, and Partners, Irvine, California, consults a panel

hardware engineer who supplies hardware that is cast into the walls to prevent breakage. The panels are sometimes braced with *strongbacks*—steel braces applied to the panels while they are being lifted and later removed. In masonry construction, heavy concrete blocks serve as both walls and support for the roof. Sometimes a layer of face brick is added on the outside of the concrete block. High-quality blocks with sufficient steel reinforcement should be used to support the ceiling joists and roof. Longer expanses of wall should contain expansion joints to prevent cracking, and weep holes should be provided at regular intervals along the bottom course of bricks to allow the brick cavities to breathe and drain properly.

Generally, a block eight inches deep by 16 inches wide by eight inches high (20.5 by 41 by 20.5 centimeters) is the basic unit of construction. Rebar can be laid in the hollow cavities of the blocks to provide additional strength. Windows and doors can be constructed using metal or wood headers. Many styles of concrete blocks are available in different textures and colors.

The preengineered metal panelized system is fabricated in a factory and shipped to the site to be erected. It consists of a steel post-and-frame structural system and a metal, panelized skin attached to the structural frame. The panels can be manufactured with a variety of surfaces, ranging from steel or aluminum skin to an aggregate or enamelized paint finish. Panelized systems offer speedy construction and low costs.

Prefabricated metal buildings, which are now more attractive than they used to be and are designed to the developer's specifications, are available from a number of companies that offer delivery directly to the site. Metal panelized systems are less costly than other types of systems in buildings where the roof beams must support more than just the roof and in which clear-story spans exceed 40 by 80 feet (12 by 24 meters). They are especially popular for traditional manufacturing facilities in which equipment is suspended from the roof.

Roof Systems. The standard industrial roof consists of three layers of tar paper and hot tar topped with a fine aggregate. Special elastic plastics and other materials that provide not only weatherproofing but also often insulation have been created for roofs in recent years. Roofs made of these materials are more expensive but last longer than the five- to seven-year span of a three-ply roof.

Different types of roof systems are popular in different parts of the country. Wood structure systems, for example, dominate industrial construction on the West Coast and throughout much of the Midwest, whereas metal truss systems are more popular in Texas, the South, and on the East Coast. The preferred system is usually the one that is the cheapest in the area.

A wood structure roof system consists of laminated wood beams and girders that support the roof, with four-by eight-foot (1.2- by 2.4-meter) wood and plywood panels. Two- by four-foot (0.6- by 1.2-meter) or larger wood purloins are nailed to four- by eight-foot (1.2- by 2.4-meter) plywood panels on the site and are lifted into place after the wood beam and girders are in place. This system is fast and economical and requires the least amount of materials.

Metal truss systems can be used to span the space between beams and walls. Plywood panels or metal panels form the roof deck. This system can provide larger bay spans than a wood structure. A metal panelized system can span the space between steel beams and girders. Manufactured metal panels are often used with preengineered wall and structure systems.

If the budget allows, some developers prefer to use four-ply built-up roofs that consist of two plies of 15-pound felt, one ply of 30-pound felt, and a 90-pound cap sheet. Others use a three-ply roof that has one layer of 15-pound felt, one ply of 30-pound felt, and a 90-pound cap sheet. A flexible cap sheet is used at all panel joints to allow for movement between panels without breaking the watertight seal.

The connection between the roof and the parapet (the part of the wall that extends above the roof) is also critical. If the parapet is no taller than three feet (0.9 meter), the roofing plies should wrap over the top of the parapet to prevent leaks. An alternative (though less recommended) method is to cast a *reglet,* the female part of a two-part sheet metal flashing that seals the roof to the building wall, into the wall about 18 inches (0.4 meter) above the roof.

Skylights are becoming standard features in warehouses. They can save tenants enormous amounts of money on electricity for lighting. Some electrical companies give rebates or special credits to developers who install not only skylights but also photocells that turn off the electric lights when natural light is adequate to illuminate the facility. In addition to skylights, roof systems must include a roof hatch and ladder to permit roof drains to be cleaned and cleared, air conditioners to be maintained, and the roof to be inspected. Smoke hatches are also required to vent smoke from the building in case of fire.

Building Systems. Power requirements have grown substantially for all industrial uses. Warehousing and manufacturing are becoming more automated; as a result, more machinery and high-tech equipment are needed, entailing a greater need for electrical power.

To support today's power needs and ensure the flexibility to adapt to tomorrow's requirements, a building should be designed to accommodate both warehouse and manufacturing functions, which typically means 1,200 amps of 480/277-volt, three-phase, four-wire power. An underground conduit should be installed so that capacity can be increased if necessary to 2,000 to 2,400 amps by changing the transformer, pulling in cable, and boosting power without major construction costs. Additional power should not be installed at the beginning of construction, however, because it is expensive. The space for future expansion should be provided so that new power can be added when needed.

Today, more and more manufacturers require air conditioning or evaporative cooling, in part because today's systems are more efficient and affordable than a decade ago. Though most warehouse and distribution facilities still do not require air conditioning unless they are handling perishable products, the buildings that serve warehouses may need to be air conditioned.

A big change in life safety systems is the introduction of early suppression, fast response (ESFR) equipment. Although traditional fire sprinkler systems react to a fire that is already burning and are designed to contain the blaze until the fire department arrives, ESFR systems can put the fire out, quickly. ESFR sprinkler heads react when they are exposed to 150°F (66°C) for only 30 seconds and then pour up to six times more water on the fire than traditional sprinklers. Adding ESFR systems to a building is expensive, because the building structure and roof must be precisely configured to accommodate the spacing of sprinkler heads and to prevent interference with the water supply.

General Advice

A metal building frame can be combined with tilt-wall sides or brick to provide a more traditional facade. To construct these combinations, the prefabricated building is lifted onto the finished slab; anchor bolts in the slab must be located so that the walls can be fastened to the foundation. Roofing systems vary depending on the manufacturer. The better systems, which include insulation, can be designed to drain into gutters or over the sides of the building.

In the 1980s, developers began using a combination of steel frame and concrete tilt-up panels to create an appealing look for R&D buildings. They typically involve the use of glass skins on the front and back facades and concrete panels on the sides to provide shear strength. Combining steel with tilt-up walls also saves money on steel.

Interior finishes are more important for R&D/flex buildings than for other types of industrial space. R&D tenants value climate control and comfort; indeed, the developer should treat an R&D building more like office than industrial space. Triple-layer insulating glass may be used to cut down noise near airports or industrial areas.

If the activities in the laboratory or warehouse space generate noise, dust, or toxic fumes, safety features are critical. Air locks may be required to protect the office area from the lab area, because a shared HVAC system would distribute unwanted dust or fumes throughout the entire building. By having two separate HVAC systems, a developer has the flexibility to seal off the laboratory area should future tenants require it.

The most frequent problems encountered in constructing industrial buildings concern drainage and roof leaks. A wall that is too thin or a column that is too small could lead to a sagging roof, which, over time, leads to leaks or roof failure.

Some other common mistakes to avoid during construction include:

- slabs that are not thick enough, causing a slab to be damaged by the crane;
- insufficient wall bracing, causing panels to fall over in high winds;
- failure to preplan the location of utilities under the slab;
- lack of a concrete area for truck and trailer storage;
- insufficient electrical service conduit (if the developer does not provide at least one extra conduit for future service, the slab and outside pavement may have to be torn up to install it later); and
- an undersized fire sprinkler system; if the system is inadequate, some prospective tenants may not be able to obtain fire insurance at competitive rates.

The market for the industrial space determines the type of construction and the quality of finishes. Cost-saving construction tips do not save money in the long run if they make a building less appealing to intended users. Industrial building techniques have been evolving more rapidly than those used for any other type of development. New materials and new systems technology often appear first in industrial structures. Beginning developers should avoid pioneering a new technique alone, but they should be familiar with current alternatives and should not fear innovation as long as experienced contractors and superintendents are working with them.

Financing

The considerations for financing industrial development are essentially the same as those for financing other income property (see Chapter 4). Equity—from the developer or from others—is invested; interim construction money is borrowed until the project is completed and leased. When the project reaches stabilized occupancy as defined in the permanent mortgage agreement, the permanent mortgage takes out (replaces) the construction mortgage. For this last step, industrial property may have an advantage over other income property: some mortgage lenders believe that industrial development is a more stable investment because its market is less volatile than other markets.

The structure of the financing for business parks is likely to be more complex than that for individual buildings, especially if the developer plans to develop both the park and some or all of the buildings in it. Land development frequently involves more than one interim loan. Separate loans for land acquisition, land development, and building construction may be required. A building project, on the other hand, usually relies solely on a construction loan that also covers part of the land acquisition cost.

Equity is required to pay for all predevelopment costs that occur before closing on the property, because construction lenders will not fund construction loans before that event. After closing, equity is still required because loans rarely cover 100 percent of a project's costs.

Interim financing is usually nonamortizing. Funds are drawn monthly to cover a percentage of the current project costs, including interest on the current loan balance. The developer submits draw requests to the construction lender based on construction completed to date. The lender's inspector verifies that the work has been done, and then the lender transfers the money into the developer's project account. The construction loan agreement specifies a deadline for repayment of principal, typically from 12 to 24 months for individual industrial buildings. When conditions for funding the permanent mortgage are met (usually based on the property's producing a given amount of NOI for one or more months), proceeds from the permanent mortgage are used to pay off the construction loan in a simultaneous closing.[20]

For business parks that combine land development with building development, funding of the permanent mortgage can occur after sufficient time has elapsed for lenders to evaluate a project's track record. The improved land is appraised and a loan equal to 65 to 100 percent of the value given, based on payments that can be supported by existing and projected revenue.

Alternatively, when a business park is partially occupied, the developer may use the cash flow from existing tenants to improve the remaining land, thus reducing the need for loans. When a building is sufficiently leased to support the debt service, the permanent lender will fund the long-term mortgage.

Construction and Permanent Loans

For industrial land acquisition and land development loans, a pension fund, insurance company, or commercial bank usually takes the first lien position. It may finance up to 75 percent of the land value and 100 percent of the land development costs, depending on the appraisal of the completed improvements and projected sales revenues.

A real estate investment trust may possibly take a secondary lien position, providing additional funds at rates typically four or five points above prime. This type of joint participation must be prearranged in a single financing agreement.

Construction/lease-up financing is arranged for individual buildings just as for other income property. Commercial banks are the primary sources for construction loans.

Developers should arrange permanent financing only when they plan to lease a building rather than sell it. If they plan to sell the building to an owner/tenant, permanent financing may hinder the sale if the mortgage has onerous prepayment conditions.

Permanent lenders look for the following items in evaluating loan requests:

- existing leases on the property, including lease rates, types of leases, and terms and provisions of the leases;
- financial capabilities and history of tenants; and
- general health of the rental market and how the leases compare with others in the market (if they are above market rates, tenants may leave; if they are below market, the property will have to be held a certain amount of time until the leases expire or rise to market levels).

Typically, industrial property must be 75 to 80 percent leased before a permanent lender will fund the mortgage. When a construction loan is taken out by the permanent mortgage, the title company is given instructions from the permanent lender to establish a title order for the new deed of trust to be recorded. Generally, 24 hours before closing, the entire sum of the permanent loan is placed in escrow in the title company's account. Upon the title company's receipt of a payoff demand and reconveyance from the construction lender, and the necessary funds and instructions from the permanent lender, the title company records the new deed of trust, pays off the construction lender, and records the reconveyance to remove the construction lender's security on the subject property.

Maintaining the value of an asset requires constant evaluation of its functional usefulness, its building systems, and its physical appearance.

Mortgages of 65 to 75 percent of value, subject to a debt service coverage ratio (DCR minus NOI divided by annual debt service) of 1.2 to 1.3, are common. In the early 2000s, cap rates for single-tenant triple net leases on industrial buildings range from 8.5 to 10 percent. The cap rate for multitenant buildings tends to be slightly higher than for single-tenant buildings.[21]

Equity Structure

Equity is always the most difficult piece of the financing puzzle to raise. Developers must use their own cash equity to fund predevelopment costs, due diligence, and other initial expenses. Beginning developers must usually look to family and friends to raise equity for their initial projects. Future tenants can also become partners in a project, an arrangement that provides equity, strength on the financial statement, and preleasing activity. Owners of private companies frequently prefer to own the property

where their company operates. Often, these individuals become joint venture partners, and their companies become building tenants. The equity partners enjoy the benefits of owning real estate and controlling one of the major tenants (their own company). This arrangement also can provide essentially tax-free income to a company owner. The rent paid by an owner's business can be expensed in the same year. The taxable income from the owner's share of that rent is usually more than offset by the owner's business deduction.

Once they establish a track record, however, institutional investors become a viable source of equity. A number of institutional investors look for opportunities to join real estate joint ventures. Although some limit their activities to prime office and retail properties, a number of them actively seek industrial properties and industrial developers to form partnerships. In the late 1990s and early 2000s, national institutional investors included pension funds, university and other private endowment funds, insurance companies, and REITs.

Dealing with Institutional Investors

Raising institutional equity for real estate deals in today's environment presents developers with a whole new set of terms.[22] Ever since Wall Street became a major player in real estate in the wake of the real estate crash of the early 1990s, developers have been faced with a variety of joint venture deal points that are new to them.

Institutional investors include pension funds, insurance companies, foundations, Wall Street funds, credit companies, and other entities that represent large pools of capital. They are distinguished from noninstitutional investors—primarily private investors—by their size and institutional character. In most cases, institutional investors act as fiduciaries for individuals, corporations, and other investors, large and small, who place their money with the institutions to invest on their behalf. Or, as in the case of insurance companies, they have funds to invest from policyholders or depositors representing many different accounts. If retirement funds are involved, institutional investors are often subject to the requirements of the Employee Retirement Income Security Act of 1974 (ERISA), which governs retirement and pension fund investments.[23] Fund managers are likely to raise money directly or indirectly through Wall Street in public and private securities offerings.

Institutional investors play a larger role today than they did in the 1980s, thanks in part to the real estate crash of the late 1980s. When money became very scarce for any kind of real estate in the wake of the S&L crisis and bankruptcy of many banks in the late 1980s, institutional investors—especially vulture funds and investors searching for high-yield investments—were among the few buyers for the problem properties and loans. Those investments were sold in unprecedented quantities by the Resolution Trust Corporation (RTC), the government entity established to work out the problems caused by the crash. During this period, Wall Street took advantage of the opportunity for high yields to become the major source of capital for the portfolios of properties and loans sold by the RTC to investors.

Vulture funds, developers, and other buyers of the portfolios, working with Wall Street capital, were introduced to a whole new set of deal structures. Although the structures themselves had been around for some time, this period marked the beginning for many real estate developers and investors to be introduced to the new structures. In particular, faced with the high-yield requirements of mezzanine debt (second and third lien debt that gave property buyers 90 to 95 percent financing), developers were introduced to the concept of *lookback returns, tiered hurdle rates of return,* and *promotes.* In essence, these deal structures shift a significant portion of the cash flow benefits from the developer to the financial partner by giving the financial partner priority for achieving certain levels of return before the developer receives a significant share of the profit.

Joint Venture Deal Points

Pension fund advisers like AEW Capital Management and Heitman introduced the concept of lookback returns in the 1980s as a means of protecting the rate of return they earned as the capital partner in joint ventures with developers. In their capacity as advisers, they act as investment managers on behalf of pension funds, endowment funds, and other institutional investors. The lookback return helps to ensure that the developer—the *operating partner*—has an incentive to manage the property carefully and to spend money on maintaining the building, because the great majority of his profit is not paid until the property is ultimately sold. A typical deal structure provides for the following priorities of cash flow distribution: 1) the return of capital, 2) a preferred return, 3) a lookback return to the capital partner, 4) an equivalent return to the operating partner, and 5) a split of the remaining profit.

In the early 1980s, operating partners often had no cash equity in the deal.[24] By the late 1980s, however, they typically had to invest at least some amount of cash equity along with the capital partner. If the operating partner were required to invest, say, 10 percent of the total equity required, its equity was treated the same as the capital partner's equity for Priority 1, return of capital, and Priority 2, preferred return. This treatment, called *pari passu,* gave the operating partner's equity the same status as the capital partner's equity. It was a point of negotiation, and it was not uncommon for the operating partner's equity to be subordinated to the capital partner's equity, in which case the operating partner received back his equity and preferred return after the capital partner received his equity and preferred return.[25]

Larger operating partners like Trammell Crow were treated on a pari passu basis, while smaller operating partners with less negotiating power were more likely to be treated on a subordinated basis (that is, their equity was subordinated to the capital partner's). Suppose, for example, that the operating partner puts up 10 percent of the equity and the capital partner 90 percent. If the preferred dividend is 10 percent and the lookback return is 15 percent, the operating partner and the capital partner simultaneously receive their capital back and the preferred return in proportion to their share of the equity. Under a *subordinated* arrangement, however, once they have received these monies, the next distribution of cash flow goes to the capital partner until he receives the lookback return of 15 percent. After that amount is paid, the operating partner may receive a catch-up return equal to 15 percent on his equity, and then the remaining cash flows may be split, say, 50/50. In this structure, the operating partner earns most of his compensation only after he delivers to the capital partner the returns projected in the original pro forma.

Tiered hurdle rates of return and *promotes* entered the developer's lexicon in the early 1990s when Wall Street became a major source of capital. The word *promote* does not have a standard definition among real estate operators, but on Wall Street and among institutional investors, it is defined as the difference between the operating partner's capital contribution and his share of the profit.[26] For example, if he puts up 10 percent of the capital in a 50/50 deal, then his equity is "promoted" by 40 percent. Basically, the equity is promoted to receive a disproportionate share of the returns. The promote is in essence compensation for sweat equity—putting the deal together and managing it. The amount of the promote becomes the first thing the capital partner asks (or demands)—the lower, the better.

Tiered hurdle rates of return provide a sliding scale under which the operating partner's promote goes up as successively higher hurdle rates of return are achieved. For example, the operating partner may receive 20 percent and the capital partner 80 percent of the cash flow up to the point where the capital partner realizes, say, a 15 percent IRR. Once that is achieved, the operating partner's share may go up to 30 percent and the capital partner's share 70 percent up to the point where the capital partner receives a 20 percent IRR. Above that, the split may be 40/60 or 50/50. In this way, Wall Street ensures that the capital partners achieve high target rates of return—something that they were able to achieve during the tight capital market of the early 1990s. As the real estate capital market normalized in the mid-1990s, Wall Street and other institutional capital providers were less able to demand very high tiered rates of return in excess of 20 percent, but the basic approach has endured to become a common deal structure with institutional partners.

The major deal points in joint ventures with institutional financial partners can be boiled down to nine main issues: 1) the operating partner's cash equity, 2) the preferred return, 3) profit share, 4) lookback return, 5) pari passu equity payback, 6) guarantees, 7) management control, 8) fees to the operating partner, and 9) fees to the institutional partner. Tradeoffs are possible among the different deal points, and the best choice for the operating partner depends on his needs and priorities. It is a mistake, however, to focus on the operating partner's share of the profit, because his actual return depends more on the investor's preferences and lookback returns and the priorities of payback than the profit split. The only way to calculate the partners' expected returns is to model the deal and to compute the operating partner's return and capital partner's return under different cash flow scenarios.[27]

Negotiating Risk

The negotiation over major deal points primarily concerns allocating risk—who takes what risk? The institutional investor tries to shift as much risk as possible to the operating partner, and vice versa.

Deal Size and Flow. One important issue is future deal flow. Charles Wu says that Charlesbank Capital Partners normally would not consider a deal as small as $3 million, but when the deal initiates a new relationship with an operating partner who can generate many more deals, it is willing to spend the time to underwrite a smaller than average investment. The prospect of a number of deals from a major local developer makes the effort worthwhile.[28]

Clawback. Another important issue is the pooling of deals with an operating partner. Charlesbank insists that all deals with a single operating partner be pooled and subject to a *clawback*. A clawback gives the financial partner the ability to reclaim profits paid to the operating partner in one deal if a subsequent deal performs poorly. Without the pooling, Wu says, "the operating partner has an incentive to 'swing for the fences' every time, because he gets the promote on good deals while Charlesbank eats the losses on the bad deals."

In arrangements involving pools of property with one operating partner, Charlesbank arranges an amount of money for the operating partner to invest over a two-year period called a *program*. The pool of properties subject to the clawback is determined by the size of the program. For example, the program may call for Charlesbank to fund, say, $30 million in equity over two years. If the full $30 million has not been invested within two years, the program duration may be extended or a new pool may be started. The operating partner would prefer to start a new pool immediately to limit the properties subject to the clawback.

Dead Deal Cost. Another important deal point is the *dead deal cost*—what happens when money is spent chasing an acquisition that does not go through. Due diligence costs on a major purchase can easily run up to $100,000. Who should bear the loss? One would expect that if the financial partner puts up 75 percent of the profit, he should bear 75 percent of the loss. Charlesbank, however, requires the operating partner to pay two-thirds of any dead deal costs, because it wants the operating partner to be careful with the money spent looking for deals.

Control. Among the major deal points, control is perhaps the most important. Financial partners have learned that the hardest part of correcting a problem property is often getting control of the asset. The buy/sell clause is intended to deal with this risk. "Capital partners love the clause; operating partners hate it," according to Wu. The operating partner is concerned that the capital partner will activate the buy/sell clause at a time when capital is scarce and steal the deal from the operating partner. The capital partner is concerned that the operating partner has much more information than he has. He may trigger a buy/sell knowing that a major tenant has decided to leave or that one is about to be signed. The operating partner's protection that the buy/sell clause will not be used indiscriminately is the financial partner's reputation for using them rarely.

John Williams also emphasizes the importance of control for the financial partner. The loan documents must let the financial partner pay the senior debt to prevent foreclosure. They also must let them come in and run the property if necessary.[29]

Deal Structure Illustrated

Figure A presents a deal structure with a three-tier hurdle rate of return. To simplify the illustration, the investor puts up all the equity—$100,000. (If the operating partner puts up part of the equity, the total cash flow for each tier would not change, assuming that total equity remains $100,000. The cash flows to the investor would simply be divided between the capital partner and the developer in proportion to their share of the $100,000 total equity.) Out of initial cash flows, he receives his money back and a 10 percent cumulative preferred return on all unreturned equity. After he receives the preferred return (because it is cumulative, it is accrued if cash is unavailable in the current year to pay it), profits are split 80/20 (with the investor receiving 80 percent) up until he receives a 15 percent IRR on all cash invested. For undistributed cash above a 15 percent IRR and less than 20 percent IRR to the investor, the profit split is 70/30. After the investor receives a 20 percent IRR, profit above that is split 50/50.

Figure B shows the computations and resulting cash flows for this deal. The overall IRR is 38.8 percent on the initial $100,000 investment. Positive cash flows total $290,000, for a net total of $190,000.

Line 13 in Figure B shows that after the equity and 10 percent preferred return

are paid, $161,900 cash flow is available for distribution. The first-tier distribution (Line 20) gives the investor 80 percent of the cash flow up to a 15 percent IRR, which is $17,533 ($9,520 in Year 2 and $8,013 in Year 3).

Line 37 in Figure B computes the cash flows required to give the investor the Tier 2 hurdle of 20 percent IRR. Because the totals for Years 1 and 2 consume all the available cash, the total to the investor for those years (Line 38) does not change. The shortfall at the end of Year 3 of $25,180 plus 20 percent interest, however, gives a required payoff amount of $30,216. The investor has already been allocated $8,013 from Tier 1, leaving a balance of $22,203. The total cash flows to the investor that give him a 20 percent IRR appear in Line 48.

Line 54 shows that after paying the investor $30,216 and the operating partner $11,519 in Year 4 for Tiers 1 and 2 combined, a balance of $108,265 is still available for distribution in Tier 3. Because the deal structure gives the operating partner 50 percent of the profit above 20 percent IRR, the $108,265 is divided 50/50.

The first-tier distribution gives the investor 80 percent of the cash flow up to a 15 percent IRR (Line 21), which

amounts to $17,533 ($9,520 in Year 2 and $8,013 in Year 3). The second tier gives the investor 70 percent of the cash flow up to a 20 percent IRR, which amounts to an additional $22,203 (the second-tier IRR is computed in Line 59). The final IRR for the investor on all three tiers of cash flow is 29.6 percent (Line 61) on total cash flows of $121,969.

The operating partner's IRR is infinite. His total cash is $68,031. Note that the sum of $121,969 and $68,031 for the investor and the operating partner equals the total cash flow available (Line 3) of $190,000.

In this illustration, the operating partner receives his profit share concurrently with the capital partner—a pari passu arrangement in which the operating partner's equity is treated exactly like the capital partner's equity. They thus receive the same hurdle rates of return and priority to distribution of cash flow. In a non–pari passu arrangement, the lookback return gives the investors *all* the profit up until they receive the hurdle IRR for that tier. After that occurrence, the operating partner receives his share of the profit for that tier. This construction places the financial partner ahead of the operating partner in receiving any share of the profit. ∎

---

figure A
Three-Tier Hurdle Rate of Return

Investor's Equity	$100,000
Investor's Preferred Return	10% cumulative
Tier 1: Profit sharing until investor receives a 15 percent IRR	
Investor	80%
Operating partner	20%
Tier 2: Profit sharing when investor's return is from 15 to 20 percent IRR	
Investor	70%
Operating partner	30%
Tier 3: Profit sharing after investor receives a 20 percent IRR	
Investor	50%
Operating partner	50%

Lookback Return with Sliding Profit Split

	Cash Flows to Investors	Input	IRR	Total	Year 0	1	2	3	4
1	**Cash Flows to Investors**	Input	IRR	Total	0	1	2	3	4
2									
3	Cash Flows		38.8%	190,000	(100,000)	0	50,000	90,000	150,000
4									
5	Beginning Balance				0	100,000	110,000	71,000	0
6	Equity Investment			100,000	100,000	0	0	0	0
7	Preferred Return	10%		28,100	0	10,000	11,000	7,100	0
8	Subtotal				100,000	110,000	121,000	78,100	0
9	Preferred Return Paid			18,100		0	11,000	7,100	0
10	Equity Reduction			110,000		0	39,000	71,000	0
11	Ending Balance				100,000	110,000	71,000	0	0
12									
13	**Cash Flow for Distribution**			161,900				11,900	150,000
14									
15	**Cash Flows to Investor—Tier 1**								
16	Equity			(100,000)	(100,000)	0	0	0	0
17	Preferred Return Paid			18,100		0	11,000	7,100	0
18	Equity Repayment			110,000		0	39,000	71,000	0
19	Subtotal			128,100		0	50,000	78,100	0
20	Profit Share 1	80%		17,533		0	9,520	8,013	
21	IRR and Total Cash Flow to Investor—Tier 1		15.0%	45,633	(100,000)	0	50,000	87,620	8,013
22	Total to Developer—Tier 1	20%		4,383		0	0	2,380	2,003
23	Total			50,016	(100,000)	0	50,000	90,000	10,016
24									
25	**Lookback Return 1**	15%			(100,000)	115,000	132,250	94,588	8,013
26	Total to Investor—Tier 1					0	50,000	87,620	8,013
27	Shortfall to Reach Lookback			204,218		115,000	82,250	6,967	0
28									
29	**Recap Tier 1**								
30	Cash Flow for Distribution			161,900				11,900	150,000
31	Investor's Profit Share 1	80%		17,533				9,520	8,013
32	Developer's Profit Share 1	20%		4,383				2,380	2,003
33	Total for Tier 1			21,916				11,900	10,016
34									
35	Cash Available for Tier 2			139,984			0	0	139,984
36									
37	**Lookback Return 2**	20%		307,016	(100,000)	120,000	144,000	112,800	30,216
38	Total to Investor—Tier 1					0	50,000	87,620	8,013
39	Shortfall to Reach Lookback					120,000	94,000	25,180	22,203
40									
41	Investor's Profit Share 2	70%		22,203			0	0	22,203
42	Developer's Profit Share 2	30%		9,516			0	0	9,516
43	Total Profit Share - Tier 2			31,719			0	0	31,719
44									
45	**Recap to Investor—Tiers 1 & 2**								
46	Total to Investor—Tier 1						50,000	87,620	8,013
47	Total to Investor—Tier 2			22,203			0	0	22,203
48	Total Required for Tier 2 IRR		20.0%	67,836	(100,000)	0	50,000	87,620	30,216
49									
50	**Recap Tier 2**			0					
51	Total Cash Flow			190,000	(100,000)	0	50,000	90,000	150,000
52	Total to Investor—1 & 2			67,836	(100,000)	0	50,000	87,620	30,216
53	Total to Developer—1 & 2			13,899			0	2,380	11,519
54	**Balance for Distribution**			108,265	0	0	0	0	108,265
55	Investor's Profit Share 3	50%		54,133				0	54,133
56	Developer's Profit Share 3	50%		54,133				0	54,133
57									
58	**Summary to Investor**			0					
59	Total Paid to Investor—1 & 2		20.0%	67,836	(100,000)	0	50,000	87,620	30,216
60	Investor's Profit Share 3			54,133					54,133
61	Total		29.6%	121,969	(100,000)	0	50,000	87,620	84,349
62									
63	**Summary to Developer**								
64	Total to Developer—1 & 2			13,899			0	2,380	11,519
65	Total to Developer—3			54,133			0	0	54,133
66	Total			68,031			0	2,380	65,651
67									
68	Grand Total for Investor and Developer		38.8%	190,000	(100,000)	0	50,000	90,000	150,000

The operating partner is naturally concerned about the events that will allow the financial partner to take over control and wants to avoid a situation where the financial partner takes over merely when the property is performing poorly. Acacia does not create economic defaults whereby a property is in default if it is less than, say, 90 percent occupied at rents of $15.00 per square foot per month ($1,935 per square meter per year). But they want to be able to insist that necessary capital improvements such as a new roof are being made. In Acacia's buy/sell agreement, the party who buys the property has 60 days to close—enough time for the operating partner to raise the cash. If he cannot close at the buy/sell price, however, the other party can buy him out at 80 percent of the price.

Cross Collateralization. Lenders like to cross collateralize properties; developers do not. If a lender is not getting paid on one property, it can foreclose on other cross collateralized properties to satisfy any deficit—which of course puts other properties at risk. Because they hold an equity position with the operating partner in their deals, institutional investors like Acacia do not like to see cross collateralization on permanent loans.

Lockout Provisions. Lockout provisions prevent the borrower on a mortgage from paying it off within a given period of time. Lockouts are particularly unpopular with operating partners, because they prevent them from refinancing a property to pull out some or all of their equity. Unfortunately, lockouts are a common—almost required—provision in conduit loans from Wall Street. Conduits represent an increasingly large source of mortgage capital funds, including mortgages originated by banks and mortgage brokers. Conduits provide capital to mortgage brokers and other mortgage originators under predefined terms. The mortgages are aggregated by Wall Street and sold to investors in the CMBS market.

Lockout provision are popular for CMBS investors because they ensure that the underlying mortgages will not be paid off during the lockout period, thus providing an assured period of return to the investor at the interest rate on the CMBS bond. In portfolio purchases of multiple buildings, lockout provisions are often unacceptable to the operating partner, who may want to sell off individual buildings to finance the rest of the transaction. If he were to sell the individual buildings, he would need to retire their mortgages (which by contract are not assumable)—an event prevented by the lockout.

Strategy and Replacement Cost. Capital partners focus on the acquisition strategy for any pool of investments. In the early 1990s, the most popular strategy was buying properties at prices well below replacement cost. Investors reasoned that no new product would be built until rents reached a level that supported new building construction (at replacement cost). As long as properties were being acquired below replacement cost, investors would have an advantage compared with new buildings, as they could be rented out profitably at lower rents. When the purchase cost–to–replacement cost

ratio became popular, land value was zero because the replacement cost referred only to improvements. Because land cost usually amounts to 15 to 50 percent of the total cost of a project, bargain hunters in the early 1990s were in fact buying properties at considerable discounts relative to new buildings.

In the late 1990s, Acacia Capital was one of a number of investors who established funds to invest in value-added real estate opportunities—properties that have conditions that must be corrected, such as high vacancies, below-market leases, or needed renovations. Such investments are risky and represent only a small portion of the endowments Acacia represents. These investments are considered to incur risk comparable with venture capital funds—high risk, high return. To achieve target returns in the high teens and low twenties (IRRs above 20 percent), the investments have relatively short duration. IRRs rise the shorter the time the money is invested. Acacia's average fund lasts for three and one-half to four years. To achieve the high returns, the focus is on the ratio of purchase price to replacement cost. As prices normalized in most markets, it became harder and harder to find properties at bargain prices. When the purchase price is equal to replacement cost, there is no advantage over new buildings and the higher target yields are not likely to be attainable. Strategies that work under certain market conditions are not appropriate when conditions change.

Marketing

Marketing an industrial project, like other types of real estate, is a multistep process that revolves around creating an identity or niche for the development, identifying target users, convincing them that the space meets their needs, and negotiating the terms of the lease or sale.

Industrial developers should start approaching potential tenants as soon as they option a site or consider developing a site already in inventory. A low-key but directed approach that takes advantage of informal contacts often works best. Targeted firms may range from major national companies to regional firms to local firms to any combination of the three. The fact that a high-quality company is attracted to the site at the outset helps to launch a park or multitenant building; the initial tenant's prestige sets the tone for the rest of the project. Developers usually begin the marketing campaign by exploiting their existing contacts, but they should also contact key brokers for leads on possible seed tenants. Because the project is still in the conceptual stage, developers will have to sell the project themselves and persuade initial tenants that the future building will suit their needs.

As development progresses, developers proceed with other aspects of the marketing program—creating a marketing plan, establishing a budget, preparing marketing materials, and creating a leasing program through in-house resources or with external real estate brokers. The marketing strategy and the tone set in printed materials must reflect the goals of the developers and target the types of tenants indicated by the detailed market analysis. Care must be taken to avoid excessive and unnecessary costs for advertising and promotion.

Los Angeles developer Gerald Katell says that local brokers tend to be the best source of market information. "They know better than market analysts who specific tenants are likely to be. You want to try to market your project to a specific type of user." Prospective tenants—users that need more space or a different type of space—often come from adjacent properties. "You should work outward from your property in concentric circles," advises Katell. Local chambers of commerce also may provide leads or find potential tenants for a project.[30]

Beginning developers can sometimes turn their lack of experience into an advantage for marketing purposes. Small developers can claim more hands-on involvement and can give more personal attention to tenants. Their costs tend to be lower because they have lower overhead than large, established development firms.

Marketing Strategy

A successful marketing program requires a clear strategy addressing what the developer is seeking in terms of types and sizes of tenants, rental rates, lease terms and conditions, and the length of the lease-up period. Marketing goals should be grounded in the realities of

A well-designed entrance to an industrial development is essential to the marketing effort.

the marketplace as determined by market analysis and any subsequent changes in supply, demand, and the competition. They must also reflect the business objectives of the owners and investors. For example, depending on their exit strategy, some investors might prefer to emphasize short-term value and thus rapid lease-up, while others might prefer to hold out for opportunities for longer leases or institutional-quality tenants that can add prestige and value when the project is sold.

Resources devoted to implementing the marketing plan must be commensurate with marketing goals. A first-year marketing budget generally ranges from 4 to 5 percent of a proposed project's anticipated gross revenues. The developer should keep in mind that the entire marketing budget must be adequate to cover the entire marketing period, not just the flurry of marketing activity that usually accompanies a project's opening.

Although the major elements of a marketing program for an industrial development are fairly straightforward, it can be difficult to come up with a hard and fast estimate of marketing and leasing expenses early in the development process. A rough estimate can be made of how much should be budgeted by compiling a comprehensive list of possible marketing activities and preparing a reasonable cost estimate for each item. The compensation scheme for marketing agents and the degree of reliance on outside brokers are important variables in marketing costs, although fees for agents and brokers typically are separate line items in the budget.

Marketing Materials

Two documents are essential to a successful marketing program: a technical services package and a sales brochure. The following discussion applies primarily to full-scale business parks, but developers of individual buildings should also have similar information available for prospective tenants.

Technical Services Package. The developer gives the technical services package to brokers. The package consists of statistical data describing the project's target market and includes information relating to population growth and other demographic statistics, statutory taxes, real estate taxes, sales taxes, interstate commerce trucking zones and rates, and public services. The package should also include information about utilities such as typical water and sewer dimensions, capacity, static pressure, and design flows as well as information on fire protection services and requirements, electrical capacity, and the name and frequency of the rail carrier, if any. The technical services package also addresses:

- details of protective covenants;
- development constraints, including setbacks, landscaping requirements, and exterior building materials;
- procedures for architectural approvals for tenant-built structures;
- locations of and requirements for parking and service areas;
- location and design of signage;

- permitted and nonpermitted uses;
- storage requirements; and
- procedures for dealing with objectionable situations such as noise, odor, vibrations, and smoke.

All procedures should be explained in a positive manner. It should be clear to prospective tenants that the restrictions will benefit their property and the overall character of the industrial park. The information may be summarized in a small pamphlet that the broker can give to potential clients.

The Sales Brochure. The sales brochure describes the ownership, location, and distinctive features of the project. Usually prepared with the help of a public relations or advertising firm, brochures usually consist of a nine- by 12-inch (23- by 30.5-centimeter) jacket with single-page literature in the jacket pockets. This design allows the contents to be updated without completely revising and reprinting the brochure. The sales brochure should include the following information:

- the developer/owner's and manager's track record, with information on previous projects;
- a list of anchor tenants;
- overall development plan that identifies the preliminary parcel configuration and proposed road network;
- technical building information;
- relevant site data, including information on utilities and infrastructure;
- a location map showing the relationship of the project to the region, immediate community, and road and rail networks;
- a detailed map showing access to the site and the immediate neighborhood; and
- a summary of community characteristics drawn from the market studies and other sources.

The quality and thus the cost of the brochure needed for successful marketing vary from place to place. In intensely competitive markets and for projects that the developer wishes to position as first class, more expensive four-color glossy presentations are warranted. In less competitive markets, black and white brochures may suffice.

Brokers

Whether or not the developer should sign an exclusive arrangement with a single broker depends on local practice. In some communities, exclusive arrangements are essential for gaining the necessary attention of any one brokerage firm, especially for smaller projects. In other communities, such arrangements are harmful, as they encourage other brokers to steer clients away from the project. In markets where competitive brokerage activity is strong, another method of marketing an industrial project may be to collaborate with the local brokerage community through an open listing. Because this informal system involves no formal agreements between devel-

oper and broker, it is important to keep brokers informed about the project and assure them that they will receive fair and timely financial remuneration as a reward for closing transactions with prospective clients.

Industrial brokers' commissions typically are expressed as a percentage of rental income. Rental income is specified in the lease and can be defined in a variety of ways, including net rent, rent plus expenses, and rent plus a portion or all of the fully amortized tenant improvements. Generally, the commission structure calls for a declining percentage of income for the later years of a lease term, usually after the fifth year. Half the amount is paid when the lease is signed and half when the tenant moves in.

Any exclusive arrangement should hold the broker accountable for promotion and sales. Inquiries from clients, direct contacts, sales presentations, and other activities should be monitored monthly.

Leads for prospects can come from a number of sources. Developers should hold regular meetings or lunches with the brokerage community to keep brokers informed of new developments, modified pricing, and current sales or leases, and they should offer regular tours. Developers should mail brochures to clients, industry contacts, and brokers known to them in other communities in the region. And they should maintain close contact with local and state economic development agencies, public departments in the community, utilities and railroads, planning commissions, and redevelopment agencies.

Advertising usually begins with heavy initial exposure in the media and then a steady, consistent marketing program to keep the project in the public's mind. Spot advertising in trade journals helps to establish an image and maintain visibility.

Leasing

Prospective industrial tenants focus on three major concerns: *effective* rent, location, and building design (especially loading areas) and amenities.

Tenants ultimately focus on the effective rent—their costs per square foot after all concessions have been taken into account (see Chapter 5). In multitenant R&D buildings, tenants focus on the costs shared with other tenants. Leases for single-tenant buildings typically are triple net or net-net. In the case of triple net leases, the tenant takes care of everything; for net-net leases, the landlord is responsible for maintaining the structure of the building—the foundations, the walls, and the roof.[31] Leases in multitenant buildings typically provide for gross rent; they resemble those for office buildings in which the landlord is responsible for building operations.

Individual tenant spaces are generally metered separately so that each tenant pays its own utilities. In addition, each tenant pays its share of common area expenses, which are allocated based on square footage. In tight markets, the developer usually can negotiate annual increases in rent based on the consumer price index. Lease terms typically range from three to five years, although two-year terms are not uncommon.

Tenant improvement allowances for office space in industrial facilities vary according to building type. The allowance is usually a small amount, say $15.00 per square foot ($160 per square meter), which the tenant can supplement if it wants.

Industrial developers should try to avoid certain lease clauses in their lease agreements:

- Clauses that require developers to rebuild the building in the event of an uninsured loss are less desirable than those that provide the option to terminate the lease.
- Rights to renew leases should be limited. Every tenant wants a five-year option to renew a five-year lease with preset ceilings on increases in rental rates.
- Rights to expand into adjacent space should be limited. Small tenants may be refused such rights altogether. Developers may give a right of first refusal to large tenants when space becomes available.
- Developers never should agree to hold space vacant by giving an unqualified right to expand into new space after a certain number of years (for example, 40,000 square feet [3,720 square meters] now, 20,000 square feet [1,860 square meters] more in five years). If a compromise must be made, developers may agree not to lease a certain space for more than a three- or five-year term. If the parties agree to such a constraint on a particular space, however, finding a tenant for that space may be difficult. For example, if the tenant in the expansion space signs a three-year lease with a two-year option, the space may need to be held vacant for the last two years.
- Short-term leases (say, for only two years) and options to terminate a lease for any reason may make financing difficult, if not impossible. Major tenants often want a right to terminate the lease if a condemnation takes place or if access to the property is impaired.
- In California, smart lessees try to negotiate a limit on tax increases so that, if the building is sold, the tenant does not pay the increase in taxes that occurs automatically under Proposition 13. A possible compromise is to limit the number of sales in a ten-year period that can raise the tenant's property taxes.

David Hasbrouck says that landlords have become much more savvy in recent years. "They do not want to pay a broker on lease options now. It has created a lot of problems in the past, especially on long-term leases with options. A tenant representative has to be very careful. There has been a shift to NNN leases with landlord-specific forms, especially for newer buildings. A tenant has to pay for everything on a NNN lease. They may not have protection against an increase in tax and insurance bases as the result of a sale. Even on a gross lease, a tenant may have to pay an impound for a change in tax basis."[32]

The abandoned United Shoe Machinery Corporation building in Beverly, Massachusetts, was turned into a $40 million office and R&D complex complete with a coffee shop and on-site elementary school.

Izzy Eichenstein points out that many industrial tenants lease older buildings. One of the favorite clauses for landlords in this case is as-is condition. Tenants have to be very careful, because maintenance of older buildings can be costly. "Lease forms have changed considerably over the last ten years. Both tenants and landlords take much more care about leases now—but mistakes still happen."[33]

Property Management

Industrial developers have become much more proactive in the management of their buildings and business parks in recent years. This attention is in response to increasingly complex operation of industrial real estate and greater concern about long-term value.

Management of industrial properties involves three stages. Priorities change during each stage.

Stage 1: Development

During the development phase, the developer's major tasks are to coordinate the installation of infrastructure and to attract seed tenants. Often, the local community is concerned about environmental issues, and, to promote the project, the developer also must display such concern. Restrictive covenants not only protect the project but also help to reassure the community that potential undesirable side effects will not be permitted.

Because of noise, dirt, and increased traffic during the development phase, the developer must foster the image of a good neighbor. Failure to respond to the community's concerns can result in time-consuming delays in approvals and inspections. On-site management is a necessity. Timely completion of infrastructure is vitally important to the seed tenant—the one that establishes an overall identity for the project. If seed tenants encounter delays in occupancy because of poor management, they are likely to convey their dissatisfaction to other potential tenants.

Gruma Corporation is the largest manufacturer of corn flour tortillas in the United States. It uses the facility in Commerce, California, for the manufacture and distribution of corn and flour tortillas under its Mission Foods and Guerrero brand names. It is the second largest plant of its kind in the United States, producing approximately 14 million tortillas a day. Operations run nonstop, 24 hours a day throughout the year.

SCIF Portfolio III, LLC, acquired the property in 1998, with the Southern California Industrial Fund (SCIF) as sponsor and developer. SCIF was founded in 1996 to acquire and reposition value-added industrial assets in southern California and to take advantage of the rebound in the real estate market at that time. It was formed by the Los Angeles–based Magellan Group, its managing member, and the Orange County–based Bascom Group. Magellan was founded in 1990 by Martin Slusser and Kevin Staley, who were partners at the Trammell Crow Company during the 1980s.

The Market
The greater Los Angeles industrial market contains more than 874 million square feet (81.2 million square meters), making it the second largest concentration of industrial space in the nation. The Commerce industrial submarket is one of the most important areas of the Los Angeles basin, consisting of approximately 83 million square feet (7.7 million square meters) of space and boasting one of the strongest infill locations in southern California. In the early 2000s, like the rest of southern California real estate, the industrial market in Commerce enjoyed high rents and an extremely low vacancy rate.

The market is strategically located for distribution, being centrally located within the region's main freeways—Santa Ana (I-5), Long Beach (I-710), Pomona (Route 60), and San Gabriel (I-605). They

provide direct east/west and north/south access to all markets in Los Angeles, Riverside, San Bernardino, and Orange counties. Proximity to the city of Los Angeles provides the advantage of servicing the Los Angeles Basin while retaining easy access to the outlying distribution areas. The location also provides easy access to the ports of Los Angeles and Long Beach. The Alameda Corridor, completed in 2002, enables the rapid transportation of goods from the ports to infill distribution hubs such as Commerce.

Gruma Corporation's Space Needs
The Gruma Corporation has been at the Commerce location since 1989. It had been running operations at this facility from three different buildings in the same city block.

The center of operations was a 150,000-square-foot (14,000-square-meter) building at 5505 East Olympic Boulevard that served as the manufacturing plant. This building, which is 17 feet (5 meters) clear, was erected in 1968 and extensively refurbished in 1989. It has an ordinary

hazard sprinkler system. Despite its age and low clear height, it has an extremely functional layout for manufacturing and is certified by the American Bakery Association.

A second building, at 5533 East Olympic Boulevard, is 27,408 square feet (2,550 square meters), has a low clear height, and is about 30 percent office space. Gruma used this building for administrative offices and for the warehousing and distribution of its Guerrero brand tortillas.

Management had been contemplating ways to consolidate operations for quite some time to produce and distribute goods more efficiently. The existing configuration, spread over three buildings, was a significant obstacle to the goal of improving efficiency, and the situation had become especially significant as the existing lease neared the end of its term in late 1998.

The circumstances triggered a debate about whether the company should re-

The office entry for the new building at the Gruma Corporation facility in Commerce, California.

Tenant Input Assumptions

Rent Roll

Tenant Name	Suite	Lease Type	Total Area (Square Feet)	Start Date	Term/ Expiration	Base/ Minimum Rent	Unit of Measure	Rent Change	Reimbur- sements	Leasing Cost	Upon Expiration
Main Building	B	Industrial	150,000	1/1997	10/2002	48,051	Amount per Month		Net		Option
Main Building	B	Option	150,000	11/2002	10 Years	0.50	Initial Base Rent	Yes	Net	Yes	Market
Building 2	C	Industrial	27,408	1/1997	2/2002	14,545	Amount per Month		Net		Reabsorbed[a]
New Building		Industrial	50,000	11/2002	10 Years	0.50	Amount per Square Foot per Month	Yes	Net	Yes	Market

Main Building

Base Rent	Rent Changes
	CPI Increase Starts after 3 Years

[a]Building demolished and replaced by new 50,000-square-foot warehouse.

locate to larger, more efficiently configured space. Given the very low vacancy rates and rising rents in the market at the time, Gruma was faced with a sharp increase in rents for the existing space. The company therefore started considering several other cities in the Los Angeles area where it might be able to lease more efficient space at a comparable price. To do so, however, meant the disruption of production at one of its most important facilities and the relocation of expensive and highly specialized equipment from the existing plant.

Supply

While the company was considering these options, the current owners of the property, SCIF Portfolio III, LLC, presented a build-to-suit plan as a possible way of retaining an important tenant while improving the overall functionality and aesthetics of its property. The development plan presented to Gruma involved the replacement of the 27,408-square-

foot (2,550-square-meter) building with a 24-foot (7.3-meter) clear, 50,000-square-foot (4,650-square-meter), spinklered concrete tilt-up warehouse. The new building would be accessible from the manufacturing plant and would be used mostly to store products awaiting distribution. While making the existing tenant's operations more efficient, the new building was designed to remain flexible so that it could be leased as a separate industrial building independent of the 150,000 square feet (14,000 square meters), should Gruma decide to vacate the premises at the end of its lease. The leasing and development team on the ownership side was led by the Magellan Group.

Leasing

Lease negotiations started in early 1999 and continued for nearly a year. The two parties finally agreed to sign a ten-year lease with two five-year options to renew at fair market value. The rent was derived based on market comparables and a

$2 million estimate for hard, soft, and financing costs for the project. The initial base rent was set at $.50 per square foot ($5.40 per square meter), net, for the 200,000-square-foot (18,600-square-meter) premises (the 150,000-square-foot [14,000-square-meter] manufacturing plant and the 50,000-square-foot [4,650-square-meter] proposed building). Building costs (hard, soft, and financing) for the owners were capped at $2 million, including a $75,000 allowance for tenant improvements. Any increases in cost would be funded by the tenant. The lease offered Gruma the option to pay such additional costs at the time of construction or to amortize them over the lease term.

Following a prolonged debate over costs and the tenant's specific requirements, new building specifications were prepared as part of the lease. Both parties decided to jointly value-engineer the process to *continued on next page* figure B

Development Budget for New 50,000-Square-Foot Building

Hard Costs, Building Shell	Budget
Earthwork	$84,357
Demolition	$118,805
Landscape	$33,000
Chain-Link Fence	$7,240
Paving	$103,856
Site Utilities	$72,827
Site Concrete and Truck Apron (65'x316')	$85,527
Cast-in-Place Concrete	$450,000
Concrete Sealer	$3,034
Structural Steel	$54,795
Rough Carpentry	$9,303
Panelized Roof	$162,910
Building Insulation (Type II Foil)	$5,390
Roofing	$35,140
Sheet Metal (Skylights)	$20,745
Doors and Frames	$3,950
Overhead Doors (24-Gauge)	$8,700
Glass and Glazing (Approximately 200 Square Feet)	$5,300
Plaster	$9,800
Gypsum Wall and Ceiling Board	$11,731
Acoustical Ceilings	$1,000
Resilient Flooring	$0
Painting (Exterior)	$14,854
Signage and Graphics	$500
Loading Dock Equipment	$1,800
Fire Protection	$111,540
Fire Protection Water Meter	$20,000
Plumbing	$24,549
Electrical	$56,900
Liability Insurance	$3,900
Subtotal: Hard Costs	**$1,521,453**
General Conditions	5%	$76,073
Profit and Overhead	5%	$79,876
Total Hard Costs, Shell	**$1,677,402**

Note: All case study financial analysis spreadsheets are produced in Argus software.

Hard Costs, Tenant Improvements		Budget
Interior Fence		$1,970
Structural Steel		
Rails, Ramps, and Stairs		$7,880
Canopies		$64,093
Rough Carpentry		$2,000
Cabinetwork		$8,165
Building Insulation		$2,165
Doors and Frames		$11,630
Overhead Doors		$5,900
Glass and Glazing		$650
Gypsum Wall and Ceiling Board		$14,955
Acoustical Ceilings		$2,854
Resilient Flooring		$3,500
Carpeting		$2,800
Painting		$2,210
Toilet Accessories, Partitions, and Marlite		$9,501
Loading Dock Equipment		$6,920
Fire Protection		$7,540
Plumbing		$34,875
HVAC		$12,950
Electrical		$32,000
Subtotal: Tenant Improvement Costs		**$234,558**
General Conditions		$0
Profit and Overhead	5%	$11,728
Total Tenant Improvement Costs		**$246,286**
Contingencies	5%	$96,184
Total Hard Construction Costs		**$2,019,872**

Soft Costs		Budget
Architecture and Engineering		
Plans/Engineering/Management		$130,000
Permits		$75,000
Planning Department Submittal		$7,500
School Fees		$0
School Fee Credit		$0
Industrial Waste Fee		$4,188
Industrial Waste Fee Credit		$0
Insurance		$50,000
Construction Management Fee	10%	$223,656
Contingencies	5%	$100,994
Total Soft Costs		**$591,338**
Subtotal: Total Development Costs		**$2,611,210**

Financing	Budget
Interest	$160,000
Escrow and Closing Costs	$75,000
Total Financing Costs	**$235,000**
Total Development Costs	**$2,846,210**

minimize costs. The first step in the process was to select a contractor, with the final selection based on pricing and several meetings of prospective contractors, the owner, and the tenant.

Financing
Fremont Investment & Loan, the existing lender, provided construction financing. Financing negotiations were carried out simultaneously with lease negotiations, and by the time financing terms were finalized, the basic layout of the new building had been agreed on. The basic terms of the financing included a 12-month, interest-only loan; initial funding to pay down existing loans on both properties; and holdbacks to fund hard, soft, and interest reserves totaling approximately $2.3 million (excluding legal expenses and closing costs), based on an approved construction budget plus leasing commissions.

Entitlements
Entitlement began when the landlord and tenant agreed on basic business terms of the lease. By the time the loan was funded, the plans had been approved by the Commerce Planning Department and been through the public hearing process.

Preconstruction
Following selection of the contractor, engineering and architectural drawings were finalized over a six-month period with input from Gruma personnel about their requirements. By the time all plans and specifications were finalized, the total estimated cost of the building had risen to approximately $2.6 million (Figure B). The complex logistics of construction without affecting the tenant's 24-hour operation also added to costs.

Based on the terms of the lease, Gruma would have to fund the additional $600,000 during construction or during the term of the lease. Even though the tenant chose the latter option, it was concerned about the magnitude of the increase in costs since lease negotiations began. Owner and tenant decided to jointly approach the city of Commerce

The office entry to the main building of the Gruma Corporation facility.

for financial assistance to help the tenant mitigate part of the additional financial burden.

A presentation to the city highlighted the importance of the tenant's business to the local community, given that Gruma is one of the largest employers in the city and its immediate neighborhood. In addition, the city would receive financial benefits through an increase in the property tax base after the new building was completed. Following the presentation and subsequent negotiations, the city agreed to provide $300,000 in financial assistance. The amount was not a lump sum but was structured in the form of tax benefits to the tenant at $25,000 per year over the ten-year lease plus an initial tax benefit of $50,000.

Because the tenant initially decided to amortize additional costs over the lease term, the owner had to fund additional equity to cover costs over the development budget.

Construction
The construction process started in March 2001 with demolition of the existing 27,000-square-foot (2,500-square-meter) building. With careful phasing and coordination with the tenant, the construction team succeeded in completing con-

struction with no significant impact on the tenant's operations; in fact, Gruma remained open throughout the process. The new 50,000-square-foot (4,650-square-meter) warehouse building was substantially completed and handed over to the tenant in November 2001.

Lease Commencement
The new lease began with Gruma's occupancy of the new building in November 2001. (The property was sold to an investment group specializing in net leased real estate investments in November 2002.) By the time all improvements were finished, including some changes in the scope of work, total hard and soft costs had increased to approximately $2,850,000. At that juncture, Gruma decided to pay a lump sum for all costs beyond $2 million.

Valuation
Based on an NOI of $1,165,916, the long-term lease, and the tenant's credit, the property's estimated market value is $13,325,000, or approximately an 8.75 percent cap rate. The financial analysis is based on an allocated cost of $7.8 million plus the $2 million cost exposure to the owners per the terms of the new lease (see Figure C). ∎

continued on next page

figure C

Schedule of Prospective Cash Flow

In Inflated Dollars for the Fiscal Year Beginning 8/1/1998

For the Years Ending	Year 1 7/1999	Year 2 7/2000	Year 3 7/2001	Year 4 7/2002	Year 5 7/2003	Year 6 7/2004	Year 7 7/2005	Year 8 7/2006	Year 9 7/2007	Year 10 7/2008	Year 11 7/2009
Potential Gross Revenue											
Base Rental Revenue	$751,152	$751,152	$678,427	$1,044,153	$1,200,000	$1,200,000	$1,262,595	$1,283,460	$1,302,315	$1,358,880	$1,358,880
Scheduled Base Rental Revenue	751,152	751,152	678,427	1,044,153	1,200,000	1,200,000	1,262,595	1,283,460	1,302,315	1,358,880	1,358,880
CPI and Other Adjustment Revenue	0	0	0	0	6,750	15,953	25,431	35,194	156,748	204,271	214,940
Expense Reimbursement Revenue											
Insurance	0	0	0	0	0	0	0	0	0	0	0
Taxes	$75,381	$76,888	$94,983	$114,215	$114,445	$116,735	$119,069	$121,451	$123,880	$126,357	$128,884
Repairs/Maintenance	1,526	1,572	1,589	1,697	1,717	1,769	1,823	1,877	1,933	1,992	2,051
Total Reimbursement Revenue	76,907	78,460	96,572	115,912	116,162	118,504	120,892	123,328	125,813	128,349	130,935
Total Potential Gross Revenue	828,059	829,612	774,999	1,160,065	1,322,912	1,334,457	1,408,918	1,441,982	1,584,876	1,691,500	1,704,755
Effective Gross Revenue	$828,059	$829,612	$774,999	$1,160,065	$1,322,912	$1,334,457	$1,408,918	$1,441,982	$1,584,876	$1,691,500	$1,704,755
Operating Expenses											
Insurance	0	0	0	0	0	0	0	0	0	0	0
Taxes	$75,380	$76,888	$96,997	$112,202	$114,446	$116,735	$119,069	$121,451	$123,880	$126,357	$128,885
Repairs/Maintenance	1,526	1,572	1,619	1,668	1,718	1,769	1,822	1,877	1,933	1,991	2,051
Management Fee (3%)	24,842	24,888	23,250	34,802	39,687	40,034	42,268	43,259	47,546	50,745	51,143
Miscellaneous Expense	1,017	1,048	1,079	1,112	1,145	1,180	1,215	1,251	1,289	1,328	1,367
Total Operating Expenses	$102,765	$104,396	$122,945	$149,784	$156,996	$159,718	$164,374	$167,838	$174,648	$180,421	$183,446
Net Operating Income	$725,294	$725,216	$652,054	$1,010,281	$1,165,916	$1,174,739	$1,244,544	$1,274,144	$1,410,228	$1,511,079	$1,521,309
Leasing and Capital Costs											
Leasing Commissions	0	0	0	$588,872	0	0	0	0	0	0	0
Reserves	$18,051	$18,593	$17,903	20,871	$22,904	$23,591	$24,299	$25,028	$25,779	$26,552	$27,349
Total Leasing and Capital Costs	$18,051	$18,593	$17,903	$609,743	$22,904	$23,591	$24,299	$25,028	$25,779	$26,552	$27,349
Development Costs											
Hard/Construction Costs											
Expansion Costs (Hard and Soft)	0	0	$2,128,950	$721,050	0	0	0	0	0	0	0
Reimbursement from Tenant	0	0	0	−850,000	0	0	0	0	0	0	0
Total Hard/Construction Costs	0	0	2,128,950	−128,950	0	0	0	0	0	0	0
Total Development Costs	0	0	$2,128,950	−$128,950	0	0	0	0	0	0	0
Cash Flow before Debt Service and Income Tax	$707,243	$706,623	−$1,494,799	$529,488	$1,143,012	$1,151,148	$1,220,245	$1,249,116	$1,384,449	$1,484,527	$1,493,960

figure D

Schedule of Sources and Uses of Capital

Equity Based on Property Value Leverage and Operating Requirements

For the Years Ending	Year 1 7/1999	Year 2 7/2000	Year 3 7/2001	Year 4 7/2002	Year 5 7/2003	Year 6 7/2004	Year 7 7/2005	Year 8 7/2006	Year 9 7/2007	Year 10 7/2008
Sources of Capital										
Net Operating Gains	$725,294	$725,216	$652,054	$1,010,281	$1,165,916	$1,174,739	$1,244,544	$1,274,144	$1,410,228	$1,511,079
Initial Equity Contribution	7,800,000	0	0	0	0	0	0	0	0	0
Net Proceeds from Sale	0	0	0	0	0	0	0	0	0	16,517,070
Defined Sources of Capital	8,525,294	725,216	652,054	1,010,281	1,165,916	1,174,739	1,244,544	1,274,144	1,410,228	18,028,149
Required Equity Contributions	0	0	1,494,799	0	0	0	0	0	0	0
Total Sources of Capital	$8,525,294	$725,216	$2,146,853	$1,010,281	$1,165,916	$1,174,739	$1,244,544	$1,274,144	$1,410,228	$18,028,149
Uses of Capital										
Property Purchase Price	$7,800,000	$0	$0	$0	$0	$0	$0	$0	$0	$0
Leasing Commissions	0	0	0	588,872	0	0	0	0	0	0
Hard/Construction Costs	0	0	2,128,950	−128,950	0	0	0	0	0	0
Capital Costs and Reserves	18,051	18,593	17,903	20,871	22,904	23,591	24,299	25,028	25,779	26,552
Defined Uses of Capital	7,818,051	18,593	2,146,853	480,793	22,904	23,591	24,299	25,028	25,779	26,552
Cash Flow Distributions	707,243	706,623	0	529,488	1,143,012	1,151,148	1,220,245	1,249,116	1,384,449	18,001,597
Total Uses of Capital	$8,525,294	$725,216	$2,146,853	$1,010,281	$1,165,916	$1,174,739	$1,244,544	$1,274,144	$1,410,228	$18,028,149
Unleveraged Cash-on-Cash Return										
Cash to Purchase Price	0.0907	0.0906	−0.1916	0.0679	0.1465	0.1476	0.1564	0.1601	0.1775	0.1903
NOI to Book Value	0.0928	0.0925	0.0653	0.0965	0.1112	0.1118	0.1181	0.1207	0.1332	0.1424
Unleveraged Annual IRR	0	0	0	0	0	0	0	0	0	0.1399

figure E

Property Summary Report

Timing and Inflation

Analysis Period	August 1, 1998, to July 31, 2008 (10 Years)
Inflation Method	Calendar
General Inflation Rate	3%

Property Size and Occupancy

Property Size	200,000 Square Feet
Alternate Size	1 Square Foot
Number of Rent Roll Tenants	3
Total Occupied Area	177,408 Square Feet
	(during first month of analysis)

Property Purchase and Resale

Purchase Price	$7,800,000
Resale Method	Capitalize NOI
Cap Rate	8.75%
Cap Year	Year 11
Commission/Closing Cost	5%
Net Cash Flow from Sale	$16,517,070

Present Value Discounting

Discount Method	Annually (endpoint on cash flow and resale)
Unleveraged Discount Rate	9 to 12% (0.5% increments)
Unleveraged Present Value	$9,050,848 at 12%
Unleveraged Annual IRR	13.99%

Stage 2: Lease-Up

Management during the lease-up stage emphasizes the selection of tenants, tenant relations, enforcement of standards, and the maintenance of the project's public image. Although the preliminary parceling of the property is the basis for marketing individual sites, the developer still should maintain flexibility. The principal concerns of the developer during this stage revolve around the compatibility of potential tenants, their locational relationships, and parceling.

The seed tenant sets the standards for the rest of the tenants. If the first tenant occupies 10,000 square feet (930 square meters) of space, subsequent tenants tend to occupy the same amount of space. If the seed tenant occupies 100,000 square feet (9,300 square meters), many subsequent tenants will occupy at least 50,000 square feet (4,650 square meters).

Site planning and the design of individual buildings are critical elements in maintaining the project's marketing appeal. The enforcement of restrictions on architecture, outdoor storage, and loading and parking ensures the project's continuing marketability. The developer should enforce the standards equally and impartially. Close supervision of architectural standards and especially exterior yard controls facilitates the financing of the project during its mature stages.

Shell buildings and multitenant spaces in partially occupied buildings can remain empty for months. If such buildings are not properly cared for (for instance, if con-struction rubble is not removed and landscaping is not maintained), they can become unsightly nuisances that lower the value of neighboring property and give the impression of poor management. Developers who lease or sell land to other builders can avoid the problem of unsightly vacant buildings by requiring builders to post a performance bond to ensure conformity to CC&Rs and design controls within a specified period of time. The bond should require that:

- exterior walls are finished and the installation of windows and doors is completed;
- all driveways, walks, parking lots, and truck-loading areas are paved;
- all construction debris is removed;
- the landscaping, including trees and shrubs planted in specified locations and sod installed, is completed and irrigation systems provided; and
- landscaped areas and parking areas are well maintained.

Stage 3: Stabilized Operations

The major objective during Stage 3 is to maximize long-term profitability. Revenues, infrastructure costs, and operating expense projections should be updated quarterly, or at least annually.

Financial management tasks include cost accounting, pricing, and keeping track of new leasing and sales information, which should cover details about prospects,

IDI's Services Group provides a host of on-site services to industrial tenants such as repairs to plumbing, lighting, electrical fixtures, and HVAC systems.

broker contacts, telephone inquiries, rental rates and available space of competitive projects, and current tenants' lease renewal dates.

The mature stage of a project occurs after it has been completely leased out or sold. Management of the completed development and enforcement of restrictive covenants are turned over to an occupants association, similar to a homeowners association. If the association is voluntary, it can be created as the developer phases out the project. If it is a mandatory association, it must be established at the beginning of the development so that all tenants and purchasers are bound by its provisions.

Associations can be a source of problems and expense for the developer if they become a means for occupants to press for services or benefits to which they are not entitled. Notwithstanding these concerns, a well-run association benefits not only the tenants and the community but also the developer's reputation by maintaining the standards of the project over time.

The main source of concern for developers during this third stage is the "residuals"—the future proceeds from the sale of buildings developed and any remaining unsold parcels. The developer plays the same role in the association as other owners: if they own buildings with triple net leases, they should inspect the property at least semiannually. These inspections are important for determining:

- how well the building is maintained;
- problems of functional obsolescence;
- the existence of restricted activities, such as the storage or manufacture of items outside buildings;
- the existence of potential problems or liabilities resulting from toxic waste; and
- the health and well-being of tenants and whether their operations are growing, maturing, or diminishing.

Various new concerns also bedevil the owners of industrial properties. For instance, in earthquake-prone areas, masonry property built before 1934 must be reinforced with steel. Dealing with tax reappraisals on existing property and trying to work out mistakes on tax bills can consume enormous amounts of an owner's time. Leaking oil tanks on properties several hundred yards away can contaminate groundwater, making it difficult to refinance nearby properties. Defense contractors insist on four-month escape clauses from leases because they do not know whether their contracts with the federal government will be extended. All such concerns demand developers' increasing attention during the operating phase of a project.

Property management for an industrial development varies considerably depending on the building type and whether it is single tenant or multitenant. Covenants play an extremely important role for maintaining a high-quality appearance. Rules with respect to on-site storage, parking, and truck parking and loading areas are just as important as landscape maintenance and trash pickup.

Truck parking in older industrial areas can create serious problems, especially if residences are nearby and the trucks impede traffic flow. If loading bays face the street, longer trucks may protrude into the street. This condition will cause continuing headaches for the owner who must contend with constant complaints from neighbors and parking tickets.

Many single-tenant buildings have triple net leases that have no provisions for an on-site property manager. Even though a lease provides for cleaning up the property and properly disposing of hazardous wastes and other sources of contamination, the owner should inspect the property regularly to ensure clean and safe storage practices.

Selling the Project

The disposition of industrial properties follows a procedure similar to that for office and retail buildings. The developer can emphasize a number of features to potential buyers:

- the building's functionality;
- the building's adaptability;
- the site's locational attributes;
- tenants' reliability and financial strength;
- the project's financial characteristics; and
- the project's future prospects.

Many industrial developers prefer to sell occupied buildings with ten-year leases during the fourth year, just before the rent steps up in the fifth year. Before that time, the rent is often so low that buyers will not pay enough for the building. In competitive markets, industrial buildings often do not become profitable until after the first increase in rents. Although sales brokers ask for the scheduled commission, commissions are usually negotiable. Smaller developers probably will have to pay higher commissions to obtain the same amount of attention from brokers as that given to larger developers who can offer more business.

Mounting concerns over toxic waste and asbestos make the sale of industrial projects more and more difficult. If the project has any kind of maintenance or fueling facility where petroleum products or chemicals collect, it probably will have to be cleaned up before it can be sold. Although everyone in the chain of title has liability for cleanup, the owner is ultimately responsible. Even though the owner may be able to recover cleanup costs from the tenant, cleanup should be done expeditiously.

Conclusion

Warehouses are far from glamorous, but good reasons exist for developing and investing in industrial facilities. They generally take far less time to build than mid- or high-rise office structures, and, as a result, developers can respond quickly to economic downturns. Moreover, warehouses and flex space become attractive affordable office locations in tight markets. The flexibility of industrial

Ongoing changes in logistics and distribution are expected to lead to larger and more complex regional distribution and warehouse centers in the future.

© 1998 Gary Knight and Associates/Courtesy IDI

space appeals to a wide range of small business, ranging from light manufacturing to storage to office uses.[34]

There are other advantages as well: capital expenditures are lower than for other product types, especially office space, and industrial property has a lower ratio of operating expenses to revenue—which means that it will perform better in up markets, because more income drops to the bottom line.[35]

Certain trends will influence industrial development in the coming years:

- The push toward greater efficiencies in logistics is leading to the consolidation of distribution centers into larger and more complex regional distribution and warehouse centers.
- The traditional role of landlord will change as tenants demand more services to run their businesses efficiently.
- Demand for high-speed connectivity and the ability to accommodate the latest technology will favor developers who build flexibility into their projects to allow for future wiring and other needs.
- The need to control tenants will make in-house management increasingly important to retain incubator tenants.
- Lower current yields will require developers to leave more equity in their projects.
- The entitlement process, which is becoming much more rigorous, will make the cost of improved land much higher; longer approval times will cause carrying costs to increase, and public exactions and development fees will raise the cost of obtaining entitlements.
- The use of nonunion contractors in most areas will be necessary to hold down costs and maintain competitiveness.

Beginning developers will continue to have many opportunities in the future, but they will have to choose their market niches carefully. Major industrial developers arguably have greater competitive advantages over small industrial developers than are found with other product types. They are in a position to respond quickly to market opportunities. Beginning developers will need to know the market well enough to sense those areas that are inadequately served by their experienced competitors, and they must be ready to pursue those opportunities aggressively.

Notes

1. The process is described in detail in Anne Frej et al., *Business Park and Industrial Development Handbook* (Washington, D.C.: ULI–the Urban Land Institute, 2001).
2. Ibid., pp. 16–17.
3. Interview with Alex Von Hoffman, visiting lecturer at the Harvard Graduate School of Design, 2001.
4. Frej et al., *Business Park and Industrial Development Handbook.*
5. Johannson L. Yap and Rene Circ, *Guide to Classifying Industrial Property* (Washington, D.C.: ULI–the Urban Land Institute, 2003).
6. Interview with David Hasbrouck, executive director, Cushman & Wakefield, Los Angeles, California, May 2000.
7. Frej et al., *Business Park and Industrial Development Handbook.*
8. National Association of Foreign Trade Zones, www.naftz.org.
9. Interview with Howard Schwimmer, Daum Commercial Real Estate Services, Los Angeles, California, 2001.
10. Interview with Raymond Bhumgara, Gannett Fleming, Inc., Camp Hill, Pennsylvania, 2001.
11. David Twist, "Determinants of Industrial Space Demand," White paper (San Francisco: AMB Property Corporation, July 2002).
12. Interview with Allan Kotin, adjunct professor, School of Policy Planning and Development, University of Southern California, and Allan D. Kotin & Associates, Los Angeles, California, September 2002.
13. Ibid.
14. Note that the term *special district* is used here to refer to a special *zoning* district. The term *special district* more commonly refers to special funding districts that are empowered to sell bonds to support infrastructure investment, primarily for water and sewer.

15. See Douglas Porter and Lindell Marsh, eds., *Development Agreements* (Washington, D.C.: ULI–the Urban Land Institute, 1989).

16. Zoning ordinances usually require three to four spaces per 1,000 square feet (95 square meters) of net rentable office area, although most lenders want to see at least four spaces per 1,000 square feet (95 square meters).

17. Interview with David Hasbrouck.

18. Ibid.

19. Interview with Izzy Eichenstein, the Oakstone Company, Los Angeles, California, June 2000.

20. The permanent lender requires that the construction loan be retired so that the permanent mortgage can assume the first lien position previously held by the construction loan.

21. Interview with Patricia Pewthers, vice president, Escrow Operations, First American Title Company, Los Angeles, California, 2001.

22. Much of this section is taken from Richard B. Peiser, "Structuring Real Estate Deals with Institutional Financial Partners," *Real Estate Review*, Winter 1999, pp. 3–11.

23. See Stanley L. Iezman, "Operating Pension Funds in Compliance with ERISA Procedures," *Real Estate Review*, Spring 1999, pp. 31–40.

24. Even then they were generally required to have some equity, but the value added through appreciation since the time of purchase in land or buildings contributed to a joint venture was treated as equity.

25. Interview with Robert Zerbst, president, CB Richard Ellis Investors, Los Angeles, California, 1999.

26. The *promote* is defined mathematically as the difference between the profit percentage and the capital contribution. If the operating partner puts up 15 percent of the capital and receives 40 percent of the profits, his promote is 25 percent.

27. See P. Gregovich, P. Lukowski, S. McSkimming, D. Morse, and P. Saint-Pierre, "Going beyond the AIMR Performance Presentation Standards: Recommendations on Distributed Income Returns," *Real Estate Finance*, Fall 1996, pp. 34–92.

28. Charles Wu, managing director of real estate investments, Charlesbank Capital Partners (formerly Harvard Private Capital Group), lecture at the Harvard Graduate School of Design, December 2000.

29. John Williams, former partner, Acacia Capital, New York, New York, 1988.

30. Interview with Gerald Katell, president, Katell Properties, Los Angeles, California, 1988.

31. Ibid.

32. Interview with David Hasbrouck, May 2000.

33. Interview with Izzy Eichenstein, June 2000.

34. Laler DeCosta II and Steve Walker, "Industrial Real Estate: Not Sexy but Solid," *Lend Lease Real Estate Investments Commentary*, No. 5, 2002, pp. 11–13.

35. Douglas Abbey, chair, AMB Capital Partners, San Francisco, California, in a presentation to the Advanced Management Development program at Harvard University, July 2001.

7. Retail Development

Overview

Retail development can range from the construction of a single store on a small parcel to the creation of a super regional shopping center covering 100 acres (40 hectares) or more. It can be the remodeling of street retail stores in older urban and suburban settings or the creation of a new town center in combination with office and residential uses. Likewise, it can be new construction or the redevelopment of an existing center or the adaptive use of a structure previously intended for another use. Typically, beginning developers who work in the retail sector will be involved in the middle range of this spectrum, developing something larger than a single-store building (such buildings are usually developed and owned by tenants) but smaller than a major regional shopping center. Increasingly, retail development is an ancillary component of other forms of development—linked and symbiotic—and thus a developer who has been associated with residential, office, and business park development might find himself involved for the first time in a retail component.

Retailing is an evolving business, and this is particularly true today with the challenges of Internet retailing, changing consumer behavior, and antigrowth and smart growth initiatives responding to urban traffic congestion and concern about the environment. Some of these challenges might seem remote from a discussion of retail development, but retail projects often become lightning rods for other community concerns.

Although all real estate development has many similarities, shopping center/retail development differs significantly from other forms of real estate development; thus, it has generated a completely distinct subset of development skills, terminology, and performance measures. Perhaps most important for the new initiate to this development type is the recognition that the success of the real estate depends highly on the success of individual and collective retail tenants. A developer new to retail development would do well to seek out an experienced partner.

Shopping centers can be classified in numerous ways —size, market served, and shape, for example—but almost all centers fit in the following definition, first set forth by ULI in 1947:[1]

> [A shopping center is] a group of architecturally unified commercial establishments built on a site that is planned, developed, owned, and managed as an operating unit related in its location, size, and type of shops to the trade area that it serves. The unit provides on-site parking in definite relationship to the types and total size of the stores.

This chapter uses the shopping center as the basis for discussion, as shopping centers encompass all the aspects of retail development, some of which might be overlooked when the project is limited to a single store, new or remodeled, or to development in an existing retail area.

Pictured at left is the CambridgeSide Galleria, Cambridge, Massachusetts.

Country Club Plaza in Kansas City, Missouri, developed in the 1920s, pioneered many shopping center concepts such as stylized architecture, unified management policies, sign control, and landscaping amenities.

Although developers have become active in the redevelopment of existing retail areas, it is important to note that these situations do not allow the same level of control as a shopping center under single ownership; redevelopment of an existing retail area relies on public cooperation and the use of various public or quasi-public entities and tools that will approximate the controls exercised by a single-owner project. Under these circumstances, many development and management rules are different and require a somewhat different set of skills from the developer.

A beginning developer usually is involved in developing a retail project smaller than 200,000 square feet (18,600 square meters) that serves a convenience, neighborhood, community, or specialty market (rather than a regional or super regional market). These small centers are often referred to as *strip centers,* because originally they were developed (as they are still) in simple linear or L shapes along arterial roads, where they were an initial response to the rapid suburbanization after World War II. In many cases, these mature and sometimes underperforming centers may represent excellent opportunities for redevelopment. Today, site configurations and strategies for locating retail stores are changing. New neighborhood centers are being developed as integral parts of large-scale residential communities. With the maturation of shopping center development experience and residential community design, newer centers often involve more varied shapes and placemaking designs. In fact, because of the increasing competition among small strip centers, standard products and shapes are giving way to more creative concepts, making the development of small centers more challenging and demanding. Older centers are receiving face-lifts to remain competitive, going through major surgery and becoming better integrated with the surrounding community in terms of land use, design, and access. Redevelopment rather than new construction on a greenfield site may well be an ideal opportunity for entry into retail development.

With the diversity that has evolved, shopping centers are increasingly difficult to categorize. Trade literature often simply divides centers broadly into regional malls and strip centers and by size and physical configuration. Considerable variety exists within each of these groups, however. A more useful way to categorize shopping centers is by the trade area they serve and the types of tenants they contain.[2]

Standard Shopping Center Categories

Shopping center categories based on market served and tenant characteristics have become standards in the shopping center industry; they have evolved over time and continue to evolve. The first distinctions drawn were neighborhood, community, and regional centers. Later additions included convenience centers at the smaller end and super regional centers at the larger end of the spectrum and a wide range of less conventional types. In all cases, a shopping center's type and function are determined by its major tenant or tenants and the size of its trade area; they are never based solely on the area of the site or the square footage of the structure. Each center category with a distinct function, trade area, and tenant mix is described below.

- *Convenience centers* provide for the sale of personal services and convenience goods similar to those of a neighborhood center. They contain a minimum of three stores with a total gross leasable area (GLA) of up to 30,000 square feet (2,790 square meters). Instead of being anchored by a supermarket, a convenience center usually is anchored by some other type of personal/convenience service, such as a minimarket.
- *Neighborhood centers* provide for the sale of convenience goods (foods, drugs, and sundries) and personal services (laundry and dry cleaning, barbershop, shoe repair, for example) for the day-to-day living needs of the immediate neighborhood. They are built

Many possible advantages—related to the market, public approvals, financing, construction, and operating results—can support the redevelopment of an existing shopping center rather than construction of a new one. But there are disadvantages as well.

Market Advantages

- Availability of Prime Real Estate—Vacant prime property for new development often is located in unproved and outlying areas without fully established surrounding markets. Older shopping centers or other retail properties, such as grocery or discount store sites, can provide attractive opportunities for redevelopment in proved and mature locations. Such locations, moreover, can be accurately analyzed for development opportunities, with less guesswork about future market changes, because the market is established and not subject to significant short-term changes. In some cases, neighborhoods surrounding older retail properties actually have become wealthier, more populous, or more intensively developed since the original development.
- An Established Customer Base—A shopping center that has been in existence for many years usually has loyal customers whose shopping patterns are already set. This built-in market provides a significant advantage for the renovated center. The location also may have nostalgic or historic significance that can provide additional goodwill.
- Fewer Competitive Sites—Developed areas usually have fewer opportunities for competitors to enter the market, limiting new competition, reducing uncertainty, and increasing the likelihood that the renovated center will be successful.

Advantages for the Approval Process

- Suitable Zoning in Place—Restrictive zoning and other development controls limit the location of new shopping centers, often because of their traffic impact. Renovation projects often require no rezoning or subdivision approvals, which can save years and translates into significant cost savings for the developer. In some cases, the project's age may allow for variances from project codes, building setbacks, or even land use restrictions. This regulatory flexibility may permit a development plan that otherwise would be impossible to build.
- Public Support—Municipal agencies and citizens groups often embrace projects that support neighborhood improvements, particularly in older neighborhoods that have been ignored by developers in the past. Some cities sponsor bond programs in which they provide funding directly or through tax recovery incentives that allow the developer to recoup part of the cost. In some areas, the development agency can aid in condemnation if some leases are difficult to cancel or additional properties must be obtained. Developers can obtain concessions on parking codes as part of negotiations with the municipality.

Advantages in Construction and Leasing

- Lower Construction Cost—The cost of buying an underperforming shopping center and renovating it is often significantly lower per square foot than building a new one.
- Faster Turnaround—Redevelopment is likely to take less time than new construction. Public approvals are often quicker, and financing is easier because the project already has a cash flow. The existing cash flow also reduces the lead time between beginning construction and closing the permanent loan.
- Established Operating Record—The history of the center can provide valuable information about what works and what does not work in that location in terms of market demand and tenant mix. This valuable information generally is unavailable in a new development project. Tenants that are not doing well or that are no longer suitable for the evolving market can be bought out, sometimes at a nominal rate, and the developer then can reposition the center with a more dynamic tenant mix.
- Affordable Deals for Anchor Tenants—Because of the lower purchase or renovation price relative to new construction, anchor tenants can be offered very competitive rental rates.

Disadvantages

- The center may be underperforming for good reasons that are not easily remedied.
- Even with redevelopment, certain layout and design factors are difficult to change and may make the center a less attractive option than a new center.
- The cost of renovations is more difficult to estimate than new construction. Renovations do not lend themselves as easily to a cookie-cutter approach as new construction, and some uncertainty often exists about the structure and what is required to renovate it properly.
- Existing tenants and leases may require buyouts, removals, and/or moves that can complicate redevelopment and add to costs. Special tenant relations programs need to be developed to ensure tenants' involvement.
- Construction usually must be managed while the center remains open, necessarily making it less efficient than new construction. Construction working hours are often restricted to nights and early mornings, and extra safety precautions are required. Expansion often requires the addition of parking structures, which are more expensive than the surface lots provided with new centers. ∎

Source: Dean Schwanke, *Remaking the Shopping Center* (Washington, D.C.: ULI–the Urban Land Institute, 1994), p. 15.

around a supermarket as the principal tenant and typically contain a GLA of about 60,000 square feet (5,580 square meters). In practice, they may range from 30,000 to 100,000 square feet (2,790 to 9,300 square meters).

- *Community centers* typically provide many of the convenience goods and personal services offered by the neighborhood center with a wider range of soft lines (wearing apparel for men, women, and children) and hard lines (hardware and appliances). The community center makes merchandise available in a greater variety of sizes, styles, colors, and prices. Many centers are built around a junior department store, variety store, super drugstore, or discount department store as the major tenant, in addition to a supermarket. Although a community center does not have a full-line department store, it may have a strong specialty store or stores. Its typical size is about 150,000 square feet (13,940 square meters) of GLA, but in practice, it may range from 100,000 to 500,000 or more square feet (9,295 to 46,500 square meters). Centers that fit the general profile of a community center but contain more than 250,000 square feet (23,235 square meters) are classified as *super community centers*. In extreme cases, these centers contain more than 1 million square feet (93,000 square meters). As a result, the community center is the most difficult to estimate for size and pulling power.

A *power center* is a type of super community center. It contains at least four category-specific off-price anchors of 20,000 or more square feet (1,860 square meters). These anchors typically emphasize hard goods such as consumer electronics, sporting goods, office supplies, home furnishings, home improvement goods, bulk foods, drugs, health and beauty aids, toys, and personal computer hardware/software. They tend to be narrowly focused but deeply merchandised *category killers* together with the more broadly merchandised price-oriented warehouse clubs and discount department stores. Anchors in power centers typically occupy 85 percent or more of total GLA.

- *Regional centers* provide general merchandise, apparel, furniture, and home furnishings in depth and variety as well as a range of services and recreational facilities. They are built around one or two full-line department stores of generally not less than 50,000 square feet (4,650 square meters). They typically contain about 500,000 square feet (46,470 square meters) of GLA; in practice, they may range from 250,000 to more than 900,000 square feet (23,235 to 83,650 square meters). Regional centers provide services typical of a business district yet not as extensive as those of a super regional center.

- *Super regional centers* offer extensive variety in general merchandise, apparel, furniture, and home furnishings as well as a variety of services and recreational facilities. They are built around three or more full-line department stores generally no smaller than 75,000 square feet (6,970 square meters) each. A super regional center typically is about 1 million square feet (93,000 square meters) of GLA. In practice, such centers range from about 500,000 to more than 1.5 million square feet (46,500 to 139,400 square meters).

All centers typically include in the site area (the gross land area within property lines) an area of sufficient size to provide customer and employee parking in relation to the GLA as determined by the accepted standard for the parking index.

Specialty Centers

A multitude of variations of these basic categories have evolved, all generally grouped under the word *specialty;* that is, they can be defined as subsets of the other, more traditional definitions. Specialty centers, in the broadest sense, are those that fail to meet, or are significantly different from, any of the above definitions. For example, a neighborhood shopping center that has a cluster of

Falls Plaza is a supermarket-anchored neighborhood shopping center in Falls Church, Virginia.

specialty food shops—gourmet food store, butcher shop, greengrocer, wine store—as a surrogate for a supermarket might be called a *specialty neighborhood center*. Likewise, a cluster of convenience uses adjacent to a major truck stop might defy normal classification. A community-scale center that has a large fitness center as an anchor with a variety of health, nutrition, and sporting goods stores or a center heavily dominated by a variety of craft-related tenants might have specialty status. It is fair to suggest that the potential for specialization is limited only by a well-conceived development strategy. On the other hand, as these less typical tenant mixes become more prevalent, their specialty status devolves most clearly as a subset of the original and traditional categories of shopping centers.

Centers that have a special architectural character or theme fall in this broad set of atypical center types. "Entertainment," "fashion," "off-price," "outlet," "power," "megamall," "home improvement," and more recently "historic" and "lifestyle" are among the terms that have been used to describe a special character, focus, or targeted retail segment.[3]

An important trend whose effect on retailing practices has been dramatic is the advent of the *big-box* or *category killer* store. A major phenomenon of the 1980s and 1990s, they began with Wal-Mart and Kmart and now include Best Buy, PetsMart, Babies "R" Us, and a number of large-format stores that sell a wide range of goods covering tenant categories that used to be relegated to smaller in-line stores, or have a huge commitment to a single category of goods that almost precludes the ability of smaller stores to compete in the same center or even in nearby centers without a special flavor that sets it apart.[4] Wal-Mart's Neighborhood Market supercenter is by any other name a neighborhood shopping center under one roof. As retailing changes, retail land use models will evolve in response. Developers will need to identify and serve new niches in the marketplace.

The integration of retailing into other real estate development categories has evolved rapidly. New formats include a significant retail component in mixed-use developments; the development of street-front-based town centers as part of larger multiuse developments and large-scale new communities; resort retailing; transportation retailing associated with air, rail, and transit hubs and stations; and support facilities for office and business parks.[5]

Project Feasibility

Project feasibility can be determined from several different approaches. In some instances, a developer has a greenfield site under control and wants to determine whether a shopping center is feasible on that site and, if so, what form it should take. Or a developer might be considering the refurbishment and repositioning of an older, obsolete center. Or a developer has retail development skills or the commitment of an anchor tenant and therefore seeks a site that would be suitable for a shopping center with some predetermined characteristics. Most often, real projects fall somewhere in the middle of these possibilities. The accompanying case study about Northfield Commons, a neighborhood shopping center with 79,000 square feet (7,345 square meters) of GLA located in Troy, Michigan, is used as the common thread throughout the chapter.

Market Analysis

A developer's initial impetus to develop a small shopping center seldom occurs without a basic knowledge of the general market. To be able to decide whether or not to proceed further and what type of project to build, however, a more in-depth analysis of the market is often required. Unlike industrial or office projects, retail markets are defined by a specific geographic trade area. The trade area for a particular site depends on demographic characteristics, street access to the site, and competition in nearby areas.

A typical market analysis, as shown in the Olney Village Mart feature box, illustrates how professional market analysts measure market potential. In all instances, a critical factor is the assumptions regarding uses that can be provided at the new retail location.

A basic foundation for market analysis is the *gravity model* or Reilly's Law of Retail Gravitation, first published in 1931 by Professor William J. Reilly, University of Texas–Austin. It states generally that when two cities (or retail centers) compete for retail trade, the breaking point for the attraction of such trade will be more or less in direct proportion to the population of the two cities and in inverse proportion to the square of the distance from the immediate area of the city or center. In effect, people will travel to the largest shopping center most easily reached, assuming the centers offer the same types of goods and services, except in the case of neighborhood centers, where customers are most interested in convenience, not size. This model has been subjected to various interpretations and reformulations over the years. One of its major weaknesses is that it does not take into consideration other important factors that influence where people choose to shop, such as variety, store quality, image, ambience, prices, and customer service.[6]

Market Factors. Similar to that for other property types, retail market analysis can be performed in two basic stages. The first stage evaluates the general characteristics of a broad market area to determine its demographic characteristics, overall economic trends, existing retail supply, any mismatches between supply and demand, and suitable development sites. During the second stage, the potential of a specific site or sites is scrutinized. After an initial concept has been developed, this stage also involves defining the primary and secondary trade areas, analyzing the demographics and buying power of the trade area, and assessing competitors in the trade area.

The boundaries of the trade areas surrounding a site are determined by a number of factors, including the anticipated type and size of the center, automobile and transit access, physical barriers, location of competing

The Area

The city of Troy is one of the fastest-growing residential, office, and retail markets in metropolitan Detroit. In recent years, most of the area's residential development has taken place in north central Troy and the adjacent portions of Rochester Hills, Bloomfield Hills, Bloomfield Township, and Auburn Hills.

Northern Troy is served by two freeways that provide unusual access to the area from other portions of metropolitan Detroit: I-75 (the major north/south commuter link) and M-59 (the major east/west commuter link). The only street in the Troy area with direct access to both freeways is Crooks Road.

The Site

Northfield Commons, which is located on approximately 12.9 acres (5.2 hectares) of land at the intersection of Crooks Road and South Boulevard, is equidistant from the Crooks Road/M-59 interchange and the Crooks Road/I-75 interchange.

Because of the area's master land use plan, no comparably sized retail development is located within three miles (4.8 kilometers) of Northfield Commons. It is ideally located to take advantage of the area's growth, and it serves a previously underserved market.

The Market

Northfield Commons serves northern Troy, Rochester Hills, Bloomfield Hills, Bloomfield Township, and eastern Auburn Hills. More than 25,000 people reside in Northfield Commons's primary market, and thousands of people work in the more than 2 million square feet (185,900 square meters) of office space that is also located in the primary trade area. Studies show that new residential development will continue the trend. Typical customers at Northfield Commons are in their middle thirties and enjoy an average household income greater than $100,000.

The Design

The design of the development was created to lend a human scale to a neighborhood shopping center. With broad covered walkways, substantial landscaping, and convenient parking, Northfield Commons is designed to appeal to shoppers as well as merchants. Major tenants are spread throughout the development, so parking demand is evenly dispersed and pedestrian as well as vehicular traffic flows easily. Unlike other retail developments in the area, restaurants are clustered together with their own separate parking area. ∎

Source: The Nelson Companies, West Bloomfield, Michigan.

figure A

Project Summary

Building Area (GLA)	79,600 SF
Parking	**468 cars**

Leasing Plan

Suite	Tenant	GLA
A-1	Little Caesar's	1,400
A-2	Mammoth Video	6,350
B-1&2	Honeyrayz Grill	3,112
B-3&4	Chinese Keno	3,200
C-1,2&3	Hallmark	4,500
D-1	Optometry on the Mall	1,500
D-2	Katherine Lynn Salon	1,500
D-3	Star Cleaners	1,500
M-1	Farmer Jack	45,000
M-2	CVS Pharmacy	10,950
Maintenance and Utility Rooms		**89**

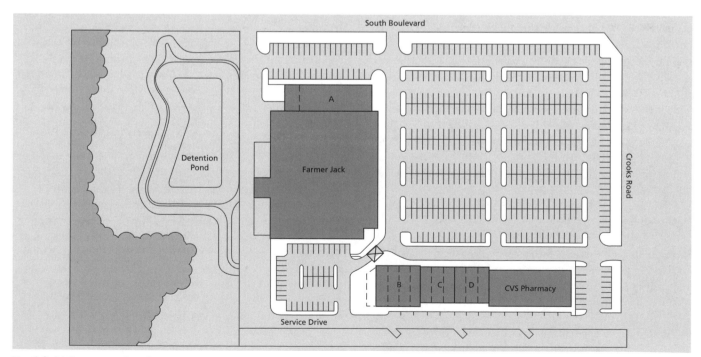

Northfield Commons site plan.

The Village at Shirlington, located in suburban Virginia just outside Washington, D.C., enjoys a market area of more than 200,000 households within a five-mile (8-kilometer) radius.

retail schemes, and population concentrations. Trade areas are usually divided into three concentric zones of influence or categories—primary, secondary, and tertiary (or fringe)—described below.[7]

- Primary Trade Area—The primary trade area is the geographic area from which the center will derive 70 to 80 percent of its regular customers. For a neighborhood shopping center, the primary trade area typically extends one and one-half miles (2.4 kilometers), with a driving time of five to ten minutes. For a community center, which is generally larger, the primary trade area is three to five miles (4.8 to 8 kilometers), with a driving time of ten to 20 minutes. At larger centers, such as regional malls, the primary trade area can range from eight to 12 miles (12.9 to 19.4 kilometers). As market areas become saturated with shopping options, driving times decline unless countered by increasing traffic congestion. In urban areas, both walking time and distance are also determinants of the primary area.

- Secondary Trade Area—The secondary trade area for both neighborhood and community centers generates an additional 15 to 20 percent of the customer base. The extent of the secondary trade area varies widely and is heavily influenced by the existence of similar centers nearby. In urban areas, the availability of transit access can dramatically expand the secondary trade area; it also has a positive impact on the size of the primary trade area.

- Tertiary Trade Area—The tertiary or fringe trade area is the broadest area from which customers might be attracted. A small but sometimes significant share of a center's customers—particularly for specialty centers, downtown centers, factory outlet centers, and entertainment centers—may be drawn from tourists and other visitors who do not live in the market area. Although customers in the tertiary trade area must travel greater distances, they may be attracted to a center because it is more accessible or provides a better merchandise mix, better value, or unusual tenants.

In addition to geographic and time/distance factors, competitive relationships, the specifics of anchor tenants, and other factors shape the reality of the trade area for a new or redefined retail facility. For example, natural physical barriers such as rivers may eliminate or reduce access to a potential site. Likewise, demographic characteristics such as ethnic diversity or economic status may affect the attractiveness of certain tenants to the perceived target population. Thus, the development concept in many cases may grow out of a general understanding of special or different characteristics of the market and thus may precede formal market analysis.

In the case of Northfield Commons, potential anchor tenants were eager to locate at the site because of its strategic location in an underserved market; therefore, an in-depth market analysis was considered unnecessary. Instead, demographic research of the areas within one-, two-, and three-mile (1.6-, 3.2-, and 4.8-kilometer) rings was conducted in conjunction with a marketing effort for the center.

Retail demand analysis focuses on a variety of key indicators; it includes the following elements:

- demographic data and employment growth trends and projections for the trade areas;
- household characteristics such as household type (families, singles, and so on), lifestyle, and age;
- income and expenditures for populations in each trade area;
- data on the size and spending patterns of any non-resident groups, such as tourists or office workers who may be expected to patronize the center.

Data on incomes and expenditures can be extracted from census data (including metropolitan area supplements), sales tax reports, consumer expenditure data

The following geographic and demographic issues and the market potential for the site and proposed retail center were considered:

- The village of Olney is situated at a key crossroads in central Montgomery County, Maryland. The road network in that part of Montgomery County favors an Olney location, with its reasonably good access. Key north/ south and northwest/southeast highways intersect in Olney and create a natural and distinct trade area for the center.

- The trade area is characterized by an affluent and growing population that is well educated and consists primarily of families. Population in the trade area grew from 137,900 in 1990 to an estimated 154,000 in 1998, an annual rate of 1.4 percent. Average household income in the trade area was an estimated $88,400 for 1998, an increase of 3.45 percent per year from the 1990 average household income of $67,300. Forty-four percent of the trade area's population have attained at least a four-year college degree.

- Floor space directly competitive to the site is appreciably lacking; thus, Olney Village Mart has an opportunity to establish itself as the primary provider of moderate to better apparel and specialty goods in the trade area. In terms of floor space and sales, the key competition's business is significantly skewed toward groceries and restaurants. Although groceries and restaurants have 40 percent of the space and 67 percent of the sales, typical retail uses such as general merchandise, apparel, home furnishings, and specialty merchandise account for only 15.3 percent of the floor space and 9.1 percent of the sales. Further, these competitive centers show relatively modest to lower sales productivity.

- The analysis projected sales of $65.7 million (plus or minus 10 percent) for Olney Village Mart for 1998 with the center expanded to 180,000 square feet (16,730 square meters). This sales volume would produce retail sales at the rate of $365 per square foot ($3,930 per square meter), adjusted for the center's 4,500 square feet (420 square meters) of office space. Of the $65.7 million in retail sales, $59.3 million in sales would be generated from within the trade area. The remaining $6.4 million in sales would be generated by shoppers from outside the trade area.

- The three merchandise groups targeted, in-line retail, grocery, and restaurants, show surplus demand. The magnitude of the surplus—$234.4 million for in-line retail, $191.2 million for grocery, and $86.5 million for restaurants—dwarfs the estimated sales for Olney Village Mart. Thus, market support is ample for remerchandising the center.

figure A

Development Sales Assumptions

Maximum Retail Development Potential

Tenants	Space (Square Feet)	Sales Productivity per Square Foot	Total Sales	Percent Sales Inflow
In-Line Retail[a]	105,800	$275	$29,095,000	15.0%
Grocery	56,000	580	32,480,000	5.0%
Outparcel Restaurants	13,700	300	4,110,000	10.0%
Total Project/Retail	180,000	$365	$65,685,000	9.7%
Total Project/All Uses	180,000	–	$65,685,000	–

[a]In-line retail space is considered to be a mix of apparel, home furnishings, and specialty merchandise.

Sources: Carl M. Freeman Associates and Kissel Consulting Group.

compiled by the Bureau of Labor Statistics, and data from local planning and economic development offices. Data may also be purchased from vendors like Claritas or CACI.

Supply analysis examines the competitive retail centers within the trade areas, focusing on those in the primary trade areas, because that is where the majority of shoppers are expected to originate. It includes the following elements:

- location, characteristics, and sales figures for competitive retail centers in the trade areas;
- estimated market share (capture rate) of existing centers and sales performance of retailers in the centers;
- availability of retail space, absorption, and sales trends by retail category;
- status and characteristics of proposed and planned retail developments and the availability of other vacant, zoned sites that could become the location of retail competitors in the future.

Existing retail centers in the trade areas should be mapped to provide a visual guide to where new opportunities may be available. In addition to published data, it is important to undertake a firsthand survey of those schemes that are expected to offer direct competition. Equally important to the documentation of existing competition is the determination of any proposed projects that are under consideration for development.

Statistics on the physical characteristics and market performance of shopping centers are available from a number of industry sources. For example, ULI's *Dollars & Cents of Shopping Centers*™ provides information on sales performance by size and type of center, based on surveys of more than 1,000 U.S. shopping centers. National and

Sales Analysis: Olney Village Mart Trade Areas

Economic Characteristic	In-Line Retail[a]	Grocery	Restaurants	Total[b]
Retail Sales Trade Area Potential	$280,972,000	$437,068,000	$144,088,000	$862,128,000
Trade Area Retail Sales (key competition)	$21,817,601	$214,977,162	$53,885,659	$290,680,422
Net Difference	$259,154,399	$222,090,838	$90,202,341	$571,447,578
Estimated Sales at Site	$29,095,000	$32,480,000	$4,110,000	$65,685,000
Percent of Sales Inflow Rate	15.0%	5.0%	10.0%	9.7%
Inflow Sales	$4,364,250	$1,624,000	$411,000	$6,399,250
Net Estimated Trade Area Sales	$24,730,750	$30,856,000	$3,699,000	$59,285,750
Required Capture Rate	8.8%	7.1%	2.6%	6.9%
Net Trade Area Surplus/Deficit[b]	$234,423,649	$191,234,838	$86,503,341	$512,161,828

[a]In-line retail is considered a mix of apparel, home furnishings, and specialty merchandise.

[b]A positive number is a demand surplus; a negative number is a demand deficit.

Sources: Claritas Data Systems, National Research Bureau, ULI–the Urban Land Institute, and Kissel Consulting Group.

Analysis

The market analysis required an examination of the following issues:

- examination of the demographics of the shopper base for the area;
- analysis of the local retail competition;
- supply/demand analysis of existing sales and potential expenditures;
- forecast of potential sales for an expanded and repositioned Olney Village Mart.

Supply/Demand Forecast

The forecast of sales was based on the following assumptions:

- Leasing will focus on merchandising Olney Village Mart with exciting and contemporary stores, principally leading national retailers in apparel, home furnishings, and specialty goods, including jewelry, sporting goods, and toys and hobbies.
- Leasing will achieve an occupancy rate of at least 90 percent for the opening of Olney Village Mart.
- A marketing campaign in the print media, including local newspapers in Montgomery County, will create community awareness of the mart.
- No new competitive centers—conventional, power, or off-price—were to open in the trade area before Olney Village Mart's opening in 2000.
- The national and local economies were expected to maintain their present level of growth or to improve.

Figure A shows projected sales that should be achievable based on the market analysis and targeted retail categories. Figure B demonstrates the probable total available sales potential for the trade area and then a required capture rate for Olney Village Mart to meet the development sales assumptions set in Figure A. All sales estimates are stated in 1998 constant (noninflationary) dollars. ∎

regional shopping center directories are published by the Chicago-based National Research Bureau (NRB). Centers are listed by state, metropolitan area/county, and municipality. NRB also publishes national and regional statistics on shopping centers in different size categories. Commercial brokers, local chambers of commerce, and business journals also prepare lists of shopping centers, with a focus on larger centers. The U.S. Census Bureau publishes monthly and annual statistics on retail sales nationally and yearly statistics for a selected number of large metropolitan areas. Additional retail sales and establishment information can be found in publications from the Census of Retail Trade.

Market Niches and the Development Concept. The objective of retail market analysis is to find a niche in the market and an appropriate development program to fill that niche. Customer surveys and focus groups are invaluable in determining shopping patterns and potential niches in the marketplace. The assistance of an experienced retail market consultant can be especially helpful in this endeavor.

The market analysis, if positive in its recommendation, should result in the identification of the following kinds of information:

- a superior site for a typical anchored strip center in an emerging area;
- an underperforming or obsolete center that has market potential;
- an area that is underserved in terms of the overall amount of retail space or a particular type of center;
- an area in which the competition is weak in terms of the quality of design, retail mix, or marketing and management;

- an anchor tenant that wishes to locate in a particular area; and/or
- a specialty concept appropriate for the area or the site.

The analysis ultimately suggests the kind of center that would be most feasible. In addition, the identified market segments may suggest a special character for the proposed center that would allow it to depart from the traditional tenant mix. For example, an area with a significant ethnic population may need different merchandise categories, services, or marketing. By 2050, according to the Hispanic Association on Corporate Responsibility, one in every four Americans will be of Hispanic descent.[8] Americans of Asian descent will

University Circle: Market Niche Strategy

Case Western Reserve University (CWRU), located on the far eastern side of Cleveland, Ohio, is a key institution in its surrounding University Circle neighborhood. A major street, Euclid Avenue, splits the crescent-shaped campus; this split and other features disrupt pedestrian flow and are major impediments to creating a unified campus. The University Circle neighborhood contains two major intersections: Euclid Avenue and Stearns Road and Euclid Avenue and Mayfield Road.

The current student union building, Thwing Center, is near the center of the campus on Euclid Avenue; it offers food service, student offices, and a Barnes & Noble bookstore. Two scenarios were considered as part of a plan that entails the redevelopment of Thwing Center:

- The subcontracted Barnes & Noble store would remain at its current site at Thwing Center. This scenario simplifies negotiations with Barnes & Noble and affirms the status quo.
- The concept of niche retailing involves the relocation of Barnes & Noble out of Thwing Center to Euclid and May-

field. This scenario has three benefits: Barnes & Noble expands its draw from the university campus to beyond University Circle, the store becomes the foundation for establishing critical mass at the intersection of Euclid and Mayfield, and the university realizes a commercial link between the north and south campuses across Euclid Avenue.

The trade area for retail development at Euclid and Mayfield is best characterized as a diverse urban market that is, not surprisingly, oriented toward well-educated young adults. This orientation of the local market derives from a higher than expected percentage (30 percent more) of 18- to 24-year-olds and a less than expected percentage (6 percent less) of those under age 17. From a retailer's perspective, 18- to 24-year-olds, primarily white, are a valuable demographic niche that is maintained by the turnover of the student population every year.

In addition, the University Circle trade area contains 34 percent nonwhites, with the white population slightly decreasing

and the nonwhite, primarily African American and some Asian, population increasing. Average household income in the trade area was estimated at $65,800 in 1999, with a higher than expected percentage of households concentrated in the household income brackets $50,000 to $74,999 (14 percent more), $75,000 to $99,999 (50 percent more), $100,000 to $149,999 (84 percent more), and $150,000 and over (133 percent more). Given the current landscape of retailing, these competitive factors contribute to a definitive retail opportunity at Euclid and Mayfield.

In addition, the relocation of the store introduces the possibility of redeveloping a former hotel for undergraduate dormitory space. Such redevelopment would inject the energy of student residents into the mix of retail, office, and existing apartment space, and the possibility of moving the student union to Euclid and Mayfield. The combination of all these uses would create the undisputed unifying element for the CWRU campus and the greater University Circle area.

Demand/Supply Forecast

A demand/supply and sales analysis for University Circle was based on the following assumptions for a development strategy:

- Leasing will focus on merchandising a retail complex in University Circle with exciting and contemporary stores centered on a core group of leading national retailers in apparel, home furnishings, and specialty goods.
- Leasing achieves an occupancy rate of at least 90 percent for the opening of a retail complex in University Circle.
- A marketing campaign of print (including local newspapers in the Univer-

figure A
Development Sales Assumptions
Maximum Retail Development Potential

Tenants	Space (Square Feet)	Sales Productivity per Square Foot	Total Sales	Percent Sales Inflow
Apparel	33,700	$321	$10,829,000	85.2%
Home Furnishings	12,500	$262	$3,278,250	91.5%
Specialty Merchandise	46,500	$313	$14,543,000	87.4%
Restaurants	17,900	$355	$6,346,975	89.2%
Entertainment	32,200	$120	$3,864,000	82.5%
Total All Uses	142,800	$276	$38,861,225	87.0%

Sources: ULI–the Urban Land Institute and University Retail Group.

have a similar impact on our demographics. The degree to which these groups will assimilate or wish to modify past shopping patterns and styles and how their presence as forces in the marketplace will or will not create niche markets is a major factor to be watched.

Although hard market data are critical in determining the feasibility of a project, an intuitive sense of the market and a creative approach are equally important. This fact is especially true of specialty centers, which require a good bit of luck as well as research to achieve success. The accompanying feature box illustrates potential retail sales for five retail and entertainment categories and provides an example of how to determine a market niche and development concept.

figure B
Sales Analysis

Economic Characteristic	Apparel	Home Furnishings	Specialty Merchandise	Restaurants	Entertainment	Total
Potential Retail Sales in Trade Area	$59,949,000	$64,231,000	$42,821,000	$85,642,000	$4,282,000	$256,925,000
Key Competitors' Retail Sales in Trade Area	$30,508,695	$15,222,643	$34,428,150	$39,635,303	$4,795,830	$124,590,620
Net Difference	$29,440,305	$49,008,358	$8,392,850	$46,006,698	–$513,830	$132,334,380
Estimated Sales at Site	$10,829,000	$3,278,250	$14,543,000	$6,346,975	$3,864,000	$38,861,225
Percent of Sales Inflow Rate	85.2%	91.5%	87.4%	89.2%	82.5%	87.0%
Inflow Sales	$1,597,713	$277,725	$1,830 475	$687,869	$676,200	$5,069,982
Net Estimated Sales in Trade Area	$9,231,288	$3,000,525	$12,712,525	$5,659 106	$3,187,800	$33,791,243
Required Capture Rate	15.4%	4.7%	29.7%	6.6%	74.4%	13.2%
Net Trade Area Surplus Deficit[a]	$20,209,018	$46,007,833	–$4,319,675	$40,347,592	–$3,701,630	$98,543,137

[a]A positive number is a demand surplus; a negative number is a demand deficit.

Sources: Applied Geographic Systems, National Research Bureau, ULI–the Urban Land Institute, and University Retail Group.

sity Circle area) will create community-wide awareness.
- No new competitive centers—conventional, power, or off-price—were scheduled to open in the trade area before the opening of a retail complex in University Circle.
- Adequate parking will be available for patrons.

With these assumptions and others, the sales analysis followed a plan based on four or five anchor stores:

- Apparel—The mix is anchored by Old Navy, which would appeal to the key age segment in the immediate vicinity of the site—18- to 24-year-olds plus the daytime workforce in University Circle.
- Home Furnishings—The emphasis in this category is on electronic goods, represented by a computer store and a consumer electronics store. A home accessories store would feature decorative and organizational merchandise that appeals to the student, artist,

and home office markets. A possible candidate for such a store is Urban Outfitters.
- Specialty Merchandise—The Barnes & Noble bookstore is the obvious anchor, with Kinko's and an athletic gear store oriented toward active young adults.
- Restaurants—The mix of eating establishments is designed to meet the needs of individuals seeking fast food, a snack or beverage break, an eating/drinking establishment, or fine dining.
- Cinema—The last key anchor designated for a retail complex in University Circle is a commercial theater.

Based on this merchandising and store plan, sales objectives and inflow ratios (the proportion of sales from inside the trade area to sales from outside the trade area) were derived for each store. The details of the merchandising plan (Figure A) were then tested against the competition and available sales potential in the trade area. The results of this analysis (Figure B) suggest that:

- a 15.4 percent capture rate for apparel is on the high side but achievable;
- a 4.7 percent capture rate for home furnishings is reasonable;
- a 29.7 percent capture rate for specialty merchandise is high if not aggressive, but the key component of this category is the Barnes & Noble bookstore, which does enjoy a monopoly over part of its business;
- a 6.6 percent capture rate for restaurants is reasonable;
- a 74.4 percent capture rate for entertainment is a very high share, but the competitive situation of the market favors an entertainment venue at University Circle.

Two additional important factors support the consultant's competitive and market analysis: the existing competition is fragmented, and the strategy to lease space to state-of-the-art operators could be achieved. ∎

Washington, D.C., residents Sarah and Shabbir Safdar asked Mindshare Internet Campaigns to help build online and offline community-based support for the expansion of an urban supermarket in their neighborhood. A small but vocal group of neighbors was behind a historic landmark application to prevent expansion of a 15,000-square-foot (1,400-square-meter) store. NIMBYists seemed to be gaining the upper hand in preventing expansion until the Safdars, at a public hearing, expressed their support for the expansion, pointing out that the store was too small to be efficiently run and that store owners might close the store altogether if they could not get permission to expand. The Safdars believed that a silent majority of neighbors considered the grocery store a vital amenity and that a larger store was badly needed.

Working with residents, Mindshare launched a site, www.wewantgiant.com, to demonstrate that the community contained many supporters of the store's expansion. The Web was used to develop a message triangle for supporters so their communications were consistent, relevant, and effective. The Web-based campaign also allowed for immediate notification and updates on issues and events, providing participants for rallies within 24 hours of notification.

Using online strategies and GIS mapping techniques, Mindshare was able to target neighborhood residents and customers and ask them to communicate their support for the store with offline action. Through online recruitment, promotion, E-mails, and phone strikes, Mindshare helped the community generate strong and effective support for the supermarket's expansion through hundreds of letters, dozens of phone calls, multiple press conferences, and other offline action.

The NIMBYists withdrew their application for historic landmark status. After some concessions in design to disgruntled neighbors, the supermarket was allowed to expand. ■

Source: Interview with Sarah and Shabbir Safdar, October 2002. For more information, see http://www.mindshare.net.

Site Selection

The following sites may offer attractive market opportunities and niches for small centers:

- newly developing suburban areas;
- jurisdictions where land use regulations or the political climate have restricted development in recent years, causing the market to become underserved. A developer with special talents or connections may be able to build a project where others could not, but the price may be high (see, for example, the Northfield Commons case study);
- older centers that have been undermanaged for years and need updating in markets where acquisition and renovation could be preferable to new development;
- outparcels at existing regional centers;
- close-in urban and suburban sites that may have changed considerably over time and are served primarily by older centers;
- inner-city areas for which redevelopment funds may be available to help make risky projects acceptable;
- growing smaller cities where retail space has not yet expanded;
- downtown locations in suburbs, central cities, and smaller cities to serve office workers and downtown residents.

Selecting an appropriate site for a retail center is critical; it depends on the market analysis and on the developer's objectives and motives. The analysis initially defines the general location and project size necessary to satisfy the desired market and meet the developer's objectives. From this point, site selection focuses on, and compares, the salient features of various sites.

The site should be good enough to preclude the possibility of a similar project's being developed in a superior market position. The selected site should not be merely acceptable but the best site available in the market. One danger to avoid is the potential mismatch between a preconceived retail concept and a site that is not the best choice simply because the developer controls or owns it.

The immediate vicinity of the site must be relatively attractive and safe so that shoppers feel secure. On the other hand, if the area is extremely quiet and secure (for instance, adjacent to a residential subdivision), neighbors may raise objections to a new shopping center. Although land use and design professionals strongly endorse access and integration with nearby residential areas, objections from nearby residents may require a buffer that tends to separate rather than integrate. Walls, solid fences, landscaped berms, or narrow, dense plantings of evergreens can be used to buffer the center's noise and nighttime lights. Even with these features, objections from homeowners may cause significant problems if the site needs to be rezoned or has been zoned but has remained vacant for many years. Any land use proposal for a site that has remained vacant while the surrounding area develops often is subject in varying degrees to NIMBYism from the surrounding population. Most often this attitude reflects residents' feeling, but it often goes deeper to the community's attitude about growth and change. Education about the advantages of an integrated design may become a necessary part of obtaining approvals, and providing buffering may still be the required solution.

Similarly, the current state of access to the site, the probable improvements needed, and present and projected traffic congestion are important factors to be considered. Resolving problems with access must be a

Site Selection Checklist

I. Location
  A. Description of location, address
  B. Map, aerial photography
  C. Site availability
  D. Regional access
    1. Existing
    2. Proposed
  E. Public transportation
  F. Neighboring land use
    1. Adjacent
    2. Beyond (within defined boundaries)
  G. Quality/stability of neighborhood
  H. Competition
    1. Location (map)
    2. Type, size
    3. Quality of tenant mix
    4. Occupancy and turnover
  I. Estimated trade area (map definition)
  J. Trade area population and distribution (densities)
  K. Community attitudes toward commercial development
  L. Proposed developments: residential, commercial

II. Site Data
  A. Plat (dimensions, size)
  B. Legal description of site(s) available
  C. Topographical features
    1. Visual
    2. Survey
  D. Subsoil conditions
  E. Problems (water, rock, fill, other)
  F. Zoning, building controls
  G. Infrastructure elements
  H. Ingress, egress
  I. Visual exposure, frontage
  J. Availability of adjacent land for expansion
  K. Current on-site improvements, if any
  L. Daily traffic counts past the site

III. Financial
  A. Asking price and terms
  B. Conditions of sales transfer
  C. Options available
  D. Property taxes
  E. Assessment fees on sewer, gas, water, stormwater drains, other
  F. Title cost
  G. Recording taxes

IV. Administrative
  A. Zoning
    1. Current zoning and permitted use
    2. Zoning authority
    3. Planning commission
    4. Local government
  B. Building department
    1. Clearances and setbacks
    2. Fire zone and fire department requirements
    3. Inspection requirements
  C. Highway department construction requirements
  D. Engineering
  E. Other, such as any local civic associations

V. Legal
  A. Legal description, title examination
  B. Easements and restrictions
  C. Filing of records

VI. Utilities and Infrastructure
  A. Location and map of:
    1. Water mains
    2. Sewer mains
    3. Gas mains
    4. Electricity supply lines
    5. Stormwater drains
  B. Special requirements
    1. Public areas
    2. Special grading: streets, slowdown ramps
    3. Curbs and gutters
    4. Sidewalks
    5. Landscaping and screens

VII. Miscellaneous
  A. Any demolition required
  B. Possible use of improvements

Source: ULI–the Urban Land Institute, "Shopping Centers: How to Build, Buy, and Redevelop," workshop manual, Spring 2001, pp. 26-27.

---

primary objective. A center built with inadequate access ultimately performs poorly, and it is often then too late to get help from government agencies or to fix the problem.

Environmental considerations may also affect a site's desirability. Vacant sites may have potential wetlands or be a habitat for endangered species.[9] Although this concern may seem ludicrous for a small site like that required for a neighborhood or community center, which may be dealt with by avoiding such sites, these issues may be why the site was overlooked in the past. At Northfield Commons, for example, this potential difficulty became an attractive feature of the development with the creation of a four-acre (1.6-hectare) wetlands/conservation area adjacent to the shopping center on part of the original total site area.

Another environmental issue that has emerged in recent years is the question of hazardous subsurface materials.[10] A site that has been used for farming might contain contaminants. A cleared site or an existing center to be rehabilitated might contain hazardous materials from an abandoned dry cleaners or other service. "In densely populated areas where land is scarce, redeveloping industrial sites and previous retail venues into new shopping centers is often the only opportunity for growth. Environmental concerns about wetland preservation are less likely to be an issue than the problems of dealing with residual contaminants."[11] Thus, it is important to obtain as much information as possible about the present and past uses of any site under consideration. It is always better to discover an impediment to development early so that the site is eliminated from further consideration or the potential cost of dealing with the impediment can be factored into the feasibility analysis.

Site Characteristics. Characteristics of the site involve questions of size, shape, accessibility, and visibility.

Size and Shape. Shopping centers can be developed at a range of densities, but the most common configuration for small suburban centers usually involves a one-story building covering 25 percent of the site, or a floor/area

BayWalk, a two-level, open-air retail center, has enlivened an area of downtown St. Petersburg, Florida. The project was planned and designed with input from the public at more than 100 forums and with city assistance in the form of an adjacent public parking garage.

ratio of 0.25. For this configuration, the site area needs to be approximately four times more than the gross building area (GBA) of the project. A rule of thumb is to build approximately 10,000 square feet per acre (2,295 square meters per hectare). Urban infill projects, however, might allow 100 percent site coverage and include no on-site parking requirement.

If the market surrounding the proposed site is expected to grow substantially over succeeding years, it may be desirable to acquire a site larger than initially necessary to serve existing market needs and then phase the project or allow for expansion over time. This strategy might also prevent encroachment from other commercial developments if the project is successful. Many jurisdictions, however, are reluctant to grant approvals for future expansion, and just because expansion space is available does not guarantee that the community will not object when an expansion is proposed. In any case, the developer should construct no more retail space than can be justified by careful market analysis. The downside of this strategy is that the project's initial profitability will be reduced if it is required to cover the carrying cost of a substantial amount of undeveloped land. Moreover, although in the past such excess land might be left essentially unimproved, today most communities require at least a minimum of landscaping and an appropriate level of maintenance. An unkempt adjacent parcel is not good development practice.

In suburbia, an ideal site should be a regular and unified shape and undivided by highways or dedicated streets. Although the term *strip center* connotes a long, narrow site, it is not always the case. A square site with an L-shaped center that wraps around a parking lot is often preferable; if the site is rectangular, its length should usually not exceed more than twice its width. Triangular sites also may be suitable, especially if they are surrounded by major arterial streets and provide good access from numerous directions. If a triangular or irregularly shaped site is used, the best solution may be to develop freestand-

ing facilities on the odd portions of the site. In urban infill locations, ideal sites are extremely rare, and an innovative design is almost always required.

Accessibility and Visibility. These factors are critical in selecting a retail site. Key measures of accessibility are the nature of the roads, the transit service, and pedestrian systems serving the site. Any shopping center site should be accessible from numerous directions, and the larger the market to be served, the more important this factor becomes. Thus, proximity to major intersections is a major advantage for any site. The traffic count on access roads is a good measure of the potential drive-by market; the volume of customers who actually pass the site and the site's orientation to the principal road serving the site or to other uses and activities that generate customers are critical. A hidden site with poor visibility is obviously at a disadvantage over one that is highly visible, but the lack of access to a site with great visibility must be resolved before it can be considered further.

Neighborhood centers should have access from collector streets; minor residential streets should not be the principal access. Community centers should be located for access from major thoroughfares. Because they have a broader array of stores than neighborhood centers, community centers should be accessible to an extended trade area via freeways.[12]

Proximity to major roads or thoroughfares and a high traffic count, however, will not alone guarantee good access. If a site is not easy to enter and safe to leave, it must have the potential to be made so. Traffic should flow freely as it approaches and enters the site. Cars moving into or out of a center can create bottlenecks at entrances or backups on major traffic routes. Designing or redesigning traffic flow at entrances to centers requires the cooperation of both traffic engineers and local highway departments. If a road cannot carry the additional traffic and turning movements generated by the center, the cost of necessary improvements and the question of who pays the cost—highway construction authorities, developers, or both—must be investigated. Developers of large shopping centers often can afford to cover the cost of major road improvements, but developers of smaller centers are less likely to be in this favorable financial position.

Good visibility improves a center's accessibility. Shoppers driving at local traffic speeds can easily overshoot the parking area entrance if they cannot see the center from the road. Even though traffic flow attracts retail business, a site that fronts on a thoroughfare with many competing distractions (including other retail stores and signs) can be less accessible and desirable than a site on a less heavily traveled arterial. In hilly terrain, a site over the brow of a hill may be largely invisible, although for a neighborhood center that needs little or no business from occasional traffic, it is not important. If the center is a community center or needs to be an attractive stop for commuter traffic, however, then both visibility and directional accessibility are important factors to consider.

Traffic patterns combined with good visibility can be very important to attracting certain tenants. For retailers whose peak business is defined by the time of day, a location by the side of the road can be crucial. For example, doughnut or bagel shops prefer locations on the drive-to-work side, while gas stations prefer to be on the drive-home side.[13]

Site Conditions. Because shopping centers usually are horizontal in nature and cover a large footprint, a flat or gently sloping site is preferable. More steeply sloping sites can be adapted for shopping centers, but they may entail higher site improvement costs and lower operational efficiency.

Sites in floodplains, on solid rock, or with a high water table require careful analysis or should be avoided. If the general area has known problems with the subsoil, whether it is rock, sandy, compressible, high density/low moisture, or low-permeability clays, the extent of these characteristics and the potential cost implications

should be estimated for each site under consideration. Although soil borings on at least a 50- or 100-foot (15- or 30-meter) grid will be taken when engineering studies are conducted, an initial assessment is necessary to avoid unanticipated development costs later. Serious subsoil conditions or an existing surface condition such as wet soil that might trigger a wetlands designation should be resolved before the site is acquired and taken into consideration when the purchase price is negotiated. Even with careful analysis, a small garbage dump, unrecorded oil or gasoline storage tanks, well heads, septic tanks, and agricultural drainage fields in the middle of a grid might be missed. Using a local soil investigation company with a long history of work in the area is a good strategy, because employees should be aware of the history of the site and its potential problems.

Several environmental problems other than wetlands should be looked for: illegal dumping, groundwater contamination, floodplains, pesticides, PCB (polychlorinated biphenyl), high radon levels, endangered species, historic structures or archeological remains, asbestos in existing buildings or in rubble from earlier demolition. All these factors can lead to costly remediation or delays.[14]

Site Acquisition. After a site with desirable physical characteristics has been identified, the developer follows the steps outlined in Chapters 3 and 4 with regard to site acquisition.

One site acquisition scenario that is especially pertinent to retail development involves acquisition of an existing center needing renovation or expansion or the consolidation of several adjacent smaller obsolete buildings into a single parcel. The key factors to look for in acquiring a small center for renovation are an outdated appearance, tired management that has not kept up with local market changes, or changing local demographics that suggest a new marketing approach. It is not unusual, particularly for aging or second-generation owners, to fail to adjust to changing demographics and thus miss the market. An analysis of a center's current perfor-

Bethesda Row covers seven contiguous city blocks in an inner-ring suburb of Washington, D.C. It encompasses renovated structures, new construction, facade improvements, and new streetscape features.

The design of Santana Row in San Jose, California, was inspired by European streetscapes.

mance against industry norms reveals the site's under-met potential. Factors to consider include the center's tenant mix and lease terms, the sales performance of individual tenants, the center's market share, the competence of existing management, the availability of adjacent or on-site land for expansion, and the appropriateness of the center's current positioning in the market. Opportunities for renovation may even include

Northfield Commons: Development Chronology

1977   Initial purchase. Property zoned B-1 for retail use.

1982   City of Troy downzones property under protest to O-1, office use.

1987   Rezoning application denied after years of seeking alternative office development.

1989   The Nelson Companies becomes joint venture partner contingent on rezoning.

1990   Request for rezoning of 8.93 acres (3.6 hectares) to *B-2—Community Business District* and the remainder to *EP—Environmental Protection District* for protection of wetlands denied. Developer initiates legal action to force rezoning.

1993   With lawsuit pending, city and developer enter into discussions that result in a court-ordered consent agreement allowing rezoning to a specific set of development guidelines (see feature box on the facing page).

1995   Grand opening of Northfield Commons.   ∎

Source: The Nelson Companies, West Bloomfield, Michigan.

acquisition of streetfront retail buildings, such as at Bethesda Row.

Regulatory Issues

The zoning provisions and public approvals required to develop a site must be studied carefully before a site is purchased. An early study should explore the attitudes toward a proposed shopping center of local residents, the city's zoning staff, and the approval body. In many cases, the site proposed for a shopping center is not zoned for commercial use when site selection begins, and in others, the existing ordinance may need a favorable interpretation or perhaps an amendment concerning provisions such as FARs, building height, parking requirements, lot coverage, setbacks, and permitted uses. In the latter case, the *avenues of relief* delineated in the ordinance must be explored. Each such method of relief has a procedural application and approval process. In most instances, the developer will have to pursue relief options sequentially rather than simultaneously. Thus, if the first route fails, another is initiated. This process can be time-consuming and offers no assurance of success. The government staff can often indicate the likelihood that the developer's desires have at least staff support, and the developer can sometimes determine whether to proceed on the basis of informal discussions. When a community is dissatisfied with the amount and quality of retailing available, a developer may find he has not just encouragement to proceed but also offers of public assistance to speed the process through the regulatory maze. A first-time retail developer is best served by identifying a suitable site where the public approval process is easy rather than arduous. At Northfield Commons, for example, the site was first acquired in 1977, but efforts to develop a shopping center did not begin in earnest until 1987. It then took eight years until the grand opening in 1995.

Among the special regulatory concerns in shopping center development are the probable impacts the project will have on traffic, compatibility with surrounding uses, environmental effects of stormwater runoff, and, in some cases, downtown retailing. Historically, developers have found that the specific standards included in the ordinances for commercial zones are difficult to meet and frequently require variances or special exceptions.

In many cities where retail centers are proliferating or are expected to proliferate, strict guidelines are implemented to control design. They may be part of the comprehensive plan or part of adopted policy statements. Often they are unofficial but underlie the way the planning staff evaluates any retail proposal for rezoning or for site plan and architectural approval for a building permit. In some communities, zoning to a planned development district may be possible. At Northfield Commons, the appearance of the center was crucial to receiving public approval; thus, specific building designs were made part of the consent agreement, in effect creating a planned zoning approval for this specific project. Although specific plan zoning may allow greater flexibility, it is likely to require much more thorough review of the project's details.

A developer unfamiliar with the community where a site has been identified should, at an early stage, consult with local planning staff and officials to determine staff and community attitudes. Awareness of these concerns will help the developer shape his plans in a way that will garner staff and official support and still meet the devel-

oper's understanding of the needs of the market. An initial negative community/staff reaction to a development proposal may be the kiss of death that will haunt any further submissions. In many situations, appropriate design requires selecting an architectural style that complements the surroundings or sets a new, higher standard of quality. Regardless of the situation, good planning and design are always assets in obtaining project approval, leasing the center to tenants, and drawing customers. Because approval times and costs have soared in recent years, developers should be aware that the more effort they expend understanding the local regulatory process and community attitudes, the less likely they will experience opposition to an otherwise well-conceived development proposal and the less likely local officials will impose excessive and unreasonable demands.

In contrast to local governments' seeking to control growth and development, the public sector in some communities actively seeks to induce development to revitalize blighted neighborhoods. These situations can provide very attractive regulatory environments. Although development under such conditions may be riskier because of the nature of the market areas to be served, the cooperation of the public sector can be extremely valuable in enhancing the development's prospects for success. In many cases, officials will not only streamline the approval process but may also provide economic incentives and public funding, locating

Northfield Commons: Consent Agreement

Subject Property: 12.9 acres net of right-of-way located on northwest corner of Crooks Road and South Boulevard.

Current Zoning: 9.7 acres zoned *R-1B—One-Family Residential* and 3.2 acres zoned *O-1—Office Building*.

Summary of Proposed Consent Judgment

1. Westerly four acres preserved as an *EP—Environmental Protection District*. Developer will provide a landscape and wetland area maintenance program, including financial guarantees.
2. Easterly nine acres may be developed as the Northfield Commons Shopping Center, *B-2—Community Business District*, with following modifications and additional land use regulations:
   A. Maximum gross floor area of commercial building space shall not exceed 79,600 square feet.

B. Buildings shall be set back a minimum of 60 feet from south property line and 75 feet from the new Crooks Road and South Boulevard right-of-way lines.
C. In addition to ten-foot greenbelt, a minimum of 15 percent of the shopping center parcel shall be landscaped.
D. Dumpsters shall be brick-walled on three sides and opaque-fenced in the front.
E. All rooftop equipment shall be screened from view from all sides.
F. Building construction shall be of materials and colors as depicted in the elevations.
G. No window signs for tenants in shopping center.
H. Pylon signs are prohibited.
I. No party stores are allowed.
J. Primary tenant to be a supermarket of like quality as Farmer Jack (A&P), Kroger, etc.
K. Second major tenant to be a drugstore of like quality as Arbor

Drugs (now CVS) or Perry's (now Rite Aid).
3. Developer may not seek variances from codes, ordinances, and design standards.
4. Developer shall construct acceleration, deceleration, and continuous left-turn lanes.
5. Developer shall construct a five-foot-high berm along south boundary of shopping center parcel, and either a five-foot-high berm or six-foot-high brick screening wall along west boundary.
6. Developer shall construct two-foot-high berms along east and north boundaries of shopping center parcel.
7. Developer to convey Crooks Road right-of-way to 90-foot line and South Boulevard right-of-way to 60-foot line.
8. Circuit Court will retain jurisdiction to insure that promises are kept. ∎

Source: The Nelson Companies, West Bloomfield, Michigan.

public facilities such as a police substation, branch library, or senior center to anchor the center and to enhance security. The redevelopment or remodeling of existing centers could mean the loss of grandfathered protection for building and zoning code requirements for parking, accessibility for the handicapped, sprinklers, noncombustible building materials, and landscaping, however.[15]

Financial Feasibility

The actual financial feasibility of a shopping center can be determined only after a specific program has been defined for a specific site, thus allowing the developer to estimate development costs and operating revenues. The generic aspects of the financial analysis process are discussed in greater depth in Chapter 4. The capital costs that need to be identified for shopping centers, some of which are unique to this real estate category, are shown in the feature box on the facing page.

Projections of income must be based on a leasing plan that represents the developer's estimate of the amounts of space to be leased to specific types of tenants. Thus, the allocation of space to the various types of tenants is a critical component of the financial feasibility analysis. Although a preliminary analysis is based on assumptions that must be proved by tenants who have signed contracts, the initial analysis and subsequent refinements are a critical step in determining the feasibility of a retail project.

The process of estimating shopping center revenues is unlike estimating revenues for other income properties. First, rental rates vary substantially, depending on the type of tenant in the space. Second, revenues may be tied to overall sales performance if percentage rents are included in the leases.

Sales forecasting typically uses one or a combination of three computer-based models:

- Analog Method—Compares the performance of existing stores having similar site and trade area characteristics;
- Gravity Method—Uses drawing power based on store size and image;
- Regression Method—Uses a statistical comparison of the factors that appear to influence sales of existing stores as a basis for predicting the performance of planned stores.

Estimating may also use less statistically based techniques:[16]

- Market Share Estimation—Uses estimates of market share based on comparable historic information;
- Competitive Redistribution—A calculation of share that might be taken from competitors and sales that are not being captured in the trade area (leakage);
- Average Productivity—A retailer's own assumed productivity for a new store based on the performance of its other stores in similar market situations.

In regional shopping centers, tenant leases for most sales-based tenants include a percentage rents clause, allowing the developer to capture additional rent above the base rent after sales have reached a certain level. Percentage rent clauses are less prevalent for smaller centers; in a sample of 251 neighborhood shopping centers, for example, only 32 percent reported collecting overage rental income,[17] and less than 25 percent of convenience centers collected overages.[18] In contrast, 54 percent of community centers in a sample of 352 paid overage rents.[19] In regional shopping centers, the percentage of tenants paying percentage rents is nearly 100 percent, although many retailers resist such clauses. The exceptions are those tenants that deliver services without sales revenue: banks are a prime example. Most analysts believe that percentage rents and overages should be excluded from the initial analyses of financial feasibility, and few lenders consider percentage rents a basis for inflating income to acquire a bigger loan.

> While overage income can hardly be discounted, the prudent entrepreneur should first measure the adequacy of the contracted income or economic benefits, in the form of minimum rents, as contrasted to the investment requirements and related risks. Only after the investor is satisfied in this regard should he apply to the figures a positive factor predicated on the likelihood of his tenants achieving "overage" levels of sales in the foreseeable future.[20]

ULI produces numerous benchmark publications providing operating performance figures for shopping centers of various types that can be helpful during financial analysis. Figures 7-1, 7-2, and 7-3, for example, provide operating results for a sample of convenience, neighborhood, and community centers, respectively. Sales per square foot, total operating receipts, total operating expenses, and net operating balance vary considerably among these three shopping center types.

Design and Construction

The detailed design of a shopping center presents many challenges. As beginning retail developers team up with experienced and qualified professionals, perhaps including a partner with retail experience, they should be aware that the architect selected should have experience in the special design requirements of shopping centers. Retail architecture is all about creating a design that meets the needs of retailers and recognizing that a more expensive or more attractive center is not a substitute for one that is not properly merchandised.

The design process passes through numerous iterations to determine the best layout and configuration, optimal access, and optional financial performance. With experience, a developer can take more control of layout, but a beginning developer should look to an experienced shopping center architect for substantial input on the first project.

Capital Costs for Shopping Centers

Land and Land Improvements

Land or Leasehold Acquisition
- Cost of land
- Good faith deposit
- Broker's fee
- Escrow
- Title guarantee policy
- Standby fee
- Chattel search
- Legal fee
- Recording fee

Off-Site and On-Site Land Improvements
- Off-site streets and sidewalks
- Off-site sewers, utilities, and lights
- Relocation of power lines
- Traffic controls
- Surveys and test borings
- Utilities
  - Water connection to central system or on-site supply
  - Storm sewers
  - Sanitary sewer connection to system or on-site disposal
  - Gas distribution connection to central system
  - Primary electrical distribution
  - Telephone distribution
- Parking areas
  - Curbs and gutters
  - Paving and striping
  - Pedestrian walkways
  - Traffic controls and signs
  - Lighting
  - Service area screens and fences
- Landscaping
  - Grading
  - Plants

Buildings and Equipment

Shell and Mall Building
- Layout
- Excavation
- Footing and foundations
- Structural frame
- Exterior walls
- Roofing and insulation
- Subfloor
- Sidewalk canopy
- Sidewalks and mall paving
- Loading docks and service courts
- Truck and service tunnels
- Equipment rooms, transformer vaults, cooling towers
- Heating and cooling—central plants or units
- Incinerator
- Community meeting rooms
- Offices for center management and merchants association
- Electric wiring, roughed in
- Plumbing, roughed in
- Fire sprinkler system
- Public toilets
- Elevators, escalators, stairways
- Contractor's overhead and profit
- Pylons
- Shopping center signs
- Mall furniture, fountains, etc.
- Maintenance equipment and tools
- Office furniture and equipment

Tenant Improvements (if paid for by developer)
- Tenant finish allowance
- Storefronts
- Window backs and fronts
- Finished ceiling and acoustical tile
- Finished walls
- Interior painting
- Floor coverings
- Interior partitioning
- Lighting fixtures
- Plumbing fixtures
- Doors, frames, and hardware
- Storefront signs
- Store fixtures

Overhead and Development

Architecture and Engineering
- Site planning
- Buildings and improvements

Internal and Financing
- Interest during construction
- Construction and permanent loan fees
- Loan settlement costs
- Appraisal costs
- Legal fees for financing

Administrative Overhead and Construction Supervision
- Construction supervision
- Field office expense
- Bookkeeping
- Home office expense
- Travel and entertainment
- Salaries and overhead of staff
- Printing and stationery

Leasing Costs and Legal Fees
- Leasing fees paid to brokers
- Salaries and overhead of staff
- Scale model, brochures, etc.
- Legal fees—leasing
- Legal fees—general

Other Overhead and Development
- Market and traffic surveys
- Zoning and subdivision approvals
- Outside accounting and auditing
- Real estate taxes
- Other taxes
- Insurance
- Advertising and promotion of opening
- Landlord's share of formation and assessments of merchants associations
- Miscellaneous administrative costs ∎

Note: Items in this list are for all types of shopping centers, including enclosed regional malls.

Source: Michael D. Beyard, W. Paul O'Mara, et al., *Shopping Center Development Handbook*, 3rd ed. (Washington, D.C.: ULI–the Urban Land Institute, 1999), p. 57.

figure 7-1

U.S. Convenience Shopping Centers: Center Size, Center Sales, and Operating Results

Number of Centers in Sample: 77

	Average	Median	Lower Decile	Upper Decile	Median	Lower Decile	Upper Decile	Number Reporting
Center Size								
Total floor space (GLA and all other floor space)	19,816	19,285	10,750	28,723				77
Owned gross leasable area (in square feet)	19,125	18,450	10,192	28,491				77
Unowned gross leasable area (in square feet)								2
Center Sales	Dollars per Square Foot of GLA							
All tenants	$243.51	$226.70	$125.93	$407.69				29
Operating Results	Dollars per Square Foot of GLA				Percent of Total Receipts			
Total Operating Receipts	**$17.14**	**$16.29**	**$8.40**	**$29.19**	100.00%	100.00%	100.00%	77
Total rent	13.61	12.77	7.28	24.73	82.25	67.83	93.41	77
Rental income—minimum	13.13	12.39	7.43	23.12	81.12	66.53	93.28	74
Rental income—overages	0.79	0.68	0.06	2.72	3.25	0.72	16.23	15
Total common area charges	**1.58**	**1.51**	**0.57**	**3.76**	8.74	4.75	15.10	67
Total other charges	**1.91**	**1.70**	**0.46**	**4.02**	9.61	3.49	21.80	50
Property taxes and insurance	1.80	1.66	0.46	3.97	8.73	3.58	21.07	51
Property taxes	1.54	1.38	0.37	3.30	7.15	2.71	18.52	65
Insurance	0.18	0.15	0.07	0.44	1.04	0.47	2.01	49
Other escalation charges	0.14	0.13			0.74			5
Income from sale of utilities	0.25	0.22	0.04	0.64	1.01	0.29	4.03	17
Total miscellaneous income	**0.16**	**0.13**	**0.02**	**0.48**	0.84	0.08	3.28	36
Total Operating Expenses	**$5.51**	**$5.12**	**$2.38**	**$9.73**	30.53%	18.80%	52.20%	75
Total maintenance and housekeeping	**1.90**	**1.72**	**0.63**	**4.87**	10.96	4.91	20.55	74
Parking lot, mall, other common areas	1.60	1.35	0.56	3.60	8.48	4.22	16.35	50
Parking lot	0.26	0.19	0.04	0.75	1.35	0.15	4.06	43
Utilities	0.39	0.36	0.15	0.89	2.16	0.63	5.50	52
Security	0.11	0.08	0.03	0.33	0.50	0.15	2.42	13
Enclosed mall HVAC								4
Snow removal	0.24	0.22	0.01	0.64	0.98	0.19	3.94	36
Trash removal	0.18	0.14	0.02	0.49	1.08	0.16	2.42	41
Landscaping	0.25	0.17	0.07	0.86	1.12	0.39	3.55	44
Elevator/escalator								1
Other	0.27	0.16	0.00	1.30	1.22	0.05	5.00	42
Building maintenance	0.34	0.22	0.05	1.02	1.55	0.37	6.34	68
Roof repair	0.08	0.04	0.01	0.29	0.34	0.12	1.82	35
Other maintenance	0.31	0.20	0.03	0.92	1.50	0.37	5.19	64
Central utility system								4
Tenant office area services								2
Total advertising and promotion	**0.07**	**0.04**	**0.01**	**0.29**	0.35	0.04	1.57	41
Advertising	0.07	0.04	0.01	0.23	0.39	0.06	1.06	25
Promotions/special events	0.02	0.01			0.11			5
Christmas decor/events	0.04	0.04	0.02	0.08	0.21	0.06	0.45	11
Marketing administration								3
Merchants association								0
Total real estate taxes	**1.72**	**1.55**	**0.65**	**3.74**	8.78	5.34	18.84	68
Total insurance	**0.20**	**0.18**	**0.06**	**0.41**	1.30	0.48	2.68	71
Liability insurance	0.05	0.06	0.01	0.09	0.33	0.07	0.87	25
Property insurance	0.10	0.08	0.04	0.31	0.76	0.32	1.96	24
Special (earthquake/fire)	0.08	0.07			0.24			9
Other insurance	0.02	0.02	0.00	0.02	0.09	0.03	0.22	13
Total general and administrative	**1.15**	**1.02**	**0.40**	**2.62**	5.88	2.54	14.69	71
Management agent fees	0.68	0.66	0.27	1.07	3.78	1.92	6.88	59
Leasing agent fees	0.22	0.16	0.01	0.64	1.29	0.07	3.92	34
Bad debt allowance	0.53	0.32			2.73			9
On-site payroll and benefits	0.52	0.51	0.13	0.94	2.24	0.94	12.46	18
Professional services	0.11	0.08	0.03	0.39	0.62	0.16	2.87	41
Other	0.14	0.08	0.00	0.99	0.44	0.02	5.24	47
Net Operating Balance	**$11.33**	**$10.35**	**$4.98**	**$21.85**	69.47%	47.80%	81.20%	75

Note: Because data are means, medians, and deciles, detailed amounts do not add to totals. No median figures are shown if fewer than five values were reported for any income or expense category, and no lower and upper decile amounts are shown if fewer than ten values were reported.
Source: *Dollars & Cents of Convenience Shopping Centers®: 2002*, p. 6.

figure 7-2

U.S. Neighborhood Shopping Centers: Center Size, Center Sales, and Operating Results

Number of Centers in Sample: 251	Average	Median	Lower Decile	Upper Decile	Median	Lower Decile	Upper Decile	Number Reporting
Center Size								
Total floor space (GLA and all other floor space)	63,734	62,531	38,038	92,784				251
Owned gross leasable area (in square feet)	61,333	59,250	36,000	91,801				251
Unowned gross leasable area (in square feet)	14,729	9,675	3,000	48,423				32
Center Sales	Dollars per Square Foot of GLA							
All tenants	$271.53	$259.08	$98.19	$472.13				120
Operating Results	Dollars per Square Foot of GLA				Percent of Total Receipts			
Total Operating Receipts	**$11.24**	**$10.61**	**$5.02**	**$20.82**	**100.00%**	**100.00%**	**100.00%**	**250**
Total rent	**8.96**	**8.54**	**4.17**	**16.28**	**82.28**	**69.04**	**91.82**	**245**
Rental income—minimum	8.93	8.76	4.11	16.18	79.84	67.10	90.26	240
Rental income—overages	0.51	0.35	0.05	1.70	2.74	0.36	12.56	81
Total common area charges	**1.15**	**0.96**	**0.27**	**3.14**	**9.28**	**3.97**	**17.69**	**233**
Total other charges	**1.01**	**0.87**	**0.35**	**2.41**	**8.67**	**4.64**	**17.05**	**178**
Property taxes and insurance	0.95	0.84	0.34	2.11	8.25	3.67	15.82	175
Property taxes	0.87	0.78	0.27	1.94	7.28	3.14	14.97	211
Insurance	0.10	0.10	0.03	0.22	0.90	0.26	2.09	174
Other escalation charges	0.33	0.11	0.02	1.25	0.92	0.11	6.78	18
Income from sale of utilities	0.28	0.22	0.06	0.81	1.58	0.63	8.17	35
Total miscellaneous income	**0.11**	**0.08**	**0.00**	**0.43**	**0.58**	**0.04**	**3.70**	**125**
Total Operating Expenses	**$3.34**	**$3.08**	**$1.47**	**$6.60**	**28.41%**	**17.12%**	**50.70%**	**249**
Total maintenance and housekeeping	**1.18**	**1.10**	**0.39**	**2.67**	**9.79**	**4.65**	**21.86**	**241**
Parking lot, mall, other common areas	0.95	0.88	0.29	2.15	7.64	3.38	17.33	189
Parking lot	0.15	0.13	0.02	0.35	1.09	0.19	4.29	163
Utilities	0.23	0.21	0.06	0.59	1.85	0.64	4.80	189
Security	0.15	0.10	0.01	0.66	0.82	0.05	3.90	83
Enclosed mall HVAC	0.03	0.03	0.00	0.07	0.17	0.02	0.76	13
Snow removal	0.13	0.10	0.01	0.33	0.89	0.11	2.81	84
Trash removal	0.12	0.11	0.01	0.34	0.82	0.08	2.34	152
Landscaping	0.17	0.14	0.02	0.48	1.29	0.28	3.30	171
Elevator/escalator	0.06	0.04	0.01	0.18	0.20	0.07	0.69	12
Other	0.17	0.10	0.02	0.76	0.95	0.13	4.10	122
Building maintenance	0.23	0.20	0.02	0.67	1.59	0.28	7.36	224
Roof repair	0.05	0.04	0.00	0.18	0.32	0.04	1.92	162
Other maintenance	0.18	0.14	0.02	0.56	1.13	0.22	5.06	204
Central utility system	0.16	0.11			1.04			7
Tenant office area services	0.09	0.07			0.59			8
Total advertising and promotion	**0.05**	**0.03**	**0.00**	**0.22**	**0.23**	**0.04**	**1.47**	**126**
Advertising	0.02	0.02	0.00	0.09	0.14	0.02	0.68	76
Promotions/special events	0.06	0.03	0.00	0.30	0.40	0.01	1.18	30
Christmas decor/events	0.04	0.03	0.00	0.11	0.21	0.04	0.51	48
Marketing administration	0.07	0.01	0.00	0.34	0.10	0.01	0.85	16
Merchants association	0.13	0.12			0.94			9
Total real estate taxes	**1.00**	**0.88**	**0.35**	**2.08**	**8.44**	**4.21**	**17.98**	**230**
Total insurance	**0.15**	**0.15**	**0.05**	**0.28**	**1.29**	**0.56**	**3.53**	**237**
Liability insurance	0.05	0.05	0.01	0.11	0.38	0.09	1.21	110
Property insurance	0.07	0.07	0.03	0.17	0.67	0.21	1.60	114
Special (earthquake/fire)	0.06	0.05	0.01	0.17	0.31	0.10	1.25	26
Other insurance	0.02	0.02	0.00	0.03	0.12	0.02	0.42	28
Total general and administrative	**0.79**	**0.69**	**0.28**	**1.94**	**5.96**	**3.26**	**15.79**	**232**
Management agent fees	0.45	0.43	0.21	0.84	4.08	2.05	5.79	201
Leasing agent fees	0.18	0.10	0.01	0.60	0.90	0.11	4.60	124
Bad debt allowance	0.18	0.13	0.02	0.56	0.80	0.20	8.46	38
On-site payroll and benefits	0.47	0.52	0.07	1.13	2.69	0.67	7.33	54
Professional services	0.09	0.06	0.01	0.37	0.55	0.09	2.70	151
Other	0.11	0.06	0.00	0.67	0.42	0.03	6.64	144
Net Operating Balance	**$7.93**	**$7.60**	**$2.48**	**$14.88**	**71.59%**	**49.30%**	**82.88%**	**249**

Note: Because data are means, medians, and deciles, detailed amounts do not add to totals. No median figures are shown if fewer than five values were reported for any income or expense category, and no lower and upper decile amounts are shown if fewer than ten values were reported.

Source: *Dollars & Cents of Shopping Centers*®: 2002, p. 201.

figure 7-3

U.S. Community Shopping Centers: Center Size, Center Sales, and Operating Results

Number of Centers in Sample: 352

	Average	Median	Lower Decile	Upper Decile	Median	Lower Decile	Upper Decile	Number Reporting
Center Size								
Total floor space (GLA and all other floor space)	195,756	182,748	112,927	380,947				352
Owned gross leasable area (in square feet)	173,338	159,404	102,371	320,840				352
Unowned gross leasable area (in square feet)	74,418	68,915	9,186	155,416				106
Center Sales	Dollars per Square Foot of GLA							
All tenants	$229.84	$223.78	$112.99	$383.71				229
Operating Results	Dollars per Square Foot of GLA				Percent of Total Receipts			
Total Operating Receipts	**$10.93**	**$10.13**	**$4.63**	**$23.06**	**100.00%**	**100.00%**	**100.00%**	**347**
Total rent	**8.48**	**7.85**	**3.67**	**17.80**	**79.99**	**64.97**	**89.72**	**343**
Rental income—minimum	8.30	7.66	3.45	17.08	78.86	62.06	87.14	338
Rental income—overages	0.27	0.16	0.02	1.18	1.57	0.18	8.87	192
Total common area charges	**1.01**	**0.83**	**0.25**	**2.63**	**8.36**	**4.25**	**15.69**	**341**
Total other charges	**1.03**	**0.87**	**0.22**	**2.96**	**9.21**	**4.04**	**18.23**	**204**
Property taxes and insurance	0.93	0.81	0.20	2.14	8.72	3.50	16.34	201
Property taxes	0.94	0.86	0.19	2.51	8.23	3.26	16.20	324
Insurance	0.09	0.07	0.02	0.22	0.76	0.25	1.84	196
Other escalation charges	0.21	0.10	0.01	0.80	0.81	0.13	6.09	40
Income from sale of utilities	0.17	0.08	0.01	1.45	0.87	0.10	5.42	94
Total miscellaneous income	**0.18**	**0.11**	**0.01**	**1.15**	**1.06**	**0.08**	**7.73**	**243**
Total Operating Expenses	**$3.44**	**$3.13**	**$1.23**	**$7.35**	**29.54%**	**16.78%**	**59.34%**	**345**
Total maintenance and housekeeping	**1.08**	**0.95**	**0.32**	**2.68**	**9.31**	**3.92**	**21.89**	**337**
Parking lot, mall, other common areas	0.84	0.78	0.19	1.97	6.64	2.73	17.82	251
Parking lot	0.13	0.10	0.02	0.35	0.97	0.18	4.27	233
Utilities	0.18	0.14	0.03	0.49	1.40	0.38	4.67	252
Security	0.15	0.08	0.01	0.63	0.82	0.09	4.37	153
Enclosed mall HVAC	0.03	0.02	0.00	0.09	0.18	0.05	1.05	29
Snow removal	0.12	0.11	0.01	0.31	1.03	0.10	3.00	142
Trash removal	0.07	0.05	0.00	0.25	0.50	0.05	1.60	196
Landscaping	0.12	0.10	0.02	0.40	0.97	0.27	2.72	239
Elevator/escalator	0.06	0.03	0.00	0.27	0.24	0.01	0.82	22
Other	0.15	0.11	0.01	0.59	0.94	0.11	4.32	178
Building maintenance	0.19	0.15	0.03	0.61	1.46	0.27	5.48	278
Roof repair	0.04	0.02	0.00	0.14	0.22	0.03	1.68	220
Other maintenance	0.15	0.12	0.01	0.49	1.05	0.12	3.90	243
Central utility system	0.28	0.12	0.01	1.36	0.82	0.25	6.98	11
Tenant office area services	0.11	0.07	0.02	0.48	0.50	0.21	2.54	20
Total advertising and promotion	**0.06**	**0.03**	**0.00**	**0.34**	**0.32**	**0.04**	**2.53**	**236**
Advertising	0.06	0.03	0.00	0.34	0.28	0.04	2.36	110
Promotions/special events	0.09	0.05	0.00	0.40	0.35	0.02	1.97	56
Christmas decor/events	0.04	0.04	0.01	0.11	0.23	0.06	0.68	74
Marketing administration	0.11	0.06	0.00	0.42	0.38	0.02	1.99	32
Merchants association	0.03	0.03	0.00	0.10	0.23	0.03	0.86	34
Total real estate taxes	**1.23**	**1.12**	**0.37**	**2.91**	**10.24**	**5.09**	**24.10**	**330**
Total insurance	**0.14**	**0.13**	**0.05**	**0.26**	**1.21**	**0.49**	**3.14**	**334**
Liability insurance	0.06	0.04	0.01	0.13	0.52	0.10	1.65	140
Property insurance	0.06	0.05	0.02	0.14	0.47	0.19	1.61	141
Special (earthquake/fire)	0.05	0.04	0.00	0.12	0.36	0.03	0.92	47
Other insurance	0.01	0.01	0.00	0.03	0.07	0.02	0.51	50
Total general and administrative	**0.71**	**0.62**	**0.25**	**1.71**	**6.05**	**2.41**	**15.21**	**323**
Management agent fees	0.39	0.36	0.15	0.76	3.50	1.73	6.00	286
Leasing agent fees	0.15	0.11	0.01	0.52	1.12	0.05	4.39	138
Bad debt allowance	0.15	0.11	0.01	0.48	0.89	0.10	4.18	110
On-site payroll and benefits	0.38	0.27	0.04	1.14	2.15	0.52	8.27	100
Professional services	0.08	0.06	0.01	0.32	0.49	0.09	2.79	208
Other	0.09	0.05	0.00	0.37	0.52	0.04	3.87	253
Net Operating Balance	**$7.56**	**$6.96**	**$2.23**	**$16.58**	**70.46%**	**40.66%**	**83.22%**	**345**

Note: Because data are means, medians, and deciles, detailed amounts do not add to totals. No median figures are shown if fewer than five values were reported for any income or expense category, and no lower and upper decile amounts are shown if fewer than ten values were reported.

Source: *Dollars & Cents of Shopping Centers®: 2002,* p. 135.

Northfield Commons: Financial Analysis

Income Analysis	Area of Store (Square Feet)	Initial Lease Rate (Per Square Foot per Month)	Annual Rent
Major Stores			
Supermarket	45,500	$10.35	$470,925
Drug Store	10,950	$14.00	$153,300
Specialty Stores			
A-1	1,100	$20.00	$22,000
A-2	6,650	$14.25	$94,762
B-1	1,600	$17.00	$27,200
B-2	1,600	$17.00	$27,200
B-3	1,600	$17.00	$27,200
B-4	1,600	$17.00	$27,200
C-1	1,500	$14.00	$21,000
C-2	1,500	$14.00	$21,000
C-3	1,500	$19.00	$28,500
D-1	1,500	$19.00	$28,500
D-2	1,500	$19.00	$28,500
D-3	1,500	$20.00	$30,000
Subtotal Specialty Stores	23,150		$383,062
Total Gross Area			79,600 square feet
Total Gross Annual Income			$1,007,287
Average Lease Rate per Square Foot			$12.65
Special Area Vacancy @ 5%			$19,153
Management Fee @ 4%			$40,291
Reserve for Replacement @ 0.01%			$10,072
Total Operating Expenses			$69,516
Net Operating Income			$937,770

Proposed Loan Data

Net Operating Income	$937,770
Coverage	1.25
Mortgage Rate	9.00%
Amortization Rate	9.66%
Amortization Term	30 years
Permanent Mortgage Term	10 years
Blended Cap Rate	10.30%
Mortgage Amount (80% of cap value)	$7,283,650
Mortgage per Square Foot	$91.50

Summary

Development Costs	$8,722,144
Contribution by Farmer Jack	$273,000
Net Development Costs	$8,449,144
Land Costs	$1,200,000
Plus CPI Adjustment	$125,000
Less Income during Construction	$180,520
Land Payment Remaining	$1,144,479
Repayment from Loan	$34,506
Net Land Investment	$1,109,972
Annual Debt Service	$703,600
Net Cash Flow	$234,169
Land Loan Repayment in Years	4.74
Initial Return on Investment	21.10%

Source: The Nelson Companies, West Bloomfield, Michigan. ■

Site Plan and Building Configuration

The initial design consideration is the creation of a preliminary site plan and building configuration plan. Shopping centers generate more people movement in and out each day than any other type of real estate project; thus, they must be designed to accommodate a large volume of customers coming and going to a variety of destinations throughout the center during operating hours. The placement of buildings, parking, circulation systems, and delivery systems must seek to optimize the attractiveness and accessibility of every store in the center for customers while meeting the functional needs of tenants. As a land use concept, a variety of retail layout schemes have evolved over many years with varying degrees of success. For small centers in suburban locations, the focus is on easy access, adequate parking, and visibility for the center and its tenants from the roadway system. In urban locations, effective pedestrian connections and access to transit and parking, which may or may not be located on site, are important. Therefore, the first design consideration is identifying the most suitable building configuration that can be applied to a specific site.

Center Configuration. The configuration of smaller neighborhood or community shopping centers depends largely on three factors: the shape of the site, the surrounding roadways, and the space requirements of anchor tenants. Most such centers are configured in some variation of one of five general shapes: linear, L-shaped, U-shaped, Z-shaped, or cluster (see Figure 7-4). The major reasons for using the L, U, or Z shapes are to restrict the length of the center, to create greater visibility for tenants, and to make the center more walkable. These basic layouts have a number of variations using setbacks, curves, and multiple buildings. At Northfield Commons, for example, the L is broken at the inside corner by the Clock Tower, eliminating the inside corner retail space that had proved more difficult to lease. A cluster provides the best pedestrian environment and lends itself to cen-

The architecture of Desert Passage in Las Vegas, Nevada, uses materials, stylized design motifs, and construction techniques from Morocco and other desert countries to create a distinctive identity.

ters that can be integrated into the adjacent community fabric or to specialty centers, as the more traditional linear center and its variations are more oriented to adjacent streets and thus to drive-by traffic. The center's concept and shape of the best available site ultimately dictate the most suitable building and site plan configuration.

The linear arrangement is still the most commonly used configuration for neighborhood centers and community centers. The linear layout is basically a straight line of stores sometimes tied together by a canopy over a pedestrian walk that passes the storefronts. Traditionally, this configuration places two major units, usually a supermarket and a drugstore or other large anchor tenant, at the ends of the center, with spaces for small tenants in between. A linear center (and its variations) is generally the least expensive structure to build and is easily adapted to most site conditions. Linear centers typically range from 500 to 1,000 feet (152.5 to 305 meters) long, including anchor tenants. When a center's length exceeds about 300 feet (90 meters), building setbacks and architectural feature need to be visually varied.[21]

From a leasing agent's perspective, shopping centers are ideally laid out with good sight lines for most of the storefronts. There should be some slight changes in setbacks and elevation to provide interesting design elements and avoid a continuous monotonous appearance. The bay depths, widths, and column spacing should provide flexibility for the types of tenants you will be targeting. Expansion and contraction areas allow a variety of store sizes.[22]

The L, U, and Z shapes are merely variations of the linear concept. For example, the L-shaped layout is best suited for a corner location, while the U-shaped configuration lends itself to a mid-block location where the site depth is greater than the required combination of store depth, parking areas, and rear building circulation. It is also most useful for a full block configuration.

Of greatest importance is the quest to maximize visibility for the retailers, including their signage, entry, and exposure for the full

frontage of the store. Because of the trend away from small shop space and toward ever-increasing large store size, L-shaped centers (with too much nonvisible area and too little parking at the inside corner of the "L") are proving less practical. The linear arrangement, with a straight line of stores, is a more successful configuration and is less expensive to build or renovate. It is easily adapted to idiosyncrasies of site shape by inflecting the straight line into slight angles or crescent shapes.[23]

Although parking is usually placed at the front of small shopping centers to allow for easy access, some centers use different configurations. Truck parking and deliveries can be relegated to the rear, where employee parking spaces can also sometimes be placed. Rear parking for employees, however, may result in security problems for personnel.

Specialty Centers and Urban Sites. Specialty centers are difficult to describe or categorize generically. They are usually "special" for a wide variety of reasons, including their site plan and building configuration. Because they typically do not include traditional anchor tenants such as supermarkets and are often more oriented toward pedestrians than automobiles, their physical layout seeks to create special character that responds both to the targeted market and the expectations and demands of tenants. Although specialty centers may in fact be developed as a variation of linear centers, they are often configured differently. The cluster design and its variations are particularly suitable for a center with an atypical tenant mix tending away from everyday needs to shopper goods.

Sites in urban areas invariably present a different set of challenges affecting site plan and building configuration. Most often the site is constrained by a variety of factors: limited size, close architectural and pedestrian relationships to adjacent buildings, historic preservation and neighborhood conservation concerns, transit access, and limitations on automobile traffic generated and/or provision of adequate parking. Thus, any attempt to discuss site planning or building configuration must of necessity be discussed in conjunction with a specific site rather than in generic terms. For example:

- Public policy and urban design considerations often favor or require the placement of buildings along the street rather than set back to enhance the city's streetscape.
- The placement and availability of parking may become a critical issue, which might be solved by maximizing the number of curbside spaces available. If the street right-of-way permits, diagonal parking best achieves this objective. If parking is in the rear, the design must provide convenient covered access to the storefronts or equally convenient rear access. Most merchants find that entrances at both ends of their establishment create security problems and conflicts between storage/administrative space and sales areas.
- In a more urban setting, it may be necessary to intermix truck delivery traffic and customer parking. If

figure 7-4
Shopping Center Building Configurations

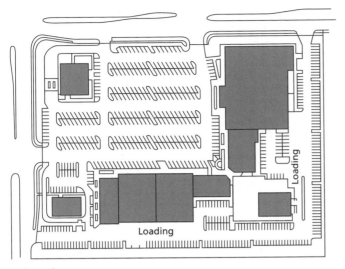

L-shaped.

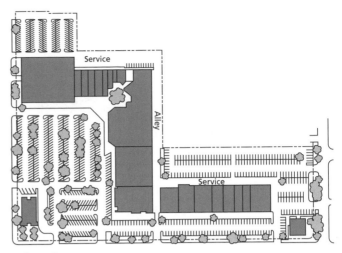

Z-shaped.

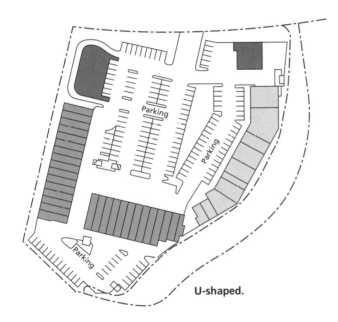

U-shaped.

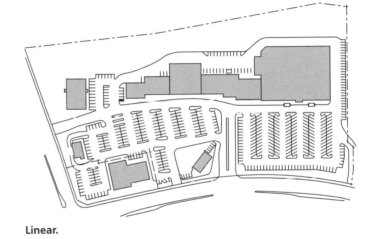

Linear.

Cluster.

so, deliveries might be limited to before or after operating hours.

- Although street-level retail is the most accessible and desirable design, tight urban sites may require a multi-level solution to produce enough square footage for financial feasibility. In some instances, this requirement has resulted in two-level stores that have traditionally been one level—for example, McDonald's among fast-food restaurants and Harris Teeter among supermarkets.
- Sites straddling a hillside may require a shopping center design that fronts two streets on two levels.

Parking, Circulation, and Access

Parking should be a positive experience, because for many, it forms a customer's first impression of the shopping center. According to the most recent comprehensive study conducted by ULI on parking requirements for shopping centers, the parking demand for a typical shopping center of 25,000 to 400,000 square feet (2,325 to 37,175 square meters) would be four parking spaces per 1,000 square feet (95 square meters) of GLA.[24] For uses such as restaurant, entertainment, and/or cinema space greater than 20 percent of the total space, an additional 0.03 space per 1,000 square feet (95 square meters) should be added. The study also determined that geographic location, an urban versus a suburban setting, and a large city versus a small city setting do not significantly affect parking demand. These standards are based on having parking spaces available for all but the 20 busiest hours of the year. Numerous other factors can affect the amount required, however, including the availability of mass transit, the walk-in trade, and tenants' demands.

Earlier studies by ULI and the International Council of Shopping Centers had set the standard at five spaces per 1,000 square feet (95 square meters) of GLA, and many communities accepted and adopted that standard. Thus, new projects may have to accept the current standards adopted by the community or go through a time-consuming process seeking variances or a change in the community's current parking standards. Many of these standards use a measure different from GLA, usually GBA or NLA (net leasable area). For example, an ordinance requiring four spaces per 1,000 square feet (95 square meters) of GBA is more or less equal to five spaces per 1,000 square feet (95 square meters) of GLA/NLA if GLA/NLA is calculated at 80 percent of GBA. In addition, based on previous studies and their own demand analyses, many anchor tenants and national chains have their own requirements for parking ratios.

The developer should carefully analyze the cost effect of providing more parking than the standard recommended above and consider seeking a modification from governmental or tenant standards that are too high or do not recognize the potential for a reduced number of spaces where walk-in trade is significant or where the site is well served by mass transit. In more urban areas, communities may require no on-site parking and may resist its provision. The lack of adequate parking can be just as damaging to a center's financial feasibility as needing to provide too much. Historically, land planned for later expansion was often paved as a least-cost maintenance strategy. This approach is not recommended, because such space often becomes commuter parking, which is difficult to retrieve later. Moreover, because paving is impervious, this excess paved area creates greater demand for stormwater management.

The design of the parking layout in relationship to storefronts requires very careful consideration. For example, parking supply needs to be concentrated near those tenants, typically anchors, who require a great deal of parking for customers. Ease of parking should always determine parking layout, but it is not always easy to achieve that objective. The circulation pattern should be continuous with no dead ends. Drivers should be able to maneuver between any subsections in the center without having to enter a public highway. If a center is, say, a combined neighborhood/convenience center, the two elements should be interconnected.

Ideally, aisles should be aligned perpendicular to storefronts to allow shoppers to walk directly from their cars to the front of stores. The aisles themselves may be curved or angled to meet physical requirements of the site or the design. Parking aisles that run parallel with storefronts should be avoided, however, because customers are then required to cut between cars, which can be hazardous.

Major tenants occupying at least 20,000 square feet (1,860 square meters) will want parking aisles to be directed toward their stores. In L-shaped centers, it may mean that aisles have to be aligned differently at different ends of the center so they align perpendicularly with the two sides of the L. This layout involves a two-way circulation route, often designated as a required fire lane, immediately adjacent to the storefront walkway and canopy. For convenience centers, however, perpendicular parking is often best placed along the storefronts. This design accommodates quick visits to the stores and fast turnover of prime spaces. It does, however, create a somewhat more hazardous situation, as shoppers can step out into moving traffic from between cars.

The layout of surface parking may be perpendicular or diagonal. Perpendicular (90-degree) parking economizes on space, facilitates circulation, and provides two-way traffic through the aisle, the safety of better sight lines, greater parking capacity, and shorter cruising distances for drivers seeking a space. Diagonal (angular) parking spaces, with 45-degree or 60-degree angles, provide one-way circulation, are easier for drivers to enter and exit, and involve fewer conflicts between adjacent vehicles when occupants open car doors. Diagonal layouts also provide greater maneuverability for sports utility vehicles and minivans. Whether to choose perpendicular or diagonal parking should depend on the generally prevailing pattern in the community that can be best adapted to site conditions.

figure 7-5

Recommended Minimum Parking Module Dimensions for One-Way Traffic and Double-Loaded Aisles

Parking Angle (Degrees)	Module	Vehicle Projection	Aisle
45	48'0"	17'8"	12'8"
50	49'9"	18'3"	13'3"
55	51'0"	18'8"	13'8"
60	52'6"	19'0"	14'6"
65	53'9"	19'2"	15'5"
70	55'0"	19'3"	16'6"
75	56'0"	19'1"	17'10"
90	60'0"	18'0"	24'0"

Note: Design vehicle = 6'7" x 17'0".

Source: ULI–the Urban Land Institute and NPA–the National Parking Association, *The Dimensions of Parking*, 4th ed. (Washington, D.C.: ULI–the Urban Land Institute, 2000), p. 46.

For perpendicular parking in general, the minimum standard bay for a full-size car is 60 feet (18.3 meters) deep, comprising two 18-foot (5.5-meter) stalls and a 24-foot (7.3-meter) center aisle to allow for two-way circulation.[25] Diagonal parking can vary from a minimum module of 48 feet (14.6 meters) at 45 degrees for a double-loaded aisle to 52.5 feet (16 meters) at 60 degrees. For retail applications, modules several feet wider make maneuvering easier, particularly for sports utility vehicles.

The standard minimum width for parking stalls in shopping centers is eight feet, nine inches to nine feet (2.6 to 2.7 meters).[26] The size of newer vehicles suggests that if space allows, a nine-foot (2.7-meter) module is preferable. A nine-foot (2.7-meter) stall is always recommended for parking areas closest to a supermarket if most customers load groceries into a parked car. If curb loading is the practice, a narrower space might be acceptable, but even with curb loading, many customers carry at least a few bags directly to their car.

Another important parking issue for shopping centers is the number and location of parking spaces accessible to handicapped individuals required by the Americans with Disabilities Act (ADA) of 1992. ADA guidelines state, "First priority should be given to measures that will enable individuals with disabilities to get in the front door."[27] For a shopping center with many front doors, this guideline can be a significant challenge. A shopping center with 100,000 square feet (9,300 square meters) of GLA would require 400 parking spaces, and ADA guidelines would require eight handicapped-accessible spaces, which need to be located next to curb ramps to walkways along the storefronts. In addition, they need to be positioned in front of or near the anchor tenants and then occasionally along the storefronts. One should always be placed in front of a convenience store. Thus, a number greater than the minimum may be required to best serve the anticipated customer base. Although not

required by ADA, the provision of designated reserved spaces for expectant mothers is a current practice for toy stores and stores selling baby goods such as Babies "R" Us.

Some experts in the field have suggested that the size of parking stalls diminish in relation to their distance from the center's building; that is, the spaces closest to the buildings would be the largest, because they are used most often. During peak hours, shoppers value the presence of a vacant space more than its size; thus, smaller spaces farther away are acceptable.

Employee parking is best placed at the rear of the stores, although concerns about security sometimes eliminate this possibility. When rear parking is used, a minimum width of 42 feet (12.8 meters) is required for the rear service and employee parking area combined. A width of 60 feet (18.3 meters) in the rear service area allows for the inclusion of a truck delivery drive and a staging area for unloading without blocking the service drive for other deliveries.

Parking and on-site circulation are part of site planning and should benefit from professional advice from design and marketing professionals. The objective is not just meeting the letter of local regulations or federal law but customer satisfaction and better overall performance for the center.

A favorable initial impression of the center and thus its success are also affected by the ease of ingress and egress. The location and number of curb cuts and the use of entrance deceleration and exit acceleration lanes should be considered. A significant issue may be the provision of sufficient stop lights to allow turns and to control traffic, thus allowing more impulse shoppers to enter the center. The ability to install curb cuts and road improvements and who will pay for them must be addressed during the feasibility study period.

Requirements for public approvals must be determined as early as possible. Road improvements are often required to make the center more functional and also to gain approval for the project. Developers should be aware that such improvements may involve significant expense.

Site Engineering and Landscaping

Design requirements for most neighborhood or community shopping centers usually dictate that the site be relatively level. An engineering firm with local experience should be employed to handle site work and assess on-site soils to determine the presence of any special problems. Foundations for most centers usually require only simple excavations to lay column footings and grade beams to support load-bearing walls, thus reducing the likelihood that soil conditions will present major problems.

If the best available site has significant slope, and this slope corresponds to the grades of surrounding roads, an opportunity may exist for a two-level arrangement of buildings and parking. For example, a sloping site with trees that must be preserved can be reshaped to accommodate a stepped but still essentially single-level center. Vehicles use a ramp, and pedestrians use wide steps with an adjacent pedestrian ramp. Other sensitive uses of a

The clock tower at Northfield Commons provides an easily identifiable symbol for the shopping center.

site's topography should make the shopping center and the site's natural characteristics compatible. A front-to-back design is also possible, but it isolates upper and lower tenants from each other. It may be a satisfactory solution if the tenant mix can be logically divided or if the less attractive level can be leased to nonretail residential or office uses. In urban areas, living over a store may be highly marketable, particularly if retail parking and residential parking can be separated.

The ideal slope for a parking lot is 3 percent, which allows for sufficient drainage but helps to prevent runaway shopping carts and difficulties with hard-to-open, heavy car doors. A slope of 7 to 8 percent is allowable in limited areas, such as entry drives. (In areas with substantial ice and snow, however, a maximum slope of 5 percent is typical.) If the site is steeper, a parking lot can effectively be broken into terraced pads separated by landscaped strips.[28]

Because large amounts of land are covered by buildings and pavement in a retail project, stormwater runoff is a major issue in shopping center design. Reducing or delaying this runoff may involve significant cost. Most communities have limited storm system capacities and often require methods to control stormwater runoff such as rooftop ponding, temporary detention basins (in portions of the parking lot, for example), detention or retention ponds, or other mechanisms for reducing the runoff rate and total runoff after development. In designing a stormwater management system, the developer should consider safety and visual appearance in addition to the primary function of water storage and should design the system as an integral part of the overall project.

Another critical site planning issue is landscaping. A surface parking lot often takes the bulk of a shopping center's open space, and such a barren expanse exposed to the public's view is usually uninviting. When properly designed and landscaped, however, parking lots can become one of a center's amenities.

In many communities, landscaping requirements are part of zoning and site plan approval. If possible, these requirements should be discussed in terms of performance standards rather than dollar amounts, percentage of total building costs, or percentage of site. Designs vary, depending on the site and the nature of the center. In general, landscaping for a parking area generally should be confined to trees and massed plantings in wells or in clearly delineated areas. Plantings should be located where they will not interfere with maintenance of the parking area or with snow removal and storage. Attractive landscape features at entrances give a good first and last impression. Landscaping should be coordinated with the location and design of center signage.

Landscaping, including land sculpture, on the edges of the center can effectively mask parking areas from the street and buffer the center from nearby residential areas. For example, screening of a certain height and density can be achieved by using a berm with shrubbery rather than a stand of trees. Regardless of the technique used, neither initial nor mature landscaping should hide the center from potential customers. Hardy ground covers, shrubs, and bushes concentrated at appropriate places in the buffers and trees that can be pruned to provide a high canopy are good solutions.

Small planting areas in the pedestrian areas of the center, next to and between buildings, and in conjunction with architectural features and landscape furniture can provide buffers from large parking areas as well as an attractive pedestrian environment. For example, fountains, pools, and seasonal plants create a cooling atmosphere and offer a series of refreshing vistas to visitors and tenants; patio areas and outdoor seating provide patrons a resting place. In areas with a homeless population, the design of outdoor spaces should avoid the creation of potential "homesites"; homelessness should not be allowed to negatively affect the shopping center environment. Good design rather than policing is the best strategy. For example, single seats can be used rather than benches and open edge landscaping rather than hedges. Again, design professionals, properly instructed, can produce appropriate designs.

Exterior lighting has also become an important design and safety feature, because a greater percentage of retail business is now being conducted during the evening. Lighting helps to protect the public, but it can also be used to create an image and character for the center. Lighting in parking areas should usually provide a minimum of about one and one-half footcandles at the pavement surface. Providing a higher level of light attracts more attention to the center at night and enhances the sense of security. But a higher level of light can also engender negative reactions from adjacent residents as well as a false sense of greater security.

An effective lighting system requires consideration of a variety of factors, including mounting height, spacing, light control, and light sources. The latter should be evaluated based on efficiency, durability, color of light, and light output.

Lighting on buildings is sometimes used to illuminate storefronts at night, particularly when the architecture is distinctive. Under-canopy lighting is needed to enhance pedestrians' vision, and accent lighting can be used to enhance the center's appearance. Frequently, under-canopy signage lights and lights from inside stores are sufficient if display windows are well lit.

Lighting in parking areas should be placed on poles located in islands at the ends of parking bays or on the dividing line between bays when they are longer than the spread of the selected fixture. In this case, a small planting bed at the base of each light standard may the logical location for a landscaped element. The mounting height of fixtures should equal approximately half the horizontal distance to be illuminated; thus, for a typical parking bay module of 60 feet (18.3 meters), a 30-foot (9.1-meter) mounting height is efficient.[29] The latest available nonglare and high-intensity lighting should be used to provide adequate illumination, reduce spillover lighting, and avoid excessive electricity costs. In surface parking lots, cutoff luminaires are recommended to minimize light trespass and to hide the light source from the view of adjacent properties.[30] In some instances, a more intimate lighting design may be desirable. This approach will be more costly than the method outlined above, however. It may also be more difficult to achieve the desired level of perceived security. The objective is to provide the customer with both real and sensed security.

Outparcel Development

Freestanding developed outparcels or pads can be attractive additions to neighborhood and community centers, but they must be placed and controlled carefully to ensure that they are marketable and do not detract from the center's overall marketability. From a financial standpoint, the sale or ground lease of outparcels can provide early cash flow to the overall financial strategy. When outparcels are planned, the developer must provide complete disclosure to the in-line tenants about the outparcel development plan so that no one will be surprised by the outcome.

Certain issues need to be considered in developing outparcels:

- Ingress and Egress—Outparcel tenants will be concerned about both direct access to the street and access easements through the shopping center.
- Control of Parking—Sometimes an outparcel may have parking in excess of its need, and sometimes it may need to share parking with the center.
- Utility Lines—Will outparcels tie into the shopping center lines or have their own lines?
- Construction—If construction on outparcels will not occur simultaneously with construction of the center, then the terms of sale or lease should seek to minimize disruption to the center or the outparcel's tenants if they proceed ahead of the center. Doing so will be to the mutual benefit of all concerned.
- Refuse Facilities—The parties should agree to the placement and screening of refuse dumpsters and outside storage.
- Sight Lines—The position of buildings on outparcels should not damage the visibility of major in-line tenants.
- Height Restrictions—Most buildings on outparcels in neighborhood and community shopping centers should be limited to one story and/or to a specific height.
- Signs—Although signage is largely controlled by local regulations, the placement and height of their signs is important to outparcel tenants. Developers must seek to ensure that signs for outparcels do not detract from, but enhance, the overall image and operation of the center, which may require a cooperative effort as well as specific conditions attached to a sale or ground lease.
- Building and Landscape Design—Although outparcel tenants frequently have corporate design requirements, even the most rigid can be modified to complement the overall center design if this concern is raised early in the discussions with potential outparcel tenants. Developers should reserve the right to review and

figure 7-6
Cutoff and Noncutoff Luminaires

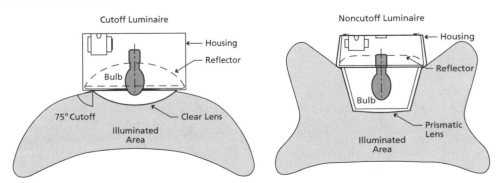

Source: ULI–the Urban Land Institute and NPA–the National Parking Association, *The Dimensions of Parking*, 4th ed. (Washington, D.C.: ULI–the Urban Land Institute, 2000), p. 45.

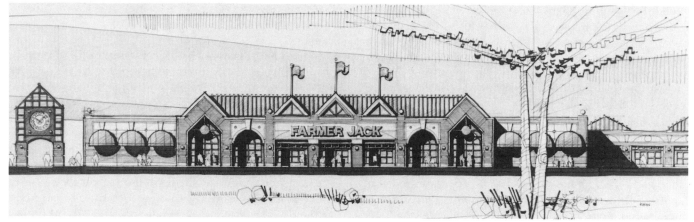

Northfield Commons east elevation.

approve outparcel tenants' plans. Although national or regional chain or franchise tenants may be required to use a standard building design, their approach to landscape design is likely to be much more flexible. An integrated landscape plan can do much to tie outparcels into the overall shopping center design.

Building Structure and Shell

Neighborhood and community shopping centers are usually highly efficient in terms of the ratio between usable/rentable space and GLA. In most instances, GBA is almost the same as GLA. Thus, the typical building design is a shell enclosing the most efficient and inexpensive bulk space possible concealed behind an attractively designed canopy and facade. In recent years, retail center design has evolved to require even more distinctive architecture to achieve a successful center. The structure must be eye-catching as well as functional. It should lend itself to future adaptation and should be a good neighbor to its surroundings. Older centers in need of repositioning may need to undergo major changes in appearance, not just re-leasing.

Structure. Small shopping centers usually are constructed of a lightweight steel roof-framing structure and tilt-up concrete walls or concrete masonry units. The design of foundations for shopping center buildings varies from region to region and from site to site, depending on subsurface conditions. Generally, however, caissons or spread footings are used to support columns and bearing walls, and a four- or five-inch-thick (10- or 12.5-centimeter) concrete slab is allowed to "float" within. For the floor slab, tolerances of movement that are set by most major tenants should not exceed three-fourths inch (2 centimeters). Likewise, the floor slab must be as level as possible. New finishing techniques using a laser screed can significantly reduce variations in flatness, but the underlying soil may require treatment with lime or cement to reduce shrink and swell and maintain level floor slabs over time. Alternatively, in some instances, on-site soils should be replaced with fill materials of higher quality to achieve the same objective.

Pouring each section of slab as a tenant finish item makes quality difficult to control. When the floor slabs

are poured in the normal sequence of building shell construction, allowances must be made for plumbing lines to serve future restrooms. A recommended technique is to place water and sanitary sewer lines parallel to, and three feet (0.9 meter) away from, the rear wall of the building and delay pouring the rearmost five feet (1.5 meters) of slab until tenants decide where to locate restrooms. Any location designated for restaurant use, however, should be constructed without a slab during initial construction because of the heavy utility needs of restaurants and the varied nature of their layouts. The slab should not be poured until the space is leased and the tenant has designed a layout for utilities. Thus, when a center has been acquired for rehabilitation and retenanting, the ideal location to locate a new tenant at least cost is a space that was previously occupied by a restaurant, supermarket, or fitness center because of their greater than normal utility requirements.

Shopping center structural frames most often consist of steel tube columns and bar joists. For main support members, joist girders offer lighter weight and more flexibility in duct locations and roof penetrations than steel or prestressed concrete T-beams. Efficient structural spans range from 24 to 30 feet (7.3 to 9.1 meters) for main support beams or girders and 30 to 42 feet (9.1 to 12.8 meters) for bar joists. Structural bays should not be planned around "typical" store widths, because "typical" will become the exception rather than the rule as tenants are acquired and positioned—and when the center is retenanted.

Shell Components. The center's exterior facing materials contribute to its image and its individuality. Using more than one material can create an attractive unified exterior and a distinctive image. Materials should be capable of being speedily assembled and erected, should be durable and easily maintained, and, ideally, should be available locally.

The choice of method for enclosing the side and rear walls of a shopping center is driven by cost. Tilt-up concrete wall panels are often favored, primarily because they can be erected by inexpensive laborers. Tilt-up walls designed for a 15- to 20-foot (4.6- to 6-meter) height are only five and one-half to seven inches (12.5 to 18 centimeters) thick and may serve as load-bearing structural walls. An alternative is to use load-bearing concrete masonry units, eight or 12 inches (20.4 or 30.5 centimeters) thick. Both these wall materials can be painted, plastered, or bricked.

Regular spacing of rear access and service doors is necessary. Spacing is generally calculated by taking the smallest average tenant size expected for the center and dividing this square footage by the depth leased. A good rule of thumb is to provide rear doors 16 to 20 feet (4.8 to 6.1 meters) apart for a 60- to 80-foot-deep (18.3- to 24.4-meter) space.

Most of the insulation for the building shell is a tenant finish item; nevertheless, insulation should be installed at perimeter walls and above ceilings. When considering reuse of older structures, stripping the building down to the shell frame may not be enough, because residual contaminants such as asbestos and lead paint may still be present.[31] For example, cement asbestos tile and sprayed asbestos insulation were common in the 1950s. Removal of these products may prove costly and could negatively affect the economic feasibility of a rehabilitation project. Another design practice that will affect the location of insulation is the current trend toward higher vertical spaces achieved by eliminating a ceiling and leaving ductwork and piping exposed. The only place for insulation in this approach is on top of the roof decking or directly on its underside.

Roof Systems. Roofs are often one of the most costly and difficult aspects of construction for shopping center developers. A typical roof lasts 12 to 15 years, but correctly installed and proactively maintained, it will last 20 years. Leaks resulting from inadequate maintenance or penetrations of the roofing are among the most common complaints from tenants. Thus, selecting the right roofing material for the specific project is an important decision.

Three principal types of roofing are used for shopping centers—built-up, single-ply membrane, and modified bitumen. Since 2000, single-ply roofs have become the dominant form, used for 49 percent of new construction, with built-up roofing at 21 percent and modified bitumen at 19 percent.[32] The elastomeric properties of these rubber-type membranes allow them to stretch and move with the deck, preventing tears. The three dominant categories of membranes are EPDM (ethylene propylene diene monomer), PVC (polyvinyl chloride), and TPO (thermoplastic polyolefin). EDPM is essentially a rubber membrane, PVC is a plastic, and TPO, the newest entry, combines the properties of both EPDM and TPO membranes.[33]

The best roof system for a particular center may well depend on the local climate. The Nelson Companies, developer of Northfield Commons, often uses a ballasted roof, that is, a single-membrane roof with washed river stone as ballast. This approach keeps the roof down in windstorms, insulates in all climates, and is inexpensive to apply. Choosing the right roof should be based on the answers to the following questions, according to Bill

Baley, vice president of operations, Pegnato & Pegnato Building Systems:[34]

- What is the cost per square foot budgeted for this location?
- How cut up is the roof system? Does it have a lot of penetrations, curbs, and equipment?
- How much foot traffic is there near the building?
- What kind of weather will the roof be subject to?
- Will the roof be subject to any contaminants (jet fuel, oils, food grease, and so on)?
- What problems have been experienced with systems used in the past?
- What is the anticipated length of ownership of the center?

White membrane roofing has been developed in response to concerns about energy efficiency and the environment. Although white membranes can cost twice as much as black membranes, cost savings in energy expenses over the life of the roof can offset the additional expense and may even generate significant savings, depending on location. For instance, a building in Florida may end up saving hundreds of thousands of dollars, while a building in Illinois may save tens of thousands of dollars over the life of a roof.[35] Regardless of the system or material used, the roof must be well designed, constructed of reliable materials, properly installed, and regularly inspected. A large percentage of lawsuits involving new construction are related to roofing failures; careful attention to roof construction is critical.

In general, roofs should slope at least one-quarter inch per foot (0.6 centimeter per 30.5 centimeters) to ensure good drainage. The future installation of rooftop-mounted HVAC units should be anticipated in designing the roof, with allowances made for their weight and prefabricated roof curbs provided to minimize random penetrations of the roof.

Front Elevation. A considerable portion of the construction budget should be spent on the front of the center, the most important facade in terms of architectural character and quality and overall image. For the front of the center, a variety of facing materials are worth considering—masonry, metal panels, wood, tile, stucco. Of these choices, masonry is the most durable and offers great flexibility in treatment. Its very durability, however, makes it more unlikely than other surfaces to be modified during future remodeling. The choice of material again depends on the character of the community. In the Midwest and East, masonry is the standard of quality, while in the West, tile, wood, adobe brick, or stucco may be more suitable. The artificial stucco EFIS is no longer recommended for store elevations, and many insurance companies will not cover the cost of replacing it because it is not durable and is easily damaged in high-traffic areas. Any of these materials may be used to build a colonnaded walk or arcade, the traditional means of sheltering customers and protecting storefronts from the weather. Canopies may be cantilevered from the building elevation or supported by freestanding columns. Their size is determined by the chosen architectural style; 10 to 15 feet (3 to 4.5 meters) is an ample width for a walkway.

The image of strip shopping centers has changed considerably in recent years as developers seek to create higher-quality centers of greater distinction. Daniel J. Fox of Regency Centers says, "The days of standard designs for grocery-anchored neighborhood centers are gone; we are spending more and incorporating upscale architecture, landscaping, and signage in our neighborhood centers. We're concerned with cost, but we're equally concerned with building a really nice shopping center."[36]

The immediate surroundings and general preferences of the region and the market dictate the appropriate project design. In a few cases, an extremely bold design might be suitable for a project, but a distinctive and attractive design that remains consistent with the character of its surroundings not only enhances the project but also receives community support. In some instances, however, a dramatic shift in the character of design is desirable and needed to overcome adverse surroundings.

Tenant Signage. Signage for shopping center tenants is an important source of a project's color, vitality, and atmosphere, and it should be an integral part of building design. Options for tenant signage available today are numerous and include:[37]

- specially shaped box signs;
- individual internally illuminated letters with Plexiglas faces;
- open-face letters with exposed neon;
- reverse-channel letters with halo effect lighting;
- bare neon, with or without special backgrounds;
- individual letters mounted on a common raceway, with or without a "receiver" channel;
- internally illuminated sign bands; and
- graphics screened onto canvas or "Panaflex" awnings.

Although tenants usually pay for their own signs, developers exercise control over what tenants can display through a declaration of permitted and prohibited signage and an approval clause in each tenant's lease. Such declarations typically forbid roof signs and large projecting signs and instead favor placement at a certain level on, above, or below a canopy, depending on a project's architectural treatment. Insistence on uniform scale, size, and placement has been practiced and is easy to administer, but flexibility is also important. In many centers today, tenants are given more freedom to design tasteful, attractive signs that fit into a center's overall image.

The design of tenants' signage should be closely linked to the architectural character that has been selected for the center. If the center's design is formal, the signs should be formal and conservative. If the center has a clear historical or cultural idiom—Spanish colonial, Key West Victorian, New England village, for example—then signage should be consistent with that character. Often,

The design for Town & Country Village in Houston, Texas, maximizes storefront visibility through the use of multiple building pads and curved streets throughout the 43-acre (17.4-hectare) site.

a design theme for a center is counter to the corporate signage of a national chain or franchise, but there are acceptable adaptations that can work for both the center and the tenant.

The optimum height of letters in shopping center tenants' signs is a controversial subject. Research on environmental graphics suggests that one inch (2.5 centimeters) of a letter's height is required for every 30 feet (9.1 meters) between the viewer and the sign. For example, a pedestrian should theoretically be able to read an undercanopy sign with three-inch-high (7.5-centimeter) letters from 90 feet (27.4 meters) away, while occupants of a vehicle passing the center should be able to read a 24-inch-high (61-centimeter) fascia sign from a distance of 720 feet (220 meters). This rule of thumb must be adjusted for the speed of the walker or vehicle and the simplicity, or lack thereof, of the typeface and the number of distractions in the immediate environment of the sign.

If signage to be permitted is not properly addressed early in the development process, problems may occur with tenants that erect inappropriate signs. In general, the allowed signage is governed by the community's sign ordinance. A developer, however, may wish to be more specific about details of the signage program and limit some things that are permissible under the sign ordinance, such as temporary signs. Although most communities have fairly restrictive sign ordinances, some may still be more liberal or flexible than the developer's market strategy for the center. Thus, the center's signage program must be developed within the limits imposed by local regulation. In some communities, a developer may be able to submit a signage program that deviates from the standard and obtain approval tied specifically to the center for which it is proposed. When a custom signage program is an integral part of the overall center design, the developer should confer with local officials. A flexible approach might be supported when the center design seeks to emulate historical architecture and historical signage patterns, particularly when the center under consideration is a specialty or themed center.

Interior Design

Tenant Space. Space leased by a tenant typically contains designated frontage, unfinished party walls separating the space from retail neighbors, an unfinished floor, and exposed joists for roof support. The architect has indicated placement of a rear door and utility stubs in plans for the shell. Both these features might be repositioned if the lease deal is made while the shell is still under construction, as is often the case.

Most developers use an allowance for finishing tenant space. The allowance, usually a dollar amount per square foot, may include floor slabs and standard floor coverings, standard light fixtures, HVAC of a certain capacity, rear doors, and a standard display window and entrance door. Tenants then pay for any upgrades to these standards over and above the dollar allowance and all other costs of finishing the space—custom fixtures, additional partitions, bathrooms, kitchen if the tenant is a restaurant, specialty light fixtures, built-in counters and shelves, and painting. To the extent that the landlord's responsibilities and the tenant's responsibilities vary from the standard allowances, they are plainly indicated on working drawings and specs and spelled out in lease documents.

To accommodate changing needs, the shopping center should be designed for structural flexibility; if possible, leasing arrangements should be flexible so that tenants can be moved to larger or smaller spaces as needed. Except for intervening fire walls, the spacing of which is governed by local building codes, partitions between tenants' spaces should not be used as bearing walls. Such partitions should be built of materials and by methods that allow for easy removal—typically, metal studs and gypsum board. To allow for flexibility in operations, structural elements such as plumbing and heating stacks, air-conditioning ducts, toilets, and stairways should be placed on end walls or on the walls least likely to be removed if the store is enlarged or the space redivided.

Store Size. Store widths for particular types of tenants are not standard. Chain store companies have studied the matter for years, and each company has employed experts to ascertain the proper width for its stores. For most modern centers, however, the design of the shell usually requires wide spans between structural columns so that stores can be inserted into modules with a minimum of conflicts with columns. When conflict occurs, columns can be disguised as part of the fixtures and often can be used as part of a store's decorative features.

For neighborhood and community centers, store depths of 40 to 120 feet (12.2 to 36.6 meters), with 70 feet (21.3 meters) a reasonable standard, are appropriate for most tenants. A key principle in deciding store depth is to use the proposed mix of tenants and store frontage they are likely to want as a basis for establishing store depth. The building could be designed with offsets at the front and rear to vary the depth. Some tenants will be satisfied and may even welcome an L-shaped

space that wraps around a small, shallow boutique space. For many tenants, store depths of 50 to 75 feet (15.2 to 22.8 meters) are ideal, while depths of 40 to 80 feet (12.2 to 24.4 meters) will satisfy most tenants (except anchors, which must be treated as a special case). In general, shallow depths are better and can accommodate a greater breadth of tenants.

Tenant spaces should be kept to the minimum size necessary, because it is better for a tenant to be a little cramped than to have too much room and insufficient sales to justify the rent. Centers with a variety of smaller tenants seem to be considerably more successful than those with only a few large stores

Ceiling Height. Although many stores have 11-foot (3.3-meter) finished or open ceilings, some small stores may have ceilings as low as nine feet (2.7 meters). Certain specialized tenants, such as variety stores and supermarkets, may require finished ceilings as high as 13 feet (4 meters). The space between the finished ceiling and the roof usually contains air-conditioning ducts, electrical wires, plumbing lines, and other utility hardware; such equipment may require as much as two to three feet (0.6 to 0.9 meter) of space between the finished ceiling and the structure. When open-web steel joists are used, much of the ductwork and other lines can be threaded between the webs. Thus, the clear distance from the floor slab to the underside of the roof varies with the structural design. In specialty centers, unusual tenants may want skylights in their stores to create a different interior volume.

Floors. Tenants usually receive an allowance for the flooring in their spaces, which is installed in accordance with criteria established by the owner and incorporated into the lease. Although a floor covering is put over the concrete slab in sales areas, it is often omitted in storage areas. Floor coverings range from tiles of various materials to carpeting. Wood flooring is not recommended for stores unless required by the tenant's decorative scheme. Even then, some of the newer synthetics that look like wood should be considered.

Northfield Commons: Tenant Finishes

The supermarket (Farmer Jack) and the drug store (CVS Pharmacy) were built as build-to-suit properties. Building heights, areas, and specific dimensions, certain finishes (special plumbing, electricity, and HVAC equipment), and interior wall, floor, and ceiling finishes were part of the lease terms. The exterior design was specified by consent agreements.

Specialty stores were built to include a concrete floor, one lavatory built to ADA standards, a ceiling, and the demising partitions between the stores. Only $35,000 was provided for tenant improvement allowances, or $1.61 per average square foot ($17.30 per square meter) of leased specialty space. ∎

Source: The Nelson Companies, West Bloomfield, Michigan.

Utilities. Leases should specify the developer's responsibility for providing vents and drains for tenants such as supermarkets, restaurants, and dry cleaners—any tenants that require large plumbing installations. Installation of the floor slab usually should be deferred until these tenant spaces are leased, because formulation of the tenant's underfloor requirements is likely to extend past the developer's shell construction schedule.

Keeping all utilities, including water lines, overhead should be seriously considered. An overhead leak may cause some damage but can be more easily located and repaired. Leaks under the slab are much more damaging and expensive to repair and disrupt use of the space. If overhead water lines are used, measures must be taken to ensure that the lines are not exposed to freezing temperatures.

Generally, a primary source of electricity provided by the developer is located at the rear of the building and individually metered. Each tenant is then required to provide the secondary electrical service from the meter, subject to the landlord's review and approval.

In strip centers, individual HVAC units typically are provided for each tenant, although in some instances, a central plant may be provided. Tenants can be made responsible for their individual units under the lease terms, or they can be maintained by the center's management. Shopping center management is always responsible for a central plant. Thus, in smaller centers, a central plant adds a management function that might be best left to individual tenants. Hybrid systems, employing large multitenant rooftop units, are also available. They may be appropriate when management retains the responsibility for maintenance. Because energy costs and energy conservation are important considerations, the selection of the most appropriate HVAC system requires the skill of a mechanical engineer familiar with the alternative gas and electric systems available to evaluate initial, operating, and maintenance costs and recommend the best system.

Construction

Proper management of the construction process is important for maintaining quality and cost control. Numerous factors dictate the correct time to begin construction, but the developer should make certain that it does not begin prematurely, because it would likely lead to problems and higher construction costs. For example, if shell construction begins before anchor tenants are committed and their space requirements known, change orders requiring costly tearing out and redoing construction may be necessary. Some communities issue building permits for foundations before approval of complete building plans. This early start can again lead to cost increases if final building design approvals are delayed or if approvals result in unanticipated subsurface requirements.

For the developer, shopping center construction involves two principal areas of concern: preparation of the site and shell, and tenant finishes. (Contracting arrangements for the site and shell, which do not differ significantly by property type, are discussed in Chapter 2.)

Tenant finishes present numerous challenges peculiar to retail development. Most important, the developer should establish and maintain close rapport with every tenant. Successful coordination involves:[38]

- a clear understanding of the deal and each person's responsibilities;
- agreement on specifications, plans, and procedures;
- follow-through enabling both parties to monitor progress; and
- communication so that exigencies are held to a minimum.

The responsibilities of each party and the specifications for construction are included in the tenant improvement schedule.

The construction of tenant finishes usually involves variations on two methods: shell and allowance, and build to suit. Each method has its own advantages and disadvantages. The simpler approach is shell and allowance, in which the developer constructs the building shell and allows the tenant a specified sum to complete all other permanent improvements to the store. In the build-to-suit approach, the developer and tenant negotiate a deal whereby the developer completes the tenant finish work and the cost is divided based on the negotiated terms of the deal. This method allows the developer to control the quality and consistency of construction, and provides a valuable service for small and inexperienced tenants. It is unlikely to be acceptable to an anchor or national chain tenant. A third alternative is also available in which the developer chooses to simply supply the shell and the tenant must bear the full cost of buildout. This approach will not work for tenants who do not have the necessary capital to do a good job. A combination of the three approaches complicates the leasing process; it is not desirable because the combination could result in widely variable allowances for tenants. In a soft market, however, tenant allowances can become a negotiating point in closing a desirable lease. Moreover, a developer may need to adjust his strategy when interest rates move up and prospective tenants can no longer afford to finish their shells.

David Nelson, president of the Nelson Companies, says, "Generally, tenant improvement allowances, at least in theory, are granted at the discretion of the developer. Most tenants expect them, but not all get them. Every developer should have a policy about the use of allowances and create a reserve in the project pro forma to cover the cost."

The Nelson Companies, in its building leases (but not ground leases) for major tenants, generally provides a build-to-suit facility or tenant allowance. The tenant allowance covers the cost of constructing the interior of the building, or it may cover the shell and finishes if the building is a prototype required by the tenant. For smaller tenants, the policy varies depending on size of the tenant, importance of the tenant to the merchandising of the shopping center, and the requirements of the tenant. According to Nelson, "We generally do not do build-to-suits or provide tenant allowances for nonnational or nonregional major or specialty tenants. In some cases, we agree to provide a minimum tenant improvement allowance or do some minor construction if it helps the deal along and we need the tenant. Because tenant allowances are often misused, we feel it is bad policy to provide funds greater than the cost of the improvements. If the developer is not careful, the tenant could be operating its business based on the developer's resources or credit. We usually insist that local specialty tenants have the operating capital to build, open, and operate their stores for approximately one year before turning a profit. Fair or not, nonchain tenants do not have the leverage to insist on tenant allowances, and we tend not to provide them. In any case, we have never provided a construction allowance for tenant improvements for a restaurant, one of the riskiest of all businesses."

The amount of the tenant allowance depends on the type and size of the shopping center, the size of the tenant, the importance of the tenant to the merchandising of the shopping center, and the tenant's requirements. For the Nelson Companies, the allowance typically ranges from $5.00 to $25.00 per square foot ($54.00 to $270 per square meter) or more. The company tries not to give a tenant allowance that exceeds the first year's rent, as local specialty tenants, regardless of lease terms and guarantees, generally do not have the capital to pay them off if they fail in the first year. If a tenant allowance is given, it usually ranges from 15 percent to 75 percent of the first year's rent. Nelson notes, "Some allowances for national or major regional tenants are worth one, two, or, in rare cases, more than two years of base lease payments from that tenant. In those cases, however, the tenant has the highest bond rating, and under the lease terms, the landlord is assured that it will at least achieve the return of its investment, whether the tenant is there or not."

Whatever basis is used, the developer must be sensitive to the tenant's needs if construction is to proceed smoothly. Supplying pertinent information and guidance will help coordination between the developer and the tenant. A data book prepared by the developer can provide the retailer and the architect/engineer with answers to many questions. The data book should contain:[39]

- an index of all the developer's architectural and engineering plans, specifications, and details;
- sections through, and details of, the leased wall construction and of any other elements of construction that may affect the tenant's planning;
- definitions of symbols used for walls, partitions, ceilings, doors, various types of electrical outlets and switches, and panel boards; riser diagrams; and door and roof finish schedules;
- definitions of standard mechanical symbols and connections;
- definitions of standard HVAC symbols;
- local design factors or criteria available to the tenant's engineer;
- excerpts of unusual building code requirements that will be helpful to the tenant's out-of-town architect/engineer; and
- work rules.

It is important to provide knowledge of local code requirements specific to retail uses. For example, a new International Building Code (IBC) published in 2000 by the International Conference of Building Officials (ICBO) mandates aisle widths of 44 inches (1.1 meters). Although in many areas of the country this requirement already exists, it is rarely enforced.[40] Local interpretation will probably decide whether this requirement applies only to main aisles or to all aisles in a store.

Congressional Plaza in Rockville, Maryland, is anchored by four stores of 20,000 square feet (1,860 square meters) or more.

In addition, the developer may provide an outline of the steps and procedures a tenant should follow to have plans and applications approved by government agencies and to file for a certificate of occupancy. The developer also should inform the tenant about any unusual jurisdictional situations and whether union labor is required.

Financing

Several aspects of financing are peculiar to shopping centers. (See Chapter 4 for a thorough discussion of the various sources and methods of financing for income property.)

Small neighborhood or community centers—often the type of project in which beginning developers are involved—can be particularly stable investments because they tend to be oriented toward the sale of nondurable consumer goods and services, those items bought regardless of changes in the economy. Supermarkets and drugstores generally can maintain relatively stable sales at all times, because they sell products that are needed regularly. Specialty centers, on the other hand, are more subject to fluctuations in the economy and are considered riskier investments. Thus, they are inherently more difficult to finance, especially if the developer has no track record.

In some instances, shopping centers can offer another attractive feature to lenders because of the amount of inflation protection they provide. "The shopping center . . . offers inflation protection [via] percentage net leases that are relatively short in duration. As the prices of consumer goods and services rise with inflation, the overage lease payments received by the landlord rise."[41] But because percentage rents are less prevalent in community centers and even less so in neighborhood centers, this feature may not be available to developers of small centers. Although percentage rents can make the longer-term financial performance of a shopping center a more attractive investment, "percentage rent is not a factor at the bank, [because] lenders look at base rent."[42]

To obtain the best financing for a shopping center, the project must have at least 75 to 80 percent of its leases with long-term creditworthy tenants. Lease terms for approximately 50 percent of the space must be for at least 20 years, with the balance of leases for creditworthy tenants a mix of ten- and 15-year terms. That is not to say that financing can be obtained only with such lease commitments, but the absence of such commitments might make obtaining favorable financing with attractive terms more difficult.

In some cases, public financing may be available for new shopping centers, especially in inner-city areas or in communities interested in economic development. Likewise, it may be possible to find lenders who consider inner-city opportunities as part of their civic responsibility. Developers interested in inner-city opportunities should explore the possibility of a joint venture with

figure 7-7

Comparison of Typical Permanent Loans from Different Types of Lenders

	Wall Street Conduit	Bank	Life Insurance Company	Credit Company
NOI	$1,000,000	$1,000,000	$1,000,000	$1,000,000
Term (years)	10	5	10	5
Type	Fixed	Variable	Fixed	Variable
Note Type	10-year Treasury bill	Prime	10-year Treasury bill	LIBOR[a]
Note Spread (percent)	2.25	1.00	2.30	3.50
Note Rate (percent)	7.50	7.75	7.55	7.25
Amortization (years)	30	25	25	30
Constant (percent)	8.39	9.06	8.91	8.19
DCR	1.25	1.25	1.25	1.20
Maximum Loan Amount (Test 1)	$9,057,783	$8,826,178	$8,981,741	$10,179,838
NOI	$1,000,000	$1,000,000	$1,000,000	$1,000,000
Cap Rate (percent)	9.00	9.00	9.00	9.00
Value	$11,111,111	$11,111,111	$11,111,111	$11,111,111
LTV Ratio (percent)	75.00	75.00	70.00	80.00
Maximum Loan Amount (Test 2)	$8,333,333	$8,333,333	$7,777,778	$8,888,889
Maximum Loan	$8,333,333	$8,333,333	$7,777,778	$8,888,889

[a]LIBOR is the rate on dollar-denominated deposits, also known as Eurodollars, traded between banks in London.

Source: Steve Bram, George Smith Partners, Los Angeles, California, 2001.

The design of Redmond Town Center in Redmond, Washington, incorporates public open spaces and a variety of specialty stores in an open-air center.

nonprofit community groups or churches, which might have capital resources, a suitable site under their ownership or control, or access to venture capital.

One means of raising equity financing for shopping center development is to sell parcels to anchor tenants or outparcels to fast-food restaurants, banks, and similar businesses after the center plan has taken shape. The value of these outparcels should increase as the certainty of the shopping center's being built increases; thus, the developer not only recaptures equity capital previously invested in the land but also can realize a substantial profit. A comparison of typical loans from various financing sources is presented in Figure 7-7.

Marketing

Leasing

Leasing for a shopping center is more complex and demanding than for any other type of development; it involves creating an effective leasing plan, obtaining commitments from anchor tenants early in the process, and then leasing the smaller spaces according to the leasing plan. The leasing plan represents the center's investment potential and is fundamental to the planning process. Every leasing plan should contain the following components:[43]

- macroeconomic overview;
- market area definition and analysis;
- strengths and weaknesses of the subject property;
- competitive outlook;
- tenant mix strategy;
- site issues and expansion potential;
- space-by-space analysis; and
- overall goals and strategy.

Prepared early in the development process, the leasing plan addresses the best tenant mix, the placement of tenants within the center, rent schedules, the pricing of store spaces, and lease specifications. The leasing plan is not cast in stone, however, and the developer must be prepared to modify it as the project evolves from concept to completion.

Tenant Mix. The most desirable tenant mix for a proposed shopping center is determined by a variety of factors, including the development concept, the size and type of center, competition in the area, the target market, and trends in consumer preferences. Preliminary determination of the preferred anchor tenant or tenants can be made after the developer has learned the characteristics of the market to be served. A shopping center's composition is ultimately determined, however, by the developer's ability to attract and negotiate with desired prospective tenants. The mix should be based on the market analysis, but the goals of the initial leasing plan may not be entirely met; tenants' preferences and resistance will almost inevitably result in a number of compromises.

In recent years, smaller centers have drawn a wider array of tenants, including many that were located previously in regional centers or prime downtown locations. Apparel stores and fashion-oriented retailers, for example, now can be found in specialty centers or even in centers anchored by supermarkets. Anchor tenants in small centers can include off-price apparel stores, home centers, movie theaters, children's stores, and health and racquet clubs.

A balanced tenant mix that meets financial credit requirements should include both strong, credit-rated national firms and good local merchants. Figures 7-8, 7-9, 7-10, and 7-11 indicate the general tenant composition of community and neighborhood shopping centers in the United States that can be used as guidelines but not absolutes when seeking out tenants for smaller centers.

In choosing stores for a center in an area experiencing new growth, the developer must secure shops that can render a service to the trade area and that have the financial stamina to weather a pioneering period. The

figure 7-8

U.S. Community Shopping Centers: Composition by Tenant Classification Group

Tenant Classification	Percent of Total Owned GLA[a]	Percent of Total Sales	Ratio: Percent of Sales to Percent of GLA	Percent of Total Charges	Ratio: Percent of Total Charges to Percent of GLA
General Merchandise (excluding department stores)	22.0%	16.0%	0.73%	12.1%	0.54%
Food	16.0	26.0	1.62	12.3	0.76
Food Service	6.0	8.0	1.29	10.7	1.73
Clothing and Accessories	10.0	12.0	1.22	11.6	1.21
Women's Wear	4.0	4.0	1.03	4.7	1.31
Children's Wear	b	1.0	1.20	0.7	1.40
Men's Wear	b	1.0	1.20	0.7	1.40
Family Wear	4.0	6.0	1.37	4.2	1.02
Shoes	2.0	2.0	1.05	2.5	1.25
Home Furnishings	6.0	6.0	0.98	7.3	1.28
Home Appliances/Music	3.0	4.0	1.45	3.7	1.28
Building Materials/Hardware	2.0	2.0	0.83	1.6	0.70
Automotive	1.0	b	0.50	0.8	1.00
Hobby/Special Interest	5.0	4.0	0.88	6.0	1.20
Gifts/Specialty	4.0	4.0	0.86	6.1	1.42
Jewelry	b	1.0	3.00	0.7	2.33
Liquor	b	b	0.50	0.5	1.25
Drugs	3.0	5.0	1.79	2.1	0.75
Other Retail	7.0	5.0	0.75	7.7	1.15
Personal Services	4.0	2.0	0.46	5.5	1.34
Entertainment/Community	5.0	2.0	0.44	4.5	0.94
Financial	2.0	b	b	2.1	1.40
Offices (other than financial)	2.0	b	0.14	2.2	1.05
Total	100.0%	100.0%		100.0%	

[a]Excludes department stores.

[b]Less than 0.05 percent.

Source: *Dollars & Cents of Shopping Centers®: 2002,* p. 255.

figure 7-9

Anchor Tenants in U.S. Community Shopping Centers

Tenant Classification	Rank	Average Number of Stores	Median GLA (Square Feet)	Median Sales Volume per Square Foot of GLA	Median Total Rent per Square Foot of GLA
Junior Department Store	6	a	33,200	$159.22	$5.35
Discount Department Store	2	0.3	69,098	173.63	4.95
Supermarket	1	0.4	48,928	370.29	6.70
Restaurant with Liquor	7	a	6,986	448.79	24.42
Family Wear	5	0.1	27,000	242.60	10.38
Sporting Goods—General	10	a	40,250	188.14	15.95
Books	8	a	25,645	225.70	18.81
Drugstore/Pharmacy	3	0.1	17,640	353.37	8.34
Office Supplies	4	0.1	24,444	243.65	10.88
Cinema—General (tickets and concessions)	9	a	32,027	60.57	6.30

[a]Less than 0.05 percent.

Source: *Dollars & Cents of Shopping Centers®: 2002,* p. 152.

figure 7-10

U.S. Neighborhood Shopping Centers: Composition by Tenant Classification Group

Tenant Classification	Percent of Total Owned GLA[a]	Percent of Total Sales	Ratio: Percent of Sales to Percent of GLA	Percent of Total Charges	Ratio: Percent of Total Charges to Percent of GLA
General Merchandise (excluding department stores)	5.0%	4.0%	0.72%	3.1%	0.62%
Food	34.0	62.0	1.82	24.5	0.72
Food Service	10.0	8.0	0.82	15.1	1.51
Clothing and Accessories	3.0	3.0	1.00	5.0	1.61
Women's Wear	1.0	2.0	1.21	2.6	1.86
Children's Wear	b	b	1.00	0.2	2.00
Men's Wear	b	b	0.50	0.5	1.25
Family Wear	1.0	b	0.33	0.5	0.83
Shoes	b	b	1.00	0.3	1.00
Home Furnishings	3.0	1.0	0.41	3.8	1.12
Home Appliances/Music	2.0	1.0	0.59	2.2	1.29
Building Materials/Hardware	3.0	1.0	0.30	1.5	0.56
Automotive	1.0	b	0.25	0.7	0.87
Hobby/Special Interest	3.0	2.0	0.47	3.2	1.00
Gifts/Specialty	3.0	2.0	0.78	3.3	1.22
Jewelry	b	1.0	1.50	0.7	1.75
Liquor	1.0	1.0	1.00	0.7	1.17
Drugs	6.0	8.0	1.38	5.5	0.90
Other Retail	5.0	3.0	0.51	5.3	1.04
Personal Services	10.0	3.0	0.33	12.7	1.31
Entertainment/Community	3.0	b	0.09	2.5	0.78
Financial	4.0	b	b	5.2	1.41
Offices (other than financial)	4.0	b	0.05	4.5	1.07
Total	100.0%	100.0%		100.0%	

[a]Excludes department stores.

[b]Less than 0.05 percent.

Source: *Dollars & Cents of Shopping Centers®: 2002*, p. 256.

figure 7-11

Anchor Tenants in U.S. Neighborhood Shopping Centers

Tenant Classification	Rank	Average Number of Stores	Median GLA (Square Feet)	Median Sales Volume per Square Foot of GLA	Median Total Rent per Square Foot of GLA
Variety Store	3	a	10,870	$115.12	$4.71
Discount Department Store	4	a	18,000	93.30	4.13
Dollar Store/Novelties	7	a	10,034		5.37
Supermarket	1	0.5	33,140	346.19	6.81
Restaurant with Liquor	9	a			
Furniture	8	a			
Home Accessories	10	a			
Hardware	5	a	20,329		
Drugstore/Pharmacy	2	0.2	10,080	381.28	8.20
Banks	6	a	4,000		

[a]Less than 0.05 percent.

Source: *Dollars & Cents of Shopping Centers®: 2002*, p. 218.

developer should also evaluate each tenant's credit rating, profit and loss experience, advertising policy, type of merchandise, type of customers, housekeeping practices, long-term operational record and merchandising policy, and integrity.

When the center is to be located on an infill suburban site or an inner-city redevelopment site, the developer's choice of tenants may be more limited. On infill suburban sites, it is a matter of identifying tenant categories that are underrepresented in the market, attracting anchors that are not presently in the local market and convincing them that the market is appropriate for them, and seeking out local merchants with a single location who might be interested in opening a second store. In some instances, such local merchants may not even have thought of opening a second store until they are approached.

One factor to consider when selecting tenants is that the resulting mix should provide balanced interplay among the stores. The success of a shopping center's tenant mix lies not in including or excluding a specific type of tenant but in selecting and combining a group of mutually reinforcing tenants that will serve the needs of the particular market.

In all types of centers, the developer must be flexible in selecting tenants and negotiating leases with them. Interior arrangements and tenant leases will be adjusted numerous times as negotiations proceed. A plan that includes at least two tenant types targeted for each space provides flexibility in leasing.

Generally, development of a small shopping center cannot move forward without commitments from anchor tenants; thus, marketing to likely anchor tenants must begin very early in the process. In fact, key tenants such as a supermarket, discount store, or drugstore should be tied in closely with the development team in planning the project. These tenants will want to influence the developer's decisions on building treatment and architectural style, parking, signage, and landscaping.

Thus, careful analysis of the kind of anchor tenant to target is one of the first steps necessary. For example, superstore centers can make the search for local tenants difficult, because the wide-ranging services of superstores can eliminate as many as ten types of tenants. Convenience stores are growing in popularity as anchor tenants in small centers and as attractive volume stores for larger strip centers, but they also may cause problems in leasing to other retailers: convenience

figure 7-12
Major Non–Department Store Anchors

Selected Store Types	Size Range (Square Feet)
1. Biggs, IKEA	>150,000
2. Warehouse Clubs (Sam's, Costco)	110,000–135,000
3. General Discounters (Wal-Mart, Target, Kmart, Venture)	100,000–130,000
4. Home Improvement (Home Depot, Lowe's)	100,000–130,000
5. Supercenters	125,000–180,000
6. Combo Stores (Kroger, Albertson's, Vons, Giant, Fiesta, Ukrops)	55,000–75,000
7. Sporting Goods (Sportstown, Oshmans, Sports Authority, REI)	50,000–60,000
8. Catalog Showroom (Service Merchandise)	50,000
9. Toys (Toys "R" Us)	45,000
10. White Goods (Linens'n Things, Bed Bath & Beyond, Homeplace)	35,000–50,000
11. Furniture (Homelife)	35,000–40,000
12. Baby Goods (Baby Superstore)	35,000
13. Home Electronics (Circuit City, Best Buy)	32,000–58,000
14. Books (Borders, Barnes & Noble)	25,000–45,000
15. Soft Goods (TJ Maxx, Marshalls, Ross Dress for Less, Steinmart)	25,000–45,000
16. Super Pet Stores	20,000–35,000
17. Computers (CompUSA, Computer City)	25,000–45,000
18. Office Supply (Office Max, Staples, Office Depot)	20,000–45,000
19. Athletic Shoes (World Foot Locker, NikeTown)	20,000
20. Music (Virgin, Tower)	15,000
21. Drugstores (Eckerds, Walgreens, CVS)	8,600–15,000

Source: Michael D. Beyard, W. Paul O'Mara, et al. *Shopping Center Development Handbook*, 3rd ed. (Washington, D.C.: ULI–the Urban Land Institute, 1999), p. 135.

stores sell a wide variety of goods and may insist on the exclusive right to sell certain items such as beer, milk, and bread. Other items sold at convenience stores—videotapes, liquor, fast food, and ice cream, for example—can also cause clashes with other tenants that sell these items. Supermarkets, drugstores, and even gas stations usually do not want to be located in a center with a convenience store.

The expansion plans of anchor-type tenants often serve as the driving force behind center development. For example, larger discount stores such as Target, Wal-Mart, and TJ Maxx are often cited as promoters of the resurgence of strip centers. The desire of food retailers to enter a new market makes them potential candidates when food retailers currently dominant in the market are disinterested. Likewise, just as the lines of traditional food retailers have progressively blurred as supercenters, category killers, convenience stores, and wholesale clubs continue to encroach upon what once was the supermarket's domain by adding food and household maintenance products, supermarkets have countered by offering nontraditional products and services such as video rentals, ATMs, and in-store banks, dry cleaning services, and even child care.[44] The presence of an anchor does not, however, presuppose the attraction of other tenants.

The intermixing of off-price and outlet tenants with more typical strip center tenants is rapidly becoming a trend. An outlet tenant can benefit from the traffic generated by a supermarket, and the other tenants in the center can, in turn, benefit from the ability of the outlet center to draw customers from greater distances.

Pricing Store Spaces. The amount of rent for a given space depends on the tenant's size, classification, and location in the project, and the amount of tenant allowance. Rent schedules should indicate clearly the tenant's classification, square footage allocation, minimum rent, and rate of percentage rent. A standard benchmark used for evaluating tenant pricing is ULI's *Dollars & Cents of Shopping Centers®*. Figures 7-13 and 7-14 summarize median GLA, median sales per square foot of GLA, median total rent per square foot of GLA, and median rate of percentage rent for different retail categories in U.S. community and neighborhood shopping centers. In neighborhood centers, for example, median total rent per square foot ranges from $4.87 for general merchandise stores to $15.90 for clothing and accessory stores. Percentage rents also can vary, from as little as 1.25 percent for food stores to 6.5 percent for entertainment venues. Some states have statutes that make it illegal for a landlord to charge or accept alternative rent based on a percentage of income for professional tenants. It is considered a sharing of income, and in those states only licensed professionals can share income with other professional businesses. Percentage rents for most large tenants range from 1 to 3 percent, while those for in-line stores cluster around 3 to 7 percent, with 6 percent most frequent.[45] In community centers, the rent for general merchandise stores might be around $6.00 per square foot, while that

Establishing a sense of community is essential to marketing and managing a shopping center today.

for jewelry stores might be more than $20.00 per square foot. Smaller in-line tenants pay percentage rents similar to those at neighborhood centers; however, larger "anchor" stores pay lower percentage rents, ranging from 1 to 5 percent.[46] (See "The Lease" below for an explanation of percentage rents.)

Tenant Placement. The placement of tenants within a center is an important and complex issue. Tenants may have strong and sometimes apparently arbitrary views about their desired position. A location that is advantageous for one type of business may be entirely wrong for another. Placement also depends on the size and depth of the space desired by the tenant. In deciding locations, developers should consider the following points:

- suitability of the tenant for the location, including the tenant's financial resources;
- compatible and complementary relationships with adjoining or nearby stores;
- compatibility of the tenant's merchandising practice with that of adjoining stores;
- parking needs generated by the tenant; and
- customer convenience.

The Lease
The way a shopping center is leased in large measure determines the center's final ambience, customer appeal, and degree of financial success. In the retail field, the percentage lease has become the most popu-

figure 7-13

Summary Tenant Information for U.S. Community Shopping Centers by Retail Category

Tenant Classification	Number in Sample	Median GLA in Square Feet	Median Sales per Square Foot	Median Rate of Percentage Rent	Median Total Rent per Square Foot	Median Common Area Charges per Square Foot	Median Property Taxes per Square Foot	Median Insurance per Square Foot	Median Total Charges per Square Foot	Median Total Charges as Percent of Sales
General Merchandise	263	30,000	$152.45	2.50%	$6.00	$0.59	$0.93	$0.10	$7.21	5.16%
Food	303	17,717	299.65	2.00	11.85	1.25	1.23	0.12	13.61	6.23
Food Service	889	2,200	289.66	6.00	19.06	1.83	1.41	0.13	22.69	10.10
Clothing and Accessories	670	3,785	193.41	5.00	14.26	1.99	1.39	0.18	18.04	9.41
Shoes	191	3,035	186.23	5.00	15.00	2.08	1.40	0.16	18.84	9.16
Home Furnishings	283	4,501	168.92	5.00	13.51	2.12	1.25	0.14	17.35	10.32
Home Appliances/Music	195	2,500	242.30	3.00	13.50	1.42	1.24	0.13	16.60	7.69
Building Materials/Hardware	58	6,070	230.07	4.00	10.26	0.93	0.80	0.10	11.70	6.38
Automotive	68	4,936	217.74	3.00	10.17	1.44	1.27	0.10	13.57	7.28
Hobby/Special Interest	261	3,459	198.47	5.00	13.50	1.51	1.34	0.13	15.57	10.23
Gifts/Specialty	303	3,300	163.23	6.00	14.52	1.86	1.34	0.13	17.48	11.40
Jewelry	93	1,200	452.97	6.00	20.48	2.49	1.36	0.11	24.77	6.82
Liquor	41	4,000	253.52	4.75	12.94	1.17	1.19	0.12	15.15	8.33
Drugs	81	12,150	366.73	2.00	8.50	0.73	0.90	0.10	9.53	2.73
Other Retail	521	1,840	243.83	6.00	15.45	1.72	1.34	0.11	18.77	10.72
Personal Services	845	1,400	146.71	6.00	15.00	1.51	1.23	0.12	18.31	14.80
Entertainment/Community	184	4,706	66.91	8.00	10.32	1.10	1.24	0.12	12.78	18.61
Financial	292	1,800			14.48	1.36	1.27	0.10	17.25	
Offices (other than financial)	353	1,600	259.14	3.34	12.33	1.15	1.24	0.12	14.42	8.97

Source: *Dollars & Cents of Shopping Centers®: 2002*, p. 16.

lar rental contract for both tenant and landlord. In the simplest form of a percentage lease, the tenant agrees to pay a rent equal to a stipulated percentage of the gross dollar volume of the tenant's sales. In shopping centers, the most common type of percentage lease is one in which the tenant agrees to pay a specified minimum rent plus a percentage of gross sales over a certain amount.

As mentioned, of the neighborhood shopping centers reporting in *Dollars & Cents of Shopping Centers®: 2002,* only 40 percent reported collecting overage rental income. In convenience centers, fewer than 25 percent collected overages. In community centers, however, more than 60 percent of tenants pay overage rents. Thus, the developer needs to determine whether percentage rates will be acceptable to prospective tenants and whether they will be a useful tool in negotiating lease terms with at least some tenants. Evidence from developers indicates that more and more national tenants are refusing to negotiate percentage rents into their leases, particularly in neighborhood, community, and power centers. An in-depth study released in 2001 by Lend Lease Real Estate Investments and PricewaterhouseCoopers suggests that shopping center industry leaders wonder whether percentage rents will survive the rise of e-retail.[47]

Various types of percentage leases exist, but the typical lease has a natural break point. For example, the lease for a 2,000-square-foot (185-square-meter) space at $12.00 per square foot ($130 per square meter) per year with a percentage rent rate of 6 percent works as follows. The minimum rent would be 2,000 times $12.00 (185 times $130) or $24,000 per year. The break point where the percentage rent begins is calculated as $24,000 divided by 0.06, or $400,000. Thus, the tenant pays a base rent of $24,000 per year plus 6 percent of annual gross sales greater than $400,000. Gross sales of $500,000 would result in an annual rent of $30,000 ($500,000 times 0.06, or $24,000 base rent plus $6,000 percentage rent). As discussed earlier, the rate of percentage rent varies from tenant category to tenant category. In some cases, steps in the rate of percentage rent go up or down as sales increase. Again, these steps vary with tenant category. With the recognition that percentage leases are declining in acceptance on the part of national tenants and that local nonpublic tenants are unlikely to accurately reveal their true sales, alternatives might include an annual increase based on the CPI or a fixed percentage increase of, say, 3 percent.

The percentage lease balances tenants' and the landlord's interests. It means, for example, that the landlord

figure 7-14

Summary Tenant Information for U.S. Neighborhood Shopping Centers by Retail Category

Tenant Classification	Number in Sample	Median GLA in Square Feet	Median Sales per Square Foot	Median Rate of Percentage Rent	Median Total Rent per Square Foot	Median Common Area Charges per Square Foot	Median Property Taxes per Square Foot	Median Insurance per Square Foot	Median Total Charges per Square Foot	Median Total Charges as Percent of Sales
General Merchandise	63	7,500	$102.96	3.00%	$4.87	$0.52	$0.63	$0.10	$6.11	4.74%
Food	191	25,313	328.27	1.25	8.00	0.89	0.87	0.10	9.96	2.37
Food Service	506	1,800	257.49	6.00	14.50	1.63	1.26	0.13	17.78	9.87
Clothing and Accessories	110	2,006	372.29	6.00	15.90	2.41	1.13	0.14	20.10	11.34
Shoes	13	2,800	225.87	5.00	9.50	1.11	1.35	0.15	11.87	6.53
Home Furnishings	55	4,700	241.42	5.50	14.00	1.75	1.38	0.16	17.50	11.30
Home Appliances/Music	73	2,000	200.72	5.00	12.65	1.36	1.29	0.15	15.58	6.90
Building Materials/Hardware	32	5,812	99.19	4.50	10.50	1.09	1.02	0.15	12.52	8.48
Automotive	29	2,800	1,122.12	3.00	11.54	1.14	1.39	0.11	14.53	4.61
Hobby/Special Interest	85	2,820	210.30	6.00	13.07	1.56	1.29	0.14	15.19	9.20
Gifts/Specialty	78	2,516	228.76	6.00	13.11	1.35	1.26	0.16	15.69	13.58
Jewelry	36	1,209	432.54	6.00	15.66	2.02	1.29	0.15	18.82	9.92
Liquor	26	2,400	277.78	3.75	13.43	1.30	0.99	0.11	15.07	5.86
Drugs	71	9,000	380.80	2.50	9.90	0.98	0.93	0.10	11.86	3.47
Other Retail	208	1,500	222.73	6.00	12.71	1.56	1.25	0.15	15.59	10.13
Personal Services	610	1,356	151.91	6.00	13.50	1.50	1.12	0.13	16.42	16.00
Entertainment/Community	83	2,495	77.03	6.50	10.00	1.28	1.30	0.13	13.19	23.30
Financial	197	1,600			12.50	1.29	1.00	0.14	14.86	
Offices (other than financial)	221	1,587	164.77	7.00	11.33	1.23	1.06	0.13	13.88	16.09

Source: *Dollars & Cents of Shopping Centers®: 2002*, p. 17.

can agree to a lower base rent for a tenant that may not be able to pay a higher rent until its sales have grown sufficiently to afford a higher rent. For the tenant, it means that if the landlord benefits from higher sales, then the landlord has an incentive to market the center to help generate those overages and to provide maintenance, management, and security that keep the center fully operating and attractive to customers.

Whether or not the lease includes a percentage rent clause, a net lease is almost always used for a small shopping center. The preferred lease is triple net: in addition to a base rent (plus overages if included), the tenant pays its prorated share of real estate taxes, insurance, and maintenance.[48] Many variations of lease terms are possible, including stepped base rent, free rent to achieve the desired base rent, lower base rent combined with a higher percentage so that the landlord takes a greater risk but has a greater gain if the tenant succeeds. This arrangement is often used for desirable first-time tenants who provide a needed special character for a center. The Rouse Company, when pioneering its festival market concept at Faneuil Hall Marketplace in Boston, wrote short-term or month-to-month leases for very small pushcarts at a percentage of sales and zero base rent. The pushcarts were the feature that made the project different, and

the risk to the Rouse Company was small because these tenants occupied space that would otherwise generate little or no rent income.

Exceptions exist for some tenant categories, most commonly financial institutions, service shops, and offices. For these tenants, the developer would be wise to consider short-term leases or leases where the base rent escalates based on a series of specified steps or on the CPI. With long-term fixed leases, the developer is not provided with enough incentive income to promote the center adequately.

The exclusive rights to sell a particular category of merchandise within a shopping center are still given in some situations in small centers. Many landlords prefer to grant these rights only when necessary—the insistence of a big retail company, for instance, or as a deal-making tool to finalize a lease agreement with a particularly attractive tenant.[49]

The center's leases function as an important management tool. Besides establishing obligations, responsibilities, and leasehold arrangements, the leases incorporate the means of preserving, over a long period of time, the shopping center's character and appearance as a merchandising complex. In effect, they establish a permanent partnership between the management and the tenants.

For example, the lease may have a buyout or cancellation clause for underperformance. A developer without significant retail development experience should retain an attorney with experience in retail leases. The novice developer also needs to have a standard lease form to use as a starting point and to make sure that all important lease elements are addressed.[50] Tenants should also use an attorney unless a court, in the absence of legal counsel for the tenant, finds that the developer has taken advantage of the tenant.

An example of where special skills are needed is the *use clause*. A restaurant lease should incorporate an attached menu that can be changed from time to time but sets an expected standard for the food style offered. A retailer's permitted uses should be limited to those agreed upon when it signed the lease to take space in the shopping center. This clause prevents a tenant from converting its store to another use or adding new merchandise lines that may conflict with those of other tenants. At a bare minimum, a chain store tenant can agree to operate its store as all the other stores in its chain. In supermarkets, for example, such businesses as pharmacies, bakeries, flower shops, coffee shops, branch banks, and laundry/dry cleaning pickup are but a few examples of new features that, if unanticipated, can affect the viability of other tenants.

From management's perspective, establishing the sharing of certain costs in the lease is very important. It must include a provision for the sharing of real estate taxes, insurance, common area maintenance (CAM), and operating expenses. Common area maintenance includes the cost of such routine activities as cleaning and maintaining the parking lot and other common areas, snow removal when needed, security, landscaping, lighting, trash removal, and utilities. Operating expenses also include the general repair and maintenance of buildings and roofs, seasonal promotional activities, general administrative and management costs, and the depreciation of machinery and equipment used to maintain the premises and reasonable replacement reserves. The developer/landlord should never accept "stops" for variable operating costs.

Organizing the Leasing Program

Agreements with leasing agents should address such issues as exclusive versus open listings, full commission to outside brokers, participation of in-house leasing staff, and incentives for the team leader. The leasing agent should be on the development team from start to finish and should provide guidance in the subtleties of tenant selection. A leasing agent with proven expertise in retail leasing in the specified market area should be chosen.

The developer must be personally involved in all stages, especially in the development of a target list for anchors that highlights priority tenants in a particular use category. Leasing is much more selective in shopping center projects than in office projects; the objective must not be simply to lease space but to lease the right space to the right tenant. Thus, setting priorities for the leasing staff and maintaining these priorities is imperative. In evaluating tenants for selection, the developer needs to consider numerous factors about each tenant:

- merchandise sold, both principal and subcategories;
- credit rating and references;
- other current locations;
- size of space needed;
- number of years in business;
- success in other stores;
- frontage needed;
- quality of management;
- business plan;
- planned date for store opening;
- compatibility with anchor;
- advertising policies;
- types of customers; and
- housekeeping practices.

Postconstruction Marketing and Promotion

A limited budget is the problem that most small centers encounter in marketing and promotion after opening. Anchor tenants, such as large grocery stores and drugstore chains, often already have their own campaigns and may refuse to participate in a center-wide effort. Smaller retailers do not have the cash to spend on promotion. Some developers believe that an owner needs four or five small centers to justify hiring a marketing staff person. Others, however, believe that a center of any size can benefit from an ongoing promotional program.

Leasing Hints for Placing In-line Users

- When leasing less than an entire block of space, always lease from the sides to the middle so that only one predetermined space is left instead of two.
- Try to assign spaces so that the last space could be divided in half and still meet minimum requirements. That is, if 15 feet (4.5 meters) is the minimum width, try to leave a 30-foot-wide (9.1-meter) space instead of a 27- or 28-foot-wide (8.2- or 8.5-meter) space.
- Try to lease the toughest space first, or if that is not possible, try to beat pro forma rents on easier space so that there is still rent flexibility for the toughest space.
- Consider what will be left to deal with—storefront width, column locations, signage area, rear or secondary access, parking—for the next tenant after each lease is made to use the remaining space for restaurant, retail, or office uses.
- On to-be-built space, try to include a provision that allows the landlord to move a tenant within a certain area up to a certain time for flexibility in lease-up. ∎

Source: ULI-the Urban Land Institute, "Shopping Centers: How to Build, Buy, and Redevelop," workshop manual, Spring 2001, p. 16.

Northfield Commons: Marketing Program

Objectives

- Articulate the vibrant personality of Northfield Commons in advertising, sales promotion, and media relations.
- Plan a proactive marketing game plan involving the strategies of Farmer Jack and CVS Drugs in the overall matrix.
- Facilitate the design and implementation of preopening direct mail/local newspaper for the grand opening.
- Coordinate the participation of VIPs, including elected officials, community leaders, and others involved in the project.
- Arrange for coverage of the opening as a news event in the print media and seek interest of radio and television stations.

- Showcase Northfield Commons as a premier community shopping center, representative of the excellence the Nelson Companies brings to all its planned developments.
- Feature the project's architectural amenities, including the brick exterior on all facings and the clock tower.

Target Audiences

- North Troy/Rochester Hills residents,
- Community leaders,
- Current and prospective tenants,
- Retail leasing agents,
- Elected and appointed officials,
- Employees of tenants,
- Print and broadcast media,
- Trade suppliers and services.

Opening Events

- Obtain lists of area business and home-owner opinion leaders; develop and distribute an individualized letter previewing the opening date.
- Collaborate with the Troy Chamber of Commerce to host an on-site walk-through a few days before the opening.
- Arrange a get-together for tenants to spotlight the grand opening marketing package. ∎

Source: The Nelson Companies, West Bloomfield, Michigan.

With a small budget, the marketing program must target a select market and reach it through a precise means. A good marketing plan extends beyond advertising, sales promotion, and special events and avoids trial-and-error approaches. It must consist of a deliberate series of actions designed to maximize a center's potential volume.

> Marketing in the 21st century is all about establishing a sense of community. Shopping centers are spending marketing dollars to promote community spirit instead of focusing ad budgets on special products and sales. The revelation that shoppers spend money where they are most comfortable has fostered a new school of thought for measuring ROI; results are evaluated in qualitative as well as quantitative terms.[51]

The concept of *positioning* lies at the foundation of a successful marketing plan. Positioning means more than creating a favorable image of a center; it consists of a careful analysis of a center's strengths and weaknesses and a close examination of the competition.

The developer should follow traditional guidelines for setting up a successful promotional program:[52]

- Financial participation in the center's promotional activities should be mandatory for all tenants, and a clause to this effect should be included in the lease.
- At least six months before the center opens (or reopens in the case of renovation or expansion), an aggressive publicity program should be instituted.
- At least three to six months before opening, a merchants association or a steering committee of merchants structured as a marketing fund should be operating —subject of course to successful preleasing. When an anchor tenant is in place, joint promotion with the owner and other merchants can stimulate substantial interest in the center.

- The center and its stores should be promoted as a single, cohesive unit. All advertising, including printed materials and radio and television spots, should seek to reinforce this perception.
- The center should be involved in community affairs to build goodwill and increase traffic to the center. For example, the center might financially support major community endeavors or plan and participate in civic events.
- The center's promotional unit and the merchants should always communicate with each other.

The size of the center determines the extent to which these activities should be pursued; small centers may find less need for many of them. If a center has a limited individual identity but is well located and attractively designed, little or no marketing may be the most cost-effective and successful approach.

If a merchants association is used in promotion, it acts as a clearinghouse for suggestions and ideas and is responsible for the programming of promotional events. Lease agreements stipulate that an association will be formed, that the tenants will pay a specified rate per square foot to the association, and that the developer will pay a certain percentage of the annual costs.[53] The developer/owner must organize and participate in the association and will also often be its guide and catalyst.

If a marketing fund, a technique begun in the 1970s and now widely used, will be created, tenants are still required to provide funds to promote the center, but the fund is totally controlled and administered by the developer/owner. The key advantage of using a marketing fund is that it allows the marketing director to concentrate on marketing and promotion rather than on details of the association.

Most small shopping centers, however, have neither promotional funds nor merchants associations. Tenants in small centers may find the ongoing costs of a promotional fund a burden rather than a sales generator, and a merchants association can be more of a problem than a solution for the developer. Nevertheless, a grand opening, seasonal decorations, and occasional special events such as a sidewalk sale are always appropriate.

Operations and Management

The effective management of a shopping center includes establishing a management approach and plan, setting up and maintaining effective financial records and accounting procedures, maintaining the property, and establishing good housekeeping practices. The objective is to minimize operating costs as a percentage of revenue while ensuring the project's long-term viability.

Perhaps the most important responsibility of the shopping center's management, however, is to stimulate merchants to create a marketplace that is above the commonplace. This objective can best be conveyed by regular communication with tenants about merchandising ideas that might be useful and further ensure the center's success. In addition, the developer/owner can use on-site maintenance personnel to observe and report activities that should cause concern. In addition to a weekly check of every store to review its condition, senior management should check stores during a monthly site visit with each tenant. When a problem arises, management should discuss it during the visit. If lease terms have been clearly violated, a more formal notification is required.

Management Approaches

Depending on the size of the center and the arrangements for operation worked out earlier during lease negotiations, the shopping center developer/owner provides maintenance and management in one of two ways: by direct supervision or employing a manager to supervise a maintenance and management staff, or by turning the center's operation over to a management firm. By acting directly as manager, the developer/owner maintains close control of the property and can influence more immediately the quality of the operation. By using an outside management firm, however, the developer may derive certain economies of scale and depth of expertise.

Owners often manage centers smaller than 75,000 square feet (7,000 square meters), because management fees charged for operating small centers are relatively high and because management of small centers is relatively straightforward. Managers who work on a fee generally get a percentage of rental income, usually 2 to 6 percent, depending on the size of the center and the scope of responsibility.[54]

The owner/manager also must decide whether or not to employ an on-site manager. For most centers smaller than 400,000 square feet (37,200 square meters), no on-site manager is needed unless the owner chooses to include offices, usually engaged in other activities, in the project.[55]

Security

Most small centers may not need regular on-site security operations. A community police substation, however, can be both a tenant and a built-in security force. Otherwise, many centers contract for a security patrol. A first step in determining security needs is to conduct a security evaluation or audit. The place to start is with the local police, who have knowledge of criminal and mischievous activity in the nearby community. Principals of nearby schools often have insight into potential problems. "Unsanctioned activities in the parking lot (vendors, a bus pickup point, [weekend private auto sales, commuter parking, student parking]) also create an unsightly nuisance at some centers."[56]

> Security has different meanings for the owner, the tenant, a shopper. To the owner, security means preserving the buildings that represent the owner's investment and maintaining peace and order so that tenants, shoppers, and the center staff are safe and are not deterred from doing business. To the tenant, security means protecting merchandise and employees, as well as providing a peaceful environment for customers. To the shopper, security means a feeling of total safety while in the center and while traveling to and from it.[57]

The center's layout and design are in themselves security tools. "No center should go 'completely dark.' But many property owners err on the side of too much lighting during closed hours and actually provide visibility for nocturnal criminals"[58] Likewise, a building design that does not have spaces for concealment or dark areas where visibility is poor provides psychological security for customers. In areas where crime against tenants is a possibility, the landlord and the tenants should consider store- and/or center-wide electronic security.

At the Martin Luther King shopping center in the Watts area of Los Angeles, developed shortly after the riots there, concerns for customers', tenants', and the center's safety led the developer to use an eight-foot-high (2.4-meter) wrought iron fence enclosing the site, video cameras, motion detectors, guards, an on-site police substation, and other security measures.[59] Although these were extreme measures, they worked in an area where riots had nearly burned out an inner-city neighborhood and where customers and tenants alike needed a strong sense of security for the center to be successful. With inner-city neighborhoods frequently underserved by retail stores but offering prime opportunities for new retail projects or revitalized street retailing, the lesson to be remembered is that security is a significant factor for success in shopping centers and requires an appropriate response after a careful evaluation of need.

Northfield Commons: Income/Expense Budget—January through December 2001

Income	
Rent	$1,056,700
CAM	
Insurance	20,000
Property Taxes	20,500
Other	184,800
Total CAM	225,300
Total Income	$1,282,000

Expenses	
CAM Expenses	
Insurance	29,000
Maintenance	
Exterminating	900
Grounds	8,900
Miscellaneous	1,200
Telephone/pager	600
On site	39,600
Parking lot	6,000
Snow removal	27,750
Supplies	4,800
Total Maintenance	89,750
Property taxes	164,000
Repairs	
Exterior	3,000
Miscellaneous	1,200
Plumbing	600
Roof	3,000
Asphalt and concrete	15,000
Total Repairs	22,800

Utilities	
Electric	16,700
Trash removal	10,800
Water	10,000
Total Utilities	37,500
Total CAM Expenses	$343,050
Operating Expenses	
Administrative Fees	$13,800
Leasing Costs	2,500
Licenses and Permits	50
Miscellaneous Maintenance	900
Management Fees	
Acquest	24,720
Nelson Properties	49,800
Total Management Fees	74,520
Professional Fees	
Accounting	4,000
Legal	4,200
Total Professional Fees	8,200
Repairs	
Miscellaneous	900
Total Repairs	900
Total Operating Expenses	$100,870
Total Expenses	$443,920
Net Income	$838,080

Source: The Nelson Companies, West Bloomfield, Michigan. ■

Financial Records and Control

To ensure success, the owner or manager must establish acceptable financial accounting and reporting procedures to collect rents (including overage rents), account for revenues and expenses, and evaluate performance. A shopping center, once completed, is like any other business in this regard.

Management's most important responsibility is to maintain accurate internal records that provide:

- control and accounting for cash and other physical property,
- data useful in policy making and decision making, and
- accurate figures for preparing tax returns.

Data produced in record keeping such as monthly information on sales figures, category performance, and productivity per square foot are critical in determining percentage rents.[60] Whereas tenants of office buildings pay only monthly rent (and perhaps expenses), rental calculations for a shopping center are more complicated and require that tenants furnish sales records and financial reports.

In the early days of the shopping center industry, the usual practice was to call for payment of the percentage overage annually in accordance with a sales report certified by an outside auditor or a responsible officer of the tenant company. More recently, leases generally have provided for uncertified overage payments quarterly, sometimes monthly, with an annual reconciliation based on an audited statement provided by the tenant. Such an arrangement levels the flow of income while keeping a tight rein on less financially responsible tenants.[61]

The Avenue at White Marsh is a 300,000-square-foot (27,900-square-meter) "main street" retail center in the heart of a 2,000-acre (810-hectare) planned community in a middle-market demographic area northeast of the city of Baltimore. The White Marsh community, under development by Nottingham Properties since 1972, consists of a regional shopping mall, residential neighborhoods of for-sale and rental attached and detached housing, a power center, hotels, office parks, and scattered pad sites, almost all on ground leases. The Avenue, completed in 1998, re-creates a five-block-long main street with angled parking, wide tree-lined sidewalks, and one-story retail shops and restaurants anchored by a 16-screen multiplex cinema. The main street is intersected by four cross streets, which help distribute parking for almost 2,500 cars among the surface lots that are out of sight of the Avenue's main street.

Site Description

Harry T. Campbell & Sons, a Baltimore County–based concrete contractor, purchased the 2,000-acre (810-hectare) White Marsh site in 1943 as a sand and gravel mine. The site, in the northeastern part of Baltimore County, was land-banked for many years. An interchange was constructed that would serve the site when I-95 went through the property in the early 1960s. With that improvement, the county designated the site a planned town center with a shopping mall and ever-decreasing densities of retail, commercial, and residential uses as they moved away from the mall. The White Marsh Mall, opened in 1981, is the largest regional mall in the Baltimore area.

Before the development of the Avenue, Nottingham started leasing ground for pad sites to national restaurant chains. The two closest to the Avenue are Red Lobster, which opened in 1992, and TGI Friday's, which leased another pad site at what is now the eastern end of the Avenue. The Avenue's 34.5-acre (14-hectare) site is located across Honeygo Boulevard—the major arterial road through the White Marsh community—from White Marsh Mall.

The Avenue at White Marsh includes several destination retailers and a major movie theater complex.

Courtesy Nottingham Properties, Inc.

In 1996, the market area's population was approximately 375,000 people within a seven-mile (11.3-kilometer) radius, representing roughly 152,000 households with a median household income of about $39,000 per year.

Development Process

By the time Nottingham was prepared to develop the 34.5-acre (14-hectare) site that became the Avenue at White Marsh, the White Marsh development was already 20 years old and had undergone a number of zoning changes. Consequently, Nottingham and the county planning commission had worked together on this development and were familiar with each other's objectives. Nevertheless, the entitlement process took 15 months.

Although the regional mall met the planners' criteria for a town center, it was surrounded by more than 80 acres (32 hectares) of parking and completely ringed by a three-lane access road and thus inaccessible to pedestrian traffic. A very active business and residential community had grown up around it, and the parking acreage isolated the community from the mall—from its own designated town center. Nottingham's conception of

the Avenue was as an alternative retail experience—a genuine town center.

The land, however, was zoned for office space only. Equally unfortunate was the county's quadrennial zoning cycle, which would not permit rezoning for another four years. Nottingham worked with the zoning commission and other county landowners to craft new PUD regulations for commercial development. Once the regulations were approved in 1994, Nottingham's was the second application to be approved in the county. The PUD regulations permit great flexibility in reconfiguring tenant use, allowing the project to change to meet the community's evolving needs.

Financing

To finance the Avenue's development costs, Nottingham put up its own cash to start, took short-term financing from a commercial bank to seal the deals, and then secured long-term financing from an institutional lender, although some deviations from this formula were allowed.

One advantage in financing is that the land was owned free and clear and thus not subject to carrying charges. As a shareholder-owned company, albeit closely held, Nottingham was answerable to equity holders who had historically supported long-range development that did not necessarily promise short-term returns, but shareholders did require that all pro formas include a valuation assessment of the land to justify the company's approach of highest and best use. An independent appraisal placed the value of the undeveloped parcel at $8.54 million, or about $250,000 per acre ($617,500 per hectare), at project inception.

Moreover, Nottingham's position was advantageous for securing debt financing. It had a longstanding relationship with its commercial bank, which had a branch in the White Marsh development area. According to the pro forma, permanent debt of $26 million was budgeted. Final debt financing approached $28 million, and loan payments were converted to equity in partnership with State Farm Life Insurance Company (another large tenant elsewhere in White Marsh), in the insurance company's first-ever land deal. Reported debt service of principal and interest was $2.6 million in 2000.

Despite these advantages and approximately 20 percent in equity (not including land valuation), project financing was difficult to obtain for an unprecedented project of this type in the weak retail market of that time. Site work could be started on a speculative basis, but construction needed to begin before having signed leases with the project's major tenants. Only by structuring the loan agreement so that construction draws could be issued once certain progressive criteria were met, with loan payments triggered by lease signings, was Nottingham able to obtain the necessary financing. This loan structure also reduced Nottingham's equity exposure during construction.

Design and Construction
The main street town center concept was still new in 1993 when planning started for the White Marsh version. Nottingham assembled a development team to ana-

lyze other examples of this type of retail center and their markets. They visited successful projects, primarily in coastal California and Florida, but they were all upscale developments not directly translatable to the middle-market demographics of the White Marsh region (although the development team was able to borrow a number of ideas that translated well to its middle-market merchandise mix and customer base).

Most obvious was the notion of a traditional main street with on-street parking. Wide tree-lined sidewalks would accommodate pedestrian traffic. Single-story retail establishments would front the sidewalks, forming massed buildings one block deep. Behind these building blocks would be conventional parking, only four bays deep. Between these building blocks, open areas would allow public gathering spaces and an inviting way to walk from the peripheral parking areas to the main street. Cross streets would aid vehicular circulation as well as provide additional sidewalks for pedestrian access to the Avenue.

Nottingham concluded that this concept could be adapted to the White Marsh

area's middle-market clientele if material costs could be kept within budget. RTKL proposed a design that adhered strictly to this strategy. For example, grade-level exterior walls were faced with durable but common materials such as ground-face and split-face concrete masonry units and brick, artfully combined and detailed.

Building blocks were designed to suggest the type of buildings that a traditional town in Maryland might have: a train station, a mill, a mercantile building, a city hall, a post office, a fire station, for example. Tenants were matched to reflect the building's thematic image—a device that was used repeatedly.

The central building on the main street is occupied by the anchor tenant, a Loews 16-screen multiplex. The main street is segmented in three parts, roughly following the curve of the arterial Honeygo Boulevard. The curve of the street slows vehicular traffic along the main street, aiding pedestrians as well as drivers backing their cars out of the diagonal parking spaces. The curve of the arc also adds aesthetic and psychological visual interest;
continued on next page

The Avenue's main street follows the curve of the adjacent major thoroughfare through the White Marsh community. Together with the head-in angled parking, the curve promotes low-speed automobile traffic.

Courtesy Nottingham Properties, Inc.

as one walks along the sidewalk, it is impossible to see the entire length of the street, and one is enticed to continue walking to see what is around the corner.

Storefronts are designed with standard-width bays, permitting flexibility as the tenant mix changes. Standard-size storefronts can be filled in with any material: doorways, fixed glass, or opaque veneers. The regularity of the bays actually promotes the thematic identity of each building block, while the variety in the storefront panels promotes the individuality of each tenant space. For similar reasons, all floor levels are identical in each building block.

Visibility of the shops' front doors is limited from the streets that ring the Avenue, but the numerous and generous vehicular and pedestrian open spaces between the blocks of buildings allow visual access to the street itself and the activity on it. The rears of the blocks are visible, but these service areas are well landscaped and screened.

Sidewalks and crosswalks are surfaced with multihued concrete pavers. A festive atmosphere is achieved by the use of kiosks, awnings, sidewalk seating, banners, signage, and graphics. Streetside cafés, fountains, sculptures, landscaping, and traditional streetlights in a custom color add to the ambience.

Three of the ten buildings at the Avenue —the multiplex theater and two freestanding restaurants totaling 88,211 square feet (8,200 square meters)— were built on ground leases by the tenants using the developer's contractors, with Nottingham providing utility stubs. These three tenants reimbursed the developer about $19.55 per square foot ($210 per square meter) for common site improvements. For retail spaces developed by Nottingham, the developer allotted an average allowance of $22.55 per gross leasable square foot ($245 per gross leasable square meter) for tenant fit-up, including tenants' mechanical, plumbing, and electrical work.

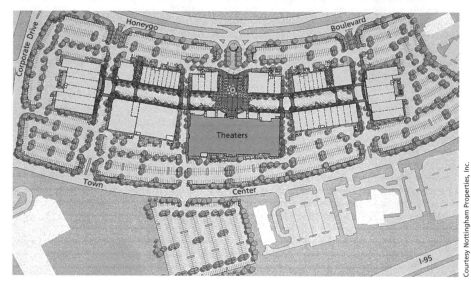

Site plan.

Tenants

Nottingham has attracted a mix of national and local merchandisers to the Avenue. Loews, Barnes & Noble, Bath & Body Works, Pier 1 Imports, Old Navy, and Chili's are the only stores one is likely to encounter in other shopping malls. Most of the other tenants at the Avenue are local, and many have their own loyal clientele.

The Avenue opened in summer 1998. During the 12 months following opening, the mall experienced a 7 percent increase in sales. The Avenue also attracted interest among businesses considering relocation to the White Marsh business district, where amenities for office workers were now close at hand.

Experience Gained

The angled parking configuration and the wide-enough but small scale of the main street were carefully studied. Pedestrian traffic in the built product, however, with 92 feet (28 meters) between faces of opposing buildings, suggests that even two feet (0.6 meter) more on each side of the sidewalk (a 96-foot-wide [29.2-meter] face-to-face dimension) would allow a better experience for pedestrians, particularly during heavy shopping days. Planting wells for trees intrude into the 12-foot-wide (3.6-meter) sidewalks, forming bottlenecks and forcing some pedestrians onto the street.

The developer underestimated the complexity of the project in approaching it as a 300,000-square-foot (27,900-square-meter) project. It turned out to be ten 30,000-square-foot (2,790-square-meter) projects, with each building having its own time schedule and demands on resources and management.

Persistence and creativity in financing and zoning were keys to the project's success. A weak retail market necessitated creative financing and the need to structure construction draws once certain progressive criteria were met. Crafting new PUD regulations not only solved a zoning problem for the project but also allowed for greater tenant flexibility and the opportunity for future changes to meet the community's needs. ■

Project Data

Land Use and Building Information

Site Area	34.5 acres
Parking Spaces	2,312 on site, 98 on public street, 227 in overflow lot
GBA	304,615 square feet
GLA	295,574 square feet
FAR	0.2

Land Use Plan

	Acres	Percent of Site
Buildings	6.8	19.7%
Streets/surface parking	19.0	55.1
Landscaping/open space	8.7	25.2
Total	34.5	100.0%

Retail Tenant Information

	Number of Stores	Total GLA (Square Feet)
General merchandise	1	24,000
Food service	9	45,920
Clothing and accessories	6	40,352
Shoes	1	4,855
Home furnishings	3	14,336
Home appliances/electronics	3	24,838
Hobby/special interest	2	2,416
Gift/specialty	7	14,037
Jewelry	1	1,633
Drugs	1	1,481
Personal services	1	1,633
Financial	1	2,640
Movie theater	1	74,035
Books and music	1	26,903
Optical	1	4,108
Vacant	1	12,387
Total	40	295,574

Development Cost Information

Site Acquisition Cost[a]	$8,540,000

Site Improvement Costs

Excavation/grading	$805,044
Sewer/water/stormwater management	806,708
Off-site costs[b]	684,733
Overflow parking lot (inclusive)	269,516
Asphalt paving	1,218,009
Curb and gutters	404,715
Site concrete	798,418
Perimeter sidewalk	115,000
Brick pavers	293,128
Parking lot lighting and site electricity	636,694
Specialty and feature lighting	698,903
Gas, electricity, and telephone service	105,745
Fountains	301,074
Site furnishings	52,943
Landscaping	483,496
Signage and special graphics	406,526
Sound and security	258,436
Total	$8,339,088

Building Construction Costs

Structure	$7,388,286
HVAC	14,598
Electrical	368,657
Plumbing/sprinkler	435,513
Fees, general conditions, and requirements	1,258,166
Total	$9,465,220

Soft Costs

Architecture/engineering	$1,386,180
Project and development management	814,040
Marketing management, consulting, and lease commissions	1,181,616
Marketing and events	412,556
Legal/accounting	498,591
Construction interest and fees	851,670
Land entitling costs	498,860
Taxes and insurance	50,567
Operating and carrying costs during lease-up	227,610
Total	$5,921,690

Tenant Improvement Allowance	$4,734,239
Tenant Reimbursement to Landlord	$1,725,000
Total Development Cost[c]	$35,275,237

Owner/Developer

Nottingham Properties, Inc.
100 West Pennsylvania Avenue
Towson, Maryland 21204
410-825-0545

Development Schedule

1943	Site purchased	11/1996	Construction started
1/1993	Planning started	6/1998	First tenant moves in
3/1996	Sales/leasing started	11/1998	Project completed

[a]Based on appraisal.

[b]Utilities and road improvements.

[c]Total project cost does not include building cost for three buildings (88,211 square feet of GBA) that were built by tenants under ground lease.

Source: Nottingham Properties, Inc., Towson, Maryland.

A balance of local and national retailers is found at Pentagon Row in Arlington, Virginia.

Maintenance and Housekeeping

The shopping center lease establishes maintenance responsibilities for the landlord and tenants. The landlord typically is responsible for the foundation, walls, roof, parking lot, and exterior open areas. Tenants are responsible for the interior of the premises. The lease serves as the groundwork for operation of the center, but beyond it, management's expertise makes the center a success.

When a shopping center is anchored by one or several major tenants, a common area operating agreement, also called a *reciprocal easement agreement,* might provide anchor tenants with certain approval rights:

- approval of the CAM budget;
- approve of any expenditures in excess of a specified amount;
- approval of any maintenance contract whose annual fee exceeds a specified amount;
- removal and replacement of the manager of common areas if they are not maintained to industry standards.[62]

These agreements are particularly important when the anchor tenants and/or freestanding tenants own their own land and buildings.

Whether the developer/owner or an outside firm acts as manager, maintenance and housekeeping in a small center usually are handled, at least in part, by independent contractors that specialize in those operations.

The developer should keep in mind that an effective schedule of regular maintenance and operations will prolong a property's life. A planned maintenance program also helps to avoid any crises that may develop as the property ages. The challenge for the developer is to balance the project's need for maintenance with costs, which may be substantial.

Proper maintenance requires regular inspections of the property. In general, every shopping center re-quires three types of inspections: standard, task, and annual.[63] The *standard inspection* is a general inspection to judge the center's overall appearance. The *task inspection* is a detailed review of the structure and common grounds. Items needing regular task inspection include entrances, vestibules, common areas, landscaping, restrooms, corridors, electrical rooms, storage rooms, vacant spaces, occupied stores, surrounding streets, signage, parking lots, lighting, the building exterior, and roofs. The *annual inspection* is an annual property evaluation of the condition of major equipment and the structure to determine the rate and degree of the property's depreciation.

In addition, the property manager should develop a standard operating procedures manual that details all specific policies, procedures, systems, and job functions

Ten Rules for Successful Neighborhood Centers

1. Determine whether an adequate number of households exists without competition.
2. Correctly define the center's trade area.
3. Avoid locations where competition can easily occur nearby.
4. Secure a strong grocery anchor of adequate size.
5. Avoid overbuilding with too many small shops.
6. Create a balanced, convenience-oriented tenant mix, and avoid excess shoppers goods.
7. Require tenants to monitor and report monthly sales.
8. In troubled times, temporarily reduce rents to keep good tenants.
9. Incorporate flexibility in design of the center.
10. As landlord, adopt the role of benevolent dictator with your tenants. ∎

Source: ULI–the Urban Land Institute, "Shopping Centers: How to Build, Buy, and Redevelop," workshop manual, Spring 2001.

relating to the property's operation.[64] The manual should specify and establish a standard for every item requiring periodic attention.

Conclusion

As population in the United States continues to grow, new neighborhood centers in newly developing suburban and exurban areas will have to match that growth. Moreover, smaller shopping centers have been aging since the suburban boom of the 1950s, and many opportunities will be available for remodeling and repositioning older obsolete centers. New immigrants from the last 30 years of the 20th century, continuing what appears to be even greater growth depending on national immigration policy, have created a new ethnic mix that offers a variety of new market conditions and opportunities for the astute developer. Continuing affluence will demand better-quality shopping centers with new tenant categories and adaptation of existing ones. Traditional anchor tenants will continue to reshape themselves and thus will seek to modify their present locations or find new, more suitable ones.

With the increase in two-career couples, single households, modified work patterns, greater mobility, new immigrant groups, and e-commerce, the way people shop will continue to evolve. Tenants traditionally found only at regional centers have moved to larger strip centers as their patrons seek closer and time-saving access through shorter shopping trips. Although most markets are saturated with regional malls, opportunities are available to fill in market gaps and target narrow infill audiences. Small centers are much easier to develop than regional centers, requiring fewer tenants, a simpler approval process, and less capital and lead time. Of the 2,172 shopping centers that opened during 1997 through 2001, 1,139 were smaller than 100,000 square feet (9,300 square meters), and 559 were between 100,000 and 200,000 square feet (9,300 and 18,600 square meters). Thus, 78 percent of total new centers added during this period were smaller centers under 200,000 square feet (18,600 square meters).[65] The growth rate during these years was significantly below the average annual growth rate for the previous 30 years.[66]

Even with continued numerous opportunities for development of small centers, competition has increased and many areas are rapidly becoming overbuilt. Other potential problems loom on the horizon. Although most analysts believe that the overbuilding that occurred in the late 1980s will not be revisited to the same extreme, real estate development has always gone through cycles and will do so in the future. In most instances, real estate slumps lag slumps in the economy, but development in the pipeline toward the end of an economic cycle suffers most from lack of market. Communities also go through cycles of pro- and antigrowth, which frequently lag an economic boom, as it is the economic boom that drives the demand for new development that

Bethesda Row in Bethesda, Maryland, features a main street retail environment oriented to pedestrians.

leads to public concerns about "rampant" growth and thus growth controls. The developer new to retail development needs to be aware of these cycles and that retail development tends to follow rather than lead. In an economy driven by consumer purchases, declines in retail sales are a key warning sign of an impending economic downturn and thus a decline in demand for new retail space. John Gerdes of L&B Realty Advisors suggests, "Neighborhood centers may be the last to feel the effects and the first to rebound because anchor tenants represent essential staples such as groceries and drug stores."[67]

Another potential problem small centers face is a lack of small tenants and a proliferation of superstores that may preclude many other tenants. In many cases, a developer may not be able to find suitable small tenants to fill a center with a large anchor tenant. If a superstore insists on the exclusive right to sell certain items, leasing space in the center to other tenants will be especially difficult.

In the first years of the 21st century, opportunities for small shopping center development have become more difficult to finance, even in cases where public approvals appear likely to be assured. When potential anchor tenants adjust their expansion plans and delay new starts, the process becomes even more difficult. But in spite of these challenges to inexperienced developers, emerging shopping patterns and new niche markets will continue to lead to opportunities for those armed with good data and an intuitive sense of the market.

Notes

1. Michael D. Beyard, W. Paul O'Mara, et al., *Shopping Center Development Handbook,* 3rd ed. (Washington, D.C.: ULI–the Urban Land Institute, 1999), p. 5.

2. *Dollars & Cents of Shopping Centers®: 2002* (Washington, D.C.: ULI–the Urban Land Institute, 2002), p. 3.

3. Many of these special types are described in greater detail in Beyard, O'Mara, et al., *Shopping Center Development Handbook,* pp. 13–16.

4. "The Changing Neighborhood Center," *Shopping Center World,* June 2000, p. 54.

5. Beyard, O'Mara, et al., *Shopping Center Development Handbook,* pp. 17–24.

6. Adrienne Schmitz and Deborah L. Brett, *Real Estate Market Analysis* (Washington, D.C.: ULI–the Urban Land Institute, 2001), p. 147.

7. Beyard, O'Mara, et al., *Shopping Center Development Handbook,* p. 46.

8. "Sites Unseen," *Chain Store Age,* October 2000, p. 153.

9. David Salvesen, *Wetlands: Mitigating and Regulating Development Impacts* (Washington, D.C.: ULI–the Urban Land Institute, 1994), provides a practical guide to development where wetlands are involved.

10. See Robert A. Simons, *Turning Brownfields into Greenbacks* (Washington, D.C.: ULI–the Urban land Institute, 1997), for a general discussion and a description of more than 50 tools and strategies to maneuver through government regulations, secure sources of financing, reduce liability, undertake remediation, and get loan guarantees and assurances for brownfield sites.

11. "Economy and Ecology Merge," *Chain Store Age,* January 2001, p. 158.

12. "Shopping Centers: How to Build, Buy, and Redevelop," ULI workshop manual, Spring 2001, p. 20.

13. International Council of Shopping Centers, *Leasing Small Shopping Centers* (New York: International Council of Shopping Centers, p. 3.

14. "Shopping Centers: How to Build, Buy, and Redevelop," p. 83.

15. Ibid., p. 66.

16. Ibid., p. 16.

17. *Dollars & Cents of Shopping Centers®: 2002,* Table 6-1, U.S. Neighborhood Shopping Centers: Center Size, Center Sales, and Operating Results, p. 201.

18. *Dollars & Cents of Convenience Centers®: 2002* (Washington, D.C.: ULI–the Urban Land Institute, 2002), Table 8, U.S. Convenience Shopping Centers: Center Size, Center Sales, and Operating Results, p. 12.

19. *Dollars & Cents of Shopping Centers®: 2002,* Table 5-1, U.S. Community Shopping Centers: Center Size, Center Sales, and Operating Results, p. 135.

20. Philip E. Klein, *Feasibility of Shopping Center Development, Shopping Center Report* (New York: International Council of Shopping Centers, 1980), p. 2.

21. Beyard, O'Mara, et al., *Shopping Center Development Handbook,* p. 100.

22. *Leasing Small Shopping Centers,* p. 71.

23. "Shopping Centers: How to Build, Buy, and Redevelop," p. 28.

24. ULI–the Urban Land Institute and the International Council of Shopping Centers, *Parking Requirements for Shopping Centers,* 2nd ed. (Washington, D.C.: ULI–the Urban Land Institute, 1999), p. 3, Table 1.

25. ULI–the Urban Land Institute and NPA–the National Parking Association, *The Dimensions of Parking,* 4th ed. (Washington, D.C.: ULI–the Urban Land Institute, 2000), p. 46.

26. Ibid., p. 45.

27. U.S. Department of Justice, "Title III Highlights," p. 6.

28. "Shopping Centers: How to Build, Buy, and Redevelop," p. 33.

29. ULI–the Urban Land Institute and NPA–the National Parking Association, *Dimensions of Parking,* p. 87.

30. Ibid., p. 86.

31. "Economy and Ecology Merge," *Chain Store Age,* January 2001, p. 158.

32. "Protecting a Major Investment," *Chain Store Age,* July 2000, p. 120.

33. Beth Mattson-Teig, "How Healthy Is Your Roof?" *Shopping Center World,* February 2000, p. 90.

34. "Protecting a Major Investment," *Chain Store Age,* January 2001, (adapted from "Choosing the Right Roof, p. 120).

35. "Energy and Performance," *Shopping Center World,* February 2000, p. 99.

36. "Groceries, Gap, and Rave Girl?" *Chain Store Age,* March 2001, p. 156.

37. "Shopping Centers: How to Build, Buy, and Redevelop," p. 56.

38. Charles S. Telchin, "How to Improve Developer/Tenant Planning and Construction Coordination," *Shopping Center Report* (New York: International Council of Shopping Centers, 1977), p. 1.

39. Ibid., pp. 3–4.

40. "New Code Affects Retailers," *Chain Store Age,* March 2000, p. 170.

41. Mary Alice Hines, *Shopping Center Development and Investment* (New York: Wiley, 1983), p. 218.

42. "Groceries, Gap, and Rave Girl?" p. 155.

43. *Leasing Small Shopping Centers,* pp. 14–26.

44. "Supermarkets Fight Back," *Chain Store Age,* August 2000, pp. 37A–38A.

45. *Dollars & Cents of Shopping Centers®: 2002,* pp. 216–249.

46. Ibid., pp. 150–195.

47. "So Long Percentage Rents," *Shopping Center World,* March 2001, p. 42.

48. Alan A. Alexander and Richard F. Muhlebach, *Operating Small Shopping Centers* (New York: International Council of Shopping Centers, 1997), p. 67.

49. International Council of Shopping Centers, *Critical Issues Facing Small Shopping Centers* (New York: International Council of Shopping Centers), p. 13

50. See Beyard, O'Mara et al., *Shopping Center Development Handbook,* Appendix 1, Sample Shopping Center Lease; and *The Library of Small Shopping Center Forms* (New York: International Council of Shopping Centers).

51. "Causes for Celebration," *Chain Store Age,* September 2000, p. 185.

52. ULI–the Urban Land Institute, "Shopping Centers II Workshop: Participant's Guide," pp. 115–118.

53. Ibid., p. 189.

54. Robert J. Flynn, ed., *Carpenters Shopping Center Management: Principles and Practices,* 3rd ed. (New York: International Council of Shopping Centers, 1984), p. 29.

55. Ibid., p. 28.

56. International Council of Shopping Centers, *Critical Issues Facing Small Shopping Centers* (New York: International Council of Shopping Centers, 1997), p. 34.

57. Alan A. Alexander and Richard F. Muhlebach, *Operating Small Shopping Centers* (New York: International Council of Shopping Centers, 1997), p. 149.

58. "Open-Air Safety," *Chain Store Age,* September 2000, p. 192.

59. For additional information, see Development Case Studies (formerly Project Reference File), Volume 16, Number 12, 1986, at www.uli.org (go to Data, then to Development Case Studies).

60. Flynn, *Carpenters Shopping Center Management,* pp. 36–37.

61. Ibid., p. 56.

62. Alexander and Muhlebach, *Operating Small Shopping Centers,* p. 134.

63. Institute of Real Estate Management, *Managing the Shopping Center* (Chicago: Institute of Real Estate Management, 1983), p. 163.

64. Ibid., p. 174.

65. Scope U.S.A. 2001 (www.icsc.org/srch/srch/scope/current/index.html) provides current statistics on shopping centers.

66. Scope U.S.A. 2001, graphs covering 1967 through 2000 (Data Source: National Research Bureau).

67. "Groceries, Gap, and Rave Girl?" p. 156.

8. Trends and Issues

Looking at the Past and to the Future

This final chapter explores changes in the real estate industry, emerging market trends, development issues, and the social responsibility of developers. This information will enable beginning developers to grasp the larger picture of real estate development and its role in society as well as identify the opportunities and pitfalls that may lie ahead as they start in the business. The chapter concludes with a discussion of the developer's special social responsibility to the community at large. Both ULI and contributors to this book are dedicated to the precept that all developers should live up to their civic responsibilities and create products and developments that make a positive contribution to their communities and the urban environment.

Changing Market Factors

To understand where the industry is going, one must understand where it has been. Many developers were baptized into the business from their first experience of recession. The industry has changed dramatically since the 1970s and 1980s, when many of today's major developers started their firms. Double-digit inflation of the

Pictured at left is Carillon Point, a mixed-use project in Kirkland, Washington.

late 1970s and early 1980s made real estate a preferred investment because it provided one of the best hedges against inflation.

The subsequent real estate crash of the late 1980s through the early 1990s has been referred to often in this book. It marked probably the most dramatic change in the real estate industry since the Great Depression. A number of factors led up to the crash:

- overbuilding of office and commercial space in most markets;
- the crisis in the savings and loan industry and a record number of bank failures;
- changes reflected in the 1986 Tax Reform Act that adversely affected real estate;
- mounting government regulation that increased the time and cost of the development approvals process; and
- regional economic recessions.

The early years following the crash were characterized by recovering real estate markets; starting in the early 1990s, the industry enjoyed an unusually long period of growth and stability. The role of the Resolution Trust Corporation, the government institution established to take over bankrupt S&Ls and to recycle their assets back into the market, marks one of the great success stories of government intervention in the real estate market. Criticized at first for selling assets too cheaply, it succeeded in rechanneling more than $300 billion in failing assets back into private possession between 1991 and 1995. Early critics charged that the rapid sell-off was hurting the recovery by placing large amounts of commercial space back on the market, depressing rents and sale prices. In retrospect, as long as the RTC owned vast amounts of property that buyers knew would eventually be sold, prices remained depressed. The speedy sell-off allowed properties to quickly reenter the market. New development did not occur until these properties were leased and prices returned to normal. Cheap commercial space also assisted the economic recovery in the early 1990s. Prices and property values quickly increased as the incipient economic boom led to rapid consumption of vacant office and industrial space.

Kenneth Leventhal argues that the government caused a 40 percent decline in value during the RTC sell-off, whereas the decline should have been only 10 to 15 percent. "In hindsight, if they had not been so draconian, more of the owners would have stayed in place, the losses would not have been so severe, and we would not have had this whole new breed of buyers— the vulture funds."[1]

Industry Restructuring

The real estate crash of the late 1980s to early 1990s led to several fundamental changes in the development industry:

- Real estate finance underwent a thorough restructuring, with more multiproduct financial providers and a homogenization of services.
- Real estate is now more *institutionalized*. Investment-grade real estate has earned the status of an asset class comparable with stocks and bonds.
- Tax reform, which virtually dried up the infusion of money from syndicators, is believed to have helped the industry by restoring the importance of traditional cash flow criteria. Along with inflation and interest rates, however, the rapid entry and exit of syndicators is one of the factors that fed the uncertainty now affecting even the stronger and long-term participants.
- Megadeals and the huge debt and equity resources they require have forced many developers to become manufacturers of products—"merchant builders"— rather than long-term owners. REITs and other institutional owners form joint ventures with developers to build new buildings that the institution buys when completed.
- To develop a strong base of consistent cash flow, many of the largest developers focused on strengthening the service part of the business, especially brokerage, asset management, and property management. Owning or managing large portfolios on behalf of institutional owners enabled these companies to build a steady cash flow stream. Wall Street valued this service-based income more highly than cyclical sources of income such as development fees.

The Demise of Small Developers?

Small developers face increasing difficulties finding money and navigating the draconian entitlement processes to put deals together. In the late 1980s, Phil Walsh, president of Emblem Development Corporation of Montclair, California, predicted some of the difficulties facing small developers, particularly in California. He noted that personal contacts with city council members no longer facilitate the zoning approval process. After Proposition 13 was passed, cities looked for new ways to raise money and turned to impact fees and exactions, creating tremendous front-end cash burdens for builders. Walsh observed that small builders and developers were being forced to the sidelines, where they were confronted with difficult options:

- Remain small and pick up projects that are not of interest to large developers;
- Joint venture with larger players or institutions;
- Build in planned communities, where the large share of profits goes to the developer of the planned community; or
- Move to outlying areas where marketing and holding costs are higher.[2]

In 1997, an article by Peter Linneman sparked a debate over whether large firms would so dominate the real estate market that small firms would not be able to compete.[3] He argued that Wall Street financing and pension fund money gave those firms that could access the public markets such a competitive advantage in their cost of funds that they would drive smaller firms out of the market. The article appeared at a time when REITs were the darlings of Wall Street. Soon afterward, REITs began to lose favor as Wall Street investors realized that they were not growth stocks and that their spectacular performance in the mid-1990s rested in large part on recovering real estate markets. Once rents and prices had normalized, the REITs' spectacular earnings growth could not be sustained. As a consequence, the cheap Wall Street equity that made REITs so formidable dried up. Without new equity capital, REITs could no longer outbid private developers in the market. Smaller real estate players were able to obtain capital while many of the larger public funds could not.

While Wall Street's interest in REITs ebbs and flows, other economies of scale increasingly favor larger developers. The largest property managers are able to buy cleaning products and replacement items cheaper than smaller companies can. New technology favors large owners who can make the sizable capital investments required for computer and Internet technology. Longer and more complicated entitlement processes make it harder for small developers to withstand the delay and cost of obtaining development approvals.

In addition, larger residential development firms have recently begun buying out other large and medium-size developers, allowing the purchasing firm the ability to grow its business and expand into new markets without

Ford's Landing in Alexandria, Virginia, is a 136-townhouse development built on the site of the former Ford Motor Company plant. Efforts to redevelop the site were unsuccessful during in the late 1980s, but new ownership and a growing economy helped to make the project a financial success upon its completion in 1999.

a three- to five-year startup. Most of the firms that are purchased are medium to large that build more than 100 homes per year, leaving the smaller developers alone.[4]

Although small developers find it hard to compete with large developers, they are not likely to disappear. Small developers will benefit from future demographic changes, because there will be no dominant groups and thus more opportunities to target niche markets. Smaller developers can target their products and develop on a smaller scale better than larger developers. "Historically, small developers have helped to ensure competition by providing tenants and buyers with alternative products. To target niche markets, developers need to think down to the lowest level of demand and do it well—for example, apartment buildings targeted to renters with large dogs. Small is beautiful."[5]

Local knowledge and contacts continue to be enormously valuable in real estate. Certain banks and equity investors are now favoring small developers with compelling ideas over larger development firms. As long as personal relationships remain central to doing business, small developers will be competitive. It is likely that their share of the real estate pie will continue to shrink, however.

Financing

REITs, securitization, and commercial mortgage–backed securities all have revolutionized real estate finance.

Although beginning developers' initial projects probably will be financed through small banks and local lenders, they should understand the bigger picture of financing real estate deals. Opportunities for cheap permanent mortgage money may come from different sources at any given time: from insurance companies or banks, or through mortgage brokers representing conduit loans (prepackaged pools of mortgages that Wall Street sells to investors). Although beginning developers most likely will find equity for their initial projects from relatives and friends, they should position themselves to be able to find institutional equity partners as soon as possible.

Robert Larson, chair, Lazard Freres Real Estate and past vice chair of Taubman Centers, Inc., emphasizes alignment of interests when Wall Street and other institutional investors work with developers. "Any investment of size needs to be made so that the interests of the company and its management are very closely aligned with interests of the investor. Any deal structure that allows for differences in incentives or objectives is bound to create problems over time. Aligning interests is critical to long-term success."[6] Lazard Freres looks for opportunities to invest in whole businesses rather than individual properties. Larson observes that investors would like a preferential position but that whether they can get one depends on the company's need for capital and the competitive market at the time. To the extent that the investor ends up with a preferred security, the possibility of divergent interests may increase.

When private companies deal with Wall Street investors, they naturally want any new investor of size to be a passive partner. This position, however, runs counter to the needs of the investor. Larson notes that structural problems exist when investors own more than 50 percent of a publicly traded company but do not have board control. If the company runs into problems, the investors need to be able to change the strategic direction of the company to protect their interests.

The trend toward consolidation over the last decade has transformed the industry so that a significant part of development has shifted from privately owned small entrepreneurs to larger public companies. Larson believes this trend increases the opportunities for well-capitalized entrepreneurs, because development is very specific to local circumstances. Large institutions in general are less flexible and nimble and less able to respond to market opportunities. Consolidation creates opportunities for smaller entrepreneurs, but in today's capital market, they must be much better capitalized than a decade ago. Opportunities for leverage are more meager. To be able to compete, developers must have a strong balance sheet or a working alliance with a capital source.

Paying for Infrastructure

Fiscal problems increasingly have forced many localities to rely on real estate development to balance local budgets and help pay for new infrastructure. Before 1980, most municipal services and infrastructure such as schools, public safety, roads, and utilities were paid for out of general revenues and general obligation bonds. Today, current residents view crowded roads and schools as a negative impact of growth and sprawl, and the costs of growth have become a contentious issue in many communities. Virtually every major city and many small cities across the country have adopted comprehensive systems such as impact fees, exactions (payments made to receive a permit to develop),[7] community facilities districts, and adequate public facilities ordinances (ordinances requiring that facilities or plans for new facilities be in place before new development is approved)[8] to address these issues. Based on the theory that development should pay its own way, communities impose impact fees—usually charged per roof or per square foot—on developers to fund roads, intersections, schools, and public safety improvements.

The trend toward higher impact fees and exactions is likely to continue as cities try to maximize revenue without significantly reducing development. Developers have turned to the legal system to resist exorbitant charges, and court rulings have limited the fees that may be charged to cover the costs imposed by new development.

Developers have much at stake when it comes to municipal finances. Local fiscal problems affect developers in several ways. First, higher fees raise the cost of development. They worsen the issue of affordable housing, which already is at crisis levels in some major cities. Second, these fiscal problems lead to cutbacks in local budgets for maintaining public facilities, causing deteriorating neighborhoods and falling real estate values. Those communities that serve predominantly lower- and middle-income households are less able to maintain public services and facilities as well as upper-income suburbs. As a consequence, real estate values do not hold up as well in some lower- and middle-income communities, reducing the attractiveness of future real estate investment in those communities.

Fiscal problems can give cities stronger incentives to work with the development community. Some of the best opportunities for beginning developers lie in working with cities on government-owned land or in redevelopment areas. If developers are willing to tolerate red tape and bureaucratic delays, cities and their redevelopment agencies will help them obtain the necessary public approvals. Public/private deals also offer opportunities for smaller developers.

The Erosion of Development Rights

The erosion of development rights is reflected in the amount of work that developers must do on a site before their right to develop it becomes *vested:* that is, the right cannot be taken away or delayed through city actions such as building moratoriums. One of the greatest risks facing developers today is that they can spend years and millions of dollars on obtaining necessary approvals to develop a site and still lose the right to develop it according to their original plans.[9] Across-the-board reductions in density and building moratoriums are becoming increasingly common in cities that are struggling to control or reduce their rate of growth.

One way for developers to hedge against the risk of losing development rights is to buy land subject to obtaining all necessary approvals and permits. Developers must spend more for land under these conditions, but the higher price is worth the reduced risk. Developers of larger projects deal with the risks of vesting by negotiating "development agreements" that require them to build certain facilities in exchange for a city's locking in existing zoning and development rights.[10] The erosion of vested development rights increases development risk significantly, but it is a trend that is not likely to be reversed in the foreseeable future.

The types and amount of regulation on development increased throughout the 20th century. Zoning and other forms of regulation have been initiated or supported by developers as a means of protecting long-term property values. It is not regulation per se but the *uncertainty* about new regulation and the time and cost of meeting existing regulatory requirements that can be the greatest risk to developers.

Every decade brings a new set of concerns. The 2000 election had more than 700 growth control measures on ballots across the country. These measures demonstrate the public's level of concern about local congestion, air and water quality, open space, and other quality of life issues. Developers should be aware of these local issues and anticipate their impact on development projects.[11]

The Technological Revolution

The technological revolution permeates every facet of our daily professional and personal lives. The implications of technology for every aspect of real estate are dramatic and have transformed how real estate professionals conduct all areas of the business, from design and construction to marketing, brokerage, property management, and financing.

Design and Construction. The Internet is changing how buildings are developed. Extranets—networks that facilitate the exchange of all forms of information, including plans, specifications, and financial data—are widely used in the design phase of development and increasingly used during construction.[12] Computer-assisted design allows all team members—architects, engineers, and developers—to use the same base drawings. Extensive use of three-dimensional imaging allows clients to visualize the project. Real-time design enables value engineering to occur concurrently with design, accelerating the process. E-mail and network conferencing over the Internet have shortened the time required to revise drawings and other documents.

The provision of high-speed Internet access is now ubiquitous in building construction, spurred by consumers' and tenants' expectations. Smart developers and landlords anticipate future technology needs and plan accordingly to install the most advanced wiring, cables, and backup generators.[13]

Marketing. Increasingly, real estate brokerage firms use the Web to market their properties. Almost all brokerage firms now have property search databases with property details and images that are frequently updated on their Web sites. These Web pages usually include an overview of the project with building and site data, floor plans, a summary of technical specifications, lease terms, and a location map. E-mails between brokers and clients, property search databases, and other Internet tools speed up deal making and allow brokers to spend more time with clients.[14]

Property Management. Dozens of software packages can help building managers use computers to make their jobs easier, put valuable information at their fingertips, and increase profits. These software packages are tailored for any type of property and are available for tenant records, lease management, maintenance scheduling, checks, taxes, profit and loss reports for one unit or an entire portfolio, payroll, and work orders. In addition, geographic information systems software can be used to provide online data, making it possible to track space tenant by tenant, including information about lease expiration dates and competitors' buildings.

Financing. The real estate industry has been notoriously slow to adapt new technology. To a large degree, the industry has watched from the sidelines as the business-to-consumer and business-to-business Internet revolution has unfolded. Traditional mortgage lenders saw Internet startup companies grab a significant share of the mortgage origination business. Not surprisingly, the greatest penetration of technology in real estate finance has been in those areas serving the largest number of consumers—home mortgage originations.

Still, real estate transactions over the Internet are predicted to be the next big item—digital transaction processing, information dissemination, financing, and closing transactions. Internet-based real estate transactions are in their infancy, but the number of mortgages, equities, leases, and sales transactions is increasing dramatically. The Internet revolution is moving faster in some areas of real estate than others. Indeed, if one lesson has been learned, it is to avoid being the first to build an Internet real estate business or to adopt an Internet-related innovation, because the failure rate is so high. Nevertheless, a revolution is occurring, and real estate professionals have no choice but to understand it and embrace it prudently.

Trends

Changes are occurring rapidly inside and outside the real estate development industry. Opportunities abound for those who are able to foresee these changes. Shifting demographic trends such as the graying of the American population, the influx of new immigrants, and the impact of new technology on American lifestyles are creating demand for entirely new types of living environments and communities. Computers, the Internet, E-mail, and cell phones provide new modes of personal and business communication that have altered lifestyle and work habits.

New Demographics

Results of the 2000 Census show that significant demographic factors will have a profound effect on the nation's economy in the future.[15] For the first time in history, the United States is predicted to have a population with a roughly equal number of people in each age group. By 2020, there will be no dominant generation or dramatic age increases, with a population that has an equal number of school-aged children, young professionals, parents, young retirees, and the elderly.[16]

According to demographer William H. Frey, new regional demographic divisions will be created that will be equally as important as our current distinctions between cities and suburbs, rural and urban. These divisions will encompass entire metropolitan areas and states, distinguishing "multiple melting pot regions," "suburban-like new Sunbelts," "heartland regions," and "new minority frontiers."[17] The multiple melting pots—California, Texas, southern Florida, the eastern seaboard, and Chicago—will become increasingly younger, multiethnic, and culturally vibrant. Heartland regions will become older, more staid, and less ethnically diverse, encompassing growing parts of the Sunbelt, economically healthy states of the new West, and declining areas of the Farmbelt and Rustbelt.

The new immigrants and their children, primarily Latin Americans and Asians, will contribute 1 million people annually to the U.S. population, accounting for more than half the 50 million additional residents during the next 25 years. As a result of current immigration laws, it is expected that incoming immigrants will choose to live in a handful of metropolitan areas, and unlike the past, these ethnic minorities will attempt to maintain their cultural lifestyles and identities. Affordable housing will be an important issue for all immigrant populations, especially Hispanic, as they cluster in areas where land and housing costs are rising and developers have difficulty providing new housing at an affordable price.

Changing Lifestyles

Playing a role in every major demographic change over the past 50 years, the aging baby boom generation continues to dominate market trends. This elderly population will increase by 80 percent over the next 25 years. Fueling this trend will be the "yuppie elderly," who have good health and high disposable incomes. They will set new standards for early retirement living.

Baby boomers are expected to have an active lifestyle and spend greater amounts on travel. Higher wealth accumulation and fewer children will permit many to enjoy an active retirement lifestyle, allowing them to stay busy and travel. It will determine where they retire and their preference for smaller and different types of housing. To cater to this market, more homes will use universal design techniques for aging in place and be wired for high technology.

Many of this generation chose to live in suburban metropolitan areas and can be expected to retire in these locations or similar locations in other states. Their retirement choices will be influenced by the quality of nearby health care facilities. This population will signal a shift in the demand for new housing. A greater share of new housing construction likely will be nontraditional types of single- and multifamily residences.[18]

Continued involvement in the workforce, either full time or part time, and their diverse lifestyles are likely to

Tierra del Rey in Marina del Rey, California, is a luxury rental community marketed toward young urban professionals and empty nesters who can afford substantial monthly housing payments.

Steve Hinds Photography

make the "active" adult communities less attractive to seniors. Unlike past decades, the elderly are not expected to relocate to the Sunbelt. Except for the well-off yuppie elderly boomers who will select high-amenity locations, most are expected to age and retire near their lifelong residences. Whether they migrate or age in place, boomers will downsize their housing.

Most retirees will enjoy a healthier, more active lifestyle, and their consumption patterns will include more travel on luxury cruises, gaming resorts, vacations in exotic locales, mountain biking, and rafting. Although many age-restricted communities remain focused on the golden years and physical fitness, new ones are being developed around intellectual or environmental themes.[19]

Lewis Goodkin notes that 77 million members of the postwar baby boom generation, born between 1945 and 1960, are moving through their 50s and early 60s and planning ahead for retirement. "That is why the U.S. Census Bureau projects that the nation's older population will reach 62 million by 2025—a peak period for seniors' housing in general. The number of people age 65 and over will remain level during the next ten years." He adds, "Retirees are increasingly opting for single-family detached homes in resort-style communities with golf, fitness centers, and jogging and swimming. They are also expected to go back to school, volunteer for community organizations, or mentoring younger professionals. Community choices are already reflecting these tendencies toward greater involvement. Most retirees now prefer to be insulated—not isolated—from working-age adults and children."[20]

New recreational activities are emerging—from rock climbing to skydiving to kayaking. Being close to nature is becoming more attractive than playing golf for some New Age baby boomers. Seniors are also the fastest-growing segment of hikers in America. For developers of resort and retirement communities, amenities such as educational programs tied in with local universities are increasingly popular. Goodkin advises developers to create more intimate and pedestrian-friendly traditional neighborhood developments, create more low-rise and mid-rise multifamily developments, and cater to specific regional or ethnic groups.

Cities versus Suburbs

The extent to which cities are on the rebound is hotly debated. Urban history during the last half of the 20th century was largely about the migration of people from cities to suburbs and the decentralization of both residences and workplaces. Census data for 2000 indicate continuing dispersion of households, and outer suburbs, exurbs, and secondary cities continue to grow faster than central cities and inner-ring suburbs. Although many cities show an increase in residents, census data also often show that three households move downtown for every five households that move out, which does not reverse cities' longstanding decline.[21] The residential future of cities may depend on how well they appeal to empty nesters and early retirees.[22]

Still, urban living appears to be on the upswing. Conversion of older downtown and near-downtown offices and warehouses to loft housing and new higher-density apartments and condominiums in and around central business districts are signs of the increasing popularity of urban life. Demand for urban living is fueled by three main groups: aging baby boomers who are moving back to the city after their children leave home; young high-tech workers who are interested in the shopping, restaurants, and entertainment of a 24-hour downtown; and immigrants who traditionally locate first in urban areas. Reduced crime levels, cheap available office space in the wake of the recession of the late 1980s and early 1990s, and changing lifestyle preferences have helped to renew the appeal of living downtown. To maintain this interest in urban living, cities need successful downtown housing programs with several common elements: committed public officials, aggressive marketing, creative financing, a flexible regulatory environment, a developer-friendly business climate, parking, amenities, and, most important, good design. Renting is the key for young professionals and minority householders to live in the city. More than 43 percent of householders aged 25 to 44 are renters, compared with 22 percent of householders aged 45 to 64 and 20 percent aged 65 and older. The majority of central city minority householders are renters.[23]

Development Issues

Smart Growth

Although growth has significant values and benefits, it is generally recognized that it can result in unintentional consequences. Recent census and other data indicate strong growth patterns will continue, challenging the balance between accommodating growth and maintaining high-quality developments and communities. In recent years, many of those involved in the development process have increasingly looked to the concepts of smart growth to strike this balance. Although it is referenced by numerous other names, including "sustainable development" and "quality growth," the term *smart growth* has become a part of the land use vernacular and will continue to influence the development process.

Popularized by state and local policies and programs, civic and environmental interests, among others, smart growth has gained national attention as one cure to the ills of sprawl. As its principles have gained popularity, they have received the endorsement of unlikely supporters, each with its own spin on what smart growth means, consequently raising the debate as to its meaning and purpose. To some, it is synonymous with no growth. To others, it is the understanding that the inevitability of growth does not dictate the type of development. It is, in fact, an umbrella term that represents a variety of issues, and to ULI, it is growth that is economically sound, environmentally friendly, and supportive of livable communities, and that enhances quality of life. Unlike the rigid growth control mechanisms used under earlier

Orenco Station is a transit-oriented development in Portland, Oregon. Built on a hillside and incorporating large historic trees, Orenco Station is close to a Portland light rail station.

growth management strategies, smart growth strives to promote a higher quality of growth that accommodates development in a way that supports the economy by generating jobs, income, and tax revenue; raises property values; provides for a variety of housing and transportation alternatives; preserves or improves the environment; and enhances quality of life.

It is likely that smart growth will continue to have a strong presence and influence over development in the future through public pressure and policies. It is a trend not entirely understood, and there remain those who are skeptical of its benefits and impacts on the building industry. To debunk such concerns and to clarify the benefits of smart growth, ULI published *Smart Growth Myth and Fact*™, the *Smart Growth Tool Kit,* and *Making Smart Growth Work*. Each publication, along with those from partnering smart growth organizations, demonstrates that smart growth concepts are desirable and economically feasible, continue to grow in popularity, and have proven, positive results.

Smart growth involves land use planning that is comprehensive, regional, and integrated with transportation planning. As local and state governments have discovered the benefits of better growth practices, they have begun to implement incentives to encourage them and have found that public, private, and nonprofit sectors can collaborate on growth and development issues to achieve mutually beneficial outcomes. The series of tools being used across the country range from tax incentives to adequate public facility ordinances. They include requirements for affordable and/or workforce housing. In some cases, zoning regulations and building codes have been changed. Such tools help those developers who want to promote smart growth do so, although in some circumstances, they require smart growth practices even by those who do not wish to support it.

For developers, the challenges of smart growth are twofold. Convincing the public that the patterns of development, especially in suburban areas, need not remain the same as the past 50 years will require education, a change in mind-set, and proof that smart growth is fiscally sound and profitable. At the same time, public opposition to growth in general will deter even quality projects that incorporate smart growth principles. The key to making smart growth the rule and not the exception is showing people real examples of how it works. Both lenders and public policies have favored single-family suburban growth, based on its proven track record, and historically, mixed-use development proposals have faced difficulties in the approval process. Changes in demographics and the public's reaction to suburban sprawl, however, are pushing lending institutions, public officials, and developers to find new ways to encourage infill and mixed-use development.

Unfortunately, it is much more difficult, time-consuming, and risky for beginning developers to undertake initial projects that are new in a community, even if the concept has been successful elsewhere. They will need to convince lenders, investors, public officials, and neighborhood groups that their new approach makes sense. Boldness should be rewarded, but beginning developers should keep in mind the experience of Doug Boone:[24]

> Pick projects that you can weather. My first projects were two suburban residential deals and one traditional neighborhood development. All three required rezoning, which took two and one-half years and significant cash to get approval. As a result, I came close to running out of cash resources and depleted my net worth. The project turned out all right, but I could have done two or three suburban projects for the same time and money and now could have five projects generating cash. Don't take questionable risks, or risk huge battles, when you're starting out.

Place Making

One thing that almost all of ULI's great thinkers agree on is the need to preserve a *sense of place*. A sense of place gives residents and workers in a community a feeling of belonging to that community. It is achieved through a combination of planning, design, marketing, and the evolution of a set of social structures and local organizations over time. Design plays a critical role, helping define boundaries, public spaces, places where people meet and have fun, character, and landmarks that people identify with that community. It does not happen overnight. Classic examples are the town centers of Sienna, Italy, and Cambridge, England. More recent examples are found in cities such as Santa Monica, Santa Barbara, and Laguna Beach, California. Ray Watson considers his foremost achievement in the design of Irvine Ranch, California, the creation and preservation of a sense of place.[25] Neisen Kasdin, mayor of Miami Beach, and developer Peter Rummell echo its importance: in Miami Beach, "The challenge is to determine how to meet future demands while preserving the sense of place that currently makes it so attractive to residents and visitors."[26]

According to Tom Lee, former chair of Newhall Land and Farming Company, "places" take many forms—from old-fashioned main streets and town squares to traditional big-city downtowns to newly developed town centers. Each creates a public realm that gives a community its heart, its character, its identity, and, most important, a place where all kinds of people can come for a wide variety of everyday activities from early in the morning until late at night, seven days a week.[27]

Why should developers care about streetscapes and public places? Such concern is part of good citizenship, but it also translates into long-term value. Streets and plazas that are pleasant to drive and walk through will increase more in value over time than less desirable neighborhoods. The surrounding buildings will likewise command higher rents and sale prices. Developers, however, cannot improve streetscapes by themselves. They are often constrained by zoning codes that mandate the width of streets, setbacks, and building heights, and lenders' biases that mandate front-door rather than back-door parking. On the other hand, early 20th century planning principles favoring the separation of uses have given way to new trends favoring mixed-use development. Many planning commissions now actively encourage mixed-use development with offices, shopping, and residences on the same or adjacent sites. And new mechanisms such as business improvement districts can help provide funding for urban design improvements and coordination of disparate property owners.

Environmental Concerns

Environmental concerns are of central importance to the general public, policy makers, and real estate developers. In the past, developers often addressed these concerns only when forced to to avoid community opposition to a development plan. Increasingly, developers recognize that a sensitive approach to the environment is good not only for the community but also for business.

Sailhouse in Corona del Mar, California, is an infill development of detached and attached luxury homes in designs reminiscent of carriage houses, bungalows, and cottages. Distinctive architecture and a pedestrian-focused site plan help provide a sense of place for its residents.

© Eric Figge

In the 1990s, perhaps the most worrisome environmental problem facing developers was liability for toxic waste. When toxic waste is found after a developer has closed on a site, development may be halted for months or even years. Developers' liability can be unlimited. Lenders' potential liability for toxic waste and asbestos has placed lenders in the unusual position of not wanting to foreclose on some loans that are in default.

Site contamination is still a major problem for developers, but the industry has slowly adopted methods for dealing with it. Both developers and lenders are slowly becoming more accustomed to dealing with contamination, partly because the majority of urban sites—and even undeveloped farms—have some contamination somewhere that must be mitigated. New laws allow lenders to lend money on sites with contamination without being automatically included in the chain of title of owners who have cleanup liability for previous contamination.

As always, new problems generate new opportunities. Some development firms specialize in properties contaminated by toxic waste or asbestos. Because the properties can usually be purchased at significant discounts, careful analysis of the removal costs and appropriate actions can generate large profits, although lenders are extremely wary of loans on such properties. Nonetheless, developers who fail to perform adequate due diligence before purchasing new properties could face financial disaster.

Programs designed to improve air quality also increasingly affect developers. Special districts in which air quality is rigorously monitored and emissions are tightly restricted are being established in major metropolitan areas. New restrictions affect not only heavy industry but also clean industry—indeed, virtually anyone who uses chemicals, sprays, cleaning fluids, fuel, or other substances that generate fumes. Districts such as the Air Quality Control District for Greater Los Angeles are empowered to impose across-the-board taxes based on the levels of air emissions currently generated by building occupants. The restrictions may ultimately force significant portions of industries, such as the furniture industry, to relocate. Developers may even be held liable for their tenants' air emissions.

Communities also are becoming increasingly concerned about the preservation of hillsides, wetlands, canyons, forests, and other environmentally sensitive areas. Developers who address these concerns in planning and designing their buildings will find communities more receptive to their projects. Those who do not will face vocal and increasingly powerful opposition.

The Need for Open Space

One of the most difficult issues relating to urban development is the creation of large, functional open space. Open space comes in many different forms, from manicured golf courses and parks to farms, forest preserves, and habitat conservation areas and nature preserves. Some open space protects views but is not accessible to the public, such as private golf courses, and other forms such as view easements prevent building but not farming or other private cultivation. Other open space is fully accessible to the public. Some areas are highly maintained, while others receive little maintenance and are left completely in the wild.

Each different type of open space is critical for the enjoyment of different people who make up a community. Open space must be specifically protected. If it is not, incremental urban development will eventually consume all potential sites and cut up habitat areas. By donating land to nonprofit conservancies, developers are able to generate charitable tax deductions that can be attractive to their investors.

Organizations like the Nature Conservancy and the Trust for Public Land provide mechanisms for developers and communities to set aside land for open space. These and other organizations serve as conservators of such land, providing access to the public while preserving natural amenities and wildlife habitats.

Cyril Paumier, of HNTB Corporation, emphasizes not only the need for more nature preserves but also for creating public open space throughout the city: "The really great cities of the world are remembered for their public realm: their parks, plazas, boulevards, squares, and pedestrian streets. It isn't about buildings alone: it's the public realm, the public environment, the connective physical fabric that sets the tone for private investment and creates the environment for human activity and habitation."[28]

Transportation and Congestion

Transportation has always been a major source of real estate value because of its impact on location, but solving the problem of overburdened roads promises to be one of the development industry's principal concerns in the next decades. Although access to transportation can create an attractive real estate market, congestion— or merely the perception of congestion—can undermine its value and motivate new and existing development to continue its move outward to more accessible locations.

According to the latest in a series of studies by the Texas Transportation Institute, traffic congestion continues to grow in American metropolitan areas of every size. The report showed "more severe congestion that lasts longer and affects more of the transportation network in 1999 than in 1982. The average annual delay per person climbed from 11 hours in 1982 to 36 hours in 1999. Delays over the same period quintupled in areas with [fewer] than 1 million people."[29]

Alan E. Pisarski, a travel behavior consultant and author of *Commuting in America,* notes that the traditional commuting pattern of suburb to city center has now changed to suburb-to-suburb travel. Of more long-term significance is the increase in travel between rural and metropolitan areas and between metropolitan areas. As jobs are located toward a region's edge, workers in rural communities or other metropolitan areas can compete for those jobs, resulting in a growth in reverse commuting, such as inner-city workers' commuting to jobs in the suburbs. Although commuting has grown signifi-

The Harrison Square rowhouse development in Washington, D.C., occupies the site of the old Children's Hospital, which had been abandoned for many decades. Such redevelopment opportunities can provide substantial returns; all of Harrison Square's 98 units were sold out within 18 months after the start of marketing.

cantly, local trips for personal business and shopping have increased even faster. Many of these trips are conducted during peak periods as part of "trip chains," as time-pressed workers take care of chores on the way home from work.[30]

The most direct method of reducing traffic congestion is to decrease the length of essential vehicle trips and eliminate extraneous trips. Developers can assist in achieving these necessary reductions by offering development in a dense, compact form with a rich mix of land uses accessible to mass transit. The inclusion of residential development, offices, retail uses, and entertainment venues in a convenient and accessible location reduces vehicle trips, spreads peak hour flows on arterial roads, makes the provision of transit modes more cost-effective, and allows more people to live closer to their place of employment. To achieve this scenario, federal and state agencies must work with the cities and counties that control land use and the developed form. Developers, who will be asked to shoulder much of the burden for improving inadequate transportation in the suburbs, would be well advised to support coordinated, collective efforts to plan transportation in their communities. Otherwise, they will be forced to pay a disproportionate share of the cost, and what they do provide will be inadequate to hold congestion constant, let alone reduce it.

Social Responsibility

Real estate development touches people in all areas of their lives—at work, at home, at school, and at play. Buildings will almost certainly outlast their developers and may endure for centuries. Therefore, developers are in a distinctive position with inherent social responsibilities. These responsibilities are at the very core of ULI's purpose, as stated in its credo: "As responsible citizens/developers, let us leave this land enhanced, . . . thereby enriching the lives of all who live on it."

Developers hold special responsibilities because their activities involve large public commitments. In many communities, developers actually build most of the urban infrastructure, including roads, sewer, and water treatment facilities, and drainage channels. In some communities, developers even provide civic facilities such as schools, hospitals, and police and fire stations.

What do communities have a right to expect from developers? In the case of subdivision development, developers function as the implementing arm of the city. As both the designers and builders, they determine land use, parks, and road layouts. Communities have a right to expect the highest possible quality of design, construction, and implementation. Developers are expected to be sensitive to community concerns, the streetscape and landscape, traffic, and other dimensions inherent in development. Developers are also expected to be good citizens of the community and concerned with protecting its long-term interests. Developers should uphold their promises—delivering buildings on time and with appropriate attention to quality.

What do developers have a right to expect from communities? They have a right to expect to be treated fairly and consistently and that decisions will be made on the basis of merit rather than politics. They have a right to expect the community to honor its commitments—to build promised infrastructure on time and to properly maintain public facilities and services. They have a right to expect the community to exercise foresight and good planning judgment in setting public policy—to ensure that new regulations are handled efficiently and do not impose unnecessary costs or delays on the development process.

The Developer's Public Image
Developers as a group suffer from a negative public image. That image is often undeserved—as when developers are identified with unwanted change. Sometimes, however, the image is deserved—when they build shoddy products, when they have been insensitive to community

needs, or when they have imposed costs on the community for which they should have taken responsibility.

In expanding communities where economic growth is desired and the environment is not threatened, it is easier for developers to overcome the stereotype of greedy hustlers. In communities with strong growth control sentiments, however, the suspicion and distrust with which community members view developers in general make conditions more difficult for all developers, no matter how good they are.

Beginning developers should understand the sources of the distrust that they will encounter. Many communities and neighborhood groups have relied on developers' promises that were never kept or on inaccurate predictions, such as a new office building that would not increase congestion. Similarly, community members have witnessed poorly maintained apartments turn into slums. Developers are the standard-bearers for the real estate industry as a whole, even though real estate brokers or property managers may also be to blame. The public approval process for new development provides the sole opportunity for most people to complain about the full array of urban ills.

Undertaking development projects in many communities has become increasingly difficult and gives developers incentives to concentrate on simpler projects. Exactions and fees are so high in many areas that developers cannot afford to provide other amenities that would benefit the community. Nevertheless, developers should remember that many of today's exactions came about because communities felt that developers were not giving adequate consideration to the impact and context of their project on the community. In economic terms, developers were not paying the full cost, including the indirect costs, of their projects.

Beginning developers sooner or later will encounter a situation where a project in which they have invested considerable time and money will go under unless they receive regulatory or financing approval. Although it is tempting to take whatever steps are necessary to save it, developers with a strong sense of character will withstand the unethical or illegal temptations to save a dying project. Developers who work closely with the community create both a successful development and a good public image. Good developers understand how their projects will enhance the neighborhood and serve the needs of the community's residents or workers. One of the most common complaints about developers is that they are insensitive to neighborhood concerns, to community concerns, to design, to the environment, and to the impact of their projects on others. Developers are sometimes justifiably criticized for destroying the fabric of neighborhoods or hastening neighborhood decline by tearing down buildings and not replacing them.[31] All developers should understand the principles of good urban design. Even though developers hire architects to design their buildings, developers must themselves be knowledgeable critics of good design, from the perspective of what is most marketable and from the community's perspective.

Ethical Structures of Major Parties to Development Decisions

- Planners—Tend to exhibit a utopian perspective, a populist orientation, a suspicion of private interests, and a belief in the irreconcilability of public and private interests.
- Developers—Utility maximizers concerned with profits, wealth, and personal distinction. Display a distrust of government typical of the private sector.
- Political Figures—Concerned about conserving their political constituencies and maximizing their political power.
- Parochial Communities (Neighborhoods, for Example)—Concerned with environmental values, property values, amenity values, congestion, intercommunity spillovers, and social values.
- Community at Large—Concerned with economic development values and the quality of the regional environment. ■

Differing Social Objectives

Every major planning decision involves at least five major parties—planners, developers, political figures, neighborhood groups, and the community at large—each with its own biases and objectives. USC professor of urban and regional planning Lowdon Wingo summarizes the attitudes of the five major parties in the accompanying feature box.

Wingo notes that although improved understanding between the groups may sometimes allow consensus to be reached, understanding and empathy can achieve only so much. The various groups seem to possess distinct and incompatible ethical codes. "If I am right," comments Wingo, "the way we actually work out of the paralysis of conflict here is by forming transitory coalitions among the five major elements of the problem."[32]

The community's interest often is at odds with that of individual community groups. For example, a homeowners association may resist road improvements that benefit the community at large because they bring more traffic through the homeowners' own neighborhood. Similarly, developers may have commitments to investors that limit their ability to provide the extra amenities that neighborhood groups demand.

Although the function of planners is to serve as neutral analysts and advisers to the city in conflicts between developers and neighborhood groups, they naturally have their own private agendas and biases. In their evaluation of projects, they may emphasize different, often contradictory, planning criteria:

- Efficiency—Making the city work better in terms of less congestion, lower-cost utilities, and lower-cost housing;
- Equity—Avoiding actions that hurt the poor, first-time buyers, renters, or other groups who end up paying for restrictive requirements;
- Income Redistribution—Favoring actions that give the poor more housing, lower rents, or better economic opportunities;

- Economic Growth—Favoring actions that encourage economic activity, industry, and job opportunities;
- Environmental Protection; and
- Neighborhood Preservation.

New development and neighborhood revitalization are the best, and sometimes the only, means that communities have available to achieve many of these objectives. The role of development in stimulating economic growth is obvious, but its role in issues of equity and income redistribution is less so. To the extent that developers build low-income housing and generate fees and taxes to the community that help subsidize other projects, developers provide one of the few sources of revenue to assist lower-income groups. In addition, although developers are often viewed as the destroyers against whom the environment must be protected and neighborhoods preserved, they are in fact more often the instrument by which environmental protection and neighborhood preservation is achieved.

Community leaders should remember that most of their goals for community improvements will be attained only with the participation of developers. Developers are the producers who initiate projects and take the risks necessary to make things happen. Because their actions have far-reaching consequences for the people who live and work near their projects, the community should have a say in the development process. Indeed, this principle underlay the evolution of land use regulation and community participation throughout the 20th century. The delicate balance between the interests of communities and of developers must be maintained if communities are to grow.

Gaining Community Support

Community opposition to growth can be one of the most difficult challenges developers face. Land use debates often begin with the question of whether or how the land is currently used. Although vacant land choked with weeds may seem to builders like a prime opportunity for development, surrounding neighbors believe that this open space is already in active use as a recreational area, dog park, or view corridor. Failing to acknowledge the presence of these existing, very-low-intensity uses can make it difficult for a developer to reach consensus with neighbors about future land uses. The situation is different when the land is already intensely used. Then citizens and developers must explore the more complex question of whether the proposed land is already intensely used, whether the proposed land use is more or less desirable than the existing uses.

A developer may insist that a proposed project will fit in with the community, but the surrounding neighbors do not view the developer as a reliable expert. The professional planner or technical land use analyst is likewise not the best choice to endorse the project's compatibility with the neighborhood. Instead, the choice should be residents who live or work near similar projects so they can easily endorse the proposed project. Although

it is important to have technical experts rationally evaluate consistency with community character, local citizens are the best source of emotional judgments about that issue.

The analysis of citizen opposition to development proposals has spawned its own vocabulary, with terms like *NIMBY* (not in my backyard) and *LULU* (locally unwanted land use) often used interchangeably. It is helpful, however, to recognize the intrinsic differences between a proposed used and the actual siting of that use.

True NIMBY disputes almost always hinge on a specific location. When a project is opposed for NIMBY reasons, citizens recognize the inherent value of the proposed use but object to the proposed site as an inappropriate location. Opponents in NIMBY disputes may directly or indirectly argue that the unique features of the property make the site unusually sensitive to project impacts. For example, opponents to a new retail project may argue that a new grocery store is desirable but assert that the proposed site is inappropriate because it contains wetlands.

Although NIMBY projects are acknowledged to be desirable as long as they are properly sited, citizens do not want a LULU anywhere. People who oppose LULUs often argue that the proposal should be rejected because there simply is not a need for the use. Recreational projects such as theme parks and convenience-related uses such as drive-through restaurants are classic examples of this kind of LULU. Opponents of LULUs may also campaign on the theme that better alternatives are available: the county should implement a crime prevention program instead of building a new jail or modify an existing arena rather than constructing a new one. Developers facing this type of opposition must fight a battle on several fronts: demonstrating the need for the proposed use, proving that the project provides that use, and showing that no other type of use can meet their need as well as the proposed use.

A significant amount of opposition to development proposals is based on citizens' misperceptions, lack of information, or exaggerated fears of project impacts. Common areas of misinformation about new projects include consistency with zoning and general plan criteria, property values, views, traffic, types of residents or commercial tenants, and changes in community character. The developer can minimize opposition based on lack of information by providing clear, credible data about the project. Most information is unilateral in nature: the builder sends messages to the public in a one-way stream outward, generally using tools such as newsletters, direct mail, Web pages, or advertising materials that can effectively educate citizens about project facts and can also help convey the sophistication, excitement, and lifestyle values of the project.

Developers and planners must satisfy, or at least address, a variety of different constituencies: local residents, including the disadvantaged such as the homeless, local merchants, preservation and arts groups, city officials, and public agency officials. Successful developers learn how to operate within their local, inevitably heterogeneous, communities.

According to Daniel Rose, community groups can, at their best, provide perspective and insight; at their worst, they can fall prey to a NIMBY or LULU mentality. "Residents often oppose the construction of a fire station in their neighborhood because they object to the accompanying noise. But the necessary services of an urban system must be located somewhere. Someone will have to work or live near a fire station or a garbage disposal site."[33]

Gerald Hines, founder and chair of the Hines real estate organization, emphasizes the role that community acceptance plays in marketability. "We look at each city as a different culture, and if we don't know the culture, we're going to have an unsuccessful project. Conferring with community boards and neighborhood associations has become a part of a project's market analysis and its later acceptance by the market."[34]

Personal Integrity

A developer's reputation for integrity is the foundation of success. The development community is a very small world. Even in the largest cities, news travels very fast and reputations precede every player. Players who lie, cheat, or break the law find that reputable companies and businesspeople will have nothing to do with them.

Years after they occur, little things can come back to haunt developers' affairs: failure to follow through on a promise, slow performance on tenant finishes, sloppy workmanship, or slow payment on contracts. Many developers will run into some form of cash flow difficulties at some time during their careers and will consequently have to renegotiate a loan or the terms of a deal. At such times, a past record of honesty and of keeping partners fully informed can make all the difference. No one likes bad news, but everyone likes surprises even less. Projects rarely go bad overnight. Symptoms develop over time—declining occupancy, delays in construction, and so forth. When partners and lenders are kept informed of the problems, they are more understanding and more willing to try to work things out. Usually, projects that get into trouble between good partners can be put back on track, or, if one partner must take over, no long-term damage is done to the other partner's reputation. If a partner has been dishonest or has failed to tell the whole truth, however, the consequences for that partner's reputation can be devastating.

Conclusion

Cities are organic in nature. Like living organisms, they experience cycles of birth, growth, and decay. Every section of every city experiences these cycles, no matter how prestigious its origins. Even Athens's Acropolis, Rome's Forum, and New York's Fifth Avenue have gone through periods of economic vitality followed by periods of economic decline. The factors that influence such cycles are very complex and include transportation, utilities,

and other infrastructure; the quality, age, and functional obsolescence of the buildings; the quality of design and public space; the age distribution and incomes of the residents and workers; and the economic health of the neighborhood, city, region, and country.

Our understanding of how to control development to create better cities and neighborhoods is far from complete. Among the greatest problems facing planners and public policy makers are how and where to invest public funds so that they will do the most to enhance improving areas or halt the fall of declining areas. Too often, massive public and private expenditures are made to rejuvenate one section of town, only to pull businesses and homebuyers away from another section of town.

In general, our performance in developing U.S. cities has been at best mediocre. It is not so much that our cities are drab and ugly as they fall short of their potential. Spaces are poorly planned; boring, repetitive designs are everywhere. Once beautiful neighborhoods are not maintained; the fabric of much of our urban infrastructure is in an appalling state of disrepair. Developing new greenfield sites is easier and cheaper than maintaining or redeveloping older areas.

No one individual or group is to blame for this situation, but all are capable of helping to remedy it. The development community must exercise stronger leadership not only in constructing and renovating U.S. cities but also in correcting the harmful aspects of the present development system. By looking after the interests of the community at large, developers serve their own interests.

Past ULI President Robert Nahas summarized the attraction of development: "The great developers whom I've been privileged to know never worked for money per se. I'm not a psychiatrist, but I think these developers want to leave a footprint in the sand. It's their particular kind of immortality."[35] Successful developers share the same goal: to create better living environments, better places, better cities. All developments must pass the test of serving current market needs or they will fail. But most developments also have a future clientele. Although individual homes and buildings may be replaced, the basic fabric of the community that developers create—street layout, parks, urban design elements—will last for hundreds of years. Indeed, one of development's greatest rewards—and the source of its greatest responsibilities—is its impact on future generations. Development offers a way to extend ourselves beyond our lifetime—to leave footprints in the sand.

Notes

1. Interview with Kenneth Leventhal, founder of the Kenneth Leventhal accounting firm, now E&Y Kenneth Leventhal, 1998.

2. From a speech by Phil Walsh to students at the University of Southern California, Los Angeles, November 1988.

3. Peter D. Linneman, "Forces Changing the Real Estate Industry Forever," *Wharton Real Estate Review,* Spring 1997, pp. 1–12.

4. Daniela Deane, "The Big Deals about Housing," *Washington Post,* March 28, 2002.

5. M. Leanne Lachman, "Our Demographic Future: A Nation of Niches. Lend Lease Real Estate Investments." Address at ULI's Washington Real Estate Trends conference, April 16, 2002.

6. Interview with Robert Larson, chair, Lazard Freres Real Estate, New York, July 2001.

7. Harvey S. Moskowitz and Carl G. Lindbloom, *The New Illustrated Book of Development Definitions* (New Brunswick, N.J.: Center for Urban Policy Research, 1993).

8. Alvin L. Arnold, *The Arnold Encyclopedia of Real Estate,* 2nd ed. (New York: Wiley, 1993).

9. In California, for example, development rights become vested after "substantial construction" has been completed, which has been interpreted to mean that a substantial portion of a building's steel or wood frame must be in place.

10. See Rita Fitzgerald and Richard Peiser, "Development (Dis)Agreements at Colorado Place," *Urban Land,* July 1988, pp. 2–5; and Douglas R. Porter and Lindell L. Marsh, *Development Agreements: Practice, Policy, and Prospects* (Washington, D.C.: ULI–the *Urban Land* Institute, 1989).

11. Phyllis Meyers and Robert Puentes, "Growth at the Ballot Box: Electing the Shape of Communities in November 2000" (Washington, D.C.: The Brookings Center on Urban and Metropolitan Policy, February 2001).

12. See www.cdi.gsd.harvard.edu, the Web site for the Harvard Design School's Center for Design Informatics.

13. Elizabeth Hayes, "Radical Changes as Worlds of Tech, Real Estate Merge," *Los Angeles Business Journal,* January 24, 2000, p. 36.

14. Ibid.

15. See William H. Frey and Ross C. DeVol, "America's Demography in the New Century: Aging Baby Boomers and New Immigrants as Major Players," *Milken Institute Policy Brief,* March 8, 2000.

16. Martha Farnsworth Riche, "The Implications of Changing U.S. Demographics for Housing Choice and Location in Cities," Discussion Paper (Washington, D.C.: Brookings Institution Center on Urban and Metropolitan Policy, March 2001).

17. William H. Frey, "Metro Magnets for Minorities and Whites: Melting Pots, the New Sunbelt, and the Heartland" (Ann Arbor, Mich.: Population Studies Center, University of Michigan, and Milken Institute, February 2002); and Frey and DeVol, "America's Demography in the New Century."

18. Ibid.

19. D.J. Burrough, "The New Golden Years," *Urban Land,* March 2000, pp. 51–53.

20. Lewis M. Goodkin, "Resort-Style Retirement," *Urban Land,* April 2000, pp. 72–77.

21. Joel Kotkin, "A Bit of a Chill for Hot Times in the Big City," *Washington Post,* March 24, 2002.

22. Riche, "The Implications of Changing U.S. Demographics."

23. Ibid.

24. Interview with Doug Boone, founder, Boone Communities, Davidson, North Carolina.

25. Interview with Ray Watson, past president of Irvine Company and chair of the Executive Committee, Disney Corporation, 1998.

26. Peter Rummell, "Preserving a Sense of Place," *Urban Land,* April 2000, p. 18.

27. Thomas L. Lee, "Place Making in Suburbia," *Urban Land,* October 2000, pp. 72–79+.

28. Quoted in William H. Hudnut III, "Open Space," *Urban Land,* October 2000, pp. 50–57.

29. David Schrank et al., *The 2001 Urban Mobility Report* (College Station, Texas: Texas Transportation Institute, 2001), p. 1.

30. Alan E. Pisarski, "Commuting in Context," *Urban Land,* May 2001, pp. 68–78.

31. It should be noted that developers never tear down buildings without intending to replace them, because the purpose of tearing them down is to increase the income generated by the property. When it occurs, a mistake, inability to get financing, or bankruptcy has almost certainly occurred.

32. See Richard Peiser, "Who Plans America? Planners or Developers?" *APA Journal,* Autumn 1990, p. 503.

33. Daniel Rose, chair of Design and Politics conference, New York City, April 1988, quoted in Maria Brisbane, "Developing in a Politicized Environment," *Urban Land,* July 1988, pp. 6–8.

34. Gerald Hines, founder and chair, the Hines real estate organization, Houston, Texas, quoted in Brisbane, "Developing in a Politicized Environment," p. 7.

35. Robert Nahas, former general partner, Rafanelli and Nahas, Orinda, California, quoted in Ed Micken, "Future Talk: The Next Fifty Years," *Urban Land,* December 1986, p. 16.

Appendices and Index

Appendix 1
Interviewees and Other Contributors

The following people generously provided insights and information on the real estate industry for this book. Their contributions are greatly appreciated.

Michelle Addington
Associate Professor of Architecture
Harvard Graduate School of Design
Cambridge, Massachusetts

Joan Betts
Vice President
Fidelity Mutual Life Insurance Company
Atlanta, Georgia

Raymond Bhumgara
Gannett Fleming, Inc.
Camp Hill, Pennsylvania

Doug Boone
Founder
Boone Communities
Davidson, North Carolina

Jamy Buchanan
Buchanan & Associates
Boston, Massachusetts

W. Stephen Comstock
Director of Communications and Publications
American Society of Heating, Refrigerating and
    Air-Conditioning Engineers
Atlanta, Georgia

Harlan Doliner
Partner
Nixon Peabody, LLP
Boston, Massachusetts

Tim Edmond
President–Capital Region
ARVIDA
Tallahassee, Florida

Izzy Eichenstein
The Oakstone Company
Los Angeles, California

Jim Fawcett
Associate Director, Sea Grant Program
University of Southern California
Los Angeles, California

Marvin Finger
The Finger Companies
Houston, Texas

Roger Galatas
President
Roger Galatas Interests, LLC
The Woodlands, Texas

Jim Goodell
President
Goodell Brackenbush
Pasadena, California

Sanford Goodkin
President
Ackman-Ziff Goodkin Real Estate Advisors
Chair
Horizon Strategies, LLC
Solana Beach, California

Vince Graham
Principal
The I'On Company
Mount Pleasant, South Carolina

Douglas Hahn
Senior Environmental Scientist
URS Corporation
Los Angeles, California

David Hasbrouck
Executive Director
Cushman & Wakefield
Los Angeles, California

Randolph Hawthorne
RGHventures
Brookline, Massachusetts

Alex Von Hoffman
Visiting Lecturer
Harvard Graduate School of Design
Cambridge, Massachusetts

Patricia Pewthers
Vice President, Escrow Operations
First American Title Company
Los Angeles, California

Douglas Porter
President
The Growth Management Institute
Chevy Chase, Maryland

James Perley
Western America Properties
Los Angeles, California

Jeannie Quintal
Title Officer
First American Title Company
Los Angeles, California

Jonathan Rose
Principal
Jonathon Rose and Companies
Katonah, New York

Scott Smith
Manager/COO
La Plata Investments
Colorado Springs, Colorado

Ronald Stenlund
President
Central Consulting Engineers
Green Bay, Wisconsin

Jim Thomas
Ware Malcomb Architects
Irvine, California

Greg Vilkin
President
Forest City Development
Los Angeles, California

Ray Watson
Chair of the Executive Committee
Disney Corporation
Los Angeles, California

Ron White
President of Residential Development
Hillwood Development Corporation
Dallas, Texas

John Williams
Former Partner
Acacia Capital Group
New York, New York

Carl Willmann
Ware Malcomb Architects
Irvine, California

Jack Willome
Former CEO
Rayco, Limited
San Antonio, Texas

John Wong
Tishman Construction Corporation
New York, New York

Charles Wu
Managing Director of Real Estate Investments
Charlesbank Capital Partners
Boston, Massachusetts

Karl Zavitkovsky
Bank of America, Real Estate Banking Group
Dallas, Texas

Leonard Zax
Partner
Latham & Watkins
Washington, D.C.

Robert Zerbst
CB Richard Ellis Investors
Los Angeles, California

Appendix 2
Sample Design Guidelines

Do This!

This home is divided into three basic parts: the base which anchors the dwelling to the ground, functioning as a natural extension of the ground plane; the middle, commonly containing a covered porch and façade walls penetrated by windows and doors; and the cap, which commonly encompasses roof elements such as hipped and gable roof forms, and chimney stacks.

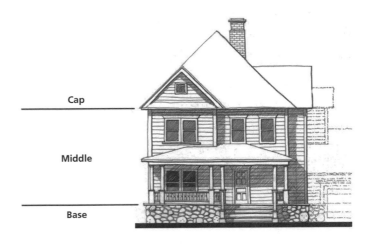

Don't Do This!

This home is composed of awkward and boxy building shapes. Walls run continuously without a change in direction. The roof profile is blocky.

Do This!

- This home is composed of complementary building shapes which taper upwards towards the center of the dwelling
- Various roof heights add visual interest to the composition of the home profile
- Large covered porch provides a platform for outdoor entertaining, socializing, and leisure while functioning as a transitional element to the second floor
- Smaller second-story building volume reduces the bulk of the garage

This sample page is from Design Guidelines for Castle Valley Ranch, Newcastle, Colorado. Courtesy Downing Thorpe & James, Boulder, Colorado.

Appendix 3
Sample Letter of Intent for an Industrial Property Purchase

Re: Dolphin Business Center
    Tampa, Florida

Letter of Intent

Gentlemen:

Pursuant to discussions with and based on the information provided to American Realty Advisors or an entity to be formed by it ("Buyer"), Buyer is prepared to enter into a written agreement for the purchase of the real property known as Dolphin Business Center, consisting of approximately 170,000 net rentable square feet of industrial space located at 10 Dolphin Way, Tampa, Florida, and personal property related thereto (collectively, the "Property"). The transaction is to be consummated based on the terms and conditions set forth in the numbered paragraphs below and to be more fully set forth in a purchase and sale agreement ("Agreement") to be executed by Buyer and _____ ("Seller").

1. *Purchase Price.* The purchase price for the Property shall be Ten Million Dollars ($10,000,000) ("Purchase Price"). The Purchase Price shall be paid at Closing (as defined below) through an escrow ("Escrow") as follows:
    1.1 Following completion of the inspection period described in paragraph 4 below, Buyer shall deliver into Escrow cash in the amount of Five Hundred Thousand Dollars ($500,000) ("Earnest Money Deposit").
    1.2 At or before the Closing, Buyer shall deliver the remainder of the Purchase Price into Escrow.
    1.3 All cash sums deposited into Escrow by Buyer, including interest on deposited funds, shall be held for the benefit of Buyer by Escrow Holder (as defined below).

2. *Escrow and Other Provisions.*
    2.1 After Seller's acceptance of this Letter of Intent, Buyer and Seller shall negotiate, execute, and deliver the Agreement, including escrow instructions, to Chicago Title Insurance Company ("Escrow Holder"). The Agreement will be prepared by counsel for Buyer and approved by counsel for Seller and shall provide for the purchase and sale of the Property on the terms and conditions contained herein and such other terms and conditions as the parties shall agree.

Upon acceptance of the Agreement by Escrow Holder, the Escrow shall be opened.
    2.2 Buyer shall order a title report/title commitment and underlying title documents through Escrow Holder. Seller shall pay all transfer taxes, fees, and charges for the real, personal, and intangible property. Seller shall pay the premium related to the standard portion of the ALTA Owner's Coverage Policy of Title Insurance and for obtaining an ALTA Owner's Extended Coverage Policy of Title Insurance, including zoning, survey and comprehensive endorsements. Buyer shall pay for all other endorsements it requires. Buyer shall pay for a satisfactory update to Seller's existing ALTA survey. Except as otherwise provided herein or in the Agreement, the Agreement and escrow instructions shall contain such other escrow provisions as are in accordance with customary practice in Hillsborough County, Florida, in connection with the purchase and sale of real property and shall provide for the Closing in accordance with paragraph 8 below. Buyer and Seller shall each pay one-half of customary escrow charges and shall negotiate their own separate fees for Escrow Holder's additional services. Prorations (including, without limitation, the proration of rents and taxes for the year in which the Closing occurs) shall be accomplished as of 11:59 p.m. on the day preceding the Closing.

3. *Title.* The transaction contemplated by this Letter of Intent and the Agreement is contingent on Buyer receiving title to the Property at the Closing free and clear of the following: (i) all monetary liens and encumbrances, except for current nondelinquent taxes; and (ii) any other liens, claims, encumbrances, easements, covenants, conditions, restrictions, leases, licenses, rights of use or possession, and similar matters, other than those approved by Buyer. Seller shall remove any liens or encumbrances violating the foregoing at or before the Closing.

4. *Inspections.* Buyer shall have thirty (30) business days after the execution of the Agreement and receipt of the information referenced in paragraphs 2, 3, and 5 of this letter to conduct, review, and approve the results of the physical, economic, and other investigations, tests, and studies that Buyer elects to perform relative to the Property. Seller shall make the

Property and all portions thereof available to Buyer and its authorized representatives for inspection. Seller, at its election, may have someone present at all times.

5. *Information from Seller.* Except as otherwise set forth herein, on or before the tenth (10th) day following the date of Seller's execution of this Letter of Intent, Seller shall have delivered to Buyer, for Buyer's review and approval, originals or copies of those items set forth in Exhibit "A" attached hereto.

6. *Conditions to Buyer's Obligations.* Buyer's obligations shall be subject to the satisfaction of the following conditions:

   6.1 The parties agree that until the Agreement is signed by all parties, any letters, drafts, or other communications or exchanges of information shall have absolutely no legal effect, shall not be used to impose any legally binding obligation on another party, and shall not be used as evidence of any oral or implied agreement between the parties or as evidence of the terms and conditions of any implied agreement.

   6.2 Five (5) days before the Closing, Seller shall deliver or cause to be delivered to Buyer a Tenant Estoppel Certificate, in a form and substance acceptable to Buyer, from each of the tenants of the Property.

   6.3 At or before the Closing, Seller shall deliver to Buyer a Warranty Deed, an Assignment of

the Leases for the Property, an Assignment of Service Contracts and Guarantees relating to the Property, and a Bill of Sale for personal property.

7. *Disapproval and Termination.* In the event that Buyer shall timely disapprove of any of the investigations or other matters referred to in paragraphs 2, 3, 4, 5, or 6 above, or from independent investigations discover a material problem, or any of the other conditions to Buyer's obligations are not satisfied, Buyer shall so notify Seller in writing. In such event, the Escrow shall be terminated, and the Earnest Money Deposit and interest earned thereon shall be returned to Buyer.

8. *Close of Escrow.* The Closing shall occur on or before ten (10) days after the conclusion of Buyer's inspection period as set forth in paragraph 4 above.

9. *Brokers' Commission.* Seller shall pay and/or defend all brokerage commission claims arising as a result of the transaction proposed by this letter and indemnify as well as hold Buyer harmless from claims for the same.

10. *Disclosure of Terms.* Except as required by law, Seller, Seller's agents, representatives, employees, and brokers, as well as the Title Company, shall not disclose any terms of this Letter of Intent, the Agreement, or any sale resulting therefrom.

Exhibit A—Checklist of Information Required

1. A copy of Seller's Title Policy with respect to the Property.
2. Copies of any surveys or maps of the Property in Seller's possession, including any ALTA surveys.
3. All leases, tenant financial statements, rental and occupancy agreements, and lease commitments relating to the Property.
4. All service contracts, maintenance contracts, management contracts, and other contracts or documents of significance to the Property or its operation, including tenants' service contracts.
5. Copies of any operating documents, contracts, and invoices related to the cost of operating the building, e.g., real property tax bill; HVAC, gas, electrical, sewer, and water bills; and any other similar contracts or invoices.

6. Copies of all insurance policies for the Property. Information regarding any insurance claims filed within the last five years. Loss history from all insurance carriers for the last five years. Certification of insurance from tenants.
7. An as-built set of the working architectural and structural engineering plans and specifications for the building shell(s), modifications, and interior improvements constructed in the building(s), including the Property's architects' calculations of the BOMA net rentable building area, together with the mechanical, electrical, HVAC, and fire protection plans and specifications, soils and geotechnical reports, environmental and ADA reports, and third-party warranties, as available.

8. Building and occupancy permits, and all other governmental permits and approvals as required to construct and operate the Property.
9. CAD files for the building core, shell drawings, and space plans.
10. A personal property inventory.
11. Any evidence in Seller's possession of toxic or hazardous materials that have been found on the Property or that are currently on the Property.
12. Any other information in Seller's possession as reasonably required by Buyer for a thorough assessment of the physical and economic aspects of the Property, including, without limitation, access to the Property's rent rolls, operating statements, annual budgets, maintenance logs, and all documents considered as books and records. ■

If the terms and conditions set forth above are satisfactory, please date and execute this letter in the space provided below and return it to Buyer by 5:00 p.m. (Pacific Time), on November 12, 2002. Upon receipt of a fully executed Letter of Intent, Buyer is prepared to begin negotiations and work toward execution of the Agreement and escrow instructions on terms and conditions acceptable to the parties.

This Letter of Intent is submitted with the understanding that it is not intended to be contractual in nature, but is merely a statement of the general terms and conditions under which Buyer, or its nominee, is prepared to purchase the Property. No contractual obligations shall be created between the parties until such time as the Agreement has been executed and delivered by both parties.

If you have any questions regarding this Letter of Intent, please do not hesitate to contact us. We look forward to working with you on this matter.

Very truly yours,

American Realty Advisors

Approved and agreed to this ____ day of _____, 2002.

_____

By:

Source: American Realty Advisors, Glendale, California.

Appendix 4
Sample Table of Contents for a Single-Family Residential Subdivision

Appendix 5
Sample Table of Contents
Declaration of a Residential Condominium

Appendix 6
Sample Commitment for an Office Building Construction Loan

Proposed Borrower
c/o Developer
5000 Locust Avenue
Anytown, USA

re: $5,000,000 Construction Loan
[name of property]

Dear Developer:

We are pleased to advise you that [name of bank] hereby offers to provide [borrowing entity] a commercial real estate construction loan on the terms and conditions set forth below:

AMOUNT: $5,000,000 (the "Loan")

BORROWER: [borrowing entity] (the "Borrower")

TERM: The Loan shall begin on the day of closing of the Loan and shall end on the day that is 18 months after the first day of the first month after closing. Interest shall accrue on the outstanding principal balance of the Loan at a rate of prime plus one (1) percent interest only. Provided that no default has occurred, the maturity date may be extended for six (6) months, at the option of the Borrower, upon 30 days written notice to the Bank and the payment of an extension fee of $[amount].

PROCEEDS: The proceeds of the Loan shall be used to pay off the existing land loan and construction escrow. The approximate use of funds is as follows:

Pay off loan	$[amount]
Construction escrow	$[amount]
Closing costs	$[amount]
Interest reserve	$[amount]
Total	$[amount]

SECURITY: The Bank will require a first deed of trust on the land and all related improvements to the Property mentioned above, together with a first lien security interest on all equipment, fixtures, and other personal property of the Borrower located on and necessary to the use and occupancy of the Property, and the Borrower's interest as landlord in all leases and contracts on the improvements and the security deposits and rents payable thereunder.

COMMITMENT FEE: In consideration for the issuance of this commitment, the Borrower shall pay to the Bank a nonrefundable commitment fee equal to [amount]% of the Loan, or $[amount], which shall be deemed fully earned upon acceptance hereof by the Borrower, and is not refundable for any reason. The Borrower has paid $[amount] on account of said fee, and the remaining $[amount] shall be due and payable at settlement. If the Loan shall fail to close for any reason other than default hereunder by the Bank, the commitment fee will be retained by the Bank as liquidated damages, not as a penalty. The Borrower agrees that as liquidated damages the amount of the commitment fee is reasonable.

ACCURACY: This commitment is subject to the accuracy of all of the information contained in your loan package and other supporting information provided to us by you or your representatives. Should any information be determined to be inaccurate, the Bank may withdraw this commitment at its discretion. The Bank will not be obliged to fund the Loan at any time when there has been a materially adverse change in your financial condition or deterioration to the subject property or improvements.

APPRAISAL: At least fourteen (14) days prior to settlement, the Bank shall have obtained an appraisal on the land and proposed improvements based on the final plans and specifications by an appraiser engaged on your behalf by the Bank. All fees incurred in connection with such appraisal shall be paid by the Borrower. The cost of this appraisal is $[amount] and must be submitted with the completed commitment letter.

EQUITY: The maximum Loan will be no more than seventy-five percent (75%) of appraised value or the amount of this commitment. If the appraised value of said Property is not sufficient to meet the 75% loan-to-value requirement, you will have the option to reduce the loan amount to meet the 75% requirement, or to post additional real estate collateral.

COSTS: The Borrower is to bear all costs of settlement including the Bank's counsel, recordation taxes and fees, mortgage title insurance, appraisal, transfer taxes, and the fees of the Bank's construction inspector for the review of the plans and specifications and construction inspections.

TITLE INSURANCE: At least three (3) days prior to settlement, the Borrower is to furnish the Bank a mortgagee's title insurance commitment for the Property from a title company acceptable to the Bank, together with true and complete copies of all documents or instruments enumerated as exceptions to title, in form and substance satisfactory to the Bank in its sole judgment. Within fifteen (15) days of settlement, the borrower is to furnish the Bank a mortgagee title insurance policy satisfactory in form and substance to the Bank and insuring the Bank's deed of trust as a first lien on the Property in the amount of the Loan.

CONSTRUCTION: No work is to commence nor is any material to be stored on the site prior to recordation of the loan documents unless the mortgagor can obtain an acceptable title policy excluding mechanics liens exceptions. Construction must begin no later than thirty (30) days after settlement as may be extended by mutual agreement. A cost analysis, in trade breakdown form, reflecting the various subcontractors and material suppliers shall be furnished by the Borrower and reviewed by the Bank's construction progress inspector prior to the first construction draw request. In the event the Bank's construction progress inspector's review determines, in his sole opinion, that the plans and specifications are inadequate or that construction costs are unreasonable, the Bank may withdraw the commitment.

DISBURSEMENT: The loan proceeds will be disbursed into a construction progress fund administered by the bank as trustee. Interest will not be charged until funds are disbursed from this account.

BUILDING AND LOAN AGREEMENT: Funds shall be advanced under the terms of a building and loan agreement as construction progresses. Requisitions in AIA form will be submitted monthly and approved by the Bank's construction progress inspector. Advances shall be limited to ninety percent (90%) of such requisition until the project is completed. The ten percent (10%) retainage payment is contingent upon receipt of the final release of liens from the general contractor and all subcontractors, final approval by the construction progress inspector, and a use and occupancy permit from the county. All disbursements are subject to a title bring-to-date satisfactory to the Bank.

REQUIREMENTS PRIOR TO THE FIRST CONSTRUCTION DRAW:

1. One set of plans and specifications.
2. Copy of the building permit and evidence that zoning requirements have been complied with.
3. Builder's all-risk insurance policy, including vandalism and malicious mischief, naming [name of entity] as mortgagee and loss payee under the mortgage clause as their interest may appear. Borrower shall provide hazard insurance during the entire term of the Loan

in amounts satisfactory to the Bank and name the Bank as mortgagee in such policy. Such policies shall require a 30-day cancellation notice.
4. Certificate of workman's compensation and copies of public liability policy for the borrower and contractor.
5. Location survey.
6. Water and sewer permit (if applicable).
7. Evidence of utility availability.
8. Soil test.
9. Copy of grading permit.

SIGN: At the expense of [name of entity], we reserve the right to erect a temporary sign at the construction site indicating financing is provided by [name of entity].

SURVEY: At least three (3) days prior to the settlement date, the Borrower shall cause to be submitted to the Bank, for approval by the Bank, a location survey of the property prepared by a licensed surveyor approved by the Bank, showing any existing improvements thereon and the locations of easements, encroachment (if any), and all other matters affecting title to the property. Such survey shall be satisfactory to the Bank in its sole discretion, and shall be deemed "current" only if it is dated within thirty (30) days of the settlement date and is otherwise acceptable to the title company for purposes of removing any current survey exception from the title insurance policy required by the terms hereof.

SITE PLAN: At least three (3) days prior to the settlement date, the Borrower shall cause to be submitted to the Bank, for approval by the Bank, a site plan showing the proposed location of the building, any existing improvements thereon, the locations of easements, encroachments (if any), and all other matters affecting title to the property.

ORGANIZATIONAL DOCUMENTS: At least five (5) days prior to settlement, the Borrower shall submit to the Bank a copy of the Borrower's Partnership Agreement, any amendments thereto, and Borrower's Resolution to borrow, which documents shall be satisfactory to the Bank in its sole judgment.

FINANCIAL INFORMATION: The Borrower agrees to furnish to the Bank, on an annual basis, the following financial information:

1. Tax returns on Borrower and key individuals.
2. Current rent rolls.
3. Copies of new leases.

GUARANTORS: The Borrower's payment of the Loan and performance of the obligation contained in the deed of trust and other documents evidencing, securing, and providing for disbursement of the Loan shall be jointly, severally, and unconditionally guaranteed by [name of entity]. The Guarantor(s) will furnish to the Bank at such time or times as specified by the Bank, such financial statements and other information concerning the financial condition of such Guarantor(s) as the Bank may from time to time require.

BROKERAGE: The Bank shall not be required to pay any brokerage fee or commission arising from this commitment and the Borrower agrees to defend, indemnify, and hold the Bank harmless against any and all expenses, liabilities, and losses arising from such claim in connection therewith, including payment of reasonable attorneys' fees.

CONDEMNATION: At the time of settlement of the Loan, no proceeding shall have been threatened or commenced by any authority having the power of eminent domain to condemn any part of the Property that the Bank deems substantial.

NONASSIGNABILITY OF COMMITMENT: This commitment is issued directly to or for the benefit of the Borrower and may not be assigned by or on behalf of the Borrower by operation of law or otherwise, without the express written consent of the Bank, which consent may be withheld by the Bank at its sole discretion.

LEASE(S): The Borrower shall submit to the Bank for its review and approval a copy of all executed lease(s) on the property. Said lease(s) shall be satisfactory in form and content in the sole discretion of the Bank. Said lease(s) shall be subordinate to the deed of trust securing the Loan. On or before the settlement date, and upon each and every request thereafter, the Borrower shall submit to the Bank a rent roll pertaining to the property certified as to its correctness by the Borrower. At settlement, we will require an assignment of rents and leases to be executed. In addition to the assignment of rents and leases [name of bank] will require the following: The building must be preleased up to 50%, or [number of] square feet, prior to settlement/disbursement of funds.

SECONDARY FINANCING: During the term of the Loan, no additional financing or refinancing by any other lender shall be secured by a lien on the Property without the prior written consent of the Bank.

SETTLEMENT COSTS: The Borrower shall pay all taxes and assessments due on the settlement date, and all recording fees and taxes, costs of title examination, title insurance premium, survey and appraisal expenses, attorney's fees, and any and all other expenses incurred by the Bank in connection with the negotiation of, prepa-

ration for, closing, and servicing of the Loan. The Borrower shall also pay all expenses incurred if the Loan fails to close through no fault of the Bank.

SETTLEMENT: Settlement is to be conducted by the Bank's counsel unless the Borrower chooses another attorney. If any attorney chosen by the Borrower is used, the Bank's counsel must approve all documents prior to settlement. The Borrower shall pay to the Bank's counsel all fees for services performed either in preparation or review of loan documents or other matters related to this transaction whether or not the loan closes.

SURVIVAL: The terms and conditions of this commitment, where applicable, shall survive the settlement of the Loan and shall continue in full force and effect, unless otherwise modified or amended in writing and signed by the Bank. No agent or broker is authorized to act in this loan transaction on behalf of the Bank. Time shall be of the essence in all matters covered by this commitment.

ADDITIONAL ITEMS: In addition, there will be other supporting documentation relating to this transaction. This documentation will contain the customary covenants and agreements pertaining to construction and permanent financing thereof that are usually required by the bank.

ADDITIONAL COVENANTS: [any additional covenants].

There are no other representations concerning this loan commitment except as set forth in writing. Any change in any terms and conditions of this commitment must be in writing by the Bank. Upon failure to comply with any requirements by the Borrower or if a requirement cannot be met for any reason, this commitment may be withdrawn at the Bank's option.

You may indicate your acceptance of this commitment by signing and returning the original of this letter, the environmental fee, and the appraisal fee for a total of $[amount] by no later than [date]. Settlement must occur on or prior to [date]. This period is extended to allow time to meet the prelease requirement. In the event these deadlines are not met, this commitment is automatically withdrawn.

Sincerely,
[signed]

Appendix 7
Underwriting Checklist for a Food- and Drug-Anchored Community Shopping Center

Tenant Information
- Rent Roll (lease start and stop dates, options)
- Leases (parent company, franchise, who signs, etc.)
- Lease Abstracts
- Tenant Size and Bay Depths
- Tenant Profile
- Sales Turnover Information
- Tenant Financials

Physical Description (Graphics)
- Site Plan Coded by Color and Labeled
  - Common Areas
  - Tenant Areas
  - Parking
  - Vacant Space
- Aerial Photographs
  - Oblique
  - Vertical
- Subject Photographs
  - Street Scenes and Adjacent Areas
  - Parking Area
  - Exterior Facade and Storefronts
  - Interior Spaces
- Maps
  - Regional
  - Area
  - Site
- Center Size
- Center Age
- Parking Ratio
- Construction Details (description and date of major improvements)

Financial Information
- Monthly Operating Statements (12 months trailing)
- Historical Operating Statement (3 years)
- Tax Returns for Most Recent Years (if available)
- Copy of Purchase Contract
- Information on Existing Loan (rate, maturity date, amortization, etc.)
- History and Details of Capital Expenditures

Environmental Issues
- Copy of Existing Phase I (if available)
- Copy of Existing Phase II (if available)
- Red Flag: Dry Cleaner on Site
- Red Flag: Gas Station on Site or Adjacent Site

Market Information
- Trade Area Demographics
- Traffic Counts for Adjacent Streets
- Area Profile
- Rental Comparisons within a 5-Mile Radius
  - Anchors
  - Minianchors
  - Shops
  - Pads
- Sales Comparisons for Similar Centers
- Recent Land Sales
- Market Graphics
  - Location Maps
  - Photos of Competitors (land sales, lease competitors, sales competitors)
- Leasing Brochures for Competitive Projects

Borrower Profiles
- Vesting of Borrowing Entity
- Trust Agreements
- Partnership Agreements
- Operating Agreements
- Financial Statement
- Résumé

Third-Party Reports
- Appraisal (if available)
- Physical Assessment Report (if available)
- Environmental Reports (if available)

Source: George Smith Partners, Inc.

Index

Note: Italicized page numbers indicate figures, photos, and illustrations. Bold page numbers indicate feature boxes.

■

Absorption: example of, 123; and industrial development, *263;* and land development, 64; and multifamily residential development, 138–39, 140; and office development, 219

Acacia Capital, 286

Accessibility: and design, 181; of industrial development, 263–64, 275; of multifamily residential development, 142–43, 181; of office development, 222–23; of outparcels, 329; of retail development, 312, 314–15, 323–27, 329

Accrued return balance, 190

Action plan, 34

Adaptive use. *See* Redevelopment/rehabilitation

Addington, Michelle, 234

Adjustable-rate mortgages, 184, 187

Advertising. *See* Marketing; Public relations

Advertising agencies, 50. *See also* Public relations agencies

Aerial photos, 98

AEW Capital Management, 282

Affordable housing, 130, 171, 173, 264; government programs, 193, 195; and immigrants, 362; and smart growth, 364

Agglomeration, 262–63

Aging population: and development industry trends, 361, 362–63; and multifamily residential development, 129, 132, 136

Agoura Hills Centre, **246–49**

Ahmanson Commercial Development, 246

Air-conditioning units, 175, 178, 279. *See also* HVAC systems

Air quality, 279, 366

Airport proximity, 263, 277

Alaska, 277

Amenities: and development industry trends, 363; and industrial development, 275, 288; and market analysis, *220;* and multifamily residential development, 174–76, 181; and office development, 218

American Institute of Architects (AIA), 37–38

American Land Title Association (ALTA), 48

American Society of Heating, Refrigerating and Air-Conditioning Engineers (ASHRAE), 233–34

American Society of Landscape Architects, 38

Americans with Disabilities Act (ADA), 327

Anchor tenants, 307, 310, 327, *338–40,* 340–41, 344, 353; reciprocal easement agreement, 352

Apartment development: condominium development versus, 179; and development process, *19;* and financing, 182, 183; leasing, 198; preleasing, 19, 197; stages of development and time line, *24;* time line for, *19, 132. See also* Multifamily residential development

Appraisers and appraisals, 46–47, 153, 184, 280

Approvals: advice about, 22; fees for, 270; of industrial development, 264, 269, 270; of land development, 80; of office development, 237; of retail development, 303, 312, 317. *See also* Regulatory issues; Zoning

Architects: compensation for, 38, 195; and energy efficiency, 233; guidelines for dealing with, **181;** and industrial development, 296; and lighting, 230, 233; and multifamily residential development, 171, 181, 195; and office development, 230, 231, 233, 238; and rentable space, 231; and retail development, 318, 333; role of, 37–38, 44, 45, 195; sensitivity to community, 368; and signs, 230. *See also* Landscape architects

Arterial streets, 100

Articles of incorporation, 120

Asbestos abatement professionals, 43–44

As-is condition, 289

Assessment districts, 78

Asset management, 250

Atlanta, Georgia, 181

At-risk capital, 22

Attorney's role, 36, 47, 193, 344

Audobon at the Branches [Reston, Virginia], *274*

Austin Ranch [Dallas, Texas], *129, 179, 180*

Austin, Texas, 77, 108

Automobiles. *See* Streets/roads; Traffic

Avalon at Arlington Square [Arlington, Virginia], *174*

Avalon Corners [Stamford, Connecticut], *174, 175*

Avco Community Developers, Inc. v. South Coast Reg'l Comm'n (1976), 76

The Avenue at White Marsh [Baltimore, Maryland], **348–51,** *348–50*

■

Babbit v. *Sweet Home* (1995), 72

Baby boomers, 129, 132, 362–63

Back-of-the-envelope analysis, 152

Baley, Bill, 331

Balloon payments, 184

Banks, 184, 238. *See also* type of bank

Baruch College, City University of New York, *39*

Bascom Group, **194**

Base maps, 98

Bass Lofts [Atlanta, Georgia], **204–7**

Bathrooms, 178, 232

Bay depths, 226, 275–77, 324

BayWalk [St. Petersburg, Florida], *314*

Beacon Centre business park [Miami, Florida], *62*

Bedrooms, 177

Before-tax computation and financial feasibility, 87

Bethesda Row [Bethesda, Maryland], *315,* 316, *353*

Beverly Hills, California, 118, 223

Bhumgara, Raymond, 267

Bidding by contractors, 44

Big-box stores, 305

Billboards, 200, 242

Birtcher, Baron, 30

Black's Guide, 219

BOMA. *See* Building Owners and Managers Association

Bonding, 48, 112

Bonds. *See specific type of bond*

Bonus clauses for contractors, 45–46

Boone, Doug, 112, 120, 121, 364

Boston, Massachusetts, 13, 114, 181

Boulder, Colorado, 225

Boundaries between municipalities, 138

Boundary surveys, 43, 98–99

Braker Center [Austin, Texas], *275*

Brick construction: of multifamily residential development, 176; of office development, 229; of retail development, 331

Brochures, 200, 288

Brokers. *See* Real estate brokers

Brown, C.W., 8–9

Brownfields, 55, 77, 267

Budgets: construction price estimator to prepare, 44; and industrial development, *292;* land use, *82,* 82–83; marketing, 115, 197–98, 199, 287, 345; and office development, 236, 250

Build-to-suits, 214, 242, 334

Building categories: industrial development, 256–59; office development, 213–15, *214;* retail development, 302–4

Building codes: for multifamily residential development, 146, 178; for office development, 216, 223, 237; for retail development, 335; and smart growth, 364

Building configuration and retail development, 323–24, *325*

Building Owners and Managers Association (BOMA), 225, 231

Building permits, 181, 237, 334

Building shape, 224, 226

Building shells/skin system, *229,* 296, 330–31

Building types: industrial development, 276; office development, 214. *See also* Building categories; *specific type*

Bullet loans, 184, *185–86,* 241

Burbank, California, 217

Bureau of Labor Statistics, 308

Business centers, 175

Business parks, 215, 255; categories of, 259; financing, 280; infrastructure, 266; site design, 272–79; zoning, 269. *See also* Industrial parks

Buyout of tenants, 303, 344

By-right districts, 269

Bylaws, 120

■

CAD (computer-aided drawing), 171

California: coastal land and development regulation, 72, 75; condominium conversions, 146–47; and development industry trends, 358, 361; energy requirements (Title 24 regulations), 235; growth controls, 76; industrial development in,

Demographic characteristics: and development industry trends, 361–62; and multifamily residential development, 137; and retail development, 307

Density: and land development, 82, 94, 104–6; and retail development, 313–14. *See also* Zero-lot-line houses; *name of specific product type*

Denver, Colorado, 181

Desert Passage [Las Vegas, Nevada], *324*

Design, 94–106; and accessibility, 272–73; advice about, 22, 238; and costs, 179; development team for, 36; example of, *123*; flexibility in, 225, 226; guidelines for, 97, *118*; industrial development, 275–79, 296; land development, 117–18; and leasing, 238; multifamily residential development, 171–82; office development, 225–38, *251*; and outparcels, 329–30; and R&D, 257, 272; and redevelopment/rehabilitation, 259–60; retail development, 330–36; sensitivity, 96–97; and social responsibility, 368–69; of subdivisions, 94–106. *See also* Exterior design; Interior design; Site planning

Design-award-build contracts, 38

Design review boards, 180

Design review committees, 117–18

Developer off-site bonds, 48

Developers: advice for beginners, **22–23**; backgrounds of, 6–8; characteristics/activities of, 3–6; definition of, 12; and homeowners associations, 120; liability of, 183, 187–88; personal guarantees of, 187–88; personal integrity of, 370; as property managers, 50–51; reputation and credibility of, 53, 55, 182; requirements for success for, 5–6; small developers, 358–59; who becomes, **8–9**

Development: types of, 4. *See also specific type of development*

Development decisions, ethics of, **368**

Development firms, 27–34; compensation, 30–33; life cycles of, 29–30; organizational structure, 30; role as development managers, 13

Development industry trends, 357–71; and changing market factors, 357–61; cities versus suburbs, 363; and community support, 369–70; consolidation trend, 358–60; cycles in, 13–14, *15*, 370; and environmental issues, 365–66; financing, 359–60; and infrastructure, 360; public image of, 367–68; restructuring of, 358; and smart growth, 363–64; and social responsibility, 367–70; and technological development, 361; and transportation issues, 366–67

Development period, 18, 148, *148*, 158

Development process: exposure over time, *24*; management of, 12–24; predevelopment, 18–19, *61*; real estate service firms' role, 46–52; and risk, 12–24; stages of, 18–23; who is involved, **36**. *See also* Getting started; *specific stage in the process*

Development rights, 360

Development team, 27, 37–46, 196; construction stage, 36, 111; participants, 36; site planning, 98. *See also specific stage of development process or specific type of member*

Dewees Island [Charleston, South Carolina], *77, 96*

Direct-mail advertising, 242, 369

Disabled persons, access for. *See* Accessibility

Discount rates, 10

Discounted cash flow (DCF) analysis: and industrial development, 271; and inflation, 86; and land development, 81, 86–94, *87–92*; level of detail for, 86; and loan repayments, 86; monthly analysis during development period, 158–59; and multi-

family residential development, 152–57, *154–56*, 165; and occupancy/vacancy rates, 157; time periods for, 86, 157–58; and timing of sales, 86

Disney Company, 217

Distribution buildings. *See* Warehouses

Dolan v. *City of Tigard* (1994), 72

Dollars & Cents of Shopping Centers®, 308, 341, 342

"Dollar stop" clauses, 245

Dominant tenement, 144

Dowe Business Park [Union City, California], *264*

Downpayment, 108

Downside liabilities, 192

Drainage, 101–2, 112, 279. *See also* Infrastructure

Draws, 182, 196, 280

Due diligence, 66, 124, 265, 283, 366

■

Eagle Harbor [Jacksonville, Florida], *78*

Early suppression, fast response (ESFR) equipment, 279

Earnest money: during development stages, 22; and land development, 108; letters of credit as, 69; and site acquisition, 66, 67

Earnout provisions, *240*, 241

Earthquake areas, 277, 297

Easements: in gross, 144; and land development, 82; and multifamily residential development, 144–45; and protective covenants, 118; reciprocal easement agreement, 352; and site planning, 105; view easements, 366

Easton Town Center [Columbus, Ohio], *11*

Echo boomers, 129, 209

Economic feasibility, 22

Economy and real estate crash of 1980s and early 1990s, 357–58

Edge cities, 252

Edgeless cities, 215

Edmond, Tim, 76

Effective rent, calculation of, **221**

Efficiency ratio, 231

Eichenstein, Izzy, 277, 289

Electric utilities. *See* Utilities

Electrical engineers, 40, 230, 233

Elevators and office development, 232

Elsinore 98 [Riverside County, California], **122–24**

Employee Retirement Income Security Act (ERISA), 282

Energy issues, *234*; green buildings, 235–36; office development, 216, 223, 234–35; retail development, 334

Engineers and engineering, 40–41, 112; advice about, 22; feasibility, 265–67; on site, 111. *See also specific type of engineer*

Enterprise zones, 270

Entrances, 100, 200, 274, 324

Environmental consultants, 41–42

Environmental impact reports (EIRs), 41–42, 77, 267

Environmental impact statement (EIS), 41, 42, 77

Environmental issues: and citizen opposition, 312, 369, 370; and development industry trends, 365–66; example of, 122–23; industrial development, 266–67; land development, 77–80, 95–96; multifamily residential development, 144; retail development, 313, 315; and site planning, 95–96

Environmental Protection Agency (EPA), 43–44, 77, 101–2

Equity, 21; advice about, 22; as compensation, 30, 31; and fees, 190, 192; and financial backing for construction, 52–53; and financial feasibil-

ity, 81; and industrial development, 280, 281–82; and joint ventures, 109; and multifamily residential development, 182, 189–90; and office development, 241–42; phantom equity, 30, 31; and retail development, 337; return on, 93, 153

Escape clauses, 297

Escrow, going into, 66

Estate houses, 104

Estimating market share, 318

Etkin, Bruce H., **16–17**

Exactions, 42, 79, 147, 360, 368

Exclusive right-to-sell listing, 49

Existing buildings, 144. *See also* Redevelopment/rehabilitation

Expense stop leases, 245

Experience Exchange Report: Income/Expense Analysis for Office Buildings, 225

Exterior design: industrial development, 258, 278–79, 296; and lighting, 230, 328–29, *329*; multifamily residential development, *176*, 176–77, *180*, 181; office development, 228–30, *230*; retail development, 330–33

■

46th Street Lofts [San Francisco, California]: market analysis, **134–35**

Fair Housing Act of 1988, 181

Fairmont Plaza office building [San Jose, California], *53*

Falls Plaza [Falls Church, Virginia]

Family firms, 29–30

Faneuil Hall Marketplace [Boston,   ﹍usetts], 343

FAR. *See* Floor/area ratio

Fast-track approach, 38, 44

Feasibility studies: development team f￠ ﹍6; and site acquisition, 67. *See also* Project 1 ﹍ibility; *specific type of study*

Federal Emergency Management Agenc￧ ﹍EMA), 101

Federal National Mortgage Association (FNMA), 117, 187, 195

Federal programs, 193, 195

Federal Reserve Board's Index of Manufacturing Output, 268

Fees: construction, 192, 270; and development industry trends, 368; and equity, 190, 192; and financing, 78; front-end, 192–93; homeowners association, 120; and land development, 78; leasing fee, 192; and maintenance, 120; and multifamily residential development, 190, 192; referral, 201; sales fee, 192. *See also* Points; *specific type of fee*

FEMA (Federal Emergency Management Agency), 101

FHA (Federal Housing Authority), 112, 117

Financial feasibility: advice about, 159, 165; and before-tax computation, 87; data for, 271; detail level in, 86; example of, 123; and go/no-go decision, 165, 171; gross versus net developable acres, 81; of industrial development, 271; and inflation, 86, 93; and joint ventures, 159; and leasing, 158, 336; and lot yield, 82; of multifamily residential development, 147–71; of office development, 225; and present value, *83*, 83–84; and quick and dirty analysis, 81, 84–85, *85*; of retail development, 318; and return, 81, 87, *92*, 93; and risk, 93; stages of determining, 147–71. *See also* Cash flow analysis; Discounted cash flow analysis; Equity

signs, 274; and site acquisition, 260, 265; site conditions, 264, 265, *272;* and site coverage, 269; and site planning, 296; and site selection, 260, 263, 264–67; and speculative development, 255; and streets/roads, *272,* 272–73; suburbanization of, 256; and supply/demand, 267–68; and target markets, 262, 286; and technological development, 258, 298; and tenant improvements/ finish allowances, 257, 289; and tenants, 257, 296, 298; and traffic, 257, 265, 272–73, *273;* trends in, 256, 298; and utilities, 264, 288; and zoning, 264, 269, 271. *See also* Business parks; Manufacturing; R&D

Industrial development bonds, 271

Industrial market and multifamily residential development, 138

Industrial parks: defined, 259. *See also* Business parks

Industrial revenue bonds (IRBs), 193

Infill sites, 180; increase in number of, 181; and industrial development, 265; and office development, 217; and retail development, 314, 340

Inflation, 10; and land development, 86, 93–94; and retail development, 336

Infrastructure: and development industry trends, 360, 367; financing of, 78–79; and growth issues, 76; and industrial development, 266; and land development, 76, 78–79; and social responsibility, 367. *See also specific type of infrastructure*

In-line users, **344**

Inspections, 55; industrial development, 297; multifamily residential development, 196; retail development, 346, 352

Installation date versus shipping date for warranty purposes, 41

Institute of Real Estate Management (IREM), 51, 225

Institutional Housing Partners (IHP), 134–35

Institutional investors, 130, 184, 238, 281–82. *See also specific type of institution*

Insurance and insurance companies, 54, 55; and construction stage, 196; office development, 240–41; and subcontractors, 196. *See also specific type of insurance*

Interest/interest rates: calculation of, *183;* and construction financing, 183, *183,* 239; and federal programs, 193; and multifamily residential development, 129, 183, *183,* 193; and office development, 239, 241

Interior design: advice about, 238; and elevators, 232; and leasing, 181; and lighting, 177, 233; and multifamily residential development, *177,* 177–78; and office development, 230–38, *231;* and retail development, 333–34. *See also* Space; Tenant improvements

Internal rate of return (IRR): industrial development, 271, 283, 286; land development, 87, *91,* 93; lookback IRRs, 159; multifamily residential development, 153, 158, 159, 190

International Building Code, 335

International Business Park [Dallas, Texas], *230*

International Council of Shopping Centers, 326

International trade zones, 263

Internet, 116, 200, 243, 361

Investment builders, 29

Investment and development, 12

Investors: concerns of, 192; as construction lenders, 54–55; joint venture with developer, 110; and multifamily residential development, 182, 192. *See also* Financing

I'On [Mount Pleasant, South Carolina], *113, 121*

IRBs (industrial revenue bonds), 193

Iron Horse Lofts [Walnut Creek, California], *60*

IRR. *See* Internal rate of return

Irvine, California: industrial development, 266; Irvine Ranch, 365; multifamily residential development, 179; planned community, 97

Issuers in conduit loans, 187

■

Jerome Frank Investments, 140, 180

Joinder, 69

Joint ventures: advice about, 23, **189;** with beginning developers, 28–29; as construction lenders, 54–55; and industrial development, 281, 282–83; and multifamily residential development, 159, 189–90, 192; and office development, 241–42; and risk, 109; structure of, 109–11

JPI, 184

Just-in-time delivery chain, 277

■

Kagan, Robert, 240, 245

Kalmuk, Bob, 124

Kansas City, Missouri, 217

Kasdin, Neisen, 365

Kassel, Dan, 96, 122, 124, 196

Katell, Gerald, 287

Katell Properties, 246–49

"Kickers," 184

Kim, David S., 194

Kimsey, Ray, 178, 181

Kitchens, 177

Kotin, Allan, 221, 268

Kramer, Marshall, 227

■

Land acquisition. *See* Site acquisition

Land development, 59–127; and absorption, 99; advice about, 80–81, 120–21; and approvals, 80; and builder precommitments, 107–8; building development versus, 61; and cluster development, 94, *95;* and commercial development, 100; and community groups/neighbors, 80–81; and construction stage, 111–12; and costs, 65, 94–95, 104; and density, *82,* 94, 104–6; and design, 117–18; and drainage, 101–2; and environmental issues, 77–80, 95–96; and exactions, 79; and financing, 78–79, 106–11; and flexibility, 80; and floodplains, 101–2; and grading, 101; gross versus net developable acres, 81; and growth issues, 76–77; industry structure, *61;* and infrastructure, 76, 78–79; loans, 81; and location, 64; and lot yields, 82; and maintenance, 116–20; and market analysis, 62–64, 69–71; and marketing, 112–16; and model/ spec houses, 114, 116; and neighborhood, 64; net developable land, 82; and planned unit developments (PUDs), 97; and platting, 103–4; predevelopment activity, *61;* and project feasibility, 62–94; and protective covenants, 64, 116–17; and regulatory issues, 60–61, 64, 65, 71–78; and return, 81; and rights-of-way, 82; and site acquisition, 65–69; and site conditions, 64, 65; and site evaluation, 64–65; and site selection, 62–69; and streets/roads, 79, 94, 100–101; subdividing land, 59–61; and titles, 65; and transportation issues, 78, 94; and utilities, 64, 65, 101–3; and zoning, 64. *See also* Subdivisions

Land notes, 68

Land planners, 40

Land use: budget for, *82,* 82–83; planning, 83–84; and retail development, 312, 323; and smart growth, 364. *See also* Zoning

Landing at Jack London Square [Oakland, California], *137*

Landowner in joint venture with developer, 109–10

Landscape architects, 38, 228

Landscaping: and industrial development, 273–75, *274,* 296; and multifamily residential development, 174–76, 200; and office development, 228, *228;* and retail development, 327–29; xeriscaping, 176

Lang, Robert, 215

Large-volume builders, 112; development industry trends, 358–60

Larson, Robert, 359, 360

Laundry facilities, 177, 178

Laurel Canyon Apartments [Ladera Ranch, South Orange, California], *59*

Lazard Freres, 359

LCOR Inc. [One Penn Square West, Philadelphia, Pennsylvania], *14*

Leasing: advice about, 23, **344;** and development industry trends, 363; and financial feasibility, 158, 336; and industrial development, 288–89, 296; and interior design, 181; and marketing, 337–44; and multifamily residential development, 197–98; and office development, 240–41, 244–45, 251; open listing, 244; and pass-through expenses, 241, 344; and pricing, 198; rates and terms, 245, 250; and renewal of leases, 289; and retail development, 318, 341–44; and tenant mix, 337–41; and termination of lease, 289; triple-net, 244, 268, 288, 289, 297, 343; types of leases, 244–45; use clause, 344. *See also* Rent; Tenants

Leasing agents, 49–50, 180, 198, 243–44, 344. *See also* Real estate brokers

Leasing office: for multifamily residential development, 175–76; for office development, 243

Lee, Chris, 32–33

Lee, Tom, 75, 365

Lend Lease Real Estate Investments, 342

Lenders: fees of, 53; and regulatory issues, 79–80; role of, 52–57. *See* Financing; *specific type of lender*

Letters of credit, 107–8; as earnest money, 69; multifamily residential development, 189; office development, 239

Letters of intent, 66–67

Leventhal, Kenneth, 358

Lewis, Ralph M., 35

Liens: mechanics liens, 40, 55; perfecting, 107; priorities, 68, 117, 183; waivers from subcontractors, 196

Life safety systems, 236

Lighting: industrial development, 279; multifamily residential development, 177; office development, 230, 233; retail development, 328–29, *329*

LIHTCs. *See* Low-income housing tax credits

Linneman, Peter, 358

Listing agreements, 49

Load factor, 231, 277

Loan commitment, 188, 239, *240,* 241

Loans. *See* Financing; *specific type of financing*

Local government: and development industry trends, 363. *See also* Cities; Government programs

Local streets, 100

Location: of industrial development, 262–63; and land development, 64; macrolocation, 140; microlocation, 140; of multifamily residential development, 140–42; of office development,

214–15, 252; of retail development, 303. *See also* Site selection

Lockout provisions, 286

Logistics parks, 259

Lookback returns, 282, *285*

Los Angeles, California: building permit process, 181; condominium development in, 147; county subdivision filing procedure, 75; environmental issues in, 366; multifamily residential development in, 142; office development in, 223, 224; retail development in, 346

Los Angeles County, subdivision filing procedure, **75**

Lot delivery, 108

Lot yields, 82

Low-income housing. *See* Affordable housing

Low-income housing tax credits (LIHTCs), 130, 193, 195

Low-rise buildings: multifamily residential development, 130, 131, 363; office development, 214, 231

Lucas v. *South Carolina Coastal Council* (1992), 72

LULU, 369, 370

Lump-sum contract. *See* Fixed-price contracts

Luxury apartments, 132, 179, *362*

■

Mackie, Don, 107

Macrolocation, 140

Mail boxes, 175

Maintenance: advice about, 23; industrial development, 288, 296; land development, 116–20; multifamily residential development, 171; office development, 234, 251; retail development, 352–53

Making Smart Growth Work, 364

Management: advice about, 23, **208;** approaches to, 346; and cash flows, 208, compensation for, 346; costs for, 250; development team for, 36; and industrial development, 289–97; and multifamily residential development, 195–96, 202–8; and office development, 250–51; and retail development, 346–53; and selling the property, 202–8; and size of project, 202; staff, 203; and tenants, 208

Manufactured housing, 94

Manufacturing, 257, 266, 268, 276

Maps, 98, 99

Market analysis: advice about, 22, **133;** and amenities, *220;* and anchor tenants, 307; on appeal of design, 104; and builder precommitments, 107–8; capture rate, 71, 139; for condominium development, 134–35; data for, 70–71, 260, 268, 307–9; definition of market, 71; employment and absorption rates, 71; guidelines for, 71; importance of, 197; for industrial development, 260, *261–62,* 262, 267–69; for land development, 62–64, 69–71; for multifamily residential development, 133–40, 197; for multitenant warehouses, **261–63;** and niches, 309–11; for office development, 213, 217–22, 226, 242; and project feasibility, 62–64; for retail development, 303, 305–11; and supply/demand, 217–20, 267–68, 307; and trade areas, 305, 307

Market approach to appraisals, 47

Market area, 136–38

Market consultants, 46

Market research firms, 139, 140

Market studies, **71**

Marketing: advice about, 23; budgets for, 115, 197–98, 199, 287, 345; computer-aided drawing (CAD)

to assist, 171; development team for, 36; example of, 123–24; and industrial development, 286–89, 296; and Internet, 116, 200, 243, 361; and land development, 112–16; larger parcels, 115; and leasing, 337–44; and location, 252; and market analysis, 197; and marketing plans/programs, 345; and marketing strategies, 197–98, 287; and model/spec houses, 114, 116, 197; and multifamily residential development, 197–202; and office development, 242–50, *243;* and outparcels, 329–30; and positioning, 345; postconstruction, 344–46; and price, 198; to the public, 115–16; purpose of, 197; and retail development, 337–46; and sales, 115; and size of project, 114; staffing for, 202; strategy, *50. See also* Leasing agents; Public relations agencies; Real estate brokers

Martin Luther King shopping center [Los Angeles, California], 346

Masonry construction, 228, 331

Massachusetts: brownfields, 267; home rule state, 74; site acquisition process, 66, 67. *See also specific cities and developments*

Massing, *118*

Materials, 228–30. *See also specific material*

Math, John, 201–2

Maturity of development firm, 30

McCaslin, Tom, 236

McDonald-York, **31**

McMansions, 104

Mechanical engineers, 40, 233, 334

Mechanics liens, 40, 55

Mercado Plaza [Palm Springs, California], *27*

Merchandising, 116, 200, 243

Merchant builders, 29

Metropolitan statistical areas (MSAs), 136

Mezzanine financing, 21, 55, 282

Michigan, 277. *See also* Northfield Commons [Troy, Michigan]

Microlocation, 140

Mid-rise buildings: apartments, 130, 131, 173, 178, 363; office development, 214

Mindshare Internet Campaigns, 312

Miniperm loans, 21, 182

Mixed-use development, 97, 365; busy streets in, 104; industrial development, 265, 267, 269; office development, 223

Mock-ups, 178

Model houses and rental units, 114, 116, 179, 197, 201

Mortgage application, **188**

Mortgage bankers and brokers, 56

Mortgage pools, 239, 358, 359

Mortgages: application package, **188;** industrial development, 280–81; multifamily residential development, 184–87; office development, 239. *See also* Permanent financing; *specific type of mortgage*

Motor vehicles. *See* Streets/roads; Traffic

Mow, Harry, 189, 193

MSAs (metropolitan statistical areas), 136

Mueller, Glenn, 14

Multifamily residential development, 129–211; and absorption rates, 138–39; and accessibility, 142–43, 181; advice about, 132, 142, 208; and affordable housing, 130, 193, 195; and aging population, 129, 132, 136; and amenities, 174–76, 181; and approvals, 180–81; and closings, 188–89; and construction costs, 131; and construction financing, 182–84; and construction stage, 195–97; and costs, 209; cyclical nature of, 129; and design issues, 171–82, **175;** and discounted cash

flow (DCF) analysis, 152–57; and easements, 144–45; and environmental issues, 144; and equity, 182, 189–90; and exactions, 147; and exterior design, *176,* 176–77, *180,* 181; and fees, 190, 192; and financial feasibility, 147–71; and financing, 129–30, 182–95; and fire codes, 145–46, 172; forms of, **173;** and go/no-go decision, 165; and government programs, 193, 195, 196; history, 129–30; and impact fees, 147; influences on, 129; and inspections, 196; in institutional property portfolios, 130, 184; and interest/interest rates, 129, 183, *183,* 193; and interior design, *177,* 177–79; and investors, 192; and joint ventures, 159, 189–90, 192; and landscaping, 174–76; and leasing, 197–98; and liens, 183, 196; and maintenance, 171; and management, 195–96, 202–8; market analysis for, 133–40, 197; market demand for, 129; and marketing, 197–202; and model/spec units, 201; and neighborhood, 140–42; and ownership, 130; and parking, 173–74; and permanent financing, 182, 183, 184–87; and pricing, 198; and private offerings, 192–93; product types, 130–32; and project feasibility, 132–71; and protective covenants, 118; and regulatory issues, 145–47; and rent, 209; and rent control, 146; and risk, 132, 187–88; scheduling of, 195–96; and site acquisition, 132; and site conditions, 143–44; and site planning, 172–73; and site selection, 140–47; and syndications, 189–90; and target market, 130; and tenants, 189; time line for, *19, 132;* and unit mix, 171–72, *172;* and visibility, 142–43; and zoning, 145, 181

Multiple jurisdictions and regulatory issues, 74

Multitenant industrial development, 258; design, 276; leasing, 288; market analysis, *261–63*

Municipal boundaries, 138

■

Nahas, Robert, 370

National Asbestos Council, 44

National Association of Realtors, 51

National Environmental Policy Act, 41, 266

National Flood Insurance Act, 266

National Real Estate Compensation Survey, 2002, *32 33*

National Research Bureau (NRB), 309

Nature Conservancy, 366

Neely, Al, 76

Negotiated-price contracts, 111

Negotiation of development agreements, 270

Neighborhood: and land development, 64; of multifamily residential development, 140–41; preservation of sense of place, 365. *See also* Community groups/neighbors

Neighborhood revitalization. *See* Redevelopment/rehabilitation

Neighborhood shopping centers, 302, 304, 336, **352;** percentage rents, 318, 342. *See also* Retail development

Nelson Companies, 331, 334, 335

Nelson, David, 334, 335

Net developable acreage, 81

Net leases, 244–45, 343

Net operating income (NOI), 148–49, 280; pro forma NOI, *149*

Net present value, 153

New urbanist approach, 97, 103, 121

New York City: condominium conversions, 146; office development, 223

Newport, South Carolina, 121

Newsletters, 198–99, 242, 369

Newspaper advertising, 200, 242

Niches, 309–11

NIMBY, **312**, 369, 370

NOI. *See* Net operating income

Noise and sound buffering, 104

Nonprofit programs for multifamily residential development, 193, 195

Northfield Commons [Troy, Michigan], 305, **306;** anchor tenants, 307; approvals, 312, 317; clock tower as symbol, *328;* configuration of, 323; consent agreement, **317;** development chronology, **316;** elevation, *330;* environmental considerations, 313; financial analysis, **323;** income/ expense budget, **347;** marketing program, **345;** overview, 306; project summary, *306;* site plan, *306;* tenant finishes, **333**

Note rates, 184, 187, *187*

"No-waste" clauses, 69

■

Occupancy/vacancy rates: calculating average occupancy rate, *157;* and discounted cash flow analysis, 157; and industrial development, *263;* and multifamily residential development, 138, 139, 157, *157,* 208; natural vacancy, 219; and office development, 219–20; stabilized vacancy, 219

Occupants associations, 297

Occupational Safety and Health Act, 266

O'Donnell, John, 30, 31

Offer to purchase, 66, 67

Office development, 213–53; and absorption, 219; and accessibility, 222–23; advice about, 221–22; Agoura Hills Centre [Los Angeles, California], **246–49;** approvals, 237; and budgets, 236, 250; build-to-suit development, 214, 242; and building codes, 216, 223, 237; and building shape, 224, 226; categorization of, 213–15, *214;* classes of, 213–14; and construction costs, 226; and construction financing, 239; corporate campuses, 217; corporate tenant with multiple location options, *20–21;* data for, 219; and design, 225–38, *251;* and elevators, 232; and energy issues, 216, 223, 234–36; and equity, 241–42; exterior design, 228–30, *230;* and FAR, 223; and financial feasibility, 225; and financing, 238–42; and flexibility/ adaptability, 222, 225, *225,* 226, 251–52; and historic landmarks, 217, 224; and HVAC systems, 233–34, 235; and impact fees, 223, 224; in institutional property portfolios, 238; interior design, 230–38, *231;* and joint ventures, 241–42; landscaping, 228, *228;* larger tenants, 221; and leasing, 240–41, 243–45, 251; and life safety systems, 236; and lighting, 230, 233; location of, 214–15; and maintenance costs, 234; and management, 250–51; market analysis for, 213, 217–22, 226; and marketing, 242–50, *243;* and merchandising, 243; and mixed-use environment, 223; and mortgage options, 241; neighborhood offices, 215; and occupancy rates, 219, 221; owner-occupied building, 214; and ownership, 214; and parking, 222, 224, 227–28; and permanent financing, 239–40; preleasing, 19; and project feasibility, 217–25; and regional economic growth, 216; and regulatory issues, 223; and rental rates, 221; and security, 228, 230, 236; selection of contractor for, 237; and selling the completed project, 251; and signage, 230; and site conditions, 222; and site planning, 227–28; and site selection, 222–23; and space modules, 226, *227,* 231; space planning for, *231,*

232, *232,* 236–37; spec building, 214; stages of development and time line, *24;* and subleased space, 220–21; and suburbanization, 216–17, *217;* and supply/demand, 217–20; and target market, 216, 222; and technological development, 216, 234, *237,* 258; and tenant improvements, 221, 236–38; and tenants, 237; and traffic, 216–17, 224–25; trends in, 216–17; types of buildings, 214; vacancy rates, 219, 221; and zoning, 223–24. *See also* Planned unit developments (PUDs)

Office/tech buildings, 258

Old Elm Village [Petaluma, California], *81*

Oliver, H. Pike, 46

Olney Village Mart [Montgomery County, Maryland], 305; market analysis, **308–9;** sales analysis, *309*

Open listing, 244

Open space: covenants for use, 118, 119; developer's donation of, 120; and development industry trends, 366; environmental concerns, 96; multifamily residential development, 172, 173; office development, 232

Operating period, 18, *148,* 158

Operations. *See* Management

Orange County, California, 120, 147

Orenco Station [Portland, Oregon], *364*

Originators in conduit loans, 187

Out-of-sequence releases, 69

Outlet shopping centers, 341

Outparcels, 312, 329–30

Overborrowing, 189

Owner-occupied buildings, 214, 217

Ownership: and development process, 12; and multifamily residential development, 130; of office development, 214

■

Pappas, Peter, **17–18**

Pari passu, 282

Parking: deferred, 224; and industrial development, 257, 258, 272, 297; and lighting, 230, 329; local streets, 100; and multifamily residential development, 173–74; and office development, 222, 224, 227–28; and outparcels, 329; perpendicular/ diagonal, 324, 326–27, *327;* and protective covenants, 119; and R&D, 272; and retail development, 324, 326–27, *327;* and security, 228, 236, 324

Parking consultants, 43

Participating mortgages, 184, *185–86,* 187, 241

Partnerships: advice about, 23; and cash calls, 192; common problems with, 28–29; and developers' integrity, 370; and organizing for development, 27–29

Paseo Colorado [Pasadena, California], *357*

Pass-through expenses, 241, 344

Patio houses, 104–5

Paumier, Cyril, 366

Pay rates, 184, 187, *187*

Payment bonds, 48

Pebble Creek at Green Valley [Henderson, Nevada], *63*

Pedestrians: and development industry trends, 363; and industrial development, 273–75

Peiser Corporation, 74, 80, 140, 180, 190

Pension funds, 54, 358

Pentagon Row [Arlington, Virginia], *352*

Percent completion, 183

Percentage rents, 318, 336, 341, 342–43

Performance bonds, 48, 296

Perley, Jim, 130, 208

Permanent financing: advice about, 22; comparison of types of, *185–86, 336;* and construction financing, 183; and industrial development, 280–81; and interest/interest rates, 183; and leasing, 239–40; and loan commitments, 188; and multifamily residential development, 182, 183, 184–87; and note/pay rates, 184, 187; and office development, 239–40; and rent, 240; types of lenders, 56–57. *See also specific type of lender*

Permits, 55. *See also* Approvals; *specific type of permit*

Pets, restrictive covenants on, 119

Phantom equity, 30, 31

Phasing of subdivisions, 75

Pisarski, Alan E., 366

Planned residential developments. *See* Planned unit developments (PUDs)

Planned unit developments (PUDs), 94, 97, 269

Planners, 368

Platting, 71–74, 103–4; and easements, 144; fees, 78; and industrial development, 271, 272; subdivision plat, 119

PMNs. *See* Purchase money notes

Point-of-sale incentives, 198

Points, 109, 183, 239

Positioning, 345

Pour strips, 277

Power centers, 304

Prairie Stone Business Park [Chicago, Illinois], *269*

Praxair Distribution [Ankeny, Iowa], *259*

Predevelopment phase, 18–19, *61*

Prefabricated buildings, 277–78

Preferred returns, 111, 190, *191,* 192

Preleasing, 19, 197, 242

Presale commitments. *See* Forward commitment

Present value, **10;** comparison with future value, 83; factors on land allocation for different uses, *83*

PricewaterhouseCoopers, 342

Pricing, 198, 341

Primary market area, 137

Privacy, 178–79

Private offerings, 192–93

Pro forma NOI, 148–49, *149*

Product type: advice about, 22; and industrial development, 256–60; and residential development, 130–32

Production homebuilders, 113

Profit. *See* Return

Profit and loss managers, 31

Project cost. *See* Costs

Project development: major parties involved in, 368

Project feasibility: of industrial development, 260, 262–71; of land development, 62–94; of multifamily residential development, 132–71; of office development, 217–25; of retail development, 305–18. *See also* Approvals; Financial feasibility; Market analysis; Site selection

Project objectives, 197

Promotes, 282–83

Property managers, 50–52; multifamily residential development, 175, 180, 202–3; office development, 250; software for, 361. *See also* Management

Property taxes, 69, 120

Protective covenants: cost covenants, 118; and design, 117–18; enforcement of, 119; and industrial development, 267, 270, 287, 289, 296, 297; and land development, 64, 74, 116–17; and multifamily residential development, 144; and retail development, 344; running with the land, 119, 144; term and revision of, 119

Public relations, 198–99, **199,** 242–43

Public relations agencies, 50, 198

discounted cash flow (DCF) analysis, 152–57, *154–56;* financial feasibility analysis, 148–71; joint venture–syndication analysis, 159; maximum loan amount, *150;* monthly cash flows during development period, 158–59, *160–63;* pro forma NOI, *149;* rental summary, *149;* return to investors, *170;* simple ratios, 152, *152*

Shell. *See* Building shells/skin system

Sheridan Plaza at Inverness [Englewood, Colorado], *218, 228*

Shipping date versus installation date for warranty, 41

Shopping centers, 301–55. *See also* Retail development; *specific type of shopping center*

Short Run facility at Phillips Plastics Corporation [New Richmond, Wisconsin], *255, 267*

Short-term leases, 289

Sick building syndrome, 234

Siding. *See* Exterior design

Signs: and industrial development, 274; and marketing, 200; and office development, 230; and retail development, 329, 332–33

Simple capitalization, 148–52, *149*

Site acquisition, 64–69; advice about, 22, 69; checklist for, 65; and closing, 66; and contingencies in purchase contracts, 67–68; and contracts, 66–69; and earnest money, 66, 67; example of, 122; and feasibility studies, 67; and industrial development, 260, 265; and land development, 65–69; and letters of intent, 66–67; and multifamily residential development, 132; and retail development, 315–16; and site conditions, 64, 65; steps in, **66;** tips, **69;** and titles, 65; and zoning, 67

Site conditions: and costs, 226; and industrial development, 264, 265, *272;* and land development, 64, 65; and multiresidential development, 137, 143–44, 176; and office development, 222; and retail development, 307, 315, 327–29; and site acquisition, 64, 65. *See also specific type of condition*

Site coverage, 269

Site engineering, 101–3, 327–28

Site evaluation, **64**

Site maps, 98

Site planning, 94–106; and absorption, 99; advice about, 22; alternative layouts, 98; base maps, 98; and boundary surveys, 98–99; and commercial development, 100; and concept development, 99–100; and costs, 94; and density, 103, 104–6; diagram of site's features, 98; and drainage, 101–2; and entrance to project, 100; final plan, 98, 181; and floodplains, 101–2; and grading, 101; and industrial development, 296; models, 98; and multifamily residential development, 172–73; and planned unit developments (PUDs), 94, 97; and platting, 103–4; preliminary, 179–81; processes, 97–98; and retail development, 323–26, 327; and site engineering, 101–3; site maps, 98; and streets/roads, 100–101; topographic maps, 98; and traffic, 100–101; and utilities, 99, 101–3; and value enhancement, 99. *See also* Density; Parking; Zoning

Site selection: checklist, 313; and development industry trends, 363; development team for, 36; and hazardous materials, 265; for industrial development, 260, 263, 264–67; for land development, 62–69; and location, 252; for multifamily residential development, 140–47; for office development, 222–23, 227–28; and regulatory issues, 65; for retail development, 309, 312–16; and site conditions, 65, 264

Size of project: and financing, 238; and first deals, 11; for industrial development, 256, 283; and management, 202; and marketing, 114; for multifamily residential development, 142; for office development, 238; for retail development, 313–14, 333

Skylights, 279

Slope. *See* Site conditions

Small developers, 358–59

Small-lot villas, 104

Smart buildings, 178, 216

Smart growth, 363–64

Smart Growth Myth and Fact, 364

Smart Growth Tool Kit, 364

Smith, Jim, 243

Smith, Scott, 75, 97, 113, 120

Social responsibility, 367–70

Soils. *See* Site conditions

Soils engineers, 41

Solid Waste Agency of N. Cook County v. *U.S. Army Corps of Engineers* (2001), 72

Space: common space, 120, 344; measurement of, 231; and office development, 231; planning of, 232; requirements per employee, *231. See also* Design; Open space

Spec buildings, 114, 214, 255

Special districts, 78, 269

Specialty neighborhood centers, 305

Specialty shopping centers, 304–5, 324–26

Sponsors in conduit loans, 187

Spot footings, 277

Spread footings, 277, 330

Sprint, 217

Stabilized operating period, 18

Standby commitments, 55–56, 241

Startup. *See* Getting started

Stebbins, Brian R., **18**

Steel construction, 228, 229, 277, 279, 330

Stenlund, Ronald, 41

Stone exterior, 229, 230

Storage areas, 119, 175, 297

Storefront system, 229

Stormwater, 144, 274, 328. *See also* Site conditions

Strategic planning, 33–34

Strategic planning and thinking, **34**

Streets/roads: and financing, 79; hierarchy of, 94, *100,* 100–101; and industrial development, *272,* 272–73; and land development, 79; and retail development, 324–26. *See also* Parking; Traffic

Strip shopping centers, 302, 313–15, 341, 353. *See also* Retail development

Strongbacks, 278

Structural engineers, 40

Stubblefield, Jo Anne, 75, 76, 116, 117, 120

Stucco, 176, 229, 331

Subcontractors, 111–12, 196

Subdivision bonds, 48

Subdivisions: definition of, 59; design of, 94–106; filing process for, 74–75; and homeowners associations, 119; and industrial development, 271; phasing, 75; process of subdividing, 59–61. *See also* Land development

Subleased office space, 220–21

Submarkets for multifamily residential development, 136–37, 171

Subordination, 69, 107, 108

Suburbs: industrial development, 256; and industry development trends, 363; office development, 214–15; retail development, 314, 323, 340; and smart growth, 364

Super regional centers, 304

Superfund, 266

Supermarkets, 341

Supplementary note procedure, 68

Supply/demand: for industrial development, 267–68; for market analysis, 217–19, 307; for multifamily residential development, 136–39, 140; for office development, 217–20; and real estate cycles, 13–14; for retail development, 307–8

Supreme Court decisions on land regulation, 72

Surety companies, 48

Surveyors, 42

Swimming pools, 174–75

Syndications, 54, 159, 189–90, 195

◼

Takeout loans. *See* Permanent financing

Target market: and design, 96, 104; example of, 124; and getting started, 14, 16–18; and industrial development, 262, 286; and marketing, 197; and multifamily residential development, 130, 133, 136–38; and office development, 216, 222, 242; and trends in development industry, 357–61

Tax credits, 130, 193, 195. *See also specific types*

Tax increment financing, 78, 271

Tax Reform Act of 1986, 54, 130, 193, 271

Taxes: increases and leasing, 289; and industrial development, 270–71, 297; and joint ventures, 110; and office development, 223; property taxes, 69. *See also* Tax credits

Technical services packages, 287–88

Technological development: and development industry, 361; and industrial development, 258, 298; and office development, 216, 234, *237,* 258. *See also* R&D

Technology parks, 259

Telecommunications, 178, 258–59. *See also* Wiring

Tenant associations, 297

Tenant finishes, 331, 333, 334–36

Tenant improvements: and industrial development, 257, 289; and office development, 221, 236–38; and R&D, 257

Tenants: credit requirements for, 208; and design, 218; escape clauses, 297; and financing, 189; and industrial development, 257, 296, 298; and management, 208; and marketing, 344; mix of, 337–41; and multifamily residential development, 208; and office development, 231; placement of, 341; and R&D, 257, 288; and rentable space, 231; and retail development, 303, 332–33, 337–41, *338–40, 342;* satisfaction of, 250–51; seed, 289, 296; selection of, 296–97, 337, 344; and signs, 230, 332–33; turnover in, 203, 208. *See also* Anchor tenants; Leasing; Rent; Tenant improvements

Tennis courts, 175

Texas: and development industry trends, 361; industrial development, 268, 278; notice to tenants of property sale, 208; regulatory concerns, 75; security systems, 179; site acquisition process, 66; subdividing land, 59. *See also specific cities and developments*

Texas Transportation Institute, 366

Third-party investors, 110

Thomas, John, 227, 230

Tiered hurdle rates of return, 282, 283, *284*

Tierra del Rey in Marina del Rey [Los Angeles, California], *131, 362*

Tilt-up buildings/walls, 330–31. *See also* Concrete structures

Time and materials (T&M) agreements, 36, 38, 42, 43